THE LIVES OF DWARFS

Two caricature renderings by artists from different eras almost twenty-five hundred years apart capture the unique features of similar dwarfing conditions. Left: *Greek cyclic, c. 450* B.C.E., *Art Resource, NY/Vatican Museum;* right: *Toulouse-Lautrec, c. 1890. Courtesy Charles de Rodat.*

The Lives of Dwarfs

THEIR JOURNEY

from

PUBLIC CURIOSITY

toward

SOCIAL LIBERATION

BETTY M. ADELSON

FOREWORD BY JULIE ROTTA

RUTGERS UNIVERSITY PRESS

NEW BRUNSWICK, NEW JERSEY, AND LONDON

Library of Congress Cataloging-in-Publication Data

Adelson, Betty M., 1935–

    The lives of dwarfs : their journey from public curiosity toward social liberation / Betty M. Adelson.

      p. cm.

    Includes bibliographical references and index.

    ISBN 0–8135–3548–4 (hardcover : alk. paper)

    1. Dwarfs—History. 2. Dwarfs—Social conditions. 3. Dwarfs—Public opinion. 4. Short people—History. I. Title.

    GN69.3.A34 2005

    599.9'49—dc22   2004016333

A British Cataloging-in-Publication record for this book is available from the British Library.

Book design and composition by Jenny Dossin

Manufactured in the United States of America

FOR ANNA
AND ALL THE REST
WHO STRIVE
TO VANQUISH RIDICULE
AND EMBRACE FULL LIVES

CONTENTS

FOREWORD

"Who Sees the Other Half of Self, Sees Truth"

My involvement with this book began as I was about to celebrate my fiftieth birthday, an event that is typically an opportunity to reflect upon one's personal journey. However, with Betty Adelson's invitation to consult with her on the graphic aspect of this book, this milestone took on another dimension. As I read the manuscript, I was struck by the fact that in my lifetime, no other work on the lives of dwarfs had ever been written. No previous study had traveled through time, as this one did, offering a new and comprehensive perspective on the lives of dwarfs from ancient Egypt to the present day.

From the obscure to the eminent, its chapters reveal the inner thoughts and public lives of individuals like me. The author's singular vision seemed to embrace the richness, diversity, and complexity of those of us who share a visible difference—dwarfism—and whose history, until now, had often been lost or overburdened with the legacy of myth, as if we ourselves were either mythological creatures or exhibiting dwarfs. For me, being viewed through this prism caused suffering in my early years far beyond the medical problems and physical limitations associated with my form of dwarfism. Because of how dwarfs were still being portrayed in mythology and the media, I had found it necessary to armor myself against stereotyped perceptions, altering even my sense of humor to guard against any possible mythic association. A seemingly daily effort of adjusting and readjusting was required for me to contend with public curiosity.

I have encouraged the inclusion of as many as possible of the vast number of illustrations unearthed by Betty Adelson because they speak powerfully to this enduring journey, taken by so many persons with dwarfism, the genesis of which is our physical appearance, our visible difference. My involvement in this work gives credence to "Who sees the other half of self, sees Truth," a maxim that has inspired my quest for many years.[1] It has reminded me to honor the dwarf part of me as well as the other parts, which are just as vital to my being Julie, and to further integrate both halves of self.

The majority of my work for this book was done between two hip replacement surgeries in 2001 and 2002. The surgeries were reminders of the travails associated with my form of dwarfism—pseudoachondroplasia. As I helped select and scan the images, I became increasingly aware that the fifty years of my life coincided with yet another milestone—the culmination of a period of extraordinary change in the lives of dwarfs.

I was born in 1951; the first meeting of the group that would become Little People of America took place in 1957. When I was born, my average-statured parents did not have an organization or any book to guide them. They felt very alone as they faced the medical ambiguities and social implications of the rare genetic disorder that affected their firstborn, my brother Steven; and two years later, myself. They seemed to be in constant motion—searching the medical establishment from New York City to China, writing to or visiting many hospitals and doctors. When I was four, they turned to their faith for hope and arranged a trip to the Vatican for a private audience with Pope Pius XII. No miracles resulted. Twelve years later, when I was sixteen, our family arrived at Johns Hopkins, where we were provided with a third, but finally definitive, diagnosis and were educated about the prospects for our form of dwarfism. I met many extraordinary physicians, notably Dr. Judith Hall, with whom I was to form a lifelong friendship. Dr. Hall's approach was holistic: I experienced for the first time a physician who viewed me as Julie first, and it was her treatment that set in motion my journey to discover the part that pseudoachondroplasia would play in the development of my other half of self.

My average-statured sister Kathy was born five years after I was. Our "big little sister" Kathy grew to be a loving, deeply empathic person in spite of the attention focused on our early medical problems. Well aware of the frailties of a society ruled by conformity, my parents were torn between their parental instincts to protect us physically and emotionally and to let go. Their encounters with the educational system were generally disastrous. While they recognized our eagerness to learn and experience with other youngsters our age, the administrators they met professed to understand, but hid behind liability concerns. At a local parochial school, they were brusquely told that at three feet four inches tall we were a "fire hazard" because of our inability to open fire doors. Consequently, my brother and I were homeschooled for the first four years of elementary education.

In 1960, after the New York City Board of Education began allocating some ground-floor classrooms for the education of the disabled, we were placed in what was called a health conservation class. It had three grade levels, one teacher, and twenty-five students with a wide range of physical and mental abilities. *Only four of us were of at least average intelligence.* By seventh grade, I had renamed the euphemistic health conservation class the "learning deprivation class." After my pleas to attend a "normal" public school with my peers were denied, I tried a sit-down strike, a common strategy of those turbulent sixties. Defeated after two weeks, I returned to complete eighth grade with a growing swell of anger at lost opportunity. In order to spare their children being forced into a poor educational setting in a local Bronx high school, my parents moved to suburban Mahopac, New York, where we attended Mahopac High School. Its progressive faculty and administration willingly made accommodations for our height of three feet six inches, walking limitations, and safety, and focused on providing equal academic and social opportunities in which we could and did excel.

Our early childhood experiences had been marked by our recognition of the stark contrast between the loving, insular world of our home and extended family, and our many brushes with public curiosity. That contrast precipitated in my brother and me a heightened awareness of stigma and stereotype. Our bodies were indeed very different. However, juxtaposed with this very real physical difference was something more—a kind of surreal connection—conjuring up associations with "ancestors" we did not recognize or want to know about. I recall in the late 1950s, when I was eight or nine, sitting on the front stoop and confronting these questions together with my older brother. I asked him, "Why were we both born dwarfs?" His answer was, "Maybe we are meant to be teachers." "Teachers of what?" We both instinctively knew the answer: "Teachers about difference."

The struggle to deal with the harshness of our physical reality persisted, along with the ever present mythic associations. We often felt as though we were on a treadmill, trying to outrun the myths and misconceptions associated with the word dwarf. The information that bombarded us in films and books, and the relentless association with the circus, discouraged any identity seeking. Even after we first learned about Little People of America, we avoided participating. We saw no positive value in claiming an "other half" associated with a community of other dwarfs. Instead, my brother and I, like most other little persons identified with family, endeavored to "fit in," to be "normal."

In the early 1960s, personal and societal forces were conspiring to change this situation. As a vocal, idealistic young person, I was influenced by the politics of those turbulent times—particularly in the area of civil rights. That generation's passionate shouts against social injustice were echoed in the cries and whispers within the insular world in which I lived as a dwarf. I recognized the similarity between the worlds of bigotry and injustices based on skin color, religion, lifestyle, and prejudice against dwarfs. While many young people were marching on Washington to protest U.S. involvement in an undeclared war in Vietnam, many dwarfs and their families, including mine, were marching to Baltimore, to Johns Hopkins, where an "undeclared war" was being fought against problems resulting from the lack of proper diagnoses and treatment of disabled persons.

Before the correct diagnosis of our type of dwarfism was made at Hopkins, my parents had endured sixteen years of erroneous information and fear-filled prognoses. During this time my interest in science and in my form of dwarfism was growing. It crystallized when I was a senior in high school, and Dr. Steven Kopits, the gifted Johns Hopkins orthopedist, after inquiring about my interests and career plans, suggested that I might consider becoming a medical illustrator. Subsequently, I decided to major in biology and minor in art at Mercy College, a small independent college with an excellent science program, an accessible campus, and an administration willing to make necessary accommodations for my short stature. However, from the time I entered college at eighteen, I had begun to feel the painful degeneration of my hips and knees, and my graduation in 1973 was followed by bilateral femoral osteotomies at Johns Hopkins Hospital—surgeries designed to realign my hips and postpone inevitable total hip replacement. After my recovery, and to prove my capability, I volunteered in my two areas of interest—art and science—and subsequently found employment in each: as a medical research technician at New York Medical College and as administrator of a local arts council. From the seed planted by Dr. Kopits, I added a third career, one that grew into a successful freelance business called Graphics for Science.

In our adult years, my brother Steven's path and mine diverged. He pursued his dreams through business, early marriage, and children, and I through college, career, and owning my own home. The women's movement fostered my desire for autonomy, the determination to take control of my own life. In 1982 I attended my first Little People of America convention. Upon meeting so many dwarfs and still feeling different, I confronted the possibility of my dwarfism being the least of all my differences. Did this other half of self define my body alone, or my being, or both? That first experience was extraordinary and stimulated me further to chase my elusive butterflies of truth, harmony, and the many halves of self within the organization as well as apart from it.

Harmony was replaced with despair at the sudden death of my brother Steven, in 1987 at age 38. He left behind two young daughters, one of whom is a dwarf. Reflecting upon his death, my life, and my niece Corynne's future, I concluded that what Steven and I first questioned together as children, why we were both born dwarfs, was now closer to being answered. Our shared life and Steven's death affirmed for me that truth and harmony could not be attained without reconciling the many halves of self. I often felt like both sculptor and stone, chiseling and being chiseled, creating and re-creating myself so that I might emerge complete, ready to unveil and celebrate the many halves of self.

The Northwest Native American precept "Who sees the other half of self, sees Truth" has given direction to my personal journey. But it also expresses the mission of this book—to offer to dwarfs and others the possibility of exploring the dwarf half more meaningfully by reading about the long, interesting history of this collection of individuals. Initially, while I was delighted to collaborate on the visual aspect of the book, I was reluctant to write about my own journey. However, I did so, because I eventually recognized how much it parallels that of many other dwarf individuals in this momentous half century. It is important to have a book like this one as we seek to affirm our prismatic lives. Betty's research, sensitive interpretation, and insightful narrative, illuminated by numerous illustrations, have widened the horizon for us all. Through this work, future generations of dwarfs and others will be encouraged to explore and embrace the transformative powers of difference.

As a gift bearer, Betty Adelson has given dwarfs what no previous work has—the opportunity to reclaim what is rightfully ours—the right to our essential humanity; the right to just be. . . .

JULIE ROTTA

PREFACE

Ever since my daughter Anna was born thirty years ago with achondroplasia, a type of dwarfism, I have recognized the need for a book about the lives of dwarfs. At that time I eagerly searched the literature and found only some specialized medical articles that were not very helpful, and sometimes alarming. Subsequently, I came upon books with titles like Freaks, Human Oddities, or Victorian Grotesque: their inadequacies and biases strengthened my resolve to offer a truer narrative to dwarfs and their families and to a society that had all too often been unwelcoming and uncomprehending. The work would be a social history that described the presence of dwarfs in other eras, in mythology and the arts, but one that would also cast light on the lives of dwarfs today and be informed by my own and others' personal experiences.

Had there been any eminent dwarfs? If so, what had their lives and those of ordinary dwarfs in other societies been? I could only imagine. But I did know that raising a child to maturity and encountering other families and individuals and professionals in the process had had a profound, transforming effect upon me. It had made me consider and develop strong feelings about such issues as disability, medical treatment, height, beauty, identity, and even the force of mythology. A book would need to touch upon all these issues.

Each issue has involved "facts" and social attitudes filtered through subjectivity, for me and for every family presented with a child who is a dwarf. Consider height, for example. The distance between five and six feet is objectively quite small. But it marks in human society the difference between a short and tall person, for example, New York City mayors Abe Beame and John Lindsay, and complex attitudes that attach to that difference. The twelve-inch difference between a four-footer and a five-footer is clearly greater than that between a five-footer and a six-footer. Because stature is a continuum, there is even disagreement about who should be referred to as a dwarf: these days, the common definition includes anyone four feet ten inches or below whose short stature involves a medical condition—individuals may be proportionate or disproportionate, and their shortness may be the result of several hundred causes or combinations of causes. Someone a bit taller but with specific skeletal features or hormonal problems, for example, may merit a dwarfism diagnosis.

The relativity of one's perception of height extends to one's ethnic group and individual family. Growing up in Brooklyn, I was always either the smallest or next to the smallest in my grade-school class. I did not mind: I liked being close to the action at the blackboard. Mostly, my height was not focused on; when it was, the attention was positive. When I reached my full height of five feet two inches in junior high school, I became the second tallest in my family, taller than my sister, who was seven years older and five feet tall; towering above my four-foot-ten-inch mother; and second only to my father, who at five feet eight inches was regarded by us all, especially my mother, as quite impressive in height. Indeed, in the community in which we lived, where most people had short, stocky East European forebears, he was.

Of all the identities I had when I was young—daughter, sister, American, Brooklynite, Jew, bookworm, mischief maker—short person was one of the least significant. When I became the mother of a dwarf, however, stature became a characteristic that would forevermore be central in my own psyche and in my family's. I felt permanently linked to dwarfs past and present, though not visibly so, and also aware that through my daughter's genes the destiny of at least some of my descendants might be joined with theirs. And I began to recognize that "dwarf identity" was largely uncharted territory.

The final decades of the twentieth century have been referred to variously as the age of anxiety or the age of narcissism. Perhaps an even more apt characterization would be the age of search for identity. One after another, first nations, then groups and individuals, have sought to chart their history and garner meaning by discovering their roots. Women, African Americans, gays, and people with disabilities, among many others, have tried to discover themselves in a history that had formerly ignored them. Until recently, few dwarfs had embarked on this journey.

Why not? Is there no dwarf history, no dwarf culture, worthy of notice? On the contrary, there is a very rich history to explore. However, those persons whose interest was piqued were apt to be daunted by the fact that most of what has been written is out of print, is not indexed under *dwarf* or *little person*, or is otherwise hard to obtain access to. These labels, which commonly evoke the stuff of myth and legend, have not been replaced, and it remains hard for profoundly short-statured individuals to find an acceptable term with which to refer to themselves. In much of northern Europe, *dwarfs* is rejected because it evokes negative images of inhuman creatures; elsewhere, *little people* is often rejected because of its association with elves and leprechauns, as well as children. These days, *midget*, once used for very small, proportionate individuals with hormonal disorders, is anathema in the United States because it is derived from *midge*, an insect; because it is associated with the world of spectacle; and because it has often been flung as an aggressive epithet in the phrase, "Look at the midget!" In this volume, I most often use the word *dwarf*, the current medical term, which is used descriptively and comfortably by individuals in the United States; I use the acronym LP, a dwarfism-community neologism that carries little historic baggage, when I refer to a member of Little People of America.

The difficulty of finding a mutually agreeable term is only one aspect of the reality that this heterogeneous group of very short individuals faces. Group identity is still a work in progress, and historically, dwarfs have felt more ambivalence than have various other minorities about claiming a group identity. One reason is that most of them are different even within their families (whose members are most often average-statured), and consequently would rather identify with these families and with the greater society than with their difference, which has so often brought stigma. On a fantasy level, however, the yearning has sometimes persisted. A good many children and some adults have even wondered whether there might be a community of "my people" existing somewhere. That fantasy is played out in Ruth Park's novel *Swords and Crowns and Rings* when a dwarf boy goes off to explore the hills where his people are supposed to be hidden.

In truth, however, except for some communities of court dwarfs, or remnants of theatrical troupes, there have been no such mysterious communities. The special case of pygmies, who because of their physical characteristics differ from medical or mythical forms of dwarfism, is fascinating in itself—but they are not the doppelgangers that dwarfs or average persons have imagined reside beyond the next hill. Because the history of various pygmy societies is so varied and complex, and has been explored in so many volumes, I have decided not to include them here, rather than to do so and simply offer a cursory synopsis that does not do them justice.

For today's young persons with dwarfism, whose self-awareness develops in a society in which they are physically different from most of their peers, finding a dwarf identity is still an elusive process. For an increasing number of persons, membership in the organization Little People of America may serve to enhance self-image and provide comradeship. It offers socialization and support, affording dwarfs from an early age the opportunity to meet others like themselves and thereby to feel less different and isolated. It helps to know you are not "the only one"—to find friends to talk to who have shared your experience. In recent years, the group has also begun to focus on providing practical resources, illuminating ethical issues, and engendering activism in areas such as promoting building accessibility and getting dwarf-tossing made illegal. (Dwarf-tossing is the "sport" in which patrons of bars pay to see how far they can throw a dwarf.)

However, the majority of dwarfs still do not belong to any dwarfism organizations, and even for those who do, obtaining information about their history has not been easy. Until recently, there were few books about dwarfs, and some of those that did exist contained factual errors and demonstrated an alienated view of their subject matter. Accounts by dwarfs themselves were extremely rare: in the eighteenth century, the Polish court dwarf Boruwlaski published an official autobiography; in the nineteenth, Lavinia Warren wrote about her life with her husband, Tom Thumb.

Finally, toward the end of the twentieth century and during the first decade of the twenty-first, there were encouraging signs. A few thoughtful, revealing memoirs by dwarfs appeared; among these works were Pieral's *Vu d'en Bas*, Angela Van Etten's *Dwarfs Don't Live in Doll Houses*, and Matt Roloff's *Against Tall Odds*, as well as Tom Shakespeare's interesting, forthright chapter in *Invented Identities*. In the 1980s Joan Ablon, a medical anthropologist, wrote *Little People in America* and *Living with Difference*, two admirable in-depth studies of dwarfs and their families, making sure that their own voices were heard. In 2003, just before this volume went to press, Dan Kennedy, a journalist who is the father of a young dwarf daughter, published *Little People;* part memoir, it includes engaging interviews and a discussion of issues relevant to dwarfs.

Three other contemporary works bear mention. *Small People—Great Art*, translated from the German, is principally an art book, with beautifully produced reproductions. It is not available in bookstores in the United States. Another German book, *Die Zwerge kommen!* contains some interesting descriptive material and rare prints, but focuses heavily on "dwarf kitsch"—garden dwarfs and comic sketches. Although the French work *Les nains* contains very valuable historical material, unfortunately it also passes on a good bit of misinformation. One important advance is that medical centers and dwarfism support groups have published valuable material for persons with a variety of diagnoses.

Some of the truest accounts so far are offered in a number of respectful, often moving documentaries that have recently appeared on cable television. These works reflect a growing interest among independent filmmakers and their audiences and have been extremely significant both for persons with restricted growth and for members of the general public who, because of their limited personal experience with dwarfs, had previously associated them either with circus performers and other entertainers or with mythological creatures—ageless and eternal beings from a different world. In addition, at least one novel with a dwarf protagonist has appeared in each of the past several years. There has recently been an enormous upsurge in interest in the situation of dwarfs in countries around the world—with organizations of "little people" forming in places as diverse as Chile and Korea. Clearly, the dramatic social changes that are occurring demand that attention be paid in new ways.

Still, thoughtless slurs occur routinely. A liberal comedian like Elaine May entitles her play about a hapless man with a midlife crisis *Taller Than a Dwarf*. Frank Rich, liberal *New York Times* commentator on contemporary culture, comments that had Elian Gonzalez been less cute—had he looked like Herve Villechaise (the dwarf actor), for example—there would have been no national political crisis about returning him to his father and Cuba. The Internet offers up inane "dwarf joke" and dwarf pornography sites. For this community, political correctness remains light years away.

As the experiences of other minority groups have shown, bigotry is relentless: struggles to diminish it resurface in each generation. Because dwarfs until recently were isolated from one another, protests of any kind were far more rare for them than for other groups. Still, one can find evidence of lone voices who have demanded just treatment. I came upon one such voice in a wonderful article called "Charles Dickens Gets a Lesson in Sensitivity: Mrs. Jane Seymour Hill's *Reaction* to *David Copperfield*," by Dr. James Gamble. The author, a Stanford University professor of orthopedics, had discovered an exchange of letters between Hill, a chiropodist who was a dwarf, and Dickens.

The correspondence had been generated by Dickens's use of Hill as a model for the character of Miss Mowcher in his monthly serialization of *David Copperfield* in 1849–1850. Mrs. Hill wrote to Dickens, confronting him about having lampooned her. At her request, he reinvented the character, transforming Miss Mowcher into an articulate, positive heroine. Jane Hill's victory may not have altered nineteenth-century readers' view of little persons, and it certainly did not rally the troops as Rosa Parks would rally African Americans more than a century later. Although nationalism was sweeping across Europe in the mid-nineteenth century, and feminist and abolitionist activity abounded in the United States, the times were not ripe for a dwarf antidiscrimination movement. How could they be? *Most dwarfs were not even acquainted with a single other person like themselves*. For the present generation, however, Hill's correspondence may serve as a rare stunning example of an early effective act of protest, and an inspiration for future activism.

Hill's is but one of the many previously "lost lives" that deserve to be brought to light. Despite the spate of recent publications by and about dwarfs, this book is the first to attempt to offer a comprehensive account of their place in history. Some chapters are more scholarly; others are more lively or discursive, in keeping with their varied subject matter. Readers need not read them in order but may skip about, favoring their individual interests. In the text I try to capture the essential nature of the many worlds in which dwarfs have lived, in an attempt to offer an informative miscellany about each.

Every one of these worlds harbors ambiguity. The history of dwarfs is a tale without a clear beginning or end. We do not know, for example, when the first dwarfs were born. Shall we mark their beginning with Lucy, the prehistoric three-foot-tall woman whose skeleton the archaeologist Donald Johanson found in Ethiopia? If we do, we are claiming that the early hominids from whom the whole human race descended are the special ancestors of dwarfs. We are probably on safer ground if we begin instead with the eleven-thousand-year-old skeletal remains of a seventeen-year-old dwarf discovered by the anthropologist David Frayer in Romito, Italy, in 1987. The oldest skeleton of a dwarf found until then, it manifested a bone disorder called acromesomelic dysplasia. There is some evidence that this boy had survived because of the special care he had received from other members of his tribe.

It is possible to speculate about prehistory, but recorded history offers a far clearer record. With enough determination and sleuthing, one can unearth stories of dwarf individuals from ancient Egypt through the twentieth century, view the paintings in which they have been celebrated, and confront a vast library of fiction with dwarf characters. The Renaissance world of court dwarfs, when they were objects of fascination and trade, is one of the most fully recorded.

In the past thirty years, dwarfs have created a new world—one in which they approach "normalcy" more closely than in any previous time—often attending college and becoming active in professions and in public life. Because dwarfism organizations now exist, and because individuals benefit from more education, easier travel, and the Internet, they are no longer isolated and voiceless, as they often were in earlier periods. They do not need to become pets at court or display themselves as curiosities in order to survive economically. Most important, new medical knowledge and surgical techniques have allowed them to be much healthier over the course of their lifetimes. Not accepting the judgments of the ignorant as the ultimate truth about themselves, dwarfs have begun to transform for the better what was previously presumed to be their inevitable unfortunate fate or destiny.

What about the future? Will dwarfs disappear? The twentieth century has brought a number of "advances" that give dwarfs choices about changing their own bodies or deciding about their children's. When given at an early age, synthetic growth hormone can now enable some children with growth hormone deficiency (a hypopituitary disorder) to grow enough inches to measure over five feet tall—to be, officially, no longer dwarfs. Similarly, techniques have been developed that can lengthen the arms and legs of adolescent dwarfs who have bone disorders, making these individuals nearly a foot taller. Tests performed in utero can enable some types of dwarf fetuses to be identified, and perhaps aborted. And because the genes for achondroplasia and several other dwarfing conditions have been discovered, the potential for gene replacement in future years exists. In some clinics, procedures are already in place that allow dwarf parents to elect not to have children who would also have dwarfism. Once gene replacement therapy has been perfected, some of the more troubling medical problems that now affect dwarfs may be ameliorated.

A few members of Little People of America have donned "Endangered Species" sweatshirts, thus displaying a barbed wit that combines apprehension and protest. Is it really possible that this new eugenics may eradicate dwarfs from the face of the earth? Not very likely: new mutations will always occur, and dwarfs born to two parents with a recessive gene for a given condition will continue to be born. All the procedures mentioned above are currently extremely expensive. These scientific developments represent dramatic changes, but ultimately they will affect only a small, typically affluent, segment of this community—those individuals with restricted growth who have learned about and have access to the treatments.

Most dwarfs who opt to be parents are equally pleased to have short or average-sized children. Most dwarf teens (making their decisions with family assistance) do not elect to alter their bodies through limb lengthening. But underlying society's offers of the option to change is the premise that it is undesirable to be a dwarf. And even when treatments are sought for medical reasons, most individuals who consider obtaining growth hormone treatment, limb lengthening, or (in the future) gene replacement tend to do so not for health reasons alone. They also want to look closer to "normal," thereby escaping a lifelong struggle with body image and society's prejudices.

Worlds without end. Apart from the historic eras in which dwarfs have lived, and the medical world that willy-nilly they must often rely on, there are also the other worlds—the worlds of myth, stigma, and unconscious psychological associations. These are the areas that represent everyone's conscious and unconscious vulnerability about being rejected by virtue of being considered different, not beautiful, inferior. The internal world without end for individual (often solitary) dwarfs in the past has been their tenacious battle to affirm their own positive self-image and ultimate worth, despite the judgments of others that shortness or irregularly shaped limbs diminish their full humanity. To this personal battle, their advocacy for society's accommodation of difference has now been joined. Because I wanted that struggle to be articulated not only by me, but through the voice of a sentient, insightful short-statured individual who had experienced it, I asked Julie Rotta, the graphics editor of this volume, to write its foreword. No renowned academic authority, it seemed to me, could better express the raison d'être for this volume.

Those of us who are dwarfs or members of their families—or merely informed, empathic human beings—recognize that dwarfs are individuals, not myths, metaphors, or comic relief. This book will offer readers a wealth of new information about their roles in history, the arts, and human consciousness. It will explore why they have inspired fascination, stigma, and abuse in the past, and why the situation has begun to change so dramatically in our own times. I hope that this will be the first of many chronicles of the "small revolution," in which the history of dwarfs is finally approached from a new, more enlightened perspective.

ACKNOWLEDGMENTS

I would like to thank the wonderful companions I met as I traveled from ancient Egypt into the present era. I am grateful, first and foremost, to Julie Rotta, who made the visual component come to life. Together we discussed which photos to include; she designed layouts, scanned images, and tended to countless details. Our discussions of content—our perspectives on dwarfs and the rest of life—added a lively dialogue to the last years of the manuscript's preparation.

Artist Bruce Johnson was a generous friend: he had assembled a marvelous collection of images of dwarfs in contemporary art that he shared with me. For two years he sent old "finds" and new, making discoveries and retrieving better copies as needed. His knowledge and efforts were invaluable in creating a rich chapter on the visual arts. I am also grateful to the executive board of Little People of America for the financial contribution that assured the high quality of the color reproductions. Many other members of the group, not specifically acknowledged here, offered assistance.

My wonderful agent, Sam Stoloff of the Frances Goldin Agency—intelligent, persuasive, and diplomatic—helped me decide to divide my original tome and found me Rutgers University Press. There I was fortunate to meet Melanie Halkias, a superb and supportive editor, who guided me through the preparation process with keen insights and editorial perspicacity. The book's final form owes much to her guidance. Her conviction that *The Lives of Dwarfs* was an important work made a real difference. For rescue missions to judiciously reduce the book's length, and further skillful editorial changes, I am grateful to my friend, poet Gretchen Primack. Writer Sheila Gordon read the manuscript in its early stages, making helpful suggestions; her enthusiasm for the book spurred me on.

Others made important contributions: Professor Mechal Sobel introduced me to Yi-Fu Tuan's *Dominance and Affection*, which helped shape my understanding of court dwarfs; she also led me to Benjamin Lay and Mary Rutherford Garrettson. Tao Jie, Professor of English at the University of Beijing, suggested original material in Chinese and translated it for me; Ethel Ruben sent me her English précis of an acclaimed Danish novel with a dwarf protagonist; John Koos unearthed several valuable, obscure bits of dwarf history; Harry Wieder, who recommended me to the Frances Goldin Agency, was a ready source of information and an indefatigable gadfly. During the final weeks, Ethan Crough assiduously tracked down vital information still outstanding. For her encouragement and friendship during respites at her deer-filled Pennsylvania acres, I am deeply grateful to Marion Leone.

Various persons generously read portions of the work and made useful comments: Dr. James Gamble, Linda Hunt, Neil Pratt, Dr. David Rimoin, Professor Nancy Romer, and Joan Weiss. Dr. David Frayer sent articles relating to his discovery of the eleven-thousand-year-old Romito dwarf. Monica Pratt, former Little People of America Administrator, was wonderfully responsive: she provided statistical information and aided my networking, as well as shared her personal experience. Demographer Berna Miller Torr guided me in interpreting database information about occupations.

I am grateful to the many individuals who contributed their stories, photographs, or both, among them Dr. Judith Badner, Billy Barty, Shawn Brush, Jacqueline Clipsham, Meredith Eaton, Arturo Gil, Ricardo Gil, Linda Hunt, Lee Kitchens, Katherine Koos, Michaela Kuzia, Tekki Lomnicki, Paul Miller, Gregg Rice, Tom Shakespeare, Scott Strasbaugh, Frank Theriault, Eric Tovey, Angela and Robert Van Etten, Corban Walker, William Wheaton, Harry Wieder, and Danny Woodburn.

Others have provided valuable information: Joan Ablon, Nancy Bruett, Steve Delano, Cara Egan, Erik and Hanna Erikson, Simon Minty, Etsuko Enami Nomachi, Natalie and Fabien Pretou, Honor Rawlings, Steve Rukavina, Bethany Jewett Stark, George Sofkin, Dr. Hae-Ryong Song, and Gretchen Worden.

A number of individuals have translated material written in French, German, Spanish, and Italian: Nura Osman, Aviva Briefel, Fay Halpern, Steven Kimball, Karl Buchholz, Lotte Adelson, Nick Weiss, Christobal Lehyt, Francesca Cecchi, and Giovanni Cozzi. Many librarians assisted me at the New York Public Library, the Brooklyn Public Library, the New-York Historical Society, the Historical Society of Pennsylvania, Adelphi University, and Drew University. Especially helpful were Beth Kushner, Assistant Librarian in the Art Reference Library at the Brooklyn Museum; Jonathan Rosenthal of the research department of the Museum of Television and Radio; Linda R. McKee, Director of Library Services at the Ringling Museum of Art in Sarasota, Florida; Janis Olson of the Center for American Studies at the University of Texas at Austin; and Stephan Saks at the New York Public Library.

I am grateful to each and every one. But most of all, I thank my extraordinary husband, Saul, who continued to love me, remained incredibly patient, tended to innumerable book-related details, and made the rest of life run smoothly while I worked and raved and anxiously brought this volume to its happy completion. My beloved children—Anna and her brother David—helped by bringing joy to my life during every stage of theirs. My final "thank you" must be to Anna, for inspiring this book and for her efforts as my formatter and CERT-computer emergency rescue team.

PART I

The Past

SOCIAL CONSTRAINTS

and the

STRUGGLE TO COPE

CHAPTER ONE

History from Ancient Egypt through the Nazi Era

The poetry of history lies in the quasi-miraculous fact that once, on this earth, on this familiar spot of ground, walked men and women, as actual as we are today, thinking their own thoughts, swayed by their own passions, but now all gone, one generation vanishing after another, gone as utterly as we ourselves shall be gone, like ghosts at cock-crow.

—G. M. Trevelyan, *"Autobiography of an Historian"*

While the allure of our distant ancestors' lives is irresistible, their inner experience is rarely accessible. When we try to conjure up previous generations of dwarfs, the situation becomes even more problematic. The early narratives available tend to have been written by casual, biased observers rather than by the protagonists themselves, and they focus almost exclusively on court dwarfs.

The history of dwarfs is embedded in the history of civilization in general. It should not be surprising, then, that along with examples of remarkable achievements, there are all too many instances of the strong taking advantage of the weak and of human differences provoking occasions for dominance and humiliation. While every society has treated dwarfs differently, a historical review leads to an extraordinary finding: the best of times for dwarfs have been the earliest period recorded—the ancient Egyptian kingdoms—and the most recent era in some Western democracies. The worst of times was the Nazi era; the intervening centuries have seen shifting attitudes and individual nuances in each society.

In a few societies, dwarfs were treated with respect and honor; in others, violence and abasement were rampant. Sometimes both treatments coexisted. Dwarfs almost always occasioned some difference in status: they might have been viewed as having a special relationship with the gods, or employed for entertainment. In

every society, there were at least a few individuals who, because of their unique personalities or family background, attained a higher social status than other members
of the group.

Court Dwarfs

For many centuries, in almost every land, those dwarfs whose history was
recorded were employed as court dwarfs—owned, indulged, exploited, traded, and
sent as gifts. Far from representing a single, monolithic experience, each of the courts
offered a milieu that sprang from the character of its monarch and its citizens.

EGYPT

The first court to be considered here is by far the most benevolent. Ancient Egypt
viewed dwarfs as having profound associations with the sacred, yet also offered them
considerable social integration in daily life. Even in this exceptional society, however,
it was the monarch who dictated the roles that dwarfs played. The oldest reference
to a dwarf at court is also one of the most evocative. It is a letter sent on behalf of the
eight-year-old pharaoh Pepi II, or Neferkare, to Harkhuf, leader of the caravans, during the sixth dynasty in Egypt, 2825 to 2631 B.C.E.:

> Thou hast said in this thy letter that thou hast brought a dwarf of divine dances
> from the land of spirits, like the dwarf whom the Treasurer of the God, Ba-ur-
> dad, brought from Punt in the time of King Ysesy. . . . And thou must bring
> with thee this dwarf, alive, sound and well, from the land of the spirits, from
> the dance of the god, to rejoice and gladden the heart of the King of Upper and
> Lower Egypt. . . .When he sleeps at night, appoint trustworthy people who
> shall sleep beside him in the tent; inspect ten times a night. For my Majesty de-
> sires to see this dwarf more than the products of Sinai and Punt.[1]

Why was this dwarf so valued by Pepi, and by King Ysesy? Historian Jean-Pierre
Hallet believes that "a living Pygmy must have seemed like the reincarnated image
of their ancestral gods."[2] When Hallet showed an Egyptian drawing of the god Bes,
protector of childbirth, to his pygmy friends, they recognized similarities to their own
harps, headdresses, and ceremonial tails.

Pepi's letter cautioning that the dwarf be well protected and guarded lends itself
to two interpretations—first, that he is valued; second, that he needs to be watched

constantly lest he escape. He is kidnapped property. This status—the combination of being highly prized, but also the property of an owner—was the defining characteristic of dwarfs' lives throughout the nearly five thousand years that they are known to have been present in the courts of Africa, Asia, and Europe. Egyptian courts seem unique in that they sometimes offered significant roles to dwarfs as priests and courtiers and also as jewelers and as keepers of linen and toilet objects.

That there also existed the potentiality for ridicule is apparent in the fact that in the Instruction of Amenemope it was found necessary to admonish the reader with these words: "Laugh not at a blind man, nor tease a dwarf."[3] But clearly, when wrong attitudes were displayed, the official policy was to attempt to extirpate them. In general, the Egyptians seemed to hold tolerant views toward disability. Physical deformity did not prevent participation in secular or religious functions, as it did in the Old Testament era.[4]

The definitive study of the place of dwarfs in the ancient world is *Dwarfs in Ancient Egypt and Greece*, by Swiss archeologist Veronique Dasen.[5] Her insightful analysis of Egyptian funerary art over the course of more than three millennia suggests that dwarfs achieved considerable respect in that society. Most depictions appear as components of funerary monuments that celebrate the deceased, with the earliest ivory dwarf figurines representing favored attendants. Sometimes their function is symbolic: four dwarfs, near a lizard, serve in later periods as a symbol of regeneration and, as Dasen suggests, protection against evil. Their symbolic association with the gods Bes and Ptah contributed to dwarfs being allowed to participate and even to officiate at religious rites. These gods were widely celebrated in the amulets and rituals of royal and ordinary Egyptians, and consequently, their human counterparts were held in some esteem.

Beginning with the Old Kingdom (2575–2134 B.C.E.), dwarfs are depicted in more than fifty tombs of high officials and royalty. There are signs that dwarfs enjoyed an affectionate relationship with those they served, often acting as personal attendants, keepers of linen, nurses, animal tenders, jewelers, and entertainers. Their elaborate pointed kilts indicate high status. Seen as too precious to perform hard labor, they are mostly shown engaged in indoor activities, though there are several representations of them as bird catchers or as navigating boats.

Probably the most celebrated Egyptian dwarf is Seneb, most likely of the Old Kingdom or somewhat earlier. His body, buried with that of his wife in a mastaba at Giza, has disappeared, but the descriptions on his tomb list twenty titles and offer some window on his career. He was, like many dwarfs, in charge of linen and weaving, overseeing the work of other dwarfs. In addition, he held several positions that put him in charge of ceremonial boats, and he also performed priestly functions. Employed by Kings Khufu and Djedefre, he participated in their funeral services. His three children's names contain parts of these kings' names, in a gesture of respect.

Seneb's advantages may have derived from his having been born into a high-ranking family and having married a woman of high rank, Senetites, a priestess. The tomb shows him in various dignified postures. The limestone statue of Seneb and his family is extraordinary in its depiction of the group—his average-statured wife's arm is around his shoulder in an affectionate pose. That even a high-status dwarf could achieve the positions he did in family, administrative, and religious realms, and be granted a fine memorial mastaba, confirms that he was accepted by the society to a degree that has rarely been achieved by dwarfs since. (See color plate 2.)

Bonnie Sampsell, a former professor of genetics, in a packed, lucid article on this subject, suggests that dwarfs were brought to Memphis and other cities from all over the kingdom.[6] Focusing on several outstanding dwarfs, she also emphasizes the importance of dance in ancient Egyptian ritual and celebrations. Although by 750–332 B.C.E. depictions of dwarfs had become more rare, the renowned Late Period dwarf Djeho was valued as a sacred dancer at festivals and funerals; he was buried at Saqqara in the same pit as his master Tjaiharpta, a high official close to the king—an unusual example of joint burial of master and servant (Fig. 1).

1. Djeho the Dwarf. Relief, 362–360 B.C.E., Egypt. Egyptian Museum, Cairo. Photograph by George B. Johnson/Egyptian Museum, Cairo.

By the time of the Middle Kingdom (1670–1640 B.C.E.), dwarfs were no longer jewelers, bird catchers, or pilots of boats. They were more apt to be personal attendants and nurses, and only rarely entertainers or animal tenders. Dasen conjectures that because of their small hands, female dwarfs may have been particularly valued as midwives. The Bes figures or Ptah-Patakoi amulets that connect them with birth, domestic protection, and craftsmanship become more common in this era. The fact that at least one female dwarf was buried with the jewels, toilet objects, and musical instruments that normally appear in tombs of the elite suggests that female dwarfs continued to enjoy respect.

During the reign of Akhenaton (1353–1336 B.C.E.), there are indications of dwarfs performing jesterlike functions, but also of their being credited with divine connections to the sun god Re. Although dwarfs tended throughout the dynastic period to be in subsidiary roles, such as attendants to the nobility, they were spared the most menial and physically demanding tasks, not just because of their size, but also because their masters' prestige would have been impaired. Dasen is aware that our knowledge of dwarfs outside the courts, and in rural areas, is limited. While some servants may have been free, it is quite possible that many were slaves or in some degree of bondage. Little is apt to become known about those who perished without tombs.

ANCIENT GREECE

Greece captured only modest attention from historians and archaeologists until Dasen's searching study. Probing the written record of Greek philosophy and literature, as well as myriad depictions of dwarfs on pottery, Dasen found evidence of considerable ambivalence in the record. While the few references to short-statured persons that do appear in Greek literature are colored by mockery, some individuals are given credit for wit and courage.

Aristotle, in several treatises, associates dwarfs with animals and children, viewing them as inferior beings. In *De Partibus Animalium,* he concludes that animals, children, and dwarf adults are less intelligent than normal-sized persons, claiming that the greater weight of the upper body interferes with reasoning. Memory is also impaired, and like children and others with large heads, dwarfs sleep too much and are easily fatigued.[7] Aristotle's statements are among the earliest example of intellectualized bias against dwarfs.

Many casual students of history have the impression that the Greeks hard-heartedly rejected physically impaired individuals. Athenian law gave the father power over the newborn; the father could decide whether the child would be accepted into the family in a ceremony or rejected and put in a public place either to die or to be rescued. In Sparta, a newborn deemed to be defective could be taken to Apotheate, a chasm at the foot of Mount Taygetus, and thrown down or abandoned.

What is not clear is how often ordinary mortals conformed to the edicts of philosophers and politicians. While both Plato and Aristotle believed that the ideal state must ensure the existence of physically and mentally fit offspring, to produce a strong elite, in reality parents made the decisions. The myth of the lame god Hephaistos, thrown from Olympus but later rescued, suggests that his "dogfaced" mother is regarded as being devoid of proper feeling.

In fact, there were many persons with congenital handicaps who did survive. Although they might not pass muster in physical selection for games or warfare, if their disability was not too severe, they might still serve in official positions. King Agesilaus, for example, was lame in one foot, and wounded war heroes were exempted from being rejected on the basis of injury or deformity. Because many kinds of dwarfism are not apparent at birth, it seems likely that the majority of dwarfs survived to maturity.

In all probability, despite some discrimination, the situation of dwarfs in Greek society was not bleak. Dasen studies the iconography of dwarfs in the arts and crafts of several periods and painstakingly distinguishes situations that reveal them as servants, entertainers, or in some instances full citizens. Although in many instances, they are depicted on Athenian vase paintings as musicians, dancers, or less frequently acrobats, in some representations they are shown in public places dressed in the manner of ordinary Athenian citizens. On the Peytal aryballos in the Louvre, a dwarf is shown as an assistant, or perhaps a patient, in a doctor's office.

Their function in a religious context is clearer. Countless vase paintings show dwarfs participating in rituals of the Dionysian cult, associated with brief states of ecstasy, sexual wildness, and inebriation. Dwarfs in these pictures are typically assimilated to satyrs—companions to Dionysos—and are depicted as bald men with exaggeratedly large penises, dancing toward female figures and expressing lascivious desire. Some commentators see the connection of dwarfs with Dionysos as positive.[8] As Dasen points out, however, despite their association with virility, satyrs are also often viewed as disappointed lovers—better known for desire than for its fulfillment. While some representations seem respectful, others, such as the vase paintings of southern Italy, offer grotesque dwarf caricatures. There are very few women dwarfs among Greek artifacts, an apparent taboo that resulted from respect, modesty, or discomfort with female deformity.

In an illuminating article, Martha Edwards challenges the stereotype of Greeks as intolerant of physical anomalies; she offers evidence that a wide variety of disabled people were integrated into Greek society, even serving as archoi—high government officials.[9] Charity was inimical to society at that time, and anyone who possibly could was expected to work. While she does not refer specifically to dwarfs, her observations allow us to speculate that at least some dwarfs did find roles in various occupations.

WEST AFRICA

While there is little written material about dwarfs in Africa in the centuries following the Egyptian dynastic period, accounts by travelers to West Africa beginning in the seventeenth century document the fact that dwarfs played significant roles in at least some African courts. Notably in the lands of the Yoruba and Ashanti, and in Benin, they were servants of the king. One seventeenth-century narrator states that the Yoruba viewed dwarfs as "uncanny in some rather undefined way, having a form similar to certain potent spirits who carry out the will of the gods."[10]

This author's description conveys some ambivalence: while he notes that dwarfs are priests and priestesses, he also terms them "unnatural beings, suffering the vengeance of the gods." The Yoruban court assigned them the name Eni Orisa, the possessions of the gods. In Sierra Leone, among the Upper Mendi people, a female dwarf accompanied the chief and was treated with great respect. Often dwarfs, some of them pygmies, served as heralds. While there is no way to prove that these ancient traditions continued uninterruptedly in West Africa over the centuries, it is striking to find similar patterns over time.

CHINA

The courts of China are a study in contrasts. Long before Alexander the Great scoured his kingdom to acquire retinues of dwarfs, the practice of collecting dwarfs as court jesters and entertainers had been introduced in China. Si Maqian, a historian of the Western Han dynasty (about 145 B.C.E.), writes about You Zan, a dwarf actor in the court of the First Emperor of Quin (259–210 B.C.E.). In one anecdote about You Zan's wit and wisdom, Si Maqian describes a banquet during which some rain-soaked guards stood shivering outside the hall: "You Zan took pity on them . . . he leaned against a balustrade and shouted, 'Guards!' When the soldiers responded, You said, 'Look. What's the use of your being big and tall? You have to stand in the rain. Although I'm short and small, I am able to stay inside the hall and have a rest. I am the lucky one in spite of my size.' The emperor heard this and ordered a change of guards so that half of the soldiers could take a rest."[11]

But dwarfs were also exploited, perhaps even sexually. Martin Monestier reports that the emperor Hsuan-Tsung created a palace harem called the Resting Place for Desirable Monsters, which included a number of dwarfs.[12] Because the Silk Road opened China to foreigners from many nations, members of China's royalty were able to seek out dwarf individuals from near and far. At least once, this practice was challenged. During the Western Han dynasty (206 B.C.E.–8 C.E.), the emperor Wu Di had imported many dwarfs to serve the royal family as slaves and entertainers. Yang Cheng, governor of Daozhou province, petitioned the emperor in their behalf, asserting that short people were the emperor's subjects, not his slaves. Moved by the appeal, Wu Di set the dwarfs free, and their grateful families deified Yang Cheng as the God of Luck.[13] Although Yang Cheng's image was worshiped during later dynasties, the practice of collecting foreign dwarfs to serve in the courts persisted, especially during the Tang dynasty (618–907 C.E.).

Even dwarfs who attained high status sometimes met with tragedy. During the Confucian era (c. 551–479 B.C.E.), Confucius himself, having bested a dwarf buffoon and counselor in debate, "to mark the triumph of right, ordered an execution. The tradition of the hagiographers maintains that he had the jesters and the dwarfs cut to pieces: was it not the best means of proclaiming the defeat of a prince who was disloyal and an enemy to the rites, who could only have a dwarf and a jester for his minister?"[14]

THE INCA KINGDOM

Only recently have archeologists begun to unravel the history of Mayan and Incan civilizations. Even accounts written by sixteenth-century Spanish invaders have only recently been carefully studied. One major work, *The Narrative of the Incas*, by Juan de Betanzos, was translated and published in English in 1996.[15] De Betanzos's chronicle contains the personal experiences and oral traditions passed on to him by his wife, Dona Angelina, an Incan princess.

In a dramatic example of the practice of using dwarfs as scapegoats, the author recounts the trials of Chimbo Sancto, a dwarf captured by Huayna Capac, one of the last of the Incan rulers. After Capac's death, Sancto was among the prisoners paraded in front of the funeral cortege. The grieving lords and ladies attacked him, with the intention of ripping him to pieces; they railed about the injustice of the Sun taking from them their wonderful ruler, who loved them all, and sending them instead a "miserable and luckless wretch who had not enjoyed the luck of being a man."[16]

Men accompanying the cortege saved Sancto from a number of women who were assaulting him. Later, however, these same men imprisoned him and his companions among tigers, lions, bears, and serpents, as was the custom, so that they might be eaten. Somehow the prisoners survived, and as a result of this miracle the men of Cuzco offered them honors and land in the Valley of Yucay. Sancto was given women so that he might produce descendants, and in fact he did have children, including two daughters and some "men of good stature."

ANCIENT ROME

In the Roman courts, dwarfs were famously prominent, employed in gratifying the appetite of royalty for both violence and lasciviousness.[17] Numerous accounts depict the participation of dwarfs as gladiators; they were forced to vie with one another and were also sometimes mismatched with Amazons. A beautiful Amazon hurled at least one dwarf across the arena for the amusement of onlookers. In the reign of Domitian (81–96 C.E.), wealthy women observed the dwarf gladiators during training and selected some to take home for a day or two to participate in erotic games.

Julia, the daughter of Augustus, is mentioned as having two dwarfs, a male named Canopas and a female named Andromeda, who assisted her in dressing. Beyond that, she is called "nymphomaniac and curious about novel experience," retaining whole troupes to draw from when she wished to satisfy her desires. She was not alone. Dwarfs, wandering naked except for jewels, were not an uncommon sight in the homes of the wealthy. In one tale Domitian pitches his stiletto at flies, and his favorite dwarf then retrieves the dagger for him. Later, that same dwarf fell into disfavor and Domitian, using a bow and arrow, shot him, piercing his arms and pinning them to the wall.

Occasionally, one reads of dwarfs in the Roman era respected for their accomplishments—among them Marcus Tublius and Marcus Maximum, both less than three feet tall, who were enrolled in a chivalric order and famed for their wisdom. But for the most part, the Roman courts collected dwarfs as oddities who could be exploited at their masters' whim. The Romans are also credited with initiating the practice of artificially crippling young children in order to stunt their growth and increase their value as freak commodities.[18] Although this practice is said to have resurfaced later in Europe, it is impossible to determine how frequently it really did occur.

ITALY

By the Italian Renaissance, violence abated but was replaced by a different sort of insensitivity, as can be seen in the court of Isabella d'Este, marchioness of Mantua (1474–1539), who owned vast collections of classical writings, paintings, sculptures, gold and silver objects, and majolica.[19]

Isabella's attitude toward her dwarfs resembled her attitude toward her other unique, valuable possessions. She created for them a group of small, low-ceilinged rooms, connected by staircases and scaled to size—designed not simply for the accommodation they afforded the dwarfs, but also to provide a proper backdrop for their display. Dwarfs were also useful as precious gifts. When Isabella's brother Alfonso was ill, she sent her favorite dwarf, Matello, to amuse him. Alfonso wrote to Isabella, saying that Matello's visit was better than receiving the gift of a castle.[20] Isabella was also interested in breeding exemplary dwarfs. In a letter to her friend Renee's lady-in-waiting, Isabella mentions having promised to give a dwarf to Renee, commenting, "She is now able to walk alone and without a guide, if the Duchess wishes to have her."[21] Isabella sent a dwarf to her daughter-in-law, Ferrante Gonzaga's wife, remarking that she was "the sweetest and gentlest creature in the world, and afforded her endless amusement."[22] There is no evidence of any royal sensitivity to how the families of these dwarfs might react to the departure of their children.

George Marek, in *The Bed and the Throne*, comments that it is difficult to assess what passed for entertainment. He describes the dwarfs as "skilled freaks turning somersaults, dancing and singing in falsetto voices, but their wit seems to have been fairly witless, at least as it comes down to us. . . . One Matello (probably a made-up name, *matto* = crazy), whom she called 'the Emperor of the madmen,' used to don a priest's cassock, waddle into the hall, and harangue the company with unctuous sermons. Typically Italian it would be even today: They were in awe of the Church but mocked the churchmen; they kissed the Pope's foot and made mouths at him behind his back."[23]

Less amusing are the antics of Isabella's dwarf "Crazy Catherine," an alcoholic who stole from time to time. Her misdeeds were overlooked because she was "merry and devoted to her mistress" and would lift her skirt and "make water" when someone in the company asked her to. "That," writes Marek, "was considered hilarious." Seeing dwarfs in ridiculous postures offered observers the chance to discharge in laughter their relief that this creature was "not us."

There sometimes did exist genuine feeling between master or mistress and servant. Isabella nursed Matello in his final illness, grieved a great deal over his death, and buried him in the family crypt. In keeping with Matello's role as the dwarf of a great patron of the arts, Antonio Tebaldeo wrote his epitaph, the poet Antonio Cammelo (called Il Postoia) composed an elegy, and Andrea di Bonsignore painted his portrait.[24] But neither his real name nor any details about his personal life come down to us; we only know how his royal audience perceived him.

One of the first descriptions I had read about Isabella d'Este referred to the apartments that she had created for her dwarfs. The Palazzo Ducale, where they resided, was in its time the largest palace in Europe. When E. J. Wood wrote *Giants and Dwarfs* in 1868, their section of the building had already long since been empty.[25] On a brief trip to Italy in 1998, I detoured to Mantua largely because I was eager to see the apartments in the Palazzo Ducale, home of the Gonzaga dynasty, and the famous Andrea Mantegna fresco *Parete della Corte Reunita*. The docent at the palazzo reported that the dwarf quarters that I had asked about were closed for repair, but allowed me to peer down into the small central lobby, containing the staircase and doorways of the rooms to the tiny, quite plain, marble suite.

Although disappointed at not being able to see more, I nevertheless found myself transfixed, and remained standing there for a long while. I was conscious of having arrived at my destination—the point of the journey being not simply the architecture, but carrying out the pilgrimage. *For they had actually lived here.* Silently, I communicated to them why I had come. Later, I walked about the Piazza delle Erbe, the charming central square nearby, and felt the vitality of this city—still in many respects the wealthy village it had always been. Among its transformations was the absence of the dwarfs who had formerly abounded there.

FRANCE

The courts of France manifested many of the same characteristics as those of the Italian kingdoms. Catherine de Médicis, queen of France in the sixteenth century, entertained a veritable passion for dwarfs—some of them, purchased in Africa, are said to have cost her dearly; others she received as gifts from the king of Poland. In a typical incident, Claire Eugenie, infante d'Espagne, traveled to France with a gentleman who brought a dwarf in a covered birdcage. He told the queen that he had a parrot that could speak in five or six languages. Only after a voice had been heard pronouncing well-turned phrases in French, Italian, English, Dutch, and Spanish did he remove the cover, revealing a female dwarf. The assembled court responded with unbridled enthusiasm.[26]

SPAIN

The court of Spain had the character of a chivalric, contentious family. Although thousands of servants were maintained there, they were typically not exposed to the public eye. Domestic ritual dominated the life of the court, and Philip IV's biographer, John H. Elliot, termed him a "prisoner of ceremony."[27]

In an excellent essay about Spanish dwarfs, Alice McVan notes that they were already well ensconced in the court by the thirteenth century.[28] She describes one elaborate banquet at which the centerpiece was a castle tower from which a dwarf appeared, waving a flag, blowing a horn, and reciting a welcoming poem. Spanish dwarfs were showered with gifts of jewelry, gold and silver, elegant clothing and furs, saddles, and the funds to pay for their weddings.

The extraordinary paintings of Diego Velázquez have made the dwarfs of Spain among the best known. In his painting *Las Meninas,* one can sense how intertwined were the lives of the royalty and the dwarfs depicted. The court's strictness and formality made especially welcome the relief that dwarfs provided. When Mariana, Philip's young second wife, arrived at the Spanish court from Austria at the age of fifteen, she laughed rudely at the antics of a dwarf, for which she was firmly reproached by the ladies of the court.[29]

Dwarfs played a part in all the significant experiences of the royal family. They escorted the queen on her convent visits; they went riding with the king; they played with the children. Dwarfs occasionally received an education that average persons did not, and some were respected for their talent and intellect; El Primo, painted by Velázquez, was assistant secretary and keeper of the king's seal.[30] The wife of the French ambassador describes Louisillo, a dwarf cherished by the king, as "having a beautiful face, with a spirit more than one can imagine; he is wise and knowledgeable."[31]

Still, brilliant dwarfs lived side by side with cretins, and there were often feuds between dwarfs and other servants. If dwarfs wanted to retain favor they had to tread cautiously, as Frances Zuñiga, one of the most famous Spanish dwarfs, was to discover.[32] Zuñiga, commonly referred to by the diminutive Francesillo, was originally a tailor. He was married, was the father of two children, and had a Jewish background.[33] He has left a rare written record of at least a portion of his experience in his letters and in his most famous work, the *Cronica burlesca*, a satirical account of the Spanish court in the sixteenth century.[34]

Some of the letters suggest that Francesillo had an easy, close relationship with many of the gentry he corresponded with; many of his writings, however, are spiked with acerbic comments. In one example, he charges that the archbishop has been occupied with the breasts of the wife of Juan de Aldana.[35] In a letter to Queen Leonor, engaged to the king of France, Francesillo teasingly threatens to challenge the king to a duel so that he may claim the fair Leonor.[36] Indeed, in the most personal part of the *Cronica burlesca*, the last will and testament, which forms the work's introduction, Zuñiga refers frequently to his amorous relationships and bequeaths the memory of his love to several women with whom he has been involved.[37] He writes, "I doubt that God will complete punishing me up there, after having begun to do it down here, for the iniquities of love that were actually not love."[38]

His writings contain several laudatory catalogs of his attributes, describing him as, among other things, "the little Frances, by the grace of God master of philosophy, bachelor of medicine, enemy of the heretic Luther, general enquirer into current affairs, friend of fickle men, reformer of hospitals for the insane."[39] At another time he portrays himself as "like one of the little men on the clock of Valdeglesias."[40] He focuses upon the physical characteristics of others, calling one man "a fat white ox fed in the middle of the country" and commenting that another's face "resembled the buttocks of the baker woman from the alcade of Bribexia."[41] One wonders how Zuñiga's own sensitivity about his body may have contributed to these assaults on others' appearance.

Zuñiga was not spared punishment for his caustic tongue. Originally a favorite, he had used his sharp wit on the emperor and offended him; the general antipathy toward his *Cronica* led to his temporary exile from court. Zuñiga had endured the beatings that were an occupational hazard and had written, "It is for their hands to give and my body to receive."[42] Always the butt of jokes because of his figure and miserable situation, he was finally cornered and stabbed to death, allegedly by Marquis de Benaventes, in an attack instigated by the very buffoonery that had constituted his livelihood.[43] Until the end, his wit did not fail him. As he lay dying, his friend Perico de Ayala approached and solemnly asked Francesillo to pray for him on the dwarf's entering heaven. "Tie a string around my finger," said the jester, "so that I don't forget."[44]

ENGLAND

There were few courts as welcoming to dwarfs as those of the British. Jeffery Hudson, one of the most famous, was born in 1619, the son of a father who was the keeper of baiting bulls for the duke of Buckingham. When Jeffery was eight, his father presented him to the duchess; the following year, when King Charles and Queen Henrietta Maria visited, Jeffery was concealed in a cold baked pie. The pie was cut open, and he was offered as a present to an overjoyed queen.[45]

The young Jeffery was apparently much spoiled at court, and there are endless tales of his antics with monkeys and with William Evans, the court giant. Whatever the truth of the statement, *Gentleman's Magazine* reported, "The ladies were very fond of him. He could make married men cuckolds without making them jealous, and Mothers of the Maids, without letting the World know they had any Gallants."[46]

Some accounts of his activities strain credulity. When he was eleven, he traveled to France to bring back a skilled midwife for the queen. The French queen, Marie de Médicis, an aficionada of dwarfs, gave him expensive presents for himself and her royal daughter. When Dutch privateers boarded his ship on the way home, he was said to have resisted valiantly; although he and the midwife did not arrive in England in time for the baby's birth, he received much acclaim. Hudson was involved in many other escapades and adventures, among them a duel in which he slew a Captain Crofts; service in the Civil Wars, in which he served bravely; and being taken prisoner by Barbary pirates. Later, he remained loyally by the queen's side when she was forced into exile in France, returning with her at the Restoration. Sir Walter Scott described some of Hudson's adventures in his novel *Peveril of the Peaks*, and numerous portraits of him exist. Hudson's adoption by the court afforded him the opportunity for a life of excitement far beyond anything that his original destiny—living out his days on his father's farm—would have granted. His story, like that of few other dwarfs from the past, continues to capture the interest of modern readers.[47]

The renowned miniature painter Richard Gibson was another dwarf at the court of Charles I.[48] As Gibson became an increasingly accomplished artist, he was

2. Peter the Great at the Marriage Feast of His Favorite Dwarf. *Engraving, c. 1712. Frontispiece in Edgar Saltus,* The Imperial Orgy: An Account of the Tsars from the First to the Last *(New York: Boni and Liveright, 1920).*

employed to teach Queen Anne to draw and was later sent to Holland to instruct her sister, the princess of Orange. In a wedding celebrated in a poem by seventeenth-century poet Edmund Waller, Gibson was married to Anne Shepherd, a woman who like himself was three feet ten inches tall. Waller focuses on this felicitous similarity in height in a poem that begins, "Design or chance, make others wive; But Nature did this match contrive . . ."[49] Horace Walpole writes, "The small couple had nine children, five of which lived to maturity, and were of a proper size." This last phrase was apparently a common one. Richard lived to be seventy-five, Anne eighty-nine, and they had a daughter, a son, and a nephew who became painters.

RUSSIA

Nowhere are dramatic contrasts in treatment more noticeable than in the courts of Russia. Although mentioned in earlier centuries, Russian court dwarfs reached their greatest prominence in the sixteenth through eighteenth centuries. Peter the Great is described as extremely fond of dwarfs, keeping up to a hundred at a time. Occasionally they were treated with tenderness; for example, when the dwarf who prepared food for and bathed the czarina fell ill, the czarina took care of her.[50]

The wedding of Peter's niece, Anna Ivanovna, and the duke of Courland was planned simultaneously with that of the royal dwarf Iakim Volkov, taking place on 14 November 1710 (Fig. 2).[51] Peter's sister Natalie invited the courts' own dwarfs as well as others gathered from all over the realm for a great ball. At the banquet for Anna, two dwarfs popped out of the centerpiece and danced the minuet on the table under the candelabra and amid the gold platters. For the dwarfs' marriage, a caravan of small carriages and Shetland ponies proceeded through the streets of Moscow accompanied by music.[52] At the church, the czar himself performed the same ceremony he had for Anna, delicately placing a wreath of flowers on the bride's head. Afterward, the group continued on to a sumptuous banquet at Natalie's palace.

One of Natalie's interests was the reproduction of dwarfs. However, after the death of the dwarf bride, it was recognized that sometimes childbirth could be hazardous to dwarfs and at other times result in average-statured offspring. As a result, Peter banned marriages between dwarfs for a time.[53] The court's capriciousness is reflected in the arrangements that were made for the 1714 wedding of the eighty-year-old jester Zotov. Four stammerers did the inviting, decrepit old people led the bride, and obese men led the groom. A mute and blind priest performed the service, and the whole wedding party undressed the couple in their nuptial chamber.[54] Clearly, the perverse amusement of the guests, not the couple's wishes, governed the celebration.

Anna Ivanovna herself did not live happily ever after. Capable, like her uncle, of strange caprices, she later married off a lover to an impoverished lady-in-waiting—a hunchbacked dwarf who loved him. The group would sometimes dine together in this ménage à trois.[55]

Peter's treatment of dwarfs was consistent with his character. Coarse and uneducated, he could show his anger at an insubordinate general by striking him furiously with a sword—and shortly afterward, all smiles, dance exuberantly. Even dwarfs who were favored could hardly expect predictable treatment from a monarch who sent his first wife to a nunnery and had his son killed. Residing in Peter's court has been described as like traveling on Mount Vesuvius, and from moment to moment waiting for the eruption of uncontrollable forces under one's feet.[56] Nevertheless, the attention given dwarfs in his court spilled into the nobility, and there was scarcely a wealthy Russian family that did not include a dwarf or two.

THE COURT DWARF AS
FAITHFUL SERVANT, WARRIOR, OR COLORFUL FIGURE

Despite the differences between the courts, there are several themes that span nations and centuries. One is the loyalty of court dwarfs, several of whom followed their masters or mistresses—among them Christian II of Denmark; Eudoxia, the wife of Peter the Great; and Marie de Médicis—to prison.[57] Marie's dwarf protected her, nursed her through illness, and begged in the streets for money to sustain her, keeping her identity hidden so as not to shame her. She died before he did, was pardoned, and was given a royal funeral. The French chronicler of dwarfs, Edouard Garnier, assumes that her dwarf met an ignominious end.

Another court-dwarf stereotype that crosses culture and time is that of the heroic warrior. The impressive Jeffery Hudson had even more formidable predecessors, such as Casan, the dwarf of Genghis Khan; and Corneille of Lithuania, who was a member of the court of Charles V of Spain.[58] Finally, there are the anecdotes about colorful personalities. Frequently mentioned are Juan d'Estrix, a Belgian who was added to the retinue of the duke of Parma in 1592 and was an excellent linguist and a ladies' man; Mr. Ramus, who accompanied the English ambassador to Vienna in 1678 and spoke so eloquently in Latin that the emperor gave him a gold chain and medal;[59] and Richebourg (1768–1858), who was in the service of the mother of Louis Philippe and who pretended to be a baby in the care of a nurse, but carried military secrets in his cap.[60]

Do we care? Most of these anecdotes involve "accomplishments" that would not merit notice had they been achieved by someone taller than four feet. Almost never revealed is the person behind the mannequin. Thankfully, there are two eighteenth-century dwarfs who have written their autobiographies. The first, Peter Prosch (1745–1789), a Tyrolean dwarf who served Prince Friedrich of Hohenlohe-Bartenstein, wrote movingly of the travails of his impoverished childhood, his interesting experiences in several European courts, and his effort, despite painful humiliations, to find comfort through trust in God.[61] Married with children and quite tiny, he was judged to have had a likely diagnosis of isolated growth hormone deficiency. Prosch's memoir is not available in English, although a brief account of it is given in *Small People—Great Art*.[62] We do have, however, an autobiography in English by one of the most interesting court dwarfs of all times, Count Joseph Boruwlaski.[63]

COUNT JOSEPH BORUWLASKI

The Polish dwarf Joseph Boruwlaski (1739–1837) was the third of six children—five boys and a girl—three of whom were average statured and three extremely short (Fig. 3). *Count* was not an official title, but one he was playfully assigned in his noble household. Boruwlaski was two feet eleven inches at twenty-five years old and three feet three inches at thirty. His short-statured brother managed an estate; his short-statured sister died of smallpox at twenty-two.

The family lived near Staristina de Caorliz, who took Joseph to live with her when he was a child, despite his mother's tears. After Staristina married, a friend suggested that the couple's child might be born dwarfed as a result of their looking at Joseph. Whether truly alarmed or not, they gave Joseph to the friend, Countess Humieska, when he was fifteen. He remained with her well into adulthood, for the most part happily. He was taught various skills, among them dancing and playing the guitar, and was well regarded. But Boruwlaski was nonetheless sensitive to the paradoxes implicit in his situation, noting that he labored under painful feelings and that he was looked upon as "an animated toy." Once, he overheard a discussion between the countess and her

3. *The Polish court dwarf Count Joseph Boruwlaski. Oil on canvas. Durham City Council, Durham, England.*

friends in which the company debated whether dwarfs could have children. The countess remarked on "how pleasant it would be to join these two little creatures, that the result might decide the question."[64]

Joseph wept bitterly upon hearing this; despite the countess's denials of having any intention to perform such an experiment, it was apparent that like so many of the aristocracy, she experienced dwarfs as merely adjacent to humanity, as somehow other and inferior—a hybrid of human and animal. When Boruwlaski fell in love with an average-statured woman, his benefactor disapproved, and he was forced to leave the court. But he had already demonstrated his strength in pursuing the courtship: while his attentions were rejected at first, he continued to pursue his Isalina with persuasive letters. He wrote, "It is very true, my dear, that at first sight, the idea of marrying a man of my stature will appear somewhat ludicrous . . . this ridicule, which affrights you, decreases very much when true love is opposed to it, and that through a mutual love we shall soon see it vanish."[65]

Boruwlaski's wisdom, force, and character won him Isalina, but it did not guarantee him an easy existence. For a time, he received a small annuity from Stanislaus II, king of Poland. He attempted to earn additional income while adventuring through Europe, offering his services as an exhibiting dwarf in a discreet and dignified way. He was introduced to the royalty of many countries, and to such celebrities as Voltaire, but he was almost always beset by financial woes. He finally settled in Durham, England, which he liked and where he had many admirers and, some say, additional amorous experiences. However, he concluded his memoir by noting that had he been formed like other mortals, he could have subsisted by means of his energy and labor and been acknowledged as "a man, an honest man, a man of feeling."[66] His health failing, he was now dependent on being rescued by patrons such as Lady Egremont and Princess Lubomirska in order to support himself, his wife, and his children. Boruwlaski has provided us with a rare enduring portrait of a dwarf who bridged a historic moment—the transition from court dwarf to exhibiting dwarf.

UNDERSTANDING THE COURT-DWARF PHENOMENON

Yi-Fu Tuan's *Dominance and Affection: The Making of Pets* is a brilliant exposition of the common characteristics of women, black slaves, fools, dwarfs, and castrati in history. Tuan points out how all these groups have functioned to aggrandize their masters. Both blacks and dwarfs are often given absurdly grandiose names, such as Socrates or Alexander the Great, that highlight their inferiority; dwarfs in particular are given such names as Bebe and Joujou (toy) or are called by diminutives ending in *illo* (little) that make it hard to take them seriously.

Tuan hypothesizes that despite their close physical proximity to dwarfs, members of the aristocracy enjoyed a social distance that allowed them to feel a mixture of charitable feeling and amusement. Had the relationship been closer, he asserts, the gentry would have found the deformity too painful—further apart, the sympathy and sense of fun would have been lost. He suggests that the profusion of dwarfs—in some courts there were as many as a hundred—can be explained as a kind of conspicuous consumption. In previous centuries, a sizable harem, a plantation overflowing with slaves, a court with a dwarf servant behind each chair were all signs of wealth and importance.

The women, the slaves, the dwarfs—all could be indulged, abused, or ignored at the master's or mistress's pleasure. Actions like the contemplated dwarf mating that was deplored by Boruwlaski must be viewed in this context. "Despite the horror of an act from a victim's standpoint, the doer may not have been aware of his own cruelty because to him the victim has little or no interest and is barely a part of his visible landscape. . . . Power, however, can be directed towards the ends of pleasure, adornment and prestige."[67]

Although the court dwarf phenomenon had largely disappeared with the decline of monarchy, much later instances have occasionally been reported of tyrants who exploited dwarfs. Joseph Stalin is said to have had a dwarf named Eyov, known as "the bloody dwarf," whom he employed in his reign of terror;[68] Joaquín Videla Balaguer, the ruthless strongman who was president of the Dominican Republic for twenty-two years, was described in 1996 as living in a strange and curious household that included "two female dwarfs, kept as mascots but who to this day are part of his retinue, and a pair of aggressive collies that, when they bit you, you had no choice but to sit there and smile."[69]

Exhibiting Dwarfs

By the end of the eighteenth century, court life was becoming less ostentatious, and court dwarfs rare. Many who would previously have served royalty turned instead to exhibiting themselves for money. Although they attained autonomy rather than being owned by others, a new question presented itself: how could the self-exhibitors come to terms emotionally with offering themselves to be gaped at publicly?

The answer is simply that it provided them with a living that was far better than obtainable through any other means open to them. And when they could, they attempted to supplement mere peculiarity with some ostensible talent, enabling them to believe that the audience valued them for their stellar performances. Whatever their skills, their popularity was quite great, achieving its height in the 1700s and persisting throughout the nineteenth and to some degree even into the twentieth centuries in traveling fairs and circuses. At one end of the spectrum was Owen Farrel, an eighteenth-century Irish dwarf who at first served a colonel in Dublin as a footman. Because he had proved himself able to perform feats of strength that were amazing for one his size—supposedly carrying four men, two astride each arm—he was persuaded to exhibit himself. His traveling days were brief, however, and he ended up ragged and unkempt, an object of ridicule, begging in the streets of London. In return for a weekly allowance, he sold his body to a Mr. Omrod, a surgeon, who placed Farrel's skeleton in the museum of the duke of Richmond; it was later removed to the University of Glasgow.[70]

At the other end of the spectrum was Matthew Buchinger, a dwarf with stunted arms and legs, who was born in Germany in 1674. Using the portion of his extremities that remained, he became an accomplished calligrapher and artist. He supported himself by selling his artwork. One of his most famous productions was an exquisite self-portrait, in which he wove within his curls several psalms. This work was later converted into an engraving that fetched the substantial sum of fifty guineas.

4. Exhibiting dwarfs Nannette Stocker and John Hauptman. From R. S. Kirby, Kirby's Wonderful and Eccentric Museum (London: London House Yard, 1804–1820), vol. 5.

Buchinger was married four times and fathered eleven children. One of his wives was supposedly insulting and abusive. Finally, Buchinger lost patience and beat her soundly, not letting her get up until she promised to mend her ways—which apparently she did. His accomplished progeny included a grandson described as the best lutenist in England.[71]

Throughout the nineteenth century, exhibiting dwarfs continued to draw crowds. Among the most renowned were three-foot-six-inch John Hauptman and three-foot-three-inch Nanette Stocker (Fig. 4). An Austrian, Stocker began touring throughout continental Europe in 1797 and was quite successful; she met Hauptman, a native of Germany, in 1798. They developed an act that featured Stocker at the pianoforte, Hauptman at the violin, and the two of them waltzing together. Well received, they traveled together for some years. Stocker is supposed to have been engaging and personable, Hauptman more reserved and stolid. According to R. S. Kirby, he proposed to her but was declined "for reasons known only to herself."[72]

There were exhibiting-dwarf couples who enjoyed more than partnerships of convenience. One exceptionally happy couple was Robert and Judith Skinner. They met while both were on tour for a week in the same town. Robert initiated a correspondence that developed into an exchange of love letters.[73] Finally, hearing that Judith was to be exhibited in London, Robert rushed there from Liverpool, and they were married the following week in the historic church St. Martin's in the Field.[74]

Since neither of them liked exhibiting, they retired to Chelsea, where they raised fourteen average-statured children. That Judith could have survived this number of births at a time when Caesarian sections—often necessary for women so small to give birth to average-size children—were not available, remains something of a mystery. But contemporary accounts attest to the fact that she did so, with all the children surviving to maturity. Only in 1742, with their savings exhausted, did it become necessary for them to return to exhibiting in London—this time with their children—making use of the dramatic contrasts in this large family in which the youngsters towered over the parents. In two years they were able to amass the equivalent of $110,000, enough to allow them to retire permanently.

There were other exhibiting dwarfs who felt a sense of shame and did not endure long in that world. They could not tolerate the ridicule, which reached its apotheosis in a poem by the seventeenth-century French poet Jean Loret, excerpts from which are translated as

These last days came to die
An incomparable cutie
Who was perceived as an admirable thing
Whom we went to see again and again . . .
The dwarf of Mademoiselle,
Whose very sickly little body
Is now among the dead . . .
In this underground grave
Lies a dwarf {more than dwarflike};
But I am wrong to speak in this way;
She no longer lies here.
This grave does not contain anything
Since two very scant earthworms
Made of her a scant meal
On the very same day as her death.[75]

The dwarf Loret refers to came to France when Marie Thérèse, the daughter of Philip IV of Spain, married Louis XIV in 1660. Today, most people would experience some discomfort at being asked to pay money to gawk at what we now term persons with disabilities, much less to pay an extra shilling to touch nine-year-old Caroline Crachimi, who, at 1 foot 10 1/2 inches, was perhaps the smallest person who ever lived.[76]

In *Memoirs of Bartholomew Fair*, published in England in 1859, Henry Morley describes English fairs, among the primary places where many dwarfs exhibited themselves from the twelfth to the nineteenth century, noting, "The Kings and Queens of Europe in the years before and after 1700, shared in the taste of all classes for men who could dance without legs, dwarfs, giants, hermaphrodites and scaley boys. . . . The taste for Monsters became a disease, of which the nation has in our day recovered with a wonderful rapidity." Fairs exaggerated their statistics and invented exotic backgrounds. A handbill at Bartholomew Fair in 1792 declared that "the Author of Nature is wonderful even in the Least of His Works," in this instance the "works" being Mr. Thomas Allen and Miss Morgan, the latter the celebrated Windsor Fairy, called Lady Morgan, a title the king and queen had conferred on her after pronouncing her "the finest Display of human nature in miniature they ever saw." Their compliment to her was returned, in phrases such as those invoked by exhibiting dwarfs through several reigns, in which they refer to themselves as "the SMALLEST subjects of the GREATEST King!"[77]

The imprimatur of royalty was much sought after, enhancing the asking price of the exhibitor. Mr. Simon Paap, the celebrated Dutch dwarf, offered his statistics—twenty-six years old, twenty-seven pounds in weight, twenty-eight inches high—and spoke of having had the honor of being presented to the entire English royal family in 1815. In the course of four days in Smithfield, England, twenty thousand people paid to see him.

In 1790, another famous Dutch dwarf, Wybrand Lolkes, a skilled jeweler and watchmaker, exhibited himself at Bartholomew Fair, after his business in Rotterdam failed. He lasted only one season at Bartholomew before returning home to try his hand at his trade again.[78] Such experiences were much more common than permanent careers, given the hardships of traveling and the degree of competition.

Not every participant was a willing volunteer, though, as a nineteenth-century account demonstrates. Its title, containing the phrase "Written By Himself" is misleading: it is a brief third-person account by an anonymous author.[79] It describes one Che-Mah, supposedly just over two feet tall, who was a musician and an excellent conversationalist and who spoke many languages. From an aristocratic Chinese family, he was abducted and brought to England. Immensely popular there, he met the Prince of Wales and Prime Minister Gladstone; later he visited the United States and

France, where he was introduced to Napoleon III and was exhibited before twenty-one thousand people in a single day. A man with family, employment, and respect in his own country, he had been turned into a curiosity. No doubt his kidnappers, like those who brought the dancing dwarf to Pepi II in ancient Egypt, rationalized their actions by praising his talents. Che-Mah's feelings go unrecorded.

Providing a comprehensive, perceptive analysis of similar cases of self-display in the United States, Robert Bogdan, in *Freak Show*, describes in great detail the growth in the eighteenth and nineteenth centuries of an industry that took advantage of the insularity of countries; he discusses the phenomenon of human exhibits, which, like those of animals, were offered to the public as exciting curiosities. In 1716 the first lion was exhibited, the first gorilla only after 1850. One of the oldest records of an American human exhibit is that of a Carolina dwarf, who is described in 1738 as having been "taken in a wood at Guinea; 'tis a female about four foot high, in every part like a human excepting her head which nearly resembles the ape."[80]

There were both "born freaks"—dwarfs, giants, and Siamese twins—and "made freaks," such as tattooed ladies. In addition, there were fake oddities, among them spurious Siamese twins who were actually two brothers in a single pair of trousers. Although human exhibits—in later years called sideshows or freak shows—have largely disappeared, there have been indications of a mild resurgence of the phenomenon. Dick Zigun, a graduate of the Yale School of Drama, regards the sideshow as an authentic American art form. He has produced his Sideshow by the Seashore in Coney Island from 1985 to the present. Among the few remnants of a long tradition, it has featured a female snake charmer, a sword swallower, a tattooed man, and an elderly man "made of rubber" who could make his abdomen do tricks, as well as a clown referred to as a "midget," a word that is anathema to most dwarfs today.[81]

Some performances, redolent of those of the past, have featured an affable individual with severe disabilities who joined the sideshow long ago when no other choice seemed possible.[82] Others display a new political correctness: instead of the old-style "fat lady," Katy Dierlan, a five-hundred-pound actress billed as "Helen Melon," assails body stereotyping.[83] Most Coney Island performances play to quite small, but enthusiastic, working-class audiences, but the producers have also introduced a traveling sideshow that performs on television and college campuses.

DIME MUSEUMS, LILLIPUTIAN VILLAGES, AND TOURING ENTERTAINERS

The phenomenon of the "dime museum," the small exhibition space and performance hall in which most dwarfs appeared in the mid-nineteenth century, developed from the desire of educators and scientists to display their artistic and natural artifacts. It reached its peak nationwide in the 1880s and 1890s. Because some of those exhibits proved to be dull, living exhibits were added.

J. Mason Warren, a physician renowned for his research in anesthesia who published "An Account of Two Remarkable Indian Dwarfs" in 1851, accepted at face value the exhibitor's statement that the dwarfs were a seven-year-old brother and five-year-old sister from an Indian tribe in South America. It is now thought that they were African Americans born in the United States.[84] Noting that they knew only a few words, he described them as resembling members of the Simian tribe or intelligent individuals of the canine race. Warren's article is not atypical of the science of his time, when exposure to aboriginal cultures was limited. In this atmosphere of ballyhoo and pseudoscience, the fame of these dwarfs spread, as did that of another pair, Waino and Plutano, known as the Wild Men of Borneo and who, like Warren's "Indian" dwarfs, were developmentally disabled.

Besides chronicling the phenomenon of freak shows, Bogdan follows developments in the wider world of entertainment, among whose most renowned figures, known by diminutive or grandiose names, are General Mite, Admiral Dot, Princess Winnie Wee, and General Grant Jr. This period has also been graphically recorded in photographs shown in Roth and Cromie's *The Little People* (1980).[85] Many groups, called "midget companies," flourished in the United States. Two of the largest and most famous originated in Europe: the Horwath Midgets appeared with the Barnum and Bailey Circus in the late nineteenth and early twentieth centuries and also toured on their own; Singer's Midgets were enormously successful, touring the United States between 1910 and 1935.[86] Dozens of others performed in vaudeville extravaganzas, which were more notable for the grand sets and costumes than for the quality of the acting—which tended toward burlesques of such historic figures as Lady Godiva and Napoleon.

Although making a steady living wage required being attached to a midget company, there were also many individuals—almost invariably men—who tried to make their fortune as private self-exhibitors and touring showmen. One of the most popular early entrepreneurs was Major Stevens. In the 1832 "as told to" autobiography—of dubious accuracy—written by Stevens's friend Robert Treat Hooten, Stevens describes himself as the son of a cobbler, as three feet tall and twenty-six years old, and as having abandoned his trade of making children's shoes to hazard his fortune performing up and down the East Coast. He eventually uses his earnings to start a business selling West Indian goods and renting rooms to "persons of low stamp," then buys a small schooner that hauls sand, and ends up painting portraits on the sidewalk. He remarks that because of his portraits "not being very correct, I abandoned this business in despair." Hooten's account, written in the first person as ostensibly by Major Stevens, describes various life-threatening adventures, as well as Stevens's flirtations with women and scenes of humiliation. Among his less agreeable characteristics are the prejudice and brutishness he sometimes displays toward individuals he refers to as Negroes.

In addition to private entrepreneurs, Lilliputian touring companies, and dime museums, a common phenomenon in the nineteenth and twentieth centuries was the midget village. In world's fairs in Europe and the United States—notably the Chicago Century of Progress Exposition in 1933—and in amusement parks such as Mamid Pier in Atlantic City, New Jersey, and Dreamland in Coney Island, New York, whole cities were constructed, containing small city halls, fire departments, and other elements. Stage shows were performed every hour. Some of the same performers that graced the touring companies turned up in the midget villages, especially after their careers had declined. Lavinia Warren (also called Mrs. Tom Thumb and Countess Magri) appeared at Dreamland in Coney Island in her later years. The Doll family was one of the most famous attractions offered by midget villages.[87]

The career of Tom Thumb, born Charles Stratton, has often been highlighted (Fig. 5). Never again would the public's fascination with dwarfs reach the heights it did with Tom Thumb and his wife, Lavinia Warren. Everyone, from Queen Victoria to President and Mrs. Lincoln, to the ordinary citizen, was eager to see the couple perform.

Charles Stratton, a native of Bridgeport, Connecticut, was discovered in 1842 at the age of five by Phineas T. Barnum and presented to the public as an eleven-year-old newly arrived from England. A prepossessing child, he proved such a popular draw at Barnum's American Museum in New York that his salary was immediately raised, and he was soon taken on the first of several international tours. The entertainments consisted of skits in which Thumb impersonated such characters as Napoleon, an Oxonian, or a Scottish Highlander; danced the polka or the Highland fling; and sang popular songs. There was apt to be a straight man, drawing Thumb out about his success with the ladies. Stratton's wife, Lavinia Warren, whose career had begun before her marriage, offered more subdued "levees," including songs, poems, and conversational exchanges with visitors.

By the time of their much publicized marriage in 1863, the couple ranked among the nation's most popular celebrities. They received expensive gifts, were feted throughout their honeymoon trip, and remained popular performers for many years thereafter. In *The Autobiography of Mrs. Tom Thumb*, Lavinia describes her domestic and international journeys during these years as well as those of her marriage to Count Magri, after Stratton's death. She offers some local color about each place she visited, but focuses mainly on anecdotes about the rich and famous whom she met along the way. Occasionally, she recounts her rebuttal to a rude questioner, but more often she relates the pleasure she took in her encounters with nobility. The book concludes: "Our itinerary involved an average one hundred and ten miles of traveling and two entertainments daily. The fact that we completed this tour without physical breakdown should be sufficient answer to the question whether we had mature bodies, whatever may be thought of our brains."[88]

The defensiveness implicit in her final sentence is common enough for dwarfs,

5. Tom Thumb with Queen Victoria and Prince Albert. From Eduoard Garnier, Les nains et les géants *(Paris; Librarie Hachette, 1884).*

performers and nonperformers alike. Although it is known that she had a happy marriage to Charles Stratton, and a less happy one to Count Magri, she reveals little of her private life in this volume. We can only imagine what it must have been like for Lavinia, plump and aging, to exhibit herself at Dreamland after years of being celebrated by royalty and presidents.

One can obtain a much more intimate picture of the lives and personalities of two other female dwarfs, the sisters Lucy and Sarah Adams, who performed between 1880 and 1900, first with the General Tom Thumb Company, and later with Barnum and Bailey and the Liliputian Opera Company (Fig. 6). Born on Martha's Vineyard, Massachusetts, they were direct descendants of Samuel Adams and indirect descendants of John Adams and John Quincy Adams.[89]

Lavinia Warren read about the musical church performances put on by the young women and contacted them. Their family reluctantly consented to the girls joining the Lilliputian Opera Company in New York, and they toured with the group. They became good friends of Lavinia's, and Lucy was later bridesmaid at Lavinia's wedding to Count Magri. The sisters successfully resisted the temptations of the wicked city; in one incident, Sarah turned away a dinner companion because she thought she smelled liquor on his breath (the offending substance later proved to be cleaning fluid he'd been using to get a stain out of fabric). The two women declined a European tour because they would have had to perform on Sundays; they remained in California for ten years, performing in churches up and down the West Coast. After their father's death, they returned to Martha's Vineyard, sometimes touring during the fall and winter. During the spring and summer they operated an antique store and tearoom. They charged a small fee for entry and for tea, entertaining customers with demonstrations of spinning and weaving wool. In addition, Lucy sang, and Sarah played a small organ.

The sisters seem to have led very contented lives, combining making a living with church work. Supposedly, they were popular in their youth, and Lucy kept pictures of six rejected suitors. Both of them seem to have had strong personalities—especially Lucy. After Sarah died in 1938 at the age of seventy-six, Lucy continued to be active in church and local issues, writing strongly worded letters to the newspaper, complaining of the desecration of Sunday by movies and golf and nostalgically praising the Sundays of her youth.[90] In an impassioned letter she invoked her ancestors, the keepers of the Martha's Vineyard lighthouse, in a plea to have it properly cared for.[91] When artifacts she had given to the Historical Society of Martha's Vineyard were not displayed prominently enough, she indignantly says she will soon come to pick them up.[92] Establishing her credentials as a member of the illustrious Adams family, a bridesmaid to Mrs. Tom Thumb, and an admired churchwoman, she declares that although only four feet tall, she is "not an imposter."

Respected if somewhat eccentric figures, the Adams sisters in their old age were viewed as more representative of an earlier time than of their own. Their activities were regularly followed in the newspapers, mostly in the *Vineyard Gazette*. Pulitzer

6. *Sarah Adams and Lucy Adams of Martha's Vineyard. From Hy Roth and Robert Cromie,* The Little People *(New York: Everest House, 1980).*

prize–winning poet Robert Hillyer, who spent boyhood summers on Martha's Vineyard, composed a poem called "The Adams Sisters" which includes these verses:

> These midget sisters sang away
> The finespun summer afternoon—
> A quavering music out of tune,
> But to a child's ear beautiful.
>
> Their dignity stood four foot tall
> In frocks of figured calico . . .[93]

The sisters' lives echo those of other dwarf performers who withdrew to quieter existences while enjoying their former celebrity. Among the best known was Admiral Dot, a member of Barnum's troupe; he and his wife retired to White Plains and ran a small hotel. The Adams sisters are both gone, but their legend persists on Martha's Vineyard. Lucy Adams, one of the last heirs of the Tom Thumb era, died in 1952.

CIRCUS DWARFS

At one time there were so many dwarfs in circuses that, beginning with the Chicago World's Fair in 1934 and continuing as late as 1958, Nat Eagle, who acted as agent for many, could make an excellent living. Although he handled other acts, the dwarfs were his favorites; he maintained a year-round company of eight or nine little people, spending much of the year with them in Sarasota, Florida. Hopeful candidates would write to him for a position, and he would visit them and their families at home and review their acts. Eagle's wife also played a part, choosing most of the special clothing required and providing piano accompaniment. Eagle's relationship with the performers was paternal and protective. According to Robert Lewis Taylor, "Fundamentally, Eagle's midgets [understood] that without him their life might be painfully dull and self-conscious; at home, in a family of ordinary size, they would receive, at best, specialized attention."[94] Taylor tries to present a sympathetic portrait of the little people—even quoting Eagle as telling new employees that smallness of stature is an identifying mark of superiority—but patriarchal condescension comes through. Like court dwarfs, "Eagle's midgets" are portrayed as less than full adults, therefore requiring a patron to shepherd their lives.

There have been many dwarf circus clowns, but probably none as famous as Michu, the Hungarian dwarf. When he finally discovered Michu in 1976, Irvin Feld, of the Barnum and Bailey Circus, had been searching for several years for a performer who would have the stature and the appeal of Tom Thumb. Michu had been born into a family of performers: both his parents were members of Budapest's Lilliputian Theatre, which presented children's plays as well as comedy. Michu, whose full name was Mihaly Mezaros, since childhood had attended a state-run school that taught such skills as juggling, acrobatics, and pantomime. For fifteen years prior to his discovery by Feld, he had worked in a traveling circus as a clown, unicyclist, dancer, and announcer.

Michu became a star at Barnum and Bailey, mostly performing in skits in which he was a David figure conquering one Goliath or another. He would disappear into a tiny phone booth and emerge as Superman; he would display great feats of strength such as bending weightlifters' bars around tough-looking clowns. But Feld was unable to deliver the re-creation of Tom Thumb's famous wedding to Lavinia Warren. He tried to match Michu with Juliana, a Hungarian dwarf performer, but bawdy Michu, who drank, smoked, and told off-color jokes, was not to her liking. Michu went on to play the title role in the television series Alf, appear in music videos with Aerosmith, play small roles in films, and make Pepsi commercials. As late as 1998 he appeared in a sideshow at Madison Square Garden in New York with Aurangzeb Khan, a Pakistani giant in sequined suit and top hat.[95]

At the other end of the spectrum from such top stars as Michu are performers like "JS," a two-foot-five-inch circus clown from Manchester, England, known in Great Britain's Brown Circus as Wee Pea. Yoram Carmeli, who has written about circuses in sociological and theatrical journals, described the clown's sorry existence: "At £25 per week in 1975, the midget was the lowest paid performer in the circus. Although salaries were a secret in the circus, everyone knew JS's salary. To supplement his low income, JS sold balloons during the show interval. . . . As JS's body was small, he was given the driver's compartment as lodging."[96]

JS was obliged to make his several costume changes a day in a urine-smelling corner of a tent that was exposed to public view. He was given physical work beyond his ability and placed by others at precarious heights to perform it. Rebelling, he muttered private nonsense words to himself.

What about JS's actual stage performance? Carmeli observes that average-statured clowns characteristically use mimicry, trickery, and slapstick to express themselves. Along with the audience, they delight in acknowledging human frailty and foolishness. Dwarf characters, however, function principally to provide contrast. They are defined by their oddity—a small sheriff threatening a large thief, or a mischievous creature pulling the chair out from under the clown. Unlike clowns who trip over their own big shoes, *these circus dwarfs exist only in relation to others.*

Carmeli's analysis of the role of the dwarf and his melancholy portrait of JS reinforce our perception of the dwarf clown as abased and self-abasing. My own recollection of circus dwarfs from childhood was seeing them dressed in clown suits, rushing about, tumbling, and being part of the general hullabaloo. In April 1995 I joined a throng at the circus, intending to observe a circus act myself, only to find just average-statured clowns in the act. Could it be that "the last picture show" had happened, and I had missed it? I thought so, when I learned that there had been no dwarfs the previous year either.[97] Curious about this, I wrote to Barnum and Bailey executive Mark Ridell; he responded by saying that dwarfs continued to be employed by the circus but had not been scheduled for the New York show: "It's just like left-handers; we don't happen to have any right now."

I decided to see if I could learn about today's dwarf clowns from the only dwarf clown with whom I was acquainted—Frank Theriault. He had been interviewed for a 1985 article about dwarfs that also featured my young daughter, Anna; Katherine Koos (the sculptor highlighted in Chapter 7); and our families. At the time, we parents felt some discomfiture at having our children grouped together with a dwarf clown in a piece in a local publication. In 2001, however, undaunted by the clown stereotype and eager to get Theriault's perspective, I searched him out in North Carolina, where he was employed as an engineer in a hotel; he also performed at parties and elsewhere and was in the midst of preparing a stand-up comedy act. Married to his wife, Melanie, for fifteen years, he had two children—a son, Jordan, hers by a previous marriage, and their daughter, Colleen Frances, a little person, then seven years old.

Frank mentioned that he had been the first dwarf to open a TV circus special. Although he had done bit parts in movies, among them *Radioland Murders*, and had appeared in commercials, he felt unapologetic about his years as a circus clown. A graduate of clown school, he saw himself as a professional and reported, "No one was exploiting me—I had a normal job; I was an entertainer like all others." He spoke of the accommodations that had been made for him in a very natural way by the circus staff. Wherever anything was above his reach, a bench or chair was installed for his convenience. He said that he had been treated and paid well and was recognized for his ability.

Theriault's performance generally consisted of four two-minute acts. Some played on the size difference, but others did not. He had found it exciting to travel all over the United States, as well as to Canada and Mexico, meeting presidents and other dignitaries. By 1988, having a wife and two-year-old son, he had decided that it was time to settle down and began working as a heating and air-conditioning engineer. He had met his average-statured wife, a journalist, when she interviewed him while he was in the circus. Devoted to his family, Theriault intends to pass on to his daughter his positive attitude about being a dwarf.

When asked why there seemed to be fewer dwarf clowns than in the past, Theriault replied that the reduction had not come from the circus administration—they were eager to find talented clowns. Rather, he said, the attitudes of parents today, the disapproving views of Little People of America, and an increase in other opportunities were responsible for clowning now being denigrated as a retrograde occupation. (Billy Barty would not speak to Theriault after learning that he was employed as a circus clown.)

The dwarf clowns whom Theriault knew came from diverse social classes. That is not the case in some non-Western societies. As *Indian Circus*, the compelling photographic essay by Mary Ellen Mark, reveals, dwarf clowns are often impoverished individuals without a place in society, who have sought out the circus as a haven. The moving 2003 film *Starkiss: Circus Girls in India* presents a similar poignant picture of indentured young girls and dwarf clowns, confined and overworked, struggling for brief moments of pleasure in a milieu very much like those that prevailed a century or two ago.[98]

THE DECLINE OF EXHIBITION

The decline of the monarchy, with its economics rooted in feudal relationships, has made ostentatious displays of dwarfs as playthings a thing of the past. Disability laws, and the greater accessibility of higher education and professional employment, account most importantly for the waning of the role of dwarfs as exhibits. The incursion of movies and television into the smallest of towns has meant that the unusual is no longer so exotic, and there are fewer "rubes" ready to be fooled by wild men of Borneo. Science has helped to explain the origins of various kinds of dwarfism, and changes in religious understanding have made it impossible for a dwarf to be viewed as a messenger of a god. Contemporary spectators, reminiscent of those who watched dwarfs battle Amazons in Roman arenas, may still pay to see dwarfs hurled across the room in Chicago bars, in a strange "sport" called dwarf tossing, but such events have become uncommon and have often been judged illegal.

The curious are still with us—but they are more likely to be interested in what dwarfs' lives are like than in merely staring at them. Hardly a month goes by without short-statured individuals appearing on *The Morey Povich Show, Montel, Jerry Springer, Oprah*, and other television talk shows. Sometimes real talent or significant accomplishments are highlighted, and sometimes the host explores quality-of-life issues. Other programs may echo the condescension of the era of "curiosities," but on balance, it seems that increased exposure has tended to enhance the general public's understanding.

An old Spanish proverb declares, "Andeme yo caliente y riase la gente" (As long as I'm warm, I don't care if people laugh at me).[99] This adage reflects the economic reality that had confronted dwarfs through the centuries. Ours is the first generation of dwarfs with the luxury of acknowledging that indeed we do care about being laughed at, that the price has been too high, and that at long last a better bargain may be driven.

Ordinary Lives: Dwarfs Outside the Courts
and the Worlds of Showmanship

Little is known about noncourt dwarfs or exhibiting dwarfs of the past. Only recently have minorities of all kinds recorded their own stories; only recently has oral
history burgeoned, with interviewers tape-recording subjects' reminiscences and historians looking in courthouses and attics for the official documents, letters, and diaries of obscure persons who lived long ago. What we do know is that the daily lives
of the majority of most dwarfs in previous eras were determined by their families and
the strictures of society. Some were artisans or tailors or helped with farmwork; others simply depended on the largesse of their families. All too often these dwarfs led
constrained lives marked by economic struggle; however, authors of some of the
older works about dwarfs do occasionally marvel at obscure or anonymous individuals who excelled at various occupations.

In 1868, for example, Edward Wood remarks of a man named Dye, "His faculties were so developed that he filled the office of bookkeeper to Hannen, a wire mer-
chant." Wood goes on to relate that Dye was irate when a stranger offered to hire his
son in order to exhibit him. He next gives an account of John Miller, a three-foot-tall
teacher who had stumps for arms. Although Miller was at one time so successful as a
teacher that he had 120 students, his work later fell off and he died in abject poverty.
Wood offers yet another anecdote, about a barrister who was cross-examining a
short-statured witness in a case and asked him what his profession was: "'An attorney,' was the answer. 'You an attorney?' said the counsel rudely. 'Why I could put
you in my pocket.' 'Very probably,' rejoined the other, 'and if you did you would
have more law in your pocket than you have got in your head.'"[100]

Elsewhere, in eighteenth-century Scotland, Hugh MacPherson and Thomas
Blair present a study in contrasts (Figs. 7 and 8). Hugh MacPherson's father was a
shepherd on a large farm. Hugh was variously employed first as a clerk at the George
Inn, in the shop of a grocer, and subsequently with J. and P. Cameron, carriers between Perth and Edinburgh. A well-dressed dandy, he was the object of mockery,
and he frequently got involved in physical confrontations when responding to the
taunts of others. Thomas Blair, however, seems to have achieved some status and
respect. He was deputy comptroller of the Stamp Office in Edinburgh, where for
many years he was able to "discharge the duties of the office with credit to himself
and advantage to the establishment." To make himself seem taller, he wore a pow-
dered wig held up by wires, one inch in height, and a high-crowned cocked hat. He
has been described as "a worthy sort of personage and a jolly companion at the social board."[101]

In all eras, many of the same pressures that affect contemporary dwarfs seem to have been in place. Particular subgroups might vary, however. The Amish, for example, who as a result of consanguinity have a greater number of dwarfs in their midst than do other groups, are known to be generally more accepting and attentive—their attitudes shaped by both their religious principles and their close community. Similarly, almost all American Indian groups have a special regard for little people. Because the spirit world is a very potent presence in their culture, they view human dwarfs as related to the little people in that world.

Previously unknown dwarf ancestors continue to emerge. As recently revealed by a family Web site, when one Charles Seaman (1797–1864) was born with achondroplasia in Bath, England, his doctor was reported to have said, "Pray God to take him, for he will never walk or feed himself."[102] However, as has so often been the case for others throughout history, Seaman's life defied all predictions. Although he was not taught to read and write until he was twelve, he went on to prepare for the ministry; he also worked as a sign and ornament painter and apprenticed as a watch-

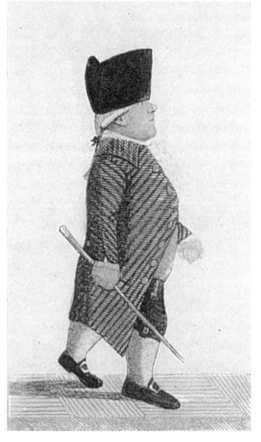

7. *Hugh McPherson, 1810. Courtesy Hy Roth Collection.*   8. *Thomas Blair, 1792. Courtesy Hy Roth Collection.*

maker. At the age of twenty, he went to Wales, where he spent four years working as a clerk, shipwright, china painter, portrait painter, schoolteacher, and conjurer. Upon returning to England, he taught school. He is said to have painted *The Battle of Waterloo*, a work admired by Queen Victoria.

In 1821, he married Elizabeth Smith, a governess, and in 1830, with their three children, they left for the United States. Seaman soon found employment in a dime museum in New York, and later as a ventriloquist performing in museums and inns and on riverboats. The couple had nine children, six of whom survived. Seaman received great praise for his performances but had many brushes with death. He walked with a cane; because of his infirmity, one of his children often accompanied him on trips.

By the early 1840s, discouraged by his meager earnings, he returned to Pennsylvania, where he had previously settled. When his application to start a school was denied, he even contemplated suicide—but he seems to have been supported by his faith. The following are two stanzas from a poem he sold for fifteen cents—a fifty-five-page work about the life of the Messiah, ending with an acrostic of his name.

Can a man by thought increase his height?
His limbs make straight by wisdom or by might?
And wherefore should the tall, the short deride,
Rise higher in their minds, and swell with pride?
Let them remember that the same wise God
Every man made of the same flesh and blood,
Some tall, some short, and all his ways are good.

Stay then; no longer boast; this truth believe:
Ere we possess, we must from God receive;
All our talents, all our powers and all
Must to the great Creator stand or fall;
And if I'm short, and others tall and wise,
Nor let me envy, nor let them despise.

The Nazis and the Dwarfs

Of all the societies in which dwarfs lived, Nazi Germany proved to be the most devastating. Many dwarfs were condemned to death because they were caught in the net that had been prepared for various groups designated as undesirables; some individuals were subjected to painful, pseudoscientific experiments simply because they were dwarfs.

According to Nazi ideology, there were classes of people—the mentally and physically disabled, Jews, gypsies, and homosexuals—who were deemed unworthy of living and propagating and therefore needed to be exterminated. The first elements in this policy were implemented in 1933, when the Law for the Protection of Hereditary Health ordained that individuals who were mentally retarded, schizophrenic, congenitally blind, deaf, or suffering from serious bodily deformity or arrested growth must be sterilized.[103] A total of four hundred thousand individuals are said to have fallen victim to the law. Deformities of head and spine—common among dwarfs—were among the characteristics that medical personnel were obliged to report.

In 1938 the German government authorized the killing of children with conditions such as those cited above; in 1939 the program was broadened to include older children and adults with disabilities. Death was administered by injection or occurred through gradual starvation; it is estimated that the adult program, known as "T4," took the lives of one hundred thousand people.[104] No figures are available on how many of these may have been dwarfs.[105] Because those individuals who resided outside institutions were not aggressively hunted down, perhaps some families who were aware of the policy took their relatives home, thereby assuring their safety, but most of those who "disappeared" from the rolls were murdered.

During World War II, Dr. Josef Mengele's infamous laboratory at Auschwitz concentration camp was established—one of many facilities directed to conduct research on matters vital to the war effort, as well as to produce basic research to fortify the position of the eugenics movement.[106] Although Mengele had been an indifferent student in his youth, he had attained degrees in medicine and anthropology and become a prominent member of Dr. Otmar Vershuer's institute at the University of Frankfurt. The institute's stance on eugenics was well known: only the genetically fit should be permitted to have children. Vershuer suspected that most characteristics, from left-handedness to alcoholism to poverty, were genetically based. Through an investigation of biological inheritance, the Aryan race could be perfected and its ascendancy assured. In spite of the enormous sacrifice of human life and the violation of sacred medical ethics, the experiments of Vershuer and his supporters added nothing of significance to human knowledge. The physicians conducting them were charged in the Nuremberg war trials, and in some cases executed.[107]

Mengele himself performed experiments on approximately three hundred twins and a small number of dwarfs. One widespread method of investigating nature/nurture controversies had been and remains the study of twins. Mengele was well aware of this and was also convinced that his study of dwarfs and their average-statured relatives could lead to dramatic new findings about heredity—as well as assure him fame. Psychiatrist Robert Jay Lifton, however, later observed that Mengele's obsession with dwarfs was closely connected to his obsession with alleged Jewish abnormality. Lifton cites the comment of Auschwitz physician Dr. Magda V.: "I think the Jews must have been freaks to him—like the dwarfs."[108]

It is now recognized that most of the dwarfs who died in concentration camps had been arrested for being Jews or other "undesirables," rather than being targeted specifically because they were dwarfs. Once in the camps, however, they might be noticed and singled out for experimentation, as happened with the Ovitz family from Transylvania, seven Jewish siblings who had formed a traveling group called the Lilliput Troupe (Fig. 9). These performers, all of whom had a rare dwarfing condition called pseudochondroplasia, were the largest such family in the world. They arrived at Auschwitz in 1944, along with their two average-statured sisters, a sister-in-law, and two young average-statured children. In addition, in order to save the lives of some average-statured friends of theirs, the Ovitzes claimed that these individuals were actually family, and they were allowed to remain in the dwarfs' barracks.

9. The Ovitz family arriving in Haifa, Israel, in 1949. © Bettmann/CORBIS.

The group's varied stature created a genetic-heredity puzzle for Mengele. Upon first seeing the dwarfs, he exclaimed ecstatically, "Now I have twenty years of material to study!" This proclamation, often repeated, did not reassure the Ovitzes about their future. Amazingly, all survived, but there were numerous occasions when one or another was close to death. Shimshon, the infant son of Leah, one of the average-statured sisters, had to manage with breast milk obtained from his severely undernourished mother, and there were times when she was threatened with separation from him.[109] The Ovitzes' pleas, and their efforts to enhance Shimshon's attraction for Mengele, resulted in his becoming the only baby in the camp who was allowed to live.

Handsome and charming, Mengele often posed as a good, loving father to the twins and dwarfs whom he used as his subjects, measuring them from fingernails to noses and photographing them. Inmate Dina Gottlieb sketched each one, as well as the Gypsies, creating a full record of his "collection." Although the dwarfs wore civilian clothes, had better bunks and washing facilities, and seemed to be better treated than other prisoners, the conditions under which they lived were still execrable: they were subject to agonizing examinations, humiliations, and a near starvation diet. Among their torments were the extraction of healthy teeth, the frequent drawing of blood, and the administration of countless X-rays; the women's uteruses were injected with drugs. In addition to enduring extreme physical pain, they were shamed by being forced to perform naked before the SS.[110]

Like many inmates, the Ovitzes had been impressed at first by Mengele's appearance and demeanor. But his erratic behavior soon disabused them of this impression. On one occasion, he confronted Dora, the tall wife of Avram Ovitz, in front of their young, average-statured daughter, Batia. Mengele shouted, "Now you will tell me if the little one is the midget's child, or did you have him with someone else?"[111] Next he demanded, "Now tell me how you lived with your midget." When Dora responded by describing her husband as good and smart, and saying that he had earned a lot of money as an entertainer, Mengele cut her off. "Don't tell me about that, only about how you slept with him," he said. As the sweat poured down her face, he continued the barrage of questions, so terrible that Sara Nomberg-Przytyk, who witnessed the scene, described them as "grotesque, inhuman torture." She concludes, "Mengele left this scene in an ill humor after being denied the intimate details."

Nomberg-Przytyk goes on to allude to the murder by Mengele of a child of one of the dwarf women, and the death of a dwarf man who was tricked by the guards and electrocuted.[112] These details, like many others offered by eyewitnesses, have proved to be false. Even a statement made by Perla Ovitz—and several others who were present—indicating that Mengele had rescued the Ovitzes from what seemed certain death in the crematorium has proved to be less than accurate. Despite Perla's vivid account, the family members seem not to have been pulled out of the gas chamber, but rather from the disinfecting sauna for new arrivals. In its atmosphere of intense, steamy heat and fumes, they experienced traumatizing conditions that might well have created the impression of being gassed.[113]

Nonetheless, the experience left Perla with the sense that Mengele's intervention had been responsible for her survival. The mixture of gratitude and anger that she felt toward him led to a lingering ambivalence that lasted all her life. Her Auschwitz experience seemed to explain her dwarf identity: "If I ever wondered why I was born a dwarf, my answer would be that my handicap . . . was God's way to keep me alive."[114]

Perla's sister Elizabeth Ovitz Moskowitz, author of the moving memoir *By the Grace of the Satan* (1987), also retained a complex, though censorious, view of her tormentor. The deepest insights into the lives of the Ovitz family can be gleaned from her book and from *In Our Hearts We Were Giants* (2004), the definitive study by Israeli journalists Yehuda Koren and Eilat Negev. The latter work includes interviews with Perla, her adult nephew Shimshon (the baby in the camp), and many other informants, including Hannelore Witkowski, the German historian and activist, whose friendship with Perla was featured in a compelling documentary made by an Israeli filmmaker.[115]

When the authors first met Perla in 1994, they were impressed by her strong voice, dignified bearing, majestic crimson dress, lacquered nails, and handsome jewelry—but most of all by her dramatic story.[116] It inspired them to do further research both in Europe and in Israel and to publish their book, which corrects many mistakes and inconsistencies in earlier published reports.

Perla was the youngest and smallest of the ten children of Shimshon (Samson) Ovitz, who was born in 1886 and died shortly before she was born. The first dwarf in his family, Shimshon was originally employed as a *badchan* (merrymaker and master of ceremonies) at weddings, but later, although he had never been formally ordained, his knowledge of rabbinical teachings and his magnetic personality led to his becoming recognized as a rabbi and healer. People believed that he had been given mystical powers by God to make up for his short stature, and he was much sought after for advice on all matters, including business, in which he had also shown his acumen and prospered.

His first wife, Blanca, had died at the age of twenty-six, leaving two daughters who were dwarfs. Bertha, his second wife, had borne eight children—five of them dwarfs. When Shimshon died of food poisoning at the age of forty-six, leaving her with ten children to support, Bertha disregarded suggestions that she institutionalize them and instead sent them all to music school for training in different instruments. Miniature cellos, guitars, drums, and violins were made for them—thereby ensuring them of a means of support. According to Elizabeth, "Mother believed in music. 'It is a fine profession, because it will enable you to be among people,' she said. 'Besides,' she would add, 'that way you can form a troupe and you'll never have to part.' That was also one of the cornerstones of her world, all for one and one for all, always."[117]

Although her mother died when Perla was only five, by then the Lilliput Troupe had been established, and her eldest brother, Avram (Abraham), who was like a father to her, helped to make it one of the most successful troupes in eastern Europe—performing variety shows that included plays, jazz, operatic duets, and stand-up comedy. The group continued performing even after the war began, using documents that omitted the fact that they were Jews. They were not captured until 1944, when they were deported to Auschwitz along with 430,000 Hungarian Jews; more than half of those in that roundup were gassed immediately upon arrival.[118]

After being liberated, and finding their home in Transylvania uninhabitable, they settled in Belgium, giving performances first in Europe and later in Israel, to which they emigrated in 1949. Despite a period of hardship following their relocation, they continued to live communally; now older and more infirm, for a time they made their living by running two cinemas and a café. Perla, the last of the siblings to survive, died in 2002, but several Ovitz children and grandchildren continue to live in Israel.

Just as the survival of Jews after the Holocaust serves as an inspiration to future generations, the survival of the Ovitz family may inspire the dwarf community. Mengele's laboratory was only the most notorious site of the quasi-medical torture and murder of dwarfs; in fact, such practices were widespread. Another instance has been memorialized at the Holocaust Museum in Washington, D.C., where a picture is displayed of Alexander Katan from Rotterdam, a dwarf with SED congenita. Katan, a nonobservant Jew, was an economist, accountant, and interpreter who spoke seven languages.[119] He was imprisoned at the Mauthausen concentration camp, where he was stabbed to death, as a pretext to study his bones. The Nazi explanation for the birth of dwarfs is offered at one Holocaust Museum exhibit: *It is the result of the mixing of Aryan and non-Aryan blood.*

Among others who perished was Lya Graf, a member of the Barnum and Bailey Circus, who had returned with her family to Germany from the United States. Earlier, in 1933, a photograph had been taken of her in the lap of J. P. Morgan—a publicity stunt designed to soften his image. She was arrested by the Gestapo in 1937 and sent to the Oranienburg concentration camp. There were three counts against her: she was Jewish; she was physically abnormal; and because of her association with Morgan, she was seen as a tool of Wall Street, which had denied Hitler a loan. In 1941, Graf and her parents were transported to Auschwitz where they subsequently were put to death in the gas chamber.[120] Many other dwarf entertainers who had been touring the United States were denied permanent visas and forced to return to Europe, despite the U.S. government's growing knowledge of Nazi atrocities.

During the Nazi era, the obscure and the famous met their fate together. In Mengele's laboratory one recognizes the ultimate nadir of the centuries-old trajectory of the utilization of dwarfs as freaks. Clearly, human moral evolution does not follow a linear, beneficent course, any more than does physical evolution.

Conclusion

In most eras, except for ancient Egypt, although individual dwarfs occasionally prospered, overall they could not look forward to respectful treatment. Social scientists have offered contrasting analyses. In his influential 1963 article, anthropologist Francis Johnston observed that dwarfs were formerly highly valued because they were believed to enjoy special relationships with the gods.[121] While this fact is undeniable, Johnston's overall assessment, which suggests that previous eras were something of a lost Eden, distorts the picture; his commentary on the position of dwarfs as royal advisors in Egypt and ancient Rome probably overstates the case. After noting that dwarfs were downgraded to functioning as pets and entertainers in the Renaissance courts, Johnston concludes that in contemporary times their situation has steadily become worse, since they have been stripped of their supernatural cloaks and made into "physical defectives" instead. Although he grants that an atmosphere of acceptance could conceivably improve their status, Johnston suggests that human fascination with the unusual makes such a turnabout unlikely in the near future. Their lack of acceptance, he concludes, has caused contemporary dwarfs to be insecure and dependent.

Johnston's perspective now seems fatalistic and at odds with recent events and growing understanding. Far more helpful is Yi-Fu Tuan's analysis. Tuan is particularly sensitive to the myths that societies use to rationalize their mistreatment of a given group. A great deal has changed since Johnston published his article, and one may certainly forgive him for not being able to anticipate the movements that were then brewing. At the same time, one must appreciate how prescient Tuan's linkage of the circumstances of various minorities has proved. We notice, for example, that those African and Asian nations that have strict rules for women—seeing them as an underclass to be dominated, infantilized, and denied control over their own lives—are the very same societies in which dwarfs enjoy the least equality and opportunity. Among dwarfs, as with most other groups, this is the first generation in which a goodly number of individuals have claimed a shared identity and are working to effect positive changes, no longer simply accepting their "place" as it has been defined by others.

CHAPTER TWO

Biographies of Eminent Dwarfs

There appears to be no reason drawn from either physiology or analogy, why the most astonishing powers of intellect, the soundest sense, the most luxuriant imagination, should not take up their abode in those abridgements of human nature called Dwarfs. Large heads, however, are almost proverbially indicative of small brains. . . . If, from speculating on the possibility of having dwarf statesmen, philosophers and poets, we proceed to inquire into the results of actual experience, we shall find less reason to expect a Locke thirty inches high, or an epic poem written by fingers no thicker than a goose-quill. Among all those human toys that have at different times amused Romans and children, carried knights' shields and ladies' love-letters, told monarchs unpalatable truths, and danced hornpipes upon tables, we cannot remember one distinguished by higher mental powers than were sufficient to produce a timely jest or smart repartee, while numbers of the dwarfish tribe have ranked yet lower in the scale of intellect. Genius, indeed, would be not be compensation for tiny stature. . . . That acute sensibility, that proud consciousness of superiority which usually accompany strong mental powers, would for ever torment and distress the tenant of a ridiculously small body.[1]

The conviction of this nineteenth-century English essayist "E. W." that small stature is accompanied by foppish vanity may seem extreme, but in fact reflects widespread prejudices and assumptions about the biologically determined inferiority of dwarfs. Two centuries after E. W.'s text was published, the absence of books documenting the lives of notable dwarfs remains a serious obstacle both to dwarfs' identity journey and to society's understanding. Some onlookers may be mystified by the "quest for roots" phenomenon. Does such documentation matter? Should individuals and groups need to prove their own worthiness by unearthing tales about their august ancestors?

Apparently, this does matter. As E. W.'s misguided commentary reveals, regard for a group is affected by society's awareness that some persons within that group have made valuable contributions. Until the appearance of Virginia Woolf's essay "A Room of One's Own," it was fashionable to suggest that women were simply intellectually inferior—and by their very nature consigned to irrationality and vapors. But given the astounding increase in the number of accomplished professional women during the past several decades, and the identification of notable women of past eras, earlier pseudobiological assumptions now seem quaint.

On a more individual level, people do commonly incorporate various social identities—personal, familial, sexual, ethnic and religious—in fashioning a sense of self. In the 1950s, the only black persons mentioned in textbooks were Booker T. Washington and George Washington Carver; the only women were Helen Keller and Susan B. Anthony—and Anthony was derided as a feminist bluestocking. Homosexuals were simply not mentioned at all. Now that the accomplishments of distinguished members of various minority groups have become widely known, the pride of individuals within those groups has grown exponentially.

Yet even in this climate, most people would have difficulty naming more than one or two accomplished dwarfs. Writers have given little attention to those who have made important contributions; often individuals described as dwarfs turn out to be merely short or of uncertain height. Writers using the same original sources have simply collected their names and uncritically transferred them. For example, journalists Walter Bodin and Barnett Hershey, in a 1934 work often cited by later authors, asserted, "There have been no less than three midget kings."[2] They mentioned Attila the Hun (whom they described as no bigger than an average twelve-year-old); Wladislaus I of Poland, who "by his exploits stands head and shoulders above his contemporary rulers despite his midget stature"; and Charles III, midget king of Sicily and Naples. Contemporary scholars indicate that Bodin and Hershey were mistaken about all three.

It is not easy to determine whether a historical figure who lived a thousand or more years ago was indeed a dwarf. Respected early authorities did not bother to substantiate their conclusions.[3] After a prolonged period of active searching, a modern researcher may still find no definitive evidence about the height or supposed dwarfism of various individuals on previous lists, and it can then be helpful to contact scholars known to have published extensively about the persons in question.[4] Such investigations often conclude with the elimination of dubious figures from the dwarf pantheon.

Aesop and Attila the Hun are among the many examples of those who had erroneously been touted as dwarfs. Although there likely was an Aesop who lived in the sixth century B.C.E. and who was responsible for several fables, no contemporary described what he looked like. His portrayal as a hunchback—ugly and deformed;

sometimes dwarfed, sometimes not—was a convention that arose much later.[5] Similarly, the inclusion of Attila as a dwarf seems to be based on a single reference in Edward Gibbon's *Decline and Fall of the Roman Empire* that, in turn, depends on several classical sources. A careful reading of Gibbon and his sources reveals that none of them aver that Attila is a dwarf.[6] Later historians agree that his ethnicity alone accounts for his short stature.[7]

Two well-known individuals who appear on more than one list may seem particularly convincing candidates at first because their names include references to their stature—Pepin le Bref (Pepin the Short) of France, and Wladislaw I of Poland, also known as Wladislaw Cubitalis or Lokietek (Wladislaw the Elbow-High). Both rulers were exceptional warriors; both conquered and unified many territories to create new national entities. They left the legacy of these nations to sons even more famous than themselves: Pepin's son was Charlemagne; Wladislaw's was Kasimir the Great.

These illustrious dwarf leaders, however, were not dwarfs at all. Pepin Le Bref, it turned out, had not been given this nickname until several centuries after his death.[8] No one really knew how tall he had been. Interestingly, Charlemagne in fact had a son who was a dwarf—Pepin II, an illegitimate son by Charlemagne's mistress who was not acknowledged as heir and was subsequently involved in an unsuccessful rebellion against his father. It is unclear whether Pepin II's illegitimacy, his personality, or his dwarfism—or all three—were responsible for the bad feeling between them, but the literature does contain pejorative references to Pepin II's stature.

In the lengthy catalogs of dwarfs cited by previous authors, there are many figures whose authenticity could not be confirmed despite extensive searches.[9] One controversial candidate is Richard III, for whom many diagnoses have been suggested, including two dwarfing conditions: hypopituitary dwarfism and Ellis-van Creveld syndrome.[10] The evidence for Richard III is sketchy and opinions conflicted. Nevertheless, Richard resonates as a historic figure transformed by Shakespeare into a consummate model for later fictional dwarfs who take revenge on a society that has rejected them for their physical shortcomings. Perhaps the most egregious error of all in books about dwarfs concerns Bertholde, described as dwarf prime minister to Alboinus, king of Lombardy. Despite Bertholde's being cited and glorified by one authority after another since 1753, with his appearance and adventures described in exquisite detail, his story has been shown to be a folk tale.[11] This revelation, from 1942, has gone unnoticed by later writers.

It is disappointing to have to scratch candidate after candidate from the list of prospects. But if merely establishing dwarf status is difficult, the search for true dwarfs about whose lives intimate details are available is even more challenging. Narratives by dwarfs themselves are extremely rare. However, distinguished dwarfs have existed in every civilization we know about: among them are the ancient poets and philosophers Alypius and Philetas of Cos; theologians John Baconthorpe and Antoine Godeau; painters Richard Gibson, Jacob Lehnen, and Henri de Toulouse-Lautrec; member of Parliament William Hay; scholar and ambassador Ferdinando Galiani; poet Alexander Pope; and engineer and inventor Charles Proteus Steinmetz. There are also a number of less prominent but equally fascinating figures: abolitionist Benjamin Lay; Methodist churchwoman Mary Rutherford Garrettson; writer Katherine Butler Hathaway; and historian and novelist Paul Leicester Ford. More recent dignitaries are Charles Lockhart, who served three terms as state treasurer of Texas, and the French notary (lawyer) Jean Brissé Saint-Macary. It is important to note that for all these figures, financial security allowed them the freedom to exercise their talents.[12]

Let us turn first to the ancients. In Alexandria in the third century C.E. lived Alypius, a philosopher and logician who influenced the philosopher Iamblichus. The writings of Iamblichus were widely known and respected until the nineteenth century, as was his biography of Alypius, which unfortunately no longer exists. Alypius has been described as "of so small and little a body, that he hardly exceeded a cubit, or one foot five inches and an half in height. Such as beheld him would think he was scarce anything but spirit and soul: so little grew that part of him that was able to corruption, that it seemed to be consumed into a kind of divine nature."[13] He had a great many disciples, with whom he engaged in private conferences and debate, but he did not leave any written records. This was left to Iamblichus, who admired Alypius's acumen and consulted him frequently. Alypius was highly regarded for his abilities, not merely as a "pygmy philosopher."

There are at least a few written fragments left by another Alexandrian dwarf, Philetas of Cos. Born in about 340 B.C.E., he was a poet, philosopher, and grammarian. He was the preceptor of Philadelphius, the young son of Ptolemy I in Alexandria. A review of early Alexandrian poetry presents Philetas as a figure "small and puny, to such a degree that his leanness became proverbial, but endowed with a lively and pleasing imagination and possessed of a curiosity that was ever on the alert, and of great perseverance in his work."[14] Fame came to Philetas first at Cos, where he had influenced such noted pupils as Zenodotus, Hermes, Anex, and Theocritus. Always in a precarious state of health, he is said to have died from overwork. Only a few remnants of his poetry, from his various epics, elegaic couplets, and love poems, survive. One line, quoting a speaker, perhaps Ulysses, reads: "I have traversed the road to Hades, whence no traveler e'er returned."[15] Anyone familiar with Shakespeare's *Hamlet* or the classical literature on which Shakespeare drew may recognize these words—but rare is the individual who knows of their association with Philetas of Cos.

Like most Alexandrian poets, Philetas had a mistress and wrote poems in her honor. While only a few lines of his poetry survive, we do know that he was considered the founder of the Hellenistic school of poetry and was celebrated in an elegy by Hermesianax of Colophon (c. 290 B.C.E.), who wrote:

> Nor is Philetas' name to thee unknown
> Than whom a sweeter minstrel never was:
> Whose statue lives in his own native town
> Hallowed to fame, and breathes in deathless brass.[16]

In the millennium or more that followed, there are few references to eminent dwarfs. Accounts by contemporaries or later writers tend to be brief encapsulations, such as the repeated citations of Licinius Calvus (82 B.C.E.–47 B.C.E.), a three-foot-tall Roman poet and orator, and Characus, identified as "the wisest counselor of Saladin."[17] New information occasionally turns up, tucked away in more general works: The writer of a work on solitude and hermits, for example, mentions Desert Father John Colobus, a hermit abbé of the fourth or fifth century C.E., also known as Saint John the dwarf.[18]

More is known about several other dwarfs who achieved prominence in the church and politics. Short stature seems not to have been an obstacle to religious appointments, and at least three figures are known to have held positions as clergymen. John Baconthorpe (1290–1346), a Carmelite scholastic, taught at Cambridge, held administrative positions, and wrote influential theological commentaries. Although many of his scholarly works have survived, little personal information about him is available. Antoine Godeau (1605–1672) was an important French cleric, writer, and administrator. The Neapolitan Ferdinando Galiani (1728–1787) was originally appointed as an abbé but achieved his greatest fame as a scholar and diplomat.

By the seventeenth century, more detailed accounts of prominent individuals begin to be available, and it becomes possible to embark upon a more revealing appraisal of these lives. The names of several are familiar—Alexander Pope, Henri de Toulouse-Lautrec, and Charles Proteus Steinmetz. Other figures are more obscure today, but were recognized during their own eras. These remarkable personalities afford us the opportunity to reflect also upon the complicated life passages of talented dwarf individuals who are not included here but who have enjoyed rich, creative lives.

Antoine Godeau

Antoine Godeau (1605–1672) is interesting for both his achievements and the discontinuity of his life story. Growing up in France, Godeau led a worldly existence.

He wrote romantic poetry, frequently fell in love, and was as frequently heartbroken. He was a habitué of the Hotel de Rambouillet, where he courted and was rejected by Julie d'Angennes, later the duchesse de Montausier, a charismatic noblewoman celebrated in verse by many poets. So public were Godeau's attentions toward her that he became known as "the dwarf of Julie."[19]

Godeau was highly regarded as a writer. Although his salon years caused some unfavorable comment when Richelieu's patronage secured an appointment for him as bishop of Grasse in 1636, he proved himself an exemplary clergyman and administrator. In 1639, he was appointed bishop of Vence, a more lucrative post, and assumed an important role in the assemblies of French clergy. Among Godeau's writings were works on church history and moral treatises, as well as poetry, which some contemporaries regarded as the greatest religious verse in France. His most recent biographer, however, finds his work inconsistent, his verse alternating between excellent and insipid. Whatever the verdict on Godeau's literary efforts, he was sufficiently important both in French church history and as a man of letters to have been the subject of several biographies. There is virtually no difference of opinion on his humanity: he has been described as passionate about intellectual pursuits, friendship, and justice. He was particularly effective in bringing together opposing forces and defusing conflicts.[20]

In earlier years, Godeau had not escaped the pain of having to defend himself because of his stature. He directed this verse against the French poet Vincent Voiture, who had made comments about his size:

> Of a more gallant dwarf than any under the heavens
> You seem by your comments to be envious
> And scorn his little being:
> But do not think that I pardon you
> I am small, but I am glorious.

Voiture seems to have reconsidered his opinion, for in a later description of Godeau he wrote: "I cannot understand how the heavens managed to fit so many things in such a small space. . . . It seems that Nature enjoys placing the most priceless souls in the smallest bodies."[21]

Ferdinando Galiani

Like Godeau, the Italian Ferdinando Galiani (1728–1787) benefited from both prodigious talent and generous patronage (Fig. 10). Galiani's father, Mateo, was a

10. Ferdinando Galiani. Engraving by Lefevre after portrait by J. Gillberg. Bildarchiv Preussischer Kulturbesitz/Art Resource, NY.

minor government official and his uncle, Celestino, was a scholar and the rector of the University of Naples, facilitating for the seventeen-year-old Ferdinando a sinecure as absentee abbé of a monastery. Galiani's biographer, Francis Steegmuller, notes that although for this post Galiani had to take a vow of poverty and submit to the tonsure, he never allowed the appointment to interfere with his uninhibited private life.[22]

Galiani's family had influence, but early signs of brilliance and erudition also contributed to his success. The fact that Galiani was four foot six inches tall was one of his least remarkable attributes (65). By the age of sixteen he had translated John Locke; at twenty-three, he had published the acclaimed 370-page *Della moneta*, containing discourses on love and money; and he and his friend Pasquale Carcami wrote a witty burlesque of the city's recently deceased official hangman, a work praised by Pope Benedict IV.

At age twenty-six, Galiani was assigned by Prime Minister Bernardo Tanucci to write the introduction for a volume of engravings of the frescoes of the ancient city of Herculaneum. Further, Galiani's intellectual brilliance and personal charm led Tanucci to select him for a sensitive diplomatic posting to France. In addition to being employed in political duties, Galiani used his time in Paris to write *Dialogues on the Grain Trade* (115), described by Steegmuller as "lively and improbably delightful"; throughout his life, Galiani would remain deeply engaged in issues affecting commerce and trade.

Although Galiani's years in Paris were the most fulfilling of his life, both his arrival and his departure would cause him humiliation. His well-known wit, like that of many other short-statured persons, was honed in part by need to defend his physical appearance. New situations offered particularly painful challenges, as did the occasion of Galiani's formal introduction to France. When Galiani was presented at court, his small, provincial appearance was met with derisive laughter (65–66). He reacted quickly, declaring, "What you see is but a sample of the secretary: the complete secretary will come later.'" His retort, though spoken with a Neapolitan accent, was admired. Steegmuller notes that Galiani's composure was likely gained through many such experiences that had trained him to absorb the pain by taking consolation in his superior mind. Tolerant of similar remarks made by friends, he sometimes referred to his small size himself.

Galiani's years in France seem to have been the most fulfilling of his life. He had close friendships with Voltaire; Denis Diderot; Friedrich Melchior Grimm; and Grimm's beloved, an extraordinary woman named Madame d'Epinay: the correspondence between Galiani and these figures is the basis of Steegmuller's book. Recalled to Naples following an indiscreet remark to his friend, the Danish ambassador to France, about the attitude of the king of Naples toward a proposed pact with France, he was disheartened but far from idle.

He remained active in political life and was appointed magistrate of privately owned lands. He also directed a comic opera, worked on a dictionary of the Neapolitan dialect, and arranged his nieces' marriages. But he never fully recovered from the disgrace of Tanucci's recalling him from his post, and he missed the stimulation of his Paris circle. His correspondence attests to his depressed state, which his friends Grimm and d'Epinay attempted to relieve, at one point initiating a relationship for him with Catherine of Russia, who bestowed upon him a gold medal and sent a gold snuffbox in recognition of his successful effort to forge a trade agreement between Naples and Russia.

From Galiani's intimate letters to d'Epinay and hers to him, we know that he had asked his friend Dr. Gatti to pay twelve francs a month to a Mme de La Daubiniere and her infant child, and had asked d'Epinay to look in on her, as she suffered from what proved to be a terminal illness. Although Daubiniere had been Galiani's mistress, and there is evidence that they cared for each other, Daubiniere seems not to have been involved with him alone. Steegmuller's description of her as *une occasionelle* helps explain why Galiani does not seem surprised or jealous that his emissary has had sexual relations with her. Despite Galiani's attachment to Daubiniere, both had surely recognized at the outset that her lesser class and his status as an abbé (publicly single and celibate) made commitment impossible (256 n. 1).

Galiani is remarkably negative toward d'Epinay's passionate feminist yearnings, though quite grateful for her attentions to him. She does not reproach him, but is liberal with the compliments so characteristic of eighteenth-century epistolary style. Her loyalty, and the closeness of Diderot and Grimm, reveal a Galiani who inspired admiration and warm personal feelings. Edward Gibbon refers to him as "the laughing philosopher"; Casanova deems him "a man of wit, a good talker, and a favorite in every circle he cared to enter" (70).

Galiani's wit never failed him. When he died in 1787 at the age of fifty-nine, one contemporary described him as "a harlequin to the end." The sensitive reader may wince a bit at this description—a familiar image of dwarf as jester—but still be impressed by Galiani's insistence that wit be entwined with dignity until the very end, when he donned his wig to accompany to the door the priest who performed last rites.

Largely forgotten by the general public until Steegmuller's 1992 book, Galiani was in his time regarded as a genius who could be mentioned in the same breath as Voltaire and Diderot. A number of recent scholarly studies of Galiani and his work have appeared in Italian and other languages. Remarkably, he continues to be respected by economists, and his writings are listed on current college bibliographies as seminal works. The *Columbia Encyclopedia* notes, "Galiani contributed greatly to the modern theory of value and to the relativistic, historical approach to economics. He opposed the physiocratic view that land is the source of all wealth."[23] Steegmuller's access to original sources provides a refreshing contrast to the hodgepodge summaries that carelessly intermix the famous, the weird, and the apocryphal dwarfs of past centuries in tantalizing three-sentence allusions.[24]

Alexander Pope

Alexander Pope (1688–1744) has been described as "the most distinguished of the classical poets of the Augustan age and the most accomplished verse satirist in English."[25] Soon after he was born, his family moved to the countryside. When Pope was ten years old he contracted what is now known to have been Pott's disease, a tubercular infection. It left him four foot six inches tall, hunchbacked, and in perpetual ill health, suffering from excruciating headaches. He did not thrive in school, and was taught for a time by priests and tutors. A voracious reader of the classics, he soon became his own teacher.

11. Alexander Pope. Portrait by J. B. Van Loo, 1742. From the collection of the Earl of Mansfield, Scone Palace, Perth, Scotland.

At age seventeen he initiated a correspondence with William Wycherly and won praise from the influential poet. By twenty he had published his *Pastorals*, by twenty-five the *Essay on Criticism* and *The Rape of the Lock*; by the time he was thirty-two he had completed his translation of Homer's *Iliad*.[26] He became not only the most celebrated poet of his age but also that rare poet who supported himself handsomely by his work. Despite frequent bouts of illness, he continued to write prolifically till the end of his days (Fig. 11).

At his idyllic retreat in Twickenham, Pope decorated "the grotto"—his study—with rare minerals. He offered his guests figs and walnuts from his carefully designed garden. Dinner might include fish from the Thames, which ran near his house. Pope employed a boatman to row him on regular trips to London and a coachman to drive him on frequent visits to the country homes of the nobility and his literary friends.

He remained an extraordinarily devoted friend to Jonathan Swift, John Gay, and others and a generous benefactor to those whose situations touched him. When Swift questioned his liberality, Pope responded that he was rich enough, that he sensed that he would not live to be old, and that he would enjoy the pleasure of giving while alive. He wrote, "When I die, I should be ashamed to leave enough to build me a monument, if there were a wanting friend above ground."[27] He died at fifty-six.

The genuineness of Pope's relationships and his generosity are indisputable, as Maynard Mack affirms in his balanced and comprehensive biography.[28] Nevertheless, what also emerges is a man who used his close friendships, his circle of noble and literary admirers, and the beauty of his environment to buffer himself against psychological wounds. The barbs of "The Dunciad," his most celebrated later work, and the deceptions surrounding the publication of his letters are but two examples of the lengths to which he went in trying to protect his fragile ego. In "The Dunciad," he castigated his personal and literary enemies, many of them made famous only by virtue of Pope's attacks. By mounting what he conceived to be an assault upon hypocrisy and mediocrity, he opened himself up to personal attack, including lampoons of his stature and deformity.

Pope's best-known feud was with the critic John Dennis, whom Pope had attacked in his "Essay on Criticism." Dennis was merciless in his response: "As there is no creature in Nature so venomous, there is no thing so stupid and so impotent as a hunch-backed toad. . . . This little author may extol the Ancients as much and as long as he pleases, but he has reason to thank the good Gods that he was born a modern. For had he been born of Grecian parents, and his father by consequence had by law the absolute

12. Caricature of Alexander Pope. His Holiness and his Prime Minister. The Phiz and Character. Grolier Club cat. 89, with papal tiara, mid-eighteenth century. Print Collection, Miriam and Ira D. Wallach Division of Art, Prints and Photographs, New York Public Library, Astor, Lenox and Tilden Foundations.

disposal of him, his life had been no longer that that of one of his poems, the life of half a day."[29] Clearly, a slight received in this Age of Manners could make its recipient exceedingly unmannerly. A particularly cruel example was an engraving used as a frontispiece to *Pope Alexander's Supremacy and Infallibility Examin'd* (Fig. 12).[30] Pope's sensitivity to personal slights increased through the years. To his friend John Caryll, he commented: "Tis certain the greatest magnifying glasses in the world are a mans own eyes, when they look upon his own person; yet even in those I appear not the great Alexander Mr. Caryll is so civil to, but that little Alexander the women laugh at."[31]

In contrast to most of Pope's biographers, who did not recognize how central Pope's appearance was to his psyche and his writing, in 1996, Helen Deutsch published an entire book on this issue, noting that the British Museum contained a four-volume bound set of pamphlet attacks on Pope, many of them mentioning his deformity.[32] Hurtful as the political and literary assaults were, the deepest wounds were probably personal: Pope's well-publicized rejection by Lady Mary Wortley Montague and, even more poignant, his abandonment of his romantic interest in the Blount sisters.

Pope's letters to Lady Montague reveal the stylized, courtly friendship of a man who is given to flattery but also hungry for acceptance and affection; her married state meant that it could be no more than a chivalric relationship. But when the relationship foundered, she, like others, mounted an attack that joined his character with his body.

> But how should'st thou by Beauty's Force be mov'd
> No more for loving made, than to be lov'd?
> It was the Equity of righteous Heav'n,
> That such a Soul to such a Form was giv'n.
>
> But as thou hat'st, be hated by Mankind,
> And with the Emblem of thy crooked Mind,
> Mark'd on thy back, like Cain by God's own Hand;
> Wander like him accursed through the land.[33]

These lines were written anonymously, but Lady Mary's authorship was known. Her attack must have been all the more painful because Pope had opened his heart to her, writing in one letter about "this Body of Mine (which is as ill-matched to my Mind as any wife to her husband)."[34]

Although tangled, this relationship was simple compared to his more openly romantic connection to the Blount sisters, Theresa and Martha. In a letter written when he was twenty-three, Pope confessed, "I am at this instant placd betwixt Two such

Ladies that in good faith 'tis all I'm able to do, to keep self in my Skin." His excitement fairly leaps from the paper; the sexual energy seems genuine, not mere hyperbole. He was in love first with one, then with the other, but he eventually reduced his visits to them.[35] As Pope's sensitivity to his appearance increased and his health declined, he abandoned all thoughts of romance and marriage. He could not hazard the ridicule or believe in a love strong enough to overcome distaste for his appearance. Pope painfully learns to subdue his nature but rails at the suggestion that art can compensate for the absence of the normal, sensual joys of life:

> . . . Heavens! was I born for nothing but to write?
> Has life no joys for me? or (to be grave)
> Have I no friend to serve . . .[36]

Still, he basked in his acclaim. Among the most highly esteemed writers of his nation and his century, he was sought after by artists: more portraits and sculptures of him were created in his lifetime than of anyone else, except royalty.[37] He would not, however, permit a full-length portrait of himself; the only such work that survives is a sketch, done from a distance without his knowledge.

Some of Pope's disappointments arose from the normal losses of his later years and from his ever more debilitating illness. Others had their origin in his position as a Catholic outsider and in his deformity in a culture that emphasized classic beauty and countenanced derision. But a significant portion of Pope's bitterness is directly attributable to his own temperament and character—which governed his reaction to his stature and deformity. He assumed a defensive critical stance that increasingly brought him into open conflict with others. The protection that his true friendships afforded him was the closest he could come to peace.

Benjamin Lay

Benjamin Lay (1677–1759), who was born in Colchester, England, was renowned for contentiousness—but his pugnacity, unlike Pope's, did not reflect personal pique or ego needs; rather, he displayed his indignation in premeditated ways in the interest of effecting social changes. Lay was one of the earliest and most vigorous abolitionists in prerevolutionary America. Although his social origins were humble and his formal education limited, he was tireless in his battle to eliminate what he regarded as one of the most profound of social ills—the enslavement of black Africans. His convictions were rooted in his Quaker upbringing, and the battle he waged took place largely within the Philadelphia Society of Friends, many of whose members were slaveholders. Lay raged against their hypocrisy and found ingenious ways to dramatize his position.

As an adolescent in England, Lay was apprenticed to a glove maker, but by the time he was nineteen he had left that position to work on his brother's farm.[38] Still restless, he became a sailor, voyaging to such remote destinations as Syria. Finally, in 1710, he returned to his native village; married his wife, Sarah, a woman described as able, intelligent, and dedicated; and temporarily settled down. For some years, the couple lived in London, where Lay earned a living as a draper. He was active in the Quaker community, but he challenged what he saw as the arrogance and vanity of the leadership, and they in turn were unnerved by his confrontational stance.[39] His membership was withdrawn, though it was later reinstated.

Roberts Vaux, Lay's nineteenth-century biographer, described Lay as "four foot seven inches in height; his head was large in proportion to his body; the features of his face were remarkable, and boldly delineated, and his countenance was grave and benignant. He was hunch-backed, with a projecting chest, below which his body became more contracted. His legs were so slender, as to appear almost un-equal to the purpose of supporting him, diminutive as his frame was, in comparison with the ordinary size of human stature."[40] Elsewhere, he has been described as having bony arms of extraordinary length.[41] We are fortunate in having an excel-lent engraving of him by Henry Dawkins, drawn from a lost oil painting by William Williams, a highly regarded artist (Fig. 13).[42] Lay's enduring popularity is revealed in the frequent imitations of this image by other engravers during the one hundred years that followed its appearance. Despite his fragile appearance, Lay seems to have been extraordinarily active—not only as a farmer and sailor in his youth, but also in later years, walking miles from his village to Philadelphia to pay visits, rarely accepting a ride.

In 1718, at the age of forty-one, Lay embarked for Barbados, where he and Sarah established a business; he remained there until he left for Philadelphia in 1732. This period crystallized his antislavery sentiments. Slave trading was particularly brutal at this historic moment in the West Indies. Lay writes:

> We had much Business in Trading, and the poor Blacks would come to our Shop and Store, hunger-starv'd, almost ready to perish with Hunger and Sick-ness, great numbers of them would come to trade with us, for they seemed to love and admire us, we being pretty much alike in Stature and otherways; and my dear Wife would often be giving them something for the Mouth, which was very engaging you that read this may be sure, in their deplorable Condi-tion. Oh! my Soul mourns in contemplating their miserable, forlorn, wretched State and Condition that mine Eyes beheld them in them.[43]

The Lays' shortness is perceived matter-of-factly by the blacks; rather than being seen as a defect, their height, like their generosity, it is regarded as merely one of their attributes. For a time Benjamin Lay dealt with his compassion and outrage by feeding the slaves as far as his resources permitted, by welcoming them to his house on the Sabbath, and by offering them basic education and religious instruction. However,

13. Benjamin Lay. Etching and engraving by Henry Dawkins after lost painting by William Wilkins, completed after 1810. Historical Society of Pennsylvania.

while the slaves respected and admired him, his fellow Quakers did not. One day, Sarah, visiting a well-respected Friend she knew, discovered the man beating a naked, bleeding slave who was tied to a tree.[44] The Friend explained that the slave had tried to run away and was being punished for his ingratitude. The Lays could not live under these conditions any longer. Sarah "wished to leave Barbados, lest by remaining there she might be leavened into the nature of the inhabitants, which was pride and oppression."[45]

Upon their arrival in Philadelphia, it became clear that Benjamin's earlier disagreements had not been forgotten. A communication was sent from Colchester, England, with the news that Lay should not have been granted a membership certificate.[46] Tactful Sarah was allowed to retain her status as an approved minister at the Philadelphia meeting even after her husband was denied membership. The Lays had had high hopes for Philadelphia, but although the conditions of the slaves were less severe, the mindset of the Quaker slaveholders proved similar to those in the West Indies. Lay found himself one of a few lonely voices opposing slavery; his friend Ralph Sandiford was another. Although he had originally planned to live in Philadelphia, he instead bought a six-acre plot in a rural setting six miles north of the city, planted walnut trees, and built a house. There Lay maintained the ascetic lifestyle he had adopted in Barbados. He was a vegetarian, spinning his own flaxen clothing because he would not wear anything that required animals to be killed, and he would use no product resulting from slave labor.

His antislavery efforts became the center of his life. In 1737 his friend Benjamin Franklin helped him to publish his rambling, impassioned, 278-page tract, *All Slave-Keepers that keep the Innocent in Bondage, Apostates*. It is addressed to all readers, but particularly to the Quaker community, whose members Lay perceived as hypocritical, and is a blend of bombastic rhetoric, reasoned refutations of Biblical pro-slavery arguments, and personal experience. Indeed, our knowledge of the Lays' happy, loving marriage derives largely from Benjamin's fond references to his wife in this lengthy tract.[47]

Lay did more than write. He carried out ingenious demonstrations of his antislaveholding beliefs. One frigid winter day, he went to Quaker meeting with his right leg and foot uncovered. In response to the astonished concern he met with, he declared, "You pretend compassion for me, but you do not feel for the poor slaves in your fields, who go all winter half clad."[48] On another occasion, he took his neighbor's six-year-old child to his house, unbeknownst to the neighbor, who came running in search of the child, whereupon Lay commented, "Your child is safe in my house and you may now conceive of the sorrow you inflict on the parents of the negro girl you hold in slavery, for she was torn from them by avarice."[49] Once, he walked the six miles from his house to Philadelphia to have breakfast with a notable citizen. When he realized that a slave was present, he unceremoniously departed, making it clear that he could not break bread with slaveholders.[50]

Perhaps his most dramatic demonstration has been referred to as the "bladder of blood" incident. Lay appeared at a Quaker meeting wearing a military coat and sword under his Quaker garments and concealing a container of pokeberry juice in a book under his clothing. During the service, he threw off his cloak and plunged his sword into the container, astonishing nearby onlookers as red liquid was sprayed on them. Lay declared, "It would be as justifiable in the sight of the Almighty who beholds and respects all nations and colours of men with an equal regard if you should thrust a sword through their hearts as I do this book."[51]

He also took positions on moral issues beyond that of slavery, among them capital punishment. He believed that criminals should be imprisoned at hard labor until they learned the error of their ways, rather than be deprived of life, often for trivial offenses. The improvements in the penal code that he recommended were adopted, making Pennsylvania an unusually progressive state in this respect. He opposed the importation of liquor because of the harm he observed resulting from its use. His interest in education brought him to the schools to explain biblical passages to the schoolchildren. His moral sense made him impatient with self-indulgence and idleness and generous to the truly needy.[52]

His good friends, including John Woolman and Benjamin Franklin, stood by him, accepting, in addition to the bountiful vegetarian meals he spread before them, his opinionated, volatile nature. However, their admiration of Lay did not prevent them from making fun of his more grandiose proposals. He met with Franklin and two other interested parties to discuss his plan of converting all humankind to Christianity, "but at their first meeting at the Doctor's house, the three 'chosen vessels' got into a violent controversy on points of doctrine and separated in ill-humor. The philosopher, who had been an amused listener, advised the three sages to give up the project of converting the world until they had learned to tolerate each other."[53]

Over time, Lay became increasingly meditative and spiritual. Although he did endure the anguish of his wife's death, he was able to end his days satisfied with the result of his efforts. In 1738 more than half the Philadelphia Friends, among them the most influential of the community, had been slaveholders. However, by the 1750s the balance had shifted, and by the 1770s only 19 percent still had slaves, and these were freed through their owners' wills.[54] Shortly before Lay's death, a friend came to inform him that the Society of Friends had made a resolution to disown those members who would not give up the practice of slaveholding. Lay reflected for a moment, then rose and exclaimed, "Thanksgiving and praise be rendered unto the Lord God. . . . I can now die in peace."[55]

William Hay

William Hay (1695–1755), who represented Seaford, England, as a member of Parliament, is the first eminent dwarf included here who had children. Beyond this, through Hay we are afforded a new, revealing perspective: his essay "On Deformity" introduces us to a historic figure who struggled with his difference and illuminated his "examined life" (Fig. 14).[56]

Hay was the second son of William Hay, also a member of Parliament for Seaford. His family was from Sussex and had once been large landowners, but their wealth had since diminished. Hay's early life was marked by tragedy: his father died the year he was born, his mother five years later. By the time he was six, both grandparents had also died, and an aunt had taken him in. Sent away to school at age ten, as was customary for boys at the time, Hay matriculated at Christ Church, Oxford, when he was sixteen and was admitted to the bar in 1723. While studying for the bar, he contracted smallpox, which seriously impaired his sight. In addition, he was several centimeters under five feet in height, with a congenital deformity that left him hunchbacked and with a body that was somewhat stooped and inflexible. Despite these disabilities, Hay was an active traveler, touring England and Scotland when he was twenty-three, writing a detailed account of his journey. Two years later he traveled through France, Germany, and Holland. He held several judicial positions until 1734, when he was elected to the House of Commons, holding a position that he retained for the rest of his life.

Hay was a Whig and a strong supporter of Robert Walpole. He is best known for introducing bills for the relief and employment of the poor and for his positions as commissioner for victualing the navy and keeper of records in the Tower. In Parliament, he was extremely hardworking, "the first in and the last out of the commons [*sic*]."

His years of travel, his decade as a magistrate, and his reputation within his community seem to have imbued in him the confidence he had lacked earlier and enabled him to court and win his wife, Elizabeth Pelham. Hay married Elizabeth in 1731 when he was thirty-six; with her he enjoyed a happy marriage and produced three sons and two daughters. This union allowed him to feel that he was a full participant in life and was vital to his well-being:

14. William Hay. From Rev. Francis Tuttle, ed., Collected Works of William Hay *(London, 1794).*

There is another Passion to which deformed persons seem to be more exposed, than to Envy; which is Jealousy; for being conscious that they are less amiable than others, they may naturally suspect that they are less beloved. I have the Happiness to speak this from Conjecture and not from experience; for it was my Lot, many Years ago, to marry a young Lady, very piously educated, and of a very distinguished Family, and whose Virtues are an Honour to her Family and her Sex; so that I never had any Trial of my Temper; and I can only guess at it by Emotions I have felt in my younger Days; when Ladies have been more liberal of their Smiles to those, whom I thought in every respect, but Person, my Inferiors.[57]

After Hay's death following a stroke at the age of sixty, one of his daughters assembled and published Hay's *Collected Works* and wrote the introduction.[58] She mentions that Hay had been involved in the business of producing silk in England, and she remembers him as kind to the tenants on his land. Although his means were modest, he managed well through "judicious economy" and was a welcoming host and a just and compassionate magistrate. His children experienced him as kind but somewhat grave and reserved when they were young, finding themselves "more observed than talked to by their father." When they became adults, he interacted with them with greater freedom, "helping them to the full extent of his power and fortune." His early losses and his British restraint may have made it difficult for him to be demonstrative, but his underlying feeling nevertheless came through.

Of his total output, including journals, poetry, and treatises on government and moral philosophy, "On Deformity" is his most enduring and most frequently cited piece. Revealing Hay as a man of intellect, compassion, and integrity, the work is erudite, filled with eighteenth-century classical references, but also passionate and profoundly reflective. Hay expresses gratitude for not having been born in Sparta, where "when I had no sooner seen the light but I should have been deprived of it; and have been thrown as a useless Thing, into a Cavern by Mount Taygetus." He protests, "Is the Carcase the better Part of the Man? And is it to be valued by Weight, like that of Cattle in a Market?"[59] He adopts a more wistful tone in discussing his family's reaction to their inability to correct his "defects": "When they could not do that, they endeavored to conceal them; and taught me to be ashamed of my Person, instead of arming me with true Fortitude to despise any Ridicule or Contempt of it. This has caused me much uneasiness in my younger Days; and it required many Years to conquer this Weakness."

Hay notes that while he is comfortable in speechmaking, he is sometimes uneasy in one-to-one encounters and must strategize when dealing with persons much taller than himself. His personal experience had engendered empathy for others, and he felt moved when witnessing abuse or a struggle against oppression; he reports that his voice changed and his eyes watered when he heard of generous acts performed by people endeavoring to influence society.[60] Hay's reflections on the world's ill-treatment of others like himself—and his struggle to overcome his own unease—are among the first considerations of these matters published by anyone with dwarfism.

Mary Rutherford Garrettson

Christian educator Mary Rutherford Garrettson (1794–1879) represents the opposite end of the spectrum from Hay's candid musings on his appearance. Several portraits painted in her own time, as well as the photographic record, reveal that she was a dwarf, but there is no evidence that Garrettson or any of her contemporaries ever referred to her short stature (Fig. 15).[61] It was not until a century after her death that her condition was mentioned, and then only in passing.[62]

Mary was the daughter of Freeborn Garrettson, a pioneer minister, and Catherine Livingston Garrettson. Freeborn was from a comfortable Anglican background. After a reportedly wild youth, he embraced Christianity, freed his slaves, and became an itinerant preacher in upstate New York.[63] One of his first converts was Catherine Livingston, the daughter of one of the most prominent families among the old colonial aristocracies. Her family was hardly pleased to see her transformed from "dear Kitty who loved parties . . . to dressing somberly and talking earnestly." But Catherine was resolute, both in her newfound faith and in her choice of a mate: she overcame the hesitation expressed by Freeborn, as well as her own family's opposition, to make a seemingly devoted marriage.

Mary Garrettson was born when Freeborn was forty-two and Catherine forty. The couple's hopes for Mary's salvation and dedicated life were more than realized when she became a prominent figure in the Methodist community, laboring indefatigably for Christian causes.[64] Through generous gifts and personal efforts, she helped establish churches in

15. *Mary Rutherford Garrettson. From Howard Morse,* Historic Old Rhinebeck: Echoes of Two Centuries *(New York: Howard Morse, 1908).*

Hillside and Rhinebeck, New York. She established a children's school; published essays on religious subjects; edited her father's papers; and after her mother's death, edited Catherine's journals.

Less well known is Mary Garrettson's authorship of two children's books, *Mabel and Her Sunlit Home* and *Little Mabel's Friends*.[65] Although these fictional works were written principally as religious instruction, they offer perceptive modern readers our best window into Garrettson's childhood, temperament, and responsiveness to nature.

Her letters reveal the pattern of her days. She writes to her many friends and relatives, showing concern about their health and extending invitations or discussing a proposed visit of her own. She corresponds with numerous clergymen, many of whom spend long periods as her guests, often conducting the services and study groups that were an integral part of life at Wildercliff, her Rhinebeck home, right up until her death at age eighty-five. Often the ministers thank her for her advice about starting a school, for her gifts of financial aid or books, or for her recent hospitality. Occasionally, Garrettson writes about her political convictions, as in a letter to her uncle about the unjust treatment of the Indians.[66]

In later letters Garrettson asserts her antislavery convictions and expresses her pain at the suffering endured by the Union troops during the Civil War, "starving in a land of plenty."[67] But more often, she focuses on religious matters. Like her mother, she had "brought souls to Christ"—although the "notorious infidel" Tom Paine, whom she tried to convert as he lay on his deathbed, proved intractable: "On all subjects but religion he conversed freely; on that he maintained sullen unbroken silence."[68]

Garrettson is described as having an exceptional memory and being well versed in science and literature; the private Mary, however, is more elusive and complex than the personality she generally revealed. Nevertheless, in her personal letters, as in her children's books, her emotionality does filter through. In one letter she castigates her beloved friend Maria Nott for having treated badly "an aged minister of Christ" in Garrettson's home; later Garrettson begs Nott to forgive her and to forget their dispute, explaining that she herself "has trained her memory to forget the unpleasant . . . I may be wrong but I think I have been happier for it."[69] Still, later, suffering from Nott's withdrawal, Garrettson reproaches herself for her own excessively loving emotions.[70]

In the letters to Nott and those to Garrettson's cousin Mary Suckley, Garrettson reveals her capacity for intimacy. She praises Mary Suckley's suitor and she refers to her own dissimilar destiny: "Our paths through life will be different. Yours will probably be varied by the duties, enlivened by the kindness and perhaps afflicted by the sympathies of domestic woes. Mine will be more solitary—unamused by the interests and unvexed by the cares of such a situation as it regards myself. I shall always feel warmly for the dear friends from whom distance separates me and if ever the selfish wish (that I had you all my own) arises (as doubtless it often will) it shall be checked by the consideration of your superior usefulness and (I hope) superior enjoyments."[71]

Mary Garrettson made her peace with her single life, but it is clear that she was often lonely and battled with moods and feelings of self-reproach. Although she repeatedly declares her affection for Suckley and mentions how she misses their time together, she can also write, "If I had a child I think I should never wish her to love as I had done. . . . I call myself fool." She asks Suckley to burn her letter as she has burned Suckley's, "leaving no record of our weakness." Given the effusive literary conventions of their time, it is difficult to judge the precise character of the "love" or "weakness" that Garrettson alludes to.

Like her mother, Garrettson admonishes herself for not knowing how to love God well enough and speaks frequently of sick headaches and depressed moods, complaints reminiscent of her mother's. Freeborn was freer in expressing pleasure, commenting that "the smiles and cheerful conversations with my lovely daughter would awaken sensibility in the mind of a hermit."[72] Mary views her father with similar enthusiasm.

Mary spent a great deal of energy editing her father's papers and her mother's diaries. Catherine's letters to Mary were often instructional in nature, and her journal mentions her prayers for her daughter, rather than revealing much about Mary's life or personality. In a 1990 doctoral dissertation about Catherine's writings, however, Diane Lobody speculates that Mary excised materials from her mother's journals that she believed might offend nineteenth-century sensibilities.[73]

If Mary Garrettson washed away the unpleasant when she could, it is also true that there was a great deal that she found positive and gratifying. Her feelings about her childhood may be discerned best from her seemingly autobiographical *Little Mabel and Her Sunlit Home*, set in "a home so delightful, that to the little girl who dwelt there it seemed like a paradise of which she never tired." Mary's memories of her relationship with her father are clearly reflected in her description of an incident in her book in which Mabel's father, a preacher, returns home and right away "his cold garments are doffed, the warm gown and slippers [are] on, [and] the little one in ecstasy is in her father's arms."[74] Little Mabel was a popular enough character to have been appropriated, authorized or not, toward the end of the nineteenth century for a lengthy poem by the Hires Root Beer Company, detailing how elfin Mabel discovered a marvelous nectar in the woods that the company now offered to the public.[75]

Clearly there was love in Mabel/Mary's childhood, but also much encouragement to contain her emotions. Mabel's mother remembers her as a girl who does not cry; her father removes the image of one skeleton from her picture book—but he keeps another in place so Mabel can "learn to conquer her foolish fear."[76] Even Garrettson's sometimes effusive language with her close friends is tempered by reserve, as in a letter to Suckley: "There are some things you will wish to know which I cannot tell you. I will not deceive you. What I may with propriety you shall hear—do not ask more."[77]

Since neither Garrettson nor others in her circle seem to mention it, we cannot assess how her dwarfism affected her sense of self or her relationships. As mentioned previously, contemporary portraits reveal that she is a dwarf, and her father's biographer, Robert Drew Simpson, uses the word, noting that she suffered from scoliosis and frequent illness.[78] The implicit compact between Garrettson and others was that no one would treat her dwarfism as a problem but all would see it simply as God's will. Neither oddity nor disabled person, she was viewed instead as a respected Christian woman of distinguished background.

One curious stratagem, however, bears mention. Members of the Rhinecliff Methodist congregation recalled that she used to sit in church holding in front of her face a fan that had a hole in it, so that she might look out without being observed.[79] One wonders whether she, like Toulouse-Lautrec and many other dwarfs, had an aversion to being stared at. This slim fact is all we have to suggest that she may have felt any discomfort about reactions to her appearance.

Mary Rutherford Garrettson is one of the rare female dwarfs we know anything at all about. She grappled with loneliness, but she could not conceive of a life for herself that included a romantic partnership; she focused instead on Christian service, friendship, visiting children, books, and nature. Although she railed at her infirmities as she aged, her stamina and her concern for others never flagged. In 1878, a year before her death, a blind Mary Garrettson dictated a sympathy note to comfort a friend. She offered to visit her the following week. Its recipient records at the top of the letter, "From my dear and precious friend, Mary R. Garrettson."[80]

Paul Leicester Ford

At the turn of the twentieth century, Paul Leicester Ford (1865–1902) was one of the most socially prominent members of Brooklyn and Manhattan society.[81] He had achieved acclaim as a historian, editor, bibliographer, novelist, political activist, and library reformer. Ford was one of a few scholars responsible for the introduction of the meticulous methods that helped make the study of history a profession, not merely a gentleman's pastime. His biographies and bibliographies of Benjamin Franklin, George Washington, and Thomas Jefferson remain in use today, and he is recognized as having humanized these important figures. Several of his novels are still in print. However, except among professionals in the fields in which he made major contributions, Ford is little known today. His rich life and tragic death deserve to be more widely recognized.

While an enormous amount of material exists documenting his professional achievements, and family letters and other works casting light on his life may be found in several libraries, the role that his short stature played is more difficult to ferret out, especially in his own writings. However, it is clear that his height did figure in the perceptions that others had of him. Several articles refer to him as a dwarf, and his biographer calls him "dwarfish"; a contemporary critic suggested that a single copy of each of Ford's works placed in a pile "would make a pyramid taller than a man of great stature."[82] A good friend eulogized him as "small in stature but great in mind" (Fig. 16).[83]

Ford was born in 1865 into a well-respected Brooklyn Heights family. He was the fourth of the seven children of Gordon L. Ford, a lawyer, book collector, and railroad administrator, who was descended from early New England settlers. Paul's mother, Emily Ellsworth Fowler Ford, was the granddaughter of Noah Webster and an author known for her hospitality and charitable activities. Born in Amherst, Emily Ford grew up near the poet Emily Dickinson remaining her close friend, and many well-known artists, writers, and musicians were guests in the Fords' Brooklyn home.

16. Paul Leicester Ford. Paul Leicester Ford Papers, Manuscripts and Archives Division, the New York Public Library, Astor, Lenox and Tilden Foundations. Photograph from Yale Collection of American Literature, Beinecke Rare Book and Manuscript Library.

Gordon Ford is probably best known for his collection of Americana, totaling one hundred thousand manuscripts and fifty thousand volumes, in its day regarded as one of the finest and most complete collections of its kind.[84] Historians from all over the country visited his home and made use of the information in his collection. Born into this family, Paul Ford gained access not only to its scholarly tradition, but also to the pleasures of residing in a grand library. But his physical condition created some constraints. His sister Emily Ellsworth Ford Skeels writes:

As my brother Paul approached the threshold of early manhood it seemed as if every avenue of activity had been closed to him. After an accident in infancy, his had been a childhood of almost constant physical suffering, with interludes of acute inflammation and fever. . . . Of schooling he had scarcely any, a few desultory months having proved his insuperable frailty. Somewhat later he shared three winters of history-study with the two sisters above and below him in the family ladder. This home-made tuition, imparted by a third—our sister Rosalie— led gaily through a course of English, French, Greek and American history. . . . From that time, as indeed before, his ardent, facile mind trained itself solely by books or in the school of life, and of both was always avid.

None the less, at seventeen a delicate physique—which gave no presage of its later endurance of work and fatigue far enduring many a strong man— and an utter lack of training in any direction, technical or otherwise, boded ill for his happiness or usefulness in life. Small wonder that he passed through a period of profound depression, known to his family chum only by his subsequent confession. . . .

At the first sign of dawn my brother wrote two little articles of mildly antiquarian content, which were accepted by *The Evening Post*. Well I remember my father's interest and participation, as well as his pride, so pleasant to see, in that first public recognition.[85]

This summary reveals some of the central elements that enabled him to prevail: the intellectual stimulation and emotional understanding that he received from parents and siblings, and his own intelligence and persevering nature. One might add to these the economic security that enabled him to devote so much time to his vocation and to maintaining his health.

At the age of eleven, assisted by his older brother, Worthington, he printed his first work, *Webster Genealogy*.[86] By his twenties he was publishing a spate of scholarly articles, reviews, and books. He then turned to fiction as a diversion from his historical writing. Ford's popular novel *The Honourable Peter Stirling* reveals the influence of his participation as an active political worker in his ward.[87] Seen as particularly instructive for youthful readers, it initially sold two hundred thousand copies, and a half million by 1945.[88] Republished in 1968 within a series of historically significant works, it is praised in the preface as among the best of American political novels. *Janice Meredith*, another extremely successful work, is a historical novel that relies heavily on Ford's knowledge of Washington and the American Revolution. His fictional efforts reveal his sentimental as well as his principled side.

Ford's accomplishments were formidable. He held important positions in many professional and social organizations. With his father and his brother Worthington, he established the Historical Printing Club, which issued books and pamphlets relating to American history. Ford was an indefatigable sleuth. An inquiry from another historian could send him searching in European libraries for an answer. Among the results of his investigations were his own *Franklin Bibliography* (1889); *Writings of Thomas Jefferson* (10 vols. 1892–1899); *Writings of John Dickinson* (3 vols. 1895); *The True George Washington* (1896) and *The Many-Sided Franklin* (1899). Ford was admired for portraying Washington not as a demigod, but as "a hearty healthy school-boy with a hot temper, a fondness for fine clothes, and a great propensity for youthful love affairs; . . .who when he was older and suffering from attacks of youthful passion wrote poetry to and about [his] love objects, which were numerous."[89] In a brief work called *Who Was the Mother of Franklin's Son*, about Franklin's out-of-wedlock son, who was raised in Franklin's household and was later governor of New Jersey, Ford warns the reader not to judge Franklin's personal life by standards of a later time and thus fail to appreciate his other virtues because of his indiscretions.[90]

Another significant interest of Ford's was drama. In a brief critical work, *The Beginnings of American Dramatic Literature, 1609–1789*, he recognizes the uneven quality of early plays but forgives the playwrights because their performances had brought pleasure to thousands. Ford's own plays were somewhat stilted. His only runaway success was *Janice Meredith*, a rendering of his earlier novel.

The background of Ford's novels owes a great debt to his social milieu. He was a frequent guest at a number of homes, but there was no place where he seems to have felt as content or welcome as he did at Stoneywolde, the home of his sister Rosalie Barr, in the foothills of the Catskills. In family letters and reminiscences one is able to discern, to paraphrase one of his titles, "the many-sided Paul Leicester Ford." Gillian, Rosalie's daughter, writes about the lighter side of her favorite uncle:

> Uncle Paul was an author of diverse abilities. . . . His fingers were unusually adept. He made all sorts of toys and tricks. We were held spellbound by the impromptu stories he improvised on the spur of the moment. A stroll with him in the woods was certain to turn into a bear hunt or an attack by savages. A drive with him along a dusty road would develop into a tour of the world; and a rest hour in the house became a game in which everyone wanted to join. He made us boats to sail and a larger boat in which we sailed. He took us fishing, shooting, and bullfrogging. . . . How we adored him. His word was our law. The hours when he shut himself in, to do his writing, would have dragged unmercifully had we not had his interest at heart.[91]

Ford's worldly successes and character were very likely among the factors that attracted his wife, Grace Kidder, but they might not have sufficed without his charm. Paul seemed a confirmed bachelor, living in Brooklyn with his sister Emily and her family, until two years before his marriage, when he moved into a separate apartment. Although the couple had known each other for some years, only after proving himself in the world did he gain the courage to propose to Kidder, a woman of ideals who cared little for fashion and was active in philanthropy.

The Fords' wedding attracted enormous attention, according to the *Brooklyn Daily Eagle*, more than any other in the previous half dozen years: "It was incontestably the marriage of the hour and not to be overshadowed, Brooklyn's foremost novelist and literarian, a man of marked social standing himself, marrying one of the most fascinating of Heights belles, a girl scarcely more than a debutante and very attractive in form and feature."[92] It was the culmination of a dream Ford had scarcely dared permit himself.

Although his correspondence does not mention his stature, a great deal of attention is given to his health in letters from his brother Worthington, his sisters, and his mother. In a valentine his mother wrote for him when he was four years old, she praises his "large brown eyes which look so kind and grave and wise," and concludes:

> I wonder if that naughty back
> Has ached and twinged with painful rack
> I wonder if that tangled harness
> Has kept you jumping, just one bar less.[93]

Ford's family doctor had prescribed day and night braces to reduce the hunchback and spinal deformity. This less-than-satisfactory effort was, at that period, a common procedure. No diagnosis seems to have been made, in his time or later.[94] While fevers and a crooked back may suggest Pott's disease, no condition should be ever be assigned retrospectively. It is worth mentioning, however, that the literature of dwarfism is full of accounts mistakenly attributing hunched, painful backs to a fall.

If Ford's stature does not seem to have been focused upon by his family, it was certainly a source of concern to Ford, whose biographer, Paul Z. DuBois, writes: "Ford's personal appearance was not unprepossessing. In spite of a hunchback and dwarfed growth which kept his height under five feet, he had strikingly handsome facial features, large brown eyes, and an attractive shock of wavy hair. Ford was sensitive about his deformity and limited public photographs to those not showing a full-length view."[95] In fact, his hypersensitivity was so acute that it led to a violent display on his wedding day: descending the church steps, he dropped his bride's hand, punched the photographer, and seized and ruined his camera.[96] Ford, rarely known to be out of control, risked public embarrassment at a peak moment because of his dismay at being photographed.

In his works, most of Ford's male protagonists are large, husky individuals. However, Donald Maitland in *The Story of an Untold Love*, who resembles Ford most closely, says, "I was not a strong boy, and my shyness and timidity had prompted me to much solitude and few friends, to much reading and to little play."[97] DuBois sees as a recurring theme in Ford's fiction the strong link between physical and moral courage.[98] Indeed, both physical prowess and moral concerns are at center stage in the final drama of Ford's life—his murder by his brother Malcolm. In this generally close family, Malcolm Ford seems to have become a pariah in later years. His brother Worthington was Paul's best man, but Malcolm was not invited to the wedding. The black sheep of the family, he was nevertheless quite famous in his own right.

Malcolm Webster Ford was the physical opposite of Paul: he was tall and strapping and was at one time the best-known all-around athlete in the United States as well as a respected authority and writer on athletic subjects.[99] Although both men's names were quite familiar to newspaper readers, only with the contest over the father's will were the two associated in the public mind as brothers. It is clear that the brothers' tensions deepened as a consequence of Malcolm Ford's having been disinherited. Gordon Ford had been displeased with Malcolm's priorities and spendthrift nature. He had wanted Malcolm to abandon his "unseemly" professional athletic pursuits. There was ambiguity about Gordon's final wishes, however, and controversy among the siblings about granting Malcolm a share—if he agreed to give up competitive sports.[100]

Paul was the family spokesman when Malcolm initiated a lawsuit claiming his father had said he wanted Malcolm provided for. After testifying that his father had died from typhoid fever as a result of nursing Malcolm, Paul said, "I do not see why Malcolm should get any of the estate, as my father had laid down his life to save Malcolm. He gave a worthy life to save an unworthy life."[101] Although the judge found Malcolm's case convincing, he ruled against him for want of evidence, and Malcolm ended up settling for a small amount. However, as his fortunes waned, he repeatedly turned to Paul for help; Paul only sometimes relented, and there were loud arguments between them. Paul Ford could excuse Benjamin Franklin and others, judging their shortcomings in context, but he could not forgive Malcolm. In the tradition of this family, status and honor were important, and Malcolm had shamed them by bringing matters to court.

Paul Ford's life ended in a drama more compelling than any he had described in his novels or nonfiction works. The disagreements between the brothers had continued to fester until 1902 when, at the age of thirty-seven, Paul was murdered by Malcolm in the library of the Manhattan mansion that Paul had built for himself and Grace when they married. Malcolm then shot himself. These desperate acts occurred after a final argument in which Paul turned down his brother's request for money.

While all were shocked by the brothers' deaths and deplored Malcolm's actions, Janet Graves Ford, in an eloquent letter to the editor, offered the most charitable view of her former husband. Janet felt that the years of brooding about being denied his property rights had unbalanced Malcolm's mind and that he was temporarily insane when he committed the murder. She describes Malcolm as a man of tender, honest impulses and successful in all but money matters; she claimed that his dire financial state after the recent failure of the magazine he had edited had been the final blow. She concludes, "Whatever may be the judgment of his friends, I am certain they will feel he is more to be pitied than blamed for being instrumental in the sad ending of the lives of two such brilliant men."[102]

Paul Leicester Ford—a genius at the apex of his life's happiness—was crushed by the combination of his brother's despair and his own unbending rectitude. The many-sided Paul Leicester Ford remains a memorable figure, having inspired in his lifetime enormous love, fatal hatred, and wide admiration—a tragic hero in his own personal drama.

Henri de Toulouse-Lautrec

Henri de Toulouse-Lautrec (1864–1901) was in most obvious respects Paul Leicester Ford's polar opposite. An energetic, sybaritic individual, his tumultuous adult years were spent creating thousands of works of art, cultivating many friends and acquaintances, traveling, and being caught up in sexual activity, drink, and playful self-display. Although a stroke led to his final illness, his congenital condition as well as syphilis, and especially alcoholism, were significant contributors to his death.

Lautrec, more famous today than in his own time, has inspired more than two hundred volumes that analyze both his life and his art. Some emphasize his life's richness, characterizing his brief thirty-six years as the typical "candle burning at both ends" existence of a consummate artist. Others emphasize his inability to resolve his psychological problems, concluding that his personal failures are reflected in his artistic weaknesses. All mention the central role that dwarfism played in his life. He had a normal-sized head and torso, but short, knock-kneed legs and short arms with comparatively long hands (Fig. 17).

Lautrec's parents personified their aristocratic lineage. They were ill-matched cousins, the children of two sisters, whose marriage was a consequence of the family's wish to preserve its wealth and traditions. The parents stopped living together by the time Henri was four years old. Much of Lautrec's character can be seen as an extension of his father's style. He resembled him in energy, gregariousness, exhibitionism, womanizing, and aristocratic aloofness. That Henri's infirmity denied him the physicality of his father, however, contributed to his focusing on his art and deepening his powers of discernment.

The consanguinity of Lautrec's parents was not unusual in their families, in which marriage between relatives was often encouraged. Although there were several instances of dwarfism in the family, Lautrec's earlier diagnosis of pyknodysostosis has been convincingly challenged.[103] Although Henri was a somewhat small child, his distinctive deformity did not occur until later. He seems to have enjoyed a pleasant early childhood in various family estates, in some respects reminiscent of Alexander Pope's, though on a grander scale. Because he was often in poor health, his mother sought to strengthen him with trips to spas on the Riviera. Neither the trips nor her prayers were to any avail. When he was thirteen, visiting his aunt and uncle in Albi, France, he broke his left femur. A year later, at a health spa in Barèges, where he had gone to strengthen his crippled leg, he fell and broke his other thigh. The growth of both legs ceased, and for the rest of his life he carried himself on his foreshortened legs with difficulty, aided by a cane.[104] When the accidents occurred it was not recognized that an underlying brittle bone disorder was responsible for his crippling. His parents wrongly blamed the doctor for setting the bones badly.

The years that followed his accidents were profoundly significant both for his character and his work. Despite considerable pain, he spent a great deal of time cultivating friendships, writing, and, especially, painting. At age seventeen he began to study painting seriously, perfecting his technique. Lautrec's aristocratic background and wealth allowed him to develop his talent without financial constraints and enabled him to find acceptance in a lively social circle. Montmartre of the 1880s and 1890s provided subject matter for his paintings as well as a haven where he could avoid the stares of the judgmental bourgeoisie. He and his friends would amuse themselves by trooping off to the country, photographing one another in Asian costumes, attending circuses and theaters, and of course, frequenting the cabarets and dance halls that became the subjects of Lautrec's paintings. Despite his slow, uneven gait, he was said to have been a good swimmer, rower, and sailor. His epicurean tastes have been cel-

17. Henri de Toulouse-Lautrec. From Charles de Rodat, Toulouse-Lautrec album de famille *(Fribourg, Switzerland: Hatier, 1985), courtesy Charles de Rodat.*

ebrated in colorful photographs of him partaking of culinary delights against a background of sensual scenes.[105]

Lautrec painted few landscapes but focused his attention on portraits and interior scenes. Among his most well known subjects were Aristide Bruant, Jane Avril, and La Goulue and settings such as the Moulin Rouge dance hall. His original use of bright color and bold pattern made him an influential figure in the world of printmaking and poster design; his portraits of friends, by contrast, exhibit a darker palette and a more traditional approach. Lautrec felt very much at home in Montmartre's cabarets, dance halls, and brothels. At one bordello, which had elegant rooms in period styles that were designed to satisfy clients' fantasies, he was a well-accepted resident, a kind of family member, eating and spending time with the women when they were not working. They called him Monsieur Henri or sometimes "coffee-pot," an affectionate nickname that telescoped his short stature and sexual virility.

In this setting, he could find relief from the slights that he had suffered in adolescence and adulthood from women of his own class.[106] His cynicism about love was fostered by such treatment and by growing up among males who loved neither the women they married nor the sexual partners they were excited by. Although Lautrec was known to have had affairs, his gallant attentions were reserved for the women of the brothel. When he visited, he brought fine food, wine, and flowers; he chatted and played cards, and was accepted as a confidant. Furthermore, he was witness to the most intimate moments between the women. Almost the only tender feelings depicted in his paintings appear in his representation of lesbian relationships in the lithographic series *Elle*.

Some critics view Lautrec as having rendered a realistic record of life in Montmartre, but as having missed out on greatness because of his narrow subject matter. Others have concluded that his limitation was the result of a lack of deep feeling and compassion in most of his work.[107] Rarely is a face portrayed clearly or sympathetically; features are often indistinct or shrouded in shadow. His subjects rarely smile or express contentment, and usually painted in profile or in frontal view but with eyes averted, they do not meet the gaze of the observer. Notice them, the artist seems to say, survey the scene, but there's no need to get too close. One does not want to belabor the point; certainly there are innumerable side-view portraits in the history of art. But considering Lautrec's tremendous productivity—735 paintings, 275 watercolors, 350 graphic works, and 5,000 drawings[108]—there are a disproportionately small number of works with a frontal view encouraging relaxed engagement between subject and painter. For most dwarfs, being exposed to a stranger's critical eye is a frequent and irksome event. Shutting out the awareness of stares becomes a practice they learn to refine to a science. Lautrec would prefer to be the critical observer, controlling the other's power to observe him. His several portraits of his beloved mother, Adele, are among the few conveying repose. Among the most moving memorabilia in the artist's record are his housemaid Berthe's poignant letters to his mother, depicting Henri's deteriorating physical condition and bizarre, drunken behavior during the period before his death, at the age of thirty-seven at the family estate at Malrome.[109]

Perhaps the most revealing evidence of the artist's inability to come to terms with his dwarfism is the fact that he painted only a single self-portrait—and that, when he was still an adolescent. Only his upper body is shown, and his expression is rather wary. All later depictions are caricatures that exaggerate the size of his head and his peculiar appearance. In one caricature, done at the age of twenty-three, he draws a disproportionately large, naked Lily Grenier performing fellatio on a tiny, fully dressed, supine Lautrec. It was left to friends to paint fuller, more affectionate portraits of him. Self-caricature is a defensive maneuver common for persons with a physical disability. As Julia Frey points out, it is an attempt to fend off unkind remarks by pointing out the deficiencies first oneself. She concludes, "By making himself 'smaller than life,' he discounted his own human value. Once he had demeaned himself in his art, his death by self-destruction was a logical conclusion."[110]

Other commentators have offered more positive appraisals.[111] Lautrec's response to his unique attributes—aristocratic entitlement, incongruent parenting, high energy level, considerable artistic talent, and ego-alien physical difference—was to leap headlong into life. He could escape ruminating about any discontents through frenetic, often sensual, activities of many kinds. His legacy is not only his art, but also the public's fascination with the joyful as well as tragic elements of his multifaceted life.

Charles Proteus Steinmetz

In Charles Proteus Steinmetz (1865–1923), research scientist, we have the example of another genius, a man of enormous professional achievement whose disability assumed a very different place in his life. None of his biographers discern in him any trace of bitterness. His relationships with others were warm, not oppositional, and although he did not form romantic attachments or have children of his own, he found an ingenious way of acquiring the family companionship he desired.

Born Karl August Rudolph Steinmetz, in Germany, Steinmetz was an only child. His father was a railway employee and his mother the widow of his father's brother. Charles had two older half-sisters from the marriage of his mother and his uncle. His deformity was congenital, with both his father and grandfather exhibiting it (Fig. 18).

Renowned for his investigations in the area of electricity, Steinmetz was responsible for 195 patents, acquired during his twenty-eight years as a consulting engineer at the General Electric Company. His reputation as a theoretician was earned through

18. Charles Proteus Steinmetz with Albert Einstein. From General Electric Company, The Story of Steinmetz *(Schenectady, N.Y.: General Electric, 1941).*

his elaboration of the mathematical law of magnetic hysteresis.[112] The magnitude of Steinmetz's contribution to electrical engineering was enormous: skilled at applying mathematical methods to practical problems, he was especially known for his investigations of lightning and its technical applications. His experiments creating artificial electricity earned him a worldwide reputation as "the modern Jupiter." Among his achievements were improvements in motors, generators, and transformers. He was also a visionary, an early advocate of atmospheric pollution control, research on solar energy conversion, and the electrification of railroads and automobiles.[113] The author of ten technical books, and faculty member at Union College, Steinmetz was as well known in his time as Albert Einstein and Guglielmo Marconi. Today, however, his name is unfamiliar to most Americans, and the few biographies that exist are fragmentary and out-of-date.

Steinmetz was a much beloved and indulged child. His mother died when he was one year old, and his father and grandmother raised him. He kept a chemical laboratory in the alcove of his room at home. His father often had the young Charles visit him at the railroad shop, where he watched and talked with the mechanics. Although he was an early scholar—starting Latin at age five, Greek and Hebrew at seven, and algebra and geometry at eight—he was also a leader at games with friends.[114]

At the University of Breslau, it was customary for the mathematics society to assign members a nickname, and for Steinmetz, who was held in affectionate regard, they chose Proteus. In Greek mythology, Proteus, god of the sea, was hunchbacked and the size of a human hand; when trapped, he could change himself into a thousand different shapes. Once he saw he could not escape he would resume his true shape and confide the secrets of the universe to listeners.[115] This nickname conveyed the admiration of Charles's friends for his flowing combination of body, spirit, and humble genius. When he became an American citizen, he changed his given name of Karl August Rudolph to Charles Proteus, fusing his American identity with his Protean self.

In Breslau, Steinmetz had become an active socialist, and eventually he was forced to flee from the authorities before receiving his doctorate in mathematics. The ever adaptable scholar journeyed to Zurich, where he studied mechanical engineering and met Oscar Asmussen, a young American student, whose family paid Steinmetz's passage to the United States and lent him money until he found work.[116] He secured employment as a draftsman with Rudolf Eickemeyer, a thriving manufacturer of machinery, who had some electrical patents. This period was followed by his "discovery" by E. Wilbur Rice Jr., chief engineer of General Electric. Rice found their first meeting memorable: "I was startled and somewhat disappointed by the strange sight of a small, frail body surmounted by a large head with long hair hanging to his shoulders, clothed in an old cardigan jacket, cigar in mouth, sitting cross-legged on a laboratory work table. My disappointment was but momentary, and disappeared the moment he began to talk. I instantly felt the strange power of his piercing but kindly eyes, and as he continued, his clear conceptions and marvelous grasp of engineering problems convinced me that we had indeed made a great find."[117] It is interesting to note the similarity of the emotional shift described here to a passage by Oliver Goldsmith about Voltaire's first meeting with Pope; when he first "perceived our poor melancholy English poet, naturally deformed, and wasted as he was with sickness and study, he could not help regarding him with utmost compassion. But when Mr. Pope began to speak . . . Voltaire's pity began to be changed into admiration, and at last into envy."[118]

Not all of Steinmetz's experiences went as smoothly as his first encounter with Rice. When a child in the street cried out, "Look at the funny midget!" Steinmetz responded, "I'm Rumpelstiltskin, I'll eat you up!" When he saw the boy's terror, he smiled and reassured him.[119] With adults, the offense could be more serious. At work, a new employee commented, "Where did they get that little monkey?" Another employee revealed that the man was the brilliant Steinmetz, and the first man feared retribution. Instead, Steinmetz invited him to dinner, defusing insult with kindness. It was easier, of course, to be magnanimous from a position of strength, but Steinmetz's benign nature and easygoing temperament were characteristic of him.[120]

In Schenectady, New York, Steinmetz first lived with two other bachelors, fellow engineers, enjoying the conviviality of their life together in a house they called Liberty Hall. There he built a conservatory where he grew desert plants, and in his yard he raised alligators. Inside, he had a private laboratory. He often ate in the boardinghouse of his friends the Kreugers. Later, he had a two-story house and laboratory built, fitted with magnetite arc lamps that he had recently developed. To run the lights, he hired Le Roy Hayden, a young engineer friend. Because most of the work took place at night, Hayden moved in, serving also as Steinmetz's assistant. When Hayden married and moved to an apartment, Steinmetz felt bereft. He invited Hayden and his bride to live with him in the spacious new residence. They seemed pleased, and a family was formed.

Eventually, Steinmetz adopted Hayden, and his three lively children became Steinmetz's grandchildren. They all lived amicably together for the rest of his life, vacationing during the summers at a rustic cabin on Viele Creek. A typical diary entry captures that period: "9 am: Just got up and had the usual breakfast of Coffee or Postum, milk and Zwieback. Went out paddling after breakfast, while Kids washed dishes accumulated. Pork chops for lunch. Cleaned icebox and burned sulfur. Finished 'Einstein's Theory of Relativity I' yesterday, working on 'Electricity and Civilization' today."[121]

Steinmetz combined a mundane and cheerful family life with various professional accomplishments. He served as head of the electrical engineering department of Union College, and was an attentive mentor of young engineers who later became eminent themselves. He became president of the Schenectady School Board in 1911 and also spearheaded a successful campaign for public parks. Although his reputation was damaged when he assumed a politically naive stance in World War I, advocating American nonparticipation and assuming Germany's victory, he recovered from this setback. From 1913 to 1917, Steinmetz served on the advisory council of the *New Review*, a left-wing publication. Among his colleagues there were Eugene Debs, Maxim Gorky, and W.E.B. Du Bois.[122] Among the articles he wrote, one expressed support for the socialist revolution. Steinmetz's sympathy for Soviet Russia led him to write to Lenin offering technical assistance with electrical engineering matters. Lenin, who had not previously heard of Steinmetz, responded warmly, declining, but thanking him for his generosity. Steinmetz was also outspoken on the protection of the environment and the reduction of industrial waste. Although he sometimes evidenced political naïveté, he could also be quite prescient.

The overarching principle that marked Steinmetz's positions, however, was humanism. He had the opportunity to acquire personal wealth, but did not because he believed that individuals, after providing for their basic needs and their families', should offer the rest for the public good.[123] His wish to share his good fortune is evident in his introduction to *America and the New Epoch*: "When I landed in Castle Garden, from the steerage of a French liner, I had ten dollars and no job, and could speak no English. Now, personally, I have no fault to find with existing society; it has given me everything I wanted. . . . The only criticism I would make is that I would far more enjoy my advantages if I knew that everybody else would enjoy the same."[124]

We don't know whether Steinmetz disavowed romantic love through lack of interest or lack of success, or whether he suffered from its absence, but his many pursuits, and his acquisition of a family, seem to have brought him considerable satisfaction.

Katherine Butler Hathaway

Thankfully, there are an increasing number of autobiographical works by dwarfs in the twentieth century. Among the earliest and best of these are the moving memoir by Katherine Butler Hathaway (1890–1942), *The Little Locksmith* (1943), and her posthumous publication, *The Journals and Letters of the Little Locksmith* (1946).[125] After the Feminist Press rediscovered *The Little Locksmith* in 2000, and republished it, adding an informative foreword and afterword, the book met with enthusiastic reviews.

Katherine Butler was born in Baltimore, Maryland, in 1890 and moved to Salem, Massachusetts, with her family when she was fifteen. By the age of five, she had contracted a form of dwarfism known as tuberculous spondylitis, or Pott's disease, the same ailment that affected Alexander Pope. Settling in bones and joints, it results in short stature and deformity, and in later years causes fatigue, pain, and serious breathing problems. Rare today and treatable, it was more common before the days of pasteurized milk and the availability of antibiotics.

No one has captured as eloquently as Hathaway the central issues that people with dwarfism confront. In a painful recognition scene, she describes how, as a teenager, she first experienced the shocking disparity between her physical appearance and her spirit. Beset by a sense of her irrevocable difference from others, she is at the same time mortified by her longing for acceptance. Most poignantly, she clandestinely harbors a dangerous wish for a romantic life partner, despite a tacit familial message that this hope is vain: "Everyone discussed the romantic futures of her brothers, sister, and their friends, but nobody ever said, 'When Katherine gets married,' or 'Why hasn't Kitty got a beau yet,' or 'We must get a beau for you, Kitty' . . . it was taken for granted that I was not to have what was apparently considered the most thrilling and important experience in grown-up life . . . the reason was so obvious that no explanation was necessary. The reason was there in the mirror for me to see. But, given the reason, nobody ever attempted to console me or to offer me any clue as to how I was to manage my life with this great thing missing."[126]

She managed through fruitful introspection and a growing talent for judicious risk-taking. Her memoir explores many universal themes. She offers, for example, an extended and tender portrayal of her relationship with her nieces and nephews and speaks about the importance of the aunt relationship to the human experience. She describes the dilemmas of artists: the competing tugs of solitary creative work and envelopment by a cherishing family; the desire for creative work and the devotion to a lover that may cause one to abandon work. Finally, she discusses her belief in a Christian God.

Some of the most compelling segments of this memoir, however, record her reflections on her physical difference. These first arose during Hathaway's long period of forced immobility from late childhood into adolescence. According to informed medical opinion of the day, by remaining in bed attached to a firm board, she could straighten and strengthen her spine. Although her spinal curvature was alleviated somewhat, other symptoms were not, and she identified with the hunchbacked locksmith who occasionally came to the family home.

She describes herself as staring at him with a strange, intimate feeling: "More a gnome than a human being," seemingly lost in his private world of "cross, unapproachable sadness," he never looked back at her. Despite her family's admonition that she should be grateful that treatment would enable her to escape the dwarf's fate, she knew of the terrible word that was used to describe him, and she felt "secretly linked" to him somehow. Her loving family, however, did not associate her with any such word, be it *dwarf, midget,* or *hunchback*.[127]

Hathaway spent her early teen years confined, often rather pleasantly, surrounded by her attentive family, books, and drawing materials. She became a thinker and a dreamer, a writer and an artist, while appreciating the visits of friends and family. Her brother Warren's support and admiration were vital and life giving—but not sufficient. She feared that because of her body she would be denied sexual love.

However, she persevered, finding friendship and romance and achieving recognition. At Radcliffe, where she had gone to study and write, she suffered at first, worried that she might be viewed as an oddity rather than the lively, intelligent woman she knew herself to be. She was reassured by friends such as Catherine Huntington, to whom she wrote the revealing letters published in *Journals*. After her Radcliffe circle dispersed, and during later periods of emotional crisis, she experienced serious depression. Her writing, her spiritual life, and her relationship with her psychoanalyst Dr. Izette De Forest, with whom she maintained a lifelong correspondence, were all instrumental in enabling her to regain her equilibrium.

Hathaway's interactions with her mother are expressed with particular skill. They could not communicate well, and when Katherine tried to express her happiness with her life, her mother did not believe her. When her daughter tried to show love in a warm embrace, her mother's New England temperament could not do the same. But when Katherine acquired her own home, her mother was quick to contribute family possessions to the enterprise. This home, called Sellenraa, was the momentous step by means of which Katherine defined herself as an autonomous person, becoming the center of her own life rather than a witness to the lives of others. The house was situated on a wooded hillside in Castine, Maine, overlooking a harbor. Hathaway spent seven happy years there, welcoming friends and family. She sold Sellenraa after she married Dan Hathaway, sacrificing for financial reasons, in order to move to Paris in 1932.

Hathaway's lyrical account of her inner life and her relationship with people and nature in *The Little Locksmith* was followed by the posthumous publication of the *Journals and Letters of the Little Locksmith,* which cast new light on her feelings about her serious romantic relationships with the Japanese artists Toshihiko and Taro and her marriage to Dan Hathaway. Although the Paris years resulted in Katherine's writing the charming 1934 illustrated children's book *Mr. Muffet's Cats and Their Trip to Paris,* they proved a difficult time for her marriage.[128] In an honest, perspicacious letter to Dr. De Forest, Katherine considers divorcing Dan:

I was horribly unhappy the first year, and I knew it, and used to wish he would die. I wanted to escape. I knew it was a mistake; but I made up my mind to make something good out of something bad. . . . It is infinitely better than it was, but still falls far short of what it should be. I have been an invalid ever since I got married. Before that I traveled alone, lived alone, took care of myself after a fashion, quite badly, but still did it, more than now. I was horribly lonely sometimes, and life didn't seem worth living, that is—after I lost Toshiko. But I did not have the heavy, unwilling body I have now. This morning, as I imagined being free again, going back to my lonely and rather dreary life, it seemed to make me young and well again, as if a frightful burden were lifted. Since I began to pride myself on creating a good marriage, I have fooled myself, and a lot of our "happiness" has been synthetic. Miraculously enough, there has been some of it that has been real.[129]

The toll of her invalidism on her relationship with her husband, her discomfort with his extravagance, and his absence as he traveled in her time of need contributed to her unhappiness: she was put in the uncomfortable position of needing to ask her brother Warren for financial assistance. Sharing her life with Dan seemed to entail at least as much sacrifice as joy. In Paris it seemed that the "normalcy" of marriage that Hathaway had sometimes yearned for was not the perfect fit for her strong-willed, artistic, sensitive nature. However, once the couple returned to the United States and purchased a beautiful old brick house in Blue Hill, Maine, tender times returned, with Dan cooking superb dinners for guests, as well as initiating their more intimate moments together in front of the fire. He energetically renovated the house and nursed her during her bouts of chronic myocarditis in the period before her death in 1942.

Nancy Mairs, in her afterword for *The Little Locksmith*, gives particular attention to the paucity of literature by women writing about the body and to the assumption that persons with disabilities will be exiles from the sexual realm. Mairs notes that this implicit message caused Hathaway to seek sublimation in her creative pursuits—to the benefit of her readers. Happily, however, it did not prevent her from claiming her right to be a fully sexual human being and sometimes even to write about that realm, with a light, deft touch. Mairs observes: "Since Katherine enjoyed both love affairs and a marriage as an adult, we may assume that the true defect lay not in her physical appearance and capacity for erotic activity but in the social attitudes that, ignoring the myriad ways in which she was a normal woman to focus solely on her physical deformity, set her apart."[130]

A wide public has now shown its appreciation of *The Little Locksmith*, a work that is especially evocative for women with disabilities; in her memoir, Hathaway echoes the feelings and experiences of these women as few authors have.

Jean Brissé Saint-Macary

Another significant memoir spans many of the same years as Hathaway's, but concludes several decades later. Jean Brissé Saint-Macary (1902–1975) was a country lawyer, doctor of law, professor of economy, advisor to the French government, and secretary of the Congress of French Notaries (lawyers specializing in contracts). As is suggested by the title of his autobiography, *1 Metre 34*, he was also a dwarf: he had a skeletal condition called SED congenita (Fig. 19).[131]

Saint-Macary's life, his attitudes toward his dwarfism, and the torment that he endured as a result of his society's attitudes contrast sharply with the less negative experience of Katherine Hathaway. But his personal misfortunes assumed historic significance when they led him to spearhead the formation of the Association des personnes de petite taille. He was the first of the individuals described here to seek out and make common cause with other dwarfs.

Born in 1902 in southwestern France to a physician father and a pious mother, Jean suffered repeated humiliations during the first four decades of his life—at the hands of adults, peers, schoolteachers, and doctors. When he was just ten years old, an elegant socialite at a banquet table remarked loudly to another guest, "I do not understand how they could have invited such an ugly runt. His presence spoils the beauty of the party." The mother of a schoolmate who had taunted and assaulted him slapped Jean to the ground, saying, "You are a little monster, you are not a man. Your mother should have killed you the day you were born." One physician, unable to explain Jean's recovery from the tuberculosis that had complicated the other symptoms associated with his diagnosis, told him, "Hurry up and die. Your condition defies medical science. We cannot tolerate it any longer." Jean underwent repeated useless stretching procedures, attached to a hospital bed with weights, in an effort to help him grow. Physicians exhibited him in amphitheaters as a specimen for discussion by medical students.

By the age of ten, he had had secluded himself with his family, his books, and his toys, venturing out only when required to do so and zigzagging his way to and from school to avoid the taunts of other children. While most of his sexual understanding was confined to fantasy, on one rare occasion a woman, in-

19. Jean Brissé Saint-Macary. From Martin Monestier, Les nains *(Paris: Jean Claude Simoen, 1977).*

tending to be generous, disrobed in front of him—the closest he came to sexual experience until his marriage.

By his early teens, he had attempted suicide, and in his twenties, he retreated to a monastery. While his family had tried to be supportive, they had offered mixed messages: his mother offered a strict religious upbringing, and his father stressed obedience and strength of character and discouraged self-pity. The elder Saint-Macary was wise about some matters but opinionated and autocratic in others. He insisted that his son become a country solicitor among people who knew him well and would grant him a good living; he made his son promise he would not pursue an academic career. Similarly, on his deathbed, he asked Jean to promise never to marry or have children, warning him that although his first child might be normal, the second would be deformed, "a monster." Jean came into his own professionally only after his father's death, becoming a solicitor four years later, in 1937. He represented farmers in their dealings with governmental agencies and helped create a rural cooperative that offered them more control over prices and fair trade. He became an economics professor at a prestigious French university as well as a valued governmental advisor.

Saint-Macary married in 1945, at the age of forty-three. He and his wife, a former nurse, had three children, only one of whom survived. Their firstborn, Marie-Antoinette, was born without deformities. Their second child, Pierre, who was a dwarf and also mute, drowned at the age of eight. After their third child, Jean-Francois, died when he was only a few hours old, they decided not to have any other children.

Despite his celebrity and appeals in the press, few potential members responded when Saint-Macary tried to form the Association des personnes de petite taille in 1973.[132] At the first meeting, there were forty photographers but only twenty dwarfs present. The French author Martin Monestier points out that the latter were all "from the world of spectacle—having already accepted their situation." Most others, he believed, did not attend because they preferred not to identify with other little persons but to remain hidden from public view.

Saint-Macary delivered a pep talk in which he told the attendees that they need not retreat from society any longer. At the same time, he painted a grim picture of how dwarfs had been abused until recently and described his own situation in these words: "When I pass before a glass, a shop window that reflects my image, I find myself ugly and hate myself." His words raised a furor: could it be, the audience wondered, that a man whose life had made him a role model for other French dwarfs actually hated himself? If so, how could others remain optimistic?

The undercurrents were not resolved at this first meeting. Madame Priatel, the mother of a child with achondroplasia, was elected president, supposedly in the in-

terest of good public relations. Some of the discussion focused on asking the government to exempt dwarfs from taxes.

This rocky inception must be understood in the context of a greater bias against
dwarfs in France than in countries such as the United States.[133] Still, it may seem
shocking that an accomplished individual like Saint-Macary, who described himself
in his autobiography as a contented husband, a doting grandfather, and a happy man
overall, could retain such negative feelings about his own body. Historically, he may
be viewed as a "bridge" figure, auguring, but not yet fully embodying, the transition
of persons with dwarfism from isolation toward community.

PART II

The Transition

CONFRONTING

MOCKERY, MYTH,

and

MEDICAL MYSTERIES

CHAPTER THREE

Stigma

I met a little elf-man once,
Down where the lilies blow—
I asked him why he was so short
And why he didn't grow.

He slightly frowned, and with his eye
He looked me through and through
"I'm quite as big for me," said he,
"As you are big for you."[1]

The audacious elf who first appeared in this poem approximately a century ago was later reintroduced to readers by the editors of *The Golden Book of Verse*. His words capture the quintessence of stigma: an atypical individual must defend his or her essential self against another's challenge. Whether that challenge stems from curiosity or aggression, the person questioned still feels called upon to justify his or her very existence.

The challenge presented to this elf-man by the curious stranger is relatively benign compared with reactions that many of those with various stigmatizing differences encounter daily. For dwarfs, this "people" that did not view itself as a people throughout history, despite the fact that references were commonly made to a "dwarf race," it was necessary to share the task of learning to deal with stigma. A recurring discussion among dwarfs concerns what to do when strangers stare, make rude remarks, or exhibit threatening behavior. Should those exhibiting such behavior be ignored, reproached, or educated? What strategies are best for friendly and unfriendly intrusions by adults? What are the best ways to respond to children?

While it is essential to develop strategies, it is also important to address the underlying question of why the stigma has been assigned by society in the first place. No recent volume has supplanted Ervin Goffman's original *Stigma*, an invaluable lode that later writers mine. His analysis may help illuminate the interaction of the elf and his questioner: even a single difference in a stranger may reduce him or her from a whole and usual person to a tainted, discounted one.[2]

Goffman divides stigma into three categories: (1) abominations of the body, that is, the various physical deformities; (2) blemishes of individual character, perceived as weak will, unnatural passions or beliefs, or dishonesty; (3) tribal markers of race, nation, and religion, these being signs that can be transmitted through lineage and that equally contaminate all members of a family. An individual who might have been viewed as acceptable is subsequently rejected for possessing a trait that overrides the claim that his or her other attributes have upon us.[3]

Usually, a person meeting a dwarf for the first time is apt to register some astonishment, whether visibly or internally. First of all, there is an obvious discrepancy between size and age: the small size suggests a child, but the facial features are those of an adult—the observer has to resolve the cognitive dissonance. Unconscious associations also play a role. The "normate" may be reminded of characters from mythology, folktales, or literature—trolls from popular legend, the dwarfs in the cartoon *Snow White and the Seven Dwarfs*, or the evil figure in Pär Lagerkvist's *The Dwarf*.[4]

Should such recollections be stimulated, all three of Goffman's stigma categories—physical, moral, and tribal—may be telescoped into one, influencing how the flesh-and-blood dwarf is judged. After the initial shock of reverberating emotionally to physical deformity, the normate may impute to this unknown person the mythological wiliness of trolls, the moral blemish of the evil-spirited dwarf, or the childlike asexual cheeriness of Walt Disney's seven dwarfs—depending on which reference is most familiar. The observer may also instinctively assume tribal associations, seeing the dwarf as belonging to an ancient dwarf race. Each response alone may cause distancing; in combination, the result can be a triple whammy. Few human differences result in so complex a stigmatizing response.

In general, among the variables causing stigma, physical disabilities tend to be the least stigmatizing; sensory disabilities more so; and developmental disability, mental illness, and alcoholism the most stigmatizing. Rarely, however, are reactions to dwarfs and hunchbacks investigated. In a 1970 study of attitudes toward difference that did include these two groups, the author found that they scored among the lowest in the preference hierarchy—fourteenth and sixteenth out of twenty-one groups.[5] They were the least preferred in the physical disabilities category. The researcher attributed the low rating of dwarfs to an aesthetic factor.

Sociobiology offers yet another explanation of prejudice toward the disabled. A large body of literature exists showing that the herd often rejects the odd-looking member. Predators choose the most deviant individuals as quarry—creatures exhibiting difference in color, motion, or other feature. Sparrow hawks, for instance, choose

atypically colored mice as prey.[6] Among humans, it is possible to cite parental or societal behavior—nurture—as the source of scapegoating and pecking orders; however, nurture cannot explain why infants are most likely to smile at facial
configurations that are familiar and regular, suggesting nature as the root cause of
such a reaction. Similarly, nature is implicated in the sensory-visceral reaction of the
nondisabled when they come in contact with persons with such disabling physical
conditions as amputation, bodily deformity, cerebral palsy, or skin disorders. These
conditions may pose a threat to the normates' sense of bodily integrity, evoking fear
of dysfunction or death.

While existential anxieties of this kind are innate, other factors are clearly
learned. The values people acquire in childhood, their familiarity with one or more
affected individuals, and their education in later years all influence attitudes toward
disability. The better educated tend to be less negative, and females are in general
more accepting than males. Societies that are heterogeneous and thus accustomed
to differences tend to be more accepting of atypical individuals. Normates in such societies are consequently less fearful of acquiring a "courtesy stigma," that is, being
seen as less worthy because of their association with a disabled person.

Further, a society's negative attitudes toward those who have diminished economic productivity may tarnish individuals who have restrictions hampering their
ability to work full time or be star performers. Most people do not have purely negative reactions, however; they are likely to struggle with ambivalence. On the one
hand, they may viscerally draw back; on the other, they may register either sympathy
or admiration for affected individuals, especially for those who have accomplished
much despite obstacles.

Two variables—beauty and height—merit special consideration because they
arouse ego-threatening feelings. Most dwarfs do nurture in themselves a liking for
their appearance, despite their recognition that they can never satisfy society's ex-
alted standards of beauty. They also find ways to affirm their own physical significance, despite being towered over by almost everyone they meet. Other dwarfs
whose appearance they find attractive can help to foster robust self-acceptance. Nevertheless, there is overwhelming evidence that both beauty and height confer enormous social privilege, thus placing dwarfs at risk of disadvantage.

Beauty

The most comprehensive and careful reviews of the literature confirm the existence of stereotyped responses to physical attractiveness.[7] Good-looking babies elicit
more emotional, engaged behavior from mothers. Attractive children are more often

chosen as potential friends by other children and elicit more frequent interaction from teachers. Moreover, the transgressions of unattractive children have been found to be judged more harshly than those of children with more pleasing looks.

Study after study confirms the existence of discrimination on the basis of attractiveness. People judge the adjustment of good-looking people as better than that of unattractive ones. A study of institutionalized troubled children found that the homelier they were, the less likely they were to be taken on trips to town. People work harder for a good-looking person and are more impelled to return an attractive person's lost possessions. Less attractive people tend to be less happy in their marriages and less self-confident. In further discouraging news, homely people are often treated poorly even by persons they have known for some time.[8]

Deluged by proof of the power of beauty in human affairs, the reader, rebelling against this injustice, may offer exceptions to the rule. There is the example of one mother, an artist, who, upon becoming accustomed to her own dwarf child, perceived the arms and legs of other infants as unappealingly elongated. Much depends on one's reference point, as well as the level of intimacy. Familiarity with different body types and our responsiveness to facial nuance and animation in people we know may lead us to make judgments of beauty that differ from those of a standardized experimental scale based on photographs. But in a culture in which the media play such a dominant role and in a society in which ideals for beauty are established by models and movie stars, the pressures are sometimes hard to withstand.

Height

The subject of height, offering less room for philosophizing, seems more straightforward than that of beauty. In the animal world, there is overwhelming evidence that size confers advantage; studies of dominance systems show that in insects, crustaceans, fish, reptiles, rodents, and ungulates (hoofed animals), size is an overriding determinant of status. Other factors such as age (notably in birds), strength, victories, and defeats may sometimes assert themselves, but size remains the most salient quality.[9]

Interestingly, although most frequently males are dominant over females, in some species, among them hyenas and squirrel monkeys, females are slightly larger than males, and thus dominate. Among some birds, such as jacanas and phalaropes, the females are larger and more brightly colored; more aggressive, they battle one another for nests, which the males tend.[10]

Compared with that of other animals, the situation for primates is somewhat complex. It is true that size and strength are crucial elements; a common order of dominance is that of mature male, younger male, and then adult female. The last two places in the hierarchy, however, may vary depending on social relationships. An immature male may defer to his sister, and the awareness of lineage is very significant in Rhesus monkeys. However, here as elsewhere among primates, a strong personality may assert itself and achieve dominance, in defiance of the "normal" order. Factors other than size—such as hormone level, complex personal relationships, and idiosyncratic traits—have been shown to influence an individual's rise within a hierarchy. Indeed, equations have been developed to assess the interaction of all these factors within given primate groups.[11]

Consequently, it is simplistic to view height in isolation as the compelling factor in dominance among primates, especially among humans. For our species, studies of influence patterns have demonstrated, to the surprise of investigators, that the tallest members of a group are not necessarily the most influential persuaders. Nevertheless, there is no question that height remains a very vital component in human dominance systems in particular, and in social interactions in general. Ralph Keyes's *The Height of Your Life*, a popular, frequently quoted treatment of the issue, contains a wealth of interesting statistical and anecdotal data.[12] With few exceptions, those who were discontented with their present height wished to be taller. In addition, most researchers have noticed that people tend to describe themselves as taller than they actually are.

Keyes catalogs the words employed to describe people of different heights; tall people are described as awesome, distinguished, formidable, hulking, imposing, and regal; small people are described as bantam, brash, feisty, munchkinish, pint sized, and spunky. The implication is that tall people are impressive by definition, and short people are awkwardly struggling to assert an importance they do not inherently possess. To be described as tall in English literature is to be credited with positive moral attributes; similarly, "a person of stature" is one with character and accomplishments. In contrast, expressions such as *shortsighted*, *shortchanged*, and *short end of the stick* connote only negative implications.

Are there no advantages to shortness? Keyes notes a few: small bodies are more energy efficient, and small women are more reproductively competent in conditions of economic stress. Small persons can be better at running marathons and at certain gymnastic feats: better balanced, they are less susceptible to serious falls. Despite Keyes's efforts at even-handedness, however, the evidence here and elsewhere tilts overwhelmingly in favor of the tall. Studies of the relationship of salary to height, when those being compared have equivalent qualifications, have revealed considerably higher earnings for taller people. Recent investigations confirm that even when gender, weight, and age are the same, investigators find a substantial salary differential, with each inch in height adding about $789 a year in pay to a person's salary.[13]

There is little doubt that height bias is rampant in the business world for both men and women. It has been reported that 60 percent of American chief executives are six feet or taller, while only 3 percent are five foot seven or shorter: every inch of height adds 2 percent to a man's income.[14] Among salesmen, taller job applicants are more likely to be hired, though their sales records may be no better; in *The Tin Men*, a movie about aluminum-siding salesmen that stereotypes shortness as associated with incompetence, the taller Richard Dreyfuss exudes confidence, while the hapless Danny DeVito evokes ridicule and pathos.

Is this bias evident only in certain societies? Unfortunately, there is considerable cross-cultural evidence of preference for taller height. The anthropologist Thomas Gregor visited the Mehinaku, a tribe of the tropical forest of central Brazil, where the height of the average male was 5 feet 3 1/2 inches.[15] The chief was the tallest man in the village; short men were referred to behind their backs as *peritsi*, a term of derision meaning ridiculously short. In a chart relating height to social success, Gregor reveals that the tallest men are the richest, sponsoring more rituals and attracting more women. A tall young wrestling champ comments, "I don't want a *peritsi* . . . for a friend. They don't make good wrestlers. I don't want people to see me walking with them. Everyone laughs at a *peritsi*." While there may be exceptions—Gregor mentions one short man who has proved successful with women—the author notes that a similar pattern prevails in other cultures.

Dissension between people of different heights occurs not only within groups, but also between groups. A particularly gruesome example of conflict between taller and shorter neighboring communities is the tribal violence that erupted in Rwanda.[16] In that country, political, rather than biological, factors were most instrumental in engendering devastating violence between tribes of taller and shorter individuals, the Tutsi and the Hutu. The Tutsi are a tall, light-brown-skinned, angular people; the Hutu are darker-skinned, stocky, and sturdy. The Tutsi, with their origins in Ethiopia, were traditionally cattle herders; the Hutu were Bantu farmers and laborers. Although revisionist history has them living in complete peace before the arrival of the Belgians, there is evidence of long-standing divisions that may sometimes have created tensions. In the film *King Solomon's Mines*, for example, the Tutsi king is shown being carried in a portable hut by the Hutus, with the Twa—the pygmies—performing as jesters, dancers, and poets (just as they had in the Egyptian courts of old). However, the relationship between the groups had never been marked by anything resembling the grisly tragedy that erupted in Burundi and Rwanda in recent decades. Hutu animosity was aroused when, during the era of Belgian colonial rule, Tutsis were given preference in educational opportunity, government positions, business ownership, and accrual of wealth, with height requirements established, for example, for scarce places in schools and colleges.

In retaliation, during a 1959 massacre in Rwanda, Hutu rebels cut off the legs of their Tutsi enemies, symbolically eliminating the privilege of height—literally cutting their enemies down to size. Since the country gained independence in 1962, there have been recurrent episodes of bloodletting. The 1990s were marked by unparalleled acts of genocide committed by Hutu against Tutsi, and Tutsi retaliation against Hutu. In the course of these battles the Twa pygmies have suffered enormous losses as well: at least 30 percent of the Twa died, leaving only eleven thousand remaining.[17] What began as sociobiological dominance of tall over short was compounded and made deadly by an outside power's granting of political privilege on the basis of height.

Examples as extreme as this are rare. More common are legal restrictions that have placed serious burdens on short persons. Until recently, most military branches and police departments have had height restrictions. Even if a case might be made for height as a physical necessity for the demands of a job such as firefighter, it is difficult to see how height could ever be justified as a qualification for a clerical position. Yet as late as 1984 in Italy, a nation of comparatively short-statured persons, a Justice Department secretary, who had placed first on her civil service exam, appealed after she was dismissed for not meeting the height requirement of five feet one inch, the minimum height for all positions in government.[18] Benito Mussolini had issued the regulation during World War II, in an effort to ensure that only Aryan males taller than five feet three inches held positions. This regulation had remained on the books, although Sandro Pertini, the president of Italy in 1984, was only five feet four inches, and the former prime minister Amintore Fanfani had been only five feet one inch.

Governmental discrimination has not stopped at employment. In l972 in Brazil, a judge refused to marry a couple, Rita Marianoleite, a professor of languages, who was ninety centimeters tall, to an agriculturalist, Ellias Jose de Souza, who was one meter, sixty-seven. Only after a press campaign did they succeed in marrying in another state.[19]

A less formal type of height discrimination is so widespread as to have become a de facto rule. In mate selection, it is an unwritten law that the male must be taller than the female; a high percentage of personal ads include the height of the advertisers. One study of married couples found that almost no males among them were shorter than their wives, despite the fact that there are many men shorter than women in the general population,[20] and despite an article in *Mademoiselle* touting short men as better lovers.[21] Some notable examples of couples in which the men are shorter occur in situations where male power is not in doubt: a Henry Kissinger may with impunity marry a taller woman; so may male movie stars. Nonetheless, Jacqueline Kennedy's marriage to Aristotle Onassis could still provoke ridicule, in part because of the differences in their stature.

If it is tough to be merely short, it is unquestionably far more difficult to grapple with the obstacles that confront dwarfs. In a magazine article published a decade ago, Cara Egan discussed her struggle to affirm herself in an inhospitable society: "'The Wizard of Oz' used to be one of my favorite movies as a child, until I got older and I realized that the munchkins were like me. Except they're not. I don't have an accelerated voice; I don't wear funny clothes; I don't have pointed ears or pointed feet. I do have achondroplasia, which is a type of dwarfism."[22] Egan described the indignities to which she had been subjected, among them walking down the street and hearing people snicker, "Hey, look at the midget." In college, she had been subjected to people picking her up and whirling her around—once by a drunk dancer, who did not desist even when Egan kicked and screamed. She resented the distorted view of dwarfs in movies such as *Willow*, in which they are portrayed as forest denizens, and in commercials in which they are presented as Santa's helpers. Having described the understanding she had attained, after considerable effort, she announced, "Now it's time for the rest of you." Ten years later, this activist stance led Egan to serve Little People of America as vice president for public relations and advocacy.

The attitudes that Egan reacted to have their origin in the distant past. In the Old Testament, Leviticus 21.20, dwarfism is mentioned as one of the physical attributes that disqualify a person from serving at the altar. In a number of later rabbinical commentaries, the Babylonian conqueror Nebuchadnezzar is said to be "as small as a midget dwarf, smaller than a handbreadth."[23] Although there is no historical evidence for his stature, this does not prevent later commentaries from calling him "the dwarf of Babel" and commenting, "Although he was the ruler of the entire world, Nebuchadnezzar did not enjoy his life for a moment; a glance at his dwarfish figure sufficed to mar his pleasure in life."[24] In contrast to these stigmatizing references, there exists an important rabbinical invocation that is to be spoken whenever a person sees a giant or a dwarf, a prayer that begins, "Blessed is God who makes man different"—taken to mean that each creation, including people who are smaller than the norm, is a miracle of God.[25]

It is much more common to come upon negative quotations than positive ones. Many of the most distasteful recent examples come from ostensibly respectable sources. A newspaper item about the Hungarian populist writer Istvan Czurka reported that in an oblique broadside against Jews, he had appealed to Hungarians to wake up to the dangers of a "dwarf minority" threatening to retake control of the country.[26] The Democratic aspirants for president of the United States in 1988 were called "the seven dwarfs," an allusion to their mediocrity. Casual pejorative comments using the word dwarf occur frequently. In her autobiography, *Body and Soul*, Anita Roddick, owner of the Body Shop chain, well known for being a politically progressive and environmentally conscious activist, wrote, "If you employ people with small thinking and small ideas you become a company of dwarfs."[27]

Negotiating Stigma

Given this background, how can dwarfs, beset by beautyism, heightism, and a succession of slights, move toward positive body images and self-esteem? The journey may not be easy, especially for those who have not had anything to do with others like themselves until adulthood. Joan Ablon, the discerning social scientist who in 1984 authored *Little People in America,* offers a cogent account of the shock of self-recognition that sometimes accompanies individuals' first encounter with Little People of America. She identifies denial as one central coping mechanism that people have relied on for coping with their dwarfism.

Here is one of the examples of avoidant behavior that Ablon describes:

RESPONDENT: If I saw another little person I'd go around the block.
INTERVIEWER: Why was that?
RESPONDENT: Because I saw myself. I just didn't want to look at that. I couldn't stand to look at myself. Because I wasn't a dwarf, [*sarcastically*] I just had rickets.[28]

Most often, denial yields to understanding once the individual is no longer dealing only with strangers but finds him- or herself making friendships with others who are similar in appearance, and self-acceptance grows.

A wealth of literature has appeared offering a fresh view of disability and stigma. In *Extraordinary Bodies,* Rosemarie Garland Thomson is particularly insightful about how people with disabilities negotiate their relationships with normates:

[Disabled people] must use charm, intimidation, ardor, deference, humor, or entertainment to relieve nondisabled people of their discomfort. Those of us with disabilities are supplicants and minstrels, striving to create valued representations of ourselves in our relations with the non-disabled majority. . . . If such efforts at reparation are successful, disabled people neutralize the initial stigma of disability so that relationships can be sustained and deepened. Only then can other aspects of personhood emerge and expand the initial focus so that the relationship becomes more comfortable, more broadly based, and less affected by the disability. Only then can each person emerge as multifaceted, whole. If, however, disabled people pursue normalization too much, they risk denying limitations and pain for the comfort of others and may edge into the self-betrayal associated with "passing."[29]

The negotiation is not one-sided. If stigma is to disappear, it also requires heightened awareness by normates of the nature and needs of persons with dwarfism and other disabilities. One sign that society has "caught on" to this is the appearance of the pamphlet *Disability Etiquette: Tips on Interacting with People with Disabilities*.[30] Remarkably, this booklet includes a section on persons with short stature—a group almost never acknowledged in the disability literature. The author, Judy Cohen, suggests not treating very short people like children—for example kissing them or patting them on the head—and advises making equipment and other items accessible and finding ways in which tall and short individuals may conduct conversations at eye level. Most important, she recommends acting in a natural manner and following the disabled person's cues. In this guide, Cohen does not view the individual with the disability as the one most in need of advice and correction. Disability is not a personal flaw, she contends; disabled people are not the "able bodied" gone wrong: disability is simply a difference that society needs to respect by adjusting its response and environment accordingly.

Such insights can be useful for dwarfs. Certainly, it does not *necessarily* follow that dealing with stigma helps us to mature as human beings. But it can be useful in challenging injustice against anyone. The lessons learned in defying our own shaming and stigmatization have the potential for creating in us broader ethical and emotional wisdom. In addition, one's view of one's body is not a problem that individuals face just because they are dwarfs: there are currently almost two million entries under the heading *body image* on the Internet, and almost half of all men and more than half of all women express dissatisfaction with their appearance.

Still, people who appear most visibly different from the norm are likely to elicit strong reactions in strangers. Dwarf individuals who discuss such matters complain about the stares and rude reactions they often encounter in public. When in a good mood, they try to educate the children and adults they meet, but often the task of doing so becomes, at the very least, tiresome, and sometimes exasperating. On occasion, encounters that have begun with teasing have even ended in threats or a measure of violence. Attitudes and behaviors that accompany the stigmatization of African Americans, homosexuals, and people with disabilities, including dwarfs, are not innocent pursuits—they may have dangerous consequences.

What a relief it would be to put on a cloak of invisibility sometimes and move about the world as one's total self, free from the stares that relate only to a single aspect of one's being. Unfortunately, cultural evolution seems to proceed at a snail's pace. The battle begins with changes in the self-perceptions of dwarfs and in the raised consciousness of the rest of society—but it does not end there. Political action is an essential part of social transformation. Because dwarfs constitute a relatively small constituency in society, their road is more difficult. They will need the participation of others, willing to join them in actualizing Mohandas K. Gandhi's dictum "You must be the change you wish to see in the world."

CHAPTER FOUR

Mythology

Because of its connection with the unconscious, mythology may have a part to play in perpetuating stigma. The very words that are most often used to describe very short human beings—*dwarfs* and *little people*—are drawn from folklore; such terms suggest that these human beings are somehow related to mythical creatures and are modern representatives of a fantasy world. Dwarfism is not the only disability with mythic resonance. Giantism brings to mind the Titans, Goliath, and Jack the Giant-Killer; it is a condition often associated with brute force and lack of intellect as well as with the human need to battle mindless bullies. Sometimes the view of a condition is polarized: Tiresias, the blind seer of Greek legend, is associated with exceptional psychic vision, while in William Shakespeare's *King Lear*, the blindness of the earl of Gloucester and of King Lear is used to symbolize their lack of moral or spiritual vision.

But there is no disability that has provided such a fertile source for myth and folktales as dwarfism. *The Motif-Index of Folk Literature* catalogs hundreds of references to dwarfs, recorded in almost every language and culture, including Russian, Norwegian, Chinese, and Yiddish, as well as African and American Indian languages.[1] Listed in the index are dwarfs with goats' feet, dwarfs dressed in every imaginable color and attire, and persons tiny enough to slip through the eye of a needle. Mythological dwarf beings possess wide-ranging powers for good, evil, and playfulness, and countless names have been assigned to them.[2] After analyzing a great many of the tales, it is possible to identify several prominent themes, each rooted in complex human beliefs and anxieties.

Gods

The popularity of the Egyptian gods Bes and Ptah was inextricably associated with dwarfs' favored position in that society. Bes was a somewhat intimidating-looking creature. A very ancient god, perhaps of Sudanese origin, he is often depicted as a sturdy dwarf with a lion's mane, protruding ears, a flat nose, bowlegs, and a tail; in addition, he is sometimes shown with a panther skin on his body and a crown of feathers on his head. His most important accoutrements often include a knife for defense and musical instruments to ward off evil spirits (Fig. 20).[3] Fond of beer, music, dance, and laughter, Bes was charged with amusing and protecting infants, especially the newborn sun god. His role as the god of childbirth was his most important one.

Bes is shown in the birth houses of temples as well as on innumerable amulets.[4] So many amulets survive that some commentators believe that every woman or child must have worn at least one. One papyrus, now in Leiden, the Netherlands, contains an incantation that is supposed to be repeated four times while placing a dwarf of clay on the forehead of the woman giving birth. Yet another prayer invokes Bes with these words: "O thou dwarf of heaven! O thou dwarf of heaven! Thou dwarf whose face is big, whose back is long, and whose legs are short!"[5] Bes functioned as patron of all the female arts, including the binding of flowers and the preparation of cosmetics and healing ointments, which were designed to protect both women's fecundity and their sexuality. His image was carved on bedsteads to drive away predatory animals

20. Figure of Bes with worshipper. Bronze, 404–343 B.C.E., Egypt. Metropolitan Museum of Art, New York.

and spirits. Sometimes he was shown with a consort, the goddess Beset. An all-important part of the culture, by the Ptolemaic period he had become the chief god of home and family.[6]

Another Egyptian dwarf god was Ptah, also called the Risen Earth. Egyptians conceived of stones and soil and vegetation, as well as creatures, as the basic elements on earth—the essential raw materials for creative work. Consequently, Ptah, supposedly the oldest divinity of all, was also the god of craftsmanship, who was said to have made the world by visualizing it. Alfred Wiedmann, an early twentieth-century authority on the religious practices of the ancient Egyptians, notes that the Khnumu, or "modelers," were thought to be the children of Ptah, with big heads, crooked legs, and long arms and mustaches. Supposedly having helped in the creation, their earthenware figures were placed in tombs in order to reconstruct the dead men in whose resting places they now resided.[7] Veronique Dasen discusses the derivation of the term Ptah-Pataikoi, which is often used in connection with dwarf figurines to distinguish them from the average-statured form of Ptah.[8]

A two-headed amulet in the British Museum depicts Ptah and Bes figures back to back, with distinctly separate heads but a single body. This association of the Egyptian gods Bes and Ptah with each other, and with birth, death, and the creative force, will repeat throughout dwarf mythology, springing up independently in disparate times and locations. One example is the ambiguous and evolving figure Hephaestus, the Greek god of smiths, depicted in some of his earlier images as resembling a person with achondroplasia. At least one critic has suggested that this representation was inspired by a connection to the Egyptian dwarf gods Bes, Ptah, and Horus.[9] In addition, Hephaestus's occupation as a smith recalls the frequent portrayal of dwarfs in later European mythology as metalworkers.

In another example, several attributes associated with the god Bes are embodied in the Nomoli figurines of Sierra Leone.[10] Mende farmers digging in their fields at times unearth small soapstone dwarf figures, with bulging forms symbolic of fertility. The farmers employ these figures to propitiate the spirits of the first farmers for a good crop. These ancestors, the original owners of the land, are conceptualized as having been dwarfs, in a synthesis of the human and nonhuman. The Nomoli figurines are a source of what the Mendes term *hale,* or spiritual force, and as a medium of contact with the ancestors, they are buried with the farmers after they die. The image of the dwarf as a bridge between the life that went before and the afterlife is a recurrent theme in many folkloric traditions.

Dwarfs are also identified with other polarized aspects of an unseen spirit world, employing the forces of nature to help or to harm people. Human and animal, god and monster, are telescoped and then interpreted as aspects of a capricious or brutal universe. Just as humans, animals, and elements embody this dual potentiality, so do many dwarf gods and dwarf servants of gods. A respect for the force of volcanoes is apparent in the legends of Pele, the Hawaiian deity of volcanoes. There are many alternative and conflicting narratives about this goddess, who is born from her mother's thighs, while two brothers, representing thunder and lightning, are born from her mother's mouth and eyes.[11] She is identified with jealousy and floods. But most prominent of all of the signs of Pele's presence is the eruption of the volcanoes, which are described even in contemporary news articles as a display of the wrath of Pele. Some sculptures of the goddess represent her as a sturdy dwarf, modeled after humans with achondroplasia.[12] In at least one version, she goes on to produce benign progeny, a daughter, Laka, and a son, Menehune, by her husband, Wahieola. Menehune's descendants are the legendary industrious little people of Hawaii.

Another elemental god—not a dwarf god, but one with whom dwarfs are associated—is Tlaloc, the Mexican rain god.[13] An deity of an earlier time, he supposedly presided over a mountain east of Tezcuco, which bears his name. His dwarf servants poured spring water from four jars—a good one, which caused crops to flourish; a second causing cobwebs and blight; a third causing frost; and a fourth causing absence of fruit. Thunder is the sound of the dwarfs smashing their jars. A horrifying cult formed around Tlaloc, using the sacrifice of children to provide a supply of rain dwarfs. This confusion of children and dwarfs is not uncommon in both real life and unconscious associations.

In a Japanese tale, the Great-Land-Master, an excellent and just ruler, is standing on the shore when a dwarf god named Suku-na-biko, "The Small Renown Man," comes in from the sea on a raft, wearing a mantle of feathers and dressed in moth's wings.[14] The dwarf tells the Great-Land-Master that he is the son of the Divine-Producing goddess and expert at the healing arts. A close friendship develops and the two collaborate at cultivating medicinal plants and curing disease. Despite being unable to walk on his tiny legs, Suku-na-biko knows everyone and goes everywhere. Ultimately, he climbs on a millet stalk, which bounces back and sends him to Tokyo, the Land of Eternity. Even today his name is often invoked for medical assistance, and he is called upon to lead people to curative springs.

Finally, there is the Indian god Vishnu (Fig. 21). In one of his avatars—descents or incarnations—he appeared as a Brahman dwarf. The gods and the giants had been locked in a terrible battle and the giants, or Asuras, were about to triumph, when the other gods entreated Vishnu to help. "Tiny, armed with nothing but his intellect, Vishnu then presented himself before Bali, the giant man of arms. 'What do you want?' said the chief of the terrible Asuras. 'Lay down your arms and grant the gods as their refuge nothing but the space enclosed by three steps of mine; the rest of the universe shall be yours.'" When the unsuspecting Bali agrees, Vishnu clears the sky in one step, the earth in another, and the lower world in the third, driving away the darkness and acquiring the name Trivikrama, meaning "of the three steps."[15] The theme of having the ability to work surprising miracles in spite of one's small size is one that will recur throughout dwarf and fairy literature.

21. Three Steps of Vishnu. Carving, twelfth century C.E., *Hoysala Temple, Halebid, India. From Volker Hansel and Diether Kramer,* Die Zwere kommen! *(Trautenfels, Austria: Verein Schloss, 1993).*

The Dwarfs of the Eddic Sagas

The origins of the Eddic Sagas have been traced to the poets of the Scandinavian Bronze Age, which spanned the years 450 B.C.E. to 1600 C.E. However, our chief written source for the mythology is the *Codex Regius,* a thirteenth-century text. Although some of the same magic powers attributed to dwarfs that are described above can be found in the *Eddas,* a distinct difference in tone and attitude is displayed in these works. While Eddic dwarfs are described as creative and knowledgeable, admiration for their gifts is accompanied by an underlying contempt. The emergence of Scandinavian and German myth in the centuries that followed is filtered through the interpretations of Christian authors in neighboring countries and relies largely on a few sources.[16]

One of the best-known facts about the Norse dwarfs is their origin. Ymir, the evil frost giant, was killed by Odin. From Ymir's flesh, Odin and his brothers shaped the earth; from his bones, the mountains; and from his teeth, jaws, and bone fragments, they made rocks, boulders, and stones. From the maggots in Ymir's flesh they made the dwarfs, giving them the intelligence and shape of humans, but consigning them to live in the caverns and grottoes of the earth.

The dwarfs' repugnant origins set the tone for the contradictions implicit in their later relationship with the gods. On the one hand, the gods granted dwarfs the powers that made them capable of miraculous accomplishments, enlisting four dwarfs— Austre, Vestre, Nordre, and Sudre—to hold up the heavens, one under each corner. The dwarfs snatched the sparks and red hot flashes cast out of Muspelheim and used them to bring light to the world, creating days, nights, and seasons. On the other hand, such wonders did not prevent the gods from viewing these light givers as little more than a necessary evil.

Despite their extreme dependency on the dwarfs, the gods devalue them. Dwarfs make indestructible fetters from impossible materials, such as the noise of a cat walking, and their magical feat enables the gods to bind the gods' adversary, the Fenris-wolf. The dwarfs slay Kvasir and mix his blood with honey, creating the mead of poetry and wisdom. Their efforts are rarely rewarded, however. When the dwarf Alvis, the all-knowing, journeys to Bilskirnir to claim Thrud, the god Thor's daughter and the bride he has been promised, he is rudely rebuffed. Thor has agreed to grant Alvis's claim if Alvis can answer all his questions, but Thor keeps the colloquy going until morning, when, smiling and complimenting Alvis's eloquence and wisdom, he declares, "But your own tongue has trapped you. The sun's rays arrest you." Dwarfs, subterranean beings, cannot tolerate the light of day, and Alvis has been turned to stone. In situation after situation, the dwarfs are exploited, deceived, and scorned; in return, they exact revenge. Greedy and often malicious, they act only in their own interests; they are master smiths and magicians who lust after women, power, and gold.[17]

The dwarfs of the Eddic sagas are all male; consequently, normal reproduction does not occur. In Scandinavian and Germanic myth, two princes make new dwarfs out of the earth when old ones die. This tradition persists through fairy tales such as "Snow White and the Seven Dwarfs" and the works of J.R.R. Tolkien, and dwarfs are still generally thought of as male. Although rare in Scandinavian mythology, helpful female little people have appeared in dreams reported by Scandinavians as early as the thirteenth century.[18] Unlike those in the Norse *Eddas,* dwarfs in these dreams relate to a mythology of benevolent elves and marvelous dwarf villages, which by then had begun to appear in diaries and fables. Often, a beautiful underground kingdom is described, with grand palaces, presided over by handsome kings. A modern fabulist, Robb Walsh, has constructed a work about this genre that may be enjoyed either as a children's book or as an entertaining spoof. His pseudoscientific account, replete with graphic documentation, describes an archaeological dig in northern England. He claims to have enlisted one Professor Egil Dvaergen (*dvaerge* means "dwarf"), who is himself both a dwarf and a specialist in Scandinavian antiquity, to take part in confirming the authenticity of a newly discovered underground Viking dwarf palace.[19] Walsh's tale is a rare light treatment of a subject that more often has inspired scholarly high seriousness. The grandfather of that tradition is Jacob Grimm, who in his *Teutonic Mythology* investigates exhaustively the fictional inhabitants of local caves and woodlands.

Teutonic Dark and Light Elves

In *Teutonic Mythology,* Grimm deals with myths and fairy tales in painstaking detail—the footnotes are typically longer than the text. At the beginning of his chapter "Wights and Elves," Grimm summarizes the characteristic features of the two groups: "These form a separate community, one might say a kingdom of their own, and are only induced by accident or stress of circumstances to have dealings with men. They have in them some admixture of the superhuman, which approximates them to the gods; they have power to hurt man and to help him, at the same time they stand in awe of him, being no match for him in bodily strength. Their figure is much below the stature of man, or else misshapen. They almost all have the faculty of making themselves invisible. And here again the females are of a broader and nobler cast, with attributes resembling those of goddesses and wise-women."[20]

In much of the literature, one finds a differentiation between "dark elves" and "light elves." Dark elves are usually not only darker in color, but also broader than light elves and gnarled, disproportionate, hairy, or all of these.[21] Humans take their distance from the dark elves, feeling quite unlike them and threatened. Light elves are more often described as attractive, proportionate though diminutive, resembling humans in all but size, and sometimes possessed of superior moral and magical qualities, but unpredictable. Females are more apt to be included in their ranks.[22] Light elves, when left undisturbed, carry on their own contented lives while providing humans with services in such endeavors as agriculture, weaving, and baking, only occasionally asking favors, for example, from human midwives. They are the secret helpers in the story "The Shoemaker and the Elves." At times, either light or dark elves can criticize human behavior.

A common tale is one in which humans visit an underground kingdom and behave badly. In one version, the twelfth-century Welsh chronicler Giraldus Cambrensis tells of the old priest Elidor, who as a child discovers a cave whose subterranean passages lead him to a beautiful green countryside inhabited by little people.[23] These playful folk dine on simple foods, respect one another, and are highly critical of the values of the people who live above. On a second visit to the underground kingdom, Elidor steals a golden ball to give to his mother. Two small men who had followed him home seize it—and the fairy kingdom is thereby forever lost to Elidor, who feels endless remorse about his misdeed.

In this and similar parables, little people are depicted as more pure than humans; they live happy, transcendent existences and tend to be physically attractive—tiny but "perfectly formed." The best-known dwarf of the Middle Ages, Oberon (also referred to as Auberon or Alberich), is the sovereign of a kingdom similar to the one described by Giraldus Cambrensis.[24] Variations abound: he may sometimes be of Germanic or Celtic origin, but the earliest works in which he appears are often French texts from the thirteenth century. Oberon turns up in Geoffrey Chaucer's *Canterbury Tales* and Shakespeare's *Midsummer Night's Dream.* Compelling myths tend not to be contained by geographical or linguistic boundaries.[25]

The character of Oberon is as remote as can be from the legends of the dark elves. Fables about these trolls and kobolds and gnomes describe them as greedy, lustful, and jealous. In contemporary terms, they would be seen as purveying id-like qualities, their creativity compromised by subterranean, instinctual forces. Within the Christian church, belief in elves and dwarfs was often associated with paganism, and so in *Beowulf,* for example, the children of Cain are said to be monsters, ogres, and elves.[26] Some of these negative associations with dwarfs have also entered into various languages.[27]

Tricksters and Helpers

Far more complex and evolving little people may be observed in the form of the trickster, analyzed by anthropologist Paul Radin.[28] The Native American Winnebago trickster gets into all sorts of difficulties because of instinctual, amoral behavior, rooted in his animal origins; but after many violent and transforming adventures, he has the potential to gain access to divine wisdom and to help humankind. A good part of the literature of dwarfs, elves, and fairies embodies aspects of the trickster myth. A trickster identity embodies duality: one may enjoy one's own virtue by disapproving of the immoral trickster or, conversely, delight in enjoying the forbidden behavior. Versions of Navaho coyote tales told to children are moralistic and include punishment; those told to adults are more likely to display pleasure in detailing the trickster's antics.

Similarly, tales of dwarfs and elves may emphasize negative elements, such as cunning and lust, in order to signal condemnation, or alternatively, playfulness and creativity, in order to indicate relishing in the freer, positive elements of impulsivity in human nature. Marie-Louise Von Franz, the eminent Jungian analyst and folklorist, in studying thousands of folktales, concluded that 85 percent of published references to dwarfs are positive; while they sometimes reflect mischievous childish impulses, most often they convey a positive *Einfall*—a good idea or hunch.[29] It is those hunches, she believes, small and easily overlooked, that lead people to creative solutions. Rather than attribute them to their own unconscious, individuals credit unseen little people.

A review of the *Folk-Motif Index* does indeed turn up a good many helpful dwarfs, as well as others who, while they may steal, play pranks, or switch children in the cradle, can be successfully propitiated. We have ambivalent accounts of the knockers, or mine dwarfs, who may be either feared by miners or seen as benevolent forecasters of danger. Brownies perform household tasks and care for animals, but when offended they may turn into boggarts and engender poltergeist-like phenomena. There seems to be no European country that does not have helpful household spirits—from the lutins and korrigans of Brittany to the domovoi of Russia. Their precursor is the Lar, a gnarled little brown man whose effigy sat on almost every Roman hearth.[30]

Kappa, a Japanese dwarf, guards the rivers and may drown travelers—but courtesy can render him harmless. Inuit dwarfs are more generally benign: the Kingmingoarkulluk bursts into song when encountering a human, and the Eeyeekalduk lives inside a stone and is a healer. The Iroquois Indians have three categories of little people—the Hongas, who protect water and rocks, the Gandayaks, who protect plants and rivers, and the Ohdowas, who live underground and prevent monsters from rising up and causing harm to people.[31] The Chinese too tell stories of elves that one can hear but not see. Under the best conditions, these creatures can be shown once how to plant flowers and they will complete the field. But if one grows rich by cheating an elf of his silver, he will cause one to grow thin and yellow and die.[32]

African tales describe a variety of dwarf spirits: the Machinga Yao, who live near Lake Nyasa, speak of the Itowe, leprechaun-like little people who can influence the ripening of crops, and in the belief system of the Thonga people, dwarfs living in the sky sometimes come down in thunderstorms.[33] Numerous varieties of little people are described by Tim Appenzeller in his volume on dwarfs, which contains illustrations by James Christensen (Fig. 22).[34]

Although we may no longer think of these mythic beings as salient or believable, many cultures still experience them as true and important. The importance of the Menehunes for the people of Hawaii is a case in point. The Menehunes, famed for their stonework, supposedly built nine or ten *heiaus* (temples) and two fishponds around Honolulu and twenty-four temples and other stone structures on various islands. Like their European counterparts in the story "The Shoemaker and the Elves," they are said to be capable of working through the night to complete a job for people they wish to help. Similarly, their displeasure is not to be risked. In 1951 some workmen who had been moving rocks at Diamond Head Crater quit, claiming that each night the Menehunes had undone work that had been completed during the day. They requested that a *kahuna*, or native seer, be called in to determine the cause of their wrath.

There are a remarkable number of stories about sightings of Menehunes by their supposed descendants, or reports of schoolchildren and their teachers who have gone in search of them. In a fascinating article, Katherine Luomala speculates that at least

22. *Mythological dwarfs. Frontispiece by James C. Christensen, in Tim Appenzeller,* The Enchanted World: Dwarfs *(New York: Time-Life Books, 1985).*

segments of this mythology may be rooted in social-class differences.[35] Just as Polynesian mythology exaggerates the beauty and heroism of chiefs and their wives, storytellers have exaggerated the smallness and deformity of common good working people. Luomala concludes that the Menehune represent a glamorized version of ordinary Hawaiians. In recent years a Menehune figure has become the mascot for the University of Hawaii football team, and Menehune images are widely employed in advertising. These playful uses need not obscure the symbolic roles they continue to play as helpful spirits who fulfill various unconscious needs for their human counterparts.

Stories of helpful little people remain very much alive in Native American culture, because they are founded in a deep, enduring belief in the existence of a spirit world. As is often the case in Native American accounts, the little people are presented in a favorable light, as is seen in this translation from the oral traditions of the earliest known Indians of Maine that encapsulates a familiar Indian creation myth: "In the beginning there was just the sea and the forest—no people and no animals. Then Koluskap came. He possessed good magic. Out of the rocks, he made the Mihkomuwehsisok, small people who dwelt among the rocks and made wonderful music on the flute."[36] For Native Americans, both nature and little people are viewed as present at the creation. Only later does Koluskap bring into being the Wabanaki, regular men and women.

John Witthoft, in "The American Indian as Hunter," writes of the beliefs of the Delaware, Cayuga, and Seneca Indians. Whereas belief has waned even in the British Isles, one of the last holdouts to give credence to unseen little people, in the Native American culture such belief still thrives:

> There is no surer way to offend an Indian than to express amusement at his quaint concept of the dwarf. He believes that such irreverent expression is as offensive to these little people as a verbal or overt insult and may incur their wrath and vengeance. . . . More than once I have had an Indian express surprise that I did not know of some detail about them. I have heard a number of descriptions of them from people who believed they had seen them, some of the descriptions being extremely detailed and precise.
>
> The dwarfs are described as generally quite friendly, guiding and helping hunters, and sheltering lost children, and offering knowledge of medicinal plants. But if seriously offended, they may take away the miscreant's mind, leaving him wandering in the woods, bereft of mental faculties.[37]

This description reflects the characteristic Native American conception of nature: it is essentially benign but requires respect or a deserved punishment may result. Indian trickster and related tales are animated in a way that distinguishes them from the more judgmental European fables. One particularly amusing account is a Métis (French Canadian–Indian) tale collected by Richard Erdoes concerning a character called Little-Man-with-Hair-All-Over.[38] Although Little-Man does kill an evil dwarf, that dwarf is merely a vehicle for Little-Man's heroism. Little-Man ("hairier than a skunk") is the ultimate troll or dark elf in appearance, but in action the ultimate heroic trickster. "Little-Man-with-Hair-All-Over was small, but he succeeded in everything he did. He was tough in a fight, so they called for him whenever there was something dangerous to do. When a bear monster went on a rampage, ripping up lodges with his huge claws and eating the people inside, Little-Man-with-Hair-All-Over had no trouble killing it. For this his grateful people gave him a magic knife." The story recounts Little-Man's victory over the dwarf and his killing of a scaly man-monster with four heads. Little-Man also has quite a way with the ladies. When one of the maidens he has rescued calls him handsome, saying, "I like a little, hairy, lusty fellow," he replies, "Then you've met the right man." He rescues and accepts three women as wives and exacts revenge on a friend who has betrayed him. But he is also a peacemaker. He resolves a dispute between a wasp, a worm, and a woodpecker. Finally, he rescues a fourth woman, by killing a slimy water monster. "'You're brave and powerful,' said the girl. 'I'm yours.' So Little-Man-With-Hair-All-Over took her as his fourth wife and carried her home to his lodge. . . . And Little-Man had been right: he was man enough for four wives, with a little left over." This tale can be enjoyed as the spirited revenge of an Indian dark elf figure over the malignant image of the Nordic and Germanic dark elf. His sexuality is neither thwarted nor decried as lust, but celebrated. His moral victory is not prim and sanctimonious, but passionate and entertaining.[39]

Fairy Tales

No discussion of northern European folklore is complete without specific attention to *Grimm's Fairy Tales,* whose stories have played such an important role in influencing the perceptions of dwarfs in the Western world. At least a dozen of the Grimms' tales mention dwarfs or thumblings. Many of the tales are essentially cautionary parables that direct children to follow a virtuous course. Dwarfs and elves are the "stand-ins" for life's system of rewards and punishment. In "The Three Little Men in the Woods," for example, a mean stepmother sends her stepdaughter out to find strawberries in winter, a seemingly impossible task. By agreeing to keep house for three dwarfs, the stepdaughter is rewarded with strawberries; enhanced beauty; and ultimately, marriage to the king. (Her quite unaccommodating sister is made to grow more ugly). In other tales, elves reward a good shoemaker; little folk give treasure to a good tailor and an extra hump to a greedy one; a dwarf, insulted by two brothers, punishes them but rewards their truthful, polite brother, winning him the king's daughter; similarly, brothers who call a dwarf a stupid runt are punished, while their good brother is given the water of life, with which to cure his father.

The analysis by George Heide of these works offers one of the simplest encapsulations of this sort of morality fable. Heide has noted that when humans and dwarfs confront each other in these legends, homespun values tend to prevail, notably the golden rule: those who treat dwarfs with respect are met with fine gifts and prosper; those who abuse them pay dearly.[40] Saddest of all, if the villagers become truly arrogant—if they ridicule dwarfs and treat them as vassals—even the kindest of dwarfs will depart forever.[41] Heide regards these narratives as echoing the oral tradition of nostalgia for an imagined blissful past and hope for a similar future.

Fairy tales also serve to warn children about the evil and deception that exists in the world. In "Snow White and Rose Red," a bear kills an evil dwarf and thereby turns himself into a prince. Rumpelstiltskin, in a parable of a dwarf's desire for intimacy that ends in self-destruction, attempts to take a human child for himself and, when unsuccessful, tears himself apart.

By contrast, some stories deal not with moral direction, but with parental anxiety about their children. In "The Thumbling," a boy born to parents who wish for a child no bigger than a thumb, resists being exhibited by two nefarious characters and instead sets forth on a series of adventures. Ultimately, his parents succeed in rescuing him from a wolf. In a story of this sort, one encounters the anxieties of parents about the survival of their undersized child. In this case, they may have wished for his smallness, but they are unprepared for the vulnerability that ensues. Still, they must permit their child to venture out and assert himself, intervening only in the most severe crises. At the end, their son safe at home again, their fears are assuaged.

This tale, with numerous variations, appears throughout Europe. A 1901 French retelling of a good number of these Petit Poucet (Tom Thumb) stories reveals certain commonalities.[42] Sometimes the child has come unbidden, but often his two childless parents have wished for him; sometimes they employ a sorcerer. The youngster is described as the same size as a grain of millet, a peppercorn, a pea, a fat finger, or a ball. Sometimes there are signs of parental ambivalence. A woman who has prayed to God for a child gives birth to a litter of infants who are the size of bugs. Her husband, frightened by how many there are, puts them in a sieve and throws them in a crossroad. After supper, the wife asks why they didn't save at least one; a voice cries out, and they are pleased to discover one of their abandoned children. In another story, the father kills two of his three tiny children, but the smallest escapes by hiding behind a broom. When his father declares that he regrets not having a child to fetch him wine, his small son yells from behind a broom that he'll go. Children are valued for their usefulness, and tiny children are under increased pressure to prove their worth.

Many Tom Thumb adventures take place in a rural setting. A child is swallowed by a cow or a wolf or captured by thieves, but he ultimately escapes by dint of his superior intelligence. In most stories he is virtuous—although in Transylvanian and Albanian stories he becomes a robber—almost always demonstrating his mastery and assuaging any doubts that his family may have had about him. Lazare Sainean believes that the dwarf's cleverness represents the effort of the imagination to compensate for a defect of birth or chance that has limited a child's heroic possibilities or made the child seem less than human.[43]

In a tale from Japan, for example, a gentle, elderly couple pray to Buddha for a child and subsequently find a baby outside their home. Although only one inch tall, he possesses the heart of a lion.[44] Issunboshi, this little one-inch boy, sets off in a rice bowl, in which are set chopsticks, to fulfill his ambition of becoming a famous samurai. Ultimately, after much magic and many conquests, he grows and grows, becomes a renowned general, and marries a princess. He invites his beloved parents to live with him happily ever after in Kyoto. Many versions of this story—one of the five best-known Japanese folktales—have been published. In this fable of simple wish fulfillment, parental ambition is rewarded, and parental belief that spirituality can magically obliterate a child's limitations proves true.

The undoing of limitations or the calming of anxieties about disability is another message that appears in many tales, most chillingly in the stories of changelings. Changelings abound in the Germanic and Slavic traditions. The Grimms' tale "The Changeling," describes a baby who is taken from his crib and replaced by a changeling with a big head and staring eyes who wants to do nothing but eat and drink. When the mother follows her neighbor's advice to boil water in eggshells, the changeling starts to laugh, and dwarfs come and take him away and return the real baby. Typically, the behavior of these changelings is lethargic; they only laugh and sing and behave like the dwarfs they supposedly are when they believe themselves unobserved. They can be exchanged with the true, desirable child by means of tricking or propitiating the dwarfs. It is very likely that changeling stories represent an attempt by parents to understand the appearance of babies with conditions such as Tay-Sachs and Down's syndrome and to find a way both to explain and to undo their unhappy situation. Their solution is to contact the dwarfs who dwell in the underground kingdom and have significant power over life, death, and illness.

The German folklorist Josef Neumann believes that the concept in astronomy of so-called dwarf stars (black, red, white, and brown) may originate in the idea that dwarfs embody the souls of the dead and that stars or light objects represent their spirits, which have ascended to the sky.[45] Indeed, primitive animistic beliefs are the basis for many beliefs about dwarfs and fairies. Human beings may wish to be invisible, to fly, to possess magic weapons and treasures, and to gain foreknowledge. In fantasy, they may fulfill these wishes by creating homunculi who possess these abilities and whose favors can be won.

There is no question that sexual themes are a significant element in dwarf mythology. Dwarfs may be the asexual, industrious helpers of Snow White or the thwarted, lustful craftsmen of the Eddic tales. In ancient literature, there are dwarfs who measure a cubit in height, with beards a cubit long, and penises a cubit and a span long. One classical scholar has discussed wordplay that connects the words *pygmy* and *phallus*;[46] other commentators have noted how curiosity about dwarfs' sexuality has resulted in their being among the most popular models used in pornographic photographs and films.

One theme that remains, but that is among the most significant, uses the dwarf to focus on all those individuals who are rejected because of their inability to meet common standards of beauty. The rejection theme, found in a number of the older fables, is perhaps best exemplified by an early nineteenth-century tale, William Hanff's *The Dwarf Nose*.[47] It describes Jacob, a tall, handsome twenty-year-old, who is changed by an old witch into a misshapen dwarf with a large, ugly nose. He is sent away by his parents, who are dismayed both by his loss of beauty and his new lack of economic viability as a seller of vegetables. Teased by children, rejected by adults, and abused physically and verbally by his father, Jacob epitomizes "everybody who, for whatever reason, is different from the norm, and for whom civilization has no place or a very low one at best. And his spiritual situation is felt more keenly because he has seen better days. The human being is a function of his pleasant outward appearance, his wealth, his power and his usefulness. Otherwise he is worthless to society."[48] This story, perhaps more than any other, captures the essence of our fear that our bodies or our children's may be judged inadequate and that ostracism and loneliness will result. There are few more profound existential anxieties than this one.

Even if it is true, as Von Franz has suggested, that most references to mythological dwarfs are positive, a real-life dwarf may find it difficult to identify with the majority of them—gods, elves, Eddic dwarfs, or deformed children—except perhaps for some of the more positive figures found in Native American tales. Even the triumphs of a thumbling may leave dwarf readers less than pleased. In spite of the fact that these stories statistically result more often in good than in ill, they remind human dwarfs that they will all too often be experienced as *other*—closer to mythological beings than to the rest of humankind.

CHAPTER FIVE

Anthropology

Reality and fantasy about dwarfs have long been jumbled in most peoples' consciousness. As late as the turn of the twentieth century, any description offered by a traveler might be believed, and the crucial distinction between ethnic populations and sporadic dwarfs was ill understood. Even when scientific and anthropological data began to become available, it was often unreliable, and disputes about where dwarf populations lived were common.

Are we all descended from giants—or from dwarfs? Clergymen, travelers, and scholars asserted with conviction, on the flimsiest of evidence, that we are descended from one group or the other. Generations of travelers asserted that there were countries in which there were races of dwarfs who were four feet tall, two feet tall, or shorter. Even today, the tabloids that claim sightings of humanoid creatures emerging from UFOs continue to print tales of explorers encountering tiny men and women, less than two feet tall, in the forests of Hungary.

Dwarf Races of Poets and Explorers

One of the earliest written references to dwarfs is at the beginning of the *Iliad*, where Homer describes the battle between the cranes and "pigmy nations"[1] This legend had long captured the attention of commentators. There were debates about whether the pygmies were human or simian, about whether the cranes were in fact ostriches, and about the exact location of the battle.

Such uncertainties were inevitable in a world that had not yet been fully explored or mapped. The earliest Greek and Roman maps did depict Africa, Asia, and southeastern Europe; but shown on the fringes of these places were illustrations of a mythical heaven—Elysium—and nightmarish regions that were supposedly home to all sorts of monsters.[2] It was not until the eighteenth century that these mythological creatures, composites based in part on exaggerations of human deformity, were widely recognized as imaginary.

Small wonder, then, that Homer, who it is now believed may have had some knowledge of the African pygmies, or "cubit-men" as he called them, should have portrayed them as smaller than the smallest persons who ever lived. The cubit, an early unit of measurement, was the distance from the elbow to the tip of the middle finger, a distance of between seventeen and twenty-two inches. The shortest man whose height has been authenticated was 22 1/2 inches (57 cm); the shortest woman was 24 inches (61 cm).[3] These were individuals with extremely rare genetic dwarfing conditions—no members of any tribe have ever been that small. The shortest groups of ethnic dwarfs in our time and in Homer's have been well over four feet tall.[4]

Cubit-men have existed, however, for more than two millennia in the imaginations of writers and travelers, among them Ctesias, Pliny, and Sir John Mandeville.[5] Readers of their accounts and later ones were typically impressed and credulous. *Purchas His Pilgrims* reported pygmies living in caves in the ground in Brazil, in mountains between Arabia and Medina, and in Greenland, where Dithmar Blefkens in 1563 discovered an area that "abounds with Bears, white Foxes, Pigmies and Unicornes."[6] As late as 1753, Pierre-Louis Moreau de Maupertuis claimed that races of giants and dwarfs existed—the dwarfs had retired to the North Pole, the giants to the South.[7]

How could such tales be believed, one wonders? Even today, there are those who believe in the Loch Ness monster and the Abominable Snowman; however, now that almost every part of the globe has been explored and anthropologists and scientists can offer reliable information, fabulous accounts are far less likely to be taken at face value.

Early Scientists and Anthropologists

Just how rudimentary knowledge about dwarfs and pygmies was in past centuries is highlighted in *A Philological Essay Concerning the Pygmies of the Ancients,* a fascinating study by the English scientist Edward Tyson published in 1699. Tyson took the position that many of the accounts of pygmy tribes that had abounded in literature and history had been based on the words of travelers who had mistaken apes for men. An early anatomist, Tyson performed a careful dissection of a chimpanzee and concluded that stories of pygmies were only "a creature of the Brain, produced by a warm and wanton Imagination."[8] It would be a mistake to undervalue Tyson's work because his conclusion was incorrect. He was capable of insights that eluded both earlier and later observers. He recognized, for example, a vital distinction that was often blurred in later commentaries—the distinction between ethnic dwarfism and individual sporadic pathological cases.

It was not until the Victorian era, an age of zealous exploration, that opinions rested on more than fragmentary evidence and hearsay. The German botanist and explorer Georg Schweinfurth (1836–1925) reported that he had found a group of pygmies called the Akka near the source of the Nile, supporting the disputed early claims of Homer, Herodotus, and Aristotle. Authentic accounts such as Schweinfurth's, however, were intermingled with doubtful ones, and it was difficult for those who had not been on the expeditions to separate fact from fiction.

Because the turn of the twentieth century saw such an extraordinary focus on discovering anthropologically novel peoples in general, and pygmies in particular, the unbelievable was often believed. And so Canadian anthropologist Robert G. Haliburton could publish articles in reputable journals and deliver to learned societies his rambling, pseudoscientific papers about the existence of dwarf races in Morocco, Spain, and the New World. Quoting an obscure paper written by a Professor Miguel Morayta (a supposed authority whose writings neither he nor others could produce) he described a community of dwarfs who lived in the Ribis Valley in Gerona, Spain: "Their height does not exceed 1 m. 10 to 1 m. 15. These Pygmies are well built and have a robust appearance. Their hair is red. Their face forms a perfect square. Their cheekbones are prominent, their jaw heavy, their nose flat, and their eyes, which are slightly oblique, resemble those of Mongols." Further, Haliburton interweaves accounts of native and British informants to prove the existence of a dwarf race in Morocco, declaring, "It is difficult to exaggerate the ethnological importance of this discovery." He predicts that the members of this race will "supply a missing link between the prehistoric cave dwellers, the brownies, and the dwarfsmiths of European folklore and fairy tales with the similar races now existing from Mount Atlas to the Kalahari desert of South Africa."[9] Haliburton's tone conveys the enthusiasm of an explorer who has discovered the Rosetta stone of dwarfs—ancient, present, and mythological.

His work was praised and taken seriously by many of his contemporaries, including Professors H. Rischbieth and A. Barrington, who authored the Galton Laboratory's definitive 1912 study of dwarfism.[10] However, a damning rebuttal by Harold Crichton-Browne in the journal *Nature* settled the issue:

> Mr. Halliburton [*sic*] begins with a statement that is at once startling and decisive. The information he has collected puts it, he says, beyond question that there exists in the Atlas Mountains, only a few hundred miles from the Mediterranean, a race of dwarfs only 4 feet high, who are regarded with superstitious reverence or are actually worshipped, and whose existence has been kept a profound secret for 3000 years. Such an emphatic assertion ought to rest on irrefragable evidence; . . . and I read Mr.

Halliburton's paper in constant expectation of the proofs of his remarkable discovery, but reached the end of it without coming on a shred of testimony in support of his contention.

Crichton-Browne goes on to point out the weakness of the "evidence" offered by Halliburton's British informants and suggests that the individual dwarfs who were seen in fact represent cases of pathological dwarfism. He knows of three dwarfs in a Scottish town, he remarks, but this does not lead him to presuppose that there is "a concealed clan of MacManikans in the Grampians." He concludes that Haliburton's dwarf story is "an instructive study in the generation and growth of myth in modern times."[11]

By the end of the nineteenth century, however, a number of scholars began to painstakingly scrutinize the available data. In one important account from 1894, the scientist Bertram Windle, a descendant of Tyson's, summarized what was currently known about where pygmies and other short-statured persons lived.[12] Windle, like Tyson, was familiar with science, history, and myth but had the benefit of reliable information. He came closer to the truth than had most of his contemporaries and any previous investigators and, relying heavily on writings by Jean-Louis-Armand de Quatrefages and Paul Topinard, was able to identify most of the dwarf populations we know about today. He clarifies and dispels some of the claims of previous writers, noting, for example, that the "little people" in the stone graves of Tennessee in fact turned out to be children.

A century of research has contributed to a better understanding of the distribution of short stature, of population migrations, of the effect of climate on height, and of the differences between pathological and ethnic dwarfism. In 1960, for example, Juan Comas broke new ground when he published a comprehensive review of South American populations titled *Pigmeos en America?*[13] By 1972, when Joseph Birdsell wrote the following summary, there was knowledge available on the major areas where the smallest human beings lived. "Turning to the other end of the scale, the populations that fall below an average height of five feet in males are primarily limited to the Negroid race and a few rain forest mongoloids. They are found among the rain forest Negrillos of the Congo, the Camerouns in tropical Africa, and among the Bushmen of the Kalahari desert in the interior of South Africa. In Southeast Asia, where populations are generally short-statured, the smallest again belong to the rain forest Negritos of the Adaman Islands, the interior of the Malay peninsula and the Island of Luzon in the Philippines."[14] Notwithstanding his use of terminology that is now recognized as both scientifically and politically incorrect, Birdsell improves on Windle, capturing in a single confident paragraph the essential facts that Windle had struggled to present almost a century earlier.

In another work, a 1991 review of current evidence, Jared Diamond identifies as

the smallest extant people the Efe pygmies of the Ituri forest of Zaire (now the Democratic Republic of the Congo), a group whose members average four feet eight
inches for men and four feet five inches for women.[15] He lists as close rivals for this
distinction certain populations in South and Central America, southern Africa, and
especially Asia, emphasizing areas in the Philippines and New Guinea. Diamond surveys the work of other investigators who have explored the hormonal and evolutionary factors responsible for pygmies being smaller than other humans, and he
touches on the complex relationship between height and climate.

Despite the efforts of scientists, however, the fanciful stories never entirely cease.
A 1989 headline in the *Weekly World News* announced, "Band of little people—only
two feet tall—attack explorers." A description followed: "A furious tribe of tiny men
and women hurled rocks and sticks to repel a group of stunned explorers who were
seeking minerals but stumbled across an ancient human race instead! . . . 'This is one
of the most incredible discoveries of our age.'" The article quoted a remark attributed
to Professor Ferenc Adony: "'We now have solid evidence that an ancient race of little people does exist—as the legends say!'" Not surprisingly, attempts to verify this
tale by contacting the University of Budapest indicated that it was pure invention.[16]
On 10 July 1990, that same publication had as its front-page attraction the picture of
"the world's smallest man, just 18 3/4 inches tall & he can sit in the palm of your
hand."[17] The issue featured a "life-size" centerfold of one Felix Barrena, who, it was
claimed, feasted for a week on a can of beans and a pork chop and could get drunk
on a thimbleful of vodka.

Are We All Descended from Dwarfs?

Before evolution was recognized as a coherent explanation of the origins of contemporary human beings, any theory could be advanced with impunity and supported with a minimum of proof. Pliny, who wrote his influential *Natural History* in
the first century, believed we were descended from a taller race than ours and had
degenerated with time.[18] Augustine, too, believed in somatic degeneracy. Although
this view had its detractors, it enjoyed considerable popularity until the Renaissance.[19] There also existed the competing view that humankind was in fact growing
taller. A great many societies maintained the belief that an earlier indigenous people,
who had been dwarfed or short statured, had ruled previously. The Picts of Scotland
and the predecessors of the hairy Ainu of Japan are among those frequently cited.[20]

A number of scholars in the early twentieth century were convinced of our
dwarf origins. Martin Monestier, in *Les nains* (1977), discusses French, German, and
Swiss investigators who believed that Europe was formerly inhabited by dwarfs.[21] He

does not challenge their evidence or reasoning. Two of the investigators whom he mentions, Antonin Poncet and René Leriche, declare in an article that appeared in a reputable publication in 1903 that dwarfs are "the vanguard of the human race, just as in animals the large variation has sprung from the small."[22] While they do call some cases "pathological" and others "ethnic," they still conclude that achondroplasia is merely an expression of ancestral pygmy genes that have become less common. Their article is illustrated with photographs; in addition, they provide the measurements of two contemporary dwarfs as well as offer references to art and folklore— both common practices in early "scientific" assessments of dwarfism. They conclude that because there were more dwarfs depicted in art in the classical era, there must have been more of them than in other periods. We now recognize that it was the nobility's infatuation with dwarfs that caused them to be collected in classical and mediaeval times and that a collection of sporadic cases does not constitute an ethnic group.

In his 1977 work, Monestier concludes that the find of "dwarf bones" at the base of the Alps confirmed that there have been dwarfs in Switzerland from earliest times.[23] It is now generally recognized that these finds and many similar ones were actually the skeletons of children or remains of somewhat short-statured persons whose smallness was exaggerated. Later, more reliable investigators pointed out that there are few authenticated European skeletons of dwarfs, and only a little New World evidence.[24] C. E. Snow in 1943 described the best-known American dwarf skeletons in detail.[25]

By 1968, the use of careful scientific methods had become the rule among physical anthropologists. Neil Huber, for example, in an early systematic study of stature, compared a variety of samples from Neolithic and medieval times, concluding that there was in fact very little difference in mean height between the groups.[26] Although the assumption that dwarf populations preceded us and developed into what we are today has been discredited, legends occasionally resurface. One prominent example is the belief that the Picts of Scotland were dwarfs. Picts is the name given by classical writers to the tribes in the far north who were among the invaders of the Roman province of Britain. Both in the early twentieth century and as late as 1988,[27] the Picts were often described as dwarfs.[28] Even now, there are people in the British Isles who fear building roads near mounds lest they disturb the peace of these spirits or ancestors. Isabel Henderson, in *The Picts*, convincingly rejects the notion that an indigenous dwarf people once inhabited Scotland (their presence supposedly "proved" by the existence of small earth dwellings).[29]

Is there any sense in which we can still be regarded as descended from dwarfs? We now know that *Australopithecus*, the prehuman biped made famous through Donald Johanson's discovery of Lucy, appeared between 3.5 million and 5 million years ago in Africa; Lucy was three and a half feet tall.[30] The individuals of the extinct species *Homo habilis* were also less than four feet in height. If one wanted to go back that far, one might perhaps think of our ancestors as dwarfs— but that would be quite a stretch. *Homo* began to exist as a genus somewhere between 100,000 and 250,000 years ago in Africa, with migration to Europe a much later development.[31] Lucy and other prehistoric examples may be similar in stature to our living dwarfs; but in all other respects, they are as different from people with the myriad types of dwarfism known today as they are from members of the general population.

Modern Exploration

This romp through human error and uncertainty makes us appreciate all the more the achievements of meticulous contemporary science. Whereas previous generations had few means of verifying incredible tales, contemporary researchers have gone on to explore and map the universe of genetic diversity.

Reports often count on collaboration. When Robert C. Bailey, a professor of anthropology at the University of California at Los Angeles, and his associates conducted a longitudinal study of growth in pygmies, he consulted physician-researchers with expertise in hormonal function.[32] When Brian T. Shaw, an associate professor of cell and molecular biology at Northwestern University, was engaged in his studies of pygmies, he turned to Bailey. Together they concluded that earlier judgments that African pygmies have features that are "archaic remnants" of evolutionary history were wrong: it was the reduced levels of an insulin-like growth hormone throughout the maturation process that had led to their short stature. The researchers also considered how these facts historically affected individuals in that society.

Increased knowledge about the genetics of dwarfism has also clarified why there are differences in the incidence of various conditions in certain geographic areas. There is, for example, an elevated incidence of cartilage-hair hypoplasia and Ellis–van Creveld syndrome in Finland and among the Amish in Pennsylvania, whereas hypopituitary dwarfism is common on Krk Island, in Croatia. Greater frequencies in certain places result from a combination of new mutations and subsequent inbreeding. Acquisition of such knowledge often requires the collaboration of researchers from many disciplines. Nowhere has this process been more tellingly displayed than in an investigation of a skeleton of a prehistoric dwarf by Professor David Frayer, a University of Kansas paleoanthropologist, and his associates.[33] In 1987, in a museum near Romito, Italy, Frayer discovered and subsequently carefully assessed the oldest dwarf remains authenticated until then. This skeleton of a seventeen-year-old-boy was determined, on the basis of radiocarbon dating, to be from the late Upper Paleolithic period—he had lived approximately eleven thousand years ago. The remains included a remarkable number of parts: a skull, as well as both left and right radius, ulna, tibia, and fibula. Only the hands and feet were missing. Frayer's discovery was regarded as quite significant and was reported on the front page of the *New York Times* and in the scientific publications *Nature,* the *American Journal of Physical Anthropology,* and *Scientific American.*[34]

Why was the find so important? First, its age extended by approximately five thousand years the earliest recorded incidence of dwarfism. That dwarfs were prominent in ancient Egypt had long been recognized; and investigators had reported instances of dwarfism in European populations. Frayer comments that these European remains, however, had all been found in large cemeteries dating from the Middle Ages. He cites other sources that mention Old World and North American cases, but he notes that these too are all from agricultural or complex—in other words, later—societies. The Romito dwarf skeleton is the only one known that derives from a hunter-gatherer society.

Second, Frayer's familiarity with skeletal remains allowed him to speculate astutely about his subjects' lives. His greatest expertise had been with Neanderthals, and he was most knowledgeable about periods several million years earlier than the Paleolithic. But for the Romito research, he familiarized himself with the work of medical and anthropological authorities in the field of dwarfism. Recognizing the limited mobility of most dwarfs, he and his colleagues concluded that if dwarfs had such daunting problems in today's world, they must have faced even greater ones in a nomadic, hunter-gatherer society. In order to survive, they speculated, the Romito dwarf must have been given assistance by others in his society.

In a piece called "Paleolithic Compassion" in the *Scientific American,* John Horgan inquired, "Did tender loving care help a Stone Age dwarf to survive?" He echoed Frayer's initial observations, noting that the youth would have tired quickly, particularly in the mountainous terrain of southern Italy. He would have had problems using his short, bowed arms in hunting and would have been a liability to his group. The case for his having survived because of the community's care seemed to be bolstered by additional evidence that this dwarf was valued. Other commentators preferred alternative explanations: they suggested that the ingenuity that is displayed by people with disabilities when they are faced with overcoming limitations, rather than the compassion of the group, could explain the dwarf's survival. He was buried with an average-statured woman, who may have been his mother, in one of the few caves in Italy that contained parietal art. Only individuals with high status were buried in caves, and this intriguing site seemed to have been an important social or ritual center.

The tale of Frayer's discovery and investigation of the skeleton is an extraordinary one. Frayer, the recipient of a National Science Foundation grant, had been in the midst of visiting sixty European museums in order to examine bones from the Paleolithic period. While he was lunching with friends at a café in Rome, they alerted him to an obscure article in an Italian journal. It described two dwarf skeletons that had been found in the same grave, supposedly locked in embrace. The tale seemed improbable, but Frayer and his colleagues—archeologist Margherita Mussi and anthropologist Roberto Macchiarelli—decided to follow up on it. They arrived at the Romito museum, where Frayer viewed the display with great excitement: one of the skeletons was indeed a seventeen-year-old dwarf, who clearly had been less than four feet tall. The figure had a bulging forehead and jutting lower jaw—his upper arm bone, the humerus, was only 58 percent as long as that of an average human skeleton, and the lower arm bone, the ulna, only 45 percent as long. Skeletal measurements of the other individual indicated that she was an average-statured woman and may have been his mother (Fig. 23).

The three researchers completed their investigation and sent articles about the find to *Nature* and the *American Journal of Physical Anthropology*. The journals expressed considerable interest in the discovery. Four of the five reviewers agreed with the researchers that the dwarf's bones represented a classic case of achondroplasia. Huffy about the fifth viewer's dissent, Frayer at first thought about sending his piece to another publication. Ultimately, however, he reconsidered and went on to seek an expert opinion about the diagnosis. He was referred to Dr. William Horton, an authority on inherited bone diseases and a physician who was actively involved with Little People of America. Horton took Frayer's photographs to an LPA conference in Philadelphia and, after consulting with other physicians, told Frayer that the dwarf had a very rare condition called acromesomelic dysplasia.

The puzzle had been solved! Without current technological devices and interdisciplinary collaboration, it would have been impossible to

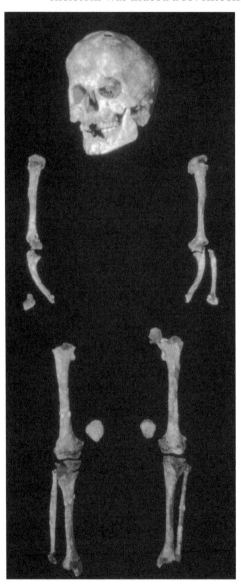

23. Skeletal remains of the Romito dwarf. Courtesy Professor David W. Frayer, University of Kansas.

assess whether the skeleton was ancient or recent, a member of an ethnic group or a specific genetic mutation, a child or an adult. The researchers would not have examined the horns of wild cattle nearby nor the artwork engraved above the burial, both of which helped to identify the date of the excavation level. They could not have conducted a radiocarbon assay to determine the age of the bone, or have had access, as Frayer did, to Horton, an authority on inherited bone diseases. (Horton has since traced the evolving designation of bone dysplasia "families.")[35]

Despite what is known, nagging questions persist. Since no information about the cause of the youth's death came to light, there is no way to determine why he did not live to an even older age than seventeen. Frayer, a decade after he completed his investigation, continues to wonder also whether the woman in the grave was indeed the dwarf's mother. Most important, after pondering the arguments that scholars advanced on both sides of the issue, he has come to reject the "compassion" theory. He notes that lots of nonhuman animals survive major pathologies without sympathetic caretakers: videos, such as PBS's *Mosu,* of severely crippled lemurs, monkeys, and apes, have helped convince him of this fact. Only the haughty opinion we have of our own species, he now believes, leads us to ascribe survival to uniquely human, cultural means of support.

In light of the inevitable lacunae that exist, interpreting prehistory remains daunting. Nonetheless, a careful analysis like Frayer's helps us avoid making speculative leaps beyond the available evidence. The mystifying case of the Romito dwarf reminds us of the dangers of coming to simplistic, premature conclusions about why a particular dwarf individual in *any* era has prevailed or come to grief. It is heartening to know, however, that a skeleton such as that of the Romito dwarf is no longer at risk of being taken for a member of an ancient dwarf race or for an ancestor of Italian fairies thought to be still roaming the hills of Tuscany. The mystery of where present-day ethnic dwarf populations reside has been solved, and the difference between these and sporadic dwarf individuals has become so plain that it is hard to remember how recently confusion reigned. Although it may sometimes appear that we have gleaned all the important answers to long-standing questions, it is unlikely that the final voyages of discovery have taken place.

In October 2004, as this book was going to press, *Nature* reported the astonishing news that skeletons of a new human species, 3 1/2 feet tall—labeled *Homo floreseinsis*—had been found on the remote island of Flores, Indonesia; the small people had lived between 12,000 and 95,000 years ago. Thus, after debunking countless false reports of dwarf species, paleoanthropologists are now eagerly tackling the scientific conundrums presented by these intriguing Floresians.

CHAPTER SIX

Medical Aspects

Early travelers and anthropologists may have appeared baffled by aspects of dwarfism, but their confusion did not have the momentous practical consequences for them that it did for physicians and their dwarf patients. Before the introduction of effective medications, sophisticated diagnostic equipment, and surgical techniques, doctors could provide little more than minimal pain relief and the comfort of their reassuring presence. It had not been only limited knowledge about the nature of their dwarf patients' conditions, however, that had held physicians back. Almost as important as progress in science and technology was the gradual improvement in physicians' attitudes toward patients whose appearance was strikingly different from the norm.[1]

Past Approaches to the Treatment of Dwarfism

A review of medical articles written during the late nineteenth and early twentieth centuries reveals that very often, transfixed by dwarfs' "abnormal" appearance, doctors focused upon it unduly. Unable to "cure" these patients and needing to do *something*, physicians recorded body measurements. As the title of one 1896 work reveals, dwarfs were of interest chiefly because they were among the "anomalies and curiosities of medicine."[2]

Physicians were as perplexed by dwarfism as were casual observers. Medical literature at the turn of the twentieth century lists case after case in which physicians merely assembled data, including such irrelevant measurements as the length of their dwarf patients' hair. Patients' complaints are rarely noted, and treatment options rarely considered. Doctors report their astonishment when they discover any talent in one so small.

Heredity was a great unknown, as attested to by such vague statements as "It may be remarked that perhaps certain women are predisposed to give birth to dwarfs."[3] Generations of doctors firmly believed in "maternal impression," the view that the

birth of a dwarf resulted from an infant's mother having seen a dwarf or an animal—
in one famed instance a turtle.[4] With only intuition and an occasional article to rely
upon, physicians lacked a research base to consult after meeting a new patient. Sometimes what they found was less than helpful, as in the case of the following information offered in *Mercer's Orthopedic Surgery*, a standard text last published in 1983. In an
entry labeled "Achondroplasia," the author lists the clinical features of the condition
and then mistakenly prints the photograph of a child who appears to have a different
condition. Under the heading "Intellect" he offers the following gratuitous and unsup-
ported observations:

> Achondroplasts are usually of normal intelligence, and frequently they are
> lively and amusing. In some cases, however, the intellect is impaired and they
> are backward for their age.
>
> Because of their deformed bodies they have strong feelings of inferiority
> and are emotionally immature, and are often vain, boastful, excitable, fond of
> drink, and sometimes lascivious. Sexual development is usually normal, but
> may be retarded. Dwarfs are very muscular and excel in feats of strength; they
> are frequently employed in theatres and circuses, partly because of their
> strength and partly because of their grotesque appearance.[5]

Before "the age of enlightenment," dwarfs died in greater-than-average numbers during every period of life: for example, both mothers of dwarfs and their infants
had high morbidity rates because of improper treatment during cesarean sections.[6]
Ignorance about the etiology of a condition also caused problems in many cases.
Dwarfism caused by nutritional deficiency was confused with skeletal dysplasias; no
one knew that extremely short proportionate dwarfs had growth hormone deficiency, originating in the pituitary gland. All conditions involving atypical bone
growth were apt to be labeled as achondroplasia, a short-limbed form of dwarfism.
By now it is known that there are more than two hundred types of skeletal dysplasias
(the number is lower if they are considered in "family" groups). Only gradually have
radiology, biochemical assays, and DNA evidence made it possible to offer precise diagnoses; only very recently have the surgical techniques that are so vital to the mobility and well-being of many dwarfs with skeletal problems been developed.

Major Treatment Advances during the Twentieth Century

People can be extremely short, with or without deformity, for all sorts of reasons.
There are congenital causes such as skeletal disorders or a growth hormone, thyroid,

or vitamin deficiency; diseases, including kidney disorders, juvenile rheumatoid arthritis, Crohn's disease, or tuberculosis; psychosocial causes such as neglect or abuse; or iatrogenic causes such as being given heavy doses of cortisone in childhood. Treating each condition properly depends on identifying its causes.

The gradual reduction of the thyroid condition called cretinism beginning around 1922, and the near disappearance of rickets after World War II, are examples of how new understanding led to treatment of dwarfing conditions. Rickets had been confused with congenital bone disorders. Only once it was learned that most cases of rickets were caused by Vitamin D deficiency and that lack of sunlight, resulting from industrial pollution, was also responsible, could the condition that plagued poor city neighborhoods in Great Britain be eliminated.[7] During World War II, Vitamin D began to be added to all milk and cod liver oil given to English children. Similarly, cretinism, now called iron deficiency disorder (IDD), was eliminated in most Western nations once its cause was recognized. Salt iodization was introduced in 1922, with amounts increasing through subsequent decades, but IDD persisted in a number of countries, among them India and Bangladesh, till quite recently. Iron deficiency can cause dwarfism, often accompanied by goiter and severely compromised mental capacity.[8]

Lest anyone think that nutritional-deficiency diseases have been conquered, a 2003 *New York Times* article will correct that impression. It describes a condition called Kashin-Beck disease that is found in the Himalayan foothills of Tibet. Research sponsored by Doctors Without Borders suggests that the disease, which affects 9 percent of the population and causes many villagers to be between three and four feet tall, is the result of bad water, poor diet, and crops grown in mineral-deficient soil—it is, in essence, a disease of poverty.[9]

Conditions causing dwarfism that have been vanquished in wealthier nations persist in poor ones. A very important development occurred in Western nations in the 1970s, with the introduction of routine screening for congenital hypothyroidism (CH), one of the most common preventable causes of mental retardation. Earlier, this condition had frequently led to dwarfism and retardation in children; it still does in areas where screening is not available. Pott's disease, or tuberculous spondylitis, the condition that affected Alexander Pope and Katherine Butler Hathaway, is now recognized as having been present in the earliest societies. Although cases continue to occur, the introduction of effective antibiotics by the 1970s made it possible to avert such sequelae as the degeneration of vertebrae, hunchback, and disabling breathing disorders.

The 1960s through the 1990s brought another major advance with the first treatment for hypopituitary dwarfism, also known as growth hormone deficiency. After dysfunctions in the pituitary gland were identified as an important cause of short stature, first human pituitary hormone, and later synthetic growth hormone (rhGH), were used to treat children with pituitary disorders. When started early, this treatment helps them to grow to normal height, sometimes enabling them to gain as much as a foot. It has been estimated that more than sixty thousand patients have been treated with synthetic growth hormone.[10]

Although dwarfism still occurs as a result of all the causes mentioned here, as well as a number of others, the skeletal dysplasias are the most visible in society overall. These disorders of bone and cartilage present some of the greatest challenges to medical treatment. Each skeletal condition is accompanied by its own set of complications; there are also variations within a particular diagnosis, whether it be called pseudoachondroplasia or spondyloepiphyseal dysplasia or by another multisyllabic name. Different symptoms may present themselves in short-trunked and long-trunked dwarfism, and special problems are associated with certain conditions, such as osteogenesis imperfecta, or brittle bone disease. Orthopedic, neurological, and respiratory difficulties are among the potential medical problems associated with most of them.

Some significant problems have been ameliorated. Through the collaboration of Dr. Richard Pauli and other experts, it has come to light that compression of the lower brainstem or cervical section of the spinal cord has been responsible for sudden infant death syndrome (SIDS) in achondroplastic infants.[11] Unlike average-size children who died in their cribs at night, these children had been more apt to die while in the sitting position in strollers, swings, or bouncers. Subsequent information provided through *LPA Today* offered advice designed to prevent SIDS and other problems resulting from compression.

Research is currently under way, notably in Israel, Japan, and the United States, for treatments that may cause children with achondroplasia, and perhaps some of the other bone disorders, to grow taller. However, practical applications of this research are some years ahead. In the meantime, partial remedies for most of the compelling problems associated with the conditions have become available. Innovative spinal and limb surgeries now offer greater mobility to patients who in earlier times would have been seriously impaired or even paralyzed. Continuous air pressure masks (CPAPs) have been developed for breathing problems, antibiotics and shunts now prevent hearing loss, and height/weight charts accompanied by counseling can make dwarfs thinner and fitter and thereby less vulnerable to joint damage. Childbirth used to be exceedingly dangerous for dwarf women. Today prospective dwarf mothers benefit from workshops given at dwarfism conferences by specialists in high-risk pregnancy. In addition, ordinary obstetricians can consult with experts to ensure safe childbirths.

The Birth of a Child
and the Search for Appropriate Care

While physicians' knowledge base is of central importance, so are their attitudes. The emotional experience of dwarfs and their families as they seek answers and real help cannot be captured by catalogs of etiology or medical discoveries. This representative account by Sandy (Clark) Leeson, the mother of a daughter with achondroplasia, can help to illuminate the great divide between the attitudes and treatment of yesterday and today:[12]

It has been almost ten years since our second daughter was born. I still remember great joy in that delivery room, but it has been a very long road since that morning. Within an hour after her birth, our pediatrician came to my room, while my husband was happily calling all the relatives. In the most matter of fact way, he asked me if anyone had told me anything about the baby? He proceeded to tell me, without my husband present, that something was wrong with her . . . she was what they called an F.L.K . . . a funny looking kid. He said he suspected that she had some sort of genetic problem and that they were getting ready to send her over to Children's Hospital for skeletal X-rays. I was literally numb. When my husband came back to the room I was in hysterical tears and he had no idea what I was talking about. Of course the doctor was gone.

If sharing these emotions with you makes you a little uncomfortable, they were meant to. Not only did that pediatrician lack compassion and consideration of my lack of medical knowledge, but his greatest fault was that even six months later he had not offered any help to us as parents. Yet we indeed had a child with certain physical handicaps requiring medical attention. When we took Katy home, all I knew was a fourteen-letter word that meant my little girl would grow only three [actually four] feet tall. That same pediatrician had mused that I really was not so very tall myself and that we should just "take her home and love her."

When her daughter was six months old, Leeson learned from an article she had searched out in a local library that Johns Hopkins University Hospital in Baltimore had a dwarfism clinic; she spent hours with Dr. Steven Kopits, who was then the orthopedic surgeon there.[13] He showed her X-rays and diagrams and gave her articles to read; he told her what to anticipate regarding when Katy might be expected to sit, crawl, and walk and what risks to watch for; he introduced her to parents and children visiting the center. Subsequently, he sent his three-page clinic notes to her pediatrician and made an appointment for six months hence—earlier if problems arose.

Many parents have described their visits to Kopits, who always made a thorough examination, answered all their questions, tickled their baby's toes, and told them what a beautiful baby they had. Reassured, they came to trust that their child had a hopeful future and that they had an expert they could always depend upon. Often, these parents had been to other doctors who behaved as if their baby had a dread disease—doctors who were either uninformed, emotionally distant, or both. More than one parent reports having been told, "Your baby is a circus dwarf."

Good care for individuals with dwarfism requires "planned management": scheduling appointments at critical developmental periods, anticipating problems, and intervening to avert dire consequences. While the situation has improved somewhat during the past decade, a combination of medical expertise and compassionate engagement is still hard to come by. Also, physicians may well be seeing an infant or adult with a condition that they have never previously encountered. If these physicians are hesitant to acknowledge the limitations of their experience and fail to make inquiries or initiate appropriate referrals, the results can be disastrous. But when doctors, patients, and family members are knowledgeable and respectful, they create an unbeatable alliance. There is no better advice to give families than to suggest that they seek out centers that specialize in dwarfism. These may be found by contacting the organization that corresponds most closely to an individual's condition or through a physician who serves on the medical advisory board of Little People of America (LPA), located on the LPA Web site (http://lpaonline.org).

The Role of Dwarfism Groups, Medical Advisory Boards, and the Internet

Most dwarfism-related organizations—the LPA, the Human Growth Foundation, the Magic Foundation, the Turner Society, the Osteogenesis Imperfecta Society, the Mucopolysaccharidosis Foundation, and numerous others—were first formed as support groups, later adding advocacy to their activities. In addition, they afford a vital bridge between affected persons and the medical community. At each national LPA conference, for example, patients from various states and abroad sign up for clinic exams, and physicians lead workshops focused on recent developments. An ongoing collaboration also exists between physicians and patients in carrying out research projects.

As of this writing, the chairman of the LPA medical advisory board is Dr. Richard Pauli, who is at the University of Wisconsin. His Midwestern Bone Dysplasia Clinic has published excellent pamphlets about the natural history of various conditions, designed to inform families about their children's situation in a positive way and en-sure better management of medical and social concerns. Neither the board nor this kind of literature existed before the early 1970s, when Dr. Victor McKusick was ac-tively training teaching fellows at Johns Hopkins University Medical Center; his stu-dents later became dwarfism specialists throughout the United States and elsewhere, and some became key board members. McKusick is the renowned geneticist who wrote *Mendelian Inheritance in Man,* the comprehensive genetics compendium, now available online. An important mentor and investigator in dwarfism research, he was also instrumental in creating the holistic model for the treatment of all genetic disor-ders that has been adopted by physicians at medical institutions worldwide. His in-fluence has been important in fostering the exceptionally positive atmosphere between patients and physicians that exists in LPA.

Although there are now several centers for dwarfism treatment in the United States and other nations, among them France, Germany, Switzerland, Belgium, Great Britain, Uruguay, Israel, and Argentina, it is still common for medical advisory board physicians to be called on to consult on difficult cases. Staff at the International Skele-tal Dysplasia Registry at Cedars-Sinai Hospital in Los Angeles, another important re-source, field inquiries and conduct research into the diagnosis, etiology, and management of skeletal dysplasias. Currently, the registry accumulates six hundred cases a year from around the world and has to date collected a total of more than ten thousand cases.[14]

While scientific articles about dwarfism can be obtained on the Internet at PubMed and Online Mendelian Inheritance in Man (OMIM), often the most up-to-date information for the layperson can be found on the Web sites of dwarfism organ-izations, including the Medical Resource Center of LPA Online.

Frequency of Dwarfing Conditions

The question of the incidence of dwarfism is a vexing one. Few studies counting the number of dwarfs within populations have been conducted. Even now, fewer than half the states in the United States have registries for medical information about the prevalence of medical conditions and diseases. Dwarfism often is not present or apparent at birth, and since calculations of incidence are most frequently based on only counting those people who have come to the attention of hospitals, even med-ical experts present their figures quite tentatively. In 1983 McKusick estimated that there were probably several million people in the world with dwarfism, taking all causes into account.[15] In the absence of definitive published figures about the inci-dence of dwarfism, a way to calculate the total is by adding the figures cited on the

Internet by major dwarfism groups and combining estimates of the incidence of such conditions as achondroplasia, Turner's syndrome, growth hormone deficiency, osteogenesis imperfecta, and Down's syndrome (these last two conditions are only sometimes accompanied by significant short stature). Using this method, it appears that there are more than two hundred thousand people with dwarfism in the United States. Efforts are currently being made by both geneticists and LPA to determine incidence more precisely.

Exact figures are available, however, for the 7,588 individuals listed as members of LPA in 2001, with 143 diagnoses represented. More than half of those who cited their diagnoses had achondroplasia, and most of the rest listed other skeletal disorders. Hypopituitary dwarfism and Turner syndrome were the only other types represented among the fifteen most common conditions listed. Dwarfism resulting from many other causes—including various illnesses, iatrogenic causes, Down's syndrome, and psychosocial dwarfism—is much harder to assess, as there is no single compendium available and for some diagnoses the incidence is unknown. Individuals whose short stature results from conditions such as arthritis or kidney disease tend to join organizations specific to their condition, rather than a general dwarfism group like LPA, and the number of dwarfs in these organizations is rarely recorded.

Controversial Procedures

If it is established that a dwarf child cannot reach average height, the majority of families work toward finding ways to ensure that their children live the best life possible as short persons. However, if they hear about safe, effective means of increasing stature, many parents are likely to explore them.

When treatments became available for hypopituitary dwarfism and congenital hypothyroidism, there was little controversy about whether to make use of them. In the 1960s, before synthetic growth hormone was available, families struggled valiantly to accumulate enough glands from human cadavers for hospitals to process and enable growth hormone–deficient children to grow. Although treatment was successful for many patients, the use of human glands was discontinued in the 1980s when it was discovered that some of those who had been treated had died from Creutzfeldt-Jacob disease, a condition akin to mad cow disease, that had been communicated in the injection process.

No such risk is entailed with synthetic growth hormone, which is currently routinely used. Despite the distress that parents experience in subjecting their children to frequent injections, they usually have little ambivalence. Especially when initiated at an early age, treatment is apt to be successful. The outcome—attaining close to normal height, and sexual maturity when that is affected—seems well worth the effort and the very considerable expense. Controversy arose when a 2003 panel advising the Food and Drug Administration (FDA) recommended that the FDA approve Eli Lilly and Company's request to use growth hormone for children who were merely short—five feet three or less—in other words, whose stature was not the outcome of a medical condition. These children were likely to grow only a few inches as a result of the treatment, which could cost between twenty-two thousand and forty-three thousand dollars for each centimeter of growth.[16] Nevertheless, as early as 1996, a survey published in the *Journal of the American Medical Association* revealed that about 40 percent of children receiving human growth hormone were getting it for uses that had not been approved by the FDA.

The introduction of limb-lengthening procedures in the United States in the late 1980s raised even greater controversy. Praised in the media and disparaged by the dwarfism community, such treatment was reported to be a miraculous solution for dwarfs with skeletal dysplasias. The *Washington Post, Time, 20/20,* and numerous talk shows featured dwarf children whose treatment would allow them to attain nearly normal stature—from a height of 4 to 4 1/2 feet (the average height of an achondroplastic dwarf), they were predicted to grow to 5 feet or more.[17]

The first reports surfaced in 1986, beginning with an article titled "Enduring Agony, a Boy's Made Taller."[18] Mary Tarabocchia, who since the birth of her son Anthony had desperately searched for a remedy for his dwarfism, took him, at the age of nine, to Italy for treatment. For eight months she slept on a cot by his bed as the doctors turned the screws each day on a system of wires and braces attached to his legs to make them longer. Seeing the pain endured by her own son and others, she had doubts, but she was reassured later when she asked her son if he was happy, and he told her that children no longer made fun of him. Anthony is now an adult; he is more than five feet tall and reports himself pleased to have had the surgery.

The procedure Anthony underwent was first introduced in Russia by Dr. Gavril Ilizarov in 1951; limb-lengthening techniques became available in Italy and other countries during the next decades, and later in the United States.[19] The International Center for Limb Lengthening at Sinai Hospital in Baltimore, directed by Dr. Dror Paley, now performs the greatest number of such surgeries. The procedure involves surgically inserting pins that, in effect, break the bones, which then heal, lengthening the limbs. Although individual practitioners sometimes perform the procedure on their own, that is not recommended, as the best results and fewest complications occur when it is carried out at major centers.[20]

Major centers performing the Ilizarov procedure attest to their safety and to individuals' satisfaction with the outcomes.[21] A different technique, the Villerubias method, was adopted by medical advisory board members Dr. David Rimoin and Dr.

Steven Isaacson at Cedars-Sinai Hospital in Los Angeles; they suggested that the procedure helped prevent spinal problems and was less painful than the Ilazorov method, and they noted that not one patient had expressed regrets about having gone through it.[22]

Is limb lengthening a modern miracle, as has been claimed, or a denial of positive dwarf identity? Physicians and those who are affected by dwarfism continue to debate whether the surgery is merely cosmetic—dictated by the pressures of a beauty-crazed society—or has legitimate medical, psychological, and health benefits.[23] For many years the reaction of the dwarfism community to extensive limb-lengthening procedures was negative. In 1988 the board of directors of LPA issued a press release emphasizing that dwarf children, when raised in a supportive environment, learned to cope effectively and that people's quality of life depended on their self-esteem and accomplishments, not on height. It cautioned that pain, surgical complications, and possible long-term effects made the procedures too risky; of particular concern to the board was that parents not make the decision while their children were still too young to give informed consent.

Because a procedure may cost about $150,000, whatever method is used is available mostly to those with good insurance coverage. By 2002, improved techniques and a new dialogue had developed, with some people with dwarfism comparing the extended limb lengthening (ELL) procedure to the cochlear implant surgery now available to the deaf and hard of hearing.[24] Having surgery for these conditions, or for blindness, they argued, need not be a repudiation of one's previous identity. Although the official position of LPA eventually moderated somewhat, the majority of the group's members rejected the treatment for themselves and their children. The limb-lengthening debate is likely to persist until the results of long-term studies of the benefits and ill effects of ELL are available.

In Utero Screening: Abortion and Embryo Choice

Unraveling the genome has raised questions about its potential consequences for dwarfs. Research efforts have identified the location, on specific chromosomes, of the genes for more than half of all bone disorders that cause dwarfism, among them achondroplasia, pseudoachondroplasia, and diastrophic dwarfism. We now have the ability to diagnose many conditions in utero. Genetic testing is now available for more than three hundred diseases or conditions in more than two hundred laboratories in the United States.[25] Diagnoses are made on the basis of amniocentesis, ultrasound, and placental chorion analysis; and parents may elect to abort a diagnosed fetus.

The primary prenatal technique used to identify short stature is ultrasound—although misdiagnosis has sometimes proved to be a problem.[26] Whether the diagnosis is accurate or incorrect, the reaction of prospective parents tends to be a state of turmoil. A good genetic counselor can be an invaluable asset in the decision-making process, but the stance of the physician is also vital. If the doctor says it is "not so bad," the parents may be more inclined to go forward with the pregnancy. If, instead, the physician is unfamiliar with the condition or seems to regard the potential birth as tragic, the parents may be more inclined to abort. What do we know about physicians' attitudes? One survey of obstetricians and geneticists, conducted in the wake of a controversial abortion of a thirty-two-week-old dwarf fetus in Australia, found considerable support for making abortion available to mothers of fetuses diagnosed with dwarfism.[27] However, LPA medical advisory board members, including Dr. Clair Francomano, who helped discover the achondroplasia gene, and other physicians have spoken out against routine screening for achondroplasia in the general population.

It is now possible for prospective parents with genetic conditions to choose in vitro fertilization, implanting an embryo without the mutant gene. They must appraise their own lives as well as struggle with the moral responsibility of deciding for their unborn child. Nondisabled adults are more liable to view disabilities as tragic than are disabled persons, even those with severe impairments. A growing number of works by sociologists, physicians, and other professionals that address prenatal testing and disability rights are now being published.[28]

The Impact of Potential Genetic Developments on the Future of Dwarfs

The announcement on 26 June 2000 by Dr. Francis Collins of the National Genome Research Institute of the National Institutes of Health (NIH), and Dr. Craig Venter, head of Celera, a private company, that the unraveling of the genome was almost complete was widely welcomed.[29] However, it soon became apparent that the complex interactions involved would be even harder to decipher than locating the genes had been, and that creating a genetic repair kit for various conditions would be the most daunting enterprise of all.[30]

Bone growth is a particularly difficult genetic characteristic to alter. Nevertheless, research with the aim of blocking the mutant genetic signals that cause conditions such as achondroplasia is currently in progress. Researchers hope that in addition to adding height, in the future genetic intervention may improve the quality of bone and cartilage, repair fractures, and prevent bone deterioration.[31]

Genetic progress represents a delicate balance. For some persons with dwarfism, it raises the specter of past eugenic abuses and the possibility of not only preventing persons who may have disabilities from being born, but also devaluing the lives of those already here. Ethical concerns and potential benefits must both be assessed. However, given the inevitable appearance of new mutations, one need not feel apprehensive about the disappearance of dwarfs from the planet. Even if it tried, no obstetrics department could field a program that would identify and alter the vast number of genetic differences. But at least on that part of the globe with resources to implement the new technology, changes, as yet unforeseeable, will occur.

The Effect of Medical Problems on the Lives of Persons with Dwarfism

No account is complete without some consideration of the physical and emotional problems associated with dwarfing conditions. A few are life threatening in infancy; others require vigilance in the early years. Some children require adenoidectomies, tonsillectomies, tracheotomies, or surgery on the cervical section of the spine. Because of ear infections, they may have shunts installed to ward off the deafness that was common in the past but rare today. Many children require osteotomies to correct or inhibit bowing. There are also a great number, however, who remain healthy with no interventions.

Children and adults with a variety of bone dysplasias must often undergo a series of surgeries. Individuals with osteogenesis imperfecta deal at all ages with unpredictable fractures, pain, and problems with mobility. Children with hypopituitary deficiency require almost daily injections given by others; by adolescence they are given the task of injecting themselves, and they often wrestle with decisions about how long they are willing to persist with this uncomfortable procedure in order to achieve their optimal height. Girls with Turner syndrome face a similar situation and, in addition, must come to terms with questions relating to their inability to bear children.

Often, problems that are present in childhood persist into adulthood. Just when personal and professional life have settled into a comfortable place, some new symptom may present itself, requiring surgical intervention—for example, as a result of spinal stenosis or deteriorating joints—or other medical attention. The life disruption cannot be overstated. Although psychological problems do sometimes occur as a result of medical and societal pressures, and depression certainly is a problem, there is little evidence that dwarf individuals experience these at a greater rate than the rest of the population.[32] Such obstacles may even foster a sense of personal strength in those who endure them, benefit, and move on.

Institutional Problems in the Medical System

Despite myriad medical advances, few are readily available to all who require them. While the dire situation in poorer nations is lamentable, affected individuals living in the United States often find themselves not much better off. Sometimes local physicians are not knowledgeable enough to refer the patient to an appropriate treatment center, and sometimes a center is so far away that families cannot manage the expeditions necessary to reach it. The greatest obstacle of all is the absence of a universal health-care system.

Treatment for Turner syndrome can cost as much as thirty thousand to forty-five thousand dollars a year; fees for the treatment of young growth hormone–deficient patients can be as little as ten thousand dollars a year, whereas the annual cost for older patients may be fifteen thousand to twenty thousand dollars or more. Complex surgeries are extremely expensive, and if patients do not have good insurance coverage, they may find themselves unable to find a competent surgeon who will accept them. Even if some coverage exists, it may leave the patient with a substantial copayment that creates financial hardship. Patients with Medicaid or with no insurance at all may have to forgo needed treatment or try to raise funds from family, friends, or their religious community. While there are expert surgeons who waive or reduce their fees for the uninsured, and some teaching or charity hospitals that adjust payment, the cost of operating rooms and hospital beds cannot always be written off. A notable exception is the Shriners' hospital system. The twenty-two Shriners' hospitals offer free care to children under eighteen who require orthopedic treatment, including surgery. But only a few European countries, notably Germany and those of Scandinavia, and in some measure Canada, make free surgery available to all who require it.

Some patients, unable to get to medical centers, communicate with experts via e-mail; knowledgeable specialists find themselves overwhelmed by the number of inquiries they receive. At a patient's request, they may spend time on the phone speaking with local physicians, who don't always welcome their counsel. Specialists speaking at an LPA conference rarely are licensed to practice in the states where the conference is being held and may therefore be subject to malpractice suits. Clearly, some form of national licensure is essential, as are agreements with managed-care companies to expedite claims on a national basis. In 2002, federal legislation was passed authorizing referrals to specialists outside a managed-care network, if the network did not include an appropriate specialist. But the process rarely goes smoothly, and many families find it a full-time job to battle the insurance bureaucracy.

Access to quality care remains as remote for most dwarf individuals in the world as it was a century ago. There is a dearth of trained specialists with sufficient expertise to treat dwarfing conditions. The federal and private monies that were available for clinical training in the 1970s and resulted in the spread of dwarfism knowledge have largely dried up, and the few excellent centers that are currently in place sometimes languish for lack of funds.

These days, when doctors embark on their medical careers in a state of debt, it is increasingly difficult to find those willing to accept modest compensation for demanding hospital schedules. The situation is not hopeless, however, and occasionally a new center opens; in 2003, for example, the Center for Skeletal Dysplasias at the Hospital for Special Surgery in New York was established.[33] Some idealists may yet be found to replace the first generation of dwarfism specialists, who are now "aging out." In the long run, however, only an overhaul of health care—perhaps a single-payer system—will ensure that treatment is available to all those who can benefit from it.

Medical knowledge about dwarfism is growing at an astounding rate. Hopefully, there are now fewer physicians who describe dwarfs to new parents as FLKs—funny looking kids—and more who have begun to see such patients not as "abnormal individuals" but as "normal little people" who, through those physicians' expertise, can be helped to attain a satisfying life. Beyond this, whether society will find the resources needed to translate medical knowledge into treatment remains the most problematic question of all.

PART III

The Cultural Mirror

IMAGES OF DWARFS

IN THE ARTS

CHAPTER SEVEN

Art

L ong before any writing appeared about dwarfs, they could be found in artwork created in every culture and in every time period. Images of dwarfs
were plentiful in the ancient world, in the stone carvings and sculptures of
Egypt, the vases of Greece, and the stone reliefs of India. They were a prominent subject in the art of the Mayas and were models for rare bronzes in Benin. Dwarfs are
portrayed in ancient Chinese ceramics and in Japanese prints, as well as in the folk
art of garden sculptures, which began to appear in sixteenth-century Europe and
have persisted into our own times. Probably the best-known representations of
dwarfs in the Western world are the religious paintings and the group and individual
portraits of court dwarfs that proliferated throughout Europe from the fifteenth to
the early eighteenth century. The lessening of this subject matter in art coincided with
the declining incidence and ultimate disappearance of dwarfs from the courts. Fantasy little people continued to be caricatured and used to accompany folktales and
children's stories, but paintings and sculptures of dwarfs became relatively scarce in
the nineteenth and twentieth centuries, with only a few first-rate portrait treatments.
In photography, images of dwarfs were more plentiful; most were of circus dwarfs
and entertainers. There are just a few remarkable and respectful modern portrait
treatments of dwarfs, as well as a number of fine photographs. Not only have average-statured artists portrayed dwarfs; there have also been a good number of accomplished dwarf artists.

According to researchers who have sought out and found and cataloged works
that depict dwarfs, they have uncovered only a small portion of the artistic productions that exist. In 1992 the volume *Kleine Menschen—grosse Kunst* appeared; two years
later, it was translated and published in English as *Small People—Great Art*.[1] Assembled in this invaluable work are more than a hundred high-quality reproductions of
artworks containing images of dwarfs; also included are detailed descriptions, background information, and tentative diagnoses of the medical conditions of the dwarfs
depicted. Almost a century earlier, the Francis Galton Laboratory for Human Eugenics in London had published a comprehensive study of dwarfism.[2] In it were listed

191 known artworks depicting dwarfs; among the artists represented were Angelico, Bosch, Veronese, Rubens, Mytens, Van Dyck, Velázquez, and Tiepolo. In addition, there are other books that deal with a variety of disabilities and include some images of dwarfs.[3]

This chapter surveys the representation of dwarfs in art, exploring what the artworks reveal about the place of dwarfs in each society and also highlighting certain pieces that are particularly accomplished or interesting. The chapter also includes a discussion of dwarf artists past and present.

Egyptian and Greek Art

The earliest examples of dwarfs as artistic subjects were found at Tel-El Amarna in Egypt and date from the fourth century B.C.E. These stone carvings give evidence of an earlier version of the "court dwarf" phenomenon that was to become widespread in many nations in subsequent centuries. Dwarfs are portrayed as the companions of princes and identified in statuary by such grandiloquent names as Pareh (the sun) and Ereh (forever) as well as "the vizier" and "the queen."[4] Despite the implicit irony in this labeling—a practice also found in the courts of Europe—there is evidence that dwarfs experienced a greater degree of respect than implied by the names they were given.

The frequency with which dwarfs appear and the variety of their roles reveal them as more integrated in the culture of early Egypt than in almost any other. Egypt has left a rich artistic legacy, notably in its funerary statuary and reliefs. Among the statuary is a small statuette of Knum-hotep, which has been praised as "a masterpiece of realism."[5] The figure's prominent head, expressive facial features, and muscular body are all modeled with painstaking care.

More than one hundred objects, including stelae, papyri, and glazed ware and works in faience and limestone, from museums throughout the world are represented in Veronique Dasen's *Dwarfs in Ancient Egypt and Greece*.[6] The images and Dasen's careful analysis assure this volume of enduring importance to any study of Egyptian art. Among the notable reliefs that show female members of the court is one of a remarkably lifelike female dwarf on an alabaster boat from the tomb of Tutankhamen (see color plate 1).

An exhibit at the Brooklyn Museum of Art in 1988 featured statuary from the temple dedicated to the goddess Hathor at Dendera. It showed Cleopatra VII and Caesarion, her son, and depicted a tiny male figure, described as representing the *ka*, or soul, of Caesarion. This example of a homunculus is only one of a variety that are found in works of many cultures, but notably in Egypt, embodying (or symbolizing) the spiritual component of human beings. This function provided a central rationale for dwarfs being highly valued in Egyptian culture and highlighted in its art. In many an exhibit of Egyptian art, the observant visitor will discover at least one portrayal of a dwarf. A 1999 show at the Metropolitan Museum of Art, in New York, offered two examples. One, from the Fourth Dynasty (2525–2465 B.C.E.) titled *Per-ni-anku,* was a painted basalt figure shown seated and holding the staff and scepter of office that revealed that he, like two other dwarfs found nearby, probably held a high position at court. The second, like the first from the Western Cemetery at Giza, was a Fifth Dynasty (2420–2389 B.C.E.) work, a smaller carving of a dwarf playing a harplike instrument. Included in a 2003 exhibit of art from Mesopotamia, also at the Metropolitan Museum, was an inlaid box known as the Standard of Ur (2500–2450 B.C.E.). This work, from Sumer, of wood, lapis, red limestone, and shell, depicts a retinue in which a dwarf leads an onager that pulls a chariot—an indication, perhaps, that dwarfs may have had roles tending animals, not only in Egypt, but also in neighboring courts.

One of the more dramatic and expressive examples of dwarf statuary is the group with Seneb, the court dwarf who has been recognized in many accounts of life and art in Egypt (see color plate 2). The atmosphere portrayed in this funerary sculpture of Seneb and his family is characteristic of that of similar works representing average-statured couples, and, like other such sculptures, illustrates the long-lasting, profound bond that evidently existed between husbands and wives.[7] In this statue, Seneb sits cross-legged on a block of stone with his small arms clasped, one of his wife's arms around him, and her hand fondly touching his arm. The space that the legs of an ordinary man would have filled is occupied by his two average-statured children, thereby, through the arrangement of masses, creating the same impression that would have been made by an ordinary seated figure.[8] The effort to make Seneb and his wife appear of equal stature is carried even further in the reliefs of the offering niche. Although Seneb is clearly depicted as a dwarf, the carvings of his retainers show them as smaller than he is, in deference to his higher status. (This pattern is common in many ancient cultures—sometimes it is hard to know whether small figures are in fact dwarfs or merely the less significant members of a court group.) Further, in this work, the modeling of the children represents an advance in Egyptian art, for their bodies are chubby—that is, rounded and childlike—unlike other depictions of children that show them as miniature adults.[9]

The Seneb statue is a triumph, for its physical beauty, its relaxed atmosphere, and its original solution to the problem of placement. But for a dwarf viewer it is particularly moving, for it is an extremely rare depiction of a dwarf and family. Typically, a dwarf is shown either alone, or as a part of a court group, or playing a role in a religious or historic drama. Occasionally there are several dwarfs in the same image;

however, they often do not relate to one another but, rather, belong to a situation being lived principally by others.

In Greek art, dwarf images frequently appear on various forms of ceramic vases. The vast majority of these portray individuals with achondroplasia, or variations on their short-limbed, muscular figures, but transformed into satyr figures. Often bald and bearded, with large phalluses, they are shown kicking up their heels, holding a wine cup, or otherwise engaged in dance or revelry. The human dwarf models have been recast as symbolic fantasy figures, captured in a moment of merriment at a feast of Dionysos. There are also representations of dwarfs in renderings of the mythical battle of the pygmies and the cranes. The dwarfs depicted on vases are generally shown in active poses.

Some dwarfs are shown attending noblemen and -women. An occasional scene has inspired speculations about the role of the dwarf in Greek society. On the vase known as the Peytel aryballos, a dwarf is shown in a clinic carrying a hare and speaking with another man. There has been considerable conjecture about his role or occupation.[10] (See color plate 3.) The dwarfs who appear on Greek vases are almost invariably shown as singletons, or occasionally as a pair of men, but almost always in subordinate or satyrlike situations, and often as caricatures. Dwarf males are occasionally shown attending average-sized females (a rare pairing in Greek iconography), possibly because their sexuality is not seen as a threat.

Dwarf women are almost never depicted. Dasen hypothesizes that their absence may result in part from women's social seclusion, but also from discomfort or sympathy on the part of artists: perhaps they wanted to prevent the type of derision that arose when a stylized dwarf woman was displayed on the vase known as the Munich skyphos.[11] The figures of dwarfs that appear in red-figure and black-figure vases are detailed and finely drawn; in comparison, the terra-cotta statuary of dwarfs that exists is rather crudely made.

Michael Garmaise has written about some lesser-known works that were produced during the later Hellenistic period.[12] He discusses several remarkable mosaics tentatively dated to the first half of the second century C.E. One panel shows an achondroplastic dwarf doing tricks with a boar; another shows a similar figure tickling a rooster (almost as big as he is) with a branch. Very likely these were performers. But one mosaic is more symbolic in nature, showing a naked male (perhaps a diastrophic dwarf) playing a flute, in the same panel as a large iconic eye surrounded by dog, bird, and crab figures. This design has an apotropaic function—the dwarf's assigned role is to ward off the evil eye.[13]

African, Asian, and Central American Art

The art of Africa, Asia, and Central America did not abound with dwarf subjects to the same degree found in the art of classical Egypt and of fifteenth-to-eighteenth-century Europe. Nevertheless, a rich tradition did flourish, documenting religious beliefs.

Because in the art of Africa, Asia, and Central America small figures are often counterposed against larger ones—these latter representing royalty or deities—to indicate status, it is sometimes difficult to determine whether an artist has depicted a dwarf or merely a person of lesser rank. A standard anthropology text uses a Yoruba bronze plaque portraying a monarch and attendants of varying sizes as an illustration of differences in status.[14] A fifteenth-century Ming dynasty silk hanging at the Brooklyn Museum of Art, in New York, shows what seems at first to be two dwarfs attending an arhat (a Buddhist monk who has reached the stage of Nirvana)—but they turn out to be merely two servants, made smaller to emphasize the arhat's importance.

Despite this ambiguity, it is possible to unearth non-Western artworks that contain bona fide dwarf subjects. As in European art, dwarfs in earlier Asian art are associated with court entertainment or religious themes. Because of the paucity of the images, an assiduous search is required to locate such representations as, for example, a striking picture by Toyokuni III (1786–1865), of a dwarf Kabuki actor (Fig. 24).[15]

Already in the Han but especially in the Tang dynasty (618–906 C.E.) in China, one finds ceramics with dwarf jesters, often in comic postures. One small, finely modeled clay figure, titled *Negroid Dwarf*, is in the collection of the Cleveland Museum of Art.[16] Another similar but less elaborate work purported to be from the same period was advertised for sale on the Internet for four hundred dollars in 1999.[17] There is no way to know with absolute certainty whether a given figure was an ordinary person or a court jester, but many have been identified as court dwarfs by cura-

24. *Toyokuni III. Woodblock print, c. 1840–1870. From P. Huard, Z. Ohya, and M. Wong,* La médicine japonaise des origines à nos jours *(Paris: Les Editions Roger DeCosta, 1974).*

tors and art experts. According to Wang Ch'ung, born in 82 or 83 C.E., dwarfs had long served as jesters. There is evidence that they continued to do so in ensuing centuries—by the eighth century they were commonly sent to monarchs as tributes.[18]

The Tang dynasty was a particularly affluent period in China in which exquisite sculptures were created, including some of entertainers who appear to be dwarfs.[19] Chang'an, the flourishing capital, was the point of departure and return for travelers on the Silk Road. Among its two million inhabitants were at least five thousand foreigners. It is not surprising to learn that the imperial court at Chang'an had contacted many nations in order to secure dwarf jugglers and actors for its entertainment. Often the faces of these terra-cotta figurines reveal them as foreigners.[20] A fine collection of fairly representative earthenware figurines from this period is on display at the Royal Ontario Museum in Toronto. It includes four dwarf figures dressed in attire that suggests they are actors or entertainers.[21] Funerary figures such as these, sometimes with cavalcades of horses and with camels, militia, and troupes of dancers and musicians, were commonly included in the tombs of prosperous officials (see color plate 4).

25. *Dwarf figures holding tray. Detail of stone gateway at the Great Stupa of Sanchi, India, c. 35 B.C.E. Photograph from* Die Zwere kommen! *(Trautenfels, Austria: Verein Schloss, 1993).*

The Amaravati region of India contains the ruins of ancient monuments that were created between 200 B.C.E. and 200 C.E. The largest of these Buddhist stupas, once the most magnificent of all, no longer exists; however, smaller ones in varying states of disrepair remain. Some of these have slabs with dwarf figures standing in each side of a gate, holding a tray on their heads; it is possible that in the original structures these statues were created to receive the offerings of visitors (Fig. 25).[22] In other scenes from the life of Buddha or Bodhisattva, dwarfs are shown either as helpers or demons.[23]

In both India and China, there are Buddhist sculptures of dwarfs as part of the capitals of temple pillars. One such sculptural element may be found at the Lianhua (Lotus) temple in Fujian province in China.[24] Typically, such dwarfs are depicted as short but extremely strong, their pleasant expressions indicating that they are happy to serve the Buddhas above them. Of a lower class, they are expected to work hard and be satisfied with whatever they get.

Dwarf figures are also prominent in Hindu art in the fourth to sixth century C.E. They appear in large reliefs and on columns and doorposts. *Ganas,* dwarfs accompanying the god Ganesh, are shown as part of the retinue of the god Shiva. Their dress is made to resemble his they have a similar hairstyle, and like him they wear a single earring and a snakelike bracelet.[25] There are some fine examples of *ganas* from the Gupta period that are on exhibit in the Baroda Museum in Sayajirao, India, and attempts have been made to identify six dwarf types, ranging from nude to elaborately clothed figures in a number of postures. Similar figures from a later period have also been found in Cambodia.[26]

The most common appearance of a dwarf in Hindu mythology is as an avatar of the god Vishnu (see Chapter 4).[27] Vishnu has been represented in a variety of Indian sculptural forms, including in pillars signifying the four directions.[28] Dwarf attendants of goddesses have been shown in other scenes throughout the Indian subcontinent, in one instance depicted emerging from crocodile mouths. Similar sculptures have been discovered in Nepal and Sri Lanka.[29] Representations of dwarfs in Indian art also occasionally appear as small terra-cotta figures. A crouching dwarf figure at the Cleveland Museum, fashioned in the form of a whistle, dates from the first century Sunga dynasty in India. Dwarfs were often accorded symbolic meaning, but sometimes they were merely ornamental devices.

Dwarfs are often portrayed on pottery as servants of gods. Linda Schele, an expert on the Maya, has compiled the largest published collection of Mayan sculptures, including superb photographs of dwarf figurines (see color plate 5).[30] These were used in ceremonies and also placed in graves of family members as beneficent escorts to the world to come.[31]

Determining whether a figure represents a dwarf is not always easy. Small clay figures from Mexico, Ecuador, Peru, and Guatemala that are featured in the book *Little People of the Earth* may or may not be dwarfs—it is possible that only some of them are.[32] Carolyn Tate, an art historian at Texas Tech, has argued that a group of sixteen Olmec figures previously regarded as crouching dwarfs are probably fetuses.[33] However, the collection in the Metropolitan Museum of Art includes an undisputed Olmec hunchback dwarf dated between the twelfth and ninth centuries B.C.E. At least *some* of the Central American statuary has represented dwarfs in their characteristic mythic roles in non-Western societies—as gods, servants of gods, protectors, and spiritual homunculi with connections to birth and the afterlife.

One of the few well-studied representations of dwarfs in Africa, outside Egypt, is the collection of Nomoli figurines of the Mende in Sierra Leone, the earliest of which date from the fifteenth century (see Chapter 4).[34] There are also photographs that confirm that "little people," both pygmies and dwarfs with a variety of constitutional conditions, were present in the courts of Benin.[35] Artistic evidence, however, is sparse. Only two handsome sixteenth-century bronze statuettes survive—one male and one female.

European Art from the Fifteenth to Eighteenth Century

In European art of the fifteenth to eighteenth centuries, dwarfs, ubiquitous in the artwork of that period, were portrayed as realistic rather than symbolic or mythic figures. Because they were such an integral part of imperial activities—serving, entertaining, and present at royal celebrations—they are almost never depicted as autonomous beings; rather, they are shown as decorative elements situated at the fringes of the lives of others more important than themselves. Their appearance in art parallels their participation in the courts; they were prominent in both. When the artists of the early Renaissance created the elaborate historical scenes that their patrons had commissioned, there was generally a court dwarf or two to use as a convenient model.

In numerous group settings, dwarfs are omnipresent, playing the role of witness. Whether a particular painting celebrates the triumph of Julius Caesar or depicts a religious scene—the tale of Moses in the bulrushes or the crucifixion of Jesus—dwarfs are often present. The implication is that all manner of men (more often men than women) were present at this extraordinary moment; dwarfs are introduced to intensify the drama and honor the central characters.

Among the many remarkable crowd scenes are several representations of *The Adoration of the Magi*. A particularly dynamic, colorful example is a painting by the fifteenth-century Florentine Botticelli (c. 1445–1510); in this work an elaborately dressed, dignified dwarf carrying two swords appears in the foreground. In *The Discovery of the Infant Moses* by the sixteenth-century painter Veronese, one of the Italian noblewomen in attendance when the baby Moses is uncovered encourages a dark-skinned young court dwarf to take notice of him.

In addition to paintings of a religious subject, there was a profusion of works that celebrated events in the lives of the royalty. Among these is Vasari's (1511–1574) *Marriage of Catherine de Medici to Henry of Orleans*, depicting the couple attended by a male and a female dwarf and surrounded by nobility and allegorical figures. In a celebrated painting by Rubens (1577–1640), *Alatheia Talbot, Countess Arundel,* with its romantic background and luxuriously clothed court figures, the court dwarf Robin appears in luxurious red and gold velvet clothing with a falcon on his wrist.

In the many paintings of dwarfs and their noble masters and mistresses, it is extremely common to find the dwarf represented as holding a dog or monkey or other animal on a lead. Indeed, the care of animals was frequently their role in cultures as early as ancient Egypt and throughout the centuries of their prominence in the courts. As playmates and trainers of animals, it was implied that they were only one step above the animals in status. Those dwarfs who had not achieved prominence in other vital roles—as artists or scribes or the like—were among the few courtiers who could be spared for this physical task. Both the small humans and the animals were expected to cooperate in providing pleasure and amusement. The dwarf's master or mistress poses with one hand on the servant's head—a posture of protection and dominance. Among the paintings that reveal variations on the hierarchical relationships between royalty, court dwarf, and animal is *Stanislaus, the Dwarf of Cardinal Granvella* by the Netherlandish artist Anthonis Mor (1517–1576). It shows an elaborately dressed, intense-looking proportionate dwarf, with a large, muscular, brown dog that is nearly as tall as he is. It is reported that the cardinal was equally interested in securing a precise rendering of his dog as he was in obtaining an accurate depiction of his court dwarf and ward.[36]

Just as intrepid visitors to exhibitions of religious art may find their eyes glazing over after a great many commonplace representations of Madonna and Child, one can tire of seemingly gratuitous and mediocre depictions of dwarf models. There are, however, extraordinary painters who have combined artistic skill and a depth of understanding of dwarf subjects to create works of superb quality. The searching portraits of Velázquez have long been properly appreciated. Three other remarkable artists, Mantegna, Tiepolo and Molenaer, merit special attention and are among my own favorites.

Giovanni Battista Tiepolo (1696–1770) was a master of perspective, "brilliant color, exuberant invention and virtuoso handling of paint."[37] Among his greatest achievements are his frescoes that cover an entire room in the Palazzo Labia in Venice: *The Banquet of Cleopatra* depicts Antony and Cleopatra at opposite ends of a table set on an elaborate dais. Struggling up the stairs leading to the banquet table is a dwarf, seen in rear view in the foreground. Also in the entourage of this couple are two black servants and a small dog (see color plate 6).

Evidently fascinated by the subject matter, Tiepolo painted many renderings of the banquet and the couple's first meeting. The physical exertion so graphically depicted in the dwarf's ascent works as a vivid parallel to the psychic struggle that is taking place behind the rather masklike expressions of the two lovers. For dwarf spectators, this painting captures the characteristic labored quality of their own gait: it is a reminder of how they may appear to others, even when the stares take place behind their backs.

26. Giovanni Battista Tiepolo, acrobatic dwarfs. Sketches, eighteenth century. From Jean Martin Charcot and Paul Richer, Les difformes et les malades dans l'art *(Paris: Lecrosnier et Babe, 1889).*

It is clear that Tiepolo had gained an intimate awareness of the physiques of his dwarf models. In his portfolio are numerous sketches of dwarfs in action, showing the shifting weights of body movement, with special attention given to perspective (Fig. 26).[38] One cannot know his feelings and attitudes, but Tiepolo's paintings suggest that he enjoyed a profound understanding of dwarfs' being-in-the-world. He often gives them a prominent position, as in *The Feast in the House of Levi,* where a dwarf is observed front and center, serving food. In at least one painting, *The Marriage of Emperor Frederick,* he painted a kneeling dwarf in a nonallegorical context, as a member of Frederick's court. The historical record, unfortunately, is silent about the sources of the understanding that fairly leaps from Tiepolo's paintings.

The artist who has been most widely acclaimed for his sensitive renderings of dwarf subjects is Diego Velázquez (1599–1660). He painted at least ten portraits of dwarfs, most displayed in the Prado in Madrid. Perhaps in no other court was the monarch as attached to his dwarf attendants as in the court of Philip IV of Spain, Velázquez's patron. In Philip's entourage, at least 110 retainers were dwarfs. This king, "wary of normal human contacts because so much depended on his personal favor, could pamper a dwarf without arousing the envy of the courtiers who were in constant attendance upon him during his peregrinations; a dwarf's life was irrelevant."[39]

Without Velázquez's portraits, we could never visualize so clearly the character of these relationships and the varied natures of these individuals who had become so important to Philip. Some, like Francisco Lezcano, were developmentally disabled. Velázquez painted him draped against a background of clouds, earth, and water; despite his obvious mental incapacity, Francisco emerges as a sympathetic figure. In another work, Velázquez painted Sebastian de Morra, a dwarf whom Philip had requisitioned from the entourage of his younger brother to serve Prince Baltasar Carlos, the future heir to the throne (see color plate 7). De Morra, painted in bright, elegant clothing against a dark background, cuts a very dramatic figure—but it is his expression that most commands our attention and has often inspired critical analysis. According to one writer, "His expression is compounded of intelligent curiosity and thinly veiled intensity. The note of assertiveness is subtly conveyed by his red, gold-trimmed smock and by the strong highlight on his forehead. His hands, rolled into tight, ball-like fists, are placed around his belt, making him seem defiant."[40] Another elaborates: "With his short legs stuck straight out and his thick hands clenched aggressively at his waist, de Morra looks like a plaything stuck up on a shelf. But one glimpse of his intense face and black, angry eyes is enough to convince the viewer that de Morra detested his role, that he wanted to be regarded as the human being he was, not as the toy the court wanted."[41]

Was de Morra really entertaining the mutinous feelings that these critics perceive? In the absence of a personal statement by de Morra or an explanation of the artist's conception by Velázquez, viewers have license to project their own personal interpretations. Another model, Diego de Acedo, or El Primo, who was rumored to have been a ladies' man, comes across quite differently. Exuding intelligence and self-assurance, and perhaps a touch of melancholy, de Acedo, a court official entrusted with the royal seal, is painted against a landscape with mountains and surrounded by large books and a pen and inkpot.[42]

It is of great importance to us here that in his paintings of dwarfs, Velázquez produced searching psychological portraits, taking the same approach that he took toward his other subjects: "The artists who preceded Velázquez at the Spanish court painted dwarfs with a cold detachment that reflected the 16th and 17th century attitude toward the handicapped. Velázquez's approach differed radically, his style was loose and evocative, and he painted the handicapped as he did the royal family, with humanity, conveying his own recognition that these unfortunate creatures were as human as their masters. He respected their dignity as human beings and delineated their individual personalities."[43]

Velázquez's masterpiece is *Las Meninas*. The painting captures the royal family in the midst of an ordinary day. Two maids of honor are tending to the infanta Margarita while she poses for her portrait. Velázquez himself is included in the image, shown painting the group. Among the characters is a young male dwarf, who rests his foot on a large dog. The king and queen survey the scene through a dim reflection in a mirror in the background, and the achondroplastic dwarf, Maria Barbola, like Velázquez himself, gazes intently at the unseen onlookers (see color plate 8).[44]

The delicate, pampered Margarita contrasts sharply with the sturdy, independent-looking Maria Barbola. How one views this contrast depends, of course, on the beholder. While Velázquez was certainly at great pains to create a very attractive presentation of the infanta Margarita, he also has treated Maria respectfully: she appears observant and thoughtful. Nevertheless, one prominent nineteenth-century chronicler of famous dwarfs found Maria Barbola "horribly ugly" and "a little monster."[45] To those of us who are accustomed to the features of achondroplastic dwarfs, Maria Barbola's face looks agreeable enough. Interestingly, unlike the faces of most of the other characters in the painting, hers and Velázquez's are shown both clearly defined and directed fully forward; their glances meet ours: artist and dwarf are alert outsiders—observers and witnesses.

Another family portrait of interest to us here is the *Parete della Corte Riunita*, a fresco by Andrea Mantegna (1430–1506) in the Camera degli Sposi in Mantua's Ducal Palace. Assembled in this painting are members of the family and court of Ludovico III Gonzaga; however, it is a female dwarf who seems to be the central feature in this huge, remarkable work. A servant of Ludovico's wife, Barbara von Brandenberg, she stands alone, a tiny, composed figure, her hands drawn together, looking straight ahead at the painter and the viewer (see color plate 9). Some of the figures in the painting are depicted conversing, others merely posing, but none seems quite as separate as she. Although an integral part of the scene, she is also set apart—a singleton in that world, though there is another dwarf in the painting. Mantegna painted other dwarfs in the familiar role of witness, notably in *The Triumph of Julius Caesar.*

Another master of the witness genre is Paolo Veronese (1528–1588). He included a good number of dwarfs in his works on biblical themes, among them *Esther before Ahasuerus, Discovery of Moses, Moses Saved from the Waters, Adoration of the Magi,* and *Jesus in the House of Levi.* Occasionally, he included them in paintings of classical subject matter, among these *The Family of Darius before Alexander.* But with the exception of the *Discovery of Moses,* in the works of Veronese, the dwarfs are fairly stereotypical and unremarkable figures, recorded as "also present."

Sometimes the same dwarf model appears in artworks by different artists, depicted in diverse ways. In a painting by Il Bronzino, a sixteenth-century dwarf named Morgante (ironically, meaning "giant"), who was owned by Duke Cosimo, is shown as Bacchus in front and back views on two sides of a single canvas. Bronzino, with stark realism, painted Morgante naked, his bowed legs and many bodily folds immortalized. A figure with similar facial features and a similar physique, a muscular achondroplast with a prominent abdomen, is portrayed in at least two sculptures. In one by Valerio Cioli, he is shown playing a pipe; in another, by Giovanni da Bologna, he rides a dragon. There remains some controversy about whether the subject for these artworks, produced about thirty years apart, is the same Morgante.[46]

Mention should be made of two significant tapestries containing images of dwarfs. In the eleventh-century Bayeux Tapestry a dwarf in the entourage of William the Conqueror holds the ambassadors' horses. In a perplexing sixteenth-century Flemish work called the Robinson Tapestry, a procession of women hold dwarfs in their arms and ride giraffes![47]

It is refreshing suddenly to encounter the Dutch painter Jan Miense Molenaar (1610–1668). In three of his paintings, dwarfs are the focus of the drama. *Dancing Couple in the Village Street* depicts a capable- and appealing-looking dwarf playing the violin while others dance or look on. *The Artist's Studio* shows that same dwarf playing with a dog while the artist paints the scene. These two are lively, cheerful representations. In the third painting, a crowd scene originally titled *Scene with Dwarfs* but now referred to as *The Taunted Dwarfs,* a male dwarf, standing in front of his female companion, is shown throwing stones at some jeering bullies (see color plate 10). The bullies flee while others look on. Here, in a deviation from the norm, one is given a view of dwarfs who act on their own behalf and are not merely peripheral to the lives of others. The figures in this painting are rare artistic examples of short-trunk dwarfism (probably spondyloepiphyseal dysplasia).

Many works that deserve mention have been omitted from this survey. Among these is a painting by Van Dyck (1599–1641) of British court dwarf Sir Jeffery Hudson with Queen Henrietta Maria and a pet monkey. There is also a realistic winter scene of shivering poor persons by Francisco de Goya (1746–1828), and others by Goya, Bosch, and Brueghel the Elder (1568–1625) that show dwarfs who look like demons or gnomes.

The work of Flemish symbolist painter Hieronymus Bosch (1450–1516) inspired many imitators. Bosch painted his dwarfs in landscapes teeming with strange creatures—all intended to portray the wages of sin and dissuade viewers from wickedness. (In his subject matter and treatment, Bosch is an early precursor of the surrealists.) In the Yale University Art Gallery is a startling painting in the tradition of Bosch, dated between 1700 and 1710 and attributed to Pseudo Bocchi of Lombardy. It depicts a witchcraft scene with dwarf figures, skeletons, owls, cats, geese, and frogs, all involved in bizarre interactions. A psychologist might use this work as part of a projective technique—it is a stunning example of how symbolic allusions have been used by artists to convey their personal feelings and their society's mindset about dwarfs.

Following the veritable explosion of varied representations of dwarfs in art that took place from the fifteenth to eighteenth centuries, dwarfs nearly disappear from the horizon, and there is a gap that lasts until the twentieth century. One peculiar genre, however, bridges the years.

Garden Dwarfs

It is difficult to know where to place the phenomenon of garden dwarfs, which has persisted from the sixteenth century into modern times. Garden dwarfs are as widespread in Western popular culture as the mythical forms of non-European art are in theirs. Short-statured persons may turn away from these statues just as African Americans turn away from black jockeys on lawns. Stronger emotions may also surface. In the film *I Don't Want to Talk About It*, Leonora, the mother of a dwarf teenager, goes out in the dead of night and smashes her neighbor's dwarf statuary to smithereens.

The popularity of garden gnomes can be traced in part to the etchings of Jacques Callot (1592–1635), although the first such sculptures appeared prior to his work. He portrayed a wide variety of types, including aristocrats, peasants, Gypsies, military men, and acrobats; his treatment of ordinary people was colored by sympathy, and he took a "delight in queer characters."[48] His *Varie figure Gobbi*, a series of dwarf figures, was first published in 1616, and his illustrations of dwarfs and other figures dancing and making music appeared in his *Capricci* series of 1617. While Callot did his illustrations from life, later imitators, notably the authors of the *Callotto Resuscitato* of 1710, were more apt to present grotesque caricatures of dwarfs.[49] Garden sculptures and porcelain statuettes that were produced in the following centuries revealed a range of attitudes, with some manifesting respectful fidelity to models and others bizarre caricature.

The fashion of installing sculptures of dwarfs in gardens has waxed and waned over time; in recent years, it has again gained in popularity. Whereas in earlier centuries such figures were designed as genuine works of art, as in the large marble dwarfs in the Mirabell gardens of Salzburg (some based on Callot's etchings), they are now mass-produced caricatures between six inches and three feet high. In Europe the production of these ceramic figures has become a competitive, multimillion-dollar business.

In 1995 Polish manufacturers began to produce copies of German garden dwarfs. Germans, who traditionally decorated their front yards with these statues, could now drive across the border and buy a Polish imitation for a fraction of the cost.[50] In 1995, German border guards seized more than thirty tons of these objects and pressured the Polish government to enforce copyright laws. While knockoffs of the dwarfs of Snow White were less salable because they were reproduced in expensive groups of seven, popular pilfered designs included a cowboy dwarf riding a pig and a gnome lying face down with a knife in his back. They remain reasonably popular in that part of Europe, where *Grimm's Fairy Tales* and Wagner's Ring Cycle are central elements in the culture.

In England, by contrast, this type of statuary has lost some popularity. The Chelsea Flower Show has rejected new garden gnomes for years, substituting figures resembling celebrities or sports stars. In France, a song called "Let's Free the Gnomes" became a hit, and four student members of a group called the Garden Liberation Front were arrested in 1997 for stealing 134 gnomes. Fritz Friedman, the Swiss president of the International Association for the Protection of Garden Gnomes, called for their prosecution. The battle has become a struggle between "horticultural correctness" and a more conventional defense of the form as an innocent expression of pleasure in the fantastic, or "an ancient human need to populate the whole world with spirits, their presence sensed in trees and boulders, caves and streams."[51]

Although garden dwarfs have not achieved great prominence in the United States, dwarf caricatures in the form of statuary can be seen at almost every large garden center. There are also occasional examples of well-wrought sculptures of garden dwarfs at estates that have been converted to public use. *Dwarf Garden,* an outdoor installation at the John and Mabel Ringling Museum of Art in Sarasota, Florida, contains stone figures that are reminiscent of the best European models. The group includes musicians and ordinary farm men and women, engagingly represented.[52] The very existence of a "dwarf walk" in a garden remains upsetting to many short-statured persons, their families, and other sensitive onlookers, but it helps that this group is artfully made and not grotesque (see color plate 11).

Dwarf Artists from the Early Seventeenth through the Mid-Twentieth Centuries

Some readers may wonder whether there have been any artists who were dwarfs. Indeed there have been. Although most seem to have been minor figures, several achieved considerable recognition and even made their living at their work—no small feat for an artist. A few are only known to us because their dwarf status was very much in the forefront, as was the case with court dwarf Richard Gibson (1616–1690). Swedish miniaturist Andreas von Behn (1655–1724), who was also a court dwarf, painted portraits in oil on copper.[53] Matthew Buchinger (1674–1740), an artist who exhibited not only his art but also himself, was born without complete arms and legs; he produced drawings and elaborate calligraphy, and at least one self-portrait is known.

More sleuthing is required to discover other artists, for example, the painters Jacob Lehnen (1803–1847) or Achille Emperaire (1829–1898), who came into prominence as a result of Paul Cézanne's painting of him and references to their friendship in biographies of Cézanne, rather than for Emperaire's own productions. Emperaire, however, was a serious working artist. The few reproductions of his work, which are available for view in libraries in the United States, are of poor quality, and although his work may appear somewhat amateurish, several of his paintings have been sold at auction. There have surely been other painters throughout the history of art who labored in obscurity. Their work may still come to light, as happened in the case of Rosa Lee (1883–1961) when Nancy Bruett, whose portrait Lee painted when Bruett was a child, remembered her and decided to transform her into a fictional character in a novel.[54]

RICHARD GIBSON

The miniaturist Richard Gibson is better known than most court dwarf artists, in part because of a famous poem about his marriage by Edmund Waller, and in part because he was described by Horace Walpole in his classic review of British painters. Recently there has been renewed interest as investigators have concluded that the D.

Gibson to whom many additional works were ascribed is actually Richard Gibson. The *D.* may have stood for Dick, but more likely for *Dwarf*: the sobriquet "Dwarf Gibson" was frequently applied to him.[55]

Gibson's peripatetic career was not unusual for a court dwarf.[56] As the page to a wealthy lady, he attracted the attention of Charles I, who commissioned many portraits from him and invited him to join the royal court. After the king's death, he entered the service of Philip Herbert, fourth earl of Pembroke.[57] He became drawing master to Princess Mary, daughter of James II, and when Mary married William of Orange in 1677, Gibson accompanied her to the Hague.[58]

To evaluate Gibson's work, it is important to understand what was expected of someone in his position. In addition to painting portraits of immediate members of the court as requested, he was assigned to make copies, in this period before photography, of portraits and other works that had been created by other artists, his copies generally taking the form of miniatures. He was often overwhelmed by the demands made on him, as shown in a note from an agent, responding to a request made by Viscount Henry Ingram: "I cannot possibly prevail with Gibson the Painter to finish my Ladies picture by express from the King he is so taken up copying 2 of the Countess of Castle Main that he will not intermeddle these 10 days with any other, and the great Picture must also waite his leisure without which he cannot worke."[59]

Gibson completed miniatures of many of the descendants of the Earl of Pembroke and the Capel and Dormer families. In later years, others assisted him, including his daughter, Susan Penelope Gibson, who herself became well known as a miniaturist under her married name of Rosse. His son Edward and his nephew William were also accomplished painters. Gibson had copied the paintings of Peter Lely; subsequently, Lely drew and painted Gibson and his wife, Anne Shepard, as did Van Dyck.

Gibson's miniatures are characterized by their thick pigment, which gives them an impasto quality and parallel striations.[60] Many of his paintings have survived, including one self-portrait on display in the British Museum, but there are several portraits of Cromwell, perhaps among his best works, whose whereabouts are unknown. Gibson seems to have had a happy family life. He was a devoted father to nine children, five of whom survived to maturity.[61] He and his wife enjoyed longevity—Gibson lived to be seventy-five, his wife eighty-nine.

FRANÇOIS CUVILLIÈS

The architect François Cuvilliès (1695–1768) was introduced to a modern public through an article in *Gourmet Magazine* in 1976.[62] Dazzling color photographs showed his ornate Amalienburg Pavilion, focusing especially on its kitchen. Cuvilliès

was born at Soignes in 1695; when he was eight years old he began residing in the
Kammerzwerg (dwarf chamber) of the elector Maximilian II of Bavaria in Brussels.[63]
When Cuvilliès was eighteen, Maximilian funded his education in Munich, later
sending him to Paris to be trained in art and architecture. After Cuvilliès returned to
the Bavarian court in 1724, the new elector, Karl Albert, appointed him ducal architect. From then until his death in 1768, he was "the greatest force in the art world
of Munich."[64]

Cuvilliès's output was great. Among his most notable commissions was the official *Residenz* in Munich, which he renovated in a formal French style, with gilt murals that displayed Oriental princesses relaxing under palm trees, chariot races, and
gold cupids, in an effect recalling Versailles. Cuvilliès also introduced the French Hotel
to Munich, which became a model for subsequent palatial hotels. His later works include the Residenztheater in Munich, an opera house with four ornamented circu-
lar tiers of boxes, magnificent chandeliers and murals, and a royal box decorated with
cupids and other figures. Operas were performed there well into the twentieth century. Cuvilliès's talents in engineering are evident in the lifting device that at one time

27. *François Cuvilliès, Amalienburg Pavilion, in the palace garden of Nymphenburg Park, Munich. 1734–1739.*
From Henry Channon, "The Frenchman, Cuvilliès," in The Ludwigs of Bavaria *(London: Methuen, 1933).*

enabled the theater auditorium to be changed from a sloping position to a horizontal one to create a dance floor.[65]

François Cuvilliès the younger published a book of his father's designs, titled *Ecole d'architecture bavaroise*.[66] Literature on the subject of Cuvilliès's architectural achievements is plentiful, but personal biographical data in English is somewhat limited.[67] Cuvilliès's Amalienburg Pavilion is his masterpiece, and one critic has wondered whether it may be the most perfect building in the world—the pinnacle of rococo elegance.[68] Built between 1734 and 1739 in the palace garden of Nymphenburg Park, outside Munich, the exterior is characterized by a classical façade with busts in medallion niches and a goddess over the door. The interior is even more compelling, with exquisite contrasts of color, texture, and detailing (Fig. 27).[69]

In the Amalienburg, Cuvilliès combined French ideas with his own use of contrasts between concave and convex shapes in the building's exterior; for the interior, he designed asymmetrical, round-cornered rooms. A perfectionist, he gave attention to every detail of embellishment in the building. His influence can be seen in his design books and his son's, as well as in the enduring interest expressed by architectural historians in his work.

JACOB LEHNEN

Lehnen was a painter of still lifes, hunting scenes, and images of wild birds and game. Born in 1802 in Hinterweiler, Germany, Lehnen is said to have stopped growing at four; he was proportionate, attaining a final height of three feet ten inches. Sent by his parents to Coblenz at the age of seventeen to finish his studies, he met a professor who encouraged his artistic interests. Next he attended the Academie des Beaux-Arts in Düsseldorf, where he subsequently exhibited widely, gained acclaim, and was elected to the Academy of Düsseldorf. He was appreciated not just as a painter but also for his personality: "He was a joyous companion, loved by all artists, his friends . . . if in a salon one could not see him well from afar, one heard him and especially listened to him. . . . He would nimbly slide into the crowd of guests and, climbing lithely on a chair, would soon make himself noticed by his joyous talk and his spirited witticisms."[70] Lehnen evidently had an easygoing temperament. When teased by children, he responded by engaging and playing with them. Many of his paintings are still exhibited in museums in Berlin and Düsseldorf, Germany; Kaliningrad, Russia; and Liège, Belgium.[71]

ADOLPH MENZEL

It is perhaps not surprising that the name of a minor painter like Jacob Lehnen should be unfamiliar. But one might expect that the name of Adolph Menzel, another short-statured artist, *should* be widely recognized (Fig. 28). Although Menzel has been called the most important artist working in Berlin in the second half of the nineteenth century and interest in his work has remained strong in Germany, only recently has his reputation soared in other European countries and in the United States. A show of at least two hundred of his drawings, prints, and paintings took place at the Fitzwilliam

Museum in Cambridge, England, in 1984; and two other exhibitions, at the Frick Museum in New York in 1990 and at the National Gallery of Art in Washington, D.C., in 1996, were well received. A catalog of the Washington exhibit was produced, and in 2002 Michael Fried published a volume, with high-quality reproductions, appraising Menzel's contribution.[72]

The sheer quantity of Menzel's oeuvre is astounding. His motto was *nulla die sine linea* (not a day without drawing).[73] He produced more than five thousand drawings; well over a thousand lithographs, woodcuts, and etchings; and innumerable oils, gouaches, and watercolors. Although he may be best remembered as a chronicler of the life of Frederick the Great and for battle scenes and historical subjects, his work shows enormous virtuosity—there are landscapes, indoor and industrial scenes, portraits, studies of household objects and of animals, and book illustrations.

A pioneer of realism who carefully researched his subject matter, he made sure every harness and uniform button was correct for its time. One of his best-known drawings is of a pair of binocu-

28. Adolph von Menzel. From Claude Keisch and Marie U. Rieman Rhegher, Adolph Menzel, 1815–1905: Between Romanticism and Impressionism *(New Haven: Yale University Press, 1996).*

lars owned by Field Marshal General Helmut von Moltke, a celebrated German commander, shown in exquisite detail that reveals a lifetime of wear. One commentator sees the fascination with the object as deriving from the fact that the "portrait" of the instrument is also a kind of portrait of the unseen owner.[74] That person may be famous, like von Moltke, or unassuming, like Menzel's cook, Lena, who left a hair-filled comb in Menzel's studio that the artist could not resist drawing.

Menzel began to sell his work as early as age twelve. He had apprenticed to his father in the latter's print shop; when Adolph was seventeen, his father died and the youth supported his mother and younger siblings by managing his father's shop and obtaining commissions for drawings and prints. A respected artist by the time he was twenty-five, he saw his international reputation grow steadily throughout his long life. He was only in his mid-twenties when he executed the four hundred drawings that Franz Theodor Kugler used to produce his wood engravings for his life of Frederick the Great, published in 1841. Just how identified Menzel had become with that character was evident in the celebration that Wilhelm II prepared in honor of Menzel's eightieth birthday: Wilhelm dressed up as Frederick, and his household as courtiers.[75]

Menzel began as a printmaker and began painting consistently only in the 1850s. A gouache he completed in 1900, *Visit to the Ironrolling Mill,* and his drawings of factories and mines affectingly convey the consequences of the Industrial Revolution. Although he became an accomplished colorist and painter in oils, he still preferred the pencil, and his drawings represent some of his best work. He is a significant precursor of impressionism, as seen notably in his *View into a Small Courtyard* (1867), with its mastery of flickering light and shadow. In his intimate interiors, he reveals an emotional and lyrical side—especially when he includes family members, such as his sister Emilie, a favorite subject.

Menzel produced several carefully drawn self-portraits, of his face only—like other dwarf artists, he avoided confronting his full-length figure in his art. A metaphorical self-portrait, *The Antiquary,* shows him holding a piece of statuary, revealing only his upper body; *Evening Gathering* offers a partial, rear view of his small figure seated with others around a table (see color plate 12).[76] A memoir by a contemporary of Menzel's contains two of his playful caricatures—a birthday sketch for an eighty-year-old friend and another showing Menzel walking, holding a closed umbrella on a sunny day.[77] In these works, Menzel's sense of self seems sturdier than that of other dwarf artists who shunned self-portrayal or who, like Toulouse-Lautrec, produced derisive caricatures. That Menzel found lighthearted ways of dealing with his height does not mean that he did not suffer. His "disproportion was a lifelong torment, and he never quite lost the feeling that strangers were laughing at him. 'If I were crippled, they'd be sorry for me,' he once said, 'but when they see the way I look, they just take it as a joke.'"[78]

In his will, Menzel wrote, "Not only have I remained unmarried, throughout my life I have also renounced all relations with the other sex (as such)."[79] He noted that he experienced a lack of *Klebestoff*—attachment—between himself and the outside world. Nevertheless, he seems to have had some measure of closeness with a few family members and friends; he lived with his sister and brother-in-law for most of his life, and in his paintings of family, there is evidence of affection.

When he died in 1905, he was given a magnificent funeral and the state bought up every piece of artwork he had left in his studio. More than six thousand items are collected at the National Gallery in Berlin and books that include excellent reproductions of Menzel's work should further secure him a place among the great artists of any era.

HENRI DE TOULOUSE-LAUTREC

Toulouse-Lautrec (1864–1901) has been discussed in detail in Chapter 2; just a brief note about his self-portraits will be added here. Lautrec completed only one youthful, somewhat blurred image of his upper body in a mirror. His other sketches are self-critical caricatures that make him look tinier than he is; and in doodles he portrays his deformity unsparingly and his face as ugly.[80] Fortunately, his reputation rests not on these images, but on his mastery of color and movement and on such paintings as *Marcelle Lender Dancing in "Chilperic"* and other depictions of the demimonde (see color plate 13).

ROSA LEE

Rosa Lee is included here as representative of dwarf artists who are little known today but enjoyed professional careers. Primarily a portrait painter, Lee received a Bachelor of Fine Arts degree from the University of Chicago and graduated from the Art Institute of Chicago. For many summers, she taught painting courses at her summer home, a rose-covered cottage in Provincetown, Massachusetts. A brochure advertising those courses shows Lee posed with her sister Jennie; between them is a portrait that Lee had painted of her sister (Fig. 29). Jennie was also a dwarf, somewhat shorter than Rosa, who was four feet one inch.[81]

One of Lee's paintings, a portrait of the town crier, is on display at Provincetown Town Hall. Although the full range of her paintings and the details of her personal life are not known, her choice of Mother Cabrini as a portrait subject suggests that she may have been Catholic. The work was favorably reviewed following a 1947

29. Rosa Lee. Personal collection of Nancy Bruett.

show at the Arthur U. Newton Gallery in New York.[82] The rest of this exhibit was made up of portraits representing "types," such as "the underprivileged type" and "the successful businesswoman." (The reviewer found the concept interesting, but the portraits not outstanding.)

As was the case for so many other accomplished dwarfs, Lee had been a performer.[83] Although she had painted for many years, she only completed her formal art studies at the Chicago Art Institute—fulfilling a lifelong dream—after her retirement. It is not only the most illustrious who provide valuable role models. The withering discouragement born of comparing oneself only to the great masters can dry up any brush.

Nineteenth- and Twentieth-Century Art

PAINTING

After this digression highlighting dwarf artists of the past, we resume the more general chronological review of how dwarfs have been portrayed in art. Ubiquitous in paintings until the end of the eighteenth century, dwarfs almost disappear from art in the nineteenth. There are occasional portraits such as one painted by Vincente Lopez in 1825 called *Aragonese Dwarf*, in which a tiny quizzical figure with a cane stands on a chair. An 1827 painting by the American artist Samuel F. B. Morse (1791–1872) called *Una and the Dwarf* depicts a scene from canto 7 of Spenser's *Faerie Queene*, in which is included a nondescript proportionate dwarf. In journals of art and antiques, one may encounter an occasional nineteenth-century work such as Erastus Salisbury Field's (1805–1900) folk art painting of a tiny dwarf with a rattle, which was put on auction at Sotheby's in 1985.[84] For the most part, these works are unremarkable, particularly in comparison with those of previous periods. .

Standing in contrast to such minor works is the portrait by Cézanne (1839–1906) of his friend Achille Emperaire, "a dwarf with shrunken limbs and a head of exceptional beauty and sensitivity." Cézanne painted it in 1868 and sent it to the Salon, where it was summarily rejected, not surprisingly, "since Cezanne detailed Emperaire's infirmities with a mixture of outrage and compassion and went on to seat him bolt upright in a thronelike armchair that was covered in a particularly blatant flowered material."[85] (See color plate 14.) Emperaire was not a curiosity to Cézanne, but a friend whose complexity Cézanne recognized and understood, and perhaps identified with.[86] A very different, but also evocative, work is *Hop-Frog's Revenge* (1898), the etching and lithograph by avant-garde symbolist James Ensor (1860–1949), inspired by Edgar Allan Poe's short story. Like Molenaar's *The Taunted Dwarfs*, discussed earlier, it is an exceptional example of a rebellion by dwarfs against abuse and humiliation.

Unique among representations of dwarfs in art is an obscure nineteenth-century work in the Galleria d'Arte Moderna in Milan. This small oil, painted in 1852 by Gerolamo Induno (1825–1890), is titled *Sciancato che suona il mandolino* (*Cripple playing the mandolin*).[87] It shows a young adult dwarf with a pleasant expression, playing a mandolin to a child—perhaps his own—close by (see color plate 15). Hans-Rudolf Weidemann, a German professor of pediatrics, came upon the work in late 1992 while attending a medical conference in Milan. Impressed by the painting, he solicited a probable diagnosis of the musician's condition from six colleagues and published his observations in a medical journal.[88] But the painting's appeal transcends its medical interest: aesthetically pleasing, the work captures the atmosphere of the dwarf's modest dwelling and the apparent pleasure he takes in his music. Even more striking is the fact that it portrays its dwarf protagonist as neither singleton nor servant, nor observer of the lives of others, but a man absorbed in his own life. He is engaged in activities of his own choosing in his own home. With the rare exceptions of the Egyptian funerary statue of Seneb and his family and perhaps Menzel's *Evening Gathering*, both described earlier, dwarfs had not been shown enjoying personal relationships.[89] Even in the twentieth century, they continued to be portrayed almost

exclusively as isolated figures or public entertainers or occasionally as abstract pro-
jections of the artist's view of "dwarfness."

Cripple Playing the Mandolin was exhibited in Rancato, Switzerland, in 2002, and
described in the gallery's catalog as personifying the popular nineteenth-century
theme of a sensitive, delicate soul captured within a deformed body.[90] Despite their
recognition of the appealing intimacy of the scene, the critics emphasize the pathos
of the dwarf's disability and his humble dwelling. The musician is described as looking skyward, transported to a musical haven—in stark contrast to his awkward, unhappy body. For some modern viewers, however, the aesthetic sophistication of this
painting is more likely to raise questions regarding assumptions about deformity.[91]
The artist's uniquely humanizing treatment of his subject suggests the possibility of a
different vision for the future.

By the first half of the twentieth century, the classical and religious themes that
were favored by the artists of the Renaissance and the Age of Reason were no longer
prevalent, and with the courts' glory days over, dwarfs were no longer as available as
models. The direction that depictions of dwarfs would take was now more uncertain,
no common theme was evident. *Dwarf of Leide,* a little-known work by Spanish-
Argentinean artist Miguel Viladrich (1887–1956) depicts a stiff, erect figure, painted
in a pre-Raphaelite style.[92] The Irish painter and illustrator Jack B. Yeats (1871–1957)
produced a more cheerful work, *The Circus Dwarf,* in which a short, attractive, colorfully dressed man in a sweater stands in front of a circus tent. The Finnish painter
Tyko Konstantin Sallinen (1879–1955), who introduced expressionism into Finnish
art, caused a stir with his 1914–1915 painting *The Dwarf.* This painting of a well-
known Helsinki man who earned his living selling cigarettes provoked a debate between two architects, one praising it as a valuable work of art, the other calling it "a
saucepan of brown sauce thrown at a tablecloth."[93]

The ambiguous status of dwarfs was generally not appreciated by artists. By the
second half of the twentieth century, however, the artists who did choose to treat this
subject began to approach it from a variety of perspectives. Marc Chagall
(1887–1985) and Paul Klee (1879–1940) introduce dwarfs as decorative elements;
Pablo Picasso (1881–1973) caricatures a plump, fully dressed male dwarf gazing up
at a tall nude model (see Fig. 30).[94]

Some paintings recall those of earlier periods. A 1988 work by the Swedish
painter Lars Anderson (b. 1957) titled merely *Dwarf* features a corpulent, aristocratic
man in an elegant black hat. This work, intentionally only partially completed, presents a melancholy figure who suggests a mood of emptiness and, as in many of Anderson's paintings, a different epoch. A work that seems at first to be merely a
quotation from literary or artistic history may turn out to have a very different objective. Jack Levine (b. 1915), a social realist painter, was inspired by the social crit-

30. Pablo Picasso, Femme et nain. *Lithograph, 1953.*

© *2004 Estate of Pablo Picasso, Artists Rights Society,*

NY. Reproduced from Helene Parmelia, ed., Picasso:

The Artist and His Model, 180 Drawings *(New*

York: Dover, 1994).

icism implicit in Ben Jonson's play *Volpone,* in which the friends of a wealthy, avaricious man seek to inherit his fortune. Levine embarked on a series of lithographs and sketches based on the play's characters. A 1964 engraving called *Venetian Lady* shows a woman looking in a mirror while a dwarf holds the train of her gown; a satirical piece, it presents the "lady" as the very image of plump, dignified narcissism; the dwarf looks bored and resigned to his role—quite different from his Renaissance ancestors.[95]

The final decades of the twentieth century saw the appearance of a number of provocative, sometimes symbolic paintings with dwarf figures. One of these is by the American Eric Fischl (b. 1948), an artist who has worked in various media and whose best-known early paintings are set in suburbia and suggest forbidden sex. His later work is more broadly inclusive of various aspects of human experience. In *Costa del Sol* (1986), an 8 1/2-by-13-foot painting of a sunlit beach, a large, muscular, androgynous-looking female bends forward in close proximity to a male dwarf. She looks beyond him, seemingly transfixed by a nude woman lounging languidly on the sand. While the sunlight falling on the two female figures highlights the possibility of a charged connection, the dwarf, a more shaded figure clad in sagging briefs, appears emotionally removed and downcast. His bearing may suggest shame, and he seems to be the outsider here in whatever events are in progress; one may speculate on the artist's intended meaning (see color plate 16).

Titles matter in Fischl's works. The title of this work translates as "The Coast of the Sun"; it does not merely suggest a place-name but intimates the sensual landscape of sea, sand, and sky, as well as the psychological landscape of the souls of the three individuals present. The visual disjuncture that appears down the center is not a mistake, but occurs because the scene was originally done as two adjacent panels. Together the panels draw viewers in, inviting them to notice the subjects' contrasting appearances and emotional states, as well become intrigued by the mysterious, erotic drama in progress. Although the image of the dwarf might be criticized as lacking in political correctness (because he is yet another isolated or melancholy little person), his situation is not unlike that of innumerable others in Fischl's abundant cast of characters: to be human is to struggle with one's life and relationships.

Neoexpressionist artist Yan Pei-Ming, born in China in 1960, moved to Dijon, France, in 1981. In his portraits, he aims to expose the "invisible man," to reflect what is "inside," to show what "may be," "will be," or "was" the individual depicted. Some are painted from the artist's imagination, while others are of people of Hawaii. One of his subjects was the dwarf artist Bruce Johnson; through a translator, Yan asked Johnson's permission to paint him.[96] The paintings, clearly done with some rapidity, are six feet by six feet. In one, Johnson's visage fills the whole canvas; his expression is serious, intense, perhaps somewhat angry, and his mouth turns down at the corners. The other painting shows a full view of Johnson on crutches, his expression softer and more reflective (see color plate 17). Yan has done several other paintings of dwarfs. One, *Trois nains,* shows three figures with exaggeratedly short lower limbs; another, *Victime, Gerald P.,* is an image of a thoughtful-looking head seen in profile.

The works of contemporary artist Alan Loehle (b. 1954) are fraught with ambiguity. Between 1997 and 2002, Loehle completed a series that included three large oil paintings and one small ink-and-brush work, all depicting the same dwarf model. In *Walking Man,* which measures 6 1/2 feet by 5 feet, an anonymous male figure walks, profiled against a desolate landscape. *The Head,* of similar size, depicts a nightmarish scene in which the same achondroplastic dwarf stands over the severed head of a pig. Reviewer Lawrence B. Chollet managed to see hope in the painting, having noticed that the pig is smiling and that the painting contains a splash of dazzling sunlight, but others may experience a sense of menace in this work.[97]

Loehle, in explaining his intentions in his work, states that the images of human figures, dogs, and meat are meant to represent the human condition, and he defines the place of the dwarf in his art: "The image of a man who is an achondroplastic dwarf is meant to elicit a shock of recognition in the viewer; his permanent, visible 'otherness' embodying the separateness we all experience and the burden this entails for the spirit."[98]

Not every modern painter identifies the dwarf figure with existential angst and loneliness. New York artist Thomas Woodruff (b. 1957) suggests the complexity of his six-by-eight-foot surrealist canvas in its title: *All Systems Go: Mission Poesy (Lil' Hot Stuff and Guardian Angel)* (see color plate 18). At the center of this compelling, mysterious work is a pensive dwarf in a red devil suit holding a raised butterfly net. One critic notes, "There is something pleasant but also very unsettling about this world, which according to the artist's own report, has to do with souls departing from this planet owing to the AIDS epidemic."[99]

The dwarf in this painting is actor David Steinberg, looking very much at home against a bucolic background of woodland creatures and flowers while a suspended "good fairy" blesses his endeavors. However, in this fairy tale scene it is impossible to overlook the centrality of the rocket, which may be seen as either a discordant, threatening element or a phallic object. The painting, created in 1988 at the height of the AIDS epidemic in the United States, balances dissonant images, and yet may be experienced as somehow reassuring. In a work that can be seen as social commentary, the butterfly net in the AIDS context becomes the central figure's attempt to capture the ephemeral beauty of his world.

Kathryn Jacobi, born in New York in 1947, is an artist who now lives part time in California and the rest of the year in British Columbia. In the 1990s she studied the old masters of the Northern Renaissance, among them Hans Holbein the Younger, Albrecht Dürer, and Rogier van der Weyden; her most recent work reveals the influence of the surrealist Max Ernst and of Paul Klee. These influences, along with her unique sensibility, have resulted in a wide-ranging body of work that marries the craftsmanship and psychological insight of the old masters with Jacobi's fascination with mythic and emotional elements in human existence. In 1987 the artist produced a series of ten paintings in which she grappled with an image of herself as a dwarf/baby, sometimes placing herself in a closet with hanging shirts, which symbolized for her the presence of her father to whom she was attached early and deeply. Jacobi observed: "I read in Leslie Fiedler's book 'Freaks' how people tend to project their dreams, fears, and nightmares onto what society calls 'freaks.' Each of us has an image of our secret selves, an image that has mythic proportions. I had always been empathetically connected with dwarfs; it was an image I'd always carried of myself. Then I found a photograph of myself in a family album. I was six months old and had the dwarflike face and proportions I'd always envisioned. So I had to paint it."[100]

Jacobi is hardly the first artist to paint herself as a dwarf. Jacques Callot did so, as did the Dutch painter Lucas van Leyden (1494–1533) and the painter and photographer George Dureau (b. 1940). All are wrestling with the "what if" of the accidental nature of the human form and with making the leap toward recognizing the commonality of people with different bodies. Jacobi probes this mystery deeply, merging baby, wise homunculus, and self into a mythic image. A photograph of Jacobi seated beneath one of her paintings is striking. Her adult upper torso is shown poised beneath the larger painting of her baby/dwarf torso: her kindly, intelligent face commingles with her younger wise/innocent self (see color plate 19).

In an 8 1/2-by-5-foot portrait from 1989, Jacobi painted the dwarf actor Tommy Madden. A photograph was also taken of the real but much smaller Tommy Madden, with a somewhat different expression, sitting on a board below. Both figures make direct eye contact with the viewer. There is an implicit challenge thrown out to the viewer of the photograph and of the painting, seen together, a challenge to relate to

Madden himself and to the questions raised by the difference in size (see color plate 20). Jacobi writes: "Getting to know Tommy was a revelation to me—I learned that while there was nothing intrinsically wise or magical about dwarfs in general, the disability itself gave him insight, courage, and compassion, and a sense of humor and sweetness that is rare in this world. I wanted the portraits of him to honor him for all that."[101]

Artists working at the end of the twentieth century do not conform to stereotypical patterns. Their acceptance of individual difference and their projection of subjective vision have led to a diversity in their approach to the subject of dwarfs that is as great as the diversity found in the lives of dwarfs themselves.

PHOTOGRAPHY

Dozens of photographers have offered memorable pictures of dwarfs: some have presented just a single photograph; others have produced more elaborate photographic essays. A remarkable number of photographs have been of clowns, reinforc-

ing the image of dwarfs as clowns in the minds of the public. The photographers' representations, however, are quite different from one another. A 1943 gelatin silver print by Arthur Fellig, known as Weegee (1899–1968), features Shorty, the Bowery Cherub; it was later included in the exhibit *The American Century: Art and Culture 1900–2000* at the Whitney Museum of American Art, in New York. Weegee was particularly well known for his journalistic depictions of murders and tenement fires and for capturing the expressions on the faces of the people involved in these events. Shorty, the cherubic dwarf dressed in a diaper, holding a beer, and wearing a 1943 party hat, is clearly intended to be an amusing emblem of ushering in the New Year; he is but one of many odd-looking habitués of the club Sammy's Bowery Follies, where

31. Weegee (Arthur Fellig), New Year's, Sammy's on the Bowery, 1943. © Estate of Weegee (Arthur Fellig). Hulton/Archive by Getty Images, NY.

32. Mary Ellen Mark, Twin Brothers Tulsi and Basant *(Great Famous Circus, Calcutta, India), 1989.*
© *Mary Ellen Mark.*

the photograph was taken (Fig. 31). This work and *A New Low in Arrests,* a photograph
of a very small dwarf (Jerry Austin) who is partially obscured by a tall, smiling, robust man who accompanies him indicate that for Weegee, dwarfs were a handy vehicle for comic photojournalism.

Mary Ellen Mark (b. 1940), in her photographic essay *Indian Circus,* which includes images of dwarfs, comments on her experiences in producing the book: "Photographing the Indian circus was one of the most beautiful, special, and joyous times
of my career. I was allowed to document a major fantasy that was, at the same time, all
so real. It was full of ironies, often humorous and sometimes sad, beautiful and ugly,
loving and sometimes cruel, but always human. The Indian circus is a metaphor for
everything that has always fascinated me visually."[102] In Mark's book, Tulsi and Basant, twin brothers with dwarfism, are shown in gorilla outfits, one with his face covered by the gorilla mask, the other meeting the eyes of the observer with force and
dignity, as if posing for Velázquez (Fig. 32). Mark quotes one of the twins: "In our
home there were four brothers. The first and the fourth were tall. The second and the
third were small. There was very little at home and we used to make people laugh so
they brought us here."[103]

The straitened circumstances of many in the twins' circus family is apparent in a
photograph of two other dwarf clowns from the Mangalore circus; they lie opposite

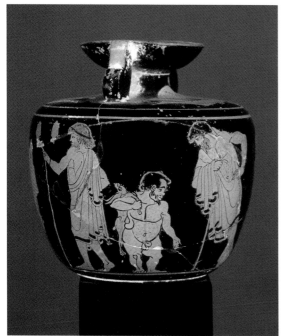

Plate 1 (top left). Female dwarf on calcite decorative vessel from tomb of Tutankhamen, late 18th Dynasty. Photograph by George B. Johnson/Egyptian Museum, Cairo.

Plate 2 (top right). Seneb and his family. Egyptian limestone statuary, c. 2320–2250 BCE. Werner Forman/Art Resource, NY. Egyptian Museum, Cairo.

Plate 3 (left). Dwarf as assistant. Ceramic, red figure aryballos, c. 480–470 BCE. Reunion des Musées Nationaux/Art Resource, NY. Louvre, Paris.

Plate 4. Tomb figurines with stone mortuary tablet, glazed earthenware. China, Tang Dynasty. Royal Ontario Museum.

Plate 5. Maya figurine. Photograph by Jorge Pérez de Lara/Museo Nacional de Anthropologia.

Plate 6. Giovanni Battista Tiepolo (1696–1770). The Banquet of Anthony and Cleopatra.
Scala/Art Resource, NY. Palazzo Labia, Venice.

Plate 7. Diego de Silva Velázquez (1599–1660). Don Sebastian de Morra. *Prado Museum, Spain.*

Plate 8. Diego de Silva Velázquez (1599–1660). Las Meninas. *Prado Museum, Spain.*

Plate 9. Andrea Mantegna (1430–1506). Parete della Corte Riunita *(Family and Court of Ludovico III Gonzaga). Fresco, c. 1487. Scala/Art Resource, NY. Palazzo Ducale, Mantua.*

Plate 10. Jan Miensen Molenaar (1610–1668). Scène met dwergen *(The Taunted Dwarfs), 1646. Van Abbemuseum, Eindhoven.*

Plate 11. Garden Dwarfs from Dwarf Walk at Ringling Museum of Art, Sarasota, Florida. Photography by Betty Adelson.

Plate 12. Adolph von Menzel (1815–1905). Evening Gathering, *c. 1847. Bildarchiv Preussischer Kulturbesitz/Art Resource, NY. Nationalgalerie, Staatliche Museen zu Berlin.*

Plate 13 (above). Henri Toulouse-Latrec (1864–1901). Marcelle Lender Dancing the Bolero in "Chilpéric." *Collection of Mr. and Mrs. John Hay Whitney, Image ©2004 Board of Trustees, National Gallery of Art, Washington.*

Plate 14 (left). Paul Cezanne (1839–1906). Portrait of the Artist's Friend, Achille Emperaire, *c. 1869. Eric Lessing/Art Resource, NY. Musée d'Orsay, Paris.*

Plate 15. Gerolamo Induno (1825–1890). Sciancato che suona il mandolino *(Cripple Playing the Mandolin), 1852. Civica Galleria d'Arte Moderna, Milan.*

Plate 16. Eric Fischl (b. 1948). Costa del Sol, *1986. Courtesy of the artist. Photograph by Zindman/Fremont.*

Plate 17. Yan Pei-Ming, Portrait of
Bruce Johnson, *1997.*
© Yan Pei-Ming. Courtesy of the artist.

Plate 18. Thomas Woodruff (b. 1957). All Systems Go: Mission Poesy (Lil' Hot Stuff and Guardian Angel)*, 1998. Courtesy of the artist and PPOW Gallery, NY.*

Plate 19. Kathryn Jacobi (b. 1947). Dwarf in a Tall Man's Closet *series, 1987. Photograph of the artist with* Self-Portrait as a Baby. *Courtesy of the artist.*

Plate 20. Kathryn Jacobi (b. 1947). Portrait of Tommy Madden, *1989. Courtesy of the artist. Photograph by Erica and Harold Van Pelt.*

Plate 21. Jan Saudek (b. 1935). Portrait of My Friend, *1992. ©Jan Saudek (www.saudek.com).*

Plate 22. Juan Muñoz (b. 1953). Dwarf with Three Columns, *1988. Photograph by Dorothee Fischer/Galerie Konrad Fischer, Dusseldorf.*

Plate 23. Andres Serrano (b. 1950). Tony Torres, model. Flaunt Magazine, *Fall 2000 Special Fashion Issue, Tom Ford for Gucci by Andres Serrano. Courtesy of the artist.*

Plate 24 (left). Jacqueline Ann Clipsham (b. 1938). Coppery Tentacle Sea Creature, *1998. Courtesy of the artist. Photograph by Hiro Ihara.*

Plate 25 (right). Katherine Koos (b. 1977) in her studio. Courtesy of the artist.

each other, head to foot, on a single narrow cot, appearing disconsolate. Prem Narayan, a dwarf clown from the Great Oriental Circus, notes that he feels bad not for himself but for his baby daughter, because "when she walks on the street, she won't look nice." He believes that he is a dwarf because his mother must have seen a dwarf the day after she conceived him and that his wife had a dwarf baby because she had looked at him. Mark, who has documented famine in Ethiopia and prostitution in India, has observed, "I photograph people who are victims of society because I care about them, and I want the people who see my pictures to also care."[104] Her approach has resulted in striking, appreciative portraits of dwarfs and other performers; her vision contains romantic elements that seem to buffer some of the more painful reality.

The work of Bruce Davidson (b. 1933), like Mark's, has both social and emotional resonance. His photographic essays include images of the impoverished inhabitants of East One Hundredth Street in Manhattan, New York; Welsh miners; and members of a teenage gang in 1960s Brooklyn, New York. He has made documentaries about a family who survived on the castoffs from New Jersey dumps and about Isaac Bashevis Singer, the Nobel Prize–winning Yiddish writer. Davidson's film *Enemies* is based on a Singer short story.

The grandson of Jewish immigrants, Davidson was five when his parents divorced.[105] Alone much of the time, he would later respond to themes associated with lonely outsiders. He found his vocation when his stepfather gave him a good camera. Despite a turbulent adolescence and a poor school record, he was accepted at the Rochester Institute of Technology, where he majored in photography. Davidson views the personal and economic struggles he confronted throughout his life as having made him sensitive to the struggles of others.

Davidson came to know his subjects intimately, and he created poignant, searching images of his characters. Jimmy, a dwarf subject of his who also became a friend, is shown in one close-up with a painted clown face (Fig. 33), and in another as a solitary Chaplinesque black-and-white figure

33. Bruce Davidson, Jimmy the Clown, *1958. © Bruce Davidson/Magnum Photos.*

34. Bruce Davidson, Jimmy in Palisades Restaurant, *1958. © Bruce Davidson/Magnum Photos.*

against a background of an empty lot and bright circus tents. These photographs contrast with another of Jimmy out of costume, eating at a diner, while a man at a nearby table stares across at him (Fig. 34). The critic Henry Geldzaler has commented that Davidson would not have been capable of his best work, including his dwarf sequence, had he not been conscious of his own role as an outsider with a need to belong.[106]

Photographs of dwarfs in magazines published outside the United States are difficult to obtain. One example of such work is a photo series in a Japanese magazine, containing dwarf subjects and with an accompanying text, that features the dwarf actor Isamu Shimizu in various settings, captured by the eminent Japanese photographer Daido (Hiromichi) Moriyama.[107] The series first shows the actor's reflective countenance, and then portrays him in performance, in a men's room, in a happy embrace with a woman, and walking about his world (Figs. 35–37). After the shoot, Moriyama and Shimizu went to a coffee shop together. Moriyama complimented Shimizu: "Mr. Shimizu, your face is really wonderful. This is my honest opinion—not just flattery, as I look at you through my viewfinder." The article concludes that Shimizu, part of a comic team, a good father of two children, a tap dancer and singer, tries to maintain a good image but there is a melancholy feeling around him, of fading away."[108]

The subject of dwarfs has attracted photographers in different parts of the world.

35. *Daido Moriyama,* Isamu Shimizu, Actor, *1967. Camera Mainichi, Mainichi Publishing Company, Tokyo. Courtesy of the artist.*

36, left. *Daido Moriyama,* Isamu Shimizu, Actor, *1967. Camera Mainichi, Mainichi Publishing Company, Tokyo. Courtesy of the artist.*

37, below. *Daido Moriyama,* Isamu Shimizu, Actor, *1967. Camera Mainichi, Mainichi Publishing Company, Tokyo. Courtesy of the artist.*

38. André Kertész, Sixth Avenue, New York, *1959. © Estate of André Kertész 2004.*

The versatile photographer André Kertész (1894–1985), born in Budapest, honed his skills in Paris and in the United States. He is known for evocative photographs of objects, like *Melancholic Tulip*; for photojournalism, as in *Displaced People*; and particularly for street scenes and "story photographs" that capture passing moments. In one such image, he photographed a blind man playing the accordion while a dwarf places money in the cup that the man's companion is holding. The presence of passersby who seem not to notice the blind musician—including a priest—enhances the effect (Fig. 38). Of this image, Kertész writes, "The little man, I remember, worked in a circus as a clown. I saw him coming down the street and I only had one picture left. I shot it at the moment he gave all his money to the blind man and his wife. He was touched by them."[109] How he knew that the little man had given "all his money" is unclear, but the detail adds poignancy.[110]

For every outstanding photograph of a dwarf clown, such as those described above, there are many others that are pedestrian and/or mirror old stereotypes. Some are the work of noted photojournalists. A number of these photographs pair dwarfs and small dogs or monkeys; others emphasize bodily contrast, as in *Sideshow* by Antonin Kratochvil (b. 1947), showing, outside a circus tent, a smiling dwarf and a heavyset man wearing a quizzical expression. Another photo that echoes circus themes is by Howard Frank (1914–2000); a tiny proportionate dwarf raises his night-stick at a policeman while a smiling crowd looks on. A 1980 photograph by Thomas Frederick Arndt (b. 1944) shows a pugnacious dwarf with his fists up in a Coney Island bar, while others take little notice.[111] In contrast to these conventional themes, in *Vitelloni, 29th Street and Second Avenue, 1954–55,* the naturalistic photographer William Klein (b. 1928) has shot a crowd scene with a man hoisting up a dwarf boy who looks as if he might be the man's son (Fig. 39). In the panoply of images in which dwarf subjects play a role, this is a rare example that documents an intimate relationship.[112]

Jan Saudek (b. 1935) is a photographer who has produced realistic photographs, as well as intentionally shocking ones, and nudes with atypical bodies. He also has set up surrealistic scenes, a number of them including dwarfs. In a series called *History of Drinking in the Czech Republic,* he devised a theatrical background with an elaborate Oriental rug and wine decanter; he posed within it a dwarf woman and an average-statured woman in antique dresses. Further photographs show these same figures nude in a variety of postures: in one scene the dwarf woman stands on an ottoman against a backdrop of clouds, wearing only a flowered bonnet. Since the photographs are labeled *Portrait of my Friend,* we may assume that Saudek intended to

39. *William Klein,* Vitelloni, Twenty-ninth Street and Second Avenue, *1954–1955.* © *William Klein/Howard Greenberg Gallery.*

celebrate his subject: the young woman's body is attractive, and the backdrop rich and sensual (see color plate 21).

Yet another beautiful dwarf woman is represented in *Daphne and Apollo* by Joel-Peter Witkin (b. 1940). Witkin is known for his carefully constructed photographic tableaux that include skeletons; broken, faceless sculptures; fetuses; and other elements that some find disturbing and others admire as innovative challenges to taboos about sex, death, and physical difference.[113] In creating the tableau *Daphne and Apollo*, Witkin reaches back to the Greek myth for inspiration. The painterly backdrop suggests a beautiful classical landscape, while the foreground contains photographic images of a goat up on its hind legs behind a terrified dwarf woman (Fig. 40). In the myth, the god Apollo, as handsome as he is unlucky in love, accosts and is rejected by the beautiful nymph Daphne. Her cries for help are answered when her father, the river god, turns her into a laurel. A sculpture by Gian Lorenzo Bernini (1598–1680), a painting by Nicolas Poussin (1594–1665), and a Dürer engraving had projected more romantic visions than are given in the Witkin image; for the earlier artists, Daphne and Apollo are attractive figures, and the statuesque Daphne is taller than her pursuer. Witkin's vision challenges previous interpretations. In making Apollo a lecherous goat and Daphne a voluptuous but pained dwarf woman, with elongated, pinlike, electrified fingers, he limns the lust of the pursuer and the horror experienced by the chaste dwarf beauty.

40. Joel Peter Witkin, Daphne and Apollo, Los Angeles, *1990. Courtesy of the artist, Ricco/Masesca, New York, and Frankel Gallery, San Francisco.*

Witkin, in an interpretation of Velázquez's *Las Meninas*, substitutes himself in the place of Velázquez, and the infanta becomes a woman with stumps for legs sitting on a metal contraption. In his enigmatic *Portrait of a Dwarf*, Witkin shows an obese, masked dwarf wearing a camisole and holding a hoop in one hand and a scepter in the other. A faceless bust with a black cameo profile is yet another significant element in this silver gelatin print. The model for the dwarf in this work was Tamara de Treaux, also the inspiration for the novelist Armistead Maupin's *Maybe the Moon*. While Witkin's bizarre or thanatotropic subject matter may be attributable to early traumatic life experiences, Witkin states that his interest in individuals who lack limbs or are otherwise physically challenged reflects his feeling privileged "to know the unique people who so mysteriously enter my life."[114]

Like Witkin, the controversial photographer Diane Arbus (1923–1971) felt empathy with her subjects. "Her ability to win their trust is legendary: When you look at these pictures, their subjects are just flowing toward her, giving up their mystery. Diane was an emissary from the world of feeling. She cared about these people. They felt that and gave her their secret."[115] Still, many viewers were shocked by Arbus's first exhibitions in the 1960s, wondering why she chose for her subject matter the developmentally disabled, the physically deformed, and others who were regarded as bizarre. By now it has become clear that her approach to such groups was the same at that toward the seemingly ordinary: she allowed their simple self-presentation to disclose a great deal. Her photographs invite—sometimes force—the viewer to feel, to think, and finally to relate to these individuals. The truth she aims to impart is the inevitability and futility of masks. Arbus's philosophy is expressed in this well-known statement: "Everybody has that thing where they need to look one way, but they come out looking another way and that's what people observe. You see someone on the street and essentially what you notice about them is the flaw. It's just extraordinary that we should have been given these peculiarities. And not content with what we were given, we create a whole other set. Our whole guise is like giving a sign to the world to think of us in a certain way, but there's a point between what you want people to know about you and what you can't help people knowing about you."[116] This double vision is evident in many of Arbus's photographs—imbedded in the images is the implicit question of how these subjects see themselves.

Arbus took many photographs of dwarfs. Most of these works have not been commercially available: until now only a small number have been reproduced in books, her estate being unwilling to allow any part of her oeuvre to be included in biographical, historical, or even most art-related publications (permission was denied for a photograph in this chapter). In September 2003, an article appeared in the *New York Times*, accompanied by many photographs, announcing that a major traveling retrospective of Arbus's work had been mounted and that a sumptuous new book on the photographer would soon be published.[117]

Among Arbus's previously published photographs of dwarfs is one that pictures three hypopituitary dwarfs sitting in a plainly furnished room. They strike us as rather plain themselves, but comfortable, and unselfconscious. In another work, Andre Ratoucheff is shown in hat and coat, diminutive against the large bed and curtained window of his room.[118] A black adolescent dwarf wearing a beseeching expression is photographed from above, his body shown in foreshortened view.

In discussing her subject matter, Arbus offered the following comments: "Freaks was a thing I photographed a lot. It was one of the first things I photographed and it had a terrific kind of excitement for me. I just used to adore them. I still do adore some of them. I don't quite mean they're my best friends but they make me feel a mixture of shame and awe. There's a quality of legend about freaks. Like a person in a fairy tale who stops you and demands that you answer a riddle. Most people go through life dreading that they'll have a traumatic experience. Freaks were born with their trauma. They've already passed their test in life. They're aristocrats."[119] Unfortunately, Arbus's final insight does not hold up: these individuals will never completely pass their test in life—they are fated to be subjected to a lifetime of testing.

As she explained, Arbus was obsessed with "freaks," over many years frequenting Times Square's Hubert's Freak Museum, which put on display Presto the Fire Eater, Congo the Jungle Creep, and a "midget" (Ratoucheff) who imitated Marilyn Monroe. She managed to win the trust of these people, photographed them endlessly, and was present to collect Hubert's glossy advertising photos when it closed in 1965. Among her most famous images is one of Eddie Carmel, "The Jewish Giant," an eight-foot-tall man whom she photographed beside his short parents—in his family's small apartment, his head almost touches the ceiling. Another familiar subject was Morales, a Mexican dwarf, whom Arbus photographed over a number of years. Patricia Boswell, Arbus's biographer, writes: "Eventually she posed him squatting bare-chested on his bed with his hat on. By that time the rapport between them was palpable, almost erotic, and you can feel it emanating from the image. 'Taking a portrait is like seducing someone,' Diane [has said]."

According to Boswell, the seduction was not only figurative. She reports that after Arbus's marriage came apart, the photographer became more depressed and her life disordered, and she would tell friends about having engaged in group sex after having photographed an orgy, or having sex with a dwarf or a couple of nudists. Boswell concludes that for Arbus, "merging with her subjects, both 'straights' and 'freaks,' was a way of giving herself to them after they revealed themselves to her camera. Such violent self-definition seemed part of her life as an artist."[120] The Arbus family did not cooperate with Boswell and disputed her commentary.

Although Arbus may have paid a price in the fallout from the dark moods that she increasingly experienced toward the end of her life, she helped both art critics and ordinary people to lose their fear of looking at individuals who are atypical and to experience difference in new ways. Her work highlights the irony in our sense of self-presentation, and she has been justly praised for her intimate investigations into the psychological.

Toward the end, however, it became difficult for some who belonged to groups that were represented in her work to trust her to project an image of them that they would find acceptable. In the last year of her life, she was dismayed when she received a letter from a representative of Little People of America turning down her request to photograph the annual convention in Florida. "We have our own little person to photograph us," the letter said.[121] Despite her enormous talent, members of this organization elected not to be immortalized in photographs by Arbus at the nadir of her despondency.

An interesting photograph to consider in conjunction with Arbus's spare hotel room scenes is one by Vivienne Maricevic (b. 1949) that shows the image of a naked dwarf emerging from behind a gossamer white curtain in a similar room (Fig. 41). This man's feet are firmly planted, his body fills the center of the space, and he looks directly at the viewer as he pulls the curtain aside. Despite the inelegant surroundings, this photograph could easily be viewed as one of simple, sensual anticipation. A very different interpretation has been offered by writer Ingrid Bengis: "But a dwarf alone in a hotel room. He comes naked from behind the curtain, enveloped in a loneliness which is final."[122] In this dispiriting scenario, an attractive single dwarf is assumed to be desolate, isolated; though Maricevic often celebrates male sexual diversity, the critic does not suspect that a welcoming partner for this man may be waiting nearby.

Another artist who has contributed memorable photographs celebrating dwarfs is George Dureau. Several of these images appear in a collection of Dureau's photographs whose primary motif is the appreciation of the male body.[123] It reflects his conscious effort to dislodge stereotypical, negative assumptions about the bodies of individuals with physical deformities. Among Dureau's dramatic photographs of amputees and other people living with physical disability are images of dwarfs (Fig. 42). Many of these

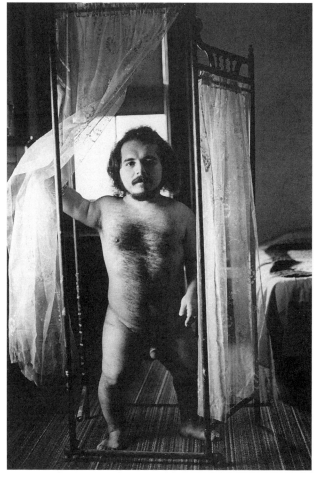

41. Vivienne Maricevic, Vince, *from* Naked Men *series.* © *Vivienne Maricevic. Courtesy of the artist.*

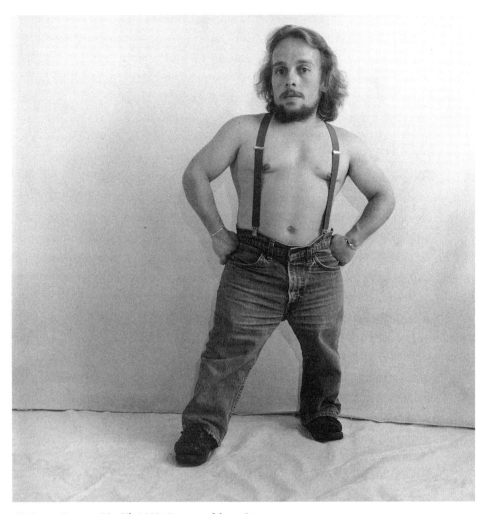

42. George Dureau, Ric Gil, 1983. Courtesy of the artist.

are shown in classical postures: one achondroplastic dwarf, a muscular black man, stands with his legs on two stone pedestals, a living statue. According to the critic Alice Hicks, Dureau, who was raised a Catholic, has produced works that exude spirituality in a different sense—that of transcendence over adversity. . . . She sees Dureau as using the principle of contrapposto in several of his pictures as well as adopting Classical poses, as can be observed in the photograph of Windell Platt, which is reminiscent of the ancient Greek sculpture *The Fallen Warrior* (Fig. 43).[124]

The men in Dureau's photographs are not mere objects of curiosity, but the medium for an appreciative artistic encounter with dwarfs. Like dwarf artist and photographer Ricardo Gil—pictured in *New Orleans* in an assertive pose, with his muscular chest and his arms akimbo—they are simply Dureau's friends or acquaintances (see Fig. 42). Both their forms and their personalities are of interest to him.

43. George Dureau, Windell Platt, *1982. Courtesy of the artist.*

During the 1980s, the decade when he did most of the photographs for *New Orleans,* Dureau painted dwarf wrestlers and, in domestic settings, dwarfs whom he knew. An artist with Classical and Romantic leanings, Dureau is recognized in the art community first of all as a painter, and only secondarily as a photographer. Unafraid of sensual or provocative material, in a show of his work at the Arthur Roger Gallery in New Orleans, he included his 1997 oil *The Flagellation Bar and Grill,* a scene with elements of both Classicism and sadomasochism that features a male dwarf on a masonry pedestal. Dureau's homosexuality influences his approach to his dwarf subjects. For artists, being the member of a minority group oneself may predispose one to create sympathetic or searching portrayals of others. Dureau's artistic gifts, combined with empathy, have resulted in unusual, evocative portraits.

SCULPTURE

The Spanish artist Juan Muñoz has created a compelling series of modern sculptures of dwarfs. Born in Madrid in 1953, Muñoz studied at the Central School of Art and Design and at the Croyden College of Art and Technology in London, and at Pratt Institute in New York City. From his home base in Madrid, he has participated in one-person and group shows worldwide; major museums have acquired his work. Much of twentieth-century sculpture, like painting, has abandoned the human figure, but Muñoz has continued the tradition of representing the figure in art. In many instances, he has created dramatic architectural backdrops that demonstrate his preoccupation with the relationship of a figure to the space it inhabits. Many artists have influenced Muñoz—including Velázquez, Alberto Giacometti, Georges Seurat, and especially Giorgio de Chirico, as well as the writers Pirandello and Borges.

Like de Chirico, Muñoz confronts his viewers with existential themes, notably the small individual in a vast, often sterile and overwhelming universe. His sculptures containing dwarf subjects for the most part date from the late 1980s and early 1990s. Among this group is *Dwarf with Three Columns,* in which a terra-cotta figure measuring three feet seven inches in height is positioned near three towering spiral columns (see color plate 22). In *The Wasted Land* (a homage to T. S. Eliot), consisting of papier-mâché, paint, rubber, steel, and wood, a dwarf figure, seated on a bench affixed to a wall, looks out at an expanse of floor space that is decorated with trompe l'oeil box-maze designs. Another mixed-media piece, *Dwarf with Parallel Lines,* is similar in conception; the same model is shown in various contexts in sculptures set on pedestals or on the floor. *The Prompter* shows a dwarf standing beneath the floor of a stage with only his lower half revealed—his head is covered by an acoustical device that hides him from view. The work evokes the historical helper-attendant role of dwarfs who were destined never to live their lives in the limelight.

Muñoz's male model is often the same dwarf, the expression on his chiseled features serious, his body solid. Muñoz has also used a female figure in at least two scenes, one work called *Sara with a Chair* and another *Dwarf Figure in a Mirror.* This second sculpture, of polyester resin and mirror, dates from 1996, when the artist was creating other scenes containing the human figure and mirrors. This tableau raises the question of how the woman will respond when she looks at herself.

The Czech artist Milan Knizak, as a member of Fluxus, was part of an international experimental art movement in which diverse media and styles were employed to support artistic spontaneity and antiauthoritarian politics. An aficionado of folk art, possessing a huge collection of marionettes, Knizak was active in fashion, design, and music, exploring such techniques as breaking and reconstituting records to create new music. Arrested and imprisoned for his activities in the late 1960s and early

1970s, in 1990, following the "velvet revolution" that led to the creation of the Czech Republic, he was elected rector of the Prague Academy of Fine Arts—where he remained a radical activist. Knizak's sculptures of dwarfs and rather elfish politicians take the form of puppets and other three-dimensional forms. He views puppets as naive and beautiful, but at the same time as functioning as small statues of people. Some are more rooted in myth and fantasy than others. Knizak comments, "Dwarfs are supposed to be kitschy, but they are not, they are just beautiful. Dwarfs are funny creatures, very dreamy. When I was young I liked the thought of having a nice small friend who would always be with me, sitting in my pocket, whispering good advice into my ear. I used them as a symbol of something childlike. Later, they developed into a symbol of something stupid, low and narrow-minded. For my next exhibition, I have decided to model [Václav] Havel's head [as that of a dwarf]."[125]

Knizak's political dwarfs include figures in which one emanates from the head of another, like Athena from the head of Zeus. Knizek pokes fun at the egotistical pretensions of politicians, avoiding cliché. He has indicated that he always tries to create pieces with double meanings. Because dwarf images can project the artists' precise intentions but are also dependent on viewers' associations, inserting a "mythic load" makes varied interpretations even more likely. He has said that so-called high art was never important to him, which is why he loves dwarfs and castles, puppets and marionettes. Above all, he sees himself as, like other artists, searching for humanity, an essence that connects people.

POP CULTURE

Representations of dwarfs are found in many aspects of pop culture. Alfred Enderle, one of the authors of *Small People—Great Art,* has assembled a remarkable collection of historical picture postcards from 1900 to 1950. There are 893 postcards featuring giants and dwarfs—742 depict dwarfs, 93 are of giants, and 58 show both. Cards displaying such subject matter have declined over the years and have now all but disappeared—the evidence shows that the majority were sent in the mail between 1900 and 1915. The characters who are pictured are elegantly dressed and often from the world of entertainment, including vaudeville and the circus. They are shown performing as musicians, acrobats, dancing couples, or soldiers, and are positioned in ways that emphasize their small stature—juxtaposed with tall people or large dogs.

Even now, mythological dwarfs continue to surface. The cartoons built around "smurfs," small characters created by the Belgian Pierre Culliford (1928–1992), led to a brisk sale in figurines and other products representing them. Smurfs can be regarded simply as children's toys or interpreted as vehicles for a utopian socialist fable.[126] Although fantasy dwarf figures have long figured in the areas of popular culture that pertain to children, and dwarf individuals have been featured as entertainers, what is new and noteworthy, in our culture, are the instances of real dwarfs being photographed in positive ways for advertising products. Several years ago, a pretty dwarf child was featured in the *New York Times* in a small advertisement for Bloomingdale's department store. In fall 2000, a series of striking photographs appeared in a special fashion issue of *Flaunt* magazine, photographed by Andres Serrano (b. 1950). They starred Nick Torres, a rugged, attractive dwarf model, in a variety of high-fashion outfits designed by Tom Ford for the Gucci fashion house; Torres's pushed-up trousers reveal that they were designed for taller men and being marketed to them as well (see color plate 23).

Dwarf Artists Today

There has been a significant increase in the number of gifted dwarf artists whose work has reached the public. It is important to clarify the label "dwarf artists," which is as controversial as the category "woman artists," "black artists," or that of any identity group.[127] Understandably, many artists, even those whose subject matter identifies them with a given group, reject this kind of labeling. Among the artists who come to mind are Mary Cassatt, who focused on the lives of women, and Romare Bearden (1914–1988) and Jacob Lawrence (1917–2000), who portrayed African Americans. The term *dwarf artists* is used here not out of ignorance or insensitivity, but mostly as shorthand. Unlike their predecessors, the five artists to be discussed here have explored their dwarf identity in their work. While in no instance has this concern shaped the entire canvas of their work, several of these artists have made important contributions to a fresh perspective on being short statured. All are professional artists who have produced a substantial body of work that would merit inclusion in art criticism of a general nature.

We know little, either from their art or their writing, about what most dwarf artists of the past felt about their difference. So it is certainly news when even a few dwarf artists address the question of how to present their own likenesses or viewpoints. Two who are close friends—Bruce Johnson and Ricardo Gil—have approached the problem in different ways.

BRUCE JOHNSON

Bruce Johnson (b. 1945), an artist now living in Hawaii, created a self-portrait in

1968 that shows him sitting on the floor among his modest possessions (Fig. 44), looking kindly. In those days, Johnson's consciousness about his being a dwarf was not quite what it was to become later.[128] Given the stares and remarks of others, he had not been oblivious to his difference, especially when at eleven or twelve years old, he saw a video of himself and was shocked to see how distinctive his body was— particularly his head and his posture when walking. The love of family and friends had tempered his self-consciousness, which he held inside, and the issue remained for some time only a personal one.

Through the years, however, coming to terms with his body became a recurrent preoccupation for Johnson. He began to wonder about the meaning of being a dwarf in different societies, especially in Western cultures. In the course of his investigations, he collected many representations of dwarfs in art, particularly those of twentieth-century photographers. During this generative period of his life, he perused these images, hoping to one day find a purpose for them.

Most of Johnson's art, however, has had little to do with dwarf themes. He regards his strongest and most consistent body of work as his nonobjective painting in acrylic and mixed media on paper. After earning a B.F.A. at the University of Hawaii, he ob-

44. Bruce Johnson, Self-Portrait in Interior, 1968. Courtesy of the artist.

tained a master's degree from the California College of Arts and Crafts in Oakland. He taught for several years at Santa Rosa Junior College in California and part time at the University of Hawaii and the Honolulu Academy of Art, and was also employed as a substitute art teacher in the Hawaii school system. Johnson earned a CETA grant through a federal program called WAPP (Works of Art in Public Places) and a Mac-Dowell Fellowship. He took part in many group shows and a number of solo exhibits.

However, making a living at his art proved elusive. There was a period when partly to support himself, and perhaps for the lure of the experience, he worked as an actor and extra, notably in the controversial *Under the Rainbow,* reviving an interest left over from an enjoyable period he had spent as a performer in a junior high school group. Serious spinal surgeries in 1976 and 1989 required his return to Hawaii, where he could receive assistance from his family. He found that he liked living in Hawaii and valued his friendships there; he and his fiancée, Leslye Sneider, now make it their home.[129]

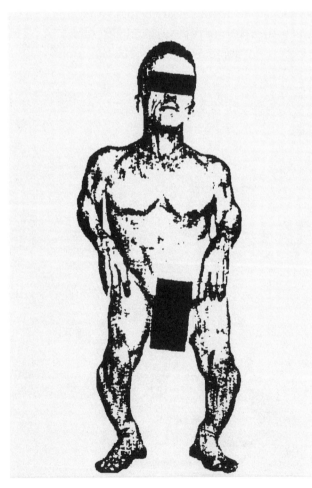

45. Bruce Johnson, Ecce Homo, *1998. Courtesy of the artist.*

Since 1989, when Johnson's disability worsened, he has managed to produce artwork only intermittently. In recent years, he has returned to looking closely at his own body in his art, as he had for a photo series he had done in the early 1970s when he posed himself in a variety of ways against a gridded wall. The human figure set against that grid was inspired in part by the work of the early photographer Eadweard Muybridge (1830–1904), who photographed people and horses in motion, painstakingly recording the changes that occurred. Johnson's series was part of his ongoing confrontation of his bodily self. He returned to that original theme later when, using a photocopy machine, he enlarged a four-by-six-foot photograph of himself to life size. That process slightly abstracted the light-dark pattern of the image and created a strong graphic quality. Because he recognized that "putting [the representation] out there as a trigger" had the power to stimulate and upset not just himself but also other dwarfs, he decided to display one of evocative images at a national conference of LPA in 1998.

The photograph was produced by Johnson as a kind of template that would have been only slightly different had it been that of another male dwarf with a similar diagnosis. Johnson placed a dark band over the eyes and genitals, making the photograph suggest a case in a medical book (Fig. 45). In a deliberate provocation, he titled the work *Ecce Homo*—both for its literal translation, "This is a man," with its religious connection to Christ on the cross, and for the resonance of the word *homo,* which he thought might jar those who associated it only with homosexuality.

The work inspired much controversy. There were some who wanted it removed, on the grounds that the "nudity" was unsuitable for children and ought not to be in a public place. The shock of recognizing themselves in stark outline bothered others. But a great many praised the piece. They recognized in it the nude photographs they themselves had been subjected to, and they saw Johnson's image and its title as a protest against the medicalization and dehumanization of dwarfs. Although Johnson recognizes that inhabiting a dwarf body will always retain its ability to "evoke a charge," his work suggests that people of short stature need both to defy stereotyping and to be able to look directly at themselves.

Johnson continues to explore themes relating to his own life. A later work on paper, shown at the 2003 LPA conference, captured a universal concern—feelings about aging. Arriving at a better understanding of his physical and emotional being has brought a measure of equanimity to Johnson, despite his difficulties, and he persists in exploring ideas involving identity.

RICARDO GIL

The photographs of Ricardo Gil (b. 1957) represent a unique contribution: his are the first images of the world of dwarfs from their own perspective, rather than that of outsiders.[130] A substantial part of Gil's oeuvre relates to his family; he is married to another dwarf, Meg, a preschool teacher, and they have a twelve-year-old daughter, Lily, who is of average stature. In this subject matter, Gil is again unusual, as only the ancient Egyptian statue of Seneb, with which this chapter began; Induno's *Cripple with a Mandolin,* and Menzel's *Evening Gathering* show a dwarf in a family setting.

Gil's photographs reveal his affection for his family in nudes of himself and a pregnant Meg—inviting the viewer to appreciate the atypical body structures of a dwarf man and woman—and in pictures of Meg and Lily together in a number of dif-

46. *Ricardo L. Gil,* Meg's Braids, *1991. © Ricardo L. Gil.*

ferent poses. It was noted earlier in this chapter that Greek vase painters almost never painted females, believing that by doing so they would cause the women shame; as this example illustrates, dwarf females have been painted much less frequently than dwarf males throughout history, and then rarely with admiration. In Gil's nude portraits of his pregnant wife, by contrast, he celebrates the beauty of her female body (Fig. 46).[131]

Gil's other major accomplishment is his manipulation of perspective. In *A Game of Frisbee* he photographs Meg and Lily in a park: Lily appears even larger than she actually is relative to Meg, and other people are seen as specks in the distance. The Alice in Wonderland world is a shifting reality. Sometimes, the world of others is seen from the subjective visual stance of a dwarf, with only the legs of average-sized adults visible to a dwarf at eye level. The dwarf must crane his or her neck skyward to see what others see—even then, he or she is confronted with such rare views as the underside of chins (Fig. 47). Some photographs offer storytelling narratives about situations familiar to persons with dwarfism. In one image, Meg struggles as she carries pajama-clad Lily, almost as big as she is, off to bed; while Meg's affection is obvious, so is the effort of her task. In another photograph, an average-statured man sinks to his knees so he may be the same size as the short-statured woman he is talking to. Anyone who has ever attended an LPA conference will recognize the attempt of the taller person to find the comfort zone required to carry on an easy communication between equals. Further, Gil's photograph of himself nude, with a halo cast on his head that was necessitated by his surgery, may elicit in the viewer symbolic associations with religious paintings. At long last a dwarf has captured individuals like himself in the midst of affirming their own important lives.

Gil's path to his current subject matter was neither easy nor direct. Born in Puerto Rico in 1957, he grew up in New Orleans; he now resides near San Francisco.[132] He had started college in New Orleans as an engineering major; only much later did he allow himself to cultivate his suppressed passion for art.[133] He left for California, where he hoped to complete his college degree. Along the way, he attempted to pursue a career in films (an area which his brother, Arturo, continues to make his vocation); while rehearsing a physically demanding scene, Gil broke his neck. He had been unaware that his condition, commonly known as cartilage-hair hypoplasia, involved cervical instability. Only after two surgeries and much time in a halo cast was he well enough to return to school, this time to study art. Because of his orthopedic difficulties and his asthma, he was often not well enough to work and had to retire on disability from his job at the National Park Service.

He enrolled at the California School of Arts and Crafts, where for a year and a half he studied sculpture and drawing, but he was forced to discontinue his studies because of financial circumstances and concern about his cervical instability. After his second surgery, he studied printmaking at Laney College and sculpture at the College of Marin. Although Gil took only a single course in photography, his interest was captured—it turned out that photography and sculpture were to become his primary fields of concentration. His bronze sculpture consists mostly of small forms; even so,

47. *Ricardo L. Gil,* Ellen's Reception, *1991. © Ricardo L. Gil.*

casting them in bronze has proved difficult because of his disabilities, necessitating assistants.[134] Three sculptures—boxlike shapes with dug-out hollows or tubular pipelike forms designed to be mounted—were inspired by a combination of stimuli, including a dream, the memory of trees he and his father had planted in Puerto Rico, and the four bolts of the halo cast he had had to wear after his surgery. Gil has worked on a sculptural rendering of orthopedic shoes, one element in the system of elaborate braces and contraptions he had worn as a child of six or seven.

An early influence on Gil was George Dureau. Dureau had invited Gil to pose for him and often invited him for simple, elegant dinners at his Victorian house near the French quarter of New Orleans. He found Dureau warm, attentive, gentle, and eccentric. Following his award of a 1998–1999 California Arts Council Fellowship, in May 1999 Gil had his first solo show, which received very favorable reviews. Like many photographers before him, notably Arbus and Davidson—but from a different perspective—Gil has grappled with the issues that confront empathic outsiders. He has considered making a documentary on some of the themes he pursues in his photography but so far has not been able to secure funding.

Gil, like Johnson, struggles with financial pressures and artistic issues, as well as the question of how much he can work given his physical limitations. Since his photographic images have appeared on his Web site, he has received mail from a number of viewers who have found the works personally meaningful. He is delighted at last to have received real recognition as an artist—and does not mind being known as a "dwarf artist," because that title is a significant part of his hard-won identity. In addition, in 2002 he resumed his theatrical career in some measure, after being invited to appear in several theatrical ventures, including the film *Cherish* and later the play *DollHouse*, Mabou Mines' stage adaptation of Henrik Ibsen's work.

CORBAN WALKER

Corban Walker (b. 1967) is best known to American audiences for his moving performance in the film *Frankie Starlight*; his appearance in this film, however, was only a temporary sabbatical from his career as an artist. Walker is a critically acclaimed Irish sculptor who received a degree in fine arts and sculpture from the National College of Art and Design in Dublin in 1992. He has won several Irish Arts Council awards and has exhibited in solo and group shows in Dublin, in other locations in Europe, and in the United States.

An important defining element in Walker's work has been his effort to deal with the relationship of his stature to his being-in-the-world. Most often, he approaches this question through the abstract rather than the figurative. Walker's perception of contrasts of scale was a central focus of his 1994 exhibit *Latitude* at the Dublin City Arts Centre. Walker explained: "Basically, four is my height expressed in feet. I started out working with the relationship between my height and what is seen as the standard average male height of six feet. The built environment is designed around this assumed norm and typical scale of six foot. . . . [In *Latitude*] I worked directly with the relationships between four and six. This came about through considering ergonomics and questions of design and scale right back through to the Renaissance and even beyond to earlier periods."[135]

Walker describes this early installation as related to "a lot of things I wanted to get out of my system about me." His later work used more involved mathematical units of four and six and their multiples, and other important concerns began to appear. He became increasingly interested in the nature of the materials—in establishing contrasts between the tough and the fragile and suggesting delicacy even in hard, minimalist structures. He also grappled with the relationship(s) between human and architectural space, and between sculpture and the other arts.

His experience in *Frankie Starlight* was influential. Working with a camera crew made him aware of the self-consciousness of the viewed, and the way things alter in appearance relative to the play of light and viewers' movements. He began to be more sensitive to these elements in his own sculpture—introducing them through the use of materials such as reflective stainless steel and silvered glass. In 1997 Walker created two large installations. In *Mapping* he used wire to trace a wave through the gallery space, along with 357 Polaroid photographs of the "details of urban objects," such as cobblestones and gratings, that he had found in different parts of Ireland; these were hung at his own height of four feet. As part of a second work, *Station (N.E.S.W.)*, Walker constructed a grid of fluorescent lights, transformers, and cables arranged vertically (Figs. 48, 49).

In reviewing these installations, Luke Clancy notes: "Although Walker has always allowed his own size to provide the key to his work, *Mapping* still registers as a notably personal, warm work. The artist has previously set himself the problem of forcing minimalist forms to give up their aloofness. Here, with the calm, ordered repetition of the Polaroid square, he has found his most convincing solution yet."[136]

In *Station (N.E.S.W.)* (the title refers to directional coordinates), Walker reveals his interest in universals through an artistic exploration—similar in focus to Gil's—of how physical position affects one's view of reality. In July 1998 the National Rehabilitation Board and Arts Council in Ireland presented Walker with its annual award given to an artist with a disability. The award included free access to a studio for a year, technical training, and the use of modified equipment.

Late in 2001, Walker became involved in a number of film projects; in addition, he received a commission from the Mitsubishi Estate Company for a site-specific, per-

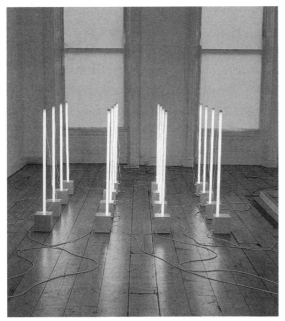

48. *Corban Walker,* Station (N.S.E.W.), *1997. Courtesy of*   49. *Corban Walker with assistants. Courtesy of the*
the artist.   *artist.*

manent installation for their new building in downtown Tokyo. He was one of five
international artists called upon to create works designed outside the gates of what
had been the Imperial Palace, damaged by earthquakes and being replaced. Walker
described his project: "The installation I am doing is a glass and light piece set in the
walls of the main staircase between the ground floor and the first level of a shopping
arcade. Above the staircase is a ten-floor glass atrium. The idea behind the piece is to
make that short journey between the two levels as interactive as possible for the person ascending or descending the stairs. The person becomes critically aware of their
own scale and their relationship to the surroundings, based on my everyday relationship to a building that is designed for someone of a different scale."[137]

Among Walker's other recent noteworthy exhibitions were two in October 2000,
one at the Ennis Festival in Ireland, where he showed a bronze called *Eye Measure*;
and another at the prestigious Pace-Wildenstein Gallery in New York, where he exhibited an installation focusing on variations in light and scale that included a forest
of turquoise-toned glass that filled the ground-floor gallery. Walker is an active participant both in the art world and in the community of other artists who are disabled.[138]
Beyond reaping the rewards of his professional activities, he enjoys a rich personal
life and a circle of good friends.

JACQUELINE ANN CLIPSHAM

Jacqueline Ann Clipsham (b. 1936), who has had a long career as a ceramic artist, chooses to keep her passionate activism separate from her artistic efforts. She has taken part in many individual and group shows, and collectors and museums have purchased her work. In addition, she has been a political activist, first in the civil rights movement and later for disability rights (Fig. 50).

Her mother was from Fort Wayne, Indiana, and her father, who emigrated from England to the United States, was a successful engineer and a self-made man. As Clipsham matured into her talented, intellectual, argumentative self, her straitlaced parents were dismayed. She was sent to Hathaway-Brown, an elite girls school in Cleveland, Ohio, with the expectation that she would go on to an elite women's college in the East. Instead she chose Carleton College, in Minnesota, where she found people she had more affinity with, and a new freedom. After a year in Europe studying at the Universities of Perugia and Grenoble and visiting relatives in England, she returned to embark on serious studies at the Cleveland Institute of Art, then obtained her master's degree from Case Western Reserve University. Her artistic talent had been recognized as early as age ten, when, while living in England, she had won a drawing prize. At Hathaway-Brown, she had begun to work in clay and had also won prizes; at the Cleveland Institute she produced ceramics and sculpture and studied life drawing.

She is comfortable in two communities— that of artists and artisans and that of activists. As a child she had often responded to the fact that black children had to endure aggressive put-downs and jeers, just as she did, and that commonality was to have a strong effect on her. When the civil rights movement burgeoned in the 1960s, she joined the Congress of Racial Equality (CORE) and went down to Sumter, South Carolina, where, while experiencing enormous culture shock, she taught art and ceramics to the local population. Back home in New York, she became a disability rights activist, working for Disabled Museum Visitors Services at the Metropolitan Museum of Art, consulting for the National Endowment for the Arts on many projects, and publishing a number of articles. In a paper on careers in the arts for people

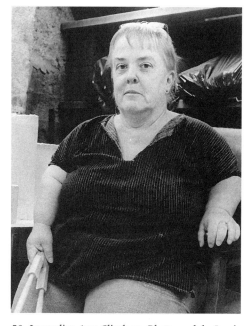

50. Jacqueline Ann Clipsham. Photograph by Lynda Greer.

with disabilities, she outlines the development of an artist's personal vision; discusses the impediments that family members and others set up when they suggest that the arts are acceptable as a hobby but untenable as a source of income; and offers practical suggestions about training and careers.[139] Clipsham taught at the Brooklyn Museum Art School for eleven years and was part of a community of artists at the Clay Art Center in Port Chester, New York, sometimes alternating periods of active political activity with her creative work, sometimes pursuing both at once. Clipsham is famously voluble, offering anecdotes about her adventures in the various movements of which she has been a part, as well as descriptions of her important and enduring friendships with obscure and famous alike.

Clipsham now lives and works in rural New Jersey. Near the entryway of her home and studio rests her collection of extraordinarily beautiful ceramics and sculptures, some her productions, but others purchased or bartered during the course of her lifetime. The kiln in her downstairs studio is custom made so that she can more easily load and fire her ceramics; she has installed a sturdy lift to get her from the downstairs to her second-floor living quarters. Before her disability became severe, she stopped using the wheel because she found handbuilt work more satisfying. Clipsham's ceramics reflect the influences of different cultures. Some of her earlier work suggests Etruscan sarcophagi and Egyptian pyramids and is a kind of homage to Eastern and Egyptian forms, informed by architecture. Other pieces refer to the jazz music that has long been one of her driving interests: a stoneware and sisal rope piece is titled *Double Chambered Blues Box* in memory of Jimmy Garrison.

Clipsham has also offered her own creative translation of some *kachina* forms in beautiful white porcelain vessels. In a series called *Narcissus,* tall porcelain triangles and short, mirrored boxes, which are made of porcelain, mirror, copper wire, resistors, and diodes reflecting female genitalia, have whimsical titles such as *Coppery Tentacled Sea Creature* (see color plate 24), *Venus Flytrap,* and *Drosophilia Melangaster.* These are a return to the sexual and biological forms that have fascinated Clipsham since her student days, when she considered science as a career. *Narcissus* also functions as social commentary.

Clipsham is proud of having created disability access symbols that alert the public to the availability of sign language, wheelchair accommodation, and Braille. Her work on this project has resulted in materials currently produced by the Graphic Arts Guild Foundation in New York. She has also produced multimedia works, among them tapes based on her feelings about the connections between jazz and visual art. In 2003, the Museum of Modern Art in New York acquired a copy of her artist book, and the Carnegie Museum in Pittsburgh added her multimedia work to its collection. On 29 July 2001, a retrospective of her forty-year career opened at the Hunterdon Museum of Art in Clinton, New Jersey.

KATHERINE KOOS

Katherine Koos (b. 1977) is a talented young sculptor who has already produced a large body of work, notably metal and wood sculptures. Koos had originally considered majoring in science, but after two years of college, she acknowledged her artistic leanings and enrolled in a B.F.A. program at the Parsons School of Design, majoring in fine arts and sculpture, and graduated with honors.

She had first worked with paper, then glass beads and spools of wire. After graduation, she rented a studio not far from her home and bought retail supplies in small quantities. One day, with her landlord's encouragement, she bought three hundred dollars' worth of wire from industrial sources. "You're young, and you'll use it!" he had said. She soon realized that his prediction was accurate—she is now producing at least one piece a month, often more, and has created more than two hundred sculptures.

Koos had demonstrated talent since early childhood. She is the daughter of John and Vivian Koos, both painters, and their Brooklyn home has always been filled with a changing panorama of artwork. Her first sculptures, featured at group shows in the New York City area, relied on the interlacing of innumerable wires into a single form. The intricate sculptures that resulted were sometimes light, sometimes quite dense, shapes when seen at a distance; they seemed to call out to viewers to draw closer to examine them and discover how the construction of the elements had led to the illusion of a single, unified whole. For a later invitational show, several hundred artists made works that measured twenty-four by twenty-four inches. The composition that Koos submitted utilized energetically spiraling wood reeds to create the sense of active, living forms, and was deemed one of the best pieces in the show.

Originally, Koos was not eager to be featured in this volume as a "dwarf artist"— she preferred to be acknowledged simply as a sculptor in her own right. She works in a sizable space in an industrial area in Brooklyn, New York, that is home to many artists (see color plate 25). When I visited, more than a dozen of her sculptures were prominently displayed—some completed, others works in progress—and a shedlike storage space in the corner of the room contained a great many more pieces. On the floor in the center of the room was a round ball four feet in diameter, formed by interlocking strips of curled wood. A large, elaborate wire sculpture was suspended on a wall. Among the smaller pieces was an open, airy wire construction with glass beads at its base; others were more closely interwoven, with involved arrangements of carefully twisted wires appearing denser and heavier. One of her pieces, ten feet in diameter, is made of kraft paper, bags, acrylic polymer, and paper clips. Another, which she made for her mother, is a set of irregular poplar squares, wider in the center, arranged as a tower, one set on another. Because her mother's vision is impaired,

Katherine built into the structure the additional element of tactile pleasure: her mother can explore the gradations of rough and smooth texture carved into each square.

Koos constructs all her pieces without the help of assistants. She explains that for her, working is like playing a musical instrument:

Notes sound different when someone else does it. In wire or wood, working with different forms, sometimes it just doesn't sound right. I use sound as a metaphor: what I mean is that you develop a different personal vocabulary, and within that vocabulary you are always building new forms—ways of putting things together, compositions. And sometimes things *do* work. My process is intuitive. Sometimes the piece changes while I am working on it, sometimes it doesn't. I like the sense of invention and discovery. It's possible that there might be a book that would show you exactly how to twist wire, but I've figured it out through trial and error.

Koos discussed the reworking process, describing it in terms of painting:

Sometimes, mixing a color, the painting doesn't work because you have a favorite section. Because that part is precious, you find that you are not willing to take a risk, take a chance. You must put it aside. Sometimes, if I buy a brush or wire, it may just sit there—till one day I just go and dive in. I don't give up easily on a piece. I try to solve it, like a riddle, looking for the right solution or balance. I consider some of my stuff as in a coma for a while. I'll ask, "Is it really finished—does it work?" So I put it away, then go back and take another look. I want to feel really secure and firm about a piece.

Much of Koos's work is constructed in modules, which she completes as an additive process. She adopted various systems of building in her early years—such as using machine screws and hex nuts in order to screw pieces of paper together. This approach enables her to not be limited by size. She had once heard an artist who was a dwarf mention size as a reason for having decided to do work on a small scale; Koos was determined that she would not be similarly limited.

Koos has appeared in a number of group shows in the New York City area. Despite extremely delicate and extensive spinal surgery at Johns Hopkins University Hospital in February 2002 and October 2003, and subsequent physical therapy, after each period of rehabilitation she returned with vigor to her studio. In March 2003 Koos was invited to contribute to an exhibition at the Belfast Waterfront Hall in Belfast, Northern Ireland, conceived of as a dialogue between American and Irish artists. Curator Linda Dennis wrote of Koos's sculptures: "Biology, anatomy, and industry all come to mind when viewing them, but something deeper and more personal is revealed as one studies them individually. There is a distinct difference between each one—even when the material is similar . . . they become recognizable as particular shapes from a distance that only reveal their true nature as a community of many particular threads on careful inspection."[140] Although Koos herself does not make this association, Dennis concludes that Koos's condition "informs her work and gives it a quiet and resonant power of reflection. . . . [I]t mirrors the artist's deep familiarity with both the strengths and weaknesses of the physical, made true by the power of connection. . . . Considered as a whole, her work is a testament to the combination of spirit and time taken to create things of enigmatic beauty, that need nothing more than themselves as explanation."

BRIEFLY NOTED

A number of other artists who are dwarfs, some recently deceased, some currently active, and others whose careers are only beginning, bear mention. Randy Bachman, who was killed by a hit-and-run drunk driver in 1987, had been a ubiquitous figure in the San Francisco rock scene for the previous fifteen years, photographing both well-known and obscure rock stars and occasionally appearing in videos himself. He was much loved by the community of performers and producers. Six years after Bachman's well-attended memorial service, Joel Selvin made Bachman's dream come true (posthumously) by collecting his work in *Photo Pass: The Rock and Roll Photography of Randy Bachman*.[141] The volume is less a fine arts publication than a bright, dramatic chronicle of the performers and atmosphere typical of club life in the era it depicts.

Mark Gash (1955–2000), a Los Angeles artist, received his M.F.A. from the California Institute of the Arts in 1982 and exhibited in many group and one-person shows in the 1980s and 1990s. Gash, whose dwarfism resulted from osteogenesis imperfecta, painted bold, colorful, sometimes fanciful works, most in acrylic on canvas. His Web site offers a good sampling of his neosurrealist paintings with storytelling elements, as well as his portraits of women. Gash was also a part-time writer and actor, receiving acclaim for his work with the North Vancouver Community Players as well as a few parts in films. A spirited, voluble man, he remained active in many spheres despite the medical condition that kept him in a wheelchair; he died at age forty-five of the complications of ear surgery.[142]

Every year at the annual conference of Little People of America, there is an exhibition organized by the Dwarf Artists Coalition, showcasing work by LPA members in the visual and compositional arts. Since its inception in 1992, more than sixty artists—professional, hobbyists, and children—have participated in the weeklong exhibit. Founded by Ricardo Gil, beginning in 2000 the DAC was headed by Irene Yuan, a 2002 graduate of the Art Center College of Design in Los Angeles.

Conclusion

The outstanding insight that emerges from this review of dwarfs in art history is that they have rarely been portrayed as at the center of their own lives, with families and personal concerns, but rather as mythic figures, singletons, servants, or entertainers. The twentieth century saw a much more diverse picture gradually emerge, with a range of realistic, surrealistic, and symbolic representations. It is impossible to know what the future will bring, but it seems likely that past characterizations will persist in some fashion alongside innovative representations of the transformations taking place today. Images of dwarfs' mythic presence are apt to endure in graphic form mostly in children's books, while visual artists—dwarfs and nondwarfs alike—depict the increasingly varied quotidian lives of dwarfs and their families. Even as social integration proceeds, a certain fascination persists, and so images of dwarfs in art seem more likely to change than to disappear entirely. Not only have the large number of both superb and commonplace works of art from the past helped to document the historical roles of dwarfs—they remain a valuable source of interest and pleasure whose attraction gives little evidence of waning.

CHAPTER EIGHT

Literature

Most persons, if asked to name a literary work with dwarfs, would prob-ably mention *Snow White and the Seven Dwarfs* and perhaps J.R.R. Tolkein's *The Hobbit* or *Lord of the Rings*. Some knowledgeable readers might recall another work or two, like Pär Lagerkvist's *The Dwarf* or Ursula Hegi's *Stones from the River*.[1] However, beyond these titles, and beyond such fairy tales as *Snow White and the Seven Dwarfs,* there exists a little-known but voluminous literature containing dwarf protagonists. While it is not possible to present a comprehensive ac-count here, an attempt has been made to highlight some first-rate works, and others that simply document the changing representation of dwarfs in literature. It has taken a millennium for their depiction to be altered from mythological figures to stock characters—sentimental or depraved—and, finally, to the rare individualized human beings that grace a small segment of modern fiction.

The Arthurian Legends

There is no strict dividing line between early folktales, whose origins are lost in prehistory, and the narratives of modern literature. However, the first writings with dwarf protagonists that were put forth as conscious, artistic creations are the hetero-geneous group of works known as the Arthurian romances. These were set out by Thomas Malory (fl. c. 1470) in *Le Morte Darthur,* a collection of these tales of courtly love, containing such larger-than-life figures as King Arthur, Guinevere, and Sir Lancelot.[2] Dwarfs appear as servants or aides-de-camp, as well as inhabitants of a dwarf kingdom of their own. The tradition of which *Morte Darthur* is a part, whose written expression first became prominent in the twelfth century in France and the British Isles, has an even richer array of dwarf characters. In his comprehensive 1958 review of the literature, Vernon Harward finds recognizable variants of dwarf figures in the traditions of Ireland, Wales, England, and Brittany.[3]

As in the original oral folktales, dwarfs in the *Morte Darthur* play both positive and negative roles. They may be beautiful or monstrous. They may be gracious hosts or hostile antagonists, conduits to the Holy Grail or betraying spies. Their kingdoms tend to be grand, underground replicas of Camelot. Harward notes a gradual progression from dwarfs' supernatural abilities in the earlier works to a more realistic representation. Clairvoyance, for example, is replaced by astrological skill. Familiar Celtic mythological characters are reframed within the courtly aesthetic. Morgan le Fay, a mysterious figure who appears in many guises, is often a short-statured fairy. Sometimes King Arthur's sister, sometimes his half sister, Morgan is almost always a sorceress, and often the enemy of Arthur and Guinevere. Like many of her dwarf predecessors, she is a healer. Morgan personifies moral complexity, and much literary criticism has been devoted to analyzing her. She is unusual for being a developed female figure in the dwarf literary canon: feminists and psychoanalysts can find projected through Morgan the female power and seductiveness that men fear, intermixed with nurturance and healing abilities.

Ysaie le Triste, another tale in the Arthurian tradition, highlights Troncq, an intriguing dwarf character who is companion and valet to two knights.[4] The hideous Troncq, who possesses attributes drawn from Celtic folktales as well as from dwarf entertainers in medieval courts, is given a prominent role—a departure from the two-dimensional dwarf aide-de-camp. After his knight Marcq succeeds in his heroic mission, Troncq sheds his grotesque shape and recaptures his previous beauty. At least one critic has viewed these characters' plight as symbolizing the human condition. The heroism of his master results in Troncq's being freed from his degraded status, just as the good works of Christians lead to their redemption on Judgment Day.[5] The transformations found in folklore—the frog-to-prince conversion—are employed here in the service of a heroic Christian theme.

During the sixteen and seventeenth centuries, both writers and readers exhibited a pervasive interest in fairies, who were the subjects of poetry and plays, one example being Shakespeare's *A Midsummer Night's Dream*. Fairies, like dwarfs, were often depicted as short-statured tricksters; however, in sharp contrast to the disproportionate dwarfs, they were generally depicted as attractive and their deeds as more mischievous than evil.

The Eighteenth Century

By the Age of Reason, interest in classical myth had grown, and the use of Celtic and Germanic folklore had declined. Dwarfs were represented less frequently in literature of the time, but in more varied ways. Oliver Goldsmith's parable *The Vicar of Wakefield* (1766) tells the story of a dwarf and a giant who become friends and agree to stick together in battle. The dwarf proves very courageous, but loses an arm, a leg, and finally an eye before triumphing. The giant remains unscathed and, adding insult to injury, marries the damsel. He importunes the dwarf: "'Come on, my little hero; this is glorious sport; let us get one victory more, and then we shall have honor for ever.'—'No,' cries the Dwarf, who was by this time grown wiser, 'no, I declare off; I'll fight no more; for I find in every battle that you get all the honor and rewards, but all the blows fall upon me.'"[6] The Vicar of Wakefield, the story's narrator, satirizes devious alliances that, in the name of heroism, wrong an innocent partner. Not until Edgar Allan Poe's "Hop-Frog" would a dwarf hero rebel so openly against victimization.

Three eighteenth-century poets offer disparate views of romance. While Edmund Waller wrote a sentimental tribute to the "match contrived by Nature" of painter Richard Gibson and his wife Anne Shepherd—both of them short statured—Alexander Pope and Christopher Smart confront a very different situation: the prospect of risking humiliation by wooing a desirable, average-statured woman. Here first is Pope's lament:

> Giants, that durst invade the Sky
> By wrathful Pow'rs were doom'd to Die;
> Shall better Fate this Pygmy share,
> Who dares attempt a Heav'nly fair? . . .
> Strike this absurd Assailant Dead,
> And make his Grave his Bridal Bed.
> This Lofty Tree to Heaven Aspires
> And who can blame his Bold Desires?
> 'Tis for that End he seems so grown,
> And therefore's wondered at by none.
> But if some humble shrub would soar,
> Meant for the ground, and nothing more,
> All this pretending Folly chide
> And laugh at its prepost'rous Pride.[7]

The four-foot-six-inch Pope feels it is hubris to contemplate a romance with a tall woman he admires. By contrast, Christopher Smart, another extremely short poet, is determined to convince the object of his desires of his own desirability:

> YES, contumelius fair, you scorn
> The amorous dwarf that courts you to his arms,
> But ere you leave him quite forlorn,

And to some youth gigantic yield your charms,

Hear him—oh hear him, if you will not try,

And let your judgment check th'ambition of your eye . . .

Say, is it wise or just to scan

Your lover's worth by quantity or weight . . .

Look in the glass, survey that cheek—

Where FLORA has with all her roses blush'd;

The shape so tender—look so meek—

The breasts made to be press'd, not to be crush'd—

Then turn to me,—turn with obliging eyes,

Nor longer nature's works, in miniature despise.[8]

The Nineteenth Century

ROMANCE, SENTIMENTALITY, AND COMPASSION

In the nineteenth and early twentieth centuries, dwarf characters fall into two general categories (which at times may overlap). In the first, they are essentially good human beings who are sinned against by society and are sympathetically and sentimentally portrayed; in the second, they are twisted in body and mind and intent on wreaking revenge.

Among the early romances is *The New Melusina* by Johann Wolfgang von Goethe, in which instead of portraying the longings of a dwarf man, as do Pope and Smart, he describes the experiences of an average-statured man as he becomes involved with a mysterious dwarf woman. This work, originally published in 1817, was later incorporated by Goethe into the second half of his *Wilhelm Meister's Travels*. It is based upon a folktale about a water sprite, Melusina, who marries Raymond of Poitiers, cautioning him that he must not see her on Saturdays. Once he breaks their agreement and discovers her secret—that she turns into a mermaid on that day—Melusina leaves him.

Goethe's story is far more complex. A young man, down on his luck, encounters a beautiful young woman and is attracted both to her and to her evident wealth. He uncovers her secret by opening a casket that he has carried for her that she has forbidden him to open. After he catches sight of her miniaturized form, she reveals that she is a descendant of Eckwald, king of the elves. Although her lover has betrayed her repeatedly and she has vowed to part from him, he prevails on her to change her mind. She agrees on the condition that he become as small as she is, and they return to her kingdom and marry. The marriage is short lived, however, and the storyteller complains, "I had an ideal of myself, and often in dreams I appeared to myself as a giant. In short, the wife, the ring, the dwarfed figure, and many other bonds made me so thoroughly and completely wretched that I began to give earnest thought to my deliverance."[9] In the end, the young man escapes, unsentimentally and without regrets.

Critical commentaries have interpreted this work as reflecting Goethe's attitude about being trapped by an inferior woman[10]—his negative view of marriage. They see the protagonist as transformed into a dwarf by his excess passion and imagination, and he is rehabilitated from his "degradation" by the same passionate impulse. To a modern reader, this "hero" might seem a dissolute, opportunistic narcissist whose grandiosity has no foundation in any actual accomplishments. But for many of Goethe's contemporaries, marriage to a dwarf, even a beautiful, wealthy, principled, charming, musical dwarf, is "marrying down."

Dwarf characters abound in the romantic novels and dramatic poems of the nineteenth and early twentieth century. A few are noteworthy; many more are commonplace. One of the more engaging novels is *The Black Dwarf* by Sir Walter Scott, who also wrote *Peveril of the Peak*, which features the real-life court dwarf Jeffery Hudson (see Chapter 1). *The Black Dwarf* was inspired by Scott's observation of David Ritchie, a dwarfed itinerant brush-maker from Edinburgh. In his introduction, Scott writes: "Tired at length of being the object of shouts, laughter, and derision, David Ritchie resolved, like a deer hunted from the herd, to retreat to some wilderness, where he might have the least possible communication with the world who scoffed at him."[11] Ritchie, three and a half feet high and with a significant deformity, had nevertheless succeeded in building a solid cottage of stone and turf with the assistance of passersby. Scott used Ritchie's actual appearance and his misanthropic nature as a model for Elshender the Recluse, or the Black Dwarf. But Scott assigned Elshender a beneficent role in the affairs of several of the novel's protagonists. Elshender's true identity is revealed as that of Sir Edward Manley, whose betrayal by a friend, along with the world's response to his deformity, had embittered him. It may be that Scott's own deformity (he had a withered leg caused by polio) led him to reinvent Elshender and portray him empathetically, thereby making his dwarf character the most memorable one in an otherwise mundane, romantic novel.

In Benjamin Barker's obscure *The Dwarf of the Channel*, John Ellery, an old deformed dwarf who is also an active and wise ship's pilot, assists two women who have confided their romantic problems to him.[12] The ensuing complicated plot contains a revelation scene in which Ellery discovers that one of these women is in fact his daughter, whose existence he had never known about. She had been born to his former wife who, unable to accept Ellery's deformity, had left him for a man who proved to be a bounder. All ends well, with Ellery's former wife begging his forgiveness, his daughters happy with their spouses, and the author affirming that inner character outweighs outer appearance.

The belated acceptance of dwarfs in a family is treated in yet another British tale, Fergus Hume's "The Dwarf's Chamber."[13] A poor fiddler, Warwick, meets Selina Lelandro, the owner of an estate that has a room that her dwarf ancestors once lived in. Lelandro, known as "Madame Tot," shows Warwick pictures of them, and then discovers that Warwick's father had been an exhibiting dwarf and that Warwick himself is in fact her grandson. With the veil of shame and secrecy lifted, so is the curse that has plagued the family since Sir James Lelandro had stolen a cup from the little people. As early as 1896, when "The Dwarf's Chamber" was written, lingering supernatural elements were being combined with naturalistic ones to produce a romantic novel whose plot questioned prejudice against dwarfs.

THE BITTER, VENGEFUL DWARF

Melodrama is more typical than romantic empathy in nineteenth-century works with dwarf protagonists. Characteristically, an embittered dwarf is shown plotting revenge when his love is rejected. Probably the most renowned of such characters had appeared two centuries earlier in Shakespeare's *Richard III* (Richard was arguably a dwarf himself). He expresses his self-hatred in the following celebrated soliloquy:

> I, that am curtail'd of this fair proportion
> Cheated of feature by dissembling nature
> Deform'd, unfinish'd, sent before my time
> Into this breathing world, scarce half made up
> . . . since I cannot prove a lover,
> To entertain these fair well-spoken days,
> I am determined to prove a villain.[14]

A gripping monologue by a vengeful dwarf occurs in James Rees's *The Dwarf, a Dramatic Poem* (1839). In this drama, the dwarf, Bartholo, is in love with his mistress; Iago-like, he betrays her beloved Paoli in an unsuccessful suit for her love. He rails:

> Ay! There they be like sheep to their destruction.
> They little deem how near their traitor stood
> That shall spoil all. I, the deformed, the mad
> Misshapen dwarf, shall sting and laugh at them.

Their ribald jests, their sneers and buffets, are
Nursed up in vengeance. Oh, 'tis sweet to turn
On the oppressor . . .
These shapeless limbs
Encase a feeling heart—How the fool man
Would hear the dwarf, misshapen dog,
The hunchback, talk of love—And yet I love,
And love so deeply, that the passion must
Be life or death to me.[15]

Such powerful, impassioned words may be moving for a general audience, but it is painful for dwarfs to encounter such intense self-hatred. Similar protagonists turn up in other nineteenth-century plays. George Darley, a minor nineteenth-century English poet and dramatist, uses a female character named Dwerga (Dwarf) in his drama *Thomas à Becket*.[16] The abused and evil representative of a malevolent mistress, she describes herself as having been raised on toadstools and mandrakes—a familiar folkloric touch.

Although less stereotyped than Dwerga and refreshingly "un-grim," Daniel Quilp, of *The Old Curiosity Shop* by Charles Dickens, is no less sinister. He is the evil foil for Little Nell's unrelenting goodness, evicting Nell and her grandfather and transforming the happy pair into homeless wanderers. With gusto, he revenges himself upon a youth who has called him "an uglier dwarf than can be seen anywhere for a penny." He describes his physical shortcomings in an ironic, mocking fashion designed to make others uneasy. He inquires of his loving, long-suffering wife: "Am I nice to look at? Should I be the handsomest creature in the world had I but whiskers? Am I a lady's man as it is? Am I, Mrs. Quilp?" And his response to her valiant efforts to locate him during a rainstorm could not be less pleasant: "'I'm glad you're cold. I'm glad you've lost your way. I'm glad your eyes are red with crying. It does my heart good to see your little nose so pinched and frosty.' . . . 'Did she think I was dead?' said Quilp, wrinkling his face in a most extraordinary series of grimaces. 'Did she think she was going to have all the money, and to marry someone she liked? Ha ha ha! Did she?'"[17]

Quilp does not try to seem lovable: instead he displays egotism, resourcefulness, and sick humor. He entertains and abuses the agreeable lot around him with his wicked tongue until consigned by Dickens to a grisly death. His misdeeds are rooted in his intrinsic mean-spiritedness rather than in how the world has treated him.

Most other dwarf protagonists have been victimized. In Hermann Hesse's 1904 story "The Dwarf," the intelligent, loyal, resourceful dwarf Filippo is enraged when his beloved lame dog is drowned by the suitor of his mistress, Margherita. Filippo prepares a poisonous potion but both suitor and dwarf die as a result of drinking it, and Margherita goes mad. Although Hesse's sympathies are clearly with Filippo, good does not triumph inexorably over evil.[18]

The revenge of Hop-Frog, Edgar Allan Poe's memorable hero in his eponymous story, is more violent and more successful. His actions are inspired by righteous indignation—and he devises a barbaric scheme to punish his tormentors. Hop-Frog, a partially crippled dwarf, is a court jester who has been given that ludicrous name by the king's ministers because of his unusual gait. His intimate friend Trippetta is a beautiful proportionate dwarf. When the king and his ministers tease Hop-Frog, making him drunk against his will, Trippetta, formerly the king's favorite, intervenes. This time, though, the king abuses her as well.

Hop-Frog comes up with an idea for a masquerade that the king and ministers have pressed him to create for them. After disguising them as orangutans, to shock and terrify others at the ball, Hop-Frog has Trippetta hoist them high in the hall, while he gloats from above and sets them ablaze. While the king and councilors are being incinerated, Hop-Frog and Trippetta make a successful escape. Readers, in spite of the horror, can exult at this triumph of justice. The dwarf characters are depicted as better human beings than their doomed oppressors. This is an unusual outcome—most of the numerous humiliation scenes in stories about dwarfs are followed neither by successful retaliation nor by happy endings.

Interestingly, when my daughter, Anna, was in the seventh grade, the teacher, who was about to read "Hop-Frog" with the class, telephoned me, concerned that because she was a dwarf Anna might be hurt or offended. I encouraged the teacher not to hesitate, but rather to discuss "Hop-Frog" with the students. She did—and Anna liked the story. I remembered how, when she was younger, I had arranged to be the accompanying mother when her elementary school class went to see *Snow White and the Seven Dwarfs* in order to deal with her response and her classmates'. I need not have worried: she felt, as the other students did, that the production was silly. In junior high school, however, Anna was terribly unsettled by *The Elephant Man;* the sadism that the central character's deformity elicited proved unbearable to watch.

I have injected this personal note in recognition that literature can never be emotionally neutral and that this chapter is not simply an objective review. It really *does* matter how these works are experienced by members of the group being portrayed, as well as by their families and friends. It is hard now to imagine that whites once laughed at Step'n'Fetchit, with no awareness of the humiliation that blacks might perceive. The following incident, brought to light in an insightful article by pediatric orthopedist Dr. James Gamble, is an example of consciousness-raising that occurred a century before that term was invented.[19]

Neither authors nor readers seem to have reflected much upon how dwarfs

51. Miss Mowcher. From Charles Dickens, David Copperfield with Forty Illustrations by "Phiz"
(New York: Oxford University Press, 1948).

might respond to being portrayed as ridiculous. Charles Dickens inserted a number
of strikingly unlikable short-statured characters into several of his works without
causing any commotion. However, in one instance, a caricature that he had created
became the occasion for a successful protest by the model for the character. In his
monthly serialization of *David Copperfield* in 1849–1850, Dickens introduced a ludicrous dwarf character named Miss Mowcher. Jane Seymour Hill, a manicurist and

chiropodist who lived near Dickens's home, recognized herself in too many details for the resemblance to have been coincidental. She initiated a correspondence that resulted in Dickens's transformation of the character.[20] She writes:

> Sir:
>
> If you had attacked me in the full time of health wealth and happiness I think perhaps I could have borne it with patience but now widowed in all but my good name you shew up personal deformities with insinuations that by the purest of my sex may be construed to the worst of purposes. All know you have drawn my portrait.
>
> I admit it but the vulgar slang of language I deny. May your Widow and Children never meet with such Blighting wit as you have poured on my miserably nervous head. Should your book be dramatized and I not protected madness will be the result. I have suffered long and much from my personal deformities but never before at the hands of a man so highly gifted as Charles Dickens and hitherto considered as a Christian and Friend to his fellow Creatures.
>
> Now you have made my nights sleepless and my daily work tearful. Tell me how I have deserved your anger. Waiting your answer I remain . . .
>
> With all due respect
>
> Yrs.
>
> Jane Hill[21]

Dickens responded, "Madam. I am most exceedingly and unfeigningly sorry to have been the unfortunate occasion of giving you a moment's distress."[22] He went on to acknowledge that his description had been based on his observation of her general manner, but that in fact Miss Mowcher's character, like others in his books, was a composite of several persons. Nevertheless, he apologized and promised that while he had not originally intended to make Miss Mowcher "a very good character," he would now do so (Fig. 51).

Within a day, Dickens received a letter from Mrs. Hill's solicitor, indicating that she would sue for libel unless the character were indeed promptly redrawn. Dickens wrote back explaining that the revised portrait would have to wait until it could be inserted in a later episode, but that he would certainly keep his pledge. He did so admirably, making Miss Mowcher's character more thoughtful and soul searching, and having her play a beneficent role in David Copperfield's life. When David proclaimed himself surprised at her expression of genuine feeling, Miss Mowcher replies, "They are all surprised, these inconsiderate young people, fairly and full grown, to see any natural feeling in a little thing like me! They make a plaything of me, use me for their amusement, throw me away when they are tired, and wonder that I feel more than a toy horse or a wooden soldier! . . . If there are people so unreflecting or so cruel as to make a jest of me, what is left for me to do but make a jest of myself, them, and everything!" She offers David a final admonition: "Try not to associate bodily defects with mental, my good friend, except for a solid reason. . . Trust me no more, but trust me no less, than you would trust a full sized woman."[23]

Dickens went well beyond his original pledge to make Miss Mowcher a good character: the author transformed her into a heroine. He seems to have reacted not only to the threat of a lawsuit, but also out of genuine empathy for Hill, which had deepened his understanding of his evolving character. Lest it be thought that Dickens was incapable of sensitive treatment of dwarf characters without prodding, the reader is directed to two other works with dwarfs. Dickens contributed a chapter to the serial "A House to Let" in *Household Words* that features a dwarf character called Mr. Chops, whom Dickens describes as having a fine and poetic mind. Confined in the fraudulent world of the freak show, Mr. Chops insists that he is "formed for society." However, he finds society as unyielding as the sideshow and, disillusioned, meets a tragic end. Mr. Chops may be seen as an prototypical artist; a paid oddity, he was like Dickens himself—their artistic sensibility and growth in wisdom caused them to feel beset by a sense of alienation.[24]

An even more important and complex character than Mr. Chops is Jenny Wren, the little "person of the house" of Dickens's last completed novel, *Our Mutual Friend*. Wren supports herself as a dressmaker for dolls; she is described as short and lame and with a hunched back, spinal curvature, extreme pallor, and bouts of severe pain—the cause of her condition has been disputed.[25] The daughter, and granddaughter, of drunkards, she must parent her father as well as cope with her own life. Although impoverished, she is nevertheless confident, capable, and nimble fingered, and she manages to provide for herself economically and emotionally.

Her physical infirmities are more than offset by her extraordinary vitality and perspicacity—she is not a sentimental figure, a pathetic and flawless cripple like Tiny Tim. In this late work Dickens has created a multifaceted dwarf character: Jenny Wren is capable of absorption in fantasy, perspicacious judgments, vengeful feelings and acts—and ultimately nurturance and close human connection. She evolves during the course of the novel, reinventing herself. First encountered as a guarded thirteen-year-old, she matures into full womanhood, overcoming many of the difficulties imposed by her physical and social constraints. This is a rare early realistic novel in which a dwarf character defies stereotype.

The Twentieth Century

HISTORICAL FICTION AND SCI-FI FANTASY

The romantic tradition is most notable in the first part of the twentieth century, but there are occasional reminders of it even during its final decades. Some of the most recent examples occur in historical fiction and science fiction, whose heroes are more assertive and less pitiable than their predecessors in earlier romantic fiction.

A poignant early example, Oscar Wilde's *The Birthday of the Infanta* (inspired by the Velázquez painting of the same name), tells the story of a young Spanish princess and her dwarf attendant. Wilde recounts the tale of a young dwarf found in the woods the day before the princess's birthday party. The youth is brought to the celebration to dance for and amuse the princess, but although his performance proves the highlight of the entertainment, the event ends disastrously. Mocked by the crowd and having become a mere plaything of the Infanta, with whom he has fallen in love, the dwarf sees himself in the mirror for the first time, recognizes his deformity, and falls to the ground sobbing. He then dies of a broken heart. The Infanta cries out disdainfully, "For the future, let those who come to play with me have no hearts."[26]

Wilde inserts fanciful elements into his drama—flowers that deride the dwarf and birds and lizards that show appreciation. While he obviously intends to satirize the court and stir in the reader a sympathetic response to the dwarf, the scene in which the dwarf recognizes his true appearance provokes a variety of reactions. The dwarf can be viewed as a tragic hero or as merely pitiable. Once again, a dwarf's self-awareness is assumed to lead inevitably to self-hatred. In spite of his attempt to impart social criticism, Wilde offers a message carrying an implicit acceptance of traditional standards of beauty, a message that precludes any chance that his dwarf character can transcend stereotype. This work continues to attract modern readers and has been adapted as a theme by composers (see Chapter 10).

The rejection theme abounds in the popular twentieth-century romantic novel. In Edith Oliver's *Dwarf's Blood* (1901), Nicholas Roxerby, the owner of a grand family estate, rejects his dwarf son, Hans, in part because Hans reminds Nicholas of his own disagreeable dwarf mother. Hans's mother, however, manages to balance the love of both husband and son. The adult Hans becomes a successful artist, his father matures, and the family rift is healed.[27]

The true masterpiece of this romantic era of dwarf protagonists is Walter de la Mare's *Memoirs of a Midget* (1922).[28] De la Mare was first and foremost a poet, and this is a poetic rendering of the consequences of physical difference for the human spirit. Its heroine, Miss M. (or Midgetina), is a young Englishwoman, the only child of bourgeois parents—an impractical, kindly father and a sensitive, sometimes emotionally distant mother. The novel is ostensibly a memoir written by Miss M.

De la Mare offers an imaginative exploration not only of diminutive stature, but also of the universal outsider role. Miss M.'s marginality can be compared to the position of the poet in society—an uneasy participant-observer with a heightened consciousness of the sensual and emotional. From early childhood, Miss M. is exquisitely sensitive to natural beauty and the nuances of others' behavior. Despite her parents' attentiveness, she recognizes that she has been "a disappointment and mischance" to them. When their deaths lead to her being thrust into the world, she proves herself a person on whom no experience is lost. She changes and grows, coming to appreciate the values of her unpolished landlady, Mrs. Bowater, and rejecting the false values of her patron, Mrs. Monnerie. Her passionate love for Fannie, Mrs. Bowater's daughter, and Fannie's volatile responses, are described with great subtlety; Mr. Anon, the dwarf whose love she does not return, is painted with murkier strokes. Even though she occasionally finds herself exhibiting pretensions similar to others in her social world, Miss M. possesses an underlying honesty that struggles to break through. She never spares herself.

The ornate style of this novel presents a challenge to modern readers. Yet the possibility that this provocative, original work featuring a dwarf protagonist may continue to be of interest to the current generation is suggested by the appearance of a new edition in 2004 and subsequent positive reviews. When *Memoirs of a Midget* was first published, novelist [Margaret] Storm Jameson called it "the most notable achievement in prose of our generation . . . a book of such exquisite and finished art that its words have the importance of threads in some tapestry of fabled beauty."[29]

A very different romantic, tragic account, featuring a dwarf couple, was presented in Aldous Huxley's first novel, *Crome Yellow* (1923).[30] Both de la Mare's novel and Huxley's are assaults on pretension. The events described in Huxley's novel take place during the weekend party of an artistic, socially elite set, reminiscent of the Bloomsbury circle, at the country home of Henry Wimbush. Wimbush reads aloud a gripping biography of the house's previous owner, the dwarf Hercules, a baronet. Despite his family's extraordinary efforts to make Hercules grow, by means of a generous meat diet, exercise, and stretchings on a rack worthy of the Inquisition, he never measured more than three feet four inches. His father rejected him, calling him an "abortion" and a "lusus naturae," Subsequently, his father avoided all company and took to drink, dying of apoplexy. Hercules' loving mother died of typhoid fever a year later, when Hercules was twenty-one.

Having the advantage of a considerable fortune, striking good looks, and intellectual and musical accomplishments, Hercules had set about fashioning a world that was made to order for him, an environment built to scale, populated with Shetland ponies and King Charles spaniels and other breeds of small animals. Gradually, he accumulated a staff of servants who were also dwarfs. Having suffered mockery when he fell in love with average-statured women, he sought a short-statured wife, finding one, Filomena, in Italy. Both beautiful and musically talented, she was the perfect mate for him, and they led an idyllic existence until their happiness was shattered when Filomena gave birth to a son, Ferdinando, who grew to be a crude, violent, averaged-statured man who ridiculed his parents and led the family to a tragic end.

During the following half century, romantic fiction in which dwarfs played a role would become less frequent; by the 1970s the genre resurfaced, typically in the form of historical novels. During the past several decades, a number of works have appeared that sympathetically portray a dwarf's struggle toward identity and acceptance.

In 1973 Francine Prose published *The Glorious Ones*, a historical novel about a group of entertainers.[31] A well-written early work by this novelist, it offers only a constricted role to its dwarf actress. As an adolescent, she is "rescued" from a school run by nuns; in the process, her rescuer, the leader of the troupe, describes her physical appearance in painfully disparaging terms. The fact that he later has a sexual encounter with her—and makes complimentary remarks about her soul—does not assuage her hurt about his ridicule of her body. Neither her effort to rationalize his nature nor the fact that she has sexual appeal for others offers adequate recompense for the heroine of this pre-identity-movement novel.

Barbara Jefferis followed with her historical novel *The Tall One* (1977).[32] After various misadventures, the tall Mary-Mary is married to Umphrey the dwarf, a member of a performing troupe. She rejects him, ultimately paying him to leave her. His character is thinly sketched and his behavior largely irrelevant: no kindness of his can reverse the truism that marriage to a dwarf is a misfortune.

Ruth Park's *Swords and Crowns and Rings* (1978) offers a rich, nonstereotyped portrait of Jackie Hannah, an Australian dwarf. The author explores Jackie's childhood, romances, and work life in evocative prose, documenting his both external and internal struggles. After a period marked by harrowing bereavements, Jackie is driven into a violent fight that begins with his being taunted about his size. Afterward, he reflects: "Grief, remorse, self-pity—he had experienced them all. Then one night he realised that what had been distilled from all these painful sorrows was purest rage. It was rage at life, fate, whatever it was that had distorted him in the womb and made his life dependent upon that fact, no matter what hopeful lies his parents had told him. For weeks, the rage trembled within him, and then it, too, came to terms with its causes. . . . It struck him then that all he had or ever would have was himself, and a moment to be himself in; and the knowledge was complete and exhausting. 'I'm me,' he said. 'And no one can take that away unless I let them.'"[33]

Another work about a sensitive young man seeking a positive identity is an English novel set in the Scottish Highlands, Vesper Hunter's *Jacon* (1989).[34] The dwarf hero leaves his family and the town where he had lived, both of which have made him feel unwelcome, and makes a life for himself, proving his self-sufficiency in the rugged, windswept environment of nineteenth-century northern Scotland. His loving connection to a young blind woman—though not always emotionally convincing—is at the heart of this novel.

Dominic (1991), by Kathleen Robinson, traces the adventures of a dwarf in fourth-century Europe.[35] While a member of a pagan acrobatic troupe, the main character is sold into slavery in Constantinople, where he studies philosophy. Finally, escaping torture in Rome, he makes his way toward Denmark. The novel contains the obligatory birth-acceptance and humiliation scenes common in books about dwarfs, but it is nevertheless of interest to us here, being a bildungsroman in which a dwarf is the central character rather than a bit player.

In contrast to the romanticism found in the works described to this point, the recently published works of George R. R. Martin and Christopher Stone are built around the actions of both heroes and antiheroes who are involved in almost constant conflict. Martin's series *A Song of Fire and Ice* is a contemporary epic fantasy about the intrigues that simmer between warring kingdoms of a feudal era, in lands where summers can last decades and winters a lifetime. The first volume of the projected six, *A Game of Thrones,* appeared to considerable acclaim in 1996; three additional volumes, also popular, have been published since.[36]

The series follows a number of interlocking dramas, filled with blunt language, warfare, sex, incest, and abuses of power; equally in evidence are heroism, cowardice, dogged endurance, and magical events. Tyrion, a dwarf character who is perhaps patterned on Shakespeare's Richard III, is a "good villain." Though he seems to be in his twenties, his intimate knowledge of events that occurred long ago mark him as much older. He is a brilliant military strategist who likes to take comfort in the bed of a good-looking, lower-class woman, whom he calls "sweetling" and treats with tenderness.

In the figure of Tyrion, Martin captures the ridicule that the dwarf must endure from persons who call him "Halfman," as well as the physical pain he experiences, as when his legs tighten and ache after he walks any distance. When a boy asks him why he reads so much, he responds:

Fourteen, and you're taller than I will ever be. My legs are short and twisted and I walk with difficulty. I require a special saddle to keep from falling off my horse. A saddle of my own design, you may be interested to know. It was either that or ride a pony. My arms are strong enough, but again too short. I will never make a swordsman. Had I been born a peasant, I might have been left to die or sold to some slaver's grotesquerie. Alas, I was born a Lannister of Casterly Rock. . . . I must do my part for the honor of my House, wouldn't you agree? Yet how? Well, my legs may be too small for my body, but my head is too large, although I prefer to think it is just large enough for my mind. . . . My mind is my weapon. . . . That is why I read so much.[37]

Memoirs of a Gnostic Dwarf by David Madsen (pseudonym of a European philosopher and theologian) is a scatological novel, recommended only for those willing to wrestle with its esoteric vocabulary and be rocked by the violence, intrigue, and pathos of its narrative of sixteenth-century Italy.[38] Anyone who gets through the opening pages, however, which describe Pope Leo being treated for anal fissures, may find that the novel does offer some rewards. It traces the conflict between the Vatican and Martin Luther and follows the shifting political alliances of the day. In addition, it exposes, through its narrator, Peppi—a dwarf much abused in childhood—the vagaries of both sideshow and court. Peppi evolves into an increasingly complex and deep character, his view of life shaped by his Gnostic philosophy.

A modest recent contribution to fantasy literature is Chris Bunch's *The Empire Stone*.[39] Its plot follows a familiar pattern: the young hero, Pierol of the Moorlands, sets out to claim and bring back the Empire Stone, a jewel with a long history, that is reputed to hold supernatural powers. Pierol, a dwarf who is an expert in gemstones, is able to wield a certain amount of magic of his own, not nearly as much as his prospective father-in-law, the wizard Abba. In the course of the novel, Pierol wages many battles; killing evil enemies in many lands, before realizing his quest for the Stone. Casual sex without much feeling is the rule. While Pierol's relationship with Kima, daughter of Abba, is a romantic one, it is not deep enough to interfere with his roving spirit.

When an interviewer asked Bunch why he had made his protagonist a dwarf, the author replied, "I like the idea of my heroes, or anti-heroes, or semi-heroes, to have some problems. So why not a dwarf? Every little person I've ever met seems to be hellaciously bad-a**ed. Their intransigence is admirable."[40] Bunch seems to have researched gemstones more thoroughly than the psychology of dwarfs. Nevertheless, many fantasy aficionados may find his book a page-turner.

BITTERNESS AND REVENGE AND DISAGREEABLE DWARFS

Until recently, sympathetic romances have been the exception. Some of the best-known and most highly respected twentieth-century novels with dwarf protagonists have perpetuated stereotypes, portraying dwarfs as either malevolent or pitiable. The authors of two such novels have received the highest honors that are awarded to writers: Pär Lagerkvist, author of *The Dwarf* (1945), won the Nobel Prize for literature; Elias Canetti, author of *Auto-da-Fé* (1946) received both the Nobel Prize for literature and the Prix International.[41]

The Dwarf is generally regarded as Lagerkvist's masterpiece. Although his antihero's personality is an invention, the novel's background is based on the court of Ludovico Moro, the Black Duke of Milan, who was a patron of Leonardo da Vinci and is depicted as Bernardo in the novel. The duke kept many dwarfs, including one called Iannici. Whereas the real Iannici faithfully followed Moro into exile in 1491, Lagerkvist's work ends with the dwarf in chains, but still seeking to be restored to his master's favor. There is no reason to suppose that the original model was evil incarnate, as Lagerkvist paints him. And although Dorothy Canfield sees the dwarf's evil nature as representing a universal element, present in us all, it is not a general philosophy applicable to all humankind that leaps out at the reader, but rather the personification of dwarf as evil.[42] Lagerkvist has the dwarf express unrelieved malevolence: "It is my fate that I hate my own people. My race is detestable to me. But I hate myself too. I eat my own splenetic flesh. I drink my own poisoned blood." In his novel, Lagerkvist perpetuates a number of myths, including that dwarfs are born old and that they are sterile, born of those "haughty creatures"—members of the detested human race: "We dwarfs beget no young, we are sterile by virtue of our own nature. We have nothing to do with the perpetuation of life; we do not even desire it. . . . We belong to that race and at the same time we stand outside it. We are guests on a visit. Ancient wizened guests on a visit which has lasted for thousands of years."[43]

A more recent work, the George Herman mystery *A Comedy of Murders* (1994), features some of the same characters as appear in *The Dwarf,* but here there is quite a different mood and purpose.[44] In this historical romp, Herman reinvents Leonardo da Vinci as an imaginative detective, and Niccolo, the dwarf, as his admiring young apprentice. Niccolo is an active, positive character with a philosophical bent; he is adventurous (he tests Leonardo's flying machine) and enjoys a romantic attachment. Apart from being based on the same characters, the two novels thus have nothing in common. Lagerkvist, a Swede, created an Italian antihero that is best understood as the spiritual descendant of mythical Scandinavian and Germanic dwarfs. The disagreeable dwarf characters of Canetti's *Auto-da-Fé*—despite Canetti's Italian nationality—and Knut Hamsun's *Mysteries* (1921), discussed below, also reflect the influence of that northern European tradition.[45]

In Canetti's *Auto-da-Fé*, Kien, a mad Sinologist and bibliophile, is inadequate to life in the real world. Wandering about the city, he encounters Fischerle, a Jewish dwarf, chess player, and pimp, who cheats the gullible Kien while pretending to be his greatest advocate. Fischerle engages in grandiose boasts about his chess-playing ability and remarks, "The miseries have got brains, that's what I say. What's the good of brains to a handsome fellow?" At the same time, he is cautious to the point of paranoia: "A Jew has to be on guard against deadly enemies. Hump-backed dwarfs and others who have nevertheless managed to rise to the rank of pimp, cannot be too careful."[46]

In yet another dwarf stereotype, Fischerle appears as a man on the margins of society, twisted in mind and body. Ironically, Canetti, who was of Jewish descent, is the creator of this large-nosed Jewish caricature. Iris Murdoch has praised *Auto-da-Fé* as one of the greatest novels of the century; while it satirizes intellectuals and materialists, however, it makes one more gratuitous contribution to the gallery of depraved dwarfs.[47]

A number of other negative dwarf characters are configured as merely pitiable. Hamsun in *Mysteries* presents a strange visitor, Johann Nagel, who comes to town inquiring about a murder. At the inn he encounters a dwarf whom he at first seems to rescue from a tormenting humiliation and befriend, but ultimately humiliates as well. It is not uncommon for a short-statured character in literature to be referred to only as "the Dwarf," encouraging a tendency to reduce the individual to the limitations imposed by physical form. In *Mysteries,* the dwarf is similarly called simply "Midget." Midget, described as ugly and of limited intelligence, eventually shows some cleverness and attains a measure of revenge, but Hamsun's intent in creating this character is not easily discernible. Like *Auto-da-Fé, Mysteries* presents an unsympathetic protagonist who is accompanied by a pitiable dwarf, serving as his foil.

José Donoso's *The Obscene Bird of Night* (1970) is another highly praised novel, the recipient of critical acclaim and literary prizes.[48] It is also a grotesque, rambling tale that in some may even inspire revulsion. The handsome aristocrat Don Jeronimo fathers a dwarf who has many deformities and, upon viewing his child, is appalled: "When Jeronimo finally parted the crib's curtains to look at his long-awaited offspring, he wanted to kill him then and there; the loathsome, gnarled body writhing on its hump, its mouth a gaping, bestial hole in which palate and nose bared obscene bones and tissues in an incoherent cluster of reddish traits, was chaos, disorder, a different but worse form of death."[49] Donoso strives to create the most shocking and abhorrent description of an infant possible, thereby setting the scene for Jeronimo's later decision to confine his son to a magnificent mansion replete with distorted images, artistic and human. Among the artworks are a statue of the huntress Diana, humpbacked and with an acromegalic jaw and crooked legs, and a nude Apollo with a harelip, disproportionate arms, and an enormous dangling sex organ. The purpose of all this is to create an artificial, monstrous world in which Boy, Jeronimo's son, never knowing normalcy, would have no standard of beauty to compare himself with that would shame him.

Another novel with odd, deformed protagonists has engendered much controversy. *Geek Love* (1989) by Katherine Dunn is ostensibly a comic novel about human peculiarity.[50] It is narrated by Olympia, a bald, hunchbacked, albino dwarf. She and her siblings are the children of Aloysius Binewski, the second-generation owner of a traveling carnival, and his wife, Lil; the pair have experimented with tetragenic chemicals in order to produce several freak offspring whom they intend to employ to make their sideshow more bizarre and lucrative. This fantastic parable exploring the grotesque on a variety of levels may alienate many readers at the outset because of its deliberately graphic descriptions of various extreme deformities. But for others, including critics parsing a postmodern philosophy of disability, it has proved to be a text with endless possibilities for discussion, among them its symbolic value as an exemplar of patrilineal capitalism.[51] Olympia's reflections on her own situation, and her encounter with Miss Lick, a philanthropist who finances the education of "physically ruined women" so that they may prepare themselves for professional careers, become a vehicle for meditations on what happens when individuals with freak identities contemplate making a leap toward "normalcy." *Geek Love* is both an original and an intentionally disturbing work.

All literary dwarfs are not required to be attractive, charming, and politically correct. Works with disagreeable dwarf characters may even approach greatness. One such work is Carson McCullers's gripping novella *The Ballad of the Sad Café* (1951), which contains a perverse dwarf character.[52] In a sleepy southern town, three lives intersect disastrously: those of Miss Amelia, the richest woman in town, who is a mannish, odd, six-foot-two-inch storekeeper and herbalist; Marvin Macy, the base ex-convict to whom she had been briefly married; and Cousin Lymon, a hunchbacked dwarf. Miss Amelia's inexplicable love for Lymon, who is depicted as mean-spirited and sickly, softens her, but she is betrayed and ruined by him when Lymon and Macy form an alliance against her.

The character of Lymon mimics the stereotype of the evil mythological dwarf—ugly in body and soul, and outside time: "When questioned directly about his age the hunchback professed to know absolutely nothing—he had no idea how long he had been on the earth, whether for ten years or a hundred!"

McCullers's fascination with the tangle of human love and hatred is at the heart of this work. Lymon, viewed only from an external vantage point, engenders feelings of revulsion; by contrast, the eccentric, emotionally crippled Miss Amelia arouses sympathy. What makes this work succeed is its vivid description of both character and landscape, its rendering of human emotion, and its understanding of the enormous influence that one's (often irrational) choice of love object exerts on one's life course.

NOVELS WITH SYMBOLIC AND MYTHOLOGICAL IMPORT

There is also a class of novels that build on dwarf mythology to deliver a moral message in a contemporary context. For example, John Gardner's *In the Suicide Mountains* (1977), while evoking folktales, has a very different modern message to deliver. Gardner creates three characters who are cast into suicidal depression by a society that has distorted expectations of them. Armida, a blacksmith's daughter, is strong and capable but is forced by her wicked stepmother to be falsely feminine. Prince Christopher the Sullen cares only about his violin and books; accused of being a sissy, he is sent on a dangerous mission. Chudu the Goat's Son is a dwarf (his father is a goat and his mother a magic fish); he is made a scapegoat for all the bad luck in the village and driven toward madness by the villagers' ostracism of him. The three companions meet on the way to Suicide Mountain, where all are determined to end their lives. Predictably, they recognize that their shared problems result from society's distortions. Christopher the Sullen and Armida marry and help each other to become their true selves; Chudu is made prime minister and, though now beloved, can still, when he pleases, frighten off enemies with his "calculated rages and crafty, sawtoothed smiles."[53]

Chudu, as the not-quite-human dwarf of myth, is disqualified from playing the romantic lead, yet he remains a prominent figure. Gardner explores how the community's misjudgment has made Chudu entertain angry and vindictive fantasies and how he struggles with his nature. *In the Suicide Mountains* is a folkloric exhortation to live one's life "in good faith" with oneself: Gardner defends his characters' right to their distinctive bodies and eccentric natures.

A work that had many admirers since its publication, and continues to enjoy a wide readership, is the trilogy *The Lord of the Rings* (1954–1956) by J.R.R. Tolkien.[54] Upon the release of popular films (2001–2003) based on the books, the author attracted an even larger public. In childhood, Tolkien had been fascinated by fairy tales and in adulthood, by works from Anglo-Saxon literature, such as *Beowulf,* and by Norse and Finnish myth; he even invented a new language based on Finnish (Tolkien was a philologist). Tolkien's Dwarves and Elves are derived most notably from Norse mythology, the Dwarves resembling their antecedents in the work they do and in their love of treasure. Tolkien's Dwarves, Elves, and Hobbits, however, are much more benign than their Norse counterparts. The battles they engage in are not glorified but portrayed in all their horror, in scenes influenced by Tolkien's witnessing the carnage of World War I.

Tolkien's gift for fantasy; his graphic descriptions of the domain he created, called Middle Earth, and of its inhabitants; and his Christian symbolism all contribute to the fascination that this work has had for critics. But it is perhaps his invention of the

Hobbits—Bilbo Baggins and Frodo, of *The Hobbit,* and Frodo of *The Lord of the Rings*—that accounts most for Tolkien's popularity. Hobbits are patterned after ordinary rustic English people, their smallness reflecting limited imaginations. Bilbo and Frodo, when they are chosen to perform knightly roles, must struggle with fear and self-doubt as they endeavor to transcend their own ordinariness. Perhaps this is why for young adults especially Tolkien's saga has such resonance: it appeals to their idealism, while allowing them to acknowledge themselves as flawed beings, vulnerable to temptation.

In contrast to the dragon Smaug and the slimy, degenerate creature Gollum—reminiscent of the dark beings of Germanic and Norse myth—Tolkien's short-statured tribes can be seen as generally pleasant in appearance. His small heroes may sometimes seem childlike, but they possess the capacity for personal growth. Devotees of fantasy will find these adventures a rich lode, with or without exegesis.[55]

In the literary tour de force by the German writer Günter Grass, *The Tin Drum* (1962), Grass deals with some of the same themes as did Walter de la Mare in *Memoirs of a Midget.*[56] In both novels, the dwarf protagonists symbolize the outsider role of the artist in society and are vehicles for social criticism. Both present in great detail the childhood and family lives of their heroes, unlike earlier works, in which dwarfs are solitary beings or simply one among many members of a tribe. Further, both protagonists sometimes earn their livings as performers. But the language that Grass uses to describe the novel's setting—the working-class town of Danzig—is often crude and incantatory: the novel's atmosphere is more redolent of cabbages than of columbines.

As H. Wayne Schow has pointed out, in *The Tin Drum* two genres coalesce.[57] One is the picaresque novel, in which the opportunistic rogue acts upon his environment and satirizes it, and the other is the bildungsroman, describing the coming of age of a reflective wanderer. This two-sided coin embossed with a dwarf image, and glittering with the patina of magic realism, results in a strange, unsettling novel. The dwarf Oskar narrates from an insane asylum, telling the tale of three generations of his family and society from 1899 to 1945 in tandem with his own quest for identity.

Like dwarfs of old, he has supernatural powers. At birth he is clairaudient—able to hear what is not present to the ear—and he has wisdom that no infant could possess. By the time he begins playing his drum at three, he can tell extraordinary tales with it and use it to disrupt or enchant his listener. In childhood, he often functions as trickster: he uses his powers (such as his ability to shatter glass) in the service of his impulses. Throughout life he maintains a precarious balance between his two exemplars—Rasputin and Goethe. They embody dwarfs' dual potential for evoking chaos or harmony. Ultimately, a single, integrated identity eludes him.

In the second part of the novel, however, Oskar decides to grow: his height increases from three feet to four feet two inches, and he achieves moral growth; unfortunately, along with these changes he also he acquires a hump. By becoming an apprentice stonecutter and contributing to his family's support, he rejects the crude materialism of post–World War II Germany, which he abhors, but he never achieves the ethical epiphany of the heroes of the bildungsroman—unattainable in this repugnant substitute for "civilization."

Oskar serves as a complex metaphor for critic, outsider, artist, tortured sensual/rational modern man. The reader may perhaps yearn for a more sympathetic portrayal of humankind, but such is not the author's vision. The volume includes many specific references to Oskar's dwarf stature. His size enables him to be an obscure observer or to be childlike, but most important, it grants him significance. As the dwarf performer Bebra puts it, "His place is on a crowded rostrum or beneath it." He must learn to deal with his difference and transcend it, becoming, as he says, "superior to my hump."[58]

The Tin Drum is a satirical puzzle that maintains an implicit respect for its hero. The film may prove harder to take: its visual imagery of squirming eels and rough sensuality, and its graphic presentation of Nazi exploitation of dwarf actors, offers a more visceral experience, with less room for reflection.

THE REALISTIC NOVEL OF THE PAST FEW DECADES

It will be a long time, if ever, before dwarf stock characters cease to make cameo appearances in works by writers seeking a certain kind of "atmosphere." Ray Bradbury, in *Something Wicked This Way Comes,* includes a dwarf among the supernatural spectral carnival figures who terrify his adolescent heroes. A homosexual dwarf with buckskin ankle boots appears in Tama Janowitz's *A Cannibal in Manhattan*; he has little reason to be in the story beyond contributing a bit of farcical noisemaking. Glocken, in Katherine Anne Porter's *Ship of Fools,* is a hunchbacked dwarf newsdealer who evokes uneasiness in the other travelers with whom he is journeying on a ship from Germany to Mexico; at one point he becomes a "symbol of degradation," the focal point for a discussion of eugenics. The dwarf character Andreev, the brilliant scientist and master sculptor whose work helps solve the case in Martin Cruz Smith's *Gorky Park,* is introduced as a specimen among specimens, sitting on a stool among sculptures of Peking and Neanderthal man. A step above pure caricature, these four novels present dwarf individuals with lives and occupations. Nevertheless, they figure as little more than props whose main function is mood enhancement.[59]

In the past thirty years, a growing number of novels have begun to appear that offer the surprise of individuality and vitality. One of the earliest of this new breed is Lilli Palmer's *Night Music* (1982).[60] The rigid, unemotional protagonist, Professor

Schulte, derives much wisdom from his elderly uncle, a dwarf referred to as Uncle Stilts. These characters may owe some debt to the Germanic tradition, but emotionally, they rebel against it. Uncle Stilts is a talented chess player and has performed clandestinely in a box—pretending to be a playing machine. Although the book contains an obligatory humiliation scene, Palmer engenders empathy. Stilts is a character who has known love, felt resentments, and gained wisdom. (His nickname, given to him by his father, is short for "Rumplestiltskin": the name suggests that Stilts has clambered up emotionally, becoming grander than his original self.) After having been physically confined within his body, his chess box, and his sickbed, Stilts becomes a potent proselytizer for liberation of the spirit.

A similar engagement with life marks one of the most dynamic, vibrant dwarf characters yet conceived—George C. Chesbro's detective hero, Dr. Robert Frederickson.[61] In a series known as the Mongo mysteries—because of the protagonist's circus name—Frederickson exhibits a multitude of talents. A former acrobat, he possesses a black belt in karate and a Ph.D. in criminology; he teaches the subject in New York City and moonlights as a private detective. The plots of these novels are set against political, religious, and scientific backgrounds, while in the foreground, rough-and-ready Dr. Frederickson and his police officer brother, Garth, drink, wrestle with criminals, wield handguns, and recover from near-death experiences in various hospitals. The author's partisanship is apparent. Government officials and cult members come in for considerable debunking, while Garth's devotion and eventual marriage to Mary Tree, a leftist folksinger, suggests his political leanings. While Frederickson may be less overtly political, both brothers are ethical activists and extremely empathic human beings. Hard drinking and iconoclastic they may be, but never cynical.

Only late in the Mongo series are there significant revelations about Dr. Frederickson's personal life. A devoted son, brother, and occasionally friend, he is not overly fond of reflection or self-revelation. He had made a stab at serious self-examination when he was younger, however, even consulting a psychiatrist, and he willingly talks about his brother Garth, whom he describes as carrying him on his shoulders, "literally and figuratively, during his tormented childhood and adolescence": "As a child I learned a thing or two about human cruelty, and it was only because of the love and understanding of my parents and Garth that I reached adulthood and took control of my own life with mind and heart, if not exactly unscathed, at least not hopelessly crippled."[62]

In an early short story, "Candala," Frederickson notes that it is "folly for a dwarf to entertain romantic thoughts of beautiful women."[63] However, with maturity and accomplishment, he finally takes a risk, not, however, through the casual escapade usually expected in a detective novel. He falls in love with Harper Rhys-Whytney, whom he first met when they both were circus headliners. A world-renowned expert in venomous snakes, she returns his affections, but work responsibilities keep them separated geographically. In a later book, *Dark Chant in a Crimson Key* (1992), the reader is finally permitted a peek at an intimate moment between them.[64] By the end of a later Mongo mystery, *Dream of a Falling Eagle* (1996), Harper has become his fiancée.

Chesbro is guilty of a few inaccuracies with respect to Mongo/Frederickson's dwarfing condition. As Chesbro sends his hero, with preternatural grace and agility, racing about the landscape, we hear nothing at all about the aches and pains, numbness, or slowness that most dwarfs experience. Frederickson drives a car, but there is no mention of the special pedal adjustments that dwarfs require. Finally, while he describes himself as "suffering from a recessive gene, three generations old," it seems far more likely, judging from Chesbro's description of Frederickson's physique, that his correct diagnosis is achondroplasia or hypochondroplasia—dominant conditions that result from new mutations, not recessive genes.

Still, these criticisms are trivial when viewed in the context of Chesbro's overall achievement. Chesbro has written a beguiling essay suggesting that his creation of Frederickson owes much to his own sense of inadequacy, his feeling "like a dwarf psychologically in the face of the awesome task of becoming a writer." He wonders whether "Mongo does not owe a good part of his success to the fact that he may strike a similar chord in many readers, for it is the rare person who does not occasionally feel like a 'dwarf in a world of giants'—giant people who press upon and threaten us in one way or another, giant problems that threaten to crush us. Perhaps Mongo, with his disdain for his 'handicap' and his indomitable will to make use of his talents, holds out to all of us the hope that, with courage, any of us may not only survive, but prevail in that very large, occasionally cold and hostile environment that is our lives."[65]

Detective story aficionados may also enjoy Ross Thomas's *The Eighth Dwarf*, a mystery that features a wily dwarf character who is, among other things, a successful womanizer; it may lack the complexity of a Chesbro novel, but it is engaging and well written.[66]

C. J. Koch's *The Year of Living Dangerously* is a novel rich in both political and human understanding. Set in Indonesia under Sukarno, it views the political situation of the country through the eyes of the foreign press corps.[67] Prominent members of that group are journalist Guy Hamilton and Billy Kwan, the Chinese Australian dwarf photographer who becomes his sidekick and guide through the labyrinth of Indonesian society. Billy's name is no accident. It is a diminutive, a nod to his boy/man stature; but more important, it carries echoes of the name Bilis, the protean dwarf figure of Arthurian legend. Bilis functioned sometimes as dwarf companion to a knight and at other times had the role of king of the Antipodes. Guy

Hamilton may be Billy's admired knight, but in reality he is "just a guy"; he lacks Billy's moral stature.

Billy offers Guy access to the corridors of power, arranging the interviews that eventually make Guy famous. He relinquishes his girlfriend, Gilly, to Guy, believing that they make a more viable couple. Although Billy is the ethical focus of the novel, his dwarfism impinges on every aspect of his personal and professional life. Despite his vision and gifts, he proves unable to overcome the tragic disparity he experiences between body and spirit, between the personal and the political.

Billy is sensitive to his genetic heritage—in addition to compiling files on friends and political figures, he has assembled a dwarf file. It contains photocopies of paintings by Velázquez and by more obscure artists. He describes the dwarf gods Vishnu and Semar, as well as King Bilis. Billy Kwan is a principled but mysterious figure whose growing personal disillusionment is interwoven with the political events of the Sukarno era. Both the novel and the movie it inspired are affecting works, among the most gripping characterizations of a dwarf protagonist created so far.

Armistead Maupin's *Maybe the Moon* is a popular novel written in a colloquial style that seriously explores social issues and offers a rare sympathetic presentation of a female dwarf, Cadence Roth.[68] Cady, a thirty-one-year-old aspiring actress, rooms with her friend Renee, a voluptuous "dumb blonde" who is her greatest admirer. In return, Cady consoles Renee when Renee gets into scrapes with abusive men.

Among the book's virtues is its depiction of the romance between Cady and her boyfriend, Neil, an attractive black musician. There is an explicit sex scene, a welcome development, although perhaps less than adequate in rendering its heroine's experience from an authentic female perspective. Only in the past decade have there been any representations of dwarfs' sexuality. Traditionally, dwarfs have been portrayed as asexual, and their attentions as unwelcome. Even contemporary writers have preferred to avert their eyes from the sex lives of persons with disabilities.

At least as central to Maupin's novel as his affirmation of Cady's love life is his sensitive treatment of her ethical conflict: should she accept humiliation and re-create her role as Mr. Woods, an E. T.–like creature in a box, or should she hold out for real acting roles, even if it means making her living in the meantime performing at children's parties? This moral dilemma is echoed in a secondary plot about a gay man's affair and his determination not to allow his lover to keep their relationship secret, to pretend to be heterosexual in the interest of his career. Whether in the closet or in the box, Maupin suggests, one is denying one's true self.

The character of Cady was inspired by Maupin's close friendship with the thirty-one-inch-tall actress Tamara de Treaux (who was among the several performers who played E. T. in the Steven Spielberg movie of that name). Maupin had first encountered de Treaux on a cruise on San Francisco Bay. In the middle of a crowded party, he had moved just a bit when a tiny woman close by said, "Watch it, Buster!" They hung out together for the rest of the trip, eventually becoming fast friends. He saw her as as "a condensed Bette Midler" and as a fellow outsider.[69] The novel that Maupin wrote to honor de Treaux after her death at the age of thirty-one became a best seller. It has been described as funny, poignant, and gutsy. Most important to us here, it is a novel that can be read with pleasure, and a sense of self-identification, by a dwarf.

In contrast to Maupin's novel, Simon Mawer's *Mendel's Dwarf* (1998) is a dark and erudite work.[70] The novel explores the ethical conundrums of eugenics through the experiences of the monk Gregor Mendel, the originator of modern genetics, and his great-great-great-nephew, Benedict Lambert, an accomplished scientist and an achondroplastic dwarf. Despite its engaging early chapters, the book does not quite fulfill its promise as a work of fiction, perhaps because Mawer, a biologist by profession, sometimes buries the reader in scientific details. It does succeed as a political statement, exploring the abuses of the Nazi era and causing the reader, through Lambert, to contemplate the issues surrounding the choice of bringing another dwarf child into the world. The author also effectively renders the fantasy life and bottled-up sexual desire that so many dwarfs, deprived of fulfilling romantic and sexual opportunities, have known. Although Lambert is an isolate, bitter and defensive, his romance with Jean Piercy Miller is the fulfillment of an adolescent dream. In describing the couple's lovemaking, Mawer reveals the problematic aspects of his characters' relationship, as well as their tenderness.

The most prominent socially conscious novel of all is Ursula Hegi's *Stones from the River* (1994), which has sold more than a million copies in the United States and has been translated into many languages. Hegi has succeeded in creating a moving portrait of Trudi Montag, a dwarf librarian in the small German town of Burgdorf during World War II, interesting in her own right, as well as a vehicle for assessing the Nazi era. The novel's first paragraph foreshadows the conflict that will be its driving force—the dramatic tension between Trudi's singularity and her yearning to be like everyone else: "As a child Trudi Montag thought everyone knew what went on inside others. That was before she understood the power of being different. The agony of being different. And the sin of ranting against an ineffective God. But before that— for years and years before that—she prayed to grow."[71]

Hegi traces Trudi's feelings about her dwarfism and the response it evokes in other people from her early childhood through middle age. Hegi is more careful in rendering these details than any previous author. She is painstakingly accurate in her descriptions of Trudi's bouts of leg pain and numbness, her internal ambivalence, and her perception of the complex social behavior of the community. She explores the nuances of Trudi's ethical dilemmas as well. As Trudi grows and her consciousness deepens, she is gradually able to resort less and less to retaliation, to going "one up" on others by exposing their secrets. She had appeared as a gossipy bit player in Hegi's *Floating in My Mother's Palm*; in *Stones from the River* she has become an embodiment of the human struggle to transcend alienation and hurt—learning not to give back blow for blow, despite the world's injustice.[72]

The pressures of the Hitler era result in moral strengthening for Trudi. She and her father hide Jews in their basement, at considerable risk. It is not incidental that they run a library. They are both symbolic and actual guardians of the town's access to enduring knowledge, antidotes to the psychology of the book burners. Is Trudi river or stone—actor or acted upon? Her force grows as the book progresses. Personally, politically, and in her existential awareness, she gathers strength, using her gifts as a seer to enhance her life and the lives of others. But despite her increased ability to form friendships and her successful struggle to trust the cherishing attentions of her lover, Max, she never succeeds in dissipating her pervasive loneliness. Inevitably, many of her closest relationships are lost to her.

Unlike most dwarfs invented by writers, Trudi is allowed to reach maturity—to gain wisdom and to have her hair turn gray. In Trudi Montag, Hegi has created a complex, believable, and sympathetic dwarf character. Unlike many dwarf characters that preceded her, she is not a paradigm of good or evil, but instead combines moral flaws and paranormal gifts; her yearnings, disappointments, ability to love, and deceptiveness intermingle to make her fully human.

Stones from the River was a selection of Oprah's Book Club, and interviews with the author on *The Oprah Winfrey Show* increased the book's success. When questioned by Winfrey about why she chose this period of time in Germany to be seen through the eyes of a dwarf, Hegi responded by saying that Trudi's angle of vision was ideal because as a little person she understood what it was like to be *other*: because people tended to separate themselves from her, she could more easily stand back and acknowledge what was happening to the Jews of Germany.[73]

Hegi, a German American who came to the United States at age eighteen, was profoundly affected by her awareness of the crimes of the Nazi era. She has also written *Tearing the Silence* (1997), a nonfiction book based on interviews with other German Americans. At readings and in interviews, Hegi has revealed that Trudi's character is loosely based on a dwarf woman who had lived in Hegi's hometown when the author was growing up. This woman was not only a gossip, but also something of an outcast. She was referred to as "Stumph Annika" (Stumpy Annie), and children were not allowed to talk to her. That woman, Hegi later discovered, had married and had two average-sized children. Hegi's beautiful evocation of Trudi's feelings about her dwarfism is the author's invention, but several dwarfs who have contacted Hegi have commented that her descriptions capture their own experience perfectly.

Few authors, apart from Hegi, have been able to conceive of anything other than a depressing or tragic ending, much less an interesting adulthood or old age for their dwarf characters. It does seem that dwarfs are almost always worse off than others. Consider the work of John Irving who, quite remarkably, has written three novels with important dwarf characters. In *The Hotel New Hampshire*, for example, the heroine, Lily, a dwarf writer, leaves a suicide note that says, "Sorry. Just not big enough."[74] A more ambitious work by Irving, *A Son of the Circus*, promises at first to offer an educated understanding of dwarfs: its hero, an Indian doctor, is dedicated to searching for the genetic marker for achondroplasia.[75] The author's obvious grasp of medical details seems to augur well for an authentic account of his dwarf characters. But the doctor's search, like Irving's novel, goes nowhere. His dwarf protagonist, Vinod, a chauffeur and former circus performer, is never developed. While Dr. Daruwalla himself, and many of the other bizarre characters, are well fleshed out in this suspenseful detective story, Vinod's character is much less so.

The title character in *A Prayer for Owen Meany* (1989) is, however, a fascinating figure.[76] A dwarf who must contend with very inadequate parents, he is nonetheless able to form significant close attachments, with a good friend and with his friend's warm, nurturing mother. Like many dwarfs in literature, Owen possesses certain supernatural powers—in his case, precognition. He is also a believing Christian and is sustained by the conviction that his life has some heroic purpose; the novel's underlying subscript is the revelation of exactly what this purpose might be. Like Irving's other dwarf protagonists, Owen is granted only a very abbreviated adulthood.

Irving's three short-statured protagonists die untimely deaths, a pattern that seems noteworthy.[77] Irving has indicated that their short stature in and of itself was not what intrigued him about his characters; rather he described them as he did because he is drawn to characters who have something missing, such as an eye in *The World According to Garp*. Loss is a recurring theme in his work, and he has explained that his short-statured characters' deaths emanated from the effect these deaths had on others who were close to the deceased—Dr. Daruwalla in *Son of the Circus* and Joe in *A Prayer for Owen Meany.*

Clearly, for Irving, it is "normalcy" that is not normal: he is engaged by difference and the outsider role and often illuminates and celebrates it. He is apt not to have recognized just how common his decision to send his dwarf characters off to an early and often a violent death has been in the literary canon. In addition to the examples already given here, in a 1993 short story by Anne Finger titled "The Artist and the Dwarf," two Jewish artists from different generations meet tragic deaths.[78] In John Sayles's *The Pride of the Bimbos*, the protagonist, a dwarf baseball player and entertainer, is harassed and humiliated and eventually commits suicide.[79] Literary dwarfs almost never marry; in one rare instance, Ruth Park's *Swords and Crowns and Rings*, when a dwarf fathers a child, the young child dies in a fire that also kills his mother.

That early deaths occur so often in literature about dwarfs is testimony to the authors' (perhaps unconscious) belief that dwarf status precludes a cheerful outcome. It may be that the nondwarf authors' sympathy for the poignancy of a dwarf's situation has prevented them from relating to the normalcy and joy that is also part of dwarf experience. But we keep getting closer. A novel with a dwarf protagonist, *The Dork of Cork* (1993) by Chet Raymo, captures the ordinariness, the pain, and the spiritual and physical yearnings of its hero—and even permits him to experience true love, though with an unconventional twist.[80] A dwarf hero, Frankie is allowed to find happiness in both work and love. This book was made into a movie, called *Frankie Starlight* (see Chapter 9).

It is difficult to keep up with the profusion of books with dwarf characters that are published. Among the most recent are the three volumes of a series by Bartle Bull. The first of these swashbuckling novels, *The White Rhino Hotel,* finds the Goan dwarf Olivio Fonseca Alavedo working for Lord Penfold in Kenya as manager, waiter, and on-call expert lover of his wife, Sissy. As the interlocking plots unfold, the novel gradually reveals Alavedo's personality, his creative forcefulness and sexual prowess, as well as his wiliness, cruelty, and manipulation of others. In passing, it also alludes to the ill-treatment that Alavedo suffered in childhood. The second novel, *Café on the Nile* (1998), set in Egypt and Abyssinia in the 1930s, is filled with safaris, poison gas, graphic sex and violence, and characters who might have inhabited Rick's Café in *Casablanca.* By now Alavedo is fifty years old and the owner of the Cataract Café in Cairo. In addition to running this lively salon, he is an aggressive entrepreneur who conducts land deals, has a loving wife and a mistress, and has seven daughters and a son. Exceedingly generous to his friends, he is a powerful, unusual figure. *The Devil's Oasis* (2001), the third installment in Bull's series, takes place during the period of Rommel's war in Africa.[81]

A lively road-trip novel, Cathryn Alpert's *Rocket City* (1995), follows Marilee, an art therapist, as she drives across the desert in the Southwest on her way to surprise her boyfriend in Rocket City.[82] She picks up Enoch, a dwarf hitchhiker, and after gradually overcoming her unease about his odd appearance and style, she is surprised to find herself attracted to him sexually as well as intrigued to discover who he truly is. This thought-provoking suspenseful novel depicts their developing relationship. Alpert expertly limns the personality of Enoch, revealing both the defensive persona he has had to create in the face of physical and emotional abuse, and the quirky intelligence that has allowed him to overcome various obstacles and emerge as an interesting, eccentric, tender, and fully realized figure.

It is unfortunate that recent foreign-language works are only infrequently translated into English. One especially great loss is Anne Marie Lon's *Dvaergene's Dans,* published to great critical acclaim in Denmark in 1998. It has enjoyed a wide reader-ship in that country and, since its translation into both French and German, in oth-ers.[83] The protagonist-narrator is Tyge Willhof-Holm, a charming thirty-two-year-old, who is 1.36 meters (4 feet 5 1/2 inches) tall—a height of which he is proud and calls "not an insignificant size for a dwarf." Like so many dwarfs who are depicted as hav-ing paranormal gifts, Tyge "is able to display all that can't be said, almost not even thought but sensed—he is gifted at sensing things."

Tyge visits the barber daily to have him trim Tyge's crew cut, which adds one cen-timeter to his height, and his goatee, which he sports to convey manliness. He wears specially made shoes and tailor-made clothes. He identifies with and patterns him-self after Giacomo Favorchi, the Italian dwarf of the prince of Sachen, who is depicted in a portrait by Karel van Mander III (1610–1670) painting in the Copenhagen Mu-seum of Art (Fig. 52).

Tyge is portrayed as a man with much insight, a clear sense of reality, and a fine sense of humor—he is optimistic and musically gifted. Born in Jutland into a noble Danish family of modest means, he has been exposed throughout his life to art, music, and literature. He is the youngest of nine unmarried siblings, who, along with his mother and his nanny, have adored and spoiled him. In Copenhagen, he holds a position as church organist, playing at funerals; he also enjoys playing the piano part time in a restaurant (although his father would have preferred him to play in the Danish royal sym-phony orchestra). His fears of rejection are al-layed when, while playing at a funeral, he meets a young woman and falls madly in love, and then discovers that she reciprocates his feelings.

52. *Portrait of Giacomo Favorchi by Karl van Mander III, c. 1650. State Museum, Copenhagen, Denmark.*

Among the novel's themes are the decline of Danish nobility and the celebration of famil-ial and romantic love. Also, as the author has remarked, her book is about living with one's limitations, developing and refining what one is, rather than being plagued by what one is not. Her protagonist's handicaps are visible, but all of us must contend with obstacles. Lon's achievement is one more signal that stereo-types have begun to be shattered.

Many works have been slighted in this re-view. There have been humorous efforts such as Philip Roth's account of two dwarf baseball competitors in *The Great American Novel* and James Thurber's 1941 tale about the ballplayer Pearl du Monville that inspired Bill Veeck, a decade later, to send in thirty-seven-inch Eddie Gaedel to pinch-hit.[84] There are also short stories such as Thomas Mann's "Little Herr Friedemann," in which a sensitive businessman is encouraged and then humiliated in his search for love. Recently, numerous other short stories with dwarf protagonists have been published by respected authors, among them Ann Beattie's "Dwarf House" and Steven Millhauser's "The Princess, the Dwarf and the Dungeon."

Some, like "Dwarf House," seem to intend to satirize a society of "normals" that is intolerant of dwarfs, but the atmosphere is so gloomy that it makes for painful reading. Others, like Harold Pinter's *The Dwarfs*, seem too tangential to merit analysis. And not everyone may concur with the jacket blurb that proclaims Kurt Vonnegut's *Cat's Cradle* "an apocalyptic tale of this planet's ultimate fate." Some of the worthy works that have not been discussed include a good number of science fiction novels in which dwarfs appear in heroic roles. Miles Vorkosigan is a four-foot-nine-inch nobleman with a brittle bone disorder in the Barrayar cycle, a collection of novels and short stories by Lois McMaster Bujold; Jack O' Shea, in *The Space Merchants* by Frederick Pohl and C. M. Kornbluth, is the first and only human to reach Venus—and he is only thirty-five inches tall.

The Paucity of Dwarf Authors

Considering the rarity of dwarfs in the general population, the number of novels with dwarf protagonists is astonishing, and it continues to grow rapidly. Some may wonder why dwarfs themselves have not produced works that dispel the negative images in this fiction. Just as Virginia Woolf speculated about the unwritten volumes by Shakespeare's apocryphal sister, Judith, we can only speculate about and regret the loss of the works never written by the generations of dwarfs whose lives were limited by social constraints. Certainly, there have been at least a few short-statured individuals who have been accomplished authors—among those discussed in this volume are poet Alexander Pope, novelist and man of letters Paul Leicester Ford, memoirist Katherine Butler Hathaway, and children's book author Mary Rutherford Garrettson. Much earlier, a fifteenth-century female Spanish court dwarf wrote poetry, of which only a few fragments survive.[85]

Additional authors may come to light, just as the following two individuals recently have. Georg Christoph Lichtenberg (1742–1749), a hunchbacked dwarf, was a professor of science at the University of Göttingen, Germany. He was esteemed during his lifetime for his essays on art and philosophy, and his enduring reputation in

Europe during subsequent centuries rested largely on his aphorisms, republished through the years. He became more widely known to the American public only after a novel based on his life, *Lichtenberg and the Little Flower Girl,* appeared in the fall of 2004. Then too, just as *The Lives of Dwarfs* was going to press, a symposium was held at Columbia University in New York in honor of Randolph Bourne (1886–1918), a radical and pacifist during World War I. Called "the forgotten prophet" by his biographer, Bourne had gained the attention of the intellectual community of his day for his writings on politics and art, as well as for a personal essay titled "The Handicapped."[86]

At least two dwarf individuals have made a mark in the world of science fiction. It is known that Raymond A. Palmer (1910–1977) was approximately four feet tall, although the nature of his short stature has not been accurately identified.[87] An inveterate reader of pulp magazines, in his twenties Palmer was successfully selling his short stories to these publications. In 1938, he was chosen as the editor of *Amazing Stories* and increased its circulation by choosing tales that appealed to its teenage audience's fascination with fantasy civilizations. Palmer was a major figure in the genres of science fiction and works involving parapsychological phenomena; he became publisher of *Fate* magazine in 1948 and *Flying Saucers* in 1977. These publications focused on tales about UFOs, the Loch Ness monster, and various psychic phenomena. Editor and publisher Judy-Lynn Benjamin del Rey (1943–1986), who had achondroplasia, has been called "a master craftsman" and "probably the greatest editor since Maxwell Perkins."[88] Many writers have expressed gratitude for her guidance in the development of their characters. Del Rey is best known to the general public for having published George Lucas's *Star Wars,* but she also discovered and nurtured the careers of many other science fiction writers, and she has been credited with having elevated the status of science fiction within mainstream literature. Isaac Asimov, the eminent science fiction writer, was a close friend of hers and writes of her in his autobiography.[89] She and her husband, Lester, were given their own imprint by Random House; they regularly had books on both hardcover and paperback best-seller lists. Sadly, del Rey died of a brain hemorrhage at age forty-three.

At least a dozen individuals are currently listed as writers in the Little People of America database. A good many individuals have published memoirs. However, in part because there are so few dwarfs compared with members of other minority groups, we will probably continue to have more dwarfs portrayed in literature than there are literary dwarfs. Interestingly, as noted in the present chapter, a good number of works about dwarfs have been written by authors who experienced themselves as outsiders or somehow aberrant. Sir Walter Scott was lame; Edgar Allan Poe was an orphan, an adoptee, and an alcoholic and was castigated for his marriage to his thirteen-year old cousin; Oscar Wilde was a homosexual, as is Armistead Maupin;

M. E. Kerr is a lesbian. John Irving has lived a lifetime without knowing the identity of his biological father; Ursula Hegi is a German American immigrant critical of the society into which she was born. George C. Chesbro taught special education students for many years. These authors' own experiences with marginality clearly contributed to their deeper understanding of their dwarf protagonists.

Children's Literature

Literature written for children that features dwarf characters has burgeoned even more dramatically than adult fiction. Just a few decades ago, the only "little people" that could be found were those who abounded in fairy tales. Unfortunately, space considerations preclude discussing these tales or mentioning more than briefly a few of the best children's books with dwarf characters.

Diane Stanley's *Rumpelstiltskin's Daughter* is a revisionist version of one of the most famous of the old folktales and offers a surprising, novel perspective. In the original Grimm tale, the miller's daughter enlists the dwarf Rumpelstiltskin's help in spinning wheat into gold—a skill that her father has falsely attributed to her. When Rumpelstiltskin agrees to perform this service for her for the third time, he extracts the promise that she will give him her firstborn child in return. However, after giving birth, she finds that she cannot bear to part with her beautiful baby, and the dwarf agrees to rescind the obligation if she can discover his name. When, with the help of a spy, she is able to pronounce his name aloud, Rumpelstiltskin exclaims, "'The Devil told you that! The Devil told you that!' . . . and in his rage he stamped his right foot so hard that it went into the ground up to his waist. Then in his fury he took his foot in both hands and tore himself in two."[90]

The traditional reaction to this ending has been to rejoice in Rumpelstiltskin's defeat and demise rather than to resonate with his despair. One need not lament the death of a homely goblin, the story suggests; his life is insignificant compared with that of a beautiful princess. His desire for parenthood is presented as hubris. Any parent or child who has found Grimm's ending distasteful will be pleased to come upon Stanley's version. She presents the reader with a character who is not a weird isolate, but rather a charming, convincing communicator. Listen to him, negotiating with the miller's daughter:

> "Okay, here's the deal," he said. "I will spin the straw into gold, just like before.
> In return, once you become queen, you must let me adopt your firstborn child.
> I promise I'll be an excellent father. I know all the lullabies. I'll read to the kid
> every day. I'll even coach Little League."

"You've got to be kidding," Meredith said. "I'd rather marry you than that jerk!"

"Really?" said Rumpelstiltskin, and he blushed all the way from the tip of his toes (which admittedly wasn't very far because he was so short).

"Sure," she said. "I like your ideas on parenting, you'd make a good provider, and I have a weakness for short men."

So Rumpelstiltskin spun a golden ladder, and they escaped out the window. They married the very next day and lived happily together far, far away from the palace.[91]

Apart from their presence in familiar folktales and their adaptations, dwarfs have secured an important place in the great number of books about children with disabilities that have been published in the past several decades. A new approach is evident. In the past, literary merit was rarely a central consideration for the authors or critics of children's stories. Rather, the narratives were seen as a means to an end, as necessary for providing simple information and for imparting moral education. Although the transmission of values remains an important goal, the values themselves have changed, and the tendency these days is to present events both honestly and artfully, inviting young readers to be active participants in the struggle to unravel complex human problems.[92]

Previously, the portrayal of disability in children's literature had been infrequent. When disabled characters did appear, they tended to be romanticized or pathetic. Often, a stereotyped character was presented who functioned as a vehicle for charitable feelings—as Tiny Tim did in *A Christmas Carol*. The character was designed to remind child readers to be grateful for the gifts that made their lives so much happier than that of the poor, unfortunate cripple or blind person: the tale became a moral injunction to be kind to others. In an early twentieth-century story, a child named Johnny Blossom revealed his superbly generous spirit by paying for his grandmother's eye surgery, comforting a man with an injured back, and inviting poor "Katerina the dwarf" to his party.[93] There are still many simplistic didactic works among books that focus on short stature. For every story written about a dwarf, there are dozens of unsatisfying others about small children who would like to be taller.

M. E. Kerr's *Little Little* is unique among both adult and adolescent novels about dwarfs in that it is a humorous work of social criticism, presenting not just one dwarf character but four colorfully drawn dwarf teenagers. Sydney Cinammon is a disproportionate, hunchbacked dwarf, who has been abandoned and raised at the Twin Oaks Orphan House: he has become a celebrity because of his performance in commercials for Roach-Killer. Little Little is the attractive, "perfectly formed" (that is, proportionate) daughter of the wealthiest family in town; Opportunity Knox, Little

Little's designated suitor, is a pompous, opportunistic young evangelist; Eloise is a pretty, snippy actress who has appeared as a lettuce leaf on television.

Sydney is the novel's narrator and also the vehicle for Little Little's protest against her mother's prejudices. Confronting her mother's rejection of Sydney, Little Little also challenges the "p.f." (perfectly formed) designation that has been assigned to her (Mrs. La Belle has dealt with her discomfort about Little Little's dwarfism by asserting her daughter's superiority to disproportionate dwarfs). Little Little exclaims, "'If Pablo Picasso had a wart on his finger, he wouldn't be the world-famous painter in your eyes, he'd be that fellow with the wart on his finger who paints! You are all caught up in a bogged down p.f.! Sydney Cinnamon has one of the best minds of anyone who's ever sat down at our dinner table, and all you see is the tooth that sticks out!'"[94]

Early in the novel, Little Little's grandfather, who is endeavoring to help her to learn to love and accept herself, communicates all he knows about dwarfs of the past. He mentions several historic figures, suggesting their importance as role models. When she asks him where the female dwarfs were, he tells her that they are buried in history with other notable ladies. "He said they were there all right, he just didn't happen to know about them." Subsequently, so that she can better identify with others like herself, her grandfather takes Little Little to her first Diminutives of America meeting. That is clearly the novel's appellation for Little People of America, and that group is satirized just a bit.

Kerr has written an inventive, spirited work that takes potshots at pretensions and bigotry of all kinds, affirming adolescents' right to take up arms against them. The cast includes other memorable protagonists: Cowboy, Little Little's mannish-looking sister; her Japanese friend, Mock Hiroyuki; and Little Little's competitor in English class, a girl named Calpurnia Dove, who is African American. These characters extend the book's significance beyond the world of dwarfs to reflect on difference overall. Despite its serious purpose, it is a wise, comic novel that allows its players to be playful.

Some additional works deserve to be briefly mentioned.[95] An expert in Indian lore, John Bierhorst has assembled twenty-two stories from diverse Native American groups in *The Deetkatoo* (1997). He writes an interesting, nuanced introduction, indicating some of the historic differences between groups, but also conveying their commonality—the affectionate portrayal of little people drawn by cultures who respect dwarfs as the physical embodiments of the spiritual world.

One of the best stories for young children is Marisabina Russo's *Alex Is My Friend* (1992), inspired by the friendship of the author's son with a dwarf playmate. Carol Carrick's *Two Very Little Sisters* (1993) is a fictionalized biography of the Adams sisters (see Chapter 1). Patty Lovell's *Stand Tall, Molly Lou Mellon* (2001) describes the efforts of a very short girl to overcome teasing and gain confidence. One of the first nonfiction works written from the perspective of a young dwarf was *Ginny's Backyard*

(1978), a book with fine photographs; it expresses Ginny Brown's personal observations about not wanting others to baby her, and her confidence in her abilities and future. Another excellent book for young readers is *Thinking Big* (1986) by Susan Kuklin; it portrays the life of Jaime Osborne, an eight-year-old girl with achondroplasia and her average-statured parents and younger brother.

For somewhat older children, Stephanie Riggs's *Never Sell Yourself Short* (2001) describes the difficulties and pleasures in the life of fourteen-year-old Josh Maudlin; it is accompanied by Bill Youmans's appealing photographs and includes pictures of talented adult dwarfs. Mary Ellen Verheyden-Hilliard's *Scientist and Teacher, Ann Barrett Swanson* (1988) features a scientist with osteogenesis imperfecta. A wide-ranging informative work for older children is Elaine Landau's *From Folklore to Fact* (1997). Among the novels written for middle school and high school students are Barbara Corcoran's *A Row of Tigers* (1969); Katherine Patterson's *Of Nightingales That Weep* (1974); Karen Rose and Lynda Halfyard's *Kristin and Boone* (1983); Jean Dixon's *The Tempered Wind* (1987); and Roman Philbrick's *Freak the Mighty* (1993). Adult works such as the Mongo mysteries of George Chesbro and *Caught Short* (1972) by Donald Davidson may also appeal to adolescents.

Conclusion

The proliferation of children's and adult literature and the rapid evolution toward realistic and diverse portrayals of dwarfs demonstrate the radical change that has taken place in a relatively short period. Repellent figures such as in Lagerkvist's *The Dwarf* have become supplanted by nuanced renderings drawing on personal experience. In the decade since its publication, Ursula Hegi's *Stones from the River* has sold more copies than any previous book containing a dwarf character. It has continued to capture the attention of readers and to be popular with book clubs; it was even featured in a successful "one book" event in Pennsylvania.[96]

Most literary works have a modest readership, and their effects are mediated by the climate of the culture overall. But one ought not underestimate the ability of popular works such as Charles Dickens's *David Copperfield* and its character Miss Mowcher to offer personal "lessons in sensitivity," or Ursula Helgi's *Stones from the River* to deepen people's understanding of dwarf individuals and the human experience.

CHAPTER NINE

Theater, Film, and Television

Dwarfs as Actors

"There are a great many professional midgets but there aren't many dwarfs who can act."[1]

Michael Dunn, the renowned dwarf actor of the 1960s and 1970s who made this remark, had good reason. From the beginning of recorded history, individuals had exhibited themselves as oddities, sometimes simply proclaiming themselves actors as well. Talent was not the first requisite—size and appearance were generally sufficient to attract an audience. As late as 1934, aspiring dwarf performers were plentiful, since performing was often the only occupation open to them.[2] At the same time, the accomplishments of serious, professional actors were often ignored or undervalued. Even today, despite an abundance of trained, accomplished dwarf actors, producers are frequently content, when seeking a short-statured actor, merely to find one who possesses a certain desired appearance. Consider, for example, this advertisement that appeared in a Little People of America regional newsletter: "Whitetail Images is currently looking for two little people to be cast in the motion picture *Seeing in the Dark*. . . . Director Robert Manganelli is looking for two men between ages 20 and 40 preferably who resemble each other. Acting experience is helpful but not necessary."[3] *Acting experience is helpful but not necessary.* Not quite any dwarf will do, but almost. Similarly, at major spectacles such as the Radio City Music Hall Christmas show, singing and dancing ability is helpful, but stature remains the chief prerequisite.

Anyone who tries to unearth information about talented dwarf actors of previous eras is apt to meet with scant success.[4] Those mentioned by writers who have researched this topic tend to be entertainers rather than professional actors: J. A.

Stranitzky (1704/5–1726) was a Viennese comedian who had also studied medicine at Vienna University.[5] Moreau was an early nineteenth-century French actor who was regarded as an excellent comedian; he played in a marionette company as the only adult among children.[6] After a brief period of success, Moreau ended his life in poverty. Harry Relph, who was better known as Little Tichborn (1867–1926), was a talented British comedian and dancer; he performed both in England and France and appeared in early films.[7] A random search of the literature on the history of the theater, ranging across several countries, yielded no specific mention of dwarf actors of earlier centuries.[8]

Other "actors" offered themselves in roles that were spectacular, acrobatic, and dehumanizing. In the 1840s, the English actor Hervey Leach (1804–1847), better known by the stage name Hervio Nano, played a variety of roles in Great Britain and the United States, appearing in performances with such titles as *The Gnome Fly, Jack Robinson and his Monkey*, and *Jocko; or, The Brazilian Ape*.[9] Leach was a dwarf who had an average-sized trunk and very small legs; because of his remarkable strength and agility, he could accomplish astounding acrobatic feats, moving from the gallery to the stage on wires and, somehow, crawling on the ceiling. He was one of the most successful of a good many "freak performers." Such novelty acts, and productions such as those in which Tom Thumb appeared, featuring persons of short stature aping their taller counterparts, were common.

In one of the few articles appraising the quality of these performances, Alvin Goldfarb notes that the celebrity of both dwarfs and giants, who often appeared together, was based largely on the sensation created by contrasts in stature.[10] Another manifestation of the performing-dwarf phenomenon was the "midget" acting troupe, which was popular in the second half of the nineteenth and early twentieth century. The best known troupe was the Liliputian Opera Company, which performed musical extravaganzas to great acclaim in capitals throughout Europe and made its American debut in 1890.[11] Among the truly gifted performers in this troupe of ten were the comedians Franz Ebert and Adolf Zink and the ingenue Bertha Jaeger. Despite their obvious talent, actors in such troupes were given only roles written expressly for them, highlighting their stature. The "compliment" proffered by one New York reviewer captures the impossible situation: "Adolf Zink was so exceptionally able that it is to be hoped he may grow up some day and act without the necessity of posing as a natural phenomenon."[12]

It has taken a long while for the theater to "grow up" and begin to welcome dwarfs in a wide spectrum of roles. Until recently, only two—Michael Dunn and Linda Hunt—had had significant careers on both stage and screen. However, when in 2003 Peter Dinklage triumphed in the film *The Station Agent*, after having distinguished himself in a number of off-Broadway plays during the previous decade, the possibility that a talented male actor who was a dwarf might finally be offered the role of leading man seemed to be approaching reality.

Cinema

Most often, it was in film and later on television that dwarf actors found employment during the twentieth century. Only in the second half of the twentieth century did a few actors assiduously hone their craft and become valued members of their profession. It is impossible to appreciate the peculiar status of dwarfs in the acting profession without viewing a range of films, including Westerns, fantasy films, and others not of the first rank.

There is certainly no dearth of films with dwarfs in them—there are literally hundreds.[13] A fair sampling reveals some dull, some embarrassing, and some even repugnant films. A number are great fun, though, and a few truly moving. It is still unusual, however, to find dwarfs cast in roles that are not limited to people of their size or that illuminate the inner experiences of a dwarf.

In the earliest silent films, dwarfs were often used to play infants or children. Then, for several decades, they were used as diminutive mimics to lend comedy to a given genre. In *The Terror of Tiny Town* (1938) they played at being cowboys; in *Little Cigars* (1973) they were pint-size gangsters. The enjoyment of the audience stemmed from its recognition that the "adult" roles had been miniaturized into bantam John Waynes or George Rafts. In early movies, especially, proportionate dwarf actors were used to create the effect of attractive miniature adult impersonators.

From *Frankenstein* to *Poltergeist,* dwarfs, particularly disproportionate individuals, were introduced to suggest an eerie atmosphere. The contemporary dwarf actor's revolt against this stereotype is tellingly depicted in the 1996 film *Living in Oblivion,* in part a spoof on low-budget independent movies. A harried director (Steve Buscemi) hires a dwarf actor, Tito (Peter Dinklage), to perform in a dream sequence, whereupon Tito protests:

T: Why does my character have to be a dwarf?
D: Look, Tito, it's not that big of a deal. Strange things happen in a dream. All I want you to do is laugh. Why is that such a problem for you?
T: Why does my character have to be a dwarf?
D: It doesn't have to be a dwarf.
T: Then why is he? Is that the only way you can make this a dream—put a dwarf in it?
D: No, Tito.

T: Have you ever had a dream with a dwarf in it? No!!! I don't have dreams with dwarfs in them. The only place I have ever seen dwarfs in dreams is in stupid movies like this. Ooooooh . . . Make it weird. Put a dwarf in it. Everyone will go whoah, whoah, whoah. It must be a dream, there's a fuckin' dwarf in it. Well, I'm sick of it! You can take this dream sequence and shove it up your ass. [He exits.]

EXPEDITOR: I can get on the phone—we can try to get another small person.

D: No—he's absolutely right. The shoot is over. I give up.[14]

Tito is reminiscent of *Toto*, the name of the dog in *The Wizard of Oz*, as well as *Tattoo*, the name of the dwarf character in the television series *Fantasy Island*. It is not uncommon for fictional dwarfs to be assigned peculiar, single names. Dinklage may have had in mind dream sequences such as that seen in the television series *Twin Peaks*, in which Michael J. Anderson plays the role of a mysterious dancing dwarf, or another in a David Lynch film, *Industrial Symphony # 1*, in which Anderson appears in Julie Cruse's dream, one in which dwarfs and other odd characters float above the landscape. In the television series *Northern Exposure*, a dwarf appears in a shaman's vision.[15]

The brief scene quoted above from *Living in Oblivion* should not be overstated as defining a completely new era for dwarfs in film, but it does hint at a changed perception. Frightened black Stepin Fetchit characters with bulgy eyes have become less common; similarly, filmmakers who offer stereotyped, condescending portrayals of dwarfs can expect to be called to task. Principled dwarf actors, too, operate from a raised consciousness that did not exist in previous decades; they now resist roles that are mere caricature, refusing to be cast as robots or extraterrestrial beings.

In assuming this stance, they are attempting to break away from the seventy-five-year history of dwarfs in film, when the niche categories they were consigned to included freaks, child impersonators, miniaturized cowboys, gangsters, purveyors of evil or the macabre, extraterrestrials, mythical or leprechaun-like figures, and mascots who sometimes identified with a full-size aggressor. The child impersonator roles tend to be most prevalent in the 1920s and 1930s, while the roles defining the individuated human being occur at the turn of the twenty-first century. In the intervening years, and into today, most of the other categories have persisted in diverse forms.

A comparison may be made, for example, between two films produced approximately forty years apart: Todd Browning's *Freaks* (1932) and Werner Herzog's *Even Dwarfs Started Small* (1968–1970). Both films emphasize the grotesqueness of their protagonists. Browning's film, set in a circus, includes "pinheads," conjoined twins, and hypopituitary dwarfs. The circus's femme fatale blonde acrobat plans to marry the dwarf, Harry Earles, and poison him for his money (Fig. 53). Seeing her humiliate Earles, and learning of her plan, the other freaks attack her, leaving her writhing in the mud, transformed into a hideous chicken. Ostensibly, Browning was depicting the just revolt of the oppressed against their oppressors. He opens the film with this didactic message: "In ancient times everything that deviated from the normal was considered an omen of bad luck and a representation of evil." He states that "the code of the freaks is the hurt of one is the hurt of all."[16]

Not everyone trusted his motives. Screenwriter Budd Schulberg, who watched him work, suspected that he was a sadist.[17] Myrna Loy and Jean Harlow both refused the starring female role, and many executives at Metro-Goldwyn-Mayer opposed its release. While some have thought the film "exploitive and tasteless," the *New Yorker* described it as "a little gem."[18] Such op-

53. *Image from* Freaks, *1932, starring Harry Earles and Olga Baclanova. Photofest, NYC.*

posing critiques reflect the contradictory nature of the film, which is at times compelling and at others horrifying. Although it lost Browning the respect of his industry, the film has retained a cult following through the years. Also, it served as an impetus for the photographer Diane Arbus's obsession with photographing dwarfs and other deformed persons.[19]

German filmmaker Werner Herzog's *Auch Zwerge haben klein angefangen (Even Dwarfs Started Small)* has provoked similarly polarized reactions. By one account, it is "ugly and completely fascinating."[20] By another, "the director imbues his misshapen characters with a sort of regal grandeur, as if to purge the German wartime atrocities against 'undesirables.'" The second reviewer also suggests that Herzog had Vietnam in mind when he made the film.[21] If these grand objectives were in Herzog's mind, only an inspired sleuth could discover them on screen.

The movie is set in a mental institution. Its loose progression of disconnected scenes depicts an inmate revolt against the institution's director and implicitly against the society that has rejected and incarcerated them. The inmates tease and mock one another, however, quite as they attack their alleged oppressor. Throughout the film, the dwarf characters titter and laugh inanely, cackling like the chickens that repeatedly materialize. Just as the critics did not question the reason for using cacophonous chickens, they did not ask why dwarfs were chosen to portray these alienated, not-quite-human caricatures. Since Herzog fails to delineate the crimes of the oppressors, and the dwarf characters are neither individuated nor likeable, any symbolic message is lost.

Such revenge themes are exceptional in dwarf filmography. In the early years, one is more likely to find, for example, Harry Earles playing in a comic melodrama such as *The Unholy Three*. Also a Todd Browning film, first produced in 1925 and remade in 1930, it portrays three circus performers—a ventriloquist, a strongman, and a dwarf—who decide to leave the circus and turn to crime. The dwarf (Earles) is motivated to leave in part because he has been made fun of and feels unappreciated; this element, however, is given only passing notice. His role in the gang is to play a baby in order to create the illusion of a normal family: mother, father, grandmother, and baby. Earles acquits himself well, both as baby impersonator and partner in crime. The movie, which also stars Lon Chaney, was deemed interesting enough to be revived in New York City in the 1990s.

The child-impersonating dwarf has largely disappeared, but crews of dwarfs, acting as miniaturized bandits or adventurers, have persisted. Advertisements for *The Terror of Tiny Town* proudly proclaimed that it consisted of an "all-midget cast," a group known as Jed Buell's Midgets. In this Western, the villain (Little Billy) engages in illegal rustling and attempts to put the blame on others; his scheme is gradually uncovered by the hero (Billy Curtis). As is typical for this genre, the cast is all male, with the exception of the female love interest (Yvonne Moray), and the movie is neither better nor worse than most Westerns. Billy Curtis appeared in similar "dwarf crew" movies in subsequent years. In 1950 Billy Barty and a largely male cast joined him in an adventure film, *Pygmy Island*, a Johnny Weismuller Tarzan movie. It was less successful than *Little Cigars*, a 1973 gangster film, in which Curtis, this time with Jerry Maren and others, forms a group of charlatans who run a medicine show as a cover-up for their car theft ring.

The adventure plot remains a fairly common formula for films employing dwarf actors. One of the best known and most lucrative is *Time Bandits* (1981), which grossed forty-five million dollars in North America; it was produced and directed by Terry Gilliam of *Monty Python* fame. The plot revolves around a boy who falls asleep and then is surprised by a band of dwarfs who enter his room by mistake. They turn out to be time-traveling criminals, moving from one era to another, and they take the boy along with them. Among those whom they visit is Napoleon, who likes them because they are small; they enjoy his favor but nevertheless steal his jewelry. A good cast of six dwarf actors, led by David Rappaport, racket about in this time-travel fantasy. Critical response was mixed—*Time Bandits* was generally viewed as more successful as adventure than as comedy and better suited to children than adults.

One small but psychologically significant subcategory of film has a dwarf acting as a mascot, achieving importance by serving the central figure. In *Saratoga Trunk,* a 1945 movie dripping with stereotypes, Ingrid Bergman is an impulsive déclassé vamp who falls in love with Gary Cooper, a resourceful Texas gambler and adventurer. She scandalizes the New Orleans gentry before setting out to find a rich husband in Saratoga Springs. Ultimately, in spite of herself, she succumbs to Cooper's charms. The foils for Bergman's flamboyant character are her two servants, a dour Flora Robson in blackface and Jerry Austin, a cheerful court jester, who is called "Cupidon." The servants' lives have meaning only through their employer, and they subject themselves to her verbal abuse without protest. Austin smiles as Bergman perches a delicious restaurant meal on his top hat, using it for a table, while he and Robson are, naturally, offered nothing to eat (Fig. 54). To prove his manliness, he joins Cooper's character in a melee between two camps in a railroad war. Despite his affection for the eager servant, whom he defends in battle, Cooper refers to him as a "half pint." Throughout the movie, the audience understands that Bergman and Cooper, two beautiful people, belong together, and it does not question their right to command lesser mortals. Jerry Austin carries off his large role well, rushing about with aplomb, but his acting cannot transcend the stereotyped writing.

In two later films, *High Plains Drifter* (1973) and *The Ballad of the Sad Café* (1991), dwarf characters are not simply mascots; they attain status through identification with an aggressor. In *High Plains Drifter* Clint Eastwood plays a powerful gunslinger who is hired to clean up a town. He succeeds, but not without a good bit of high-handed, vicious behavior of his own. Mordecai (Curtis) is at first mistreated by Eastwood but then hangs around until he is accepted as his helper. After becoming the gunslinger's right-hand man, and even mayor, Mordecai is the only townsperson besides the gunslinger who has the courage to wield a gun against the outlaws. Within the limits of this suspenseful film's formulaic elements, Curtis's acting is competent, but the role does not make great demands.

The Ballad of the Sad Café is based on a novella by Carson McCullers (see Chapter 8). In a dreary, lonesome southern town, the wealthy Miss Amelia (Vanessa Redgrave) is respected for her carpentry skills and herbal wisdom; however, she has no facility with words or people until her (probably spurious) cousin Lymon (Cork Hubbert) shows up one day. He is a hunchbacked dwarf, bedraggled, odd, and self-pitying, an idler with a malevolent streak. But Miss Amelia loves and indulges him. He convinces her to open a café in her store, and the people of the town come to life a bit. Lymon and Amelia develop a kind of intimacy, and she displays a lightness of spirit she has never experienced before.

Then, when Marvin Macy, Miss Amelia's former husband, arrives, everything changes. Lymon turns on Amelia, humiliating and abandoning her, for Marvin's sake, crushing her spirit permanently. Love's irrationality and its power to enhance or demolish a person are aptly realized in the marvelous acting performance of Vanessa Redgrave and the creditable work of Cork Hubbert as Lymon, though it lacks the fine language of the original novella and the exceptional acting ability of Michael Dunn, who achieved critical and popular acclaim in the 1974 Edward Albee play.

54. *Jerry Austin in* Saratoga Trunk, *1946. Photofest, NYC.*

Lymon, though a familiar "evil dwarf" character, is transformed by McCullers into a provocative figure, capable of surprising reversals.

Space restraints preclude surveying the enormous number of horror films and adaptations of fairy tales in which dwarfs have performed. Suffice it to say that it is not unusual for the résumés of dwarf actors to include the title role in *Rumplestiltskin* or an appearance as an extra in a Frankenstein movie. Perhaps the nadir of the portrayals of the dwarf as scary monster is the dwarf character in the much acclaimed *Don't Look Now* (1973), starring Donald Sutherland and Julie Christie. A married couple whose young daughter has died by drowning travels to Venice, where Sutherland, an architect, is working. A blind, clairvoyant woman convinces Christie that her daughter's spirit is restlessly wandering the city. At first disbelieving, Sutherland ends up chasing a small hooded figure through the streets of Venice—only to discover, when he catches up with her, that she is not his daughter at all, but a grotesque dwarf.

This scene does not end merely with the architect's disappointment at not finding his daughter. Instead—inexplicably—the dwarf murders him with an ax! No motive is supplied to explain her vicious act—her terrifying appearance is explanation enough. Adelina Poerio, who plays the dwarf, is not required to act, but rather to deliver one moment of sensational shock value. *Don't Look Now* won a 1973 nomination for best film from the British Academy Award committee.

Although dwarfs continue to appear in horror films, they are now less apt to be cast in negative roles. In *Poltergeist* (1982), dwarf actress Zelda Rubinstein, playing an exorcist and clairvoyant, is hired to cleanse a house of rampaging spirits. Rubinstein delivers a convincing performance in this film, but is later typecast in spin-offs such as *Teen Witch* (1989) and *Guilty as Charged* (1992), the latter a comedy-horror film with Rod Steiger. Occasionally, Rubinstein does get the chance to play a small but ordinary role, as in the award-winning television series *Picket Fences* (1992–1996), in which she played the sheriff's secretary—a decent woman with some extrasensory powers.

No survey of the dwarf in film is complete without *The Wizard of Oz* (1939). It is this movie and the cartoon *Snow White and the Seven Dwarfs* that are frequently named when people are asked to recall films in which dwarfs appear. The majority of dwarfs in *The Wizard of Oz* were not professional actors, and their appearance in the film represented a moment of unforgettable glory.[22] Among those who came to the film with acting experience were Billy Curtis, Jerry Maren, and Yvonne Moray; Meinhardt Raabe, who played the Coroner, was chosen for this coveted speaking role because of his dignified presence and educated speech. (He had a B.A. in business administration from Northwestern University but had been rejected for accounting positions because of prejudice; he had worked in midget shows at the Chicago World's Fair and had been touring as Little Oscar for the Oscar Mayer Wiener Company.)[23]

55. *The Munchkins, in* The Wizard of Oz, *1938. Photofest, NYC.*

Many of the remaining 124 Munchkins had been unemployed when they were recruited for the film, and the fifty dollars a week they received seemed generous—though it was a small fraction of the salaries that were given to the stars of the film. The dwarfs who were chosen were assembled by the opportunistic and paternalistic Leo Singer of Singer's Midgets. He employed his own troupe, adding nine other performers from a group called Harvey Williams and his Little People and other individuals whom he located by canvassing the entire country for candidates. Almost all were hypopituitary dwarfs (referred to as *midgets* before the term was seen as pejorative). Few persons with achondroplasia (disproportionate dwarfs) were included, and the single black applicant was the only candidate who was rejected. Several children were added to achieve the required number of Munchkins. Producer-director Mervin Le Roy is quoted as saying that he hired only "little people who were little and cute and looked perfect," and the technicians, who regarded the Munchkins with affection, spoke of them as "little toys" and "little dolls."[24]

Those who had played the Munchkins were generally enthusiastic about their experience, although some were not pleased with the remarks that Judy Garland made about them on the *Jack Paar Show* in 1967, two years before her death. She called them "little drunks" and described a forty-year-old participant in the film whose dinner invitation she had declined as "two inches high." The Munchkins, she reported, "all got smashed every night and they picked them up in butterfly nets."[25]

This was not the kind teenager the older Munchkins remembered, and they felt that the carousing that she reported had been vastly exaggerated (Fig. 55). Moreover, these accounts led to the making of *Under the Rainbow*, a 1981 farce starring Kevin Kline and Carrie Fisher and dwarf actors Billy Barty, Cork Hubbert, Pat Bilon, and Gary Friedkin, with Pam Ybarra as production assistant. The movie portrayed the little people, in rehearsals for *The Wizard of Oz*, hanging from chandeliers and destroying the hotel where they stayed. A love scene with Cork Hubbert was cut from the final version. Rejected by the public and critics alike, it quickly became unavailable in most video stores. Many dwarfs were dismayed by the film's poor quality and its perpetuation of the stereotype of dwarfs as cavorting goofballs; they had trouble forgiving the immortal line "You are bad little people, you deserve to be short!"[26]

The Wizard of Oz itself was tremendously popular. Often called America's favorite fairy tale, it extols the vision of home, the joys of adventure, and the theme of finding one's strength within. The Munchkin scenes—little more than ten minutes in length—are memorable. Tiny, elegantly dressed personages from a fictional world, they function as a Greek chorus and an audience. It is they who celebrate the triumph of good over evil—everyone who has seen the film remembers them jubilantly singing, "Ding, dong, the wicked witch is dead!"—and the marvelous moment that the gray of Kansas turns to color, when Dorothy arrives in Munchkinland.

The Wizard of Oz is one of a number of movies that include a fictional village in-habited only by dwarfs. Another such fantasy, a "sort of *Star Wars* meets the *Wizard of Oz*," is *Willow,* which tells the tale of an elf who has been selected to protect a small baby who is destined to end the reign of an evil queen and thereby bring peace to the world.[27] The British actor Warwick Davis stars as the endearing, virtuous elf hero, and Billy Barty appears in an effective supporting role as the community's High Al-dren. Davis successfully confronts the difficult set of challenges in this peripatetic, sometimes amusing adventure. Unlike in *The Wizard of Oz,* the dwarfs are not pre-sented exclusively en masse; several have speaking roles and reveal their individual personalities. Despite these improvements, the film continues to suggest to children that dwarfs are to be found living together in the woods.

A common role assigned to dwarf actors is that of extraterrestrial, in a category of movie that could be called the "dwarf in a box" film. Two actors are particularly known for such roles. The first is Michael Patric Bilon, the thirty-four-inch, forty-pound actor who played the title role in *E.T. The Extra-Terrestrial* (1982); the second is Kenny Baker. Born in England, Baker worked in variety shows as a member of the troupe Burton Lester's Midgets, in music halls and ice capades, and in his own musi-cal-comedy act.[28] He then entered the world of films, appearing in *The Elephant Man, Mona Lisa, Amadeus, Time Bandits,* and the *Star Wars* films, in which he played R2-D2. Baker sweltered unseen and unheard within a small metal box, knowing when a take was over only when someone banged on his costume with a hammer.[29]

Most serious dwarf actors would find roles like these demeaning, in spite of their appeal for the public, and many have declined them. Cadence Roth, the actress hero-ine in Armistead Maupin's novel *Maybe the Moon,* is based on Maupin's good friend, Tamara de Treaux, a thirty-one-inch-tall actress who had played E. T. (see Chapter 8).[30] In Maupin's novel, Cadence Roth accepts an assignment to present an award to Bette Midler. Instead of remaining in the confining guise of an elf, as instructed, she presents the award divested of her regalia. Her protest resonates for all dwarf actors who have felt they did not have the luxury of rejecting such assignments.

Challenging parts for dwarfs have remained few and far between. Even when a desirable role appears, those who are responsible for casting may decide that no dwarf is suitable. When *Moulin Rouge* was made in 1952, José Ferrer, a tall actor, was cast as Toulouse-Lautrec—his height had to be disguised by his playing the role on his knees. Dwarf stand-ins were used for long shots in the film, but no dwarf actor was trusted to play the artist until 2004 when Mark Povinelli appeared in *Belle Epoque* at Lincoln Center in New York. Baz Luhrman, director of the 2001 version of *Moulin Rouge,* had given the Toulouse-Lautrec role to average-statured John Leguizamo. These examples help to illustrate why no dwarf actor is included as a star on any of the hundred-best-films lists.

Despite this, there have been some memorable performances among the dozens of dwarf actors who have earned their livings in the film industry. Harry Earles (aka Doll) was among the few notables in the 1920s and 1930s; the French actor Pierre Pieral was prominent mostly from the late 1940s through the 1970s; Michael Dunn in the 1960s; and Billy Curtis from the late 1930s into the 1970s. Linda Hunt, who has been active since the 1970s, has had the longest and most illustrious career.

Departing briefly from American movies, we turn to dwarfs who have been cast in foreign films, some of these films becoming classics. The dwarf actor Delphin was cast as the headmaster of a boys' school in French anarchist Jean Vigo's celebrated drama *Zéro de conduite* (1933); Delphin was symbolic of the establishment: stunted in body and spirit. Jesus Fernandez, who played the lonely disciple of the Christ-like protagonist of Luis Buñuel's extraordinary film *Nazarin* (1958) and appeared also in Buñuel's *Tristana* (1970), has had a considerably longer and more varied career than did Delphin. Fernandez has acted in thirty other films as well as on television and has been a scriptwriter, director, and casting agent.[31] Jimmy Karoubil, who had a small part as a terrorist in Jean-Luc Goddard's *Pierrot le fou* (1969), had earlier been cast in a substantial role in *A Woman for Joe* (1955), a British film about the circus whose characters and plot are rife with explicit "antimidget" bigotry.[32] Although roles that convey such content continue to be created, there is reason for a glimmer of optimism a half century later, in both American and foreign films.

Until recently, productions had not shed much light on the lives that dwarfs lived. Although the dwarf narrator in *Ship of Fools* (1965) plays a vital role in the film as a social critic, the audience is afforded only limited insight into his own experience and feelings. Among the few ambitious films by serious directors that offer a more subjective perspective is *I Don't Want to Talk about It* (1994), produced and directed by Maria Luisa Bemberg, some of whose other thoughtful films have feminist themes. This film tells the story of an older man (Marcello Mastroianni) who falls in love with Charlotte, a fifteen-year-old achondroplastic dwarf played by Alejandra Podesta. Luisina Brando delivers an outstanding performance as Charlotte's mother, Leonora, who is determined to shape her daughter into her own perfect creation. She provides Charlotte with tutors for piano, languages, and horseback riding, making sure that any reminders of her dwarfism are removed from sight. Leonora burns the books *Gulliver's Travels, Snow White,* and *Tom Thumb* and destroys a neighbor's garden-dwarf statuary in the dead of night. After Charlotte's marriage, Leonora is no longer able to control her. Charlotte escapes the golden prison created by her mother and her worldly husband by riding off with the circus.

Bemberg introduces her film as a tale "dedicated to all the people who have courage to be different in order to be themselves." Clearly well intentioned, she remarks that in making the film, her greatest fear was of humiliating Podesta: "For her, unfortunately, fiction and reality are dramatically connected. . . . And when she goes back to her home, she's still the character." Bemberg seems to support the love between Charlotte and her much older suitor, despite it being unusual and socially disapproved. But for Bemberg, "the film is really about Charlotte's possessive mother, an arrogant, absolutely horrible woman, who for me is a metaphor of repression and intolerance. She could represent any one of the many South American dictators we've had."[33]

One may wonder why Charlotte's route to freedom must be the circus—a throwback to a past world no less constraining than the life Charlotte has left. Another troubling element, the dispassionate romance between the cosmopolitan Mastroianni character (perhaps fifty years Charlotte's senior) and Podesta's barely sketched, more innocent character, is less than convincing. Nevertheless, despite Charlotte's sometimes annoyingly compliant nature, the audience gets to see, probably for the first time in cinematic history, an attractive female dwarf making choices that she perceives as expanding her universe.

In *Frankie Starlight* (1995), a film version of Chet Raymo's *The Dork of Cork*, the emotion has a truer ring. The drama unfolds through the perspective of Frankie himself as the film follows him from boyhood to manhood (Fig. 56). The romantic elements are beautifully realized, as is his struggle for self-acceptance. As is the case in so many of the novels previously discussed, Frankie is without one parent (as was Charlotte), and there are tragic elements in his situation. But here there is some relief from the sadness; Frankie's temperament and personality in childhood are endearing, and his relationship with his mother has a lyric quality. As he prepares to journey to Texas with his mother's boyfriend, Terry, he asks, "Are there dwarfs in America, Terry?" "Sure, there are dwarfs everywhere," comes the response. As an adult, Frankie struggles with his identity and surrounds himself with photos of famous dwarfs. One day,

awash in liquor and upset after an interview about the book he has written, Frankie knocks over a table and his drink in despair. But unlike so many dwarfs in literature and film, he is not destined to remain angry and isolated: he finds a partner he loves, and in a realistic and touching scene, he is shown dancing with his tall bride on the roof. The adult Frankie is

56. Corban Walker in Frankie Starlight, *1995. © Ferndale Films.*

wonderfully acted by Irish sculptor Corban Walker, and his younger self by thirteen-year-old Alan Pentony.

Podesta, Walker, and Pentony are not the only nonprofessionals hired by directors for acting roles. Ian Michael Smith, eleven years old when he played the title character in *Simon Birch*—the cinematic version of John Irving's *A Prayer for Owen Meany* (see Chapter 8)—portrays a character very much like himself, a bright, thoughtful young dwarf: one reviewer noted Ian's "curiosity, his passion for meaning, [and] his emotional openness."[34] But Smith (who has a condition called Morquio's syndrome) has been praised also for his acting ability: "His comic timing is instinctive and lucid, and he doesn't go for cute; instead he underplays. At its best *Simon Birch* takes its lead from its young star's performance."[35]

The film adaptation brings Simon Birch to only age twelve and therefore loses the more subtle nuances of the book's revelation of his emerging adult consciousness. Simon is a preternaturally wise twelve-year-old, who prophesies that he is destined to perform a courageous deed, but that he will die prematurely. Anyone familiar with the many novels in which dwarfs die young may be struck once again by writers' inability to conceive of an adult life for their heroes.

Nevertheless, the film succeeds as a touching "buddy" movie. In a presentation at the 1999 convention of Little People of America, Ian Smith spoke about his experience making the film, and both Ian and his father discussed their reaction to the responses it had evoked. His father said that he was particularly pleased that critics Gene Siskel and Roger Ebert had found the film personally meaningful, Siskel judging it one of the year's ten best movies. Parents of dwarfs reported that the film helped their children feel better about themselves, and parents of children with Morquio's syndrome felt encouraged by seeing an outgoing, active child with this condition. Poised, intelligent, and confident at thirteen, Ian expressed enthusiasm for the experience and good feeling about his relationship with the other actors. His family indicated that they would consider another role only if it fit into his busy and rewarding schedule, and served him emotionally.

Just when a few enlightened films augur progress, other movies are released that demonstrate the worst aspects of dwarfs in cinema. The Austin Powers trilogy and the film *The Red Dwarf* revive regressive stereotypes of dwarfs.

The Austin Powers series (*International Man of Mystery* [1997], *The Spy Who Shagged Me* [1999], and *Goldmember* [2002]) had considerable popular appeal. Its critical reception was more mixed, however; one reviewer called *The Spy Who Shagged Me* "less a James Bond parody than a celebration of hedonism and the redemptive power of shamelessness." The dwarf character in the films, Mini-Me (played by Verne J. Troyer), is described as "a thirty-two-inch dwarf who bites and generally terrorizes the staff at world domination headquarters. . . . So let us be clear about this: even as we acknowledge what Mike Myers has added to the world in the way of good cheer, let us acknowledge that this is a movie in which a midget bites the star in the crotch and then gets picked up, swung around, and bashed into a pole . . . the different parts of a messy comedy at least have to be good, and much of this movie is terrible."[36]

The sensibilities of dwarfs who find themselves offended by the portrayal of Mini-Me are not likely to be assuaged by the fact that another character, a bizarre Scotsman called Fat Bastard, played by Myers, is also an object of merciless ridicule. Sharing victimization does not attenuate its force. In Mini-Me, Myers has created the archetypal dehumanized dwarf of literature and film: Mini-Me has no identity of his own; he is mute, he mimics his master, and he is an evil and infantile creature whom most people do their best to avoid.

For Troyer, playing Mini-Me was an opportunity to act in a major role. Previously he had largely acted in costume, playing an alien baby in *Men in Black* (1997); a monkey in *Mighty Joe Young* (1998); and a baby panda bear and a dog in home video productions. (That last job was the worst because Troyer had to be on all fours in the heat, and the dog's head was so big that he kept falling down.)[37] Apart from acting, his only employment had been in a disagreeable job in customer service. So his large role in the Austin Powers films, working with stars he liked, was exhilarating. He got a sense of having "made it" when a talking Mini-Me doll and an eighteen-inch plush toy were created in his image. How could it not be exciting for this young man—who had grown up in a sheltered Amish community—to suddenly be so famous and sought after? In his interviews, the question of image did not arise, and the role was justified: "Verne Troyer is an amazing actor and an amazing acrobat," said Myers. "I told him, 'You have to remember you're one eighth Dr. Evil's size, so therefore you're that much more evil. You're compressed evil, so basically you go to the part of his heart that is very dark and black.'—And he did!"[38] No doubt Myers knew when he undertook to make Austin Powers that his characterizations were less than politically correct. He was merely having fun, albeit at the expense of groups whom he did not expect his targeted audience would care about offending.

What may be even more surprising than the mockery in *Austin Powers*, however, is the misguided effort of a serious filmmaker who creates an atavistic dwarf character, all the while believing that he is offering a positive, universal figure. *The Red Dwarf* (1998), a feature debut by the Belgian director Yvan Le Moine, has been described by him as a metaphor for the human condition. He explains further: "The idea behind the film was to talk about the small man locked up inside each and every one of us, about the fact that there is always suffering. Fed up with the humiliation and vexation of it all, the small man will seek revenge. He will want to become the biggest of all men. And the day he actually becomes the biggest man on earth, he will realize as any one of us would, that it's better to be prince of one's own kingdom and to be generous and loving to those who are close to him than to be part of the world of the big."[39]

Unfortunately, this grandiose conception bears little resemblance to the final film. Based on a story by contemporary French writer Michel Tournier, it presents a weird, depressed dwarf named Lucien whose job it is to create false evidence of adultery in divorce cases. Feeling rejected and unappreciated at his workplace, he has an affair with a wealthy, corpulent, over-the-hill opera singer (played by Anita Ekberg of *La dolce vita* fame). When she rejects him, he drunkenly makes himself up as a female clown and murders her. Lucien then takes refuge with a circus troupe; although reviled by some of the other performers, he experiences tenderness with a pubescent female acrobat named Isis. The ending, unsurprisingly, is tragic.

Lucien is played by the experienced French actor Jean-Yves Thual, who won the Molière award (the French Tony) for his performance in Gilles Sebal's *Mr. Schpill et Mr. Tippeton* (1996). Despite his handsome appearance, Thual's acting cannot rise above the writing—little variety of expression is asked of him. Although film's first scenes intimate a break with stereotypes, it does not realize this vision. *The Red Dwarf* received a fifteen-minute ovation at the 1998 Cannes Film Festival, but when it was shown in New York in 1999, it won little favor with either critics or audiences.

Other foreign films that have offered prominent roles for dwarfs include *Le franc* (1994), an amusing yet poignant, Senegalese-Swiss short (forty-six minutes) about a clever dwarf who guides a poor fellow, who had robbed him, through the paces of buying a lottery ticket and claiming his prize. *Guimba the Tyrant* (1995) is a full-length feature, a collaboration of filmmakers from Mali, Germany, and France. An allegorical tale based on an old legend, the film contains elements that that suggest parallels with Malian dictator Moussa Traoré, and thus it can be appreciated on various levels. It features a prosperous tyrant, Guimba, and his lascivious dwarf son, Jangine; through these characters, the film explores the interaction of despotic political power and irrational sensual appetites.

Italian director Matteo Garrone's controversial 2003 film, *L'imbalsamatore* (*The Embalmer*), centers on Peppino, a middle-aged, short-statured taxidermist who has not come to terms with his own homosexuality. He uses money obtained from the mafia to catch the attention of Valerio, a handsome twenty-four-year-old. Peppino hires Valerio and carouses with him, but when Valerio is attracted to a young woman, melodramatic and at times gruesome elements ensue. The film has had both good and bad reviews from critics; gay people and short people have attacked it for expressing malice toward their groups.[40]

Six Eminent Dwarf Actors

The careers of six actors—Billy Barty, Michael Dunn, Pierre Pieral, Herve Ville-chaize, David Rappaport, and Linda Hunt—will be discussed not only to set forth their experiences, but also to illuminate those of other short-statured actors. Linda Hunt is the only actor in this group of six who is still alive and active in her profession.

BILLY BARTY

The career of Billy Barty (1924–2000), who died at the age of seventy-six, spanned the greater part of the twentieth century. A consideration of his career path affords an opportunity to view both the accomplishments and the difficulties that confront dwarf actors. First appearing as a child actor in the *Mickey McGuire* silent comedies of the late 1920s, Barty in an unparalleled feat remained steadily employed into the 1990s, appearing in more than two hundred films and hundreds of television shows.[41] Nevertheless, his name may be unfamiliar to many moviegoers: throughout the early years of his career, as was the case for the majority of dwarf actors, he was rarely listed in the credits. In addition, his movies were never widely popular or critically acclaimed, although his performance, when reviewed, was often praised.

The enormity of his achievement, however, should not be underestimated; his career was long and his roles were varied. Few viewers realize that the mischievous child who appeared in *Alice in Wonderland, A Midsummer Night's Dream,* and Busby Berkeley musical extravaganzas in the 1930s is the same actor who appeared in *Foul Play* and *The Day of the Locust,* his own favorite role, in the 1970s (Fig. 57), *Willow* in the 1980s, and *Life Stinks* in the 1990s.[42] He also had roles in children's features, including *Pufnstuf* (1971) and *Rumpelstiltskin* (1986). His contribution to the movies was recognized at the 2001 Academy Awards ceremony, in which he was among those honored as important actors who had died during the past year.

Born William John Bertanzetti in Hillsboro, Pennsylvania, with a dwarfing condition called cartilage-hair hypoplasia, Barty was an unusually energetic youngster. During his early years in vaudeville, he traveled around by car with his parents and two sisters, an experience he remembered fondly. Physical comedy was prominent in his routines early on—a favorite quip of his was that standing on his head got him into show business.[43] Some of his earliest work traded on his size: he played an infant who became a pig in *Alice in Wonderland*, a lascivious baby in several Busby Berkeley musicals, and a small boy who bit Frederic March in the leg in *Nothing Sacred*. (That scene has been cut from recent videotapes.) Always well-known for mimicry, Barty received his greatest acclaim for his singing, dancing, and impersonations on the Spike Jones TV variety shows in the 1950s—especially for his imitation of Liberace.[44]

He gave a brief but memorable performance in "The Glass Eye," a 1957 episode of *Alfred Hitchcock Presents*, in which he played a ventriloquist's supposed dummy. In fact, he is the ventriloquist and the "ventriloquist" is a dummy. In the 1960s, he hosted *Billy Barty's Big Show*, which ranked as one of the most popular children's television shows for three years in a row. At first, the managers of the station in Los Angeles that was approached to carry the show, KTTV, were reluctant, unaccustomed to working with people of Barty's size, but Barty enlisted the influential program director Jim Gates to help him get on the air. In later years, he occasionally played film roles, like the breezy huckster in *Foul Play*, that, although the characterization was enhanced by his size, might just as easily been performed by a taller person. Barty gave a convincing, amusing performance in this film, which starred Chevy Chase, Burgess Meredith, Rachel Roberts, and Dudley Moore.

A founding member of Little People of America and of the Billy Barty Foundation, Barty was also an energetic advocate of equal opportunity and fair treatment for dwarf actors. He inspired considerable controversy, nonetheless, when he sup-

57. *Billy Barty in* The Day of the Locust, *1975. Photofest, NYC.*

ported and appeared in *Under the Rainbow* (1981), which was viewed negatively by the "antidefamation" wing of Little People of America and panned by reviewers.

Barty seems to have enjoyed his life immensely. While in college, he participated in several sports as well as serving as sports editor of the school paper. Told he was too small to play golf, he had special clubs made and became quite proficient, later running a golf tournament that raised money for the Billy Barty Foundation.[45] Barty was married for forty years to Shirley Bolingbroke, a woman he had met at a 1960 Little People of America convention. His wife and daughter are short statured; his son, who is average statured, learned very early to shrug off the stares and rude remarks of others.

The most notable aspect of Barty's later career was his steady development, as both a professional actor and a disability activist. His style of acting was direct and broad, not studied, and contained many elements of the old vaudeville style. He noted with pride that he and Rod Steiger never rehearsed their scene for *W. C. Fields and Me.* He was quick to contrast himself with Anthony Quinn, who was trained in Method acting, and with the young Tom Cruise, who discussed with Barty how best to grasp a coffee cup when before the camera. Barty advised him not to think about it, but to just do it. Barty declared forcefully, "I don't like to rehearse—I just like to shoot!"[46]

At the end of his career, Barty came to the conclusion that the movie industry had become less hospitable to dwarf actors than it had been in the past as a result of the increased emphasis on beauty and glamour. But there had always been some resistance to employing dwarfs, and Barty remembered W. C. Fields's comment that "you don't want to work with children, animals, or midgets"—the implication being that they steal the spotlight. Barty could think of no reason for the enormous disparity between the number of male and female actors in the industry, but he did note that talented actresses such as Patty Maloney had been stymied by lack of opportunity. He was hard pressed to come up with the names of any up-and-coming dwarf actors whom he expected might become eminent.

Barty can be remembered for his versatility and his unique "niche" achievement. He regarded himself as unusually fortunate—happy with his marriage, his children, his friendships, his career, and his role in the dwarfism community. The overflowing crowd at his funeral attested to all these accomplishments.

MICHAEL DUNN

Fame is notoriously fleeting, as is epitomized by the career of Michael Dunn (1934–1973). Dunn was a serious actor, much admired a generation ago but little known today. In 1964 he achieved Broadway stardom in the role of the hunchback dwarf, Lymon, in *The Ballad of the Sad Café*. Critics, in a *Variety* poll, chose Dunn as best supporting actor. Reviewing a performance of *The Inner Journey* at Lincoln Center in New York, Clive Barnes wrote, "Michael Dunn as the dwarf is so good that the play may be worth seeing just for him."[47]

Dunn was born in Oklahoma as Gary Neill Miller.[48] He was three feet ten inches tall and had a rare dwarfing condition—probably spondyloepiphyseal dysplasia (SED)—that resulted in bone deformities and other complications.[49] Extremely intelligent and articulate, he attended the University of Michigan and the University of Miami; while at Miami, he performed in the theater group and served as editor of the campus magazine. Later he held a variety of jobs, including hotel detective, before

58. *Michael Dunn with Colleen Dewhurst in* The Ballad of the Sad Café, *1962. Photofest, NYC.*

becoming an actor. Determined to dissociate himself from the anonymous crowd of dwarf performers, Dunn remarked: "The fact that there are no dwarfs around who are actors—there are a great many professional midgets and some dwarfs who can speak lines—means there's not a lot of competition for roles, and I was conscious of this when I went into acting."[50]

Nevertheless, Dunn did not have an easy time of it. Despite excellent notices for his first performance off-Broadway, in *Here Come the Clowns* (1960), he was given only a few minor roles before appearing as Lymon in the 1964 production of *The Ballad of the Sad Café* (Fig. 58). Following his success in the play, he teamed up in a cabaret act with Phoebe Dorin, drawing positive reviews for his witty delivery and fine baritone. Dunn and Dorin performed in clubs in New York and San Francisco, along with Joan Rivers, Bill Cosby, Woody Allen, and others.[51] But despite these successes, and an Emmy nomination for his role as Dr. Miguelito Loveless in the 1960s TV series *The Wild Wild West*, his movie roles generally made scant use of his talent. Only in *Ship of Fools* (1965), for which he garnered an Academy Award nomination for best supporting actor, was he given a role in which he could exercise the force of his personality and the full range of his acting skills. He plays the narrator, a self-aware outsider whose critical outlook provokes his telling commentary on the Nazi ambience of the ship. The extraordinary cast includes Oscar Werner and Simone Signoret; Dunn seems very much at home in this august company. *Ship of Fools* is a rarity: it is a first-rate movie, composed of sophisticated characters and themes, in which a talented dwarf actor has been given the opportunity to deliver a superb performance.

Dunn had his share of demeaning roles, notably in the pedestrian comedy *You're a Big Boy Now* (1966), and unremarkable parts, including as Midget Castiglione in the detective story *Madigan* (1968). In a very brief, and unconvincing, performance in *No Way to Treat a Lady* (1968), he falsely confesses to a crime, maintaining that he would have been believed had he not been a dwarf. Things only went from bad to worse for Dunn. In 1970 he appeared in a poorly made French film called *Trop petit mon ami*. In a moderate-sized role in *Murders in the Rue Morgue* (1971), he is forced to endure negative reactions to his stature; he inquires of the female lead, "Do I disgust you? I didn't disgust your mother." This film was followed by roles in other movies with titles like *Doctor Frankenstein's Castle of Freaks* (1973), *Freakmaker* (1973), and *Teen Alien* (released in 1978, after his death).[52]

Charming and effervescent onstage and off, Dunn would wake late and then frequent Downey's steak house on Eighth Avenue in New York City, where he would pass the hours socializing and drinking. There, in a 1965 interview, he asserted that he could drive, fly a plane, and handle a gun—and on a dare had made a parachute jump.[53] Although he certainly did drive, some of the other claims he made to interviewers and reporters have since been challenged.[54] There is no doubt that he was an avid reader and an amateur sculptor. Dunn was married for two years to Joy Talbot, who in the opinion of Dunn's cabaret partner Phoebe Dorin was gorgeous but opportunistic: Dorin blamed Talbot for "taking [Dunn] for everything he had" when he and Talbot divorced.[55] Dorin suggested that Dunn had married Talbot so he could be like other men, able to display a beautiful woman on his arm.

While filming *The Abdication* in London in 1973, Dunn was found dead under mysterious circumstances, presumed by some to have committed suicide. The full story did not emerge until years later, when medical writer Elisabeth Thomas-Matej published her very thorough investigation of his death. Although alcohol may have contributed, his death was determined to be related primarily to medications he'd been taking. To relieve his severe pain so that he could manage to perform, Dunn had sought help from a physician, who prescribed painkillers and barbiturates that were unsuitable for someone with pulmonary vasoconstriction, a complication of his SED.[56] Dunn's health problems had not been adequately addressed, in part because the nature of his condition was not generally well understood in the 1970s and effective surgical treatments were not yet available. In addition to his severe physical problems and attendant mental distress, Dunn struggled with the psychological aspects of his dwarf identity and, perhaps to avoid pain, had minimal contact with others who had similar conditions. Catching sight of himself once in a full-length mirror, he felt a sense of disconnection: "There I am . . . a dwarf. It shocks me. I just can't believe it's me. I don't feel like a dwarf inside."[57]

PIERRE PIERAL

The French actor Pierre Pieral (1923–2003), born Pierre Aleyrangues, appeared in more than thirty films and is better known to European moviegoers than in the United States. He is best recognized for his performance as the dwarf Achille in Jean Cocteau's *L'éternel retour* (1943). In this modern version of the Tristan and Isolde story, the star-crossed lovers, here named Patrice and Nathalie, meet their undoing through the actions of the amoral and unrepentant Achille (Fig. 59), whose covetous parents are as culpable as he is: they blame each other for his dwarfism, and while they baby and indulge him, they give him neither love nor moral strength.

In a later film, *La Princesse de Clèves* (1960), Pieral once again plays a character who is responsible for the calamities that befall the drama's protagonists, but he was not always consigned to the role of evil dwarf. An accomplished comedian, he played the small but significant role of Grand Duchess Antoinette, cross-dressing to do so, in the farce *Voyage surprise* (1947). He was active from the 1940s through the 1980s: his film-

59. Pierre Pieral and Jean Marais in The Eternal Return, *1943. Photofest, NYC.*

ography includes minor roles in *La corona negra* (1950); *Hunchback of Notre Dame* (1957), and *Le crime d'amour* (1982). One of Pieral's last prominent appearances was in Luis Buñuel's final film, *That Obscure Object of Desire* (1977). In a small and unchallenging role, Pieral plays a psychologist who converses with other passengers on a train.

Pieral wrote one of the few extant autobiographies by dwarfs, *Vu d'en bas* (Seen from below), an emotional commentary on his life, in which he volunteers insights into his dwarf identity and, to a lesser degree, his homosexual and bisexual identities. He writes of his excitement at becoming an actor and having Cocteau offer him film and theater roles and of his disappointment at the paucity of parts for dwarf characters in the theater, noting that it never seemed to occur to anyone to allow him to play any other roles. Despite these limitations, he viewed his acting career as vital to his personal development and was grateful for the opportunity to escape the fate awaiting so many others. "What would I have been had I not benefited from exceptional fortune? One of the ten thousand French dwarfs, rejected by society, mocked, abandoned, objects of derision and repulsion. No one pitied dwarfs. They were laughed at or feared."[58] The memoir details Pieral's struggle against feelings of rejection and inferiority, alcoholism, and suicidal thoughts, offering a glimpse into the consciousness of a sometimes tortured but always passionate and reflective man.

HERVE VILLECHAIZE

It is unfortunate that the autobiography that Herve Villechaize (1943–1993) had planned to write never materialized, for his was an eventful life; his reflections would have been of considerable interest. Instead, only the outline of his family life and some of the more lurid details of his divorces are known to the general public. Born in Paris, the son of a surgeon, Villechaize was one of four brothers; a gifted artist, he entered the prestigious Ecole des Beaux-Arts in Paris at age sixteen. After arriving in New York to continue his studies in the visual arts, he began, instead, to act in films and the off-Broadway theater. By the 1970s and 1980s, he had appeared in more than a dozen movies.[59]

Villechaize is identified mainly with a single television series in which he costarred, *Fantasy Island*. In the series, Mr. Roarke (Ricardo Montalban), a millionaire, enables petitioners to fulfill their fantasies; Villechaize played Tattoo, the millionaire's assistant. On the set, Mr. Roarke treated Tattoo as confidant and pet, with both affection and condescension. The show, which played on an audience's delight in observing people who had complex problems finding a *deus ex machina* that made their dreams come true, ran from 1978 through 1984. After he left *Fantasy Island* in 1983, Villechaize had difficulty finding employment, despite attempts to refine his speech, eliminate his French accent, and improve his acting. Besides making commercials for Dunkin' Donuts and Coors beer, he appeared only briefly on television, on the *The Larry Sanders Show*.

Villechaize was chosen for the *Fantasy Island* role on the strength of his performance as Nick Nack, the house servant of James Bond's villainous adversary in *The Man with the Golden Gun* (1974). Although deceptively pleasant, Nick Nack proves as wily and destructive as his employer. Villechaize offers a very convincing performance and has a chance to be physically active, as well as full of psychological tricks.

But in *Two Moon Junction* (1988), the

60. *Herve Villechaize with his wife, Camille Hagen. Photofest, NYC.*

rambling story of a wealthy young woman and a man who works in a carnival, he has a meaningless, wooden role in which he does little more than swear repeatedly. In the bizarre comedy *Forbidden Zone* (1980), in which two beloveds compete for his affections, he lies atop one, briefly simulating lovemaking. "Your nipples stiffen when I touch them with my fingertips," he says. This often pointless movie contains Jewish jokes and other content leading to cornball moments; it is unfortunate that a film that finally provides a dwarf with a romantic role turns out to be such a poor one.

Like many other dwarf actors, Villechaize was also cast in a fairy tale, *Rumpelstiltskin* (1982), skillfully adapted by screenwriter Shelley Duval, who wanted to render in film the magical spirit of the childhood fairy tales she loved. Although Villechaize plays the role convincingly, there is one problem that his acting cannot prevail over: when the king declares at the film's end that "we shall all be happy as long as we all shall live," Villechaize's character is not included among "all" the happy individuals. It is true that in this film he is not presented as a grotesque or evil character, and thus is not maligned as in other versions of the story, but dwarf individuals and other sensitive viewers are apt to notice that neither is Rumpelstiltskin's loss mourned.

Villechaize's private life received a good deal of publicity. His first wife was Anne Sadowski, an artist; his second, Camille Hagen, an actress (Fig. 60). At the time of their divorce in 1982, she accused him of pushing her into a fireplace and firing a pistol at her. In other instances, he had run afoul of the law for illegal gun possession. Finally, on 4 September 1993, he had dinner and went to a movie with his assistant/girlfriend, Kathy Self; then, at 3 a.m., he went out on the patio of his North Hollywood home and shot himself. In a note, he explained that "although he 'loved everybody' he could no longer bear his ailments."[60] His medical problems had included breathing difficulties resulting from undersized lungs and bouts with pneumonia, ulcers, and a spastic colon.[61]

Actress Sue Rossitto had known Villechaize well. He had called her the day before his suicide but not reached her. The moment she met Villechaize, Rossitto felt that he was a candidate for suicide.[62] Often unhappy, he had never made his peace with his stature; he was attracted only to tall women but his relationships did not go well. He lost his role on *Fantasy Island* not only because of a much publicized salary dispute but also because he often appeared on the set drunk and in bad humor. For years, he had carried a derringer in his pocket.

His first wife believed that Villechaize's greatest difficulty was being confined in a body that wasn't doing him any good. According to Billy Barty, "He was fighting a battle of denial, and that tears at you." But the most telling comment of all was one Villechaize himself made in 1988: "I am a man trapped in a boy's body. I accept it. But I do not have to like it."[63]

DAVID RAPPAPORT

A man of extraordinary intellectual brilliance, the British actor David Rappaport (1951–1990) acted and also played accordion and drums semiprofessionally in his native England while studying psychology at the University of Bristol. In 1975, Rappaport, who was three feet eleven inches in height, married his average-statured college sweetheart, Jane, who was a midwife; a year later they had a child.

While in college, Rappaport acted in a revue that received rapturous reviews at

61. David Rappaport as Rinaldo and Clancy Brown as Viktor in The Bride, *1985. Photofest, NYC.*

the Edinburgh Festival, but despite this early promise, after a hitchhiking trip to the United States, he returned to England to teach grammar school. He vacillated about a permanent career choice, accepting radio roles and in the evening, after teaching, acting in *Volpone* at the National Theater alongside Sir John Gielgud and Ben Kingsley. Finally, battling his fears about the financial insecurity of an acting career, he took the leap. "It was the worst possible time to become an actor," he said. "I had a wife and a kid. But it seemed now or never, so I went with it."[64]

Rappaport had appeared in numerous television shows in Great Britain before meeting Terry Gilliam at a benefit show for Amnesty International in London. Gilliam suggested the idea for *Time Bandits* (1981), and Rappaport was chosen for the leading role, with Sir Ralph Richardson, John Cleese, and Katherine Helmond featured in the cast. Rappaport had also begun to write, and he produced a one-man show called *Little Brother Is Watching You*, which he took on tour in England. As a result of his performance in *Time Bandits*, he was gaining recognition in the United States, and he decided to embark on a full-fledged movie and television career there.

In addition to acting in *Time Bandits* and *The Secret Policeman's Ball* (1981), he had a leading role in the Dutch film *Mysteries* (1984) with Rita Tushingham; that year he also appeared in *Unfair Exchanges* on television, which was followed by the films *The Bride* (1985) and *Luigi's Ladies* (1989). He was probably best known to general audiences as the crafty, loquacious lawyer Hamilton Schuyler on *L.A. Law*, who sometimes triumphs over his opponents by playing on his short stature. Steven Bochco, the creator of that show, admired Rappaport and chose him for the role, as well as another in a spin-off called *Hooperman*. The first dwarf to have a television show of his own, Rappaport played a good-natured inventor, Simon McKay, in *The Wizard* in 1986–1987 and appeared in *Peter Gunn* in 1989. His most challenging film role was that of Rinaldo, the acrobatic, intellectual companion of a slow-witted giant, Viktor, in *The Bride* (1985). In this film, a takeoff on the Frankenstein story, he and Viktor journey to Hungary, where they join a circus (Fig. 61).[65]

Rinaldo expresses great joie de vivre throughout, while protectively running interference for his companion; in return, he is befriended, loved, and protected. In the end, he falls prey to grasping circus entrepreneurs who maliciously cut the string of his trapeze. Viktor is left only with Rinaldo's resounding rallying cry, "Follow your dream." Rappaport did his own difficult stunts for this show and survived a near-fatal fire on the set.

Rappaport's character is at the same time complex and endearing. Both Rinaldo and the monster, Viktor, are humanized, while the villains are depicted as outsiders. Despite its origins in a classic tale, *The Bride* rises above stereotype, in part through the intelligence and energy that Rappaport brought to the role. The actor took pride in this performance. He also was positive about his work in *The Wizard*, the television show he created in the 1980s, as were others: "Rappaport gets a chance to show a 'little person' as a fully rounded human being. He uses his brain, exhibits a fine sense of humor and even does some nifty physical stunts."[66] The series, however, did not last.

Rappaport's conception of himself as an actor is revealed in the roles he did not accept. He turned down the part of R2-D2 in *Star Wars.* Although he did not anticipate that it would be the smash hit it turned out to be, he did know that spending "six months in a Tunisian desert in a tin can" was a horrible prospect. Even when he realized that had he taken the role, his percentage of the profits would have amounted to a quarter million dollars, he had no regrets: "I'm proud I turned it down. That role only called for a dwarf, not an actor. Besides, my ambition isn't to make a lot of money. I just want to be a good actor in a very good movie."[67]

Despite some setbacks, Rappaport enjoyed professional recognition and desirable acting opportunities—more than most. An intellectual, an excellent cook, and a man with diverse interests, he appeared to have a satisfying personal life: though he was divorced, he had become involved in a new romantic relationship. When he committed suicide on 2 May 1990, public shock was less great than it might have been because there had been a much-publicized failed attempt previously. The tragedy of his death was deeply felt by those who knew him, but neither his obituaries nor references in the press have as yet illuminated the source of his despair, or adequately appraised his considerable accomplishments.

LINDA HUNT

Linda Hunt (b. 1945), who has been recognized as one of the outstanding actors of her generation, is still actively engaged in her profession, performing in film and theater, narrating documentaries, and doing voiceovers. She represents a bridge between the experiences of the previous generation and the one now reaching maturity. Her reflections on acting, and on the influence of her short stature on her life and art, have much insight to offer others entering the profession.[68]

Hunt was born in Morristown, New Jersey, her family moving soon afterward to Westport, Connecticut. When she was a baby, doctors noticed something odd about her; one physician at Babies Hospital at Columbia Presbyterian in New York labeled her a cretin and advised her parents to institutionalize her. Hunt's mother refused to believe him, and she worked with her daughter, rigging up graspable toys in her crib. A year later, she returned to the hospital with her thriving child and made the doctor eat his words.[69]

In her teenage years, Hunt was diagnosed as having hypopituitary dwarfism, but her treatment was ineffective. Musing on her experiences, Hunt comments, "I think

I felt indicted by that doctor at the hospital, by that world of authority that perceived me in the first months of my life as a freak of nature. But there was this other voice, encouraged by my parents and compounded by my reasonableness, that said I should explore the alternatives." When she was twenty-five, she decided to suspend these emotionally difficult and unproductive efforts to alter herself through hormone therapy. Describing a subsequent encounter with an average-statured actor, a hypopituitary patient for whom the treatment had worked, she tried to imagine what would have happened if the outcome had been similar for her. She concluded, "If you ask me if I liked going through all this and being the way I am, the answer is yes. That's the answer. What I've been through is like a spring rain compared to what other people have had to deal with. And no, I can't 'imagine' if the treatment had worked."[70] A decade after she spoke these words, she could smile wryly at her earlier characterization of her experiences as "like a spring rain," but she continues to recognize that one important salvation was her commitment to the theater.[71]

At age seven, Hunt was captivated by the performance of Mariette Hartley, then twelve years old, in a children's theater production of *Little Women*. Hunt went on to study acting at the Interlochen Arts Academy, a school for the performing arts in Michigan and, beginning in 1964, spent two years at the prestigious Goodman School of Drama in Chicago. Her father volunteered to pay her expenses for the following two years so that, in lieu of attending college, she could try to break into the theater in New York. Unable to achieve recognition there, she returned to Westport, so discouraged that she was on the verge of giving up. Robert Lewis, one of the founding members of the Group Theatre with Stella Adler and Lee Strasberg, was teaching in Westport at the time. Struck by Hunt's imposing presence and ability, he helped rekindle in her the determination to succeed as an actor.

Hunt's strong sense of self is apparent in all her roles. Her most celebrated film role, as the male dwarf photographer Billy Kwan, in *The Year of Living Dangerously* (1982), won her an Academy Award for best supporting actress (Fig. 62). Mel Gibson and Sigourney Weaver played the romantic leads; Hunt represented the conscience and soul of the drama. Peter Weir had looked long and unsuccessfully for an actor to cast in the pivotal role of Kwan, an Australian Chinese dwarf outsider, and had rejected a number of male applicants. Only when he cast Hunt did the movie come together.[72] Through Hunt's moving performance, Kwan's complex character— at once grandiose, empathic, and hidden—is superbly rendered. When Hunt was out of work in her twenties, her father had suggested that perhaps she give up acting, get a degree, and teach. This suggestion Hunt had resisted, and instead, was able to give her parents the pleasure of witnessing her accepting an Oscar in a two-thousand-dollar gown.

Who would have expected in 1982 that despite the accolades she received, Hunt would never again be given a starring role in a first-rate film? Although denied this opportunity, she acted in eighteen movies and provided voiceovers for a number of others. Her first small part was as a prizefighter's mother in Robert Altman's *Popeye* (1980), a comedy-musical adaptation of the classic comic strip, with Robin Williams and Shelley Duvall. Among her most notable roles were a fine cameo performance in *The Bostonians* (1984), in which she plays Mary Prance, a workaholic physician who is understanding of others' romances but intolerant of too much "togetherness" with her feminist companions. In *Silverado,* she plays Stella, a saloon manager. She was given a special step to stand on, so she could see over the counter, remarking to Kline, "The world is what you make of it, friend. If it doesn't fit, you make alterations."

62. *Linda Hunt as Billy Kwan in* The Year of Living Dangerously, *1983. Photofest, NYC.*

In almost all of Hunt's roles, she is strong and wise—and she is single. When she first met her agent, Nicole David, in Los Angeles, David asked her if she had a vision of the television roles she would play if she remained there. When Hunt shook her head, David said, "You would play schoolteachers and nurses, and maybe career women. You would play unattached women."[73] Few producers and directors are imaginative enough to transcend typecasting based on looks, as Peter Weir did for *The Year of Living Dangerously.* Hunt appears in *She Devil* (1989), with Meryl Streep and Roseanne Barr, as the authoritarian Nurse Hooper. In *Kindergarten Cop* (1990), with Arnold Schwarzenegger, she is Miss Schlowski, the firm but understanding principal; in *The Relic* (1997), she is a courageous and encouraging curator; in *Eleni* (1985), she is a rebellious Greek woman; in *Rain without Thunder* (1992), as the pragmatic head of the Atwood Society, she fights to decriminalize abortion; and in *Dragonfly* (2002) she plays a resolute nun. In Robert Altman's *Pret-à-Porter* (1994), she is one of three fashion editors who are toyed with by a photographer, Steven Rea—but clearly not a contender for his affections.

The only movie in which she played a romantic role is *Waiting for the Moon* (1987), an American Playhouse film made for television.[74] The film sets the loving lesbian relationship of Gertrude Stein and Alice B. Toklas against a background of

French cottages and countryside and touches on their association with Pablo Picasso and Ernest Hemingway. This slow-moving drama, featuring Hunt in a subtle, under-stated performance as Toklas and Linda Bassett as Stein, has an almost home-movie quality. The film received an award for the best dramatic feature at the Sundance Film Festival in 1987; both Hunt and Bassett received awards for best actress. Hunt was in her early forties when the film was made; given the norms of Hollywood, had her stature not eliminated her from consideration for other romantic roles, her age would have. A decade earlier, Arthur Miller had wrestled with the question of the obstacles confronting individuals who did not measure up to society's benchmark when he wrote a part for Hunt in *Fame* (1978), a Hallmark Hall of Fame television drama.[75] Miller admired Hunt's talent: "Seeing Linda, I immediately wished I could have her in something. Anyway, I insisted that she play Mona, and there was no ar-gument. I still think the only person to do her justice would be Fellini. With lesser ac-tors, who are less complicated, it's easy to identify their particular gift, but when you get someone who is full of secret energy, a persona that's not the sum of its parts, it's a different kind of algebra."[76] In *Fame,* an Italian director proposes to a playwright that Mona, a jockey with a doctorate, be given the starring role in his play. The ensuing conflict in this drama—Miller's critique of superficial beauty—foreshadows Hunt's actual experience in film. During most of her career, Hunt viewed herself as a theater actress, and she was more successful in obtaining challenging roles in theater than in film, although, again, these were not romantic ones.

From early on, playwrights have created works with her in mind—George Trow wrote *The Tennis Game* (1978); Emily Mann, *Annulla: An Autobiography* (1988); and Wallace Shawn, *Aunt Dan and Lemon* (1985). She has accepted major roles in an as-sortment of both classic and experimental plays: Bertolt Brecht's *Mother Courage and Her Children* (1984), Anton Chekhov's *The Cherry Orchard* (1988) and *The Three Sisters* (1996–1998; Fig. 63), Lavonne Mueller's *Little Victories* (1983), and Caryl Churchill's *Top Girls* (1983). She has won two Obies for her performances. In the Peter Brooks production of *The Cherry Orchard,* Hunt communicates both her character Charlotta's charisma and the hopelessness of her situation.

Emily Mann's *Annulla* (1976) is the one-woman monologue of an elderly Holo-caust survivor. Hunt played that role to sold-out audiences for four weeks. Mann re-marked, "Why would Linda Hunt come and do it in Brooklyn for twenty cents a week? But she did. Here she is, a Wasp, and she understands this little Jewish lady, and she knows how it was to be a Jew in the thirties."[77] Her decision to appear in *An-nulla* is but one instance of Hunt's penchant for seeking interesting vehicles with laudable themes. She has narrated and provided voiceovers for a good many docu-mentaries, including the IMAX film *Amazon* (1997), with Dr. Mark Plotkin and Ma-mani, a Buddhist shaman, and *Out of the Past* (1998), the account of a gay-straight alliance in a Salt Lake City, Utah, high school. Her cultivated, resonant voice can also be recognized in many commercials.

Over several seasons, beginning in 1998, television audiences viewed Hunt in the recurring role of the forceful Judge Zoey Hiller in the award-winning series *The Practice*. However, in the absence of starring roles in first-rate films, her name remained less familiar to the general public than might have been expected in light of her long career and critical acclaim.

Although Hunt is often described as diminutive, she is rarely referred to as a

63. Linda Hunt as Olga with Mary Stuart Masterson as Irina in Three Sisters, *1992. Photofest, NYC.*

dwarf: in fact, as late as 2003, a journalist could assert that she was not a dwarf.[78] Because she is four feet nine inches tall and proportionate, her dwarfism is often not recognized. This marginality contributed to the length of time it took for Hunt to fully come to terms with her dwarf identity.[79] Although she now speaks freely of that process in private conversation, it first revealed itself publicly in 1998 in a letter she wrote in response to a piece by Lisa Abelow Hedley in the *New York Times Magazine*.[80] Hedley, the mother of a baby daughter with achondroplasia, had written about her feelings during the year that followed her daughter's birth; her description, while indicating her distress at others' reactions, intimated that she was also still grappling with her own. Hunt's letter to the editor was printed two weeks later:

> I was born with hypopituitary dwarfism in 1945, when doctors understood little about my condition. As a result, it wasn't actually diagnosed until I was 12. As a child I suffered from an acute sense that something terrible and secret was wrong with me. I was very small for my age (I'm now 4 feet 9 inches), my head was large for a little girl and my nose, which had no cartilage, spread insistently across my face. In retrospect, I realize how much easier it might have been for me to know, from an early age, that I had a specific hormonal disorder.
>
> It's such an odd thing to be challenged this way. Dwarfism, after all, isn't like cancer or heart disease. It isn't fatal, and it isn't even an illness. It is physical, though, and inescapable. Unlike some diseases, there is no possibility of a magic cure. You don't get over it. It is you. But you aren't it, and that's an important distinction.
>
> Hedley's response to her friend's observation, that it might be best to put her daughter up for adoption, is incomprehensible to me. "Even if we were to consider putting her up for adoption," she writes, "it would surely be in the privacy of our own home and minds." Her friend's offense, I can only conclude, is that he spoke her thoughts out loud.
>
> Nothing the world dishes out could be more harmful to LilyClaire than her mother's suppressed shame and disappointment. I hope that by now Hedley and her husband realize that the catastrophe they imagine has befallen them with the birth of their daughter is entirely in their minds.[81]

Hedley, a filmmaker, had already begun to be active on her daughter's behalf and later went on to produce the thought-provoking documentary *Dwarfs: Not a Fairy Tale* for HBO.[82] As for Hunt, writing to the *Times* had marked a milestone, as she wrote me a year later: "My letter to *The New York Times* was momentous for me, a real 'coming out' if you will. As a lesbian I hardly know which front is more important to be out on. Discovering a fluid identity that embraces my dwarfism and my gayness, and everything else in the mix, feels the only possible way to live now. I fall far short of it (forgive the pun) a lot of the time but not all of the time."[83]

I met Linda Hunt first in Los Angeles and later in New York.[84] She was warm and empathic, with a fine sense of irony and a wonderful laugh; she listened thoughtfully and spoke eloquently, quite willing to discuss her Pilgrim's Progress toward full acceptance of her dwarf identity. She had not thought of herself as a dwarf until she was about twenty. When she was a teenager, her doctor and her mother spoke to her about joining Little People of America, but she wanted nothing to do with it. In adulthood, she was asked by the Human Growth Foundation to serve on their board of directors, but as she was not clear about the group's function, or the value of becoming associated with it, she declined. She had not had any friends who were dwarfs and did not know other short-statured persons in the acting profession.

More than thirty years earlier, however, she had seen Michael Dunn on stage in *The Ballad of the Sad Café*; she had thought that his performance was great—and that he had a magnificent face. More recently, she had met Ursula Hegi, author of *Stones from the River,* a book she really liked; though she is convinced that Hollywood would never make such a movie, she could have seen herself performing in it had she been younger.

In one of the most telling moments, Hunt spoke of how when she was young she had thought of herself as pouring all her energies into her work—being a nun or angel for her art. From adolescence on, she had not expected that life's ordinary intimacies and milestones would come to her. Only gradually did that idea change. But she found herself "growing up—growing and getting larger inside. Because you take up more room in your own life, more of your own psychic space, your priorities are reconfigured."

She could not pinpoint exactly when she had begun to have that larger life, but a central element in it was her very satisfying intimacy with her partner, Karen Klein. They had been together since 1986. While Klein had encouraged the move to Los Angeles, Hunt, at first doubtful, had ultimately found the move restorative. She came to love the quotidian pleasures of her life—closeness to work, friends, and natural beauty—and now prefers not to be away from home for very long.

Most of the time Hunt is able to subdue the messages of others that suggest that short stature, being a lesbian, or not being surrounded by family and children disqualify one from achieving full status in our society. Instead, she has used her marginality to enhance her insight. In the best of moments, she appreciates that she is still a *rara avis,* an actor who earns a good living in her chosen profession.

Heightism and Sexism

It is not only dwarf actors who face prejudice when attempting to secure meaningful roles; heightism also affects actors who are not dwarfs, but merely short, like Danny DeVito, who is five feet tall. In most of his films, he has played comic roles as short-tempered mavericks. In *Living Out Loud* (1998), he was finally cast as a gentler, supportive figure and offered a better chance at love. But this did not spare him hostile judgments. One reviewer commented: "I cannot watch Danny DeVito in a love scene without barfing. Dwarfs should not be permitted by law to have love scenes in movies. I know I'm going to hear from a lot of dwarf support groups and I suppose the midget groups will come after me too. But look, I'm entitled to some prejudice. I don't have anything against these people. I just think they should stay the hell out of the movies I patronize. Or at least we should have a dwarf warning: You know, WARNING; THIS MOVIE WILL SHOW DANNY DEVITO IN A LOVE SCENE."[85]

Extreme as this response is, similar attitudes have prevented dwarfs, particularly those with bone deformities, from being cast in parts that do not specify a dwarf character—much less romantic roles. Short women have faced the greatest discrimination; there are far fewer female actors than male in the film industry. Since exceptional, youthful beauty is the sine qua non for most movie roles for women, female dwarfs are automatically ruled ineligible, and only those—such as Linda Hunt— who meet the criteria of being highly talented, proportionate, and "just a bit short of the mark" are even considered for a realistic role not specifically written for a dwarf.

One rare exception to the rule was the part of "Tiny Woman," played by Judy Wetzell, in *Being John Malkovich* (1999). Generally, even capable dwarf actresses such as Debby Carrington, Patty Maloney, and Sue Rossitto have found themselves limited to costume or stunt roles. When Maloney was offered a guest appearance on *Little House on the Prairie* (1982), her peers regarded the event as a significant coup. Rossitto has remarked that 95 percent of roles are designed for males—whereas men might audition three or four times a week, women are lucky to do so three or four times a year. She protested, "Why could we not be cast in normal roles—even just as the neighbor next door?"[86] She was subsequently delighted to hear about Meredith Eaton being cast in a starring role in *Unconditional Love* (2003).

In 1999 there were 102 members in the Screen Actors Guild (SAG) listed as "Little People."[87] Most were employed in science fiction or action films, some of them as performers of stunts. Few were female; many were underemployed.[88] SAG has shown its concern for diversity in the media by conducting studies of the portrayal of women and members of minority groups. Although a 1998 SAG report did not discuss dwarfism specifically, it noted and deplored the fact that the percentage of characters with disabilities had declined to approximately half the 1993 figure, and when they did appear, disabled characters did not play "normal" roles—the plot focused on their disabilities.

Even in the last decade of the twentieth century, most people would have been hard put to name a single dwarf actor, though they may have known about Hank the Angry Drunken Dwarf, who, until his death on 4 September 2001 at the age of thirty-nine, was a frequent guest on *The Howard Stern Show.* Hank's role was to appear there while inebriated, allowing himself to be queried by Stern about his prodigious drunkenness, his varied sexual experiences, and his indiscriminately bigoted views.[89]

Revisiting Fantasy Roles: Arturo Gil

The demeaning performances of such individuals as Hank (Henry Nasiff) are at one end of the spectrum; the achievements of the few uniquely gifted and fortunate dwarf actors who are able to obtain high-profile roles in serious drama or comedy are at the other. In between are many capable actors who enjoy their work and are sometimes even among the more sought after and financially successful. Most of them perform in fantasy roles, in costumes that hide their bodies, and at times even their faces. Their names are listed far down among the film's credits, if at all, and they are not generally known to the public.

Actors who play fantasy characters have engendered criticism from a segment of the dwarfism community. However, there are many others who argue that since most roles available to dwarf actors *are* in science fiction films or woodland fantasies and the like, it makes no sense to proffer negative judgments about performers who accept such assignments. Only when the role itself is repellent, these advocates believe, should one pass judgment.

It is easy to see why this subject is controversial. At a time when an increasing number of dwarf actors have

64. *Arturo Gil. Photograph by Rick Hustead.*

perfected their craft and are campaigning to secure realistic, meaningful roles, high-lighting these mythological figures may be viewed in a sense as undermining the public's ability to perceive human dwarfs as the varied adults they are. Actor Arturo Gil, who has played parts in every fantasy category, takes a nuanced point of view (Fig. 64). He has appeared in twenty films with titles such as *Leprechaun, Ghoulies IV,* and *Bill and Ted's Bogus Journey;* he has also had similar roles on two dozen television shows and been featured in many commercials. Almost all his parts required him to perform in costume—as a rabbit, a baby, a leprechaun, and so forth.

Gil appears blessed by a sunny disposition. Although he is cognizant of the limited opportunities available to him, he prefers to focus on the rewards he does have.[90] He enjoys doing costume work and finds it a challenge to portray the imaginary characters. He says that he finds the parts rewarding because they enable him to put a smile on peoples' faces. In the process, he is able to meet and spend time with interesting people. Occasionally, he has even been pleased to garner a role that has allowed him to interact with a major character, as was the case in *Monkeybone* (2000), starring Bridget Fonda, Whoopi Goldberg, and Brendan Frasier. Gil played Rat Guard, capturing Frasier's character and throwing him in jail. Because he had worn an elaborate costume, he would not be recognized on the street—an advantage, as he values his privacy. The part was a small one, but that also did not bother Gil—he describes himself as the "king of bit parts."

Even bit parts are not easy to come by. Although there is some camaraderie among the actors who play these "little people roles," they face the same competition for the few parts available that is endemic to the rest of the industry. Gil has had several movie roles in recent years and has appeared on television, in *Providence* and on Comedy Central. Some of the material on the latter, he recognizes, could be seen as politically incorrect but not truly offensive. He appreciates the good money, the health benefits, and a schedule that allows for a relaxed family life that his current work offers. At a San Jose regional Little People of America meeting, he met his wife, Dawn, to whom he is happily married; they have an adopted daughter, Gabrielle, who is a great joy to both parents.

Like many of his peers, Gil had not originally intended to be an actor and had not taken acting lessons. He was employed as a disc jockey in a New Orleans nightclub and as a radio engineer before taking a computer job in Los Angeles. After occasionally filling in for a friend at shoots, he got his SAG membership working in Billy Barty's remake of *Snow White and the Seven Dwarfs,* after which he committed himself to acting. Gil feels that he has used his size as an asset and believes that for the most part he has not received disrespect from LPA members for his choices. Although he does not mind playing elves and woodland creatures—he regards them as legitimate entertainment—he is eager for other opportunities. He looks forward to finding a venue for a script that he and others have been working on and would be open to appearing in mainstream roles. In April 2001, Gil garnered a starring role in an episode of the popular sitcom *Ally McBeal*. There he delivered a strong performance as a young man who was being sued for fraud for not having identified himself as a dwarf during a courtship that he and an average-statured woman had conducted by e-mail. Gil was pleased to have the chance to deliver a few speeches affirming his sense of self-worth.

Aware of the slow progress of other minority groups in obtaining desirable media roles, he feels an affinity with them: his Web site contains a link to the SAG disability rights site. The gulf between actors who are cast in costume roles and the very few who attain challenging, nonfantasy parts still exists, but it has grown just a bit narrower with the emerging trend toward more realistic roles. Increasingly, Gil and others like him reflect on how to strike a balance between supporting their families and obtaining parts they are proud to play among the limited number available.

Television

Most of the early television work available to dwarfs was in vaudeville or on children's shows or sometimes in roles playing bizarre characters. Roles that were neither fantasy nor retrograde were almost nonexistent until the 1980s. In that decade, two shows depicted a dwarf in a significant, ongoing role. The first was *The Magician*, which for two years was hosted by David Rappaport; the second was *Diff'rent Strokes*, starring Gary Coleman. Coleman was a dwarf child actor (he was four feet tall as a result of a kidney disorder) who played the adopted black son of a wealthy, sophisticated white couple. This popular series employed Coleman's short stature and race as springboards for both conflict and comedy.

As in the case of Herve Villechaize, however, once the series was canceled, Coleman had difficulty obtaining work. The adult Coleman worked as a bouncer, and he was arrested for assault. More recently he has worked as a columnist for Ugo.com and has appeared occasionally on Comedy Central, while still yearning for more significant film roles than the bit parts open to him.[91] In 2003, seemingly as a publicity stunt, he joined the crowded field of candidates vying for a place on the ballot in the race for governor of California. How lightly his candidacy was taken was made apparent when Jay Leno invited all 135 aspirants to appear on his show and remarked, "And Gary Coleman, don't worry. We will have a booster seat."[92]

The tales are legion of average-statured actors who have brief periods of celebrity after which they are beset by rejection, substance abuse, or serious depression. There is no reason to think that this pattern is more common among dwarfs, but a dearth of starring roles and nonstereotyped characters historically has made their situation more difficult. To some extent this situation still pertains. Dwarfs are most evident at Christmastime, when armies of elves populate commercials and seasonal shows. Even an accomplished actor such as Cork Hubbert (who played Lymon opposite Vanessa Redgrave) could be cast in a 1998 production of *ER* as an obese, disagreeable dwarf who demands to be released from the emergency room to return to his job as one of Santa's elves.

Fantasy figures were common on television throughout the 1990s. In 1993 Phil Fondacaro played a "little green man" on *Northern Exposure*. Ed, a shaman-in-training, perceives him as an evil spirit and is alarmed. The dwarf protests that he has come only because he has been called, and an experienced shaman explains to him that Ed himself has created the spirit, who is in fact his demonic low self-esteem.[93] It is surprising that this series, noted for its nonstereotyped characters, employed a dwarf as a negative symbol. In *Twin Peaks*, a cult series that appeared in 1990–1991, a dancing-dwarf dream (with Michael J. Anderson) was featured that seemed entirely gratuitous. Average-statured comedian Julie Brown commented, "Any show that ends an episode with a vibrating dwarf is my kind of TV."[94]

In the 1990s there were encouraging signs of change. Zelda Rubinstein's appearances in *Picket Fences* have already been mentioned. In another episode of that same series, a dwarf character, skillfully played by Michael J. Anderson, rescues an abused elephant from a circus.[95] In the process of being put on trial for his action, he meets and courts the sheriff's attractive deputy. Although she ultimately rejects him, there is one kiss, and a hint of romance, before she explains her decision not to get any more involved. The relationship is less convincing than it might be, but the show does make a serious try at exploring a potential romance between a dwarf and an average-statured person. Anderson displayed his considerable talent in Julie Taymor's *American Playhouse* version of Poe's "Hop-Frog."[96] In this production, which starred Moreille Moss as Tripetta and Anderson as Hop-Frog, Taymor used rubberized puppets to depict the courtiers in a rendering of the story that some viewers found innovative and others less than successful.

By the turn of the twentieth century, positive, realistic portrayals of dwarf characters on television became more common. Phil Fondacaro, in *Touched by an Angel*, played a dwarf father who was raising an average-statured son.[97] The son at first hid their relationship from his friends and pretended that another man was actually his father. After considerable struggle, the son overcame his shame and the two were shown moving toward a warm, loving relationship. Although the script stereotypically made the father a clown, it still showed real persons working out the tensions in a father-son relationship. Playing this role was a departure for Fondacaro, who had previously been in more than thirty movies, playing an Ewok in *Return of the Jedi* and acting in many low-budget horror films.[98]

A real breakthrough occurred when a dwarf character named Mickey, played by Danny Woodburn, was introduced on *Seinfeld* as Kramer's sidekick. Woodburn's *Seinfeld* role is the rare example of a dwarf appearing regularly as a real person on a popular show. His appearances were positively received, and he was sought after for other parts. In 2001, Meredith Eaton, in the role of spirited lawyer Emily Resnick, became first a guest star and then a regular performer in another series, *Family Law*; the character had been created with her in mind. Unfortunately, both shows were discontinued, but they signaled the potential for a new era.

In the spring of 2001, within a few weeks of each other, dwarf actors were featured on two popular sitcoms—*Becker* and *Dharma and Gregg*. On *Becker,* Danny Woodburn plays a deliveryman—an ordinary character—but Becker himself expresses his conviction that "the dwarf brought bad luck." Despite other characters' pooh-poohing Becker's superstition, subsequent events seemed to prove his point, evoking audience laughter. In a very different scenario, Dharma, of *Dharma and Gregg,* is forced to confront her own prejudices when a dwarf couple visits—Gregg's school chum (Mark Povinelli) and his wife (Meredith Eaton), an oral surgeon. The episode dramatizes Dharma's embarrassment at her recurrent social blunders and contrasts them with her genuine effort to change.

Such shows at least represent pioneering efforts to raise average-statured people's consciousness about dwarfs. The fact that pop culture is taking notice of the group suggests that we have arrived at what may be a historic moment; positive changes are sometimes noticeable in serious drama as well. In 2001, Danny Woodburn appeared on the cable channel Showtime in a made-for-TV film titled *Things You Can Tell Just by Looking at Her,* a drama in which several fine actresses, among them Glenn Close and Holly Hunter, played interlocking roles that revealed the lives and loves of seven women. In one of the segments, called "Someone for Rose," a writer played by Kathy Baker surprises herself by first being curious about, and then falling in love with, a forthright, appealing dwarf accountant, played by Woodburn.

In fall 2003, two other actors made television news. In *Carnivale,* an HBO series scheduled to last at least three years, Michael J. Anderson was cast as Samson, a former sideshow performer who had been elevated by management to a position running a traveling carnival during the Great Depression. *Carnivale* offered Anderson, a veteran performer whose previous appearances had been mostly in fantasy roles, "one of the greatest experiences of my life."[99] For most of his twenty-year career, except for a few roles mentioned earlier in this chapter, he had been consigned to non-speaking parts, as elves, leprechauns, and small creatures, once playing a penguin. *Carnivale,* interlaced with magical realism and fraught with the characters' complex battles between good and evil, represented an unexpected coup for Anderson, and his performance received positive attention.[100]

Martin Klebba, at twenty-nine years old, appeared as Hank Dingo in *Knee High PI*, a Comedy Central made-for-TV show. Billed as the world's smallest detective, Klebba, who had had a few small parts in films previously but whose résumé was heavily tilted toward his activities as stuntman, offered a good acting performance and performed spectacular physical feats; some reviewers, however, described the writing as tasteless and corny and built mainly around the gimmick of Klebba's stature.[101] Finally, on 16 December 2003, NBC announced that it would be presenting Verne Troyer, Ellen Fondacaro, and Phil Fondacaro in a half-hour reality comedy show about their lives together in their specially built San Fernando Valley home.

Current Theater

Once Michael Dunn and, later, Linda Hunt, were no longer active on the New York stage, few other short-statured actors appeared on Broadway or off. Amateur and even professional dwarf actors were still most apt to be found in whimsical costumes, earning a month's salary in Radio City's annual Christmas extravaganza. At the turn of the twenty-first century, however, there seemed to be a sudden burst of activity, most notably in the performances of Peter Dinklage.

In May 2000, Dinklage starred as Bobby Lemondrops in Mark Spitz's *I Wanna Be Adored*, a dark comedy about the British rock band Joy Division. During the previous six months he had played "the handsome and hardhearted Prince Charming" in *Poona the F**k Dog* and a "cynically honest commedia clown" in Brandon Cole's *Imperfect Love*.[102] His off-Broadway credits included performances in a half dozen other plays. However, in October 2004, after his success in the film *The Station Agent* (2003), Dinklage was cast in the title role in Shakespeare's *Richard III* at the Public Theater in New York, providing him with a challenge he had long coveted.

Only a few other dwarf actors had garnered interesting roles during this period. In April 2001 there had been a performance of a witty, disturbing existential drama called *Killer Midgets* at the Pelican Studio Theater in Manhattan. Despite its off-putting title, the play, written and directed by John Dapolito, had some thought-provoking elements. David Steinberg, Mark Trombino, and Ethan Crough were extremely effective in contrasting roles as Mafia characters who happened also to be dwarfs.

But it was not until November 2003 that a major production with dwarf actors was mounted. Mabou Mines' *DollHouse*, an innovative adaptation of Ibsen's *A Doll's House*, opened to much acclaim at St. Ann's Warehouse, a small theater in Brooklyn.[103] The play cast actors Mark Povinelli, Ricardo Gil, and Kristopher Medina in the male parts, and average-statured women in the female roles. This unusual casting of three short-statured males was not simply a gimmick. The staging, which featured doll-like puppets and a scaled-down entryway, symbolized the emotional trap that marital relationships often posed for both males and females. The sexually charged performances of the male actors contributed significantly to this absorbing reinterpretation of Ibsen's work. While the play's positive portrayal of dwarfs' physicality was something new, so was the casting of Povinelli as Toulouse-Lautrec in an original musical play about the artist's death, titled *Belle Epoque,* which opened in New York's Lincoln Center in 2004. (The famously short Lautrec had previously been played on both stage and screen by tall actors.) At least for a few physically atypical gifted actors, the barriers about being cast in classic or romantic roles seemed finally to be coming down.

TEKKI LOMNICKI

Many dwarf actors have wanted to create opportunity by writing their own material. The unique theatrical achievement of Tekki Lomnicki, a Chicago writer, director, and performer, demonstrates that this is possible. Lomnicki considers herself a writer first, and then an actor and director.[104] After majoring in English in college she spent many years working for corporations, writing, and managing creative people, but finally began freelancing in order to make room for more pressing interests. She is currently artistic director of the Tellin' Tales Theatre in Chicago.

Lomnicki grew up in a Chicago suburb with her parents and two brothers. Not quite three and a half feet tall, she walks with the aid of crutches. Her diastrophic dwarfism meant that her childhood was marked by a good many orthopedic surgeries and hospital stays. (Recently, she has used these experiences in presentations she performs at hospital workshops and symposia for doctors and patients.) Apart from medically necessary interruptions, she sees herself as having been treated as a normal child. Her father's attitude is typified by a line of his that she has included in one of her performances: "Just throw the ball to her and she'll catch it!" The comfort and confidence that this kind of rearing conferred has enabled her to put people at ease.

In 1994 her life changed dramatically, when she and her colleagues Michael Blackwell and Nancy Neven Shelton collaborated on a play called *When Heck Was a Puppy: The Living Testimonies of Folk Artist Edna May Brice.* Its success with audiences and critics led the three to form Tellin' Tales Theatre, which was incorporated in 1996 after receiving a grant from the City of Chicago's Department of Cultural Affairs. In 1997, a storytelling musical that Lomnicki and Laura Dare were commissioned to write and act in was produced at the theater. Her quirky originality as a writer showed itself in *Alchemy*, produced in 1996, for which she invented four female characters—among them a lesbian sculptor and an astronomer-nun—who manage to turn what is troublesome or "base" in their lives into gold. Subsequently, Lomnicki wrote and produced *Genetic Material* and performed in it in 1999 and 2000. She collaborated on the show with her average-statured friend Lotti Pharris.

Although Lomnicki had always been careful not to do comedy hinging on her height, feeling that it might get stale very fast, some of her most successful stand-up routines do refer to her own experience. Her keen wit is evident in a monologue from *Genetic Material* about her evolving sense of self: "I used to think that if I found the perfect purse everything would be okay. Maybe if it had enough pockets, there'd be room for everything—my confidence, the right words, potions to make men fall in love with me, salary raises. . . . Maybe if I changed my hair, people would be talking about that and not how short I was."[105] After describing a number of other vain stratagems that she had tried—wearing a certain lipstick and a blue suit with a circle pin— she finally recognizes that "I was such a fake!" With her "perfect boyfriend" and "perfect boss" gone, she is forced to confront herself, in a climax that elicits enthusiastic audience response: *"I had no choice but to finally be real."*[106]

Lomnicki's theater career has frequently generated personal insights that she has later incorporated into her writing and interactions:

> I have found that the times I've felt discouraged have been because I am limiting myself in some way. Last year, for instance, I was in a very beautiful play called *The Sleepwalker's Ballad*, an adaptation of a poem by Federico Garcia Lorca, and for the first time on stage I played the ingénue. She was supposed to be beautiful, romantic, hopeful, and especially young. The director cast me in the role; she didn't limit me. It was me who couldn't get at the beauty inside myself.
>
> Disabled or not, I think that's a part of the human condition. We all struggle to set our souls free and it hurts—it's scary to be who we really are. But when we do that, that art transcends any disability.[107]

Tellin' Tales has given diverse individuals a venue to invent and present shows on themes of their own choosing; participants both with and without disabilities have been encouraged to write and perform their own works. Another important aspect of the theater is its work with children. In the fall of 1998 a mentoring program called Six Stories Up was initiated in which distinguished Chicago storytellers were paired with middle school children. The project is now an annual program. A racially diverse crew of children with and without disabilities work together with mentors to craft a theatrical production. One ten-year-old, Emily Benz, paid tribute to this experience when she told her mother that she would never feel shy around a disabled person again (Fig. 65).[108]

Lomnicki has been able to facilitate others' telling their stories because she is so much a master of her own, beginning with the story of how she was born. Lomnicki's breech birth had been a difficult one and she had stopped breathing. Sister Mary Thecla, whose job it was to baptize babies who might not survive, was in attendance. Lomnicki describes the outcome: "St. Thecla is invoked for a long and happy life, and for a happy death. Sister Mary Thecla decided, because it was St. Thecla's feast day and that was her name also, she would baptize me in that name so I would have a happy death. But as soon as the baptismal water touched me, I began to breathe. So instead of having a happy death, I've ended up having a happy life."[109] *Happy,* however, does not mean problem free. In childhood and adulthood, Lomnicki has had

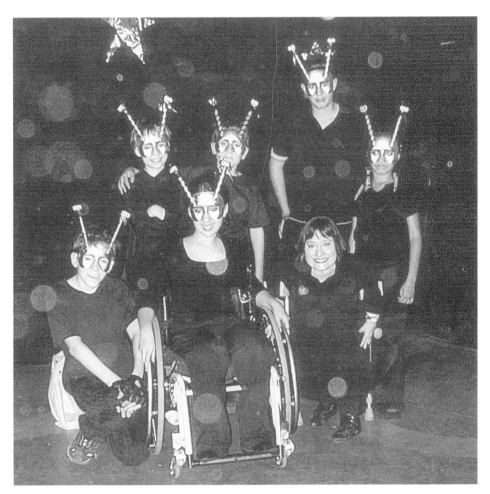

65. *Tekki Lomnicki and apprentices from her Tellin' Tales Theatre Company's performance of* Six Stories Up in Outer Space. *Photograph by Dolores Lomnicki.*

more than her share of struggles—physical, spiritual, and financial. But she has fashioned for herself a unique role as a writer, director, and social activist who is also a dwarf—authentically portraying and influencing the lives of persons with disabilities. Lomnicki approaches the human experience with depth and humor.

Documentaries

Reality has proved more compelling than most of the fictional plots involving dwarfs. The late twentieth century saw the proliferation of dwarfs as atmospheric novelties in MTV videos and in the "midget porn" explosion described in the media.[110] These exploitive operations still persist, but they have been counterbalanced in some measure by the production of an increasing number of high-quality documentaries about dwarfs. Independent American filmmakers produced at least a dozen such films between 1984 and 2004, most portraying dwarfs' lives thoughtfully and truthfully. Almost as many have been produced by foreign filmmakers and shown in countries as widespread as South Korea and Chile. The fact that this genre surfaced at the same historic moment as better opportunities became available for some dwarf actors in popular cinema and television seemed to augur a new era in realism.

The majority of the documentaries that emerged, in a great rush, highlighted the difficulties and joys in the lives of dwarf children, adults, and their families, many of them members of Little People of America. The earliest, and still one of the best, is *Little People: The Movie*, produced by Jan Krawitz and Thomas Ott in 1982.[111] Krawitz's interest in dwarfs was stirred by reading an account of an LPA conference in Florida. She decided to feature this community because she recognized that she had come upon an intriguing, little-known subject. She saw dwarfs as "historically reviled in the culture; theirs is a disability that no one has any sympathy for." As she worked on the film, she came to see them as representing an interesting paradigm of the "other" in our culture; at the same time, she quickly acquired an easy familiarity with her subjects. "If you hang out with a bunch of dwarfs for the weekend," she remarked, "average-size people begin looking strange to you."[112]

Little People, like several later efforts by other filmmakers, was made in part at an LPA conference and captured the exuberance of a group boat ride. In addition, it followed a number of individuals in their daily lives, notably student Mark Trombino as he made his way around classroom and gymnasium, wondering aloud how best to manage in this large-sized world. Ron Roskamp and his wife discuss their courtship and marriage, and Len Sawich, a psychologist and humorist, jokes pointedly about how our society, not he, is out of joint. Krawitz's device of closely framing the faces of the people she is filming results in the audience meeting them eye to eye and thus experiencing them as individuals, not objects. In 2004 she released another film, *Big Enough*, in which she followed the lives of some of her original subjects through the next two decades.

In the twenty-year period between *Little People* and *Big Enough*, many other films appeared, most of them in the United States, but several in other countries. Two notable British films were Lord Snowdon's *Born to Be Small* and Tom Shakespeare's *Ivy's Genes*. The approach of these and most of the other documentaries is thoughtful, their delivery engaging, and their content informative.

Peter Mauro's *Four Foot Ten* was filmed at the Los Angeles LPA conference in 1998 and focuses on a number of people who were attending their first convention: two lively, likable individuals, each with missing limbs, are shown as they get to know each other and eventually fall in love. A family from Ireland in which the son has a rare disorder, metatropic dysplasia, finds assistance through a Web site after years of searching. They benefit from meeting a warm, experienced family whose adult son has the same condition, and they encounter an excellent doctor who recommends crucial surgery.

Most of the documentaries, including Robert Byrd's *Short Stories* (2000), tend to be structured around three to five individual dramas.[113] Byrd, an African American filmmaker, revealed in an interview that he identified with this other minority group and felt that observing members of the community would help him understand his own place in the world. The families featured are followed for a year, their lives skillfully and movingly photographed. Unlike most of the other documentaries, this film presents families in crisis, which in the eyes of at least one reviewer results in an "unrelentingly bleak" and "disquieting" effect and makes the film best suited to provoking discussion within the dwarfism community, rather than to being an introduction for the general public.[114] Similarly, a 1993 Israeli film titled *You Just Can't Hide It* offers a mixed picture: although it features a woman who is a microbiologist at the Weitzman Institute, a man in the computer field, and a comedian, individuals' problems with self-acceptance and discrimination are more in the forefront than in most American documentaries.[115]

Gerard Issembert's *Dwarf: Standing Tall* (1999) covers a great deal of ground and offers much variety. It begins with the image of an achondroplastic dwarf walking in the city and exposes the difficulties of living in a physically unaccommodating world. After offering a bit of history, Issembert focuses on a number of family dramas, including the birth of a child to a dwarf couple and the interactions of average-statured parents and their dwarf children. Among the other segments included in this remarkably packed film are interviews with Lee Kitchens, engineer and LPA elder statesman, as he moves about his specially constructed home, and with Paul Miller, then a commissioner at the U.S. Equal Opportunity Commission in Washington, D.C. Miller describes the discrimination he had to overcome during his career.

Issembert received an award at the LPA Toronto conference in 2001. The documentary, which has frequently been shown on the Discovery Channel during the past several years, has attracted attention and had some impact on understanding and attitudes. At the channel's request, Issembert produced a sequel, *Little People, Big Steps* (2002). It demonstrates that "even without medical complications, life is a daily battle for dignity." The film includes a lengthy presentation about human growth hormone and the aging cast members of *The Wizard of Oz* and explores the evolving attitudes and experiences of members of the Restricted Growth Association, the British dwarfism group. In one compelling segment, Dr. Jennifer Arnold, a three-foot-two-inch primary-care pediatrician at Children's Hospital of Pittsburgh, goes about her rounds, winning the respect and affection of patients and staff.

Certain themes and individuals are treated in more than one documentary. Martha Holland, photographed as a child in Krawitz's 1984 film, reappears as an adult in Lisa Hedley's provocative *Dwarfs: Not a Fairy Tale* (2001). There she is shown skillfully teaching and relating to her students; anxiously entering a romantic relationship; and finally, along with her friends and family, expressing elation at her wedding. That film's four other segments highlight episodes about average-statured parents with a dwarf infant; a teenager's limb lengthening; a lonely older motel worker who had been given up by his wealthy parents as a child; and orthopedist Dr. Michael Ain, who had battled prejudice to become a surgeon at Johns Hopkins. Hedley dedicates the film to LilyClair, her daughter, then four years old.

Particularly moving is the treatment in *Medical Mysteries: Little People, Big Lives* of Tim Rodman, a teenager with Jantzen Type MTC, a rare form of dwarfism that progressively and mercilessly causes his legs to twist. Tim's strength, his family's sensitive care, and the extraordinary surgical skill and vision of their doctor, Steven Kopits, coalesce to effect a successful outcome. In addition, the film features photographer Ricardo Gil and his family. Ricardo's wife, Meg, responds to uninformed questioners who ask how the Gils will manage their average-statured daughter, Lily, as she grows taller: "We don't parent with our bodies," Meg responds. "It is out of respect and compassion that we parent." Lily is heard lovingly "sticking up" for her parents.

Recent television productions have been aimed at diverse audiences. In 2001 the music cable channel MTV, which is watched by young people, broadcast a show called "I'm a Little Person" in its *True Life* series. It focused on Robyn Watson, a first-year college student; Wee Man, a skateboarder; and Terra Odmark, an aspiring singer. What was notable in this instance was that hip young adults, who may never have watched educational channels, responded to this program on the station's bulletin boards, expressing their appreciation of this presentation of the lives of dwarf individuals, a topic of which they had previously been unaware. Still more documentaries are in progress, including one by Steve Delano, currently titled *No Bigger Than a Minute*. The film represents a breakthrough—it is the first documentary produced and directed in the United States by a dwarf filmmaker.

Liebe Perla (1999) and *Starkiss: Circus Girls in India* (2003) are two documentaries that feature dwarfs in countries outside the United States. In *Liebe Perla,* we view the dramatic unfolding of a relationship between two dwarf women—one an Israeli survivor of Auschwitz born in Transylvania, and the other a younger German woman who becomes her friend. Created through the cooperation of an Israeli filmmaker, Shahar Rozen, and his German assistants, this well-received documentary had its American premiere at the Margaret Mead Festival's disability film series in November 2000 at the American Museum of Natural History in New York. A few months later, it was shown at a Jewish film festival in New York to positive reviews.

The film documents the German disability activist Hannelore Witkowski's quest to locate the "research" footage of the films that Nazi doctor Josef Mengele had made about his pseudoscientific experiments on dwarfs during World War II. Most important, it presents a fascinating portrayal of Perla Ovitz, the last of the Ovitz family, on whom Mengele had experimented (see Chapter 1). The film follows the developing affectionate friendship between Ovitz, a tiny, elegantly dressed woman who makes most of her own colorful clothing, and the legally blind, down-to-earth, intellectual Witkowski, who is decades younger. Witkowski queries Ovitz about her concentration camp experience, whereupon Ovitz intimates the horror of that time but refuses to condemn Mengele absolutely: in her mind, her family's lives were saved through his intervention. Witkowski found this reaction understandable, believing that Ovitz was forced to exercise denial in order to live with her memories. Witkowski, by contrast, in this moving, uplifting film, sought to raise the consciousness of Germans and others about the eugenic terror perpetrated in the Holocaust, so that the attitudes that had led to it could be quashed before they again became a threat. (She noted the contrasting reactions of German and American audiences in a discussion following the premiere.)[116]

Starkiss: Circus Girls in India (2003), by Dutch filmmakers Chris Relleke and Jascha de Wilde, captures the drama of the circus and also exposes its abuses. The film centers on the lives of the indentured young daughters of impoverished families in Nepal who have been imported to India to work in the circus. The plight of two dwarfs is also revealed, with one, named Johnson, expressing mixed feelings about his situation. Although he is grateful to have been rescued from poverty and social abuse, he feels the strains of his confinement and yearns for marriage and a "normal life." In the film's final segment, Johnson has a look of resignation as members of the audience either pull away from him or pat him on the head. At its New York premiere, the filmmakers reported that while walking with Johnson outside the circus, they had seen bystanders throw stones at him. This excellent documentary offers the modern audience an education about a phenomenon that is reminiscent of the exhibition of dwarfs in previous eras.

Most documentaries described here have been seen only by limited audiences. A major exception is *Dwarfs: Not a Fairy Tale* (2001), shown on HBO, which opened to critical acclaim and reached two million viewers when it first appeared in 2001; its rebroadcasts are reaching still more. This rash of recent productions suggests that documentary filmmakers are responding to social forces that are now in the air.

Three Talented Actors and New Opportunities

DANNY WOODBURN

Best known for his portrayal of Mickey Abbott, Kramer's friend on the television series *Seinfeld*, Danny Woodburn (b. 1964) studied film and theater at Temple University and worked in the theater in Philadelphia and New York before moving to Los Angeles. Woodburn made appearances on *Seinfeld* for five years, ending in 1998, and was depicted in the show as an appealing, oddball character, much like the others. He goes on double dates with Kramer and gets into a variety of scrapes with him. In one episode they share a goofy scene in an audition that culminates in an acting role for Mickey, and afterward Kramer gets Mickey to pose as a child he is babysitting for, after the real child has run away.[117] In another episode, Mickey ends up marrying a woman named Karen; Jerry Maren, a veteran dwarf actor, plays Karen's father.[118] Mickey is volatile and combative, but this behavior is translated into a winning assertiveness that Woodburn has characterized as positive for little people (Fig. 66).[119]

Woodburn's own assertiveness is quite evident. Once when he heard a producer using the expression "stunt midget," he insisted that *stuntman* be used instead. He has often spoken out against the practice of identifying people by their stature, comparing this practice to the insulting treatment of other minority groups: "If I were to refer to every Jewish person everyday [*sic*] of my life as, 'Oh there's Bob the Jew,' I would think people would get tired [of it]."[120]

Woodburn has a reputation for rejecting offensive roles. Several years ago, he was offered a script for a late-night murder mystery show. Dismayed to discover that the role for which he was being considered was for a character that could only be described as weird, pathetic, and self-abasing, Woodburn sent the author a critical two-page review. Instead of rejecting him for the role, the writer revised the script, taking all of Woodburn's objections into account. Woodburn was then hired for the part, which became one of his best roles.[121] He believes that Hollywood attitudes are improving, with producers more interested in depicting little people in a positive way—as characters with feeling, depth, and personality.

When Woodburn played Otli in the syndicated fantasy-adventure series *Conan the Adventurer,* he worked with the writer to produce a realistic character, rather than a standard-issue comical sidekick. While the 1997–1998 series in general was not very well received, Woodburn's performance was. In *Special Unit 2,* a comedy-action series containing elements of the paranormal, he plays Carl, the unit's informant Link to that universe. He plays "a gnome who has a compulsive armed robbery habit he doesn't really want to kick."[122] In response to questions about the risk of typecasting, Woodburn has noted that he is selective and at times turns down dehumanizing roles, even when doing so results in periods of unemployment, but that as a fortunate result, he is offered bigger and better parts, which are not specifically written for a little person.[123]

Woodburn's versatility and emotional range have been demonstrated in more than a hundred television performances, as well as in film and on the stage. In the television film *Things You Can Tell Just By Looking at Her,* mentioned earlier, he played the thoughtful romantic lead; in the film *Death to Smoochy* (2002) he was the kindly supportive friend of the disagreeable title character; in other roles he has displayed his unique belligerence and his gift for physical comedy. For eight years, he performed stand-up comedy, winning awards and taking advantage of that venue to challenge notions about dwarfs. He is not afraid of playing offbeat, somewhat controversial roles. In several skits on *Tracy Takes On* (HBO) he played Mitch, a stuntman, married to Rayleen (Tracy Ullman), a stuntwoman. She does most of the talking: "People want to know what it's like between the sheets," she says. "He's bigger down there. He's got a wenger like a king kangaroo. Sometimes I let him sleep on me—he's nice and light."[124] In a later episode, Ullman has the two of them making love while hang gliding

66. Danny Woodburn. Photograph by Mark Husmann.

—Rayleen's dream is to get this James Bond–like episode reproduced in *Penthouse*. As the couple is shown floating into the sky, she exclaims, "Like two very large insatiable pelicans, we go up in an orgy of flight! The world was our brother, friction our friend!"[125] One may question the taste, but these skits are no more absurd or politically incorrect than Ullman's other send-ups, and Mitch has an appealing personality and comes across as well loved by Rayleen.

Both his professional and personal life are currently on an upward trajectory: in 1998 Woodburn married his love of seven years, actress-playwright Amy Buchwald, and they have a home together in Los Angeles. Woodburn has had to endure fifteen operations and corrective surgeries, mostly on his hips, knees, and ankles, and he is well aware that in a previous time his aspirations could not have been realized.[126]

PETER DINKLAGE

The most successful dwarf actor on the scene today, Peter Dinklage (b. 1969) is active on stage, on the screen, and in television. Dinklage grew up in Marchtown, New Jersey, and then attended Bennington College in Vermont, where in 1991 he received a B.A. in drama and a Libby Zion award for dramatic excellence. While in college he embarked on several lifelong close friendships with theater people, which helped to shape his professional career. After Bennington, Dinklage attended the Royal Academy of Dramatic Arts in London and the Welsh College of Music and Drama in Cardiff. Returning to the United States, he settled in Brooklyn, where he became a part of the New York theatrical community, performing mostly off Broadway, in the plays noted earlier, and in television, on the shows *Third Watch, Oz, As the World Turns, The Street,* and *The Beat.*[127] In an interview in 2000, Dinklage commented, "I seem to play a lot of wisecracking, cynical characters . . . but what I really want is to play the romantic lead and get the girl."[128]

His desire seems closer to being fulfilled than those of his predecessors. In the roles he has played in ambitious, quirky films, he has not necessarily got the girl, but he has established himself as a sexually attractive male. He appeared as the former boyfriend of Christina Clark in *Safe Men* (1998) and as Rosie Perez's boyfriend in *Human Nature* (2002), a dark comedy about nature and civilization; in *Never Again* (2002) he rejects a lonely woman (Jill Clayburgh) whom he meets online; and he has a small role in Fischer Stevens's *Just a Kiss* (2002), a romantic comedy-drama about the ripple effect of infidelity.

As early as 1996, in *Living in Oblivion,* Dinklage had demonstrated that he could steal the show. However, *The Station Agent* (2003) is the first film in which his considerable talent is given a chance to take center stage. Tom McCarthy both wrote the screenplay and directed the film, which features an eccentric aficionado of trains named Finbar McBride (Dinklage) who inherits an abandoned depot in a rural New Jersey town. In the film, three appealing individuals with contrasting personalities— each lonely in a distinctive way—overcome their outward differences and become friends. In the cast with Dinklage are Bobby Cannavale, who plays a hot dog vendor, and Patricia Clarkson, a depressed artist (Fig. 67). This unique "buddy" movie through a series of comical, empathy-inducing incidents evokes deep, universal resonance in its audience.

McCarthy, who had already worked with Dinklage, saw him on the street one time and was "struck by his movie-star ability to ignore the constant stream of attention, good and bad, that comes his way."[129] That ability is put to good use in a number of the movie's first scenes, when casual observers stare, show shock, or make clumsy or hostile remarks. McCarthy recognized that casting Dinklage in the role would help explain the character's reserve and heighten his erotic appeal. McCarthy has come to regard Dinklage as a "pure leading man" and has compared him to Gary Cooper.[130]

Dinklage sees the character of Fin as neither shy nor bitter, but perfectly comfortable in the path he's chosen: "He just doesn't know what he's missing, and he finds out midway through the movie."[131] *The Station Agent*, a critical and popular success, won several prizes at the Sundance Film Festival in 2002 and opened to great acclaim in art theaters in October 2003. The irony is compelling: the same actor who, as Tito, had walked offstage in *Living in Oblivion* in 1995, railing against theatrical ploys that stereotyped dwarfs, was now taking center stage as the first dwarf actor to play a romantic lead in a major first-rate film.

Throughout his career, Dinklage has rejected offensive roles, especially in commercials: "You know immediately when something's not right—even if the money's good. I'd rather get an office job. Acting is what I love to do, and I won't taint that."[132] When asked whether he would like to play roles in which he is not a dwarf, he responds by saying that he *is* a dwarf, and so that possibility does not exist. Nevertheless, he registers his appreciation of writers and directors who allow his stature to take a backseat to the character he projects. Like Dunn and Hunt, Dinklage numbers among the few dwarf actors to have sought and found major roles in the theater, and he has begun to be cast in parts not necessarily written with a dwarf in mind. Since the success of *The Station Agent*, he has been the subject of many interviews, which are worth reading for insight into his perspective on his acting career and for his revealing responses to queries about his dwarfism. There has been only one false note in the chorus of huzzahs: in a throwback to an earlier time, a *New Yorker* columnist, seemingly unaware of the actor's theatrical background, wrote, "Now there is talk of Dinklage becoming a star, though it is not clear if this is because he is a curiosity or

67. Peter Dinklage with actors Patricia Clarkson and Bobby Cannavale and director Tom McCarthy, of The Station Agent, *2003. Photograph by Jeff Vespa/Wire Image.com.*

because he is good."[133] The era of curiosities is fading, however, and indeed, Dinklage is more than good: he is a superb actor who is generating audience excitement at the prospect of his being cast in challenging roles not previously open to dwarfs. If indeed a new chapter in the history of dwarfs in the acting profession is about to be written, Peter Dinklage will deserve credit for his central role in freeing coming generations of actors from "living in oblivion."

MEREDITH EATON

Meredith Hope Eaton (b. 1974) is a relative newcomer to the acting scene. Her career has been unique in that both her first film appearance and her most notable television performances have been in starring roles (Fig. 68). Eaton is best known for playing the "spitfire" lawyer Emily Resnick on the CBS prime-time television series *Family Law* (2001–2002), for which she received a MAC (Manhattan Association of Cabarets and Clubs) award nomination for best supporting actress. She also attracted attention for her role as Maudey Beasley, Kathy Bates's daughter-in-law, in the film *Unconditional Love*, shown on the Starz channel in August 2003.[134]

Eaton had been involved in theater during her high school and college years, but because she was well aware of the limited opportunities in the field, she had not pursued that path with vigor. Instead, she obtained a master's degree from Adelphi University's prestigious program in psychoanalysis and subsequently became one of the few students accepted into Adelphi's doctoral program. Then lightening struck: hearing about an open casting call for a short-statured actress to play a major role in *Unconditional Love*, in which Kathy Bates and Rupert Everett would be the stars, she decided to try for the part. She found herself remarkably secure during the crowded auditions: "I read Maude and felt her in my bones: I knew I could make her loveable and spunky, and I knew it was going to be my part. I left the first reading feeling, 'This is it—my

68. Meredith Eaton. Photograph by David Kriegel.

parents are going to kill me.'"[135] Eaton's fiancé, Michael Gilden, said, "Meredith, we *all* think we got it [the part we tried for]." An actor with many years of experience, who also has a career in business and marketing, he had been afraid of Meredith's getting her hopes up. But when Eaton did get the part, her parents and Michael were delighted for her.

Meredith has never regretted her decision to choose acting over psychology. She finds much flow back and forth between the two areas: "I use psychology every day of my life—on sets and in family life," she asserts. What matters these days is not whether there is any chance that she might change careers later, but that she loves her work now: "It's where I feel most alive," she says.

Unconditional Love is a campy comedy/drama written by Australian writer and director P. J. Hogan and his wife, Jocelyn Moorhouse. Kathy Bates is an endearing middle-aged housewife whose husband has just told her that he's leaving her. She jettisons her humdrum life and embarks on a series of adventures, sparked by her adoration of a singer whom she idolizes. Eaton plays Bates's daughter-in-law, a dwarf whose husband has left her, in part because of his fear of having a dwarf child. Besides Bates, Eaton, and Rupert Everett, who plays the singer's gay former lover, the film also offers engaging cameo performances by Barry Manilow, Julie Andrews, Sally Jesse Raphael, and Lynn Redgrave.

Critics were unanimous in praising the acting of Kathy Bates and the "scene stealing" comic performance of irrepressible Meredith Eaton. The film's promos, which show Bates, Everett, and Eaton cheerfully posed together, may be seen as embodying visually one of the film's underlying themes—the joyful celebration of difference. No matter how quirky the characters or their aspirations may seem, the three companions—dwarf, gay, and female—ultimately prove true to themselves and to each other. Interestingly, the script explicitly mentions the scary, murderous little person from the film *Don't Look Now* (1973); Eaton is deliberately dressed in a red raincoat similar to the one worn by Adelina Poerio in the earlier movie. Through these reminders, the filmmakers contrast Poerio's stereotypically evil dwarf with the assertive, comical character played by Eaton, highlighting recent changes in attitude.

Eaton was born in 1974 in Long Island, New York. Her father is an administrative law judge and her mother a clinical psychoanalyst; she has an older brother. Many factors, including her temperament and her parenting, seem to have contributed to the assertive personality that is evident in all her performances. Eaton especially credits the influence of her mother, who like Eaton has pseudochondroplasia: "My mother is a little person—the most wonderful role model, an educated, warm, loving woman. When I was younger, she gave me the opportunity to join LPA but I was not ready for it. I was always outgoing and had a large group of friends; I was not isolated or lonely. In college I was in a sorority and in groups, and I had long relationships with average-sized men."

Eaton's approach to her dwarf identity began to change significantly when she was about twenty-two and received a computer while recovering from one of many surgeries. Whereas previously when she saw a dwarf character on television she had changed the channel, now she instead began researching dwarfism. In a chat room, she encountered Michael Gilden, her future husband; later, she met him in person at an LPA conference and found him the most charismatic, sensitive man she had ever met. Married in May 2001, they now live in Los Angeles. As a result of Eaton's joining LPA, she also met Leila, a kindred spirit from Ohio—her first LP friend—with whom she shares a deep bond, a shoe size, and the comfort of being able to discuss such problems as what it feels like to traverse the mall with painful hips.[136]

Apart from *Family Law,* Eaton has made other television appearances as well as made a pilot for a comedy show for NBC called *Mister Ambassador,* starring Rupert Everett and Derek Jacobi.[137] Despite her early good fortune, Eaton has been around long enough to be aware of the possibility of not finding acceptable work in the industry, and she acknowledges the hazards of being typecast as "feisty" but also notes that since she just happens to be feisty and "sassy," portraying those characteristics is not difficult.[138] Besides offering her own input into the scripts of all her roles, she has also been writing some of her own. In the meantime, she takes pleasure in her work and in the fan letters she has received about being a role model for young little people.

A FEW MORE ACTORS — AND THE PROBLEM OF DIGITIZING

TanyaLee Davis (b. 1970) is a three-foot-six-inch comedian who describes herself as the Ferrari of comedy—low to the ground and kind of racy. Born in Canada, she has lived in Los Angeles and currently lives in Las Vegas. She is the winner of the 2003 Norman G. Brooks Standup Comedy Competition at the Melrose Improv, a Hollywood comedy club at which the most high-powered comedians have performed. She has toured cities throughout the United States; in 2001 she headlined her own show at the Melbourne Comedy Invasion at the Edinburgh Festival. Her humor sometimes includes anecdotes about encounters with outsiders' perceptions of little persons, or her loving marriage to six-foot-tall Marty Hiebert. Through her raunchy jokes, she aims to convey that "being sexy" comes from within.

Another young actor is Mark Povinelli, whose theater credits include the role of Feste in *Twelfth Night* at the Will Geer Theatricum Botanicum, Heckler in *Standup Shakespeare* at the Oddyssey Theater, Nano in *Volpone* at the Shakespeare Theatre, and Sancho Panza in *Man of La Mancha* at Self Family Arts Center. He spent a year with the national tour of *The Wizard of Oz*; his television credits include *Frasier, Dharma and Gregg, Bob Patterson*, and *The Hughleys*. Most recently, he starred as Torvald in *Doll House*, Mabou Mines' adaptation of Ibsen's *A Doll's House,* and as Toulouse-Lautrec in *Belle Epoque* at Lincoln Center in New York.

Actor Brian D. Kline, who had experienced frustration bordering on despair during his many years of dealing with the film industry, recently decided to take a major step toward changing the overall situation for LPs in the industry. Even though he himself had recently been cast in several films, in 2002 he decided to assume a more proactive role in filmmaking and invited other dwarfs to join him in the effort. He wrote an original screenplay and established connections with producers, aimed at putting together and distributing projects with non-stereotyped roles. Other LPs, for example, Nancy Adams, have been active in the technical part of filmmaking; Adams helped to re-create the camera motion essential for the computer graphics in the *Lord of the Rings* trilogy.

Lord of the Rings caused a great stir when it cast average-statured actors and used digital methods to reduce their size. Kline and other dwarf actors who had auditioned for and coveted these roles were up in arms. They felt that they not only looked the parts, but also had more than enough talent to play them well. Digital technology and unsympathetic directors could now conspire to exile dwarf actors even from the mythological roles for which they had previously been typecast—and criticized. Ironies piled on ironies.

Some actors were not undone by the *Lord of the Rings* casting. Warwick Davis, who tried out for Gimli the Dwarf, felt that the casting of average-statured actor John Rhys-Davis to fill the role was understandable—that there might not have been enough accomplished short actors to play the twenty or so roles available, compared with the pool of thousands of average stature. Davis, who garnered two coveted roles, of Professor Flitwick and a bank teller, in *Harry Potter*, has played many other-worldly characters; in addition he runs an acting agency in England that specializes in little people. He sees progress: "We used to be treated as a commodity, with six or so little people hired in a bunch as if they were bananas."[139] He strives to see that actors are chosen as individuals and paid fairly.

Conclusion

Dwarfs cannot alter their physical selves onstage any more than they can in the world outside. But an increasing number of gifted actors have learned to use those physical selves to advantage. Linda Hunt explains: "My size totally informs my feelings and attitudes. . . . I think that's true of all of us, in living inside of the bodies we live inside of; it totally colors who we are. . . . When you look at someone who is crippled or deformed or very small, you immediately feel their sense of difference, of isolation. To be able to reveal, in the course of a film or play, the way we are all connected—not only our separateness, but our mutuality, our commonness—is very exciting to me."[140]

Critics in the past have noted that an "immense chasm exists between disabled people and their screen counterparts," and they have called for a truer representation.[141] As both *Unconditional Love* and *The Station Agent* make clear, the unique, the seemingly atypical, are in fact the norm, and drama explores how characters reveal themselves in the context of their relationships. Liberation does not result from having filmmakers depict affected individuals in a consistently positive manner, which is "in reality a call for only pseudo-normal images of abnormality." Rather, the "call should be for the valuation of difference (abnormality) in itself, as only then will the illusion that normality is a reality be laid to rest."[142]

CHAPTER TEN

Music

To some degree, the same great chasm between society's perspective and that of dwarfs that has existed historically in literature, theater, and art has prevailed also in music, with some differences. From dwarfs' first recorded history in ancient Egypt until the present, music has frequently turned up as a significant element in their lives. However, under *dwarf* in histories of music, one finds mostly a lengthy list of instrumental works with that word in the title, or vocal pieces with dwarf characters. These are usually works that confine themselves to myth and legend, with dark mood music serving as background for the antics of grotesque figures, or arpeggios that accompany texts about lighthearted fairies. Any historical references to dwarfs as musicians are apt to describe exhibiting dwarfs—individuals from dime museums, carnivals, or "chatauquas."

The common image of dwarfs in music has tended to be limited and stylized. A typical description from the eighteenth or early nineteenth century might highlight an exhibiting dwarf such as three-foot-three-inch Nanette Stocker, who played the pianoforte while three-foot-six-inch John Hauptman played the violin; how well they played is not known, but their routine required that they conclude by dancing a waltz. In the mid-nineteenth century, the most memorable representations were offered by the evil dwarfs of Wagner's *Ring of the Nibelungs*; in the twentieth, the Munchkins of *The Wizard of Oz* and their engineered, accelerated voices were so entrenched in viewers' consciousness that it was not uncommon for the parent of a newborn dwarf to inquire whether that child would sound like a Munchkin; and in Martha's Vineyard, Massachusetts, as late as the 1940s, one could still visit the diminutive Adams sisters, who served tea, sang, and played the organ for tourists in search of a novel experience.

Further inquiry, however, illuminates an interesting history. There have been a remarkable number of talented performers, including a few truly great ones in our own era. In addition, music has provided a vital means of expression for many short-statured persons who have never performed professionally.

Musical Compositions with Dwarf Characters or Themes

Although most pieces with dwarf themes are not well known, a good many such compositions have been written. In "Zwerge in der Oper," Clemens M. Gruber mentions more than two dozen works that feature dwarfs in musical theater—including opera, ballet, and folk pieces—written in the nineteenth and twentieth centuries.[1] Most of his references are to German works, but a good many are English, and Jules Massenet's 1909 instrumental piece, "Perce-Neige" (Snow White), is French. The most famous is Richard Wagner's cycle of operas, *Der Ring des Nibelungen* (1876). In the first opera of that cycle, *Das Rheingold* (1869), the Rhinemaidens, who guard the gold, tease and flirt with the dwarf Alberich. They inform him that anyone who forges the gold into a ring can achieve world domination; the Rhinemaidens believe that the gold will be safe, because to possess it, one must renounce love, and given Alberich's obvious tendency to lust, they cannot believe that he will be tempted. When they rebuff him, Alberich indeed grabs the gold, renouncing any hope of love, and goes off to forge it into the powerful Ring.

Beyond the complex plots of *Das Rheingold, Die Walküre, Siegfried,* and *Götterdämmerung,* the four operas of the *Ring,* it is their characterizations that have left an indelible mark on operagoers, with dwarf protagonists among the most memorable. Alberich and another prominent dwarf, Mime, are represented as evil, mendacious figures who dream of love, but are consigned to pursuing power and revenge instead. Laura Eppy, an opera lover now living in Queens, remembers having seen many performances of the *Ring* cycle in her native Germany in the 1930s. The dwarf characters, she said, were made up to appear as ugly as possible, hunchbacked and with eerie gray makeup, consummately "scary, nasty little people." In Germany during that period, Wagner's *Ring* was viewed by adherents of the Nazi ethos as confirming the superiority of the "Aryan race," in such figures as its golden hero, Siegfried, and, at the same time, the worthlessness of inferior creatures such as dwarfs.[2]

There have been many complicated analyses of Wagner's dwarfs.[3] One biographer sees every aspect of the hyperactive Mime—his odor, his gait, his high-pitched voice—as reflecting Jewish stereotypes. Others find Mime sympathetic, and the conductor Colin Davis believes that Alberich is the most compassionately drawn *Ring* participant. Gustav Mahler, the composer, identified himself with Mime, remarking, "I know of only one Mime and that is myself. . . . You wouldn't believe what there is in that part, nor what I could make of it."[4]

Novel and surprising interpretations of elements from the *Ring* have been presented. Pulitzer Prize–winning composer Christopher Rouse was inspired by the character of Alberich to write *Der gerettete Alberich* (Alberich saved; 1997). (Unlike those of most of the other characters, Alberich's fate is not spelled out by the end of

Wagner's cycle.) Rouse views Alberich's cruel deeds as the result of the dwarf's mistreatment at the hands of others and concludes that it is possible "to recognize the inherent evil of his nature and deeds and yet still discern some measure of humanity in him and, in the process, to feel compassion for his plight."[5] The piece, first performed in Cleveland in 1998, was written for Scottish percussionist Evelyn Glennie, who is deaf, and includes a segment in which Alberich is reincarnated as a rock drummer.

Another source of inspiration for composers is Oscar Wilde's *The Birthday of the Infanta* (see Chapter 7), which has been translated into ballets and operas, among them a children's opera by Richard Stoker (1963), as well as a musical fable by Joseph Wagner (1946) and a work for string quartet by Maria Newman (1994). In Wilde's tale, the dwarf, who has been given to the young Spanish princess as a birthday present, at first believes himself her worthy suitor. After she mocks him, however, he looks in the mirror, is aghast, and in despair falls unconscious and dies. One may conjecture that this dwarf protagonist, like so many others, has served as the projection of the beliefs and emotions of these many composers. Alexander Zemlinsky's *Der Zwerg* (1921), for example, is animated by the composer's deep affinity for the dwarf protagonist. Zemlinsky is known to have denigrated his own appearance and is said to have identified strongly with the dwarf. Alma Schindler, who had an affair with Zemlinsky, described him in starkly pejorative terms: "[He] cuts the most comical figure imaginable—a caricature, chinless and short, with bulging eyes." The piece has recently been revived and reviewed: "The score of [*Der Zwerg*], . . . is rich, colorful and fascinating . . . it makes all of Zemlinsky's other orchestral works sound like rough drafts. Its central character, too, is a brilliant and moving creation. At first the Dwarf is seen largely from the outside, as the orchestra portrays his awkward movements. But soon the opera accepts him at his own valuation. The crooked slips and syncopations give way, and he opens out into a heroic vocal style: having been introduced as a Nibelung gnome, he becomes a Siegfried."[6]

The libretto, written by Georg C. Klaren, introduces some tension by having the chief chambermaid, Ghita, show compassion for the dwarf, while the chambermaids' chorus offers society's contrapuntal view that he is ugly and unacceptable. The Infanta sings, "Are you insane? Love you, as one would a man? Well now, you are ugly, a dwarf and misshapen! You are so ugly that you are funny. You are a monster, not a man!"[7] The dwarf's expressions of self-loathing, his tragic death, and the Infanta's later reference to him as merely "a broken toy" contribute to the opera's dramatic intensity and the audience's empathic response.

The *Infanta* tale has a power over audiences that most other musical pieces involving dwarfs lack. Many of the British works were created for children and tend, like the French composition "Perce-Neige" by Massenet to be more ornamental, less serious, and based on fairy tales. Almost all the characters in them are male, as they are in the operas. A fairly typical instrumental sequence is apt to resemble the one in Leo Ornstein's *Dwarf Suite for Piano* (c. 1892). Its movements are titled "Dwarfs at Dawn," "Dance of the Dwarfs," "Funeral March of the Gnomes," "Serenade of the Dwarfs," "Dwarfs at Work," and "March Grotesque." Among other compositions with similar themes are Edvard Grieg's *March of the Dwarfs,* Heitor Villa-Lobos's *Dance of the Merry Dwarfs,* and Georges Bizet's *March of the Dwarfs.* The majority of works with *dwarf* in their titles are obscure, fantasy-inspired pieces that are rarely performed.

Musician-Performers: The Old Tradition

Dwarfs have shown up everywhere in the entertainment world for want of other employment, though it was difficult for a dwarf to succeed on musical talent alone. Occasionally, a single dwarf musician might join an average-statured group (as Little Sammy Bryant did, joining Aretha Franklin and her father when, early in her career, they toured with a gospel group), or else become part of a "midget" troupe.

To tap into this odd amalgam of music, it is useful to scan obscure articles such as those published in an eclectic music "zine" called *Roctober,* whose October 1995 issue was titled *Comics and Music, Large and Small.*[8] In a piece called "Midget Rock and Roll," accounts of talented performers are intermixed with others that describe persons who are little more than atmospheric props. The article recalls acts of the nineteenth and early twentieth centuries, among them the Doll Family, the Del Rio Midgets, Singer's Midgets, and Tom Thumb. Their abilities varied: Paul Del Rio, who performed with his two sisters, was "a great pianist, despite his small hands," while Tom Thumb was more of a performer than a singer. The Singer Midgets, prominent among the Munchkins of *The Wizard of Oz,* performed entire operas as part of their stage shows. Their musical extravaganzas were uneven, as were those of The Liliputian Opera Company, organized by Tom Thumb's wife, Lavinia Warren, after his death.

Johnny Puleo, a four-foot-six-inch harmonica virtuoso, played with Borrah Minevitch's world-famous Harmonica Rascals; Puleo's own group was called Johnny Puleo and the Harmonica Gang. He also appeared in the movies *Always in My Heart* (1942) and *Trapeze* (1956). The less talented "harmonica midgets" with whom Minevitch replaced Puleo when he went on to solo work wore floppy hats and harmonica holsters and were sometimes mistaken for Puleo. He himself made frequent television appearances, notably on *The Milton Berle Show;* his recordings continue to be respected, with some available on CD. As late as December 2000, Puleo's work was played on the New York City public radio station WNYC. His performances, however, often employed his stature for comedic accent—in a typical Las Vegas act, an attractive showgirl rebuffs his advances until he wins her by playing a seductive tune on his harmonica; she follows him into a swimming pool, where both disappear beneath the water.[9]

Dwarf Musicians from the 1930s to the Present

Only rarely has a dwarf musician achieved the recognition that he or she deserved. Some of those who did—four-foot-eight-inch Edith Piaf (1915–1963) comes readily to mind—were not thought of as dwarfs but as simply diminutive. Piaf was given her name, which means "little sparrow," by the nightclub owner who was responsible for starting her career; her legacy of affecting ballads, "La vie en rose" and "Non, je ne regrette rien" among others, continue to have a strong emotional resonance for listeners. Piaf's heartrending childhood and turbulent personal life have been explored in several works of memoir and biography.[10]

THE JAZZ WORLD

A good number of outstanding dwarf musicians made a mark in jazz. Even here, however, there were some who were only peripheral, colorful characters. Pee Wee Marquette (whose real name was William Crayton Marquette), one of the best known, was three feet nine inches tall and a mediocre singer. In the 1940s and 1950s he served as a master of ceremonies at Birdland, where Dizzy Gillespie and others played. He tended to overpraise big tippers in his introductions, setting off arguments that ended with insults alluding to Pee Wee's stature, as when Lester Young exclaimed, "Listen here, half a m-f!"[11] Pee Wee ended up as a doorman at the Hawaiian Kai Rest.

By contrast, Baltimore-born William Henry Webb (1909–1939) achieved fame and influence well beyond his thirty years. Hunchbacked from congenital tuberculosis of the spine, he was just over four feet tall, giving him the name Chick. As a toddler he had been injured by a fall down a flight of stairs, resulting in partial paralysis of his legs. Despite his physical limitations, he went on to become one of the great drummers and bandleaders of the 1920s and 1930s. Perched on a high platform and assisted by custom-made pedals and gooseneck cymbal holders, he created "thundering solos of a complexity and energy" that influenced other great drummers such as Buddie Rich and Louis Bellson (Fig. 69).[12]

Although Webb could not read music, he was able to memorize intricate arrangements perfectly, playing a twenty-eight-inch bass drum and various percussion instruments. While still a teenager, he began playing in bands on pleasure boats;

after moving to New York in 1925, he spent the following six years leading bands in clubs. He achieved his greatest celebrity at the enormous Savoy, "the World's Most Famous Ballroom." The highlights of the Savoy era were the regular contests between the greatest bands of the day. The Webb musicians had become the unofficial house band, and they served as reigning champions. They alternated with the competing bands, each playing similar sets with abandon as the crowd danced and finally indicated its choice of winner. On only one occasion was Webb's band vanquished, losing to the great Duke Ellington on 7 March 1937. On 11 May 1937, in one of the most famous competitions, Webb defeated Benny Goodman and his band, then at the height of their popularity, with Gene Krupa on drums. Of Webb, Krupa was to say, "Chick taught me more than anyone. . . . He worked those cymbals with great facility and freedom and taste. The sound he got from his drums was marvelous. His playing, so clean and fast and technical, had the kind of drive that is impossible to describe if you weren't there to feel it. The records don't do him justice. Chick was the guy who made big band playing an art, a great craft."[13]

The night of the competition with Goodman, more than four thousand people crowded into the Savoy, and five thousand gathered outside.[14] Webb's lead singer

69. *Chick Webb. Photofest, NYC.*

that night was Ella Fitzgerald. Two years earlier, he had taken a chance and had hired the gangling, scruffy teenager after she had won a number of singing contests in Harlem. He began by paying her $15 a week; by the time Webb's band defeated Benny Goodman, Fitzgerald was earning $125 a week. Throughout their time together, until he became too ill, he took responsibility for her well-being. Despite requests to join other groups, Fitzgerald remained loyal to Webb, and after his death she assumed leadership of his band.

Webb proved to have considerable business acumen. Most music broadcasts in the 1930s were live; Webb saw this as an opportunity and sought exposure through this medium. He was given eight slots a week, which was more time than any other band was able to secure. His weekly program for NBC elicited more than five thousand fan letters a week. The grandeur of Webb's reign as King of the Savoy behind his custom-finished four-piece set of Gretsch-Gladstones is gone, along with his drums, decorated with inlaid designs of baby chicks and sprinkled with gold sparkle, but many of his recordings have been remastered and are now available on CD.

After Webb's physical condition deteriorated—the intense pain interfering with his ability to perform—he ceased touring. On 16 June 1939, he died of pneumonia at Johns Hopkins Hospital in Baltimore. Fitzgerald, in the most moving part of his funeral, paid tribute to Webb by singing "My Buddy." Traffic was blocked for his funeral procession, and thousands mourned.

Six decades later, another jazz great, French pianist Michel Petrucciani, died at the age of thirty-six, of a complication of osteogenesis imperfecta, the brittle-bone condition that had given him a height of just over three feet and a weight of sixty-five pounds. He was eulogized on both sides of the Atlantic by such dignitaries as French president Jacques Chirac and by music lovers and critics. Stuart Nicholson of *Jazz Times* was among them: "Despite the unqualified admiration of just about everyone who counts on the international jazz circuit, recognition that Michel Petrucciani had been perhaps the finest of all the young musicians who swept into jazz during the last 20 or so years was only really forthcoming after his death on January 6, 1999."[15] In his trenchant assessment of Petrucciani's career, Nicholson notes the array of gifted musicians who played with Petrucciani, making up a "who's who" of bassists and drummers and including the violinist Stephane Grapelli, with whom Petrucciani made the album *Flamingo*, which sold more than one hundred thousand copies. Petrucciani was aware of the double takes that his appearance provoked: "At concerts he paused for people to gawk at his tiny frame and for photographers to photograph, his contribution to dispelling embarrassment and misunderstanding the disabled are still forced to struggle against, saying 'I just get tired of people saying this guy is three feet tall, weighs 50 pounds and plays like a mother-fucker. I'm like anybody else. I may look different but I'm a normal musician.' But as soon as he started to play, audiences, and perhaps even Petrucciani himself, lost any sense of physical handicap. A romantic at heart, his expansive imagination led him down unexpected improvisational byways with an open kinetic joy you could almost reach out and touch" (Fig. 70).[16]

Petrucciani's internal organs were cramped into his small trunk, and he had long suffered from asthma. In childhood, he could not risk rough outdoor play, instead spending up to six hours a day at the keyboard, having begun to play the piano when he was four. His father, Antoine (Tony), was a jazz guitarist, and the family jazz band, which Michel became a part of while still a child, included his brothers Louis, a bassist; and Philippe, a guitarist. In addition to introducing Michel to jazz, his father insisted that his son receive extended training in classical music. He studied for eight years before deciding that his talents were better matched to improvisational jazz. Petrucciani observed that his father's encouragement "saved my life."[17]

As early as his first album, which he recorded at age sixteen, Petrucciani enjoyed commercial success. In the twenty years between that debut and the posthumous release in 2000 of the live album *Trio in Tokyo,* Petrucciani played to enthusiastic audiences, in 1998 alone performing close to 140 concerts. At age seventeen, he astonished a group of older, more experienced colleagues when he played John Coltrane's "Giant Steps" at breakneck speed.[18] His long fingers, unaffected by the fragility that diminished the mobility of the rest of his body, spanned a tenth on the keyboard, the minimum span for great pianists.

Besides his prodigious talent, he had personal qualities that engendered respect from others: "Petrucciani reminded people of Dostoyevsky's 'Idiot'—the 'wholly beautiful man' whose function it was to disseminate a new state of being. He led them to reevaluate their definitions of ugliness and beauty and of bad and good luck. He was a redeemer. Charles Lloyd

70. *Michel Petrucciani. Photograph by David Redfern/Retna Ltd.*

called him an 'avatar.' It can be said without rhetoric that he was the personification of the victory of the spirit over the flesh."[19]

Lloyd and Petrucciani helped invigorate each other's careers, eventually touring together, and recording *Montreux '82*. Their performance at the Montreux International Jazz Festival won them the Prix d'excellence. Admired in the United States as well, when Petrucciani first performed at the Vanguard, he was immediately recognized as an important new voice, and his performance at Carnegie Hall as part of the Cool Jazz Festival in 1983 was lauded. Settling in Brooklyn, New York, for most of the following five years, he played concerts in the United States, Canada, Japan, and Europe. An excellent video shows him in concert. In the virtuoso trio that Petrucciani toured with, Eliot Zigmund played the drums and Polly Davidson the bass. After several years, Davidson left and Keith Jarrett joined the group. Zigmund has described Petrucciani as "a live wire, who lived fast and furious,"and spoken of the incredible spirit that Petrucciani had radiated in his youth. In addition to his astounding talent, he communicated both openness and vulnerability. He brought his full physical being to his music, injecting his performances with enormous energy, often ending up wringing wet after a performance. Although Zigmund referred to Petrucciani as "a beautiful person, with something magical about him," he did qualify his assessment of Petrucciani's career just a bit, noting that the pianist had become more commercial with the years and, like many stars, had sometimes allowed his career interests to impair his personal relationships.[20]

Petrucciani was married and divorced twice. With Mary Lordes, he had two children, Alexandre and Rachid Roperch, of Paris, one of whom was a child from Mary's previous marriage and whom Michel adopted. His biological son, like Petrucciani, was affected by osteogenesis imperfecta, though in a milder form. Michel had two other significant relationships, of several years each; his last companion, Isabelle, survived him. Petrucciani was a man with considerable charm and had had little difficulty drawing attractive, intelligent women to him. He drank, smoked, and enjoyed the club scene, persisting in this pattern despite doctors' advice. One aspect of his mystique for others was his Italian and French origins that allowed Petrucciani and friends to sojourn in medieval castles. Another was his disability—although he did not invite that kind of attention, he was aware that people were interested in him because of it. Petrucciani had minimal contact with other dwarfs, but he did perform a concert for the Osteogenesis Imperfecta Foundation at their national conference in 1989, evidence of his recognition that he might be of value as a role model.[21]

In the early years, because of his limited mobility, it was not uncommon for band members and others to carry him, and rather than minding this, he seemed to welcome the assistance. In later years, he walked with crutches. There were difficult occasions when Petrucciani's weak legs gave way and he broke a hip, a tibia, or an arm.

Petrucciani dealt with pain and crises well, maintaining a positive outlook. Perhaps he knew that he needed to live his life at high speed and fully because it would not be a long one.

The vocalist Little Jimmy Scott might seem to be out of place in a discussion of jazz artists of short stature, as his final height reached five feet seven inches (Fig. 71). However, the rare condition from which he suffered, Kallman's syndrome, is a disorder of the hypothalamus and pituitary glands. Besides resulting in a high-pitched voice (usually ranging from soprano to contralto), affecting sexual development, and causing depression and mood swings, it significantly inhibits growth. A significant figure in the history of jazz, rhythm and blues, and popular music, Scott had been four feet eleven inches tall or less when, in his thirties, he experienced a growth spurt—something that happens spontaneously to a minority of dwarfs with similar conditions; Tom Thumb, for example, experienced this sort of change. Despite this gain in height he is still called Little Jimmy Scott and referred to as diminutive or slight. His short stature during his early years significantly influenced his sense of self and interactions with others throughout his life.

Scott has resurfaced and become prominent during the past decade. He had been active in the jazz world principally in the 1940s and 1950s but then had lapsed into obscurity, playing only occasionally at small local clubs. Discouraged, Scott left the East Coast and moved back to Cleveland, supporting himself by working as an aide in nursing homes and as a shipping clerk. When an old friend of his, Earlene Rogers, called the jazz station WBGO in Newark in 1984 to ask why they never played his work, she was told that he was dead.

His comeback began with this phone call (which eventually also resulted in his marriage to Earlene, who was to be his fourth wife). Recognition came gradually, but in August 2000 his comeback seemed assured when his photograph appeared on the front page of the *New York Times Magazine*.[22] By

71. Little Jimmy Scott. Photograph by Lawrence Lucier/Getty Images.

then he had recorded several new albums, and much of his old work was being reissued. He finally found good management, and was sought after for jazz events internationally. In sold-out engagements at Birdland in New York and the Kennedy Center in Washington, and in appearances in Japan, he received standing ovations.

Scott was one of ten children in an extremely poor family. His mother was killed in a car accident when he was thirteen, and because his father was a gambler and unable to cope, the children were split up among several foster homes.[23] Although Scott was deeply troubled, he held on to the values and musical interests that his upbringing had offered. His mother's home was filled with music: "Singing was the thing in my family. It was a company-keeper for everybody. Late in the evenings, my mother would come in and play different songs on the piano that she knew we could sing. . . . Two sisters and another brother and myself had a quartet, and we'd sing in church."[24]

While still in his teens Jimmy met a mentor, Estelle Young, and joined the troupe she was shepherding through African American theaters and clubs in the Midwest. He moved on to the Lionel Hampton Orchestra and won a contract with the Savoy, but management difficulties, problems with alcohol, and violent marital conflict contributed to a decline in his career. Despite some unevenness in the recordings that do survive, there is unanimous agreement that Scott has exhibited, and even now continues to exhibit, a prodigious talent. On his recent album, *Mood Indigo,* Scott, backed by first-rate musicians, sings classic love songs at his trademark slow tempo in his unique voice: "A one-of-a-kind vocalist, Jimmy Scott has always eluded easy classification. His distinctive infusion of romantic elements with blues and jazz elements places him in a category all his own. Vocalists ranging from Ray Charles to Nancy Wilson to Lou Reed have paid tribute to the power of Scott's singing. Extending notes—and emotions—to the breaking point, he has expressed infatuation and heartbreak with a naked intensity usually associated with female singers, notably Judy Garland and Edith Piaf."[25]

Many of Scott's reviewers mention the startling contrast between Scott's diminutive size and his "soul-stirring" sound. His personal struggles have been cited as the source of the powerful authenticity of his renditions. Scott movingly performs the old standards, such as "Someone to Watch Over Me," "Sometimes I Feel Like a Motherless Child," and "Everybody's Somebody's Fool" (his greatest hit). In "The Talk of the Town," he sings, "I can't show my face / Can't go anyplace / People stop and stare / It's so hard to bear."

Like most dwarfs, Scott has been subjected to stares all his life. Although he is heterosexual, and capable of sex, he is incapable of reproduction. He has a feminine or androgynous appearance and has experienced shame in a variety of ways. Made fun of in childhood and "hit on" by gay men in adulthood, he has had both his age and his sex erroneously perceived throughout his life. "Even today," Scott says, "cats in the grocery store say, 'Miss, what do you want?'"[26] In his earlier years, Scott may have reacted with a curse or a threat of violence; these days he is more likely to ignore such a comment.

Scott communicates warmth and a lack of pretentiousness toward people from all social levels, and he is particularly generous toward young musicians. His guiding principle is that it matters to tell a beautiful story in a song and sometimes in the process to touch people who may feel hurt or lost. In this he seems to be successful: the performer Madonna has said that he is the only singer who ever really made her cry. Repeatedly, in discussing those who have influenced him, Scott mentions Paul Robeson: "He expressed a dynamic way of putting truth in song. He knew how to handle a lyric and put the meaning in the song. I always wanted to be a singer who could tell a story the way he could."[27]

CLASSICAL MUSIC

Bass-baritone Thomas Quasthoff is one of the great lieder and oratorio singers active today. "Vocally, Mr. Quasthoff has everything: a deep, rich tone, the power to project with apparent ease in a hall as large as [the Avery] Fisher, and the imagination and personality to enliven the work at hand." He has been described as projecting emotion with nuanced humor, a palpable sense of drama and tension, and affective pathos.[28]

Just over four feet tall, with handsome, expressive features, Quasthoff performs on a raised podium in order to compensate for his short stature: much of the time he sits or leans against a chair. A "thalidomide baby," he was born with serious deformities—his malformed hands are attached to his shoulders, and his short legs require the support of special shoes. Although newcomers to his concerts may react to these differences when he first walks onstage, his easy presence and intelligent, passionate voice soon overarch all else. His natural vocal ability manifested itself very early. When he was a baby, lying in a hospital ward in Germany, he astonished his nurses by singing back one of the melodies they had just played. Despite his exceptional voice and musical aptitude, he had to battle hard to arrive where he is today. His family had to contest the government's view that he ought not to live at home. Then, after painful limb therapy in childhood, he had been placed in an unchallenging school setting with youngsters with cerebral palsy, before his parents managed to get him transferred to a regular school. When, at age fourteen, he sought admission to the Musikhochschule in Hannover, he was rejected because he could not meet the school's inflexible requirement that he be able to play the piano. Despite his remarkable vocal range—which spans from the low C of a true bass to the middle C of the majority of tenors—the school was unwilling to make an exception. The rejection turned out to be beneficial: his family arranged for him to take daily lessons from Charlotte Lehman, which continued for the following seventeen years. Quasthoff realized only in retrospect that had he been accepted, he might have had only one lesson a week. This way, he received years of daily voice and musicology lessons.

In 1988, when he was twenty-eight, Quasthoff won a prestigious international music competition in Munich and the baritone Dietrich Fischer-Dieskau commented on his "wondrously beautiful voice." Quasthoff had some doubts about whether the prize had been conferred out of pity. "But I will never forget what the jury chief told me," says Quastoff. "He said: 'You can be absolutely sure you didn't win the competition because of your disability. If you hadn't earned it, that would be a much bigger problem for you." It would, the head of the jury explained, have been cruel to raise hopes and expectations that could not later be fulfilled.[29] Quasthoff was still not certain that he could be successful as a full-time musician. At first, following the recommendations of his parents who wanted him to have a dependable occupation to fall back on, he studied law and then went on to work fourteen-hour days in a bank. Well aware that he had no affinity for these occupations, he became a radio announcer for the following six years, supplementing his income by singing jazz and cabaret music.

Only when Claudio Abaddo asked him to sing the aria "O, Freunde!" for a recording of Beethoven's Ninth Symphony and Seiji Ozawa requested him for Bach's *Saint Matthew Passion* did his career really take off. Now in his forties, he has an exclusive recording contract with Deutsche Grammophon and receives more invitations to perform than he can handle. Quasthoff has mastered a wide range of classical material, performing in the United States and Europe with the conductors Kurt Masur, Sir Colin Davis, Daniel Barenboim, and Riccardo Muti. The versatile Quasthoff also appeared at the Oregon Festival in 2000, performing a collection of spirituals and works from pop and jazz, including novel renditions of Ella Fitzgerald, George Gershwin, Robeson, and Bobby McFerrin songs. He was met with rapturous applause.[30]

Having been told frequently that his physical limitations would preclude his performing in opera, it was only in April 2003 that Quasthoff performed with Simon Rattle and the Berlin Philharmonic, singing the role of Don Fernando in Beethoven's *Fidelio*. In January 2004 he sang four arias by Mozart in a Live from Lincoln Center concert broadcast by PBS stations nationwide.

Quasthoff had the satisfaction of being invited to teach at the same Hanover *Hochschule* that rejected him so many years ago. He is now Professor for Life at the Music Academy in Detmold, Germany, where he maintains a full schedule and is held in high regard by students. He lives in the town where was born, near his parents and an older brother; he schedules no more than fifty concerts a year, reserving some time for family and his girlfriend, a voice teacher with two children who lives two hundred miles to the south. Quasthoff is able to manage without assistance even when traveling and has only housekeeping help when he is at home.

He becomes impatient with the constant focus on his deformities. In an interview in 2004, when asked if he saw himself as a role model, he replied, "'If it's true it's a nice side effect.' But the danger of focusing on this, he added, is that he could start to play a role as a representative for the disabled. The only role he wants to play, he said, is that of 'serious artist.'"[31] Earlier, he insisted that critic Steven Moss not portray his life as "a brave struggle against fearsome odds": "For me, my disability is a fact and not a problem. For sure, I have to handle some things differently from other people. But it's not so different from the life of someone who is not disabled. In any case, who is really not disabled? I am in the lucky position that everyone can see it. But if you are never happy, if you are only concerned about money and success, this is in my opinion also a kind of disability."[32] Similarly, he believes that persons with disabilities should not be held to a low standard. He has criticized the work of blind singer Andrea Bocelli, whom he regards as inexpert and not a classical artist.

He acknowledges that there were difficult times.[33] His parents had not sheltered him, and he had grown accustomed to people's intrusive curiosity. However once, when an inquisitive woman lifted his cape to look at what was underneath, he spat at her. His mother, exiting a store, viewed the encounter and said, "Come, spit again!" Although he and his mother have never discussed her guilt about having taken thalidomide, he expresses empathy for her situation, noting that no one but a mother herself can know what it feels like to bring into the world a child with a disability. Pleased that he was born with a sunny disposition, he hopes that by demonstrating his enthusiasm for life, he can prove to her that things are all right.

While journalists may at times seem to focus excessively on Quasthoff's disabilities, more often they extol his voice, in agreement that he has "all those qualities which make him a master of Bach singing—nobility of tone and manner, consummate breath control, thrilling sense of drama, and sensitive understanding of the text. This brand of singing, full of reverence yet brimming with warmth, humanity, and consoling strength, affectionately phrased, dramatically gripping, yet warmly intimate, is an art which makes us glad to be alive."[34]

POPULAR MUSIC

The rap artist Bushwick Bill (Fig. 72) was born Richard Shaw in Kingston, Jamaica, in 1967 and raised in the Flatbush section of Brooklyn, New York. In 1987, he

72. *Bushwick Bill. Photograph by Barry Brecheisen/© Rolling Stone.com.*

moved to Houston, Texas, where twenty-two-year-old James "L'il J" Smith invited him to join the Geto Boys, a group that Smith was organizing. Shaw first joined the band as a dancer, but Smith encouraged him to take up rap and helped him to get the training he needed to develop recording skills.

Although their personalities and musical backgrounds varied, all the members of the Geto Boys had experienced significant trouble of one sort or another. Willie D had done time for robbing a gas station; Scarface (Brad Jordan), a talented musician who played piano, violin, guitar, and drums, had been raised in a middle-class neighborhood and had recorded his first single, "Big Time," at sixteen, but a manic-depressive episode had led to two years in a psychiatric ward. One of the group's hit songs, "Mind Playing Tricks on Me," was based on Scarface's experiences.[35] Bushwick Bill had also suffered from psychological problems in the past, which in his case had led to a particularly dramatic and violent episode. In 1991, when he was twenty-one and his girlfriend only seventeen, he had been in a drunken, depressed state when, threatening to kill their child if she refused, he persuaded her to shoot him. He ended up losing an eye. The cover of the group's next album, the platinum *We Can't Be Stopped* (1991), showed a photograph of the band members pushing Bushwick Bill, with his ghastly empty eye socket, on a hospital gurney. Although that album contained the soulful song "Mind Playing Tricks on Me," some of their work achieved a new high for recorded violence. Bushwick Bill, along with Gangsta Nip, who was on the same label, introduced the style that would later be known as "horror-core" into his music and lyrics.

The group's notoriety escalated when, after making two albums with Rap-a-Lot, their own label, they signed with Def American. When the president of Geffen Records refused to distribute their album because of its content, they accused the label of bigotry toward African Americans, pointing out that the company had not rejected other albums with similarly raunchy content by white artists, even those employing misogynist, racist, or homophobic material.[36] One of the group's songs, "The

Mind of a Lunatic," referred to necrophilia, murder, and other violent acts, stimulating an ongoing debate about the appropriate role of the music industry in screening or censoring content.

By 1993 the group had disbanded, and Bushwick Bill embarked on his own separate career. In 1992 he had already aroused strong reactions with his album *Little Big Man*, on which he described the gory details of the shooting incident, as well as more of the sexism, wild tales, and violence that characterized the Geto Boys' releases. Among his later albums were *Phantom of the Rapra, No Surrender . . . No Retreat,* and *Universal Small Souljah,* which appeared in 2001.

Bushwick Bill identifies first and foremost with rap's heroes, those who are lashing out, proud of their resilience in overcoming racial and other obstacles. His dwarf identity merges seamlessly with his rap stance, in part because as a young person he often needed to fight physically. He has talked with documentary filmmaker Steve Delano about how he needed to be tough in order to walk down his block in Brooklyn: "I love my mom and dad—I'd die for them—but when my dad told me not to go outside because people would make fun of me, I couldn't listen. I want to be part of that great big world out there."[37]Although he had encountered only a few other dwarfs, show business people, before meeting Delano, Bushwick Bill described himself as "down with little people"—he felt comfortable around them. But the best way to grasp his connection with his dwarfism would be to listen to "Who's the Biggest," on the album *Phantom of the Rapra,* or "Size Ain't Shit":

> Yo Bushwick, whaddya do when m'fuckers underestimate your size man?
> First of all I laugh
> (then what?)
> Smash their ass like a goddam car crash.[38]

Bushwick Bill claims that the shooting incident made him stronger: "I see the world from a whole different perspective, and I realize that there is too much to strive for to go out over something stupid."[39] Now the father of several children by different mothers, he loves his children, whom he describes affectionately as "butter."[40]

During his career as a member of the Geto Boys and as a solo performer, he has been a writer and rapper on three gold and platinum records. Close to three million copies have been sold, and his albums and singles frequently hit the top of a variety of charts. He is now "one of the most recognized and respected artists in rap music."[41]

In a very different vein, the material performed by the singer Nelson Ned has progressed from love songs to gospel. Born in Uba, Brazil, in 1947, Ned is called "the little giant of song." With a repertoire that consisted mostly of romantic ballads, in the 1960s he began to attract huge crowds throughout Latin America and in the United

States. He produced gold and platinum records and also wrote for such major artists as Moacir Franco and Antonio Marcos.

His phenomenal artistic success, however, was accompanied by what he now views as a chaotic personal life. Ned has published an autobiography, titled *Pequeño gigante de la canción* (Little giant of song), in which he discusses his regret about past sexual escapades and his abuse of alcohol and cocaine, apologizing to his wife, children, and friends for past failings.[42] Since his very public conversion to Christianity in 1993, he has focused on his spiritual and evangelical concerns and the promotion of his gospel albums, including *Christ Es Vida*. (Some of his earlier recordings continue to be available on CD, including *El romantico de America* [1993] and *Selecao de Ouro—20 Successos—Nelson Ned* [1998].) One interviewer, remembering his past concern about sales and public recognition, asked whether Ned did not fear that his shift to Christian music would reduce his popularity. He replied that he had received gold records for his Christian recordings as well and that although he still likes recognition, his spiritual concerns and his sensitivity to the people he meets have become central.

In the world of folk music and bluegrass, Shawn Brush, born in 1969, is one of Canada's most respected young musicians—an accomplished singer, songwriter, and guitarist (Fig. 73). After attending a bluegrass festival with his father in 1985, he began playing the guitar, learning from both local musicians and the recordings of the greats, especially Willie Nelson, Johnny Cash, John Prine, Doc Watson, and Woody Guthrie.[43]

After a stint with Timberline, a bluegrass band, Brush embarked on a solo career, releasing his first recording, *The Wooden Hill*, in 1994, which was followed by four more albums: *The Adrian Gail* (1995), *In the Land of the Giants* (1995), *1999 Plus Shipping and Handling* (1999), and *SteAl Town* (2000). *The Adrian Gale* featured country music, but also reggae, blues, and ballads. Brush appeared on the cover of *Canadian Blue Grass Magazine*; he won the Bluegrass Composer of the Year award in 1991 and again in 1994, and he has produced a total of ten albums in ten years.

Despite his exceptional talent, the road has not been easy for Brush, personally or professionally. Brush has Morquio's syndrome, a condition produced by a missing enzyme, and is just over four feet tall. He required eight corrective surgeries before the age of sixteen and since then has had to contend with a number of fractures: some years ago, as a result of a fall, five lumbar vertebrae were compressed. One reviewer, praising Brush as a brilliant guitar player with a strong voice and dozens of original songs, also notes, "Every morning he wakes up in pain. It can hurt to cough. The blues are in his bones."[44] Since his condition is such an important part of his identity, Brush has developed a character called the Krooked Cowboy to communicate ideas that might otherwise make audiences uncomfortable. He describes this alter ego as "charismatic, mysterious, inspirational, funny, and a wicked guitarist."[45]

Brush is proud to say that he has played and still plays for anyone who will listen—in concert halls; at folk festivals and folk clubs, parties, and homes for the elderly; on radio and television, "and even [in] the odd bowling alley."[46] Because setting up in bars was physically demanding and not very lucrative, Brush for a time gave up doing gigs he formerly accepted. When his first albums were released, he discovered that com-

73. Shawn Brush. Photograph by Jinny Ollmann.

mercial radio gave them almost no play. He was only temporarily discouraged; his love of music led him to persevere, and by September 2003, his career had reached a new high point. He scheduled concerts in Hamilton and Burlington, Ontario, to celebrate the issuing of two new CDs: *You Asked for It,* a compilation of his most frequently requested solo work, and *Shawn Brush and Friends,* a collection of his best performances with other artists. Some pieces have a universal theme; others allude specifically to his difference (the "Wooden Hill" refers to the staircase that he remembers climbing with difficulty as a child at home); a few are lighthearted or comical. He comes across as a man familiar with love and a wide range of intense emotions.

Brush's reputation continues to grow: his guitar playing has been called "awesome," his presentations praised for their sincerity and intimacy, and Brush himself referred to as a "Canadian National Treasure."[47] Although his music has been aired on the radio in many European nations, the United States, Australia, and Japan, Brush is not as well known outside Canada as he is in that country, because he has mostly been limited to playing in local venues. These days, however, despite walking with two canes and feeling considerable concern about his health, he has spoken about "traveling to the Big Apple." An outgoing person, he sees himself as living a normal life most of the time, loving music, working when he is able—he is focused "not on what I can't do, but what I can."[48] With John Farrington, he is writing his autobiography, partly as a vehicle to promote his music, but also to share with others his remarkable life and his reflections upon it.

74. *The Little Kingz. Photograph by Steve Truglio. Courtesy of Commodity Oddity Entertainment.*

Many efforts to achieve prominence in the music world are short lived, and this is as true for dwarfs as for anyone else. The band called the Little Kingz was significant because of the talent of its members, because it was a rare modern *group* of dwarfs—recalling similar groups in the past—and because of the controversy that surrounded the band's formation (Fig. 74). Early in 2001, the online Dwarfism List thrummed with arguments about the Little Kingz.[49] A recently formed rock band, its four members were lead singer Scotty F-Word, guitarist Pauly J, bass guitar player Stevie D, and drummer K-Roc. When an interviewer from the *New*

York Press first questioned them about the size of the guitars they played and about their influences, his queries engendered the crude exchanges and seemingly misogynist remarks typical of the hard-rock world.[50] Similar banter marked the group's appearance on the *Opie and Anthony* radio show.

Scotty felt he had to defend himself : he explained in an online post that he had always wanted to be in a rock band, had been in a few before the Kingz, and loved every minute of it. He had songs in his head about life, love, downtime, and his love for his daughter and his wife. Although he was aware that he might act a little crazy at times, joke, speak his mind, and do things to grab attention, he remained positive about being an LP and respectful of his LP brothers and sisters—but he could not change his nature.[51]

The controversy that the Little Kingz evoked is characteristic of similar ones that abound in the dwarf community. To what degree are performers responsible simply to their art and themselves, and to what degree must they be model citizens, representing their community? Some LPs felt that the group's gimmick—featuring themselves as the dwarfs they were—paled beside those of others in the music industry, where posturing is common; only rock fans, these advocates said, were qualified to judge their talent. The Little Kingz achieved some recognition during the two years of their existence, performing mostly in small clubs in towns along the East Coast, as well in major venues such as Manhattan's CBGB, where they played for a responsive young crowd. In 2001 and 2002 they performed for a crowd estimated at between thirty thousand and fifty thousand people at the HFStival, at RFK Stadium in Washington, D.C., an annual event organized by the radio station WHFS. They shared the stage with the Black Crowes, StainD, Linken Park, Eminem, and the Mighty Mighty Boss Tones; in addition they were featured in the movie *Zoolander*.

Most of the songs on the group's album, *Revolution*, are original. Scotty's lyrics for "What's the Big Idea" speak for themselves: "I get your unsigned hate mail that you deliver; I'll just cut you down to size. So now that you try, but you don't understand the evolution, why am I so surprised? What are your other motives, and how would you know, if you have never met my kind?" This piece was Scotty's response to Randy Newman fans who have used his song "Short People Deserve to Die" (which Newman claims is well-intentioned irony) to denigrate dwarfs.

On 27 April 2003, before a capacity crowd in Tampa, Florida, the Little Kingz gave their last performance. Scott Strasbaugh (Scotty F-Word) said that they had disbanded because the guitarist had had to leave for health reasons, and he was impossible to replace. Scott is now the singer in a band called Buck 20 and is continues to write music.

There is ambiguity about certain other musicians. Lorenz Hart, who, along with Richard Rodgers, was responsible for some of the greatest American musical comedies, while not generally referred to as a dwarf, was barely five feet tall in elevator shoes and was rejected for military service for reasons of height. His biographer, Frederick Nolan, wrote that although "his head was of normal proportion, his body, hands and feet were not much larger than those of a child"; he had a "gnomelike face and body, and a very explosive personality." He was the butt of jokes: "'What's Larry Hart up to these days?' 'Oh, about my belt-buckle.'"[52]

Among the many talented musicians not yet noted are drummers Joe Gnoffo, previously active in Chicago and now in Los Angeles, and Mike Lipsky, a drummer with a band called Blues Daddies in San Francisco. Keyboardist Chris Errera had some success with a Chicago band called the Sine. Two gifted vocalists are rousing popular singer Grace Oliver and Carolyn Boursse, a singer and a member of the San Francisco Bay Area Chamber Choir, which specializes in a cappella work and has made ten European tours.

It is not uncommon in this community to find individuals who have worked as both actors and musicians. Michael Gogin, for example, who has emceed many events for LPA, has filled a variety of roles in the entertainment industry. In addition to acting in movies and on television, he plays the guitar, sings, and composes music ranging from folk to rock to symphonic pieces, to works with jazz overtones. He has appeared in several operas and has completed his first album, a compilation of eleven original songs. While he feels that the music world, especially the jazz world, is more accepting of physical difference than many other fields, he knows that competition makes it difficult to achieve recognition.

75. Michaela Kuzia. Courtesy of Michaela Kuzia.

A promising younger musician is Michaela Kuzia, who plays the piano, sings, and composes (Fig. 75). Kuzia has stirred large crowds with her songs about love and loss. Her material ranges from love songs to an original song about rainforest destruction and a reflective ballad about her relationship with an older sister on the eve of her sister's wedding. Songwriting is Kuzia's great passion; she composed her first formal song at fourteen and others since then for piano and voice, often in a style similar to those of Sara McLaughlan and Tori Amos.

Having grown up in a musical family, with three sisters who played instruments including violin, cello, lyre, and piano (one of her sisters is an opera singer), Kuzia is currently taking her first steps toward a professional career. A music major first at Florida State University and currently at the prestigious Berklee College of Music in Boston, she has had her songs played on two radio stations, been interviewed on live broadcasts, and performed at The Lion's Den, a popular bistro in the Berkshires. Her first CD appeared in October 2003.

Music in the Lives of Dwarfs

Apart from the "star performers," the ordinary folks also merit notice. A good many short-statured persons today play musical instruments, frequently going to great lengths to obtain scaled-down instruments and to find teachers who will help them accommodate to their unique limitations. Parents inquiring about whether their children will be able to play a given instrument are often encouraged by performers such as Michaela Kuzia:

> I am an achon and I've played [piano] for 13 years now, and I can personally reach over an octave, but I honestly think that is because my fingers were worked out at a young age when I first started playing. If you start 'em early their fingers will become more flexible over time. It will help in the development of them as well. It's not about the length of your fingers, it's about the width of your hand. For the feet, it's pretty essential to have something that you can put your weight into when playing. . . . I use pedal extensions that have a platform. They are especially made for the piano and I guess were designed for children, but hey man, they totally work. . . . It would have been a joke if I had come to the music school in college and not been able to work the pedals—it's a big part of playing. If you want further info, let me know. . . .
>
> I totally encourage you to have your son start playing.
>
> Check ya later—Mickay[53]

Because dwarfs may be less able to engage in strenuous physical activities, the mountains they climb must be of another sort. Unlike art and writing, which are solitary activities, music affords a variety of formal and informal combinations. Unlike in theater, an institutional structure is not required; two individuals, a quartet, a band, a chorus, or an orchestra—all these configurations work. In addition, appearance is not as great a barrier as in many other professions. Professional success can be elusive, but the pleasures of the shared activity often prove their own reward.

PART IV

Lives Today

TRANSFORMING

DESTINY

CHAPTER ELEVEN

Lives Today

It is a peculiar sensation, this double consciousness, this sense of always looking at oneself through the eyes of others, of measuring one's soul by the tape of
a world that looks on in amused contempt and pity.

—W.E.B. Du Bois

Anatomy is destiny.

—Sigmund Freud

You must be the change you wish to see in the world.

—Mohandas K. Gandhi

Seeing Oneself through the Eyes of Others

Among the most stirring dramas of the twentieth century were the struggles of
one minority after another to demand justice and social inclusion. Although dwarfs
have been latecomers to the identity procession—their demands for respect and
recognition building only toward the turn of the twenty-first century—Du Bois's
statement, originally referring to African Americans, rings true for dwarfs. Constantly
subjected to stares and disparaging comments, they have known well the looks of
"amused contempt and pity."

A vital point in any stigmatized group's pilgrimage toward self-affirmation is its decision to shed "identification with the aggressor," that is, seeing oneself through the
eyes of the dominant other and trying to emulate that authority. An identification with
or yearning for "bigness" is evident in the titles of works about dwarfs, for example, Discovery Channel's *Dwarf: Standing Tall* and *Little People, Big Lives*; *Walking Tall* (by three-
foot-eight-inch-tall motivational speaker Peggy O'Neill); and children's writer Susan
Kuklin's *Thinking Big*. These titles suggest a familiar tension, with dwarfs' positive self-
identity held hostage to society's judgment. But there has been progress: Think Big, the
original motto of LPA, is now rarely used, and the title of Jan Krawitz's 1994 documentary, *Big Enough*, is an explicit rejoinder to those who disparage shortness.

"We are a contradiction in packaging," says Julie Rotta, "for encased in our small bodies are not small minds, not small needs and desires, not small goals and pleasures, and not small appetites for a full and enriching life."[1] But "small is beautiful" is still an elusive concept for many individuals, whose inner voices may express exasperation with the medical and social problems that accompany being a dwarf. For such moments, self-affirmation is necessary, but not sufficient. A real reprieve would necessitate society's evolving beyond "biological instinct"—the rejection of the different ones in the herd—and accepting dwarfs as individuals, thus easing their path through life.

"Anatomy Is Destiny" Revisited

The aspirations for a full life expressed by Rotta were seldom fulfilled in earlier times. Society's beliefs about dwarfs had long reflected the biological determinism implicit in Freud's assertion above (intended to explain women's limitations). Whether they were regarded as links to the gods or sources of amusement, dwarfs' physical appearance was viewed as the sole explanation for their constricted roles in society.

But nowadays in at least a handful of nations, the expectations of dwarfs resemble those of the general population, and they feel freer to shape their own future. As a result of medical advances, most are healthier and more mobile than before. At least in the Western world, greater prosperity has brought with it opportunities for dwarfs. In the expanding economy that followed World War II, dwarf individuals found themselves equal to newly created positions that required more brains than brawn, and recent developments in computer technology have created further opportunities. The educational establishment also grew, and ramps and other accommodations for disabled veterans that a grateful society had created on college campuses now benefited dwarfs as well.

The civil rights movement blazed a trail through the courts in the 1960s, and in the following decade disability rights advocates did the same, these efforts culminating in the passage of three major pieces of antidiscrimination legislation.[2] Families of dwarf children have benefited significantly from individual educational programs (IEPs) that ensure that students' special needs are met. Improved scooters and Access-a-Ride systems allow people with limited mobility to secure gainful employment. Accessible air travel allows people to develop friendships and work lives that span continents and oceans. Finally, the Internet provides access to medical and practical information about dwarfing conditions, as well as facilitating networking and mutual support. The changing situation of dwarfs can be discerned from the contrasting findings of several studies of dwarfs conducted between 1981 and 2003. The most recent studies suggest that social barriers are at least as important as health issues in lessening or enhancing dwarfs' quality of life.[3]

Dwarfism Organizations and the Emergence of a Shared Dwarf Identity

Although dwarf individuals' quality of life has not yet caught up with that of their average-statured relatives, considerable improvement has occurred. In addition to new economic opportunities, the self-help movement that began to flourish in the United States by the 1970s has been extremely beneficial for those with rare medical conditions. Although LPA became part of the movement, it did not start out that way. The first meeting of the group, then referred to as Midgets of America, originated as a publicity stunt in Reno in 1957. Nick Bourne, of the Riverside Hotel, where Billy Barty was performing, had the idea to advertise Reno as "the biggest little city in the world," and he thought of inviting a group of dwarfs to his hotel and offering them free rooms and inexpensive meals. That gathering drew only twenty-one people; three years later, in Las Vegas, one hundred attended. Most of that second group were entertainers; performers continued to predominate for many years. By the time the group gathered for the Los Angeles conference in 1998, however, there were sixteen hundred attendees from twenty countries, with a wide range of occupations. (By then, their numbers included average-sized family members and medical professionals as well.) LPA is now composed of many local chapters, regional districts, and an executive board that arranges for national conferences and sets policy.

The magnitude of the historic difference that the growth of LPA made in the lives of dwarfs cannot be overstated. The growth of this group, whose membership spans every political, religious, class, and personality difference imaginable, caused this "people that was not a people" to become one. Although less than 10 percent of dwarfs in the United States are members of LPA—and the percentage may be even smaller in some other nations where equivalent groups exist—media attention to the organization has increased public awareness and inspired social change.

From the beginning, the group had a public relations objective: Billy Barty stated that he planned to demonstrate to society that little people were worthy individuals, capable of a wide range of endeavors. By the year 2000, when its membership had expanded to nearly eight thousand, the group undertook more advocacy work, stressing health legislation issues, campaigning for greater accessibility of automatic teller machines (ATMs) and gas pumps, and lobbying against dwarf tossing. LPA also provided a much greater array of services, including a medical advisory board, an adoption committee, a Dwarf Athletic Association, and a Web site.

The International Scene

The international character of the dwarfism community was first examined in the work of a young anthropologist, Bethany Jewett, in 1987. After graduating from Swarthmore, she received a Watson fellowship and traveled to twelve countries with the intention of learning about the lives of dwarfs in each society. Her report centered on national differences in attitudes toward disability and the nomenclature of extreme short stature. She discovered only a handful of groups, with sizeable ones only in Australia, New Zealand, and nations in Western Europe. It was in these locations that dwarfs were best off socioeconomically. Her informants in Asia were fewer, and they tended to speak of their isolation and of families that had hidden them away as a result of shame. Some Asian cultures also seemed to have different attitudes toward independence—it seemed more natural simply to ask others for help.[4]

By 2003 dwarfism groups had been organized in twenty-eight countries. Currently, there are organizations in Argentina, Australia, Austria, Belgium, Brazil, Bulgaria, Canada, Chile, Colombia, Denmark, England, Finland, France, Germany, Holland, Ireland, Israel, Italy, Japan, Kosovo, Malaysia, New Zealand, Nigeria, Norway, Scotland, Slovenia, South Korea, Spain, and Switzerland. Many of these groups have been formed in the past decade.

Often, these organizations were formed by individuals from other nations who had been inspired by attending an LPA conference. The media is playing an increasing role in the growth of international groups. In 1999, after Chilean television highlighted the lives of dwarfs, membership in the Chilean group more than doubled (its medical advisor, geneticist Gabriella Reppeto, trained at Johns Hopkins). A similar turn of events followed the efforts of the Korean Broadcasting Company (KBC), which filmed the July 2000 LPA conference in Minneapolis to show the Korean public that dwarfs could live a vital and fulfilling life. In 2000 and 2001, KBC presented the resulting fifteen-episode documentary serial—to an audience of five million viewers. The media campaign touched viewers, changed attitudes, and created a viable organization with amazing speed. Pediatric orthopedic surgeon Dr. Hae-ryong Song, who had studied in the United States, helped form the group in South Korea.

The situation in South Korea is quite different from that in other Asian nations, which see anomalies as punishment for misdeeds of the affected individuals' ancestors. In China, despite the efforts of Deng Xiaoping's disabled son to raise social and governmental consciousness, discrimination remains widespread. Disability and short stature are still used to block candidates' admission to colleges and such fields as foreign service; in 2001, thousands of women and some men, most of them college educated, were spending large sums for limb-lengthening surgery to enhance their chances at obtaining good positions.[5] There are some signs, however, that a searching assessment of the situation of Chinese women throughout history is now taking place and that cooperation has been increasing among scholars, advocates, and government representatives toward improving women's lot in the future. Since the fates of various subjugated identity groups tend to be related, it becomes increasingly possible that positive developments for dwarfs and disability groups may also ensue.[6] In Japan, the homogeneity of the population and the long-standing isolation of the disabled meant slow progress, but recently, there has been some evidence of the elimination of physical barriers and the popularity of books by individuals with disabilities.[7] Although Little People of Japan has been formed, so far it has only about twenty members.[8]

George Sofkin of Bulgaria, who first visited the United States in 1995 to attend the Denver LPA conference, was struck by the contrast between the cheerful atmosphere there and the dismal situation of dwarfs in his own country. He helped create Little People of Bulgaria, the first such group formed in a post-Soviet country.[9] Bulgaria has much poverty and little history of recognizing the needs of persons with disabilities. However, the organization has been able to attract two hundred members, a high percentage of Bulgarian dwarfs, and its media campaigns have improved public attitudes. There have been several successful fund-raising ventures, and, despite little government support overall, persons with dwarfism are now eligible for free care in the best hospital in Bulgaria.

The Little People of Kosovo was formed in 2002 and currently has seven hundred members. It is unique in that it must appeal to previously warring Albanian and Serbian communities and also in that it is a part of an umbrella group of persons with various disabilities. Hiljmnihmnijeta Apuk, who has economics and law degrees and is employed as district financial officer, is the group's president.

It would be a mistake to conclude that even Western nations have been universally benevolent toward people of short stature. There are about ten thousand short-statured persons in France. Despite the efforts of the dwarfism group Personnes de petite taille (the equivalent of LPA), which currently has five hundred members, the situation for dwarfs in France, described as rather bleak in the works of Monestier, Pieral, and Saint-Macary, has improved only slightly. However, some signs of change can be seen: for example, the group's president, Patrick Petit-Jean, was denied a teaching license in earlier years, but has since seen that regulation overturned. Nevertheless, Natalie Pretou, a woman with diastrophic dwarfism, and Fabien Pretou, her average-statured husband, report that besides fending off mockery and cruelty, most French dwarfs rely on minimal social assistance payments, and only the most enterprising find employment. In the Pretous' judgment, southern countries such as France and Spain are worse off than northern countries like Great Britain and Switzerland; Romania, still reverberating from the policies of Nicolae Ceauşescu, is worst of all.[10]

It is certainly true that the United States, the Scandinavian countries, and the United Kingdom have taken the lead in disability rights legislation and allied issues. In the United Kingdom, good medical care is available, and the Access to Work program enables people with disabilities to earn a full wage in an appropriate environment.[11] The government of Denmark provides the most comprehensive services: not only does it reimburse for surgical care, it pays caregivers for aftercare, subsidizes those who are able to work only part time, and helps pay for home improvements. The Danish group has 150 dwarf members (50 of them adults) and a greater number of average-statured members.

In 2003 the first dwarfism group in Africa, the Dwarfs Association of Nigeria (DAN), was formed. In that country, where dwarfs are active as entertainers, prejudice remains extreme: many still see dwarfs as a bad omen and run away from them in the street.[12] In Hyderbad, India, in 2003, eighty dwarfs made public their dire state, threatening suicide if their demands for accommodations given to others with disabilities were not met. Elsewhere, dwarfs are still viewed as endowed with magical properties. In 1999 infertile couples from the West, in hopes of conceiving children, attended a fertility festival in Bhutan that featured four dwarfs in puffy skirts and two dancers dressed as cows.[13]

Life Passages

The milestones and problems of dwarf children and adults merit a lengthier discussion than there is room for here. Fortunately, valuable material is available in Dan Kennedy's *Little People: Through My Daughter's Eyes;* Betty Adelson's *Dwarfism;* and especially in Joan Ablon's *Little People in America* and *Living with Difference.*[14] In the latter work, Ablon offers examples of how individual families respond to the birth of a child who is different. In general, if the parents enjoy a good relationship with each other, have access to a medical facility with knowledgeable staff, and are fortunate enough to have supportive family and friends, they are apt to do well. However, quite often even when they lack some of these advantages, many manage and even thrive. Economic insecurity, however, may present a formidable problem. Competent medical care, basic life amenities, and leisure time pleasures are often out of reach. Dwarfs in poor neighborhoods often report that they have experienced considerable ridicule and bullying, especially from teenagers who have been poorly socialized and subjected to abuse themselves.

Even in the most felicitous environment, some difficulties are inevitable: by perhaps five or six, in response to teasing or other frustrating situations, a child may protest, "I don't want to be a dwarf!" (Upsetting as hearing this declaration may be

for parents, they must accept their child's feelings and respond with understanding.)
Parents discover that the problems that come with being a dwarf must be handled
again and again, in changing, age-appropriate ways, just as discussions about sex are
approached differently depending on the age of a child. Accepting one's identity is a
gradual process, and it involves allowing negative as well as positive aspects to be
voiced. Much to the surprise of many new parents, however, the child is apt also to
receive significant positive attention from those in his daily life.

Various identity issues arise, such as dealing with having been adopted (a frequent occurrence among dwarfs). Some teenagers rely heavily on their families during this period; others focus on new interests and skills. Some join LPA and others
leave the group, taking a moratorium from dwarf identity. Young adults tend to leave
home later than average, because of either physical disabilities or emotional needs.

There have been few studies reporting the marriage rates of dwarfs, and their results, from small, nonrandom samples, cannot be assumed to be representative. In
general, the investigators have found rates below 50 percent, in some cases as low as
22 percent; in one large study, however, higher figures are documented.[15] In April
2000, LPA administrator Monica Pratt reported that approximately 30 percent of
short-statured members had been married or were currently in a conjugal relationship; her figures included those currently married, cohabiting, widowed, or divorced.
It is important to keep in mind that these statistics do not count people who are in
committed relationships but live apart from a partner, or gay men and lesbians. This
last group has only recently begun to "come out" within the organization. Nevertheless, the LPA 30 percent figure affords the best estimate so far of the current marriage
rate.

It may come as a surprise that LPs are as likely to have a spouse of average height
as of short stature. Non-LPA members are even more likely to have average-statured
mates; there has been prejudice within LPA against relationships with average-
statured partners, but this is now declining. Dwarfs who are married, whether to a
short- or an average-statured mate, are not automatically more happy than unmarried people, but Ablon has commented that every dwarf she has met has placed a
particular emphasis on marriage: "Marriage serves as a legitimization and normalization rite for a population disenfranchised from many of the taken-for-granted social
rituals of society."[16] In the final analysis, society's attitudes must continue to change
if finding a mate among the average statured is to become commonplace.

Approximately four hundred members on the 2003 LPA database have children.
Among those who are the children of married couples, two-thirds as many have parents who are both short; the other third have one short- and one average-statured
parent. A smaller number are the children of cohabiting, widowed, divorced, or single parents. Given the difficulties of childbirth, adoption is a useful option for women

of short stature; approximately 180 children of LP parents have been adopted, and there are additional adopted dwarf children whose parents are of average height.

Not all LPs elect to have children: some speak about their concern about not putting their children through the physical and emotional pain that they have endured; others feel that their disability would make caring for children too difficult. Still others prefer to use their available energies for personal enjoyment and projects that offer service to others. But many do long for the joys of family life, and they are sanguine about the outcome for their children, feeling that, somehow, their children will manage well, just as they have. Most who do have children have no more than two, but a few have as many as four. There may be national differences within the dwarfism community in attitudes toward having children at all.[17]

In the middle and later periods of life, issues of work and community are preoccupations for dwarfs, as for the general population. As people of short stature age, disruption caused by medical problems is often a concern, sometimes demanding major changes. For example, those who have lived far from family may move closer in order to secure help.

Vocations

In 1934, the following assessment of the employment options for dwarfs appeared: "What are they to do with their lives? Their choice is decidedly limited. Unlike normal children, they cannot plan careers at will. Innumerable doors are closed to them. They cannot be aviators, policemen, engineers, electricians, chefs, laborers, bus drivers, clerks. The professions are closed to them. A doctor, a lawyer, a schoolteacher no taller than a small child, not only would be laughed out of countenance, but would probably starve to death."[18] Walter Bodin and Barnet Hershey, who made this statement in *It's a Small World*, mention later that there are "midget" shopkeepers, clockmakers, jewelers, salesmen, and architects. Still, they cannot imagine that dwarfs are capable of a very broad range of activities. (In fact, all the occupations that they describe as impossible choices are now among those that include dwarfs.) Bodin and Hershey's book, marred by inaccurate information and clear bias, was nevertheless frequently quoted by later writers.[19]

The earliest reliable information about occupations was E. T. Morch's respected 1941 study of seventy-seven dwarfs in Denmark. He found that most of the thirty-nine men in the study were artisans and laborers, some were tradesman and clerks, one was a musician, and one was a clown.[20] A number of women worked as housekeepers or seamstresses, and most of the others were described simply as "untrained women." In the United States, the situation changed slowly. Only 6 of the 143 persons attending the 1960 convention of LPA were professionals.[21] A 1977 survey of adult little people found 25 percent unemployed and 60 percent making low annual salaries, twenty-nine thousand dollars or less (in 2001 dollars).[22] In the least prosperous nations, unemployment remains extremely high; in others countries, occupations vary widely. Members of the Restricted Growth Association in Great Britain, for example, include physicians, bakers, university lecturers, employees of McDonald's, and a vicar; the Danish group includes social workers, a physician, and a watchmaker.

The LPA 2003 database offers the most complete vocational profile available so far; it lists the occupations of 3,189 adult LP members. Not all listed their occupations, so these results must be taken as provisional, and since LPA may not be representative of the wider population of dwarfs, we cannot extrapolate to that group. Nonetheless, it is interesting to compare the profile of the database group with that of the general public. The 2000 U.S. census showed 33.1 percent of the employed population in management, professional, and related occupations; for LPA respondents the figure was 41.9 percent. In the general population, 41.7 percent worked in service-, clerical-, and sales-based jobs; for LPA members it was 45.9 percent. The main categories that were substantially different for the two groups were construction, production, farming, and maintenance, in which occupations the general population totaled 24.1 percent and LPs only 10.8 percent. LPs in this category include a couple of boilermakers, a forklift driver, a logger, and a good many mechanics, welders, and maintenance workers.

Approximately 26.3 percent of dwarfs are in professions. This category includes one hundred teachers, many social workers, a number of artists (fine artists, graphic artists, and designers), several architects, and ten writers, journalists, and editors. Science-related professionals include nurses, physicians, engineers, biologists, an astrophysicist, an archaeologist, a marine biologist, and a chemist. Those in managerial and finance-related occupations include forty-six accountants, several bankers and actuaries, and administrators in both business and public-service sectors. There are thirty computer specialists. Office, sales, and service occupations are well represented. There are 164 homemakers, of whom 28 are unemployed and 56 have disabilities, some working part time. The incidence of dwarfs with disabilities who are not in this group, or who did not enter any occupation on the database, is unknown.

Only two LPA members are listed as "clown," another as a "rodeo clown," and one as a "ringmaster assistant." Circus clowns have always represented only a minute fraction of the total dwarf population; because they were once so prominent in the public eye, they have mistakenly been seen as representative. A good number of individuals, however, worked at least part time in some aspect of the entertainment world: there are more than a hundred actors and entertainers; several musicians, drama teachers, and comedians; and a number of television, radio, and music producers and promoters. Many members are employed in more than one occupation, and many younger people identified as actors have day jobs. Particularly among older members, it is not uncommon to find transitions from a physically demanding job to a job that requires, instead, intellectual or interpersonal skills. Despite workplace discrimination, members of LPA have found employment at a significant rate. One statistic augurs well: 381 individuals in the database are college students. Statistics tell only part of the story; to offer a fuller sense of what is possible with increased opportunities, what follows are profiles of a selection of individuals who have benefited from them.

LEE KITCHENS: ENGINEER, INVENTOR, ROLE MODEL

Lee Kitchens (1930–2003), a respected elder in the American dwarfism community, was deeply mourned upon his death in June 2003 and celebrated at the following month's annual LPA conference—the only one in forty years that he had not attended. He was a former LPA president and had served on the board of the Human Growth Foundation.

Kitchens was born in Fort Worth, Texas, the son of average-statured parents and brother of an average-statured sister, who was six years younger.[23] The first dwarf in his family, he had spondyloepiphyseal dysplasia (SED). He attended public schools and then studied electrical engineering at Southern Methodist University. He worked for Texas Instruments for thirty-eight years in positions of increasing responsibility; Kitchens's contributions number among some of the major scientific achievements of the late twentieth century. Active in the creation of early transistors, he participated in the development of the first scientific calculator; later he played a part in the production of computers. For several years he trained local managers in Europe; he remembered this period as one of the best times of his life. Over the years, he toured thirty-two countries, later teaching for seven years at Texas Tech.

Kitchens, who besides being an inventor was an airplane pilot and community activist, valued his family life as one of his principal sources of pleasure. In college, where he had made his first efforts to meet other little people, he met and dated his future wife, Mary, and, upon graduation, married. Their life together was an extraordinarily happy one; they were married for 26 1/2 years (he did not forget to count that extra half year!). After her death, Kitchens set up a fund in her honor so that people without the means to do so could attend their first LPA conventions.

Lee and Mary adopted two children. Their son, who, it was originally believed, was a dwarf, grew to five feet seven inches; their daughter was a little person (Fig. 76). In addition, she married another person with dwarfism, and they had two children, one average sized and one with achondroplasia. Kitchens faced a tragic loss when his daughter died in 1991, leaving her young son and daughter. Because of the father's health problems, Kitchens raised his adolescent grandson in the small bedroom community of Ransom Canyon, located on a lake outside Lubbock, Texas. He was mayor of this town of eleven hundred inhabitants, and when he retired from office in the late 1990s, the appreciative town named a street after him.

Kitchens was well aware that his birth must have been a disappointment to his father, a rancher, who would have liked a strapping son to join him in his physical labors. He knew that his father, though in some ways a positive influence, doubted that his son would ever be able to support himself, and Lee was determined to prove him wrong. In adulthood, Lee was to derive great pleasure from having his father, the state's expert on the sheep business, seek his advice, and when he became aware that his father must have been dyslexic, he grew to understand his shortcomings.

Although both parents tended to be somewhat overprotective, his mother, a librarian with two years of college, was better able to appreciate Lee's talents. Soon after Lee's birth, Charles Lockhart, who was a dwarf, was elected Texas state treasurer. Lee's mother kept a newspaper photo of Lockhart; it convinced her that her son

76. *Lee Kitchens family. Courtesy Little People of America.*

too could succeed in life.[24] She encouraged him to build airplanes, and while others were out dating in the high school years, he was in his darkroom, honing yet another skill. Kitchens felt that he had benefited from the highly disciplined household in which he had been brought up—a grade of C in English resulted in his being grounded for six weeks; if a child in the house complained about dinner, he or she prepared the next one—but during his childhood he had never been able to talk about being a dwarf. Until he spoke with a friend, an older married man, in college, he had kept his feelings to himself. Once he met Mary, he no longer had to bear them alone.

"I feel fortunate in being a little person," he remarked. "Once people meet you, they'll always remember you." He felt lucky to have worked for a progressive company, and to have been born at a time in history when things were changing for persons with disabilities. Although grateful for the progress that had been made since the Americans with Disabilities Act, Kitchens noted that it takes two or three generations to address social wrongs—because parents continue to teach children what they believe, and discrimination does not yield easily. In part through his invention and marketing of the Kitchens' Kart, a specially adapted scooter for dwarfs, Kitchens was a role model who helped dwarfs to better manage their physical world; and through his personal example and insight, he offered them guidance in negotiating their emotional world.

WILLIAM A. WHEATON: ASTROPHYSICIST

Bill Wheaton (b. 1942), the child of average-sized parents, was born in Oklahoma City, Oklahoma; his family moved to California in 1951. Originally misdiagnosed as having achondroplasia, he was later correctly diagnosed as diastrophic. Because his younger brother was not born until he was nine, and his younger sister when he was twelve, his parents were better able to devote themselves wholly to his care in the early years. He had clubfeet as a baby and required several operations, casts, and braces before he was eight; he developed major hip problems a few years later. He walked on crutches from 1952 to 1979, had six operations in four years, and spent a total of seventeen months in residence at Shriner's Hospital. Somehow, despite all he had to put up with, his parents managed to make him feel "simply wonderful" as a child; "self-esteem was almost bullet-proof by age 5."[25] He describes his mother as "very brilliant, radical, articulate, and beautiful," and his father as "mellow, domestic, and sweet as anything." His father was a general practitioner in McFarland, the fifth-poorest town in California—*Grapes of Wrath* country. The family lived mostly in Delano, Cesar Chavez's starting point, where his mother was considered the town Red. Later, she attended law school, and in 1976 she took her bar exam. Wheaton at that time had a newborn son, David, and his mother cared for the baby to allow Wheaton to complete his doctoral dissertation.

Wheaton had become interested in space in the third grade. The idea of weightlessness was a prime motivation—his feet hurt! His academic performance was mediocre until that grade, when a teacher persuaded him that he was the smartest kid in the class. Her confidence in him was a crucial factor, as was a *Collier's* series that introduced the idea of space travel as not simply a fantasy, setting him on his trajectory toward a career in science. He soon started designing rocket engines. Wheaton was a prodigy. He describes being smart as his "power base, his ecological niche," but, viewed as arrogant, he was once beaten up by other children. In an effort to diminish the risk of such treatment, during one stay at Shriner's Hospital he assessed and reshaped some of his behavior, subsequently becoming more popular among teachers and peers. He continued to succeed in his studies, and in the tenth grade, he learned enough calculus to understand trajectories and orbits and to estimate rocket performance. He shot through school and was granted early admission to Harvard after three years of high school.

Wheaton's curriculum vitae includes the following passage: "He took a position at MIT in April 1976 working on the UCSD/MIT gamma ray experiment (A4) flown on HEAOI 1. During this period he was the discoverer of the strong 20 keV cyclotron absorption feature in the 3.6 s transient pulsar 4U0115+63." Despite the obviously arcane nature of this text and of the seventy-five astrophysics articles on his Web site, all attesting to a brilliant, sophisticated mind, Wheaton was plagued for many years by self-doubt and intermittent bouts of serious depression:

> For most of my adult life I have thought of myself as a cripple; but the physical problems you see were not what I meant. . . . I had a B- in college, and it felt like being dragged by a horse. It took me 11 years to finish grad school (maybe a UC record?!), without a break; even though I got the highest score on the 12 hour qualifying exam, and my advisor told my mother (this is probably not the most reliable source!) that my Ph.D. defense was the most brilliant he had ever seen. Even though I have been a high-spirited person all my life, from HS on into the mid 1980s I was driven by fear and the sense that I had absolutely no choice but to slog on, through a swamp, or die.[26]

Following a great struggle, he has largely emerged from his depression, with the aid of a good psychiatrist and antidepressant medication. In recent years, he has had to deal with repeated hip replacement surgeries; displaying his fortitude, Wheaton refers to these ordeals as merely "nuisances" (Fig. 77).

77. William A. Wheaton. Photograph by Duane Gruber.

Wheaton met his wife, Georgia, between his junior and senior year at college, when he taught math and science in a school for refugees in Tanganyika. They married in 1974; their son, David, has grown to six feet three inches tall. For Wheaton, David's birth was the peak of a lifetime full of positive experiences. His loving relationship with his wife assuaged his earlier shyness, his fear that he was unacceptable to women. His participation, beginning in 1989, in "a fantastic church" affords a fulfilling sense of community. He is grateful that they accept "a poor believer and worse Christian, an agnostic like him."

Wheaton is involved in ongoing space research at the Infrared Processing and Analysis Center at Caltech. He has an interest in the possibilities of discovering other beings in the universe—he has had more familiarity with dwarf stars than with his dwarf peers. His current height is approximately four feet eleven inches; it never occurred to him until recently that the term *dwarf* might apply to him—he thought of himself only as disabled. But several years ago he signed on to the Dwarfism List on the Internet and began to communicate with others, a thought-provoking exploration for this surveyor of unrevealed universes.

HARRY WIEDER: DISABILITY AND GAY RIGHTS ACTIVIST

Social revolutions require catalytic figures who are smart, abrasive, eccentric, demanding—and fun-loving. Harry Wieder (b. 1953) was destined to be just such a firebrand. Born in the conventional, middle-class community of Forest Hills, Queens, in New York, Wieder was not raised by his parents to be a troublemaker. In fact, one of the major sources of friction between them has been Harry's challenging of society's rules.

His parents are Jewish World War II survivors; at least half of their relatives perished at the hands of the Nazis. His mother's experiences have taught her to be wary, worrisome, and deferential. One of her regular admonitions to her son was that he must avoid behaviors that might prove embarrassing. But of course, she could not foresee that those behaviors were precisely the ones that would serve a budding revolutionary well. Erving Goffman's *Presentation of Self in Everyday Life* had been an important influence in shaping his thinking and behavior.

Early in the administration of President Bill Clinton, a coalition he had joined hoping to revolutionize the health care program fell apart, but Harry was not disillusioned.[27] He had learned a great deal during his years in Act Up, the gay rights organization that became known for its militancy during the height of the anguish about AIDS in the gay community. He participated in many actions and was once arrested for blocking the Queens Midtown Tunnel. Besides being part of Act Up, he worked with Queer Nation and Housing Works (a group that provides housing to people with AIDS). His time with Act Up taught him to put up a good fight and strive for the maximum—"If you ask for ten percent you may end up with five," he frequently observes. "But if you ask for 150 percent, you'll get 110!" (Fig. 78).

Wieder has gained both fame and notoriety. In 1993, *New York Newsday* columnist Jimmy Breslin wrote a Runyonesque article about Wieder, inventing some details, but capturing his combative, roguish nature and his penchant for truth.[28] *OutWeek,* a gay publication, published a picture of Wieder posing in a G-string with a tall black man—another prominent gay activist—a photo that Wieder delights in displaying. When others allowed his shortness to exclude him from full participation at the "love-in" of a Queering the Streets demonstration, he threatened to protest by unzipping the fly of some taller person who ignored him (Wieder's head would reach just that level).

His dramatic stratagems represent, in part, a victory over an earlier shyness. His time as an undergraduate at New York University was a turning point for him. An English major with a minor in political science, Wieder also studied Greek literature and acted in Euripides' *The Frogs.* He made some good friends and felt a part of things for the first time in his life. Law school at Temple University, however, ended in some bitterness after a dispute with a difficult faculty member; he then failed his bar exam. Unable to practice law, he became a kind of unpaid professional advocate. By 1983 he required surgery for back trouble; he has continued to have problems with his spine and gets around on crutches. He also has a significant hearing loss,

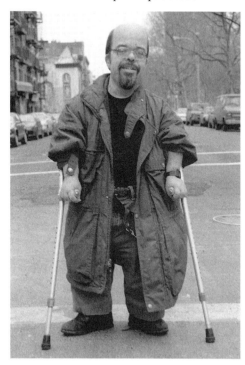

78. Harry Wieder. Photograph by Kristin Sabena/© 2001 Community Media, LLC.

which qualifies him for a pleasant one-bedroom apartment in a Manhattan residence for the deaf where flashing lights signal a bell ringing and a concierge provides security. On weekends he drives to Forest Hills to visit and help his elderly parents.

When his father was in better health, they drove and camped in every state but Hawaii between 1968 and 1982. Although he values those experiences, Wieder recognizes that they substituted for experiences that he was not having. In 1986, after reading David Levin's *Family Dancing*, he "came out of the closet like a cannonball!" Since then, he has grappled with his body image. "I couldn't understand how others could find me attractive," he says. He has had to overcome these feelings in order take pleasure in his sexuality.

Wieder, through the years, chose not to be active in LPA, expressing criticism of the group for not interacting more with the disability community, but he has recently attended a number of LPA events. He nurtures his dwarf identity through books, movies, and friendships.[29] Because he realizes that his body makes him conspicuous already, he delights in standing out in the service of a good cause. He is active in the Independent Living Center where he resides, Disabled in Action of Metropolitan New York, and the 504 Democratic Club (named after Section 504 of the 1973 Rehabilitation Act, which mandates that federally funded programs provide accessibility for persons with disabilities). The club honored Wieder in 2003 for his long career as a disability activist. At that event he gave an impassioned speech, deploring the disability community's timidity and advocating resistance to the administration of President George W. Bush, whom he blames for a reduction in social services and diminishing of civil liberties. He also recommended a closer relationship between the disability and dwarfism communities.

Relying on an income derived from disability insurance and modest family backing freed Wieder to be a vigorous, almost full-time advocate. Despite his health concerns and limitations in mobility, Wieder's spirit is indomitable, and he is always ready for a new project. He has written plays and is currently working on short stories with dwarf protagonists.

TOM SHAKESPEARE:
SOCIAL SCIENTIST AND DISABILITY RIGHTS ACTIVIST

Tom Shakespeare (b. 1966), respected social scientist and disability activist, is the son of a British physician (William Shakespeare, profiled below) and a mother of Sri Lankan heritage. In addition to Tom's many valuable scholarly contributions, he has contributed a reflective autobiographical piece to *Invented Identities? Lesbians and Gays Talk about Migration*, a volume on the subject of confronting attachments to two worlds—the community of origin, in which one is reared and learns one's intrinsic values, and the community that allows the affirmation of one's sexual identity.[30]

For Tom Shakespeare, the contrasts are particularly great. He was raised in a world of privilege, counting among his prominent ancestors the poet-playwright William Shakespeare himself. His average-statured mother, Sue, was of Sri Lankan Burgher background (that is, her family was descended from Dutch colonists), and she maintained such traditions as serving curry for Sunday lunch. Both parents adhered to traditional values and conventional expectations. Tom satisfied some of these expectations by becoming a successful academic (his younger brother, James, is a priest, and his older half brother, Matthew, is an artist). Although the family was not overtly homophobic, neither were they comfortable relating to the gay community. As for the achondroplasia that affected both father and son, according to Tom it was "implicit, and ignored, taken for granted."[31] In aspirations, lifestyle, and dress, it was understood that each person would endeavor to fit in.

However, Tom was constitutionally and temperamentally not a conformist. He never felt fully at home at boarding school or at Cambridge University, where he received his doctorate in sociology, though "the rigidity, discipline, and expectations of the school gave me something to fight against, and something against which to define myself."[32] His definition of himself was strengthened when he became involved with REGARD, the British organization of gay persons with disabilities, through which he experienced a true sense of belonging. His association with the group also encouraged him to take pleasure in performing, in making people laugh (Fig. 79).

Tom is the father of a son and a daughter, Robert and Ivy, each born in 1988 to different mothers. Although he has expressed some regret about the impetuousness that led to their births, he does not regret his fatherhood. He originally moved to Tyneside, England, so that he could coparent Ivy; she now also has a half sister and stepsister. Robert lives in Cambridge with his mother. In *Invented Identities,* Shakespeare speaks about his migration from Cambridge to Tyneside, the former an upper-class environment, the latter a working-class community. He now lives in nearby Hebburn. In 2002 he married Caroline (Cas) Bowditch, who trained as a primary school teacher and genetic counselor and currently works for a community arts project in North Tyneside.

79. Tom Shakespeare. Courtesy Tom Shakespeare.

Shakespeare is director of outreach for the Policy, Ethics, and Life Sciences Research Institute (PEALS), a Newcastle-based project developing research and debate on the social and ethical implications of the new genetics. Before this, he was a lecturer in sociology at the University of Sunderland and worked as research fellow in the Disability Research Unit of the School of Sociology and Social Policy at the University of Leeds. He has published and edited a number of books and articles on issues relating to adults and children with disabilities, sexuality, older persons, and the ethics of genetics.[33] In addition, he produced documentaries, including *Ivy's Genes* (Shakespeare's children also have achondroplasia).

In addition to his serious scholarly research, Shakespeare generally has several frivolous balls in the air. He has published two popular works, *Choose to Change,* a book about overcoming fears and enjoying life, and *Coral and Pearls,* containing quotations for every day of the year from various thinkers. He has also produced a board game, Hogwarts, based on the Harry Potter books. Among a number of unfinished projects is a comic novel about disability, titled *Man of Steel,* and a play about the disabled Italian Marxist Antonio Gramsci, a collaboration with Tom Philips. He remains active in REGARD and in the Northern Arts Board, the National Lottery Charities Board, and the Restricted Growth Association, the British group for short-statured persons.

Both Tom and his father before him were responsible for bringing the lives of British dwarfs to public attention. Tom has become a television celebrity, offering commentary on issues relating to disability, sexuality, and genetic decision-making. In an article titled "Last Words Mmmm Mmmm Mmmm: More Thoughts on Monogamy," he discusses bisexuality, monogamy, and open relationships in the context of his own experience; having found open relationships simpler to manage in theory than in practice, he analyzes the various alternatives.[34] Shakespeare's work grows from his own personal experience, not only in such a controversial field as sexual behavior, but also in disability theory and eugenics. Aware of the changes he has experienced in his own journey, he calls himself an "identity nomad." For his latest exciting expeditions, consult his Web page.

COLLEEN FRASER: DISABILITY RIGHTS ACTIVIST

Colleen Fraser (1950–2001), who was vice chair of the New Jersey Disabilities Council and an advocate for people with disabilities for more than twenty years, was a passenger on United Airlines Flight 93 when it was hijacked and crashed in Pennsylvania on 11 September 2001.[35] Colleen identified with the disability community, not specifically with the dwarfism community: because she was proportionate and her condition caused by rickets, she did not think of herself as a dwarf. Although I had never met her, I attended her memorial service at the Trinity United Methodist Church in Ewing, New Jersey; I felt personally moved to do so, but also, because I regretted that the lives of so many important short-statured individuals had gone unrecorded, I wanted her to be known to a wider public once the media moment was over. The service had been organized by the Progressive Center for Independent Living (PCIL), where Fraser had been executive director. The group of approximately fifty people gathered there reflected the diverse community that she had served. One of the few short-statured persons present was Christine Fraser, Colleen's four-foot-eight-inch sister.

Huntley Forrester, the board president of PCIL, spoke of Fraser as the driving force behind the organization that they had started six years earlier. Fraser rebelled against a world in which people were known as *cripples* and *midgets* and *dumb*. Forrester, who is African American, compared Fraser's dreams—removing barriers and improving job opportunities and transportation—to those of Martin Luther King Jr. One of Fraser's closest friends, Ethan Ellis, executive director of the Developmental Disabilities Commission, spoke of her as comrade-in-arms, mentor, and role model. He admired her fierce commitment to making others listen, even when what she said was difficult to hear (Fig. 80).

Lydia Kirschenbaum, chairperson of the New Jersey State Independent Living

80. Colleen Fraser with Gov. Jim Florio of New Jersey. Courtesy Christine Fraser.

Center, referred to Fraser's various positions, from former chair and current vice chair of the Developmental Disabilities Council, to president of Community Access Unlimited. More important than her titles, however, were the ways in which she loved and ministered to and fought for all those she served, gaining in strength through the years. After mentioning that Fraser was a member of a class of persons previously consigned to roles as public curiosities because of their height, Kirschenbaum recited a poem by Emily Dickinson containing the line "Your stature touched the sky." More than one speaker referred to Fraser's passionate nature—she was not a person who sat by and watched. They imagined her using her cane to assist the people on the airplane who had intervened against the hijackers to prevent the plane from being flown into the White House.

When I later contacted Fraser's sister, Christine, she explained that both she and Colleen had been born with congenital rickets, and in childhood Colleen had broken a number of bones and undergone many surgeries. Colleen was four feet six inches; Christine was knock-kneed, but Colleen was bowlegged, like her father. When Colleen was seven years old, and her sister eight, Colleen had corrective surgery, but her walking was still impaired. The sisters remained close all their lives and had lived together. Christine, one year older, had been more of a caregiver in the earlier years, but during the past decade she had developed chronic fatigue syndrome and relied on Colleen. They had sometimes ended up working for the same agencies.

Christine said that Camp Merry Heart in Hackettstown, New Jersey, a camp for disabled children, had made an enormous difference in their lives. A social worker had helped their father arrange for them to leave their public housing development for three weeks at Merry Heart, where they returned for part of every summer for ten years. Not only did the experience offer them freedom and enjoyment, it also helped them identify with the disability movement in a positive way. By the time Colleen accepted an invitation to one LPA event, out of courtesy, her identity within the greater disability community was already central. Christine mentioned her sister's empathy, especially for persons who were in institutions or nursing homes or who had otherwise been cut off from full engagement with life.

Christine reminisced about how Colleen testified in Washington, D.C., and "blew people away," proving herself once again "a small presence to be reckoned with!" Colleen had railed at the Work Incentive Act, which helped people only after they reached the bottom economically, and at the governor of New Jersey, who had sued to prevent the Americans with Disabilities Act (ADA) from being applied to state government. She suggested forming alliances with groups such as the American Association of Retired Persons (AARP) that have the money to affect policy; she also spoke about the need to find ways to monitor compliance with the ADA—"Nobody is looking at doctors' offices to see if we can get in," she observed.[36]

Fraser was famously impatient with sluggish bureaucracy, commenting: "I can see all the way from my handicapped class in the third grade to here. We have come a long way, but, when you consider the rapidity of change in other areas of society, we have been chugging along in mud up to our waists. . . . A social marketing consultant from Canada once asked me if I was willing to wait for ten years for the changes I want. I am not willing to wait for ten minutes. I will work for ten years, though."[37] Tragically, she was not given that chance.

ANGELA MUIR VAN ETTEN: LAWYER, ACTIVIST, AUTHOR; AND ROBERT VAN ETTEN: INDUSTRIAL ENGINEER

The *Miami Herald* announced the Florida wedding ceremony of Angela Muir (b. 1953) and Robert Van Etten (b. 1949) with the headline "Prince and Lady of Little People Exchange Vows" (Fig. 81). Muir had been president of the Short-Statured People of New Zealand, and Van Etten president of the Little People of America.

Angela Muir came to the United States from New Zealand in 1981 on a Winston Churchill Fellowship to study how public recognition of the rights of individuals with disabilities was influenced by education and legislation. Although her goal was professional, she recognized that this opportunity might also offer personal advantages. In her engaging memoir, *Dwarfs Don't Live in Doll Houses,* she writes about the emotional growth she attained from her early romantic experiences: "Through all these heartaches and soul-searchings, I had acquired a sense of confidence. I knew the depth of love I was capable of giving and was strong enough to offer it even knowing it wouldn't be returned. I also knew I was worthy of love and should not be surprised if someone paid attention to me. There was no reason why someone shouldn't love me. Somehow, once I started believing that, I was no longer consumed with the desire to find a husband. I had found my own value and knew I was able to live happily ever after as a single person. I could only marry if I found a man who was worthy of my love; one who would love me in return."[38]

By the time these reflections had crystallized, Angela had completed law school and proved herself as a law clerk, barrister, and solicitor in New Zealand. She had spent four years with firms that handled criminal and family cases; she often had occasion to appear in court. Her book details a number of her encounters with prejudice—unnerving, amusing, or both. Just as these experiences and the internal battles she had fought and won had matured Angela, Robert's experiences had matured him. In elementary school, he was the class clown—not an uncommon role for a little person. He soon tired of this, however, and with the encouragement of his mother and demanding sixth-grade teacher, he changed.

College was a particularly rich period: Robert majored in industrial engineering and was active in a variety of extracurricular activities, organizing a coffeehouse run by the Catholic Newman Club, serving as coxswain for the rowing team, and acting. He was elected president of the Men's Residence Association and the Handicapped Students' Council and was a senator in the student government.[39] All these positions would prepare him for his later role as LPA president from 1980 to 1982 and 1984 to 1986.

Robert and Angela found each other at an optimal moment for both, when each was enjoying a sense of confidence and achievement. Robert had dated both average- and short-statured women and had overcome much adversity. He had had many reconstructive surgeries and had at various times before and since their meeting mastered scooters, crutches, and other mobility aids. In graduate school, his engineering class responded to his difficulty in walking by developing a small bicycle with stabilizer wheels, powered by a helicopter battery donated by General Electric. These experiences helped inspire his interest in developing rehabilitation strategies for others.

Both Angela and Robert have devoted significant parts of their work lives to improving the world for persons with disabilities. Once in the United States, Angela earned her J.D. at the University of Maryland and worked as an attorney, legal editor, and writer. Her unofficial assignments have been at least equally important, how-

81. Robert and Angela Van Etten. Courtesy Robert and Angela Van Etten.

ever: she has been a powerful, seemingly irresistible force in the service of disability rights—especially for little people.

Robert's efforts have been directed toward the more technical aspects of this endeavor. Early in his career, he published a rehabilitation sourcebook about appliances marketed in 1979–1980 for disabled persons. In Washington, D.C., he served as a communications engineer for the Architectural and Transportation Barriers Compliance Board. In 1982 he was selected Outstanding Young Man of America by the Junior Chamber of Commerce and subsequently was employed by Dr. Steven Kopits at Johns Hopkins Medical Center, programming patient and research files.

The couple moved to Cleveland, where Robert worked at Cleveland Metropolitan/Highland View Hospital, helping physicians and therapists analyze and design products used in rehabilitation; next they moved to Rochester, where Angela had a good job offer. At that time, Robert established his own business as part-time rehabilitation consultant for government and private agencies. He also designed a chair especially for little people, with a shallow seat and footrest.

In Rochester, Angela completed and published *Dwarfs Don't Live in Doll Houses.* While almost all previous works about persons with dwarfism had been written by average-statured authors, Angela's book is a rare first-person account of what it is like to come to terms with and manage one's dwarfism. Designed also to increase public understanding, the book includes a vivid description of the anti–"dwarf tossing" campaign, in which she played an important role. After being rebuffed by trade publishers on the grounds that there would be insufficient interest in such a book, Angela published the work in 1988 with Adaptive Living, Robert's company. It received a positive review in *Library Journal,* and has found its way into many public libraries. The dwarfism community views its appearance as an important milestone.

Angela has led LPA's effort to lower the height of ATMs, gas pumps, vending machines, and public pay phones. In 1991 the Access Board—the agency Congress designated to see that buildings and facilities are accessible to the disabled—resolved to enforce a forty-eight-inch side-reach standard for new or renovated ATMs. After the banking industry applied pressure, however, the board reversed its decision. Seven years later, with the side-reach standard remaining at fifty-four inches, the board was still dragging its heels and calling for further research—which Van Etten interpreted as code words for "not in your lifetime." She was pleased to become a mentor to Tricia Mason, who became the principal advocate at the American National Standards Institute (ANSI) in 2001, traveling from Montana to Washington, D.C., to attend meetings. With the aid of Oregonian David Bradford, Mason took part in a successful effort to make gas pumps more accessible, and she is now encouraged to see progress toward accessibility of elevator buttons and lavatory-faucet controls.[40]

A forceful, eloquent speaker with considerable charm and humor, Angela has made approximately one hundred appearances on television and radio programs in more than a dozen cities in the United States as well as in New Zealand and Australia. Her disability rights efforts have been highlighted in many articles. The Van Ettens also enjoy a rich personal life close to their families and friends. Recently, they moved to Florida to be near his family. Robert, with the aid of computer-generated building plans, translated the couple's ideas into reality and designed a home with reachable faucets, cabinets, and other accommodations.

Spirituality has long been a central force in their life. Robert, who still runs Adaptive Living and markets his Ergo Chair for Little People, is employed part time as a computer instructor at Samaritan House, a Christian residential school for boys with learning difficulties and from troubled homes. He serves as LPA district director in Florida and has also organized his college's thirtieth reunion. Angela first held a job doing legal research, writing, and editing for the Christian Law Association, but when that position was defunded, she was hired as an advocacy specialist by the Coalition for Independent Living Options in West Palm Beach. She advocates for people with disabilities in areas such as employment and housing and teaches them to navigate bureaucracies. In 2004 she was also elected vice president of membership in LPA.

Several years ago, a twenty-six-year-old man of extremely short stature wrote to the *San Francisco Chronicle*, reporting that a local realtor would not hire him because potential homebuyers would view him as "a small infant." Columnist Ilana DeBare responded to the man's letter, citing Angela Van Etten's experience of having been advised by law firms to seek behind-the-scenes work because clients might not have confidence in her; DeBare wrote that Angela had persevered and become a successful trial lawyer. Angela suggested this strategy for the man: "He could say something like, 'Let me work out of your firm's office for three months. If I don't sell anything, then I'll move on.'" She advised him to demonstrate his sales personality and let it be known that he had a positive outlook and was not easily rebuffed.

WILLIAM SHAKESPEARE: PHYSICIAN

It is interesting to compare the autobiographical writings of Dr. William Shakespeare (1927–1996) and his son Tom, profiled earlier, noting the generational and temperamental differences that distinguish the two men. William's unfinished memoir, *Walking through Leaves*, offers the recollections of a reserved, nature-loving, upper-class man who minimizes the role of disability in his life.[41] He praises his "caring, enlightened" family and the opportunities granted by his social background. Only rarely does he expose problems, and he does not discuss any difficulties he may have encountered in raising his own children (Fig. 82).

Readers of *Walking through Leaves* may be curious about how this William Shakespeare may be related to his more famous namesake. Dr. Shakespeare reports that he and the poet-playwright have a common ancestor, the latter's grandfather Richard, and that the younger William is thus a first cousin fourteen generations removed. Dr. Shakespeare's memoir is less than a hundred pages long, but it brims over with descriptions of his childhood, courtship, and medical career, including also his service as vice president of the Restricted Growth Association. Given his family's connections with aristocrats, politicians, writers, and artists, it seems natural for him to introduce the names Lloyd George, Sarah and Diana Churchill, and Lord Mountbatten as well as the actor Sam Wanamaker, who was responsible for the rebuilding of the Globe Theatre.

Beloved by friends and family, Dr. Shakespeare was also a respected physician who played an important role in the disability rights movement in Great Britain. Leadership qualities run in the family: his grandfather John had been head of the Free Church General Council of the Anglican Church. William's father, Sir Geoffrey, had been a Liberal member of Parliament and served as parliamentary secretary in the Ministry of Health and the Ministries of Education and the Admiralty.

Shakespeare was raised by loving parents on "a fine street in Chelsea." His idyllic childhood was interrupted by a period in Bavaria where his parents took him for medical treatment. The therapy was a waste of time and potentially dangerous—to stimulate growth, he was given thyroid extract by mouth, a treatment that could have caused permanent damage. Such misadventures, unfortunately, were not uncommon in the 1930s.

At Cambridge University William studied natural sciences and coxed the rowing team. He graduated with honors, but his last year at the university was blighted by two tragic events. In 1949, his average-statured younger sister, Judith, committed suicide at the age of eighteen; his beloved mother died of a massive stroke less than a year later. Judith had been treated for severe intermittent depressions for several years previously, having a predisposition that ran in the family. Despite this, and his good relationship with Judith, William wonders if his disability played a role, noting, "It is regrettably common in a family who have an affected child that this child is over-protected and cared for to the detriment of the normal siblings."[42]

He remembers his mother as a bright, kind

82. *Dr. William Shakespeare. Courtesy Tom Shakespeare.*

person with whom he had a loving relationship. He recounts an anecdote about the time when, looking for him, she asked the barber whether anyone was inside the shop. When the barber responded that there was one gentleman inside, she asked, "A small gentleman?" William understood that to her he was "a small gentleman, nothing more, nothing less."

After a period of strain working in a brick factory, Shakespeare enrolled in a medical program at St. George's Hospital. He found his studies demanding but pleasurable, and he enjoyed traveling during breaks. When he was thirty-five, as he was recovering from a bout of pneumonia, one of the staff nurses in his ward introduced him to Susan Raffel, another nurse, whose family was from Sri Lanka and of Dutch Burgher background. The couple's friendship deepened, and within a year they decided to marry. While his family approved of the match, hers did not, because of his physical disability and their difference in backgrounds.

He eventually became a senior partner in private practice and served on the general staff of Manor House Hospital, an institution for the mentally disabled, developing a special interest in that field. Sue was parish councilor and chair of the local

83. *The Shakespeare family: Tom Shakespeare's daughter Ivy with (*from left to right*) grandfather Dr. William Shakespeare, great-grandmother Sheila, and grandmother Sue. Courtesy Tom Shakespeare.*

school governors organization for many years, in addition to performing many other good works for her village and her church. The couple had two children; Tom had achondroplasia, whereas James grew to more than six feet tall. Tom is an academician, James a priest and theologian. The brothers have remained close through the years.

Dr. Shakespeare was invited to the first annual conference on achondroplasia in Italy in 1986. In an article published subsequently, he suggested that limb lengthening was being performed more frequently in Italy, Spain, and Russia than elsewhere because those countries were less accepting of disabilities; he also made recommendations for positive child rearing.[43] Shakespeare was active both in the Restricted Growth Association and as vice president of Physically Handicapped and Able Bodied (PHAB), a national body that encourages unaffected individuals to assist those with disabilities. His friend Lord Snowden made a film called *Born to Be Small* that depicted Shakespeare at his house and in his medical office. Shakespeare was also featured on television, in newspaper articles, and in the film *Ivy's Genes,* made by his son Tom.

In his final years, Shakespeare was forced into retirement by a number of health problems. He ultimately died of a heart attack. In *Walking through Leaves,* he concludes: "I have enjoyed my time" (Fig. 83).

JUDITH BADNER: GENETICIST AND PSYCHIATRIST

Dr. Judith Badner (b. 1960) is a distinguished research scientist, a geneticist, and a practicing psychiatrist at the University of Chicago. She thrives on combining research and treatment. Dr. Badner was born in Silver Spring, Maryland, the daughter of Julius Badner, a meteorologist, and Margaret Badner, a senior meteorological technician. Judith was the youngest of three children. She was slow to walk and talk, and she was diagnosed at the Easter Seal Center as mentally retarded (the center's term). This common misdiagnosis was later corrected when her hearing problem was discovered; once this was treated surgically, it became clear that she was an exceptionally bright child.

Her intense interest in medicine and genetics was perhaps stimulated by her experience of spending years as a patient at Johns Hopkins's Moore Clinic, where she observed physicians who treated genetic disorders. Beside regular checkups, she underwent difficult but ultimately successful osteotomies to correct her bowleg deformity. Although Badner majored in biology at the Massachusetts Institute of Technology (MIT), she also had a strong interest in mathematics and sought a career into which she could incorporate both interests. She entered a program in human genetics at the University of Pittsburgh, receiving her M.S. in genetics two years later,

84. *Judith Badner. Courtesy Judith Badner.*

and was admitted to the University of Pittsburgh's Medical School. Her fears about affording the program were assuaged through an unexpected inheritance and financial assistance from the Pennsylvania Vocational Rehabilitation program. She obtained her Ph.D. in human genetics in 1988 and her M.D. in 1990 (Fig. 84).

Badner won admission to a four-year residency at the prestigious McLean Hospital, a Harvard affiliate. She wanted a career that would also allow her to combine her research interests with her desire to work with people, and a research specialization in the new field of psychiatric genetics afforded not only this, but also the possibility of making a significant scientific contribution. As a senior staff fellow at the National Institutes of Health (NIH) from 1994 to 1998, she continued to pursue both research and clinical interests. In 1998 she was awarded the NIH Fellows award for research excellence.

In 1998 Badner and several other members of her group moved to the Department of Psychiatry at the University of Chicago, where NIH principal investigator Elliot Gershon had relocated. Badner has been featured in a volume about notable women in science and engineering,[44] and authored or coauthored more than forty articles, frequently on genetic linkage or allied studies in the areas of bipolar disorder and schizophrenia. As a genetic statistician, she analyzes data to identify the locations of genes that are contributing to the development of a trait or disorder, using existing programs or creating her own. Early genetic research sought to identify single genes that were responsible for medical conditions; now, however, there is a new emphasis on the interaction of genes with one another and with environmental factors. Badner works to illuminate the complex interactions involved in psychiatric diagnoses. She sees approximately thirty outpatients, most suffering from depressive or anxiety disorders, and a number from bipolar disorder or some other condition. She enjoys her work, experiencing a particularly great reward in helping those who believed they could not be helped. She has encountered few problems in her professional life because of her dwarfism. Only once during her residency did she have a negative experience, when a well-known psychiatrist told Badner's supervisor to pull her off a VIP patient's case. "If you were psychotic," he said, "would you want someone who looked like that?" In fact, she has very rarely had difficulties with patients themselves because of her difference in appearance. Once a new patient said, "I don't want this doctor." The physician in charge responded, "I could give you a less competent doctor who isn't a dwarf." By the time the deadline for transfers arrived, the patient opted to continue treatment with Badner. Indeed, Badner's patients tend to view her dwarfism positively. She theorizes that when psychiatric patients first encounter a mental health worker, they often wonder how that privileged person can begin to understand them; in the case of Badner, they recognize at once that Badner must have faced and overcome difficulties herself in order to arrive at her current position.

Badner grew up in a supportive family, and she in turn is supportive, taking the role of nurturing aunt to her several nieces and nephews, among them an autistic niece. She enjoys a close friendship with her roommate, a freelance writer and disability activist who has Asperger's syndrome, a high-functioning type of autism. Badner had considered adopting a child, probably a dwarf child, but she has since concluded that given her heavy professional workload, she would do best not to venture the responsibilities of a single mother. She will content herself for now with the areas of generativity already in place, as well as reading, relaxation, and personal pursuits.

ROBERT REICH: SECRETARY OF LABOR, ECONOMIC ADVISOR, PROFESSOR, AUTHOR

The word *dwarf* has rarely been used in reference to Robert Reich (b. 1946). Nevertheless, after Reich declared his candidacy for governor of Massachusetts, the *Washington Post* devoted much attention to Reich's stature and to his frequent humorous references to it.[45] The *Post* writer concludes that because Reich is 4 feet 10 1/2 inches tall, he is not a dwarf: the commonly accepted definition states that the person measures 4 feet 10 inches or less and has a medical condition. The journalist had researched the matter thoroughly, noting that Reich's shortness was associated with the congenital condition Fairbank disease (multiple epiphyseal dysplasia). In fact, this condition is a mild form of dwarfism that is inherited as a dominant trait, resulting in an average-sized trunk but shorter-than-usual legs.[46] While its symptoms are often not apparent in early childhood, the condition is marked by developmental abnormalities of bone that can cause pain in the hip, knee, and ankle joints. Although Reich jokes about his height, he has also discussed it seriously, at least once, on a late-night television program in which he advised young people not to let their shortness compromise their dreams. When told of his having been written about in *The Lives of Dwarfs,* he said that he had no objection to being included in the book, which he characterized as "about short-statured individuals."[47]

Why did the *Post* journalist, as have others, conclude that Reich was *not a dwarf*? A semantic dilemma may have been created because commentators understood that being saddled with a stigmatizing term would not be helpful to Reich's political ambitions. In fact, the four-foot-ten-inch boundary is arbitrary—if Reich lost another half inch in late middle age, as people frequently do, would he only then become a dwarf? As an outstanding achiever who happens to be short, whether he is called a dwarf or not, Reich is an exemplar for people of any height—but particularly for those who are also short statured (Fig. 85).

Reich was secretary of labor during Bill Clinton's first term and recognized as an ethical, impolitic, often dissenting liberal voice. In his surprise best seller *Locked in the Cabinet,* a memoir based largely on the journals he kept from 1992 to 1996, Reich interweaves politics and personalities.[48] He offers insights into the Clinton administration and into his own character. Like playwright Eugene O'Neill, Reich has a keen eye for hypocrisy, and he attempts to discover the real person behind the masks he encounters during his "Strange Interlude" in government service.

His intimacy with his wife, Clare, and his trust of her perspicacity helped him to maintain his own integrity. Apparently, Reich had a difficult time learning the rules of the game in Washington, although he had served there earlier in a number of capacities. Because "deficit hawks" helped to persuade Clinton to place a single-minded emphasis on balancing the budget, many innovative programs that Reich had envisioned as helping the working poor and middle class were shelved. Nevertheless, he achieved four hard-won victories: the increase in the minimum wage; progress in the fight against sweatshops; a law requiring companies to fully fund their promised pensions; and the school-to-work apprenticeship program, which enrolled a million young people.[49]

A devoted husband and father, Reich eventually could not tolerate the schedule that life in Washington, a place that he felt did not respect families, had imposed upon him. He had met his British wife, Clare—who is seven inches taller than he is—at Oxford soon after he met Bill Clinton, who, like Reich, was a Rhodes scholar there. She had taken two years off from her work as a law professor and founder of an advocacy program for battered women to be with him in Washington. At the end of that period, she and her children left for the life they loved back in Boston, with Reich commuting on weekends. Finally, Reich decided to resign, saying that he had decided to choose family over what he considered the best job of his life.

Perhaps he was also tired of being a gadfly in the Washington wilderness and was discouraged by his limited influence in matters such as welfare legislation. He became University Professor at Brandeis University and resumed writing, lecturing, and delivering regular commentaries on National Public Radio on matters affecting working people in the economy. (Although his background is in history and philosophy, he has published eight books and innumerable articles that relate to labor and economics.) He has not stopped being a social critic. In *The Future of Success,* a searching examination of the difficulties of balancing work and a meaningful personal, family, and civic life, and another called *I'll Be Short,* he discusses the fault lines that threaten the well-being of our entire society.[50]

85. *Robert B. Reich addresses crowd in 1993. © Reuters/CORBIS.*

This second title is evidence of Reich's humorous approach to his size; with such wit, he is able to defuse a situation and make others comfortable. Once, when introducing new appointees, he found himself at a lectern that was scaled to Clinton's height, but only reached Reich's nose. Peering over the top at reporters, who seemed embarrassed by his situation, and imagining television viewers unable to view his face, he joked, "Modesty aside, I've known for months that I was on Bill Clinton's short list."[51]

When an examining sergeant rejected Reich for service in Vietnam, the sergeant remarked, *"Maybe someday you'll grow, and then you can serve your country."* Another time, after Clinton made an emotional address in which he echoed Reich's views about expanding middle-class opportunities, Clinton reached down to give him a bear hug, while Reich reached up and hugged his chest. "We must look odd," thought Reich, "this huge panda bear of a president locked in an embrace with this organ-grinder's monkey of a labor secretary. But for this one brief moment . . . I feel as though we're on exactly the same track, the one we should be on."[52]

Not surprisingly, it can be a pleasure for Reich to encounter another powerful short person. Allan Greenspan, head of the Federal Reserve Board, is someone with whom Reich feels affinity, despite their ideological differences. Reich has written a playful, imaginary account of an argument with Greenspan:

REICH: *Well, you can take your crummy lunch and cram it, you robber-baron pimp.*
GREENSPAN: *Go suck on a pickle, you Bolshevik dwarf.*[53]

Besides humor, another tactic he used, when he was young, was enlisting the aid of taller friends; among these was Michael Schwerner, the civil rights worker who later was murdered in Mississippi.

This grab bag of memories relating to size is only a small sample of those that Reich proffered in *Locked in the Cabinet.* An article about the Massachusetts governor's race, in which Reich came in second in the Democratic primary, quoted his closing punch line: "I am not a big man. But it is not the size of the dog in the fight. It is the size of the fight in the dog."[54]

PAUL STEVEN MILLER:
LAWYER AND EQUAL OPPORTUNITY COMMISSIONER

In 1997, when I came upon an announcement in the *New York Times* of the marriage of Paul Steven Miller and Jennifer Coletti Mechem, I was delighted, as I knew the groom and liked him, though we had lost touch.[55] My next thought was, "How wonderful it is to read about an individual who is a dwarf—without the focus being on his size!" (The article gave details typical of wedding announcements.) Not quite three years later, Miller's Web page announced the arrival of Naomi Whitney Mechem-Miller, born 26 January 2000.

In his younger days, Miller was ubiquitous at LPA conferences. At age twenty-five, he was bright, good looking, personable, and a Harvard Law School graduate. Paul was allied with the most progressive elements in LPA, and in addition to valuing it as a social organization, he foresaw it becoming an advocacy group; while having a good time himself, he seemed preternaturally aware of the needs of others.

In 1994 President Clinton appointed Miller commissioner of the Equal Employment Opportunity Commission (EEOC), for a five-year term, with the power to administer the ADA. In 1999 he was reappointed until 2004. Prior to his appointment, Miller served as director of litigation for the Western Law Center for Disability Rights, a nonprofit legal services center, and taught at several law schools. He had also been deputy director of the United States Office of Consumer Affairs and White House liaison to the disability community. He has served on a number of committees and task forces, working to establish national policy to raise the employment rate of adults with disabilities (Fig. 86).[56]

Miller has also published articles about disability rights issues. In one commencement address, he revealed that despite his achievements, his own professional path had not been without significant roadblocks: "As a law student, I found that the very law firms that had pursued me based on my resume would immediately lose all interest in employing me as soon as they met me or learned of my size. It pained me to see my classmates, even those with lower grades and less experience, receive offer after offer, while I received forty-five rejection letters from law firms without a single callback. . . . [One law firm said] they feared that their clients would think that they were running "'a circus freak show.'"[57]

Miller is well aware of the value of the connections he developed at college. When potential employers rejected him, a law school friend mentioned Miller to the friend's brother, Mickey Kantor, who was then a senior partner in a Los Angeles law firm; saying that Miller was exceptionally brilliant, the friend convinced Kantor to hire him. Kantor, who later became a prominent figure in the Clinton administration, helped put Miller on the road that eventually led to the EEOC job. While Miller was employed at Kantor's firm, one of the firm's clients was Steven Bochco, creator and executive producer of the popular television series *L.A. Law*. Bochco used Miller as the model for the dwarf lawyer on this show.

Less than a decade later, Miller attained his powerful national position that allowed him to take up arms against blatant discrimination. One of Miller's great accomplishments at the EEOC was his introduction of conciliation procedures, which

reduced pending cases by nearly 33 percent. In an EEOC case concerning a developmentally disabled man who was fired by the restaurant company Chuck E. Cheese
and then awarded damages, Miller made it known that such vulnerable individuals
in the American workforce would be aggressively protected by the agency.[58] Arguing before the Senate Committee on Health, Education, Labor and Pensions, he urged
protection from genetic records being used along with résumés to disqualify someone from a job, so that workers could seek early detection and treatment of serious
medical conditions without the fear of negative consequences.[59] Perhaps his own
bout with cancer in 2000, when he required chemotherapy and radiation treatments,
intensified his strong convictions on health issues.

In 2002, when I met with Commissioner Miller at his Washington office, he had
just returned from a lawyers' meeting in New Orleans, where he became keenly
aware that there were few legal academics with disabilities.[60] The ADA had recently
suffered a number of setbacks in the courts. How, he wondered, could lawyers advocate for the goals defined by the act when the faculties of law schools included so few

86. Paul Steven Miller with former president Bill Clinton. Courtesy Paul Steven Miller.

affected individuals? He began to think that once he completed his stint with government, he might perhaps play a significant role as a law professor.

Miller spoke of the transformations he had noticed taking place in LPA in recent decades. When he was growing up, almost the only professionals in the group were schoolteachers—they were seen as special, and looked up to. Many members were glad simply to have jobs at all. Miller was finding it especially exciting to witness the tremendous difference in the current generation's sense of self-esteem and life expectations. Even when he was growing up, however, there had been a few young people who had stood out and had ambitious goals, which they had since realized: Michael Ain had gone on to become an orthopedic surgeon, Joe Roach became a council member in Texas, and Ruth Ricker became a disability activist and LPA president. All these "vanguard" teenagers had had parents who encouraged them to lead full lives. Miller himself had received encouragement at home:

> My parents gave me the kind of confidence in myself that I needed—not just to assimilate and have the same dreams. But also to recognize that I *was* different—there *is* a difference—and to have the understanding, no matter how perfect or imperfect that was then, that this was something that needed to be developed. . . .
>
> Both sides are important. Some people choose to live in one world: "You're exactly the same, no different—you don't need to be in LPA!" That leaves a child empty and confused. On the other hand, to have your whole existence involved in the dwarf world, and absent yourself from all the rest, misses the point. One particularly needs the supportive teachers and friends there, and some lucky breaks along the way. But if you don't explore that part [the difference], ultimately it will bite you in the ass. My relationship with Johns Hopkins was crucial—with the doctors and with people like [social worker] Joan Weiss. It was not something that anyone said or did, but the knowledge that I was part of the greater community. I was sometimes plugged in, and sometimes not—but I always knew it was there.

Ultimately Miller wanted to use his opportunities, including his attendance at Harvard Law School, "to do something good." He did not want to be "a regular old lawyer that blended into the woodwork." It was important to use his difference: "One of the compelling factors in my personal and professional life related to my sense of belonging—being different and not different. Having all the right credentials, having my ticket punched in all the right places, but ultimately still being different." His initial rejection for employment had made him reevaluate his parents' message that if you worked hard toward your potential, you would be protected in life as a dwarf.

He resonated with this younger generation in his determination to endow disability with a sense of empowerment.

Looking back on what had influenced his thinking, Paul reminisced about childhood experiences: one special event had been meeting with Don Davidson, a dwarf who had become general manager of the Atlanta Braves. The experience had helped give Paul tremendous confidence—the feeling that one did not have to settle for less, but could pursue one's potential. (Davidson opened his memoir, *Caught Short*, with a letter from Miller's father and closed it with lines about Miller. For both men, role models were vital.)

Miller takes much delight these days in his family. His wife, Jennifer, who is partially deaf, had been an advisor to the governor of Washington and worked on disability policy issues at the Department of Education. His daughter, Naomi, he described in 2002 as "a reflective, thoughtful two-year-old, very self-possessed." She had unexpectedly uttered the words "Daddy little, Mommy big!" demonstrating an early recognition of their difference.

A couple's difference in stature routinely provokes curiosity in others. Miller, questioned on this point in an interview for *Ha'aretz*, discussed his relationship with Jennifer, with whom he had fallen in love at first sight:

> [Interviewer:] Was it hard for her to go out with a little person?
> [Miller:] I don't think it was any harder for her to go out with me than it was for me to go out with her. Look at me: What's not to love?
> [Interviewer:] Didn't her parents object to her wanting to marry you?
> [Miller:] Of course not. She told them, "I'm going out with a senior federal official, a Harvard graduate." Why shouldn't her mother love me?
> [Interviewer:] What's the secret?
> [Miller:] The secret is to be yourself. But you should think of it this way, too: I wouldn't have gotten into a relationship with a woman who had a problem with my height to start with.[61]

Naomi is average-statured. Before her birth, Paul and Jennifer had known that there was a 50 percent chance that their child would be a dwarf, but they had rejected prenatal testing. Seeing both advantages and disadvantages of having a short-statured child, he compared his situation to that of other minorities: "Do you want to say that because Jews have harder lives than Christians in the United States, American Jews shouldn't have children?"[62] For Miller, the personal and the political are never far apart. His unique perspective is valued highly by colleagues and students at the University of Washington School of Law, which he joined as professor in 2004.

GREGG AND JOHN RICE: ENTREPRENEURS

Given the barriers that exist, it is not easy for people of short stature to amass wealth. A number are struggling financially, while more fall somewhere along the continuum that is the middle class. Therefore, when I first heard about Gregg and John Rice (b. 1952), I was intrigued. I knew only that they are listed in *The Guinness Book of Records* as the world's smallest twins, recorded as 86.3 centimeters tall, and that they were wealthy entrepreneurs. Subsequently, I viewed them on a television infomercial, as they told their life story and attempted to convince viewers that if the Rice Brothers could overcome obstacles and become real estate entrepreneurs, anyone could (Fig. 87).

When I telephoned Gregg Rice, he extolled his life in West Palm Beach with the same enthusiasm and cadences I recognized from his television presentation.[63] He and his brother John were born in 1952. He told me that the enterprising pair had accumulated much of their fortune in real estate but that since 1990, they have been doing marketing and advertising for a West Palm Beach, Florida, pest control firm; sales at this twenty-year-old business improved by 800 percent under their management. Their lives had not always been a success story. Shortly after the twins' birth, they had been abandoned. When they were nine months old, they were adopted by a working-class couple who had recently lost a child and were the parents of two other children. "We were blessed that they accepted us," said Gregg, "and did not try to overprotect us. These people instilled in us the desire to go out and try." When the twins were in the eighth grade, their mother died, followed by their father a year later, at age fifty-two. The two boys then lived with their sister and brother-in-law until they were out of high school and had entered junior college. They began selling products door to door; their employer, recognizing their abilities, recruited them for the home office and further sales training, and they worked for that company for the following six years. Their unique com-

87. John and Greg Rice. Courtesy John and Greg Rice.

bination of remarkable size, outgoing personalities, and salesmanship had made them invaluable assets to the firm.

In the mid-1970s they decided to go into real estate. Their success in that endeavor brought both large financial rewards and much publicity: "Everyone enjoys a good human-interest story," Gregg explained. After they received an award from the Board of Realtors, they found themselves responding to requests from firms such as Century 21 to speak to groups outside the immediate area. By the late 1970s, their fame had spread: they were being interviewed on television talk shows and were featured on current affairs programs, among them *20/20* and *Regis and Kathy Lee Live.* In one of their frequent appearances on the *Morey Povich Show,* on a show that featured twins and other multiples, the thirty-four-inch-tall Rice twins were joined by Michael and James Lanier, who, at seven feet four inches, were the tallest identical twins in the world. Gregg Rice says that he has not encountered any condescension or other untoward treatment during his appearances in the media. On the contrary, he feels that because he and John came across as witty and warm, the atmosphere of the presentations has been overwhelmingly positive.

The twins have formed a multi-million-dollar company, called Think Big, that promotes motivational speaking and offers seminars on creative problem-solving. In a display of showmanship, they generally begin the meetings by driving their identical custom-made Porsches into the room. In addition, they do charitable work for young people and are active in their community, serving on the boards of various nonprofit organizations. "People should pay their civic rent," Gregg comments. "Most don't." Although it seems that work and community interests are central to Gregg's life and leave little room for leisure, he does not hesitate when asked what is most important in his life: "My son," he says. "I was married and have a twelve-year-old son in the seventh grade."

The worst time had occurred when John Rice broke his neck in an automobile accident and almost died. His recovery was brought about through the felicitous intervention of Dr. Steven Kopits, whom the twins had met many years earlier, in the mid-1980s, at an airport. Kopits had been fascinated by them; he told them about his background as an orthopedic surgeon specializing in dwarfism, and he inquired into their understanding of their conditions. They volunteered that they had achondroplasia. Kopits recognized that their correct diagnosis was SED congenita, and he invited them to come to Baltimore to participate in his research. The twins were unable to do so because their schedules did not permit it, but their doctor did contact Kopits. In 1990, after John Rice's catastrophic accident, he was flown to Baltimore for surgery, and he remained under Kopits's care for fifteen months until he recovered. Expressing his deep gratitude, John spoke at Kopits's memorial service in 2002.

TOMMY McINTOSH AND OTHERS: MEMBERS OF THE CLERGY

The Reverend Tommy McIntosh did not set out to be a prison chaplain, but certain factors prepared him to be particularly empathic toward people who had experienced struggle and defeat. Growing up in an impoverished family in government-subsidized housing, he was the son of an alcoholic father who was eventually committed to a mental institution. McIntosh found comfort and role models at the Baptist church he attended in Birmingham, Alabama, and beginning in childhood he wanted to be a minister.[64]

After graduating from Southwestern Baptist Seminary in 1978 and following four years in youth ministry, he was ready to assume a leadership position. However, organized religion being no less susceptible to prejudice than any other institution, he could not find one. Subsisting through odd jobs and soon to be a father, he waited for a call that never came. Finally, encouraged by his wife, Julie, he took a more active role, first volunteering as a hospital chaplain and then enrolling in a clinical pastoral-training program. Part of the program was an internship at the Travis County Correctional Complex in Del Valle, Texas. At first he was depressed by the experience, but gradually he began to perceive it as a God-given opportunity to make a difference in the lives of others through his faith.

He is now senior chaplain at the facility. He and one other chaplain deal with approximately seventeen hundred inmates in Del Valle and another five hundred at a jail in Austin. McIntosh works with prisoners of diverse faiths, an aspect that pleases him. Testimonials of former inmates reveal the influence that he has had on their lives. Wynn, who is recovering from cocaine addiction, first thought, "This is a chaplain? This little bitty man?" Now he credits his relationship with McIntosh as a transforming influence on his life. Straight for six years, he supports his family as a truck driver and volunteers at the correctional facility, leading church services and ministering to inmates. "When you're an ex-con, people expect you to fail," he said, "But Tommy expected me to succeed."

McIntosh is strengthened by the support he receives from his wife, and by his family life with his daughter, Shaina, and son, Timothy. Being a good father is a central driving force for this man who suffered from the absence of one. His earlier fears about how his children would respond to ridicule for having "a little daddy" have given way to a conviction that responding to that difference has made everyone in the family more compassionate.

Increasingly, dwarfs are entering the clergy. That should not be surprising—people who have had to grapple with existential questions themselves are often better prepared to help others confront similar issues. Among persons of short stature who serve congregations is Paul Stevens Lynn, who after two decades in the ministry is now the pastor of the seven-hundred-member Christ Lutheran church in Dubois, Pennsylvania.

Another member of the clergy, the Reverend Stella Dempski, was the first little person to be ordained in the Presbyterian Church.[65] Acceptance did not come easily for Dempski. The more than sixty congregations she sent her résumé to, after she received her Master of Divinity degree and her Master of Arts in Christian education, were impressed with her background. At the interview, however, they were oddly quiet. "The process tested my patience but not my faith. I knew I would find a church. God had called me to pursue ordained ministry. The ministry is my life choice—not a job but a way of life." Dempski eventually secured a position at the First United Presbyterian church in Westminster, Maryland, where, on 12 October 2002, she was married.

James Putney, resident chaplain on the oncology unit at the University of California, Los Angeles, Medical Center has Morquio's syndrome, a rare condition; he feels that the painful corrective surgeries he underwent throughout his childhood and the pain caused by his arthritis have made him better able to empathize with the physical and emotional distress of patients. Dahlia Kronish, the daughter and granddaughter of rabbis, is completing her studies at the Jewish Theological Seminary in New York and will soon be ordained as a Conservative rabbi.

FIGURES IN SPORTS

On 18 August 1951, St. Louis Browns owner Bill Veeck arranged to have the three-foot-seven-inch performer Eddie Gaedel jump out of a seven-foot birthday cake between games of a double header. Then, in the first inning of the second game, he sent Gaedel in to pinch hit, instructing him not to swing: with a strike zone of only one and a half inches, it was inevitable that he would be walked. The stunt worked, and when Gaedel, who received one hundred dollars for his appearance, reached first base, the crowd went wild.

The American League banned future pranks of this kind, but Gaedel's jersey, with a "1/8" on it, ultimately landed in the Hall of Fame. The incident inspired a short story by James Thurber and may have influenced Philip Roth's depiction of the dwarf pitchers in *The Great American Novel*. Decades of references to the stunt in the press and on the Internet have ensued, sometimes reflecting a change in attitudes. When in 1999 Veeck's son Mike hired David Flood—billed as David the Dwarf—as a greeter at games, a critical article appeared, titled "How Demeaning: Devil Rays Dropped the Ball on Dave."[66]

In the intervening years, dwarfs have found respect in sports, participating as umpires or administrators, and a number of short-statured college students are now enrolling in sports-management programs.[67] The earliest and best-known baseball official was Donald Davidson, general manager of the Atlanta Braves, whose memoir, *Caught Short,* was published in 1972.[68]

Many dwarfs refuse to be consigned to lives of physical inactivity. The founding, in 1985, of the Dwarf Athletic Association of America by Len Sawich and others represented a dramatic breakthrough, with competitions in swimming, basketball, bocci, volleyball, powerlifting, and track and field among the highlights of annual conferences.[69] Dwarf athletes have taken part in international competitions since 1988. Erin Popovich, four feet two inches tall, won gold and silver medals in swimming at the 2000 Paralympics and was selected as its torchbearer in 2001. For those who do not compete but wish to keep fit, exercise videos have been produced that feature workouts designed for short-statured individuals.[70]

THE UNRECORDED OTHERS, BRIEFLY NOTED

Among public figures, there are some who are extremely short yet typically not identified as dwarfs, and who prefer not to be so characterized. One such individual is sex therapist Dr. Ruth Westheimer, four feet seven inches tall, who is well known for her appearances on radio and television, and for her cheery sign-off, "Have good sex!" Westheimer is a refugee from the Holocaust. In her engaging autobiography, *All in a Lifetime,* she describes her turbulent childhood and young adulthood, her three marriages, her successful struggle to obtain education and professional training, and her ultimate happiness as wife, mother, and grandmother.[71] As an adolescent, she had written, "Everything is difficult. I have to fight for everything all alone and it hurts. . . . I want to be young and happy like the others. Is it only because I'm small and ugly?"[72]

Diastrophic dwarf John Paterson, an urban economist who became head of Australia's Department of Health and Community Services, was a powerful and controversial figure in Australian politics. Married twice and survived by four children, he died in 2003.

Matt Roloff, a successful computer professional and entrepreneur, lives with his wife, Amy, and four children in Portland, Oregon, on a farm that contains fantastic structures of his own design and construction. President of LPA from 2002 to 2004, Roloff provided dynamic leadership to the organization in the midst of its burgeoning outreach and activism. His autobiography, *Against Tall Odds,* traces his path to personal maturity and a position of influence in the dwarf community.[73]

Unfortunately, *The Lives of Dwarfs* has not included profiles of individuals in working-class occupations. These persons nevertheless have a part to play, and the lives of several have been described by Joan Ablon in her in-depth study of twenty-four members of LPA.[74] It is to be hoped that in the future, other writers will pursue the inquiry further, casting light on the life stories of a far broader segment of the dwarf population.

Echoes of the Past: Sombrero Service, Midget Wrestling, and Dwarf Tossing

There still remain some activities that arouse controversy because they seem a reprise of eras when dwarfs often had little choice but to accept their roles as performing curiosities. These varied activities inspire both powerful protests and passionate defense.

SOMBRERO SERVICE

Steve Vento has held conventional jobs as a car salesman and bar owner in Las Vegas. In addition, since the age of eleven, he has worked in nightclubs and carnivals and has been hired by advertisers to play characters such as Hamburglar, Big Boy, and Mr. Yuk. In the early years, his activities excited little public comment. He provoked controversy, however, when in January 1999 he began to work at Nacho Mama's, a Mexican restaurant in Milwaukee, mingling with customers and offering them salsa and chips, which were served from his enormous sombrero. "People eat off my head," Vento unabashedly announced. "I'm a walking buffet." He professed to enjoy parading about, as well as doing balloon and magic tricks, regarding these activities as natural manifestations of his being a "people person." For him, the matter was simple: "What I have is not a disability or a handicap. It's a gift God gave me. I make people happy with my job. What's wrong with making people happy?"[75]

By contrast, for Anthony Soares, then LPA's vice president for public relations, Vento's Nacho Mama role was "barbaric," "humiliating," "degrading," and "disgusting." Other LPA members took issue with Soares's statements. He did not speak for the organization, they protested, especially the 9 percent of members who had some connection to the entertainment field. Danny Black, a professional clown and talent agent, found nothing amiss in Vento's performance and expressed an affinity with people who "made an advantage out of a disadvantage."

Black runs an agency advertised on the Internet as called shortdwarf.com, which provides short-statured entertainers for local parties, corporate events, and television programs, including *The Maury Povich Show*, mentioned earlier.[76] He has carved out a niche for himself in a field previously run almost exclusively by average-statured agents. Although he does turn down some listings that he sees as disreputable, Black disagrees with the position taken by Soares and others that provocative comic roles based on stature alone necessarily inflict damage. In his view, LPs who are secure in their own identities can accept that a percentage of their group earns their living this way, while those who are insecure will be unduly upset.

In August 2003, Vento, who refers to himself as "Milwaukee's Favorite Midget" and who relishes uttering "politically incorrect" statements and telling midget jokes in media appearances, opened a downtown dance club, Ripples on Water, catering to twenty-one- to forty-year-olds. Although he faults long hours for his failed marriage, which produced his twelve-year-old son, in whom he takes delight, he is satisfied with the life he leads.

Are Vento's antics merely good-natured fun? Soares, who is an art director at a Manhattan advertising firm and now also president of the city council of Hoboken, New Jersey, thinks not. Once a talent agent, not dreaming that Soares might be a respected Hoboken figure, spied him on the street and asked if he would like to make a few extra bucks performing. Soares rebuffed his approach and enlightened him. Little people are found to be humorous, Soares feels, as a result of their previous accepted roles as jesters and freak show performers, but also because performers today accept similar parts. Noting that individuals in wheelchairs don't evoke the same response, he concludes, "They laugh at dwarfs because it's been made to be okay."[77]

The question is this: do members of minority groups have a responsibility to refuse positions that may invite criticism or ridicule of the group and thereby revive a history of discrimination and oppression? A documentary called *True Life: I Am a Little Person,* which aired on MTV in January 2002, addressed this question. Terra Odmark, an attractive, talented young woman, was featured in the film exuberantly loading up her car and taking off for Los Angeles to make her fortune as a singer. When she arrives in the city, she seeks employment. After hearing that she is a dwarf, a prospective employer, who had previously shown interest in her, denies her an interview. She is next offered a job as a stripper, which she turns down. She finally agrees to join several other short-statured people in an Ozzie Osborne road tour. (Rock videos with dwarfs have become a "hot" product.) In the role of a gremlin, Terra is made to cavort foolishly, wearing makeup that distorts her features, and she comes to feel painfully compromised. "I've learned from this," she says, and she vows not to repeat the experience. Later, on the Dwarfism List and the MTV electronic bulletin board, several offers are extended to Terra to help her gain genuine musical opportunities. In addition, a young, prepossessing college student and diastrophic dwarf named Robyn Watson was highlighted on the show, and she received a positive response from many young people, who expressed admiration for her.

MIDGET WRESTLING

When radio journalist Steve Rukavina noticed that there was a midget-wrestling match touring Regina, Saskatchewan, in Canada, in 1999, he was intrigued. The event was one of the many scheduled on the "B"-grade wrestling tours that crossed the Canadian prairie. Rukavina made a seven-minute tape of the performance, including both the comments of the wrestlers and those of an LPA member, with the aim of offering a balanced report.[78]

To learn about the attitudes of dwarfs, he posted an inquiry on the LPA Internet bulletin board. He received a number of responses; one especially articulate statement came from Martha Davis-Merritts, a three-foot-eight-inch medical researcher at the University of Michigan, who made a convincing case that midget wrestling perpetuated an outdated view of dwarfs, who no longer had to demean themselves. Rukavina noted that the word *midget* is currently out of fashion in the dwarfism community, as it is commonly viewed as a term of derision, equivalent to a racial slur. That is certainly not the opinion of midget wrestlers themselves; it is for them a purely descriptive term, and one in which they take pride.

Rukavina's tape conveyed the spirits of the performance of two wrestlers, the Little Reaper and Sweet Thing, and the response of two hundred boisterous onlookers in the packed Regina Exhibition Hall. The Little Reaper hobbled in wearing a black shroud and ghostly makeup; Sweet Thing made a dramatic entrance accompanied by music of the heavy metal variety. There was much clowning and teasing of the referee until, fifteen minutes later, Sweet Thing pinned the Little Reaper to the mat. The crowd responded with more energy to this bout than to the average-sized wrestlers who fought—though one fan commented that he didn't take midget wrestling seriously as a sport. Following the match, the Little Reaper spoke with Rukavina about how he used to love watching wrestling as a child. When he finally got into the ring professionally his family was proud of him; twenty years later, he still sounded full of enthusiasm. Sweet Thing (Chris West), who'd been active in the profession for five years, expressed similar sentiments: his family enjoyed watching him, and his nine-year-old niece brought her friends over to get his autograph. Chris had wanted to be a wrestler since he was seven years old and was happy that he had made his dream come true. When not wrestling, he worked at a golf course.

Anthony Condello, the Winnipeg promoter who arranged the bout featured in Rukavina's tape, had seen the sport become less popular, with perhaps ten full-time midget-wrestling professionals remaining and with events held in more isolated places. The activity no longer emphasized athletic skill but rather entertainment value. A midget wrestler these days was more of a "stuntman." Although a wrestler could make between one hundred and five hundred dollars a night, depending on reputation, payment was typically on the low end, and midget wrestlers made much less than average-sized wrestlers.[79]

The legendary Lord Littlebrook (Eric Tovey) is one of the few remaining luminaries of the midget-wrestling world (Fig. 88). Two of his contemporaries, who have been called the greatest midget wrestlers of all time, passed away not long ago, Little Beaver (Lionel Giroux) in 1995 and Sky Low (Marcel Gauthier) in 1998. Active in his field in one capacity or another for a half century, Eric Tovey has long been recognized as one of the true greats: in the seventies he held the World Midget title, and he has served as a promoter and trainer of midget wrestlers. He has trained many of the wrestlers still active today. Tovey rails against the changes that have taken place in midget wrestling: "When I started in the fifties, there was no such thing as paint on the face—I'm disgusted, I really am. . . . I want midget wrestling, I don't want midget comedy."[80]

Friendly and garrulous, he spoke to me from his home in St. Joseph, Missouri about his life and the transformation of wrestling. Born in England in 1928, he was one of seven children of a hardworking father: "My dad worked his butt off support-

ing us," he said.[81] Tovey's childhood was disrupted by World War II, resulting in his having little schooling. When he was offered the opportunity to become part of a circus, he jumped at it, quickly learning everything he could: he became an acrobat, a trapeze artist, and a bareback rider. He was happy to be part of "one big family," living together and eating in a big mess hall. When the Cole Circus left for the United States in 1949, Tovey joined them. He ate his first steak on the boat: incredulous at its size, he knew that back home it would have fed his whole family.

A year after his arrival, the circus went bankrupt, and he was forced to seek whatever employment he could find, in circuses, carnivals, and nightclubs. When a friend told him about midget wrestling, Tovey didn't know a thing about it, but he proved a quick

88. Eric Tovey, aka Lord Littlebrook. Greg Oliver Collection.

study. At first he made between three and seven dollars a performance; he complained to management and was eventually given a living wage. His handlers dubbed him "Lord Littlebrook" but he was uncomfortable being identified as an aristocrat.

Tovey remembers the old days as hard, but friendlier than the present: "Many people won't admit how hard it was. But eventually, I was rated as the best. One year I traveled one hundred thousand miles—the IRS questioned me and couldn't believe it. I'd fly out of L.A. to Australia and New Zealand; I spent two or three years in Europe."

Tovey decries the changes he sees, saying that in 1951 the business had exciting tag matches, not clowns like today. He went to the gym daily and practiced real holds and wrestling. He was a promoter and trainer in Canada for 12 1/2 years, working with eighteen wrestlers; these days he's down to four. In spite of the reduced opportunity, two sons have chosen to join the family business, under the names Beautiful Bobby Dean and Little Kato. Although one of his sons recently had to take a month off because of two injured vertebrae, Tovey minimizes the risks of the job. He was brought up in an era when, if a wrestler was hurt, he just worked through the pain and made the best of it. Tovey's children include a son who is more than six feet two inches and a daughter who is five feet two inches. Tovey seemed glad to have progeny who have chosen his calling. He rarely watches matches on television, except when his sons are on.

What stands out is Tovey's pride in himself and his work—his satisfaction in being small but unusually trim and robust, able to "keep up with the big boys." In his view, he had been able to go them one better by being active and naturally faster moving. Tension sometimes existed between wrestlers with different kinds of dwarfism: proportionate individuals of Tovey's type sometimes disparaged disproportionate wrestlers, referring to them as "the ones with the big heads."

The pressures that affect midget wrestling today are substantial. There is not likely to be another performer like Quebec-born Claude Giroux, who once did two hundred shows a year but now runs a landscaping business and wrestles rarely. As public interest has waned, typical whirlwind tours are apt to be in places like Montana, the Rocky Mountains of Wyoming, and the Black Hills of South Dakota.[82] Some towns show enthusiasm, others disapproval. Political correctness also plays a role now. In one instance a match was canceled because it was felt to be inappropriate for a school to endorse a fight between two people of short stature. "The ironic thing is that both midgets are card-carrying members of LPA," co-promoter Keith Heilbronner noted, "This is what they chose to do."[83] In the end, the match was canceled after pressure from the American-Arab Anti-Defamation Committee on the grounds that a wrestler was called the Iron Sheik. There have not been any formal protests about midget wrestling from LPA.

In February 2000, a television program featured two average-statured females who wrestled and lost to two professional midget wrestlers, with Verne Troyer (the actor best known for his performance as Mini-Me in *Austin Powers*) acting as one of the two referees.[84] One of the women commented, "I was afraid I might be beat by a midget"—up front was the fact that he was a midget, not that she, who had never wrestled, was competing against a skilled professional wrestler.

DWARF TOSSING

Dwarf tossing first achieved prominence in Australia in 1985 when bouncers at a Queensland nightclub entertained customers in bars by competing to see who could throw a dwarf the farthest.[85] The activity quickly spread to other countries. The dwarf, wearing a jogging suit and a crash helmet, was picked up and thrown by a harness into a pile of mattresses. In England, four-foot-four-inch Lenny the Giant was the best known. He was also part of a four-man comedy act called the Oddballs; its highlight was a striptease dance performed with balloons.[86] Lenny was twenty-nine years old, and his family had emigrated from India twenty years earlier. Before joining the Oddballs he had worked in a computer factory making circuit boards; he found his current activities more lucrative and enjoyable.

But dwarf tossing soon evoked consternation, from both officialdom and the dwarf community. European government officials decried it as a new form of exploitation, and British member of Parliament John Hannam found it appalling that such a practice should be considered entertainment. Pam Rutt, acting chairman of the Restricted Growth Association, cautioned that "if people get the idea that dwarf-throwing is all the rage and just for fun, thugs and drunks on the street at night will say 'let's throw the dwarf.'"[87]

Such comments were heard everywhere. The pastime failed to spread through Europe as its sponsors had hoped, and although it caught on in the United States in a number of cities, campaigns were mounted almost immediately to bar the practice. After Mike Royko, a Chicago journalist, publicized and joked relentlessly about dwarf tossing, trying to get tavern owners in the area to introduce it, the local chapter of LPA as well as others expressed their dismay. Beth Wason Loyless, a Chicago teacher who was then membership chair of LPA, assumed the role of radio and television spokesperson against dwarf tossing. Eventually, Mayor Harold Washington declared such contests "degrading and mean-spirited, repugnant to everyone truly committed to eliminating prejudice against any group" and took a tavern owner, who was to have hosted an event, to court; the event was canceled. Another tavern owner jokingly explained his decision not to schedule an event: "Ees too dangerous. Maybe somebody get keeled—I don't mean the dwarf get keeled—what if dwarf heet a regular customer and keel him. How do I tell his wife what happen? And what do the wife tell her keeds? Hey keeds, I got bad news. Your daddy got keeled by a flying dwarf."[88]

In the years that followed, LPA mobilized and, bolstered by letters from members of its medical advisory board, emphasized the danger of this activity for dwarfs, who because of narrow spinal cords may risk paralysis by being thrown. When a Clearwater, Florida, bar instituted a dwarf-tossing contest in 1988, and put a huge sign on the U.S. Highway 19 publicizing the event, the dwarf community was quick to respond. In a strongly worded letter to the *St. Petersburg Times,* Beth Tatman, the LPA district director, and Nancy Mayeux, the parent coordinator, commented that the situation obscured the reality that dwarfs have careers in a wide range of ordinary occupations. They added: "Our parents now fear for their children's safety. Our dwarf children have enough problems today with older children who try to pick them up 'because it's fun.' These older children may now feel it's okay to try tossing them as well."[89]

LPA's board of directors published a lengthy document detailing why the practice needed to be outlawed, and its membership rallied to see that it was. Newspapers all over the country published editorials opposed to the activity. In 1989 dwarf tossing was made illegal in Florida; in 1990, with effective leadership and lobbying spearheaded by Angela Van Etten (profiled earlier), it was banned in New York. LPA proved that it could be a successful, even militant, advocacy group. The following year, French interior minister Philippe Marchand banned dwarf tossing in France, calling it an intolerable attack on human dignity. Consequently, a French company was forced to cancel its contract to stage dwarf tossing in about forty establishments.[90]

Still, even today, in states where it is outlawed, such as New York, events occasionally occur. In August 1999, Frank the Jolly Dwarf appeared at Scooter's Pub on Long Island and allowed himself to be tossed by three-hundred-pound Big Mike Forstbauer. "I can't believe that I'm tossing a dwarf," he said. "This is great."[91] The event was discontinued after LPA members informed the bar owner that his license was in jeopardy. But in 2001, three-foot-two-inch David Flood, aka "Dave the Dwarf," filed suit in U.S. District Court in Tampa, Florida, challenging the ban on dwarf tossing as unconstitutional, claiming that it illegally discriminated against people with dwarfism.

Some little people themselves have questioned why LPA was taking such a strong stand on dwarf tossing, when it takes a hands-off approach to certain other forms of entertainment—even those considered objectionable—in which LPs participate. Doesn't being an adult in the United States confer the right to pursue happiness in one's own fashion? Former LPA vice president Cara Egan issued a succinct response reiterating previous points and stating her belief that there is an association between dwarf tossing and hostile working environments for dwarfs. In the 1980s, when dwarf tossing originally surfaced in Florida, LPA members had reported a significant increase in the incidence of ridicule on the job.

An obituary of James S. Moran, who was described as "master of the publicity stunt," noted that he had been enraged by not being granted a permit to carry out one of his cleverest schemes. "It's a sad day for American capitalism," he said, "when a man can't fly a midget on a kite over Central Park."[92] Philosopher Peter Suber of Earlham College considers rules against dwarf tossing to be paternalistic, and he questions whether "protecting people from themselves" is just or wise.[93] In another tightly reasoned set of statements, Robert W. McGee concludes that there are no valid legal or philosophical arguments to justify restricting the practice, which he describes as a win-win situation: those who watch are entertained, and dwarfs on tour can earn an excellent income.[94] One cannot call a person exploited if he or she is being given the opportunity to earn a six-figure income: in that case boxers and other athletes are also being exploited. Further, McGee advances the opinion that persons engaged in this activity have seldom been hurt.

A brief item on the Internet reports that a thirty-three-year-old man died of brain damage after being tossed too many times, but there appears to be no definitive evidence of the immediate cause, and no one has studied those who have been tossed. The battle continues, but the international community has rendered its decision: in September 2002 the U.N. Human Rights Committee affirmed a French ban on dwarf tossing and said that it was "necessary in order to protect public order, including considerations of human dignity."[95]

You Must Be the Change You Wish to See in the World

While specific issues like dwarf tossing, limb lengthening, genetic screening, and public access have claimed attention, only recently has there been a serious effort by people of short stature to forge an alliance with the wider disability community—an effort that had been impossible while dwarfs were endeavoring to prove that they were "just like everyone else," only shorter. Now LPA acknowledges that many individuals in the group have legitimate disabilities and that acting on that fact represents strength, not a call for pity. Consequently, LPA supported the efforts spearheaded by the National Organization for Rare Diseases (NORD), which resulted in the passage of the Rare Diseases Act of 2002. That act increased government investment in the development of diagnostics and treatments for rare diseases and disorders; it established regional centers for clinical research and doubled funding for the Orphan Product Research Grant Program. On 13 October 2003, the U.S. Senate voted unanimously to pass the first federal bill aimed exclusively at safeguarding genetic privacy—thereby barring companies from using genetic information to deny health coverage or employment. Opposed by insurance companies and stalemated in Congress for the previous six years, its passage was fought for by EEOC commissioner Paul Miller and supported by the dwarfism community.

Cara Egan, former LPA vice president, has detailed the growing efforts of LPA to take political action. The organization expresses zero tolerance these days for media representations of dwarfs as a pitiable, handicapped minority or as sideshow curiosities. After reading a laudatory profile in a newspaper about the "successful" career of Lester Green, also known as Beetlejuice, Egan expressed dismay in a letter to the editor.[96] She noted that Green, who had appeared as one of Howard Stern's "Wack Pack" and offered himself for dwarf tossing and striptease events, was a person with a mental impairment severe enough to prevent him from conducting an interview with the newspaper. Therefore, she concluded, he could not make a sensible choice about participating, and was "trapped in a modern version of the circus sideshow."

LPA leadership and members encourage media outlets to present more authentic portrayals. The word has got out that the opinions of the dwarf audience matter. On one occasion, an account executive for a bank consulted Egan in advance to get "an honest take" on whether LPA would view a commercial that showed a dwarf working inside an ATM machine as negative or hurtful. Producers still in the planning stages of an upcoming film attended a regional meeting to question LPA members about various sensitive issues.

Increasingly, the leadership of the organization recognizes the commonality that little people and other stigmatized groups have. Egan has compared the dilemma facing the African American characters in Spike Lee's film *Bamboozled* with the situation of dwarfs in the media. Because the numbers of adult members in LPA are modest compared with those of other organized groups, however, assembling enough activists to translate insights into effective advocacy is easier said than done (Figs. 89, 90, and 91).

Conclusion

To appreciate just how much our understanding of dwarf history has changed, consider this passage from the 1977 work *Les nains*:

Pursued, adulated, dwarfs have had a choice place in the history of civilization. The most important people of their epoch have sought them out, lent an attentive ear to their counsel, or simply loved to keep them. The dwarfs were in-

89. *Little People of British Columbia—Society for Short Stature Awareness.*

90. *Little People of Korea. Courtesy Little People of Korea.*

91. Former Little People of America president Matt Roloff (center) and his wife, Amy, with members at an LPA gathering. Courtesy Matt Roloff.

tegrated with the rest of society, finding employment, amusing the public, thereby finding their reason for being. But in the twentieth century, the most eager for normalcy and rationality, the dwarfs saw themselves as little and destitute of their function and forced to assume the sad role of handicapped beings. . . . In the past they were phenomenons, possessed of pride—today they are considered infirm or monstrous. . . .Victims of tragic persecution, they have formed themselves into organizations.[97]

In another popular account, Daniel P. Mannix, a writer who worked for several years in a carnival, composed a paragraph in which he lumped together "midget" airplane mechanics, Texas state treasurer Charles Lockhart, and a variety of circus sideshow performers, concluding with self-satisfied benevolence, "It would seem to me that all these freaks were happier and more useful than they would be locked up in institutions."[98]

A more enlightened perspective is one thing; altering reality is another. One must never forget that the successful individuals described in this chapter are not representative of the total population of dwarfs. There is a man named David in my own neighborhood whom I would pass on the street occasionally, or observe picking up papers in the lobby of the local bank, before he became disabled. Others had spoken to him about seeking treatment at one of the specialized medical centers, or coming to LPA meetings, but he had rejected these suggestions. I last observed him at a distance, leaning on a rickety walker, which he hardly had the strength to move. I later learned that he was no longer able to leave his house.

One eighty-two-year-old nursing-home resident discussed her life with me, albeit with some wariness. She believed that the reason for her dwarfism was that a caregiver had dropped her. She had lived with her parents until their deaths. Although she had had a few friends, she had never worked, she said, because she had sometimes needed braces and had worn glasses; in the nursing home, she kept to herself.

In 1999, LPA's recognition that there were still many little people who were lonely, shy, or otherwise shut off from normal peer relationships and needed educational, psychological, or social assistance led the executive board to work with the University of Cincinnati to develop a peer support and outreach program.[99] Although this effort did not obtain the needed funding, its aims were not forgotten. In 2003, Leslye Sneider, LPA's first director of development, took on the task of attracting monetary support for such ambitious goals.

The changing image of dwarfs is stimulated both by the new activism and by exposure in the media of successful people of short stature. For example, pediatrician Jennifer Arnold is featured in documentaries and on talk shows, and former LPA president Matt Roloff has appeared on *The Oprah Winfrey Show*.[100] The focus may be on a local schoolteacher, perhaps, in a segment on the nightly news—it appears to astound TV reporters that short persons can succeed even in ordinary occupations.

The pace of progress sometimes seems dizzying, and sometimes frustratingly slow—especially but not only in less-developed nations. And the evolution described here does not alter the fact that for each short-statured individual, the process of achieving self-actualization remains a lifelong challenge and that the echoes and abuses of the past will not soon disappear. But we are closer to the horizon—where the value and beauty of difference is acknowledged—and we are limping, and sometimes even leaping, toward it.

A Reverie

Coming to the end of the journey that is this book, I find myself adrift in reverie, the faces of people I knew personally, and others met only in books, passing before me. I imagine a *Twilight Zone* scenario in which generations of dwarfs, past and present, are gathered together. On the dais sits Boruwlaski, the brilliant court dwarf who made his living exhibiting himself and in old age was forced to scrounge for handouts from benefactors. Seated beside him is Jane Hill, the chiropodist activist who gave Charles Dickens a lesson in sensitivity. Quaker abolitionist Benjamin Lay can be overheard arguing with scientist-socialist Charles Proteus Steinmetz about how to solve society's most urgent problems. Dwarf orators of all eras are assembled: Licinius Calvus of 82–47 B.C.E.; William Hay, the eighteenth-century member of Parliament; contemporary disability activists Angela Van Etten, Paul Miller, and Colleen Fraser. All are getting ready to deliver rousing speeches to the cheering crowd. The audience includes many of the court and exhibiting dwarfs who made their living amusing the gentry and who were led into ignominious dependency. There are also obscure figures from the past whom no one recognizes. Big people and small can be seen eating, drinking, and dancing, wheeling about on agile legs or on crutches or Kitchens' Karts, while in the back of the room a few conspirators plot strategies to elect the first dwarf president of the United States.

This last event would represent a much higher Everest than electing the first Catholic, the first divorced man, the first African American, or even the first woman. In the past, almost invariably, the taller candidate has won. James Madison, our shortest president at five feet four inches, was first elected in 1809, almost two centuries ago. Perhaps, too, given the problems and obloquy that currently attach to the presidency, no dwarf will chose to run for office and trade one stigmatized role for another. But what a pleasure it would be to rewrite the old sociobiology of height and power! While we give fantasy full rein here, why should we not dream?

AFTERWORD

My daughter, Anna, was a teenager when I first began to do serious research into dwarfism in the late 1980s, burrowing among obscure references in the New York Public Library and querying scholars about whether individuals described as dwarfs by earlier writers indeed *were* dwarfs. I knew that comprehending material from many disciplines—the social sciences, the arts, and the medical world—would be a formidable task, but since no one had written a book of this kind and there was an urgent need for it, I felt I ought to try. I had previously written a few scholarly pieces—a thesis for a master's in English about initiation rites in the works of Mark Twain and Christian symbolism in Henry James, as well as a dissertation about moral judgment in women for my doctorate in psychology. Until I began this volume, however, there had never been a subject that I had felt passionately enough about to consider writing a book.

Because of the daunting scope of this project, I wanted to share the work and exchange ideas with an LP coauthor. My credentials as the mother of a dwarf meant that I was marginally one of the family, but I also wanted the book to offer the prism of subjectivity that only being a dwarf oneself could grant—also expressing to the dwarf community that I was committed to seeing that, at last, insiders rather than outsiders were contemplating their experiences. Although a talented individual expressed interest, other obligations made him unavailable. I next considered but rejected the idea of separate authorities for each chapter, deciding that what I lacked in initial expertise might be compensated for by diligent research. A garden designed by a committee is rarely the most interesting, and a personal vision can enhance insights into both nature and human nature.

After retiring from my practice as a psychologist in 1997, I focused most of my energies on the book: I looked at reproductions of art from many time periods, viewed countless films, and read dozens of novels. Each chapter proved an extraordinary adventure. The "eminent persons" whom I found were never listed under *dwarf* or *little person* in the card catalogs or on the Internet but were found serendipitously or through friends' recommendations. The chapters about the arts were particularly engaging. I began without preconceptions, but I found that the mass of material led to a single conclusion: dwarfs had rarely been portrayed as thinking, feeling individuals who were at the center of their own lives, but rather were presented as adjuncts to the lives of others. In literature, they were typically depicted as unhappy—whether comical or pathetic or vengeful—and defined largely by disappointment in their bodies. In visual art, until recently, they were shown as isolates, without viable families, or mere witnesses to history. In theater and film, they were cast as mythological figures or comic sidekicks.

Remarkably, during the final decade of my research, exciting changes occurred. Old constraints loosened for dwarfs, and their contributions to many fields increased. Each time that I thought I was nearing completion, a dozen events cried out for inclusion: new films and documentaries appeared; new Little People organizations formed; gifted individuals in various professions came to my attention. Colleen Fraser's contribution to the disability movement was celebrated in 2001; in 2003, Peter Dinklage, after years of off-Broadway theaters and bit roles in films, suddenly became a star.

During the final years of my project, I came to see the inadequacy of the graphics I had been collecting, these being gray photocopies, many carelessly reproduced in libraries with poor copy machines. Involved in the text as I had been, I had neglected this aspect of the book. I contacted Julie Rotta, a graphic artist with a background in the medical field, who lent her professional expertise and insights to the project. Between two hip replacement surgeries in 2001 and 2002, she initiated her prodigious labors and did marvelous work—helping to collect new material and refining and preparing what I had gathered, including the images of modern art that Bruce Johnson generously contributed.

Julie and I engaged in endless discussions, constantly found new material that we wanted to include, and regretfully had to leave much of it out. In the process, we talked about our own lives and the lives of dwarfs in other times and places, and we became close friends. At last, after well over a decade of research, the original tome was completed in 2002. Because of its great length, it had to be divided into two books, and then cut and revised appreciably between 2002 and 2005. The chapters on the historical and artistic aspects became *The Lives of Dwarfs*, published by Rutgers University Press; the other chapters, on medical aspects, psychology, families, and dwarfism groups became *Dwarfism*, published by Johns Hopkins University Press.

Of course, without Anna's being part of our family, these books would never have been written. Some readers may surely have wondered why, if she was its inspiration, I have not written more about her. There are two reasons: although in the early days of her life, I had read every memoir I could get my hands on that had been written by a person raising a child with disabilities, I never conceived of my project in that light. Had I done so, there were excellent models that I might have emulated, such as Robert and Suzanne Massie's *Journey,* which alternated chapters about the history of hemophilia with chapters about their experiences raising their son. But I felt that my personal experiences should not take center stage here. Other writers' works would be published, I thought, illuminating the personal parts of their lives as dwarfs and families of dwarfs. (Dan Kennedy has just published an excellent, wide-ranging memoir of this kind, interweaving the personal with issues affecting dwarfs.) My own book was designed to be social history.

Furthermore, and very importantly, when I first discussed with Anna the possibility of writing this book, she was fourteen. She responded, "You're not going to write about me, are you?" I assured her that I was not. However, once I began, I was eager to have her approval. I got it one day when, returning home, I was surprised to find a two-tier filing cabinet in place, with a red ribbon around it. "You need to get yourself organized, Mom," she said. I felt happiness, both for the gift and for the endorsement of my work that it symbolized.

Recently, I asked her how she would feel about my writing about her now, in this Afterword. I explained that readers would certainly find it strange if I made no mention of her life. "Fine," she said, and we went on to discuss the parameters of my narrative. In spite of her offering me freedom, I felt strongly that I did not want to appropriate her life story—it should remain hers, simply to keep private for herself and her friends, or to present more fully later if she chose to. For my part, I would write just a brief account telescoping some of the significant details. Here it is:

Anna, from the start, was an effervescent, spirited child, energetic and determined. As a toddler, she careened down the block on her Little Wheels; she climbed to the top of the jungle gym that her father had built for her in the back yard and said delightedly, "Grandma would be scared if she saw me way up here, wouldn't she?" She wanted to do everything, and most often was able to—she sliced strawberries deftly when she was only three. Her early years were generally pleasurable, and she always had close friends and ideas for fun.

We lived in a Brooklyn neighborhood with old houses that were being renovated; our block association planted trees on our street, and neighbors and their children were constantly in and out of one another's homes. Anna and David, her average-statured brother who is four years older, were close, and they benefited from the liberal atmosphere of our community, which welcomed groups with diverse ethnicities, religious preferences, and sexual orientations. We could shop on our short main street and be assured of meeting friends; the children could walk to school. My husband, Saul, and I shared child care. When Anna was born, I had been working as a counseling psychologist at Queens College; when she was two I opened my own private practice and worked three days a week in an office fifteen minutes away, thereby leaving ample time for family life. Saul, an architect employed in hospital renovation, was generally home by 5:00 P.M. We had excellent part-time babysitters and loving grandparents to indulge the children on weekends. Saul took care of them on the two evenings that I worked, and if the children were ill on my workdays, he stayed at home to care for them. We were reassured about Anna's health by our regular trips to the Moore Clinic at Johns Hopkins, where she had bowleg osteotomies at the age of four, done by Dr. Kopits. Our family was active first in a group called Parents of Dwarf Children and then in the Mets chapter of LPA.

Anna did well in her public elementary and intermediate school: when her intermediate-school principal gave her a hard time about getting permission to go on a class ski trip, I went to school to negotiate the matter and subsequently obtained medical notes to support her request. Anna, for her part, avowed, "If he still says no, I'll get my friends to picket!" She had strong feelings about many social issues—including being a vegetarian, which she became at the age of twelve. Her academic record was good enough to ensure her admission to a selective public high school, but she had by then become less at ease with her schoolwork. Her late high school and early college years proved the most difficult because of both social and academic pressures. She dropped out of Skidmore College at the end of her sophomore year and worked at an after-school center, with children and in the office; she was well regarded by the children, their families, and other staff members.

Later, she increased her salary and responsibility by working as an office manager at the Brooklyn Bridge Park Coalition, a community liaison group that successfully shepherded through the governmental bureaucracy a plan to build a public waterfront park. She left that position because she had fallen in love and moved to Indiana to be with her girlfriend; there, she initially had difficulty finding a job, but eventually was employed in the human resources department of a casino. As in her other jobs, she earned much praise. After her relationship ended, she returned to New York. The following period included gigs touring Europe with Pokemon and acting in the Radio City Music Hall road show in Chicago, for both adventure and financial reasons. She is currently a coteacher of four-year-olds, a job she likes very much; she lives near us in a studio apartment.

An important piece of Anna's story is the fact that she left LPA in early adolescence, preferring to remain only in the world of her average-sized friends and family. She returned to the organization in 1999, at the age of twenty-five, when she attended her first annual conference as an adult in Portland. Since then, she has become increasingly at home in that world and is an active participant in LPA. She views having reclaimed her dwarf identity as an essential and very significant part of her maturation.

My husband and I have found enormous pleasure in each stage of our children's lives, both Anna's and David's. He is now a Reform rabbi with a Manhattan congregation. Recently married, he lives a few blocks from us with his wife, writer Lynn Harris. He was always an affectionate, caring brother. There is no doubt that we have also experienced significant anxieties about the well-being of both children. In late adolescence and young adulthood, especially, we resonated to Anna's struggles, physical and emotional. But we have also delighted in the person she has turned out to be—in the good feeling that exists in our family, and in the stimulation and pleasure that our children's friends have brought into our lives. Their temperaments are quite different, but the values of both are excellent, and that pleases us very much.

This journey began with Anna, but it has also affected my personality and values more broadly. My friendships within the dwarf community, and my growth in understanding human differences, have enriched and transformed me. In the turbulent early days after Anna's birth, I wept and felt anxiety about her future. From the moment I reached Johns Hopkins when she was four months old, and was encouraged by Dr. Kopits and social worker Joan Weiss to feel more sanguine about Anna's future, I began to feel more peaceful. Still, at the very first Johns Hopkins symposium I attended, when Anna was not quite a year old, I found myself looking out my hotel window at the little people in the swimming pool below and was embarrassed by my staring. I stepped back, but later returned to the window. By the time the day was over, however, I had met many of the dwarf adults and children who were present. They had become individuals whom I was beginning to know and some of whom I already liked. I will always remember that symposium as the day that I crossed the line that had divided us.

By now, no dwarfs look strange to me. My years as Anna's mother and part of the dwarfism community have deepened me, making me more comfortable with differences of all sorts and clearer about what really matters in life. I see beauty in a broader array of possibilities. Not only do these persons no longer seem "odd and peculiar"; they have become individuals, some of whom I love and could even envision falling in love with. That recognition and similar epiphanies gained through parenthood, friendship, and my intellectual labors make me grateful for having been granted experiences that have enriched my appreciation of life and people.

This book represents my effort to pass on some of what I have learned and perhaps to stimulate in others the drive toward further research and advocacy that its contents inspired in me. I hope that short-statured readers will enjoy the material that illuminates their own identity journeys. I hope that the disability community will appreciate the solidarity of one more interesting minority group that is rejecting exploitation and circumscribed roles and replacing them with lives formerly unimaginable. I hope that "normates" may acquire familiarity with worlds that they have previously observed only as outsiders. Long as this volume is, it contains but a fraction of what has already been uncovered about the lives of this interesting, heterogeneous group of very short persons. The journey that confronts them is much longer, and the road is uphill.

NOTES

Foreword

1. Cam Hubert, *Dreamspeaker* (N.p.: Clarke, Irwin, 1978), 77.

Chapter 1. History from Ancient Egypt through the Nazi Era

1. Margaret Murray, *The Splendor That Was Egypt* (1949; New York: Praeger, 1972).
2. Jean Pierre Hallet, *Pigmy Kitubu* (New York: Random House, 1973), 92.
3. W. R. Dawson, "Pygmies and Dwarfs in Ancient Egypt," *Journal of Egyptian Archaeology* 24 (1938): 189.
4. Leviticus 21.16–23: God told Moses to inform Aaron that a blind or lame man, a dwarf, or a person with a broken foot or hand, a flat nose, scurvy, or other blemish ought not to serve at the altar.
5. Veronique Dasen, *Dwarfs in Ancient Egypt and Greece* (New York: Oxford University Press, 1993).
6. Bonnie M. Sampsell, "Ancient Egyptian Dwarfs," *KMT: A Modern Journal of Ancient Egypt* 12 (Fall 2001): 60–73.
7. Dasen, *Dwarfs in Ancient Egypt and Greece*, 206–221.
8. Alfred Enderle, Dietrich Meyerhöfer, and Gerd Unverfehrt, *Small People—Great Art*, trans. Karen Williams (Bremen, Germany: Artcolor Verlag, 1994), 93–94.
9. Martha Edwards, "Construction of Physical Disability in the Ancient Greek World: The Community Concept," in *The Body and Physical Differences: Discourses of Disability*, ed. David T. Mitchell and Sharon L. Snyder (Ann Arbor: University of Michigan Press, 1997), 35–50.
10. H. U. Hall, "Dwarfs and Divinity in West Africa," *Museum Journal* (Pennsylvania University Museum) 18 (1927): 305.
11. Si Maqian was an eminent historian and philosopher of the Western Han dynasty. I am indebted to Tao Jie, professor of English at the University of Beijing, for bringing to my attention and translating this anecdote, from Si Maqian's *The Historical Record*, vol. 126.
12. Martin Monestier, *Les nains: Des hommes différents* (Paris: Jean Claude Simeon, 1977), 71. Monestier mistakenly writes "Hsuan-Tsang," the name of a Chinese monk and spiritual leader from another era. Monestier is probably referring to Tang dynasty (713–756 C.E.) emperor Hsuan-Tsung. Unfortunately, Monestier does not cite his source here or in most other instances. Still, if read with some caution, his book is an invaluable resource.
13. Vivien Sung, *Five-fold Happiness: Chinese Concepts of Luck, Prosperity, Longevity, Happiness, and Wealth* (San Francisco: Chronicle Books, 2002), 30.
14. Marcel Granet, *Chinese Civilization* (New York: Meridian Books, 1958), 295.
15. Juan de Betanzos, *Narrative of the Incas*, trans. and ed. Roland Hamilton and Dana Buchanan (Austin: University of Texas Press, 1996).
16. Ibid., 190.
17. Monestier, *Nains*, 68. For anecdotes about the Romans, see 68–70.
18. Dasen, *Dwarfs in Ancient Egypt and Greece*, 247–8.
19. Julia Cartwright, *Isabella d'Este, Marchioness of Mantua, 1474–1539: A Study of the Renaissance* (New York: E. P. Dutton, 1923).
20. George K. Marek, *The Bed and the Throne: The Life of Isabella d'Este* (New York: Harper and Row, 1976), 39.
21. Cartwright, *Isabella d'Este*, 363–364.

22. Ibid., 81.

23. Marek, *Isabella d'Este,* 39.

24. Cartwright, *Bed and the Throne,* 134.

25. E. J. Wood, *Giants and Dwarfs* (London: Richard Bentley, 1868), 260–261.

26. Monestier, *Nains,* 100.

27. John H. Elliot, "Philip IV of Spain, Prisoner of Ceremony," in *The Courts of Europe: Politics, Patronage, and Royalty, 1400–1800,* ed. A. G. Dickens (London: Thames and Hudson, 1977), 169–189, 175.

28. Alice J. McVan, "Spanish Dwarfs," *Notes Hispanic* 2 (1942): 97–129; for background, see 97–98.

29. Ibid., 120.

30. Ibid., 117.

31. Monestier, *Nains,* 112.

32. See Fernando Videgáin Agós, *Francesillo de Zuñiga, bufon del emperado* (Pamplona, Spain: Disputacion Foral de Navara, Direccion de Turismo, Bibliotecas y Cultura Popular, n.d.), 6. Agós was born in 1940 and this pamphlet is probably fairly recent. Francesillo claimed to be related to the noble Zuñiga family, but in fact had only been a jester for Duke Alvaro de Zuñiga.

33. Ibid., 5, 23–24. Since Jews had been expelled from Spain in 1492, Zuñiga's ancestors were apt to have been *conversos.* Agos demonstrates racial stereotyping, declaring that Zuñiga was Jewish in blood and sophistry, adoring anyone from whose hands would fall bread and clothing, and attacking others.

34. Pidal Juan Menendez, "Don Francesillo de Zuñiga, bufon de Carlos V," *Revista de archivos, bibliotecas y museos,* 3 epoca, 21 (July–August 1901): 72–96.

35. Ibid., 93.

36. Ibid., letter #1 to Queen Leonor, February 1526.

37. Francesillo de Zuñiga, *Cronica burlesca del emperador Carlos V: Edicion introdiccion y notas de Jose Sanchez Paso* (Salmanica, Spain: Editionos Universidad de Salmanica), 1989. First published in the sixteenth century.

38. Francesillo de Zuñiga, *Cronique plaisante de don Francesillo de Zuñiga,* trans. and with an introduction by Paul Redonnel (Paris: J. Bernard, 1930), 27.

39. Ibid., 125–6

40. McVan, *Spanish Dwarfs,* 100.

41. Zuñiga, *Cronique plaisante,* 37, 41.

42. Agos, *Francesillo de Zuñiga,* 4, 25.

43. Redonnel, introduction to Zuñiga, *Cronique plaisante.*

44. McVan, *Spanish Dwarfs,* 101.

45. Wood, in *Giants and Dwarfs,* provides one of the more detailed descriptions of Hudson's life (274–284); this account is based on his.

46. R. S. Kirby, *Kirby's Wonderful and Eccentric Museum; or, Magazine of Remarkable Characters, including all the curiosities of nature and art from the remotest period to the present time* (London: London House Yard, St., Barnard and Sultzer for R. S. Kirby, 1804–1820) vol. 3, 406–408.

47. See Nick Page, *Lord Minimus: The Extraordinary Life of Britain's Smallest Man* (London: HarperCollins, 2001). Although longer than most, this account does not offer a fresh perspective.

48. Horace Walpole, *Anecdotes of Painting in England* (London: J. Dodsley, 1782), vol. 3, 116–118.

49. Edmund Waller, "On the Marriage of the Dwarfs," in *The Poems of Edmund Waller,* ed. G. Thorn Drury (London: Laurence and Bollen, 1893), 92.

50. Monestier, *Nains,* 89. In this rare instance Monestier cites his source: Villebois, *Memoires secrets pour servir a l'histoire de la cour de Russie* (Paris: E. Dentu, 1853).

51. Lindsay Hughes, *Russia in the Age of Peter the Great* (New Haven: Yale University Press), 288.

52. Rosalynd Pflaum, *By Influence and Desire: The True Story of Three Extraordinary Women—the Grandduchess of Courland and Her Daughters,* ed. A. G. Dickens (New York: M. Evans, 1984), xv.

53. Monestier, *Nains,* 91.

54. Ibid., 92. The accounts offered by Monestier and Hughes differ, but the atmosphere described is the same.

55. Pflaum, *By Influence and Desire,* xvii.

56. M. S. Anderson, "Peter the Great, Imperial Revolutionary?" in *The Courts of Europe: Politics, Patronage, and Royalty, 1400–1800* (London: Thames and Hudson, 1977), 264.

57. Edouard Garnier, *Les nains et les géants* (Paris: Librarie Hatchette, 1884), 113, 135.

58. In the early thirteenth century, Casan, a young Tartar dwarf, successfully led an army of two hundred thousand soldiers, helping Genghis Khan to conquer China (Garnier, *Les nains et les géants,* 137); another respected warrior was Corneille of Lithuania, the dwarf of Charles V of Spain, who helped conquer the Turkish armies (Garnier, *Les nains et les géants,* 79–80).

59. Walter Bodin and Burnet Hershey, *It's a Small World* (New York: Conrad-McCann, 1934), 196. A longer account is available in Jean-Alexandre Havard, *Les nains célèbres depuis l'antiquité jusques et y compris Tom-Pouce* [par A. Albanes (pseud.) et Georges Fath] (Paris: G. Havard, 1845) as well as in Wood, *Giants and Dwarfs,* 274–276.

60. Monestier, *Nains,* 102.

61. Peter Prosch, *Lebnis und Ereignisse des Peter Prosch* (Munich: Anton Franz, 1789; reprint, with an introduction by Walter Hansen, Pfaffenhofen, Germany: W. Ludwig Verlag, 1984).

62. Enderle, Meyerhöfer, and Unverfehrt, *Small People—Great Art,* 255–257.

63. Joseph Boruwlaski, *Memoirs of the Celebrated Dwarf, Joseph Boruwlaski, a Polish Gentleman,* trans. Mr. Des Carrieres (London, 1778).

64. Ibid., 31–33.

65. Ibid., 117–119.

66. Ibid., 247.

67. Yi-Fu Tuan, *Dominance and Affection: The Making of Pets* (New Haven: Yale University Press, 1984), 2.

68. Monestier, *Nains,* 95.

69. Sarah Kershaw, "Joaquín Balaguer, 95, Dies; Dominated Dominican Life," *New York Times,* 15 July 2002, B7.

70. James Caulfield, *Portraits, Memoirs, and Characters of Remarkable Persons from the Revolution in 1688 to the End of the Reign of George II* (London: J. G. Barnard, 1813), vol. 3, 230–231.

71. Ibid., vol. 2, 22–25.

72. Kirby, *Kirby's Wonderful and Eccentric Museum,* vol. 5, 228–229.

73. The whereabouts of these letters are unknown.

74. Bodin and Hershey, *It's a Small World,* 222–224.

75. Garnier, *Les nains et les géants,* 116.

76. Gaby Wood, *The Smallest of All Persons Mentioned in the Records of Littleness* (London: Profile Books, 1998), 7.

77. Henry Morley, *Memoirs of Bartholomew Fair* (London: Chapman and Hall, 1859), 315–316, 462, 476.

78. Wood, *Giants and Dwarfs,* 383.

79. Che-Mah, *A True Life and an Interesting History of Che-Mah, the Celebrated Chinese Dwarf, Smallest of All Dwarfs, Written By Himself* (New York: New York Popular Publishing, 1882).

80. Robert Bogdan, *Freak Show: Presenting Human Oddities for Amusement and Profit.* (Chicago: University of Chicago Press, 1988), 25–26.

81. *Smithsonian,* December 1996, 8.

82. Bogdan (*Freak Show*) has described his embarrassed attendance at a Coney Island sideshow. In 1993 I too visited a sideshow there, in order to experience such an event. One of the performers was the same Otis Jordan whom Bogdan had seen. For one dollar, Jordan offered a "carte de visite," similar to those provided by previous generations of exhibiting dwarfs. Previously having billed himself as the "frog man," he had changed his title to the more scientific "ossified man." His body was almost entirely paralyzed and locked in a seated position. His card described his childhood in a family of seven children in Barnesville, Georgia, and—until the circus came to town in 1963—his inability to find a job despite his high grades at school and skill in crafts. In 1993, at the age of seventy, he presented an act that consisted of rolling cigarettes and lighting them with his toes. His card's message concluded, "To you, my friend, I say, 'Never give up.' I never have."

83. Douglas Martin, "The Weirdest Show on Earth," *New York Times,* 3 April 1998, E45. See also advertisements for Sideshow by the Seashore at "Coney Island Circus Sideshow," www.coneyisland.com/sideshow.shtml.

84. J. Mason Warren, "An Account of Two Remarkable Indian Dwarfs Exhibited in Boston under the Name of Aztec Children," *American Journal of Medical Sciences* 42 (1851): 285–293.

85. Hy Roth and Robert Cromie, *The Little People* (New York: Everett House, 1980).

86. Bogdan, *Freak Show,* 161–163.

87. For accounts of these events and of the life of Tom Thumb, see Roth and Cromie, *Little People;* Frederick Drimmer, *Very Special People* (New York: Amjon, 1973); Bogdan, *Freak Show;* and in primary sources, available at the Brooklyn Historical Society, the New-York Historical Society, and circus museums.

88. Lavinia Warren, *The Autobiography of Mrs. Tom Thumb* (Camden, Conn: Archon Books, 1979), 179.

89. Henry E. Scott, *The Adams Family of Martha's Vineyard* (Rutland, Vt.: Mercury, 1987), 41.

90. Letter to the *Vineyard Gazette,* 27 October 1950, Adams sisters collection at the Historical Society of Martha's Vineyard, Mass.

91. Letter from Lucy Adams to Admiral H. G. Bradbury, 20 March 1952, ibid.

92. Letter from Lucy Adams to Lloyd L. Shepherd, 27 May 1939, ibid.

93. Robert Hillyer, "The Misses Adams." *Vineyard Gazette,* 31 December 1954.

94. Robert Lewis Taylor, "Last of the Great Carnival Talkers," *New Yorker,* 26 April 1958, 72.

95. Douglas Martin, "The Weirdest Show on Earth." *New York Times,* 8 April 1998, E35, 45. Khan said that the chance to make a spectacle of himself gave him money and prestige he could not find in menial jobs.

96. Yoram S. Carmeli, "Wee Pea: The Total Play of the Dwarf in the Circus," *Drama Review* 26 (Winter 1989), 130. See also Yoram S. Carmeli, "From Curiosity to Prop: A Note on the Changing Cultural Significance of Dwarves' Presentations in Britain," *Journal of Popular Culture* 26 (Summer 1992), 69–80, 130.

97. For the general effects of changes in circuses, see Marcello Truzzi, "The Decline of the American Circus: The Shrinkage of an Institution," in *The Sociology of Everyday Life* (Englewood Cliffs, N.J.: Prentice-Hall, 1968), 314–321. For the article about Frank Theriault and the Koos and Adelson families, see Eric Sherman, "It's Heart Not Height That Counts," *Staten Island Sunday Advance,* 26 May 1985, sec. 3, 1.

98. Mary Ellen Mark, *The Indian Circus* (San Francisco: Chronicle Books, 1993), *Starkiss: Circus Girls in India,* produced, directed, and written by Chris Relleke and Jascha de Wilde, in English, Hindi, and Nepalese, with English subtitles. At the film's premiere on 11 June 2003, Relleke and de Wilde spoke of the appealing aspects of the world of spectacle, but they were also clearly aware of its abuses in parts of the world.

99. This evocative saying expresses the painful choice that so often shaped the roles of dwarfs in history. See Sheila Ackerlind, *Patterns of Conflict: The Individual and Society in Spanish Literature to 1700* (New York: Peter Lang, 1988), 132.

100. Wood, *Giants and Dwarfs,* 421, 423, 445.

101. The descriptions of MacPherson and Blair and the quotations are from the legend accompanying original etchings in the collection of Hy Roth, Evanston, Illinois.

102. See the Seaman family Web site, http://www.geocities.com/kwseaman2000/Reunion2000a.html. I am grateful to Dan N. Rolph of the Historical Society of Pennsylvania, of whom Charles Seaman is a distant ancestor, for bringing Seaman to my attention.

103. Yehudah Koren and Eilat Negev, *In Our Hearts We Were Giants: The Remarkable Story of the Lilliput Troupe—A Dwarf Family's Survival of the Holocaust* (New York: Carroll and Graf, 2004), 94–95.

104. "The History Place: World War II in Europe, Nazi Euthanasia," http://www.historyplace.com/worldwar2/timeline/euthan-bio.htm.

105. According to Drimmer, the Nazis sent approximately ten thousand "dwarfs, midgets, and other short people" to the gas chambers (*Very Special People,* 259). It is unclear, however, where Drimmer obtained these figures, and none are available for dwarfs' deaths in institutions. That there were a great many, however, is reflected in the fact that Mengele's colleague, Hans Grebe, had abandoned his dwarfism research by 1943 because dwarfs had disappeared from institutions (Koren and Negev, *In Our Hearts We Were Giants,* 95).

106. Elie A. Cohen, *Human Behavior in the Concentration Camp* (London: Free Association Books, 1988), 81–114.

107. Alexander Mitscherlich, *Doctors of Infamy: The Story of the Nazi Medical Crimes* (New York: Henry Schuman, 1949), 146.

108. Robert Jay Lifton, *The Nazi Doctors: Medical Killings and the Psychology of Genocide* (New York: Basic Books, 1986), 348.

109. Elizabeth Moskowitz [Moshkovitz], *By the Grace of the Satan: The Story of the Dwarves Family in Aushvitz in Dr. Mengele's Experiments* (Ramat-Gan, Israel: Rotem, 1987).

110. Yehudah Koren, "Size Matters: Survival in Auschwitz," *Hadassah Magazine*, November 1999, 33–34.

111. Sara Nomberg-Pryztyk, *Auschwitz: True Tales from a Grotesque Land* (Chapel Hill: University of North Carolina Press, 1985). While Nomberg-Pryztyk describes the scene, she does not name the mother, who is identified by Koren and Negev (*In Our Hearts We Were Giants*, 170).

112. Later writers repeated Nomberg-Prystyk's inaccuracies about the child's death and the dwarf's electrocution. See, for example, Gerald Astor, *The Life and Times of Dr. Joseph Mengele* (New York: Donald I. Fine, 1985), 101–102.

113. Koren and Negev, *In Our Hearts We Were Giants*, 81.

114. Koren, "Size Matters," 34.

115. Shahar Rozen, *Liebe Perla* (Israel and Germany; in Hebrew and German, with English subtitles), 1999.

116. Koren, "Size Matters," 31–34.

117. Moskovitz, *By the Grace of the Satan*, 12. The family history included in this section is drawn from her personal account and the research of Koren and Negev.

118. "The Death Marches of Hungarian Jews through Austria," www.yad-vashem.org.il/download/about_holocaust/studies/lappin_full.pdf.

119. Koren and Negev, *In Our Hearts We Were Giants*, 173

120. Drimmer, *Very Special People*, 259.

121. Francis E. Johnston, "Some Observations on the Roles of Achondroplastic Dwarfs through History," *Clinical Pediatrics* 2 (1963): 707.

Chapter 2. Biographies of Eminent Dwarfs

1. E. W., *New Monthly Magazine and Literary Journal* 4 (1822): 49.

2. Walter Bodin and Barnet Hershey, *It's a Small World* (New York: Coward-McCann, 1934), 193.

3. Among the nineteenth-century texts on which most later authors have relied are Garnier, *Les nains et les géants*; George M. Gould and Walter L. Pyle, *Anomalies and Curiosities of Medicine* (Philadelphia: W. B. Saunders, 1896; reprint, New York: Bell, 1956); Jean-Alexandre Havard, *Les nains célèbres depuis l'antiquité jusques et y compris Tom-Pouce*, [par A. Albanés (pseud.) et Georges Fath (Paris: G. Havard, 1845); and Wood, *Giants and Dwarfs*.

4. Professor Aleksander Gieysztor of the University of Warsaw noted that Wladislaw was only a short man and that the nickname the Elbow expressed a sympathetic familiarity of his subjects with him (letter to the author, 15 February 1990); Professor Walter Goffart of the University of Toronto, an expert on the canonized sixth-century bishop Gregory of Tours, said it would be as charming for Gregory to be a dwarf as for Attila, but that there wasn't the slightest basis for such an idea (letter to the author, 5 June 1986); Professor Averil Cameron of Oxford University, who has written on Procopius, has no evidence of his being a dwarf (letter to the author, 13 June 1996). Joan Slomanson in *A Short History: Thumbnail Sketches of Fifty Little Giants* (New York: Abbeville Press, 1998) claimed that Alfred Moore, U.S. Supreme Court Justice from 1800 to 1804, was four feet five inches tall; however, the administrator at the Moorefields Foundation in North Carolina, and a researcher at the Supreme Court Historical Society in Washington, D.C., were convinced that Moore had been five feet four—there had evidently been an error in transposition. These are but a few of the mistakes I discovered.

5. Noted by Maximus Planudes, c. 1300, in *Encyclopaedia Britannica*, s.v. "Aesop."

6. See Edward Gibbon, *The Decline and Fall of the Roman Empire* (New York: Peter Fenelon Collier and Son, 1901), vol. 3, 344.

7. See Katherine Scherman, *The Birth of France: Warriors, Bishops, and Long-Haired Kings* (New York: Random House, 1987), 30; and J. Otto Maenchen-Helfen, *The World of the Huns* (Berkeley and Los Angeles: University of California Press, 1973), 361. Note also that dwarfs are listed as members of Attila's entourage—with no association made.

8. Scherman, *Birth of France*, 268.

9. Doubtful candidates include Admiral Gravina, who led the Spanish navy against Lord Nelson; Husain Pasha Kucuk, a diminutive Georgian slave who became a vizier under Selim III and reformed the Ottoman navy; Eugene of Savoy, who in the service of Austria was one of the great military strategists of his time; Charles Durazzo (Charles III), king of Naples and Hungary in the fourteenth century. See Wellbore St. Clair Baddeley, *Charles III of Naples and Urban VI* (London: W. Heineman, 1894) for his portrait; an accompanying legend notes only that he is short and ruddy.

10. K.T.L. Fu, "The Healing Hand in Shakespeare's Literature: Shakespeare and Surgery," *Hong Kong Medical Journal* 4, no. 1 (1998): 85.

11. Alice Jane McVan, "Spanish Dwarfs," *Notes Hispanic* 2 (1942): 104.

12. The celebrity of other well-known dwarfs—the Egyptian Seneb, the British Jeffery Hudson, the Polish Count Boruwlaski, and the American Tom Thumb—is inseparable from their stature, and they have been included in the History chapter.

13. Nathaniel Wanley, "Of Dwarfs, and Men much below the common Height," in *The Wonders of the Little World; or, a General History of Man in Six Books* (London, 1678), book 1, chap. 23, 47.

14. Auguste Couat, *Alexandrian Poetry under the First Three Ptolemies, 324–222 BC* (New York: G. P. Putnam's Sons, 1931), 71.

15. Ibid.

16. Alfred Körte, *Hellenistic Poetry* (New York: Columbia University Press, 1929), 96.

17. Poet and orator Licinius Calvus (Licinius Macer Calvus Gaius) was described as an "eloquent Lilliputian" by the poet Catullus, his acclaimed contemporary.

18. Peter France, *Hermits: The Insights of Solitude* (New York: St. Martin's Press, 1996), 25, 35, 37, 43, 47–8.

19. *Encyclopedic Dictionary of Religion*, 1979, s.v. "Godeau, Antoine."

20. Yves Giraud, "'Nain de Julie' et homme de Dieu," in *De la galenterie à la sainteté*, ed. Yves Giraud (Paris: Klincksieck, 1975), 42, 38, 27. I am grateful to Aviva Briefel for her assistance in selecting and translating the quotations in the Godeau section.

21. Ibid., 13.

22. Francis Steegmuller, *A Woman, a Man, and Two Kingdoms: The Story of Madame d'Epinay and the Abbé Galiani* (New York: Alfred A. Knopf, 1991), 54. Further page references to this work are cited parenthetically in the text.

23. *The Columbia Encyclopedia*, 6th ed., 2001, s.v. "Galiani, Ferdinando."

24. For example, many works include the following quotation, first published in Henry Richard Vassall Fox, Lord Holland, *Foreign Reminiscences* (London: Longman, Brown, Green, and Longmans, 1850), 146: "The Duke of Altamira, Marquis of Astorga, was the least man I ever saw in society, and smaller than many dwarfs exhibited for money. He was president of the Junta, and drove about with guards like a royal personage. They called him Rey Chico, a name formerly given to a King of Granada, and it was an allusion to that name that the small club or knot of men I have mentioned gave themselves, that of Junta Chica." This group, which got its ideas from the Encyclopedists of France, was active in attempting to promote liberal laws and popular government in Alcaza.

25. *Encyclopaedia Britannica*, s.v. "Pope, Alexander."

26. Among the works for which he is best known are "Moral Essays," "Essay on Man," "Epistle to Dr. Arbuthnot," and "Satires" and "Epistles of Horace," as well as his volumes of letters.

27. Letter from Alexander Pope to Jonathan Swift, 9 October 1729, in *The Correspondence of Alexander Pope*, ed. George Sherburn (Oxford: Clarendon Press, 1956), vol. 3, 57–58.

28. Maynard Mack, *Alexander Pope: A Life* (New York: W. W. Norton, 1985).

29. Ibid., 183–184

30. William K. Wimsatt, *The Portraits of Alexander Pope* (New Haven: Yale University Press, 1965), 70.

31. Mack, *Alexander Pope*, 152.

32. Helen Deutsch, *Resemblance and Disgrace: Alexander Pope and the Deformation of Culture* (Cambridge: Harvard University Press, 1996).

33. Lady Mary Montagu, *Verses Address'd to the Imitation of the First Satire of the Second Book of Horace, By a Lady* (London: A. Dodd, 9 March 1733); see also Deutsch, *Resemblance and Disgrace*, 2.

34. Mack, *Alexander Pope*, 304

35. For a thoughtful overview of Pope's relationships with women, especially the Blount sisters, see James Anderson Winn, *A Window in the Bosom* (Hamden, Conn.: Archon Books, 1977).

36. Alexander Pope, "An Epistle to Dr. Arbuthnot," in *Alexander Pope: Selected Works* (New York: Modern Library), 180.

37. Wimsatt, *Portraits of Alexander Pope.*

38. Roberts Vaux, *Memoirs of the Lives of Benjamin Lay and Ralph Sandiford; Two of the Earliest Public Advocates for the Emancipation of the Enslaved Africans* (Philadelphia: Solomon W. Conrad, 1815). The biographical account above is drawn largely from this work and from Benjamin Lay, *All slave-keepers that keep the innocent in bondage, Apostates,*" first published in 1737 by Benjamin Franklin. Excerpts from that work appear in Roger Bruns, ed., *Am I Not a Man and a Brother: The Antislavery Crusade of Revolutionary America, 1688–1788* (New York: Chelsea House, 1977), 46–64. See also archives at the Historical Society of Pennsylvania.

39. Robin K. Berson, *Marching to a Different Drummer: Unrecognized Heroes of American History* (Westport, Conn: Greenwood Press, 1994), 197–201.

40. Vaux, *Memoirs,* 20.

41. *Friends Intelligencer,* Philadelphia, 18 Twelfth Month, 1869, in *Quaker Scrapbook,* Am 12780, Cox-Parrish, Whalen Collection, I, 295–301, collection Historical Society of Pennsylvania.

42. Wilford P. Cole discusses the history of this work at length in "Henry Dawkins and the Quaker Cemetery," *Wintherthur Portfolio* 4 (1968): 34–46, collection Historical Society of Pennsylvania.

43. Lay, *All slave-keepers,* 52.

44. Berson, *Marching to a Different Drummer,* 198.

45. Ibid., 20.

46. Minutes of Friends' Quarterly Meeting of Colchester, 12 April 1732, collection Historical Society of Pennsylvania.

47. This three-by-six-inch volume, *Lay's Address to Slavekeepers, 1737,* was one of the earliest and most influential eighteenth-century abolitionist documents. Lay's disjointed text is marked by great passion; his references reveal his erudition.

48. Vaux, *Memoirs,* 28.

49. Berson, *Marching to a Different Drummer,* 199.

50. Ibid., 37.

51. Vaux, *Memoirs,* 27.

52. An article in the *Quaker Scrapbook* at the Pennsylvania Historical Society praises the rebel the Friends formerly viewed as a heretic: "Twenty-eight years of his life were spent in Pennsylvania, and because of his singular appearance, and persistent labors among all classes of people, in town and country, it is probable that every man and woman, and almost every child in the State was familiar with Benjamin Lay, the friend and protector of the oppressed" (*Friends Intelligencer,* 18 Twelfth Month, 1869).

53. John G. Whittier, "The Journal of John Woolman: An Appreciation," http://www.strecorsoc.org/jwoolman/appre1.html.

54. Jean R. Soderlund, *Quakers and Slavery: A Divided Spirit* (Princeton: Princeton University Press, 1985), 15.

55. Vaux, *Memoirs,* 51.

56. This section is drawn from three sources: *The Dictionary of National Biography,* s.v. "Hay, William"; William Hay, *The Collected Works of William Hay, Esq.* (London: J. Nichols, 1794), vol. 1; and William Hay, "Deformity," in *Fugitive Pieces* (n.p: R. Dodsley), 1765.

57. Hay, "Deformity," 124.

58. Hay, *Collected Works.* Both facts and brief quotations are drawn from his daughter's introduction; her name is not given.

59. Hay, "Deformity," 95–96.

60. Ibid., 117.

61. I am indebted to the historian Mechal Sobel, who knew of Mary Garrettson and directed me to the Methodist archives at Drew University in Madison, New Jersey, holding Garrettson's correspondence as well as other manuscripts and books relating to her. In hundreds of letters and in the other material by her contemporaries, I found no reference to her dwarfism.

62. See Robert Drew Simpson, ed., *American Methodist Pioneer: The Life and Journals of the Rev. Freeborn Garrettson, 1752–1827* (Madison, N.J.: Academy Books, 1984), 251.

63. Diane Lobody, "Lost in the Ocean of Love: The Mystical Writings of Catherine Livingston Garrettson"

(Ph.D. diss., Drew University, 1990), 49–50. Just how wild was "wild" is a good question. Pioneer ministers often married late and described their earlier behavior as licentious. "Kitty's" transformation was verified.

64. R. Wheatley, "Obituary of Miss Mary R. Garrettson," *Christian Advocate,* 27 March 1879, 198–199. Also published in J. F. Richmond, ed., *Minutes of the Methodist Episcopal Church* (New York: Nelson and Phillips, 1876).

65. *Little Mabel and Her Sunlit Home, By a Lady* (New York: Carlton and Porter, 1860) and *Little Mabel's Friends: A Sequel to Little Mabel and Her Sunlit Home* (New York: Carlton and Porter, 1862). Although the frontispiece of *Little Mabel and Her Sunlit Home* identifies it only as "Written by a Lady," the Drew catalog lists both this work and *Little Mabel's Friends* as written by Mary Garrettson. For her to have openly professed authorship of these works, written for Sunday school use, would have been to display vanity that was unseemly for a pious Christian.

66. Mary Garrettson to uncle (name not noted), 11 February 1830: "We have been so interested on behalf of the poor Indians whose fate is depending on the decisions of the Congress now in session, that we should feel most guilty not to write to you on the subject, although our sentiments can add nothing to the scale, which seems to us to be fearfully balanced between justice and humanity on the one hand, and interest and expedience on the other" (Garrettson collection, Methodist archives, Drew University).

67. Mary Garrettson to Susan and Anna Warren, December 1864, Garrettson collection, Methodist archives, Drew University.

68. R. Wheatley, "Obituary of Miss Mary R. Garrettson," 198.

69. Mary Garrettson to Maria Nott, 17 March 1821, Garrettson collection, Methodist archives, Drew University.

70. Mary Garrettson to Maria Nott, undated. The full account reads, "I cannot, will not believe that your love for me has subsided. . . . Oh toward you my own beloved Maria? Impossible—my own fear is that I feel for you an excess of affection which perhaps my duty to a higher power should check— not that I think religion calculated to dry up the warm spring of love" (Garrettson collection, Methodist archives, Drew University).

71. Mary Garrettson to Mary Suckley, 11 July, 1800, Garrettson collection, Methodist archives, Drew University.

72. Simpson, *American Methodist Pioneer,* 359.

73. Lobody, "Lost in the Ocean of Love," 6. References to Catherine Garrettson's rage against her mother, for example, have been obliterated.

74. Garrettson, *Little Mabel and Her Sunlit Home,* 82.

75. "Little Mabel," in Harris Collection, Brown University Library, Providence, Rhode Island. We don't know whether she authorized Hires's adoption of Little Mabel, but the drawings are of the same appealing little girl.

76. Garrettson, *Little Mabel and Her Sunlit Home,* 136.

77. Mary Garrettson to Mary Suckley, n.d.

78. Simpson, *American Methodist Pioneer,* 15.

79. Robert Simpson, personal communication to the author.

80. Mary Garrettson to friend identified only as Frances, 18 May 1878.

81. I thank John Koos for drawing to my attention the sale of Ford's Manhattan home, announced in the *New York Times* Real Estate section (22 February 1998), in which it was mentioned that historian and novelist Paul Leicester Ford was a hunchbacked dwarf. Ford material may be found at the Brooklyn Public Library, the New-York Historical Society, and the New York Public Library, which has Ford family collections. Yale University also has a Ford collection.

82. Paul Z. DuBois, *Paul Leicester Ford: An American Man of Letters, 1865–1902* (New York: Burt Franklin, 1977).

83. Victor Paltits, quoted in DuBois, *Ford,* 154.

84. *National Cyclopedia of American Biography* (Ann Arbor: Xerox Microfilms), vol. 13, 105.

85. Preface to Emily Ellsworth Ford Skeels, *Mason Locke Weems, His Works and Ways in Three Volumes: A Bibliography Left Unfinished by Paul Leicester Ford* (Two hundred copies self-published, 1929), vol. 1, vii.

86. The work is described thus: "Compiled for Presentation by Noah Webster, New Haven, 1836. With

Notes and Corrections by His Great-Grandson, Paul Leicester Ford, Brooklyn, N.Y. Privately Printed, 1876, 250 copies" (*National Cyclopedia of American Biography,* s.v. "Ford, Paul Leicester").

87. Paul Leicester Ford, *The Honorable Peter Stirling* (New York: Henry Holt, 1894; reprint, with a preface by Wilfred A. Ferrell, Ridgewood, N.J.: Gregg Press, 1968).

88. DuBois, *Ford,* 63.

89. *Home Magazine,* Binghamton, New York, February 1897, n.p., clipping in Paul Leicester Ford Collection, New York Public Library.

90. Paul Leicester Ford, *The Many-Sided Franklin* (New York: Century, 1899).

91. Gillian Webster Barr Bailey, "Recollections of Gillian Webster Barr Bailey," typescript recorded for her dependents, 61–62. Also quoted in DuBois, *Paul Leicester Ford,* 137–138. Gillian Bailey's warm recollections are echoed in letters between them and between other family members included in the New York Public Library collection. Letters to and from Paul Ford reveal him as a devoted uncle and loving brother and son.

92. *Brooklyn Daily Eagle,* 9 May 1902, 8.

93. Emily Ellsworth Fowler Ford to Paul Leicester Ford, 1870, New York Public Library Paul Leicester Ford Collection. Also quoted in DuBois, *Ford,* 14.

94. Ford's family and friends describe his condition as resulting from a fall early in life. The circumstances remain murky. Ford's friend Hugo Palsits says that Ford fell from his nurse's arms in infancy; his niece Gillian Bailey, however, writes that he fell from a barn loft much later. DuBois, his biographer, notes these contradictions (*Ford,* 13–15), but he fails to conjecture further about the nature or origin of the condition.

95. DuBois, *Ford,* 21.

96. *New York Evening Journal,* 19 September 1900, clipping in New York Public Library Paul Leicester Ford Collection.

97. Paul Leicester Ford, *The Story of an Untold Love* (Boston: Houghton-Mifflin, 1897), 4.

98. DuBois, *Ford,* 69.

99. *Brooklyn Daily Eagle,* 9 May 1902, 8. An accomplished sportsman, Malcolm was once examined by a prominent physician and athletic authority, who said of him, "He is undoubtedly the greatest combination of strength, activity, and endurance that has yet come before the public" (ibid.).

100. He said that Gordon Ford had told his children, who were ranged around his deathbed, that he could not feel satisfied unless Malcolm was provided for. According to Malcolm, his siblings reneged after he made a wealthy marriage, later denying they had ever thought of dividing the estate with him "because I had not led a proper life" (ibid., 3).

101. *Brooklyn Daily Eagle,* 9 May 1902, 3.

102. Ibid., 12 May 1902, 5.

103. Julia Frey, *Toulouse-Lautrec: A Life* (London: Weidenfeld and Nicolson, 1994), 71. In 1962, French physicians Lamy and Maroteaux diagnosed it as pyknodysostosis; Frey claims that their diagnosis was based on caricatures. More recent genetic evidence and testing of his relatives calls the original diagnosis into question.

104. Julia Frey, "Henri de Toulouse-Lautrec: A Biography of the Artist," in *Henri de Toulouse-Lautrec: Images of the 1890s,* ed. Riva Castleman and Wolfgang Wittrock (New York: Museum of Modern Art, 1985), 24.

105. Genevieve Diego-Dortignac, Jean-Bernard Naudin, and Andre Daguin, *Toulouse-Lautrec's Table* (New York: Random House, 1993), ostensibly a cookbook featuring the dishes the artist prepared and enjoyed, offers a colorful portrayal of the sensual aspects of his world.

106. See Pierre Paret, *Lautrec: Women* (Lausanne: International Art Book, 1970).

107. Frey, "Henri de Toulouse-Lautrec," 18; Lawrence Hanson and Elizabeth Hanson, *The Tragic Life of Toulouse-Lautrec* (New York, Random House, 1956).

108. Michael Kimmelman, "Toulouse-Lautrec, Stripped of the Cliches," *New York Times,* 6 June 1995, H31.

109. *Unpublished Correspondence of Henri de Toulouse-Lautrec: 273 Letters by and about Lautrec Written to His Family and Friends in the Collections of Herbert Schimmel,* ed. Lucien Goldschmidt and Herbert Schimmel (New York: Phaedon, 1969), 226, 232, 240.

110. Frey, "Henri de Toulouse-Lautrec," 35.

111. Even Hanson and Hanson, who, in *The Tragic Life of Toulouse-Lautrec,* eloquently document his short-

comings, nevertheless conclude by extolling "a lifelong display of courage so resolute, so unfailing and disguised with such gaiety, that, contemplating it, one is astounded" (263).

112. According to his colleagues, his contribution did for the magnetic circuit what Georg Simon Ohm had done for the electric circuit.

113. A more detailed summary can be found in Charles Gillespie, ed., *Dictionary of Scientific Biography* (n.p.: American Council of Learned Societies, Scribners, 1976), 24.

114. Henry Thomas, *Charles Steinmetz* (New York: G. P. Putnam's Sons), 11.

115. Ibid., 16.

116 General Electric, *The Story of Steinmetz*, nineteen-page pamphlet, New York Public Library.

117. John T. Broderick, *Steinmetz and His Discoverer* (Schenectady, N.Y.: Robson and Adee, 1924), 15–16.

118. Mack, *Alexander Pope*, 447.

119. Thomas, *Charles Steinmetz*, 40.

120. Ibid.

121. John Anderson Miller, *The Story of Charles Proteus Steinmetz* (New York: American Society of Professional Engineers, 1958), 196.

122. For Steinmetz's activism, see Sender Garlin, *Three American Radicals: John Swinton, Crusading Editor; Charles P. Steinmetz, Scientist and Socialist; William Dean Howells and the Haymarket Era* (Boulder, San Francisco; Oxford: Westview Press, 1991), 49–96.

123. John Winthrop Hammond, *Charles Proteus Steinmetz: A Biography* (New York: Century, 1924), 478.

124. Garlin, *Three American Radicals*, 58.

125. Katherine Butler Hathaway, *The Little Locksmith*, illustrated by the author (New York: Coward-Mc-Cann, 1943; reprint, with a foreword by Alix Kates Shulman and afterword by Nancy Mair, New York: Feminist Press, 2000); Katherine Butler Hathaway, *The Journals and Letters of the Little Locksmith* (New York: Coward-McCann, 1946). Both texts were published posthumously; Hathaway had the pleasure of seeing the first chapter of *The Little Locksmith* serialized in the *Atlantic Monthly* before her death.

126. Hathaway, *Little Locksmith*, 167–68.

127. The unspeakable word (15) is never actually mentioned by Hathaway herself. I wrote to her nephew Anthony Butler, asking for a photograph of his aunt and for any recollections he had. An engaging, amiable man, he was happy to talk about her. Butler had known nothing about her emotional struggles, but on the contrary had found her warm, cheerful, and generous. For him, as for so many others, dwarfs are people of extreme short stature and short limbs; because his aunt was proportionate, and just somewhat shorter than average, she was "normal" in his view. It is therefore not surprising that Butler and his sisters felt strongly that Hathaway's photograph should not appear in a book about persons with dwarfism and did not give permission for one to be reproduced. He was willing, however, to share some memories: he recalled the nieces and nephews encouraging "Aunt Kitty" to get married; he remembered her showing him her manuscript when he was in college and asking his opinion. A physically active person himself, he replied that the book needed more action! After mentioning how affectionate she was, he said that he had a picture of her with her arm around him. It is to be regretted that readers of this volume will not have the pleasure of viewing that photograph.

128. Katherine Butler Hathaway, *Mr. Muffet's Cat and Her Trip to Paris* (New York: Harper and Brothers, 1934).

129. Hathaway, *Journals and Letters*, 303.

130. Mairs, afterword to Hathaway, *Little Locksmith*, 252.

131. Jean Brissé Saint-Macary, *1 Metre 34*, as told to Etienne de Monpezat (Paris: Julliard, 1975). Fay Halpern translated the work and provided the English summary on which my account is based. My description of the first meeting of the Association des personnes de petite taille relies on my translation of Monestier's account.

132. Monestier, *Nains*, 183–84.

133. Monestier's prejudices are sensed in some of his comments elsewhere in *Les nains*. See also Pieral's memoir *Vu d'en bas* (Paris: Laffont, 1976) and Natalie and Fabien Pretou's e-mail comments in Part 4 of this volume. They reinforce the impression that France offers a less-than-benign atmosphere for its dwarf citizens.

Chapter 3. Stigma

1. John Hendrick Bangs, "The Little Elf," in *The Oxford Book of Children's Verse in America,* ed. Donald Hall (New York: Oxford University Press, 1985), 190.
2. Erving Goffman, *Stigma: Notes on the Management of Spoiled Identity* (Englewood Cliffs, N.J., Prentice-Hall, 1963), 3.
3. Ibid., 4–5.
4. The neologism *normate* appears to have first been used by Rosemarie Garland Thomson, in *Extraordinary Bodies: Figuring Physical Disability in American Culture and Literature* (New York: Columbia University Press, 1995).
5. J. L. Tringo, "The Hierarchy of Preferences toward Disability Groups," *Journal of Special Education* 4 (1970): 295–306.
6. Joseph Lopreato, *Human Nature and Biocultural Evolution* (Boston: Allen and Unwin, 1984), 177–8.
7. See, for example, C. Peter Herman, Mark P. Zanna, and E. Tory Higgins, *Physical Appearance, Stigma, and Social Behavior: The Ontario Symposium,* vol. 3 (Hillsdale, N.J.: Lawrence Erlbaum Associates, 1986).
8. One of the best reviews may be found in Edward E. Jones et al., *Social Stigma and the Psychology of Marked Relationships* (New York: W. H. Freeman, 1984), esp. 52–56.
9. See, for example, Edward O. Wilson, *Sociobiology: The New Synthesis* (Cambridge: Belknap Press of Harvard University Press, 1975), 291–294.
10. Peter J. B. Slater, *The Encyclopedia of Animal Behavior* (New York: Facts on File, 1987), 73.
11. Wilson, *Sociobiology,* 294.
12. Ralph Keyes, *The Height of Your Life* (New York: Warner, 1981).
13. "Want a Raise? Stand Tall, Survey Says," *MSNBC News,* http://msnbc.com/news/981402.asp?0dm =C16MB. This account is based on T. A. Judge and D. M. Cable, "The Effect of Physical Height on Workplace Success and Income," *Journal of Applied Psychology* 89 (2004): 428–441.
14. Nancy Etcoff of Harvard Medical School, cited by Gina Kolata, in "What We Don't Know about Obesity," *New York Times,* 22 June 2003, Week in Review, 12. .
15. Thomas Gregor, "Short People," *Natural History* 88 (February 1979), 14–20.
16. Jane Perlez, "The Bloody Hills of Burundi," *New York Times Magazine,* 6 November 1988, 90–125; Alex Schoumatoff, "Rwanda's Aristocratic Guerillas," *New York Times Magazine,* 23 December 1992, 42–48.
17. "Twa Women Cultivate Healthy Communities in Post-War Rwanda," *Raising Our Voices: News from the Global Fund for Women,* August 2003, 7.
18. "Who Measures Up in Italy," *Newsweek,* 23 January 1984, 33.
19. Martin Monestier, *Les nains: Des hommes différents* (Paris: Jean Claude Simeon, 1977), 164–65.
20. J. S. Gillis and W. E. Avis, "The Male-Taller Norm in Mate Selection," *Personality and Social Psychology Bulletin* 6 (1980), 396–401.
21. Julie V. Iovine, "Do Short Men Make Better Lovers?" *Mademoiselle,* November 1987, 92.
22. Cara M. Egan, "The Seven Dwarfs and I," *Newsweek,* 9 September 1991, 8–9.
23. Genesis Rabba, 16.4. This text was written before the sixth century C.E.
24. Louis Ginzburg, *Legends of the Jews* (Philadelphia: Jewish Publication Society of America, 1959), 422.
25. Tosef, Ber vii, 3.
26. Celestine Bohlen, "A Survival of the Past, Anti-Semitism Is Back," *New York Times,* 20 February 1990, A10.
27. Anita Roddick, *Body and Soul* (New York: Crown Trade Paperbacks, 1991). Quoted in review in *Economist* 321 (12 October 1991), 92.
28. Joan Ablon, *Little People in America: The Social Dimensions of Dwarfism* (New York: Praeger, 1984), 91.
29. Rosemary Garland Thomson, *Extraordinary Bodies* (New York: Columbia University Press, 1997), 15, 13.
30. Judy Cohen, *Disability Etiquette: Tips on Interacting with People with Disabilities,* 2d ed. (New York: Eastern Paralyzed Veterans Association and Access Resources, 2003), 24.

Chapter 4. Mythology

1. Stith Thomas, ed., *Motif-Index of Folk Literature*, 6 vols. (Bloomington: Indiana University Press 1955–1958). This invaluable reference work was published in a revised edition in 1989 and appeared on CD-ROM in 1993. It classifies and summarizes narrative elements in folklore.

2. Brian Kline, a member of Little People of America, posted a rich, descriptive list of approximately one hundred mythological figures on the Dwarfism List on 2 April 2002; his link is on LPA Online.

3. Manfred Lurker, *The Gods and Symbols of Ancient Egypt* (New York: Thames and Hudson, 1974), 32–33.

4. Barbara Watterson, *The Gods of Ancient Egypt* (New York: Facts on File, 1984), 127.

5. Warren R. Dawson, "Pygmies and Dwarfs in Ancient Egypt," *Journal of Egyptian Archaeology* 24 (1938): 185–189.

6. Margaret Murray, *The Splendor That Was Egypt* (London: Sidgewick and Jackson, 1963; reprint, New York: St. Martin's Press, 1987), 115–116. Page numbers are from the 1987 edition.

7. Alfred Wiedmann, *Religion of the Ancient Egyptians* (New York: G. P. Putnam's Sons, 1897), 137.

8. Veronique Dasen, *Dwarfs in Ancient Egypt and Greece* (Oxford: Oxford University Press, 1999). For the etymology of the names Ptah and Ptah-Pataikoi, see 84–85; for the two-headed amulet of Bes and Ptah-Ptaikos (at plate 2b), see 41.

9. K. Aterman, "From Horus the Child to Hephaestus Who Limps: A Romp through History," *American Journal of Medical Genetics* 83 (1999): 53–63. Aterman explores evidence that connects Hephaestus to an Egyptian dwarf god; he also speculates that the smith's lameness may result from his exposure to the toxic metals used in his work.

10. William T. Hommel, *Art of the Mende*, exh. cat. (College Park, Md.: University of Maryland Art Gallery, 1974), 7–8.

11. Martha Beckwith, *Hawaiian Mythology* (Honolulu: University of Hawaii Press, 1970), 167–179, offers a summary of some of the very different versions of Pele's history.

12. Sheila Sawhill, *Pears Encyclopaedia of Myths and Legends* (London: Pelham Books, 1978), 100.

13. Hartley Burr Alexander, *Latin American Mythology*, vol. 11 of *The Mythology of All Races*, ed. L. H. Gray and G. F. Moore, 13 vols. (Boston: Marshall Jones, 1916–1933), 71–2.

14. John Ferguson and Masaharu Anesaki, *Japanese Mythology*, vol. 8 of Gray and Moore, *Mythology of All Races*, 229–230.

15. J. Hackin et al., *Asiatic Mythology* (1932; reprint, New York: Thomas Y. Crowell, 1963), 130–131.

16. For a general historical background and sources, see H. R. Ellis Davidson, *Scandinavian Mythology* (London: Paul Hamlyn, 1969). See also John Arnott Macculloch, *Eddic Mythology* vol. 2 of Gray and Moore, *Mythology of All Races*; and Kevin Holland, *The Norse Myths* (New York: Pantheon Books, 1980). Holland's primary sources are *Saxo Grammaticus*, the Latin work of a twelfth-century ecclesiastical authority who is critical of these "heathens"; the *Prose Edda*, of the Icelandic thirteenth-century poet and historian Snorri Sturluson, who offers a poetic and sympathetic rendering of the myths; the *Codex Regius*, a manuscript written in the thirteenth century and found in an Icelandic farmhouse in the seventeenth century. The information in the following paragraphs is drawn largely from Holland's account.

17. Holland, *Norse Myths*, xxxii.

18. Georgia Dunham Kelchner, *Dreams in Old Norse Literature and Their Affinities in Folklore* (Cambridge: Cambridge University Press, 1935), 40. In one instance, an elf woman directs a dejected shepherd boy to a wishing stone; another elf woman helps searchers, through a dream, to find a boy under a cliff.

19. Robb Walsh and David Wenzel, *Kingdom of the Dwarfs* (New York: Centaur Books, 1980).

20. Jacob Grimm, "Wights and Elves," in *Teutonic Mythology* (1883; reprint in 2 vols., New York: Dover, 1966), vol. 2, 439.

21. Ibid., 444. They may be called *Erdmannlein* or *Erdmanneken* in Germany, *Hardmandle* in Switzerland, and *underjordiske* in Denmark, all in recognition of their connection with the earth. They are also called dwarfs, brownies, kobolds, gnomes, and trolls.

22. Walter Kafton-Minkel, *Subterranean Worlds: 100 years of Dragons, Dwarfs, the Dead, Lost Races, and UFO's from inside the Earth* (Port-Townsend, Wash.: Loompanics Unlimited, 1989), 31–39. The light elves are the English elves or fairies, the Irish *sidhe* or gentry, the Scottish *sith*, the French *fées*, and the korrigans of Brittany. For other terms, see Grimm, "Wights and Elves, 456.

23. Kafton-Minkel, *Subterranean Worlds,* 30–31.

24. For a detailed account of Oberon's origins and alternate forms, see Claude Lecouteux, *Les nains et les elfes au Moyen Age* (Paris: Editions Imago, 1988)

25. The French tales are *Huon de Bordeaux* (1220–1260) and *Roman d'Auberon* (1260–1311). Claude Lecouteux, a French expert in the mediaeval period, proclaims that Oberon is the dwarf granted the most powers in Western literature.

26. *Beowulf: A Verse Translation,* trans. Michael J. Alexander (New York: Viking, 1973).

27. The word for *nightmare* is still *Alpdruck* (elf force) or *Alptraum* (dwarf dream). The English expression "Go to the deuce" has its origin in the vulgate *duse,* meaning *dwarf.* In Old English, a word for *insane* is *ylfig* (elfish); and *epileptic* is translated as *dveorg* (dwarf).

28. Paul Radin, *The World of Primitive Man* (New York: E. P. Dutton, 1971), 3.

29. Marie-Louise Von Franz, *Patterns of Creativity Mirrored in Creation Myths* (Dallas: Spring, 1972), 170–187.

30. Georges McHargues, *The Impossible People: A History Natural and Unnatural of Beings Terrible and Wonderful* (New York: Holt, Rinehart and Winston, 1972), 47–73.

31. Ibid.

32. Wolfram Eberhard , ed., *Folktales of China* (Chicago: University of Chicago Press, 1965), 93–95.

33. Alice Werner, *African Myths,* vol. 3 of Gray and Moore, *Mythology of All Races,* 259–226.

34. Tim Appenzeller, ed., *Dwarfs: The Enchanted World* (Alexandria, Va.: Time-Life Books, 1985).

35. Katherine Luomala, "Menehunes, the Little People," in *Voices on the Wind: Polynesian Myths and Chants* (Honolulu: Bishop Museum Press, 1986), 123–136.

36. Displayed at the Abbe Museum of Stone Age Antiquities, in Acadia National Park, Maine.

37. John Witthoft, "The American Indian as Hunter," *Pennsylvania Historical and Museum Commission Reports in Anthropology* 6 (1953).

38. "Little-Man-with-Hair-All-Over," in *American Indian Myths and Legends,* ed. Richard Erdoes and Alfonso Ortiz (New York: Pantheon Books, 1984), 185–191. The following quotations are from these pages.

39. For an overview of dwarfs in legends across cultures, see Gray and Moore, *Mythology of all Races*; Ruth Manning-Sanders, *The Book of Dwarfs* (New York: E. P. Dutton, 1969); *The Complete Grimm's Fairy Tales,* introduction by Padraic Colum, folklorist commentary by Joseph Campbell (New York: Pantheon Books, 1972); John Bierhorst, *The Deetkatoo: Native American Stories about Little People* (New York: William Morrow, 1998).

40. George Hans Heide, "Dwarfs in German Folk Legend: An Inquiry into the Human Quality of These Creatures" (Ph.D. diss., University of California, Los Angeles, 1976), viii.

41. Ibid., 218.

42. Lazare Saineanu, "Les géants et les nains: D'après le traditions roumains et balkaniques." *Revue des Traditions Populaire* 14 (1901): 304–310.

43. Ibid., 310.

44. Junko Morimoto, *The Inch Boy* (New York: Viking Kestrel, 1986).

45. Josef Neumann, "Der Zwerg in Sage und Märchen: Ursache oder Abbild der Missgestalt des Menschen?" *Gesnerus* 43 (1986): 223–240. Neumann credits these ideas to Adelbert Kuhn, in *Mythologische Studien* (Frankfurt am Main, 1902).

46. Frederic Ahl, *Metaformations: Soundplay and Wordplay in Ovid and Other Classical Poets* (London: Cornell University Press, 1985).

47. William Hanff, *The Dwarf Nose* (New York: North-South Books), 1994.

48. Eugen Swartz, quoted in Neumann, "Der Zwerg," 237.

Chapter 5. Anthropology

1. Homer, *Iliad,* trans. Alexander Pope (Norwalk, Conn.: Easton Press, 1979), book 3, line 48.

2. Frank Spencer, *Ecce Homo: An Annotated Bibliographic History of Physical Anthropology* (New York: Greenwood Press, 1986), 11.

3. These are the measurements of Gul Muhammed, who was examined in New Delhi in 1990 and

found to be the world's shortest man, and Pauline Muster (1876–1895), the world's shortest woman, as reported in *Guinness World Records* for 2002.

4. Jared Diamond, "Why Pygmies Are Small," *Nature* 354 (1991): 11.

5. Pliny (first century C.E.) placed the Pygmaei Spithamaei in India, following an earlier description by Ctesias (fourth century B.C.E.) about black men called Pygmies, who were described as a cross between apes and humans and as a cubit and a half tall. For Pliny reference, see H. Rieschbieth and A. Barrington, "Dwarfism," in *Treasury of Humans Inheritance* (London: University of London, Francis Galton Laboratory for Human Genetics, 1912), vol. 1, 355. For Ctesias, see Bertram C. Windle, introduction to Edward Tyson, *A Philological Essay Concerning the Pygmies of the Ancients* (1699; reprint, London: David Nutt in the Strands, 1894), 42. See also the compilation of Mandeville, who traveled in Asia and Africa between 1322 and 1356 and combined his own experiences, those of previous travelers, and a liberal dose of invention. He described men and women three spans long, served by giants, who lived only six or seven years. John Mandeville, *Mandeville's Travels,* edited by M. C. Seymour (London: Clarendon Press of Oxford University Press, 1967), 152.

6. Samuel Purchas, *Haklutus Postumus; or, Purchas His Pilgrims* (Glasgow: James MacLehose and Sons, 1906), vol. 13, 513.

7. Spencer, *Ecce Homo,* 84.

8. Tyson, *Philological Essay,* 99.

9. R. G. Haliburton, *Survivals of Prehistoric Races in Mount Atlas and the Pyrenees: Memoir Delivered to the 10th Session of the International Congress of Orientalists* (Lisbon: National Printing Office, 1892), 1, 5.

10. Rischbieth and Barrington, "Dwarfism," n. 6.

11. Harold Crichton-Browne, "Dwarfs and Dwarf Worship," *Nature* 45 (1892): 269–271.

12. Windle, introduction to Tyson, *Philological Essay.* Among the groups mentioned by Windle are the Mincopies of the Adamon Islands; the Aetas of Luzon; the Karons of New Guinea; short-statured populations in India, Borneo, and Ceylon; the Wambutti Congo pygmies; and the Bushmen of South Africa. He examines links between contemporary dwarf populations and those mentioned by philosophers and travelers. See especially 1, 36, 104.

13. Juan Comas, *Pygmeos en America?* Publicaciones del Instituto de Historica (Universidad Nacional Autonoma de Mexico, Mexico), ser. 1, no. 58 (1960). Comas discusses conflicting evidence about the existence of pygmies in South America and concludes that there are aboriginal tribes in northwest South America where males range in height from 150 to 159 cm and females from 140 to 148 cm.

14. Joseph Birdsell, *Human Evolution: An Introduction to the New Physical Anthropology* (New York: Random House, 1972), 461.

15. Diamond, "Why Pygmies Are Small," 11.

16. Ruth Clark, "Band of Little People—Only Two Feet Tall—Attack Explorers," *Weekly World News,"* 21 February 1989. Because the article strained credulity, I wrote to the University of Budapest to determine whether the article may have represented a distortion of an article that originated in Hungary. The chair of the anthropology department reported that he was unable to find a Professor Adony or Stefan Miklos at his university or elsewhere. Not surprisingly, neither Ruth Clark, the article's author, nor the editor of the *Weekly World News* responded. The modern mythmakers in Lantana, Florida (the home of this tabloid), who dream up such tales do not want interlopers spoiling their fun.

17. "The World's Smallest Man," *Weekly World News,* 10 July 1990.

18. Pliny, *Natural History,* quoted by Spencer, *Ecce Homo,* 25.

19. George M. Gould and Walter L. Pyle, *Anomalies and Curiosities of Medicine* (Philadelphia: W. B. Saunders, 1896; reprint, New York: Bell, 1956), 324.

20. Elizabeth Andrews, "Traditions of Dwarf Races in Ireland and Switzerland," *Antiquary* 45 (1909): 369–375. This is one of many articles that explain fairy traditions by positing an ancient dwarf people, the Pechts (or Picts). See also Cyril Dieckhoff, "The Position of the Iberians and the Dwarfish Races in the Ethnology of the British Isles," *Transactions of the Inverness Scientific Society* 9 (1918–1925): 83–109. For another review of the supposed continuity between present dwarf races and prehistoric pygmies, see D. Gath Whitley, "Present Day Dwarf Races and Prehistoric Pigmies," *London Quarterly Review* 12 (1902): 139–152.

21. Martin Monestier, *Les nains: Des hommes différentes* (Paris: Jean-Claude Simeon, 1977), 35. Monestier's major sources are Professor Julius Kollman and Professors Antonin Poncet and René Leriche. Their

work contains flawed scholarship and wild deductive leaps. Poncet and Leriche assert that the existence of pygmies in France is well established by skeletal evidence; that ethnic dwarfs can be distinguished through X-ray evidence; and that dwarfs still exist whose anatomy is a replica of ancient pygmies, who ruled the world. The German scholar, Kollman, makes similar claims, offering photographs of skulls and other bones of both smaller and larger individuals from several continents and providing inaccurate maps of stature. This same Kollman advocated the hypothesis of an Aryan race, which was later employed by Nazi theoreticians. Poncet and Leriche, citing the excavations of Kollman in Switzerland and Léonce Manouvrier in France, argue that dwarfs have existed since Neolithic times.

22. Antonin Poncet and René Leriche, "Nains d'aujord' hui et nains d'autrefois," *Revue Scientifique* 20, ser. 4 (1903): 587–593. The article was translated from the French by Nura Osman.

23. Monestier, *Nains,* 36. Monestier seems to accept the evidence of these investigators (referred to only by their last names, Nuesch and Guttman) as authentic.

24. William A. Horton, Robert Macchiarelli, and Margherita Mussi, "Dwarfism in an Adolescent from the Italian Late Upper Paleolithic," *Nature* 330, no. 5 (1988): nn. 16–18.

25. C. E. Snow ("Two Prehistoric Indian Dwarf Skeletons," Alabama Museum Paper no. 21 [1943]) found the skeletons during two separate excavations, one in 1934 and the other in 1939. One was male, the other female. I have not found any later evaluation of these important remains.

26. Neil M. Huber, "The Problem of Stature Increase," in *The Skeletal Biology of Earlier Human Populations,* ed. Don R. Brothwell (Oxford: Pergamon Press, 1968), 67–102.

27. Early in the twentieth century, papers were published in *Antiquary* and in the *Transactions of the Inverness Scientific Society* that attempt to prove that in the British Isles, Switzerland, and Lapland dwarf races existed. The existence of low earth houses, which supposedly could only have been inhabited by extremely short-statured people, was cited as evidence. In a more far-fetched example of conjecture, a 1919 presentation to the Inverness Society, a Father Cyril Dieckoff quotes an introduction to a collection of West Highland tales to demonstrate that fairies and Laplanders resemble each other and once lived side by side.

28. Humphrey Carpenter, review of *Family Memories* by Rebecca West, *New York Times Book Review,* 31 July 1988, 26. Carpenter wrote that the Picts "were, if anybody does not know it, the dwarfish primitive people which inhabited Scotland until the advent of the Celts." In a subsequent letter to the editor, Donald Souden challenged this statement, noting that it was only because the Picts left behind small, dark, and mysterious structures that they themselves were assumed to be small, dark, and mysterious. "Whatever they may have been, they were most assuredly not dwarfs" (letter to the editor, *New York Times Book Review,* 18 September 1988, 52).

29. Isabel Henderson, *The Picts* (New York: Praeger, 1967). Henderson dismisses "evidence" that the Picts lived in tiny earth dwellings. In fact, the *souterrains,* or earth houses, the majority or which were built in the second and third century B.C.E., varied in size. Some larger ones may have been used for dwellings, but the truly small ones were likely used for cattle shelters, storage, or sepulchers, for which cavelike structures have typically served.

30. Donald Johanson and Martland A. Edey, *Lucy: The Beginnings of Humankind* (New York: Simon and Schuster, 1981).

31. Stephen J. Gould, "This View of Life: Honorable Men and Women," *Natural History* 97, no. 3 (1988): 18.

32. See Robert C. Bailey, "The Comparative Growth of Efe Pygmies and African Farmers from Birth to Age Five Years," *Annals of Human Biology* 18 (1991): 113–120.

33. Frayer was helpful in providing his original slide of the Romito dwarf skeleton and an article that described his research odyssey (Roger Martin, "Dwarf Star," *Explore,* Summer 1988, 11–15).

34. David W. Frayer et al., "Dwarfism in an Adolescent from the Italian Late Upper Palaeolithic," *Nature* 330, no. 5 (1988): 60–62; John Horgan, "Paleolithic Compassion," *Scientific American* 258 (1988): 17, 20.

35. W. A. Horton, "Evolution of the Bone Dysplasia Family," *American Journal of Medical Genetics* 63 (1996): 4–6.

Chapter 6. Medical Aspects

1. The material in this chapter is discussed in much greater detail in my *Dwarfism: Medical and Psychosocial Aspects of Profound Short Stature* (Baltimore: Johns Hopkins University Press, in press).

2. George M. Gould and Walter L. Pyle, *Anomalies and Curiosities of Medicine* (Philadelphia: W. B. Saunders, 1896; reprint, New York: Bell, 1956).

3. Gould and Pyle, *Anomalies,* 337.

4. Theophilis Parvin, "The Influence of Maternal Impression upon the Foetus," *International Medical Magazine* 1 (1983): 487–493. Ninety similar cases attesting to maternal impression were published in reputable medical journals between 1853 and 1886. See Josef Warkany, *Congenital Malformations* (Chicago: Yearbook Medical Publishers, 1971), 12–14.

5. Robert B. Duthee and George Bentley, *Mercer's Orthopedic Surgery,* 8th ed. (London: Edw. Arnold, 1983), 207.

6. "Transactions of the Obstetrical Society of Philadelphia," *American Journal of Obstetrics,* October 1879, 766–770.

7. James G. Gamble, "Charles Dickens: His Quaint Little 'Person of the House' and the English Disease," *Pharos* 59, no. 4 (1996): 24–28.

8. C. S. Pandav and K. Anand, "Toward the Elimination of Iodine Deficiency Disorders in India," *Indian Journal of Pediatrics* 62, no. 5 (1995): 545–55.

9. Jim Yardley, "Stunted by Illness, Tibetan Villagers Ponder Flight," *New York Times,* 29 September 2003, A8.

10. M. M. Grumbach, B. S. Bin-Abbas, and S. L. Kaplan, "The Growth Hormone Cascade: Progress and Long-Term Results of Growth Hormone Treatment in Growth Hormone Deficiency," *Hormone Research* 49, supp. 2 (1998): 41–57.

11. R. M. Pauli, et al., "Apnea and Sudden Unexpected Death in Infants with Achondroplasia," *Journal of Pediatrics* 104, no. 3 (1984): 342–348.

12. Sandy Clark, "My Story," http://www.gisselmann.dk/Websites/website_story-02.htm.

13. Dr. Kopits, an orthopedist who was greatly admired in the dwarfism community, died in July 2002. Research using statistics and videos he assembled during his years at Johns Hopkins and St. Joseph's Hospital is being prepared for publication; details can be obtained from the *Little People's Research Fund* in Towson, Maryland.

14. International Skeletal Dysplasia Registry, www.csmc.edu/genetics/skeldys/default.html.

15. Susan Lawrence, "Solving Big Problems for Little People," *Journal of the American Medical Association* 250, no. 3 (1983): 323, 328–330.

16. Patricia Callahan and Leila Aboud, "A New Boost for the Vertically Challenged," *Wall Street Journal,* 11 June 2003, D1.

17. For a brief account, see University of Maryland Medicine, "Maryland Center for Limb Lengthening and Reconstruction," 1–2, http://www.umm.edu/mcllr. The method was devised in 1951 by Gavril Abramovich Ilizarov in the small industrial city of Kurgan in Siberia. It has been estimated that more than a million patients have been treated using his methods—most of them not dwarfs, but individuals with congenital limb deformities or bones severed or crushed in accidents. Most of the surgeries have involved pinning a fixator—a metal framework that runs the length of the section being stretched—onto the bone and stretching them daily over a period of months or years. Newer, less painful procedures are currently being developed. At first limb lengthening was performed mainly on teenagers and even children; now it is sometimes offered as late as young adulthood. The surgeries can cost between $80,000 and $130,000 and are sometimes covered by insurance.

18. Michael Winerip, "Enduring Agony, a Boy's Made Taller," *New York Times,* 30 December 1986, B1.

19. For greater detail, see R. Gross, "Leg-Lengthening," *Lancet,* no. 9190 (1999): 1574–1575; A. J. Herbert, J. E. Hertzenberg, and D. Paley, "A Review for Pediatricians on Limb Lengthening and the Ilizarov Method," *Current Opinion in Pediatrics* 7, no. 1 (1995): 98–105. For a discussion of outcomes and complications in European patients, see R. Aldegheri and C. Dall'Oca, "Limb-Lengthening in Short-Stature Patients" *Journal of Pediatric Orthopedics B* 10, no. 3 (2001): 238–4.

20. This procedure, with variations, has become much more common in the United States, notably at Paley's Maryland Center. Dr. Mark Dahl at the Minneapolis Limb Lengthening Center and Dr. C.

Robert Rozbruch at New York's Hospital for Special Surgery are two other physicians with expertise in this procedure. A small number of patients have been treated successfully with the Villerubias method at the Cedars-Sinai Medical Center in Los Angeles. Botched surgeries by individual doctors who are not based at major centers have been reported.

21. Herbert, Herzenberg, and Paley, in "A Review for Pediatricians," reported that there had been very few patients with permanent sequelae, and a growing number of accounts note patient satisfaction with the procedure.

22. D. Rimoin, "Extended Leg Lengthening," *LPA Today,* January–February 1991, 7–8. After studying the work of Villarubias in Barcelona, Rimoin concluded that the Villarubias method was the most benign, least painful, and most helpful in reducing the problems of the back and spine. See also "Experimental Surgery Helps Dwarfs Stand Tall," http://www.mahidol.ac.th/mahidol/sc/sclg/exper.htm.

23. Limb lengthening was predominantly adopted in countries where beauty was a central concern (Italy) and where the procedures were paid for by the government (Denmark) and to some degree in England, where it was viewed less negatively than in the United States.

24. When Heather Whitestone, Miss America in 1995 and an important representative of the deaf and hard of hearing community, underwent cochlear implant surgery, many in that community took a critical view of her decision.

25. *NORD Orphan Disease Update,* Summer 2000, 3.

26. P. Modaff, V. K. Horton and R. M. Pauli, "Errors in the Prenatal Diagnosis of Children with Achondroplasia," *Prenatal Diagnosis* 16, no. 6 (1996): 525–30.

27. "Doctors: Don't Want No Short People Round Here," *Dateline,* 7 May 2000, wysiwyg://31/http://pro-life.about.com/n...library/archives/news/aa070500news.htm. Support was 100 percent for abortion at thirteen weeks. It fell to 14 percent at twenty-four weeks, but remarkably, 70 percent of geneticists and obstetricians who specialize in obstetrical ultrasound thought abortion should be available at twenty-four weeks if dwarfism is diagnosed. (The physicians were commenting on availability, not necessarily on whether abortion should be done, but their responses were assumed by many to be associated with a negative view of dwarfism.)

28. See Erik Parens and Adrienne Asch, eds., *Prenatal Testing and Disability Rights.* (Washington, D.C.: Hasting Center Studies in Ethics, Georgetown University Press, 2000).

29. For a survey of the genome enterprise and the questions it raises, see "Now the Hard Part: Putting the Genome to Work," *New York Times,* 27 June 2000, F1–8.

30. "Gene Therapy: What and Why," *March of Dimes Research Annual Report,* 1997–1998, www.modimes.org/research2/Research AnnReport/genetherapy.htm.

31. *LPA Today,* July–October 1998, 38. Since 1998, a number of items have appeared about research being done at the Weitzmann Institute in Israel in the laboratory of David Givol, who is studying dwarf mice that share many features with human counterparts. Prochon Biotech is a privately owned Israeli biotechnology company founded in 1997 with the aim of finding a "cure" for achondroplasia. For updates about developments in this area, see EntrezPubMed (www.ncbi.nlm.nih.gov/entrez/query.fcgi) and other online sources.

32. For deeper discussion, see the chapter on psychology in my *Dwarfism.*

33. Geneticist Jessica Davis and pediatric surgeon Cathleen Raggio became its codirectors. The founding of the center was supported by the hospital administration; Alan Greenberg, a private benefactor; and local dwarfism groups.

Chapter 7. Art

1. Alfred Enderle, Dietrich Meyerhöfer, and Gerd Unverfehrt, *Small People—Great Art,* trans. Karen Williams (Hamm, Germany: Artcolor Verlag, 1994).

2. H. Rischbieth and A. Barrington, "Dwarfism," in *A Treasury of Human Inheritance* (London: University of London: Francis Galton Laboratory of Human Eugenics, 1912) vol. 1, 355–573.

3. See Jean Martin Charcot and Paul Richer, *Les difformes et les malades dans l'art* (Paris: Lecrosnier et Babe, 1889); Erica Tietze-Conrat, *Dwarfs and Jesters in Art,* trans. Elizabeth Olson (Phaidon 1957); J. Kunze and I. Nippert, *Genetics and Malformations in Art* (Berlin: Grosse Verlag, 1986); Hansel Volken

and Diether Kramer, eds., *Die Zwerge kommen!* (Trautenfels, Austria: Verein Schloss Trautenfels, 1993).

4. Wolfgang Born, "Monsters in Art," *Ciba Symposium* 8 (1947): 686.

5. Ibid.

6. Veronique Dasen, *Dwarfs in Ancient Egypt and Greece* (Oxford: Oxford University Press, 1993).

7. Jon M. White, *Everyday Life in Ancient Egypt* (New York: Putnam, 1963; reprint, New York: Peter Bedrick Books, 1991), 169.

8. William Smith, *A History of Egyptian Sculpture and Painting in the Old Kingdom,* 2d ed. (London: Oxford University Press, 1948), 57.

9. Werner Forman and Bedrich Forman, *Egyptian Art* (London: Peter Nevill, 1962), 49.

10. Dasen, *Dwarfs in Ancient Egypt and Greece,* plate 44b and pp. 221, 229–30, 233–34.

11. Ibid., plate 51 and p. 244.

12. Michael Garmaise, "Studies in the Representation of Dwarfs in Hellenistic and Roman Art (Greece, Egypt)" (Ph.D. diss., McMaster University, Canada, 1996).

13. Ibid., 2. For mosaic panels D, E, and ii, see 234 and 235.

14. E. Adamson Hoebel, *Anthropology: The Study of Man,* 4th ed. (New York: McGraw-Hill, 1972), 365.

15. P. Huard, Z. Ohya, and M. Wong, *La médecine japonaise des origines à nos jours* (Paris: Roger Dacosta, 1974).

16. Tietze-Conrat, *Dwarfs and Jesters in Art,* 10, 86.

17. An "unusual Tang dynasty model of a dwarf," was advertised in July 1999 on the Trocadero Web site by the Dah Wey Gallery of Bethesda, Maryland. Online offerings of Chinese and Pre-Colombian dwarf images are not uncommon.

18. Tietze-Conrat, *Dwarfs and Jesters in Art,* 86.

19. Dagny Carter, *Four Thousand Years of China's Art* (New York: Ronald Press, 1948), 78–79.

20. "The Fall of the Silk Road," in *The Silk Road,* http://china.pages.com.cn/chinese_culture/silk/fall.html.

21. Sherman Lee, *A History of Far Eastern Art,* 5th ed. (New York: Harry N. Abrams, 1994), 308.

22. Devaprasad Ghosh, "The Development of Buddhist Art in South India," *Indian Historical Quarterly* 4, no. 4 (1928): 727; available at http://pears2.lib.ohio-state.edu/FULLTEXT?JR-ENG/gho.htm.

23. Enderle, Meyerhöfer, and Unverfehrt, *Small People—Great Art,* 78.

24. Professor Tao Jie to the author, e-mail, 19 June 2003.

25. Enderle, Meyerhöfer, and Unverfehrt, *Small People—Great Art,* 76.

26. T.V.G. Sastri, "Dwarfs from Samalaji in Baroda Museum," *Picture Gallery Bulletin* (Baroda India Museum, Baroda, India) 15 (1962): 21–29 and plates 18, 19.

27. Alain Danielson, *The Myths and Gods of India* (Rochester, Vt.: Inner Traditions International, 1991), 169, 170.

28. See Jane Turner, ed., *The Dictionary of Art* (London: Macmillan; Grove Dictionaries, 1996), s.v. "Deori Kalan." The oldest example of an Indian temple dedicated to Vishnu in the form of Vamana is a ruined fifth-century temple at Deori Kalan in Madhya Pradesh.

29. Turner, *Dictionary of Art,* s.v. "Nepal: Sculpture before c. AD 800"; "Stupa: Sri Lanka"; "Sri Lanka: Other arts: Terracotta." For further information about original sources, see "Indian subcontinent: Sculpture, 4th–6th centuries AD, Late phase in central India and high phase in central India"; "Indian subcontinent: Sculpture: 2nd–1st century BC: South"; "Namakkal"; "Karle."

30. Linda Schele, *Hidden Faces of the Mayas* (Poway, Calif.: ALTI; Impetus Comunicacion S.A de C. V., 1997).

31. Ibid., 150–161.

32. Gillet G. Griffin, Robert Stroessner, and Marlene Chambers, *Little People of the Earth: Ceramic Figures from Ancient America* (Denver: Denver Art Museum), 1990.

33. Carolyn Tate and Gordon Bendersky, "Olmec Sculpture of the Human Fetus," *Perspectives in Biology and Medicine* 42 (1999). See also "What the Olmecs Knew," *U.S. News,* http://www.usnews.com/us-news/issue/970623/23out.htm.

34. William L. Hommel, *Art of the Mende* (College Park, Md.: University of Maryland Art Gallery, 1974); "Form and Meaning of Masks in Three Mende Societies" (Ph.D. diss., Indiana University, 1981).

35. Enderle, Meyerhöfer, and Unverfehrt, *Small People—Great Art,* 70–75.

36. Ibid., 132.

37. Michael Levey, *Giambattista Tiepolo: His Life and Art* (New Haven: Yale University Press, 1986), 1.

38. Charcot and Richer, *Les difformes et les malades dans l'art,* 32–33.

39. Dale Brown, *The World of Velázquez* (New York: Time-Life Books, 1969), 120.

40. Jonathan Brown, *Velázquez: A Painter and Courtier* (New Haven: Yale University Press, 1986), 174.

41. J. P. Dominguez, "El buffon don Sebastian de Morra," *Journal of the American Medical Association* 261, no. 5 (1989): 671.

42. Enderle, Meyerhöfer, and Unverfehrt, *Small People—Great Art,* 199–200.

43. J. P. Dominguez, "El niño de Vallades [Francisco Lezcano]," *Journal of the American Medical Association* 261, no. 4 (1989): 496. It is not uncommon for ostensibly well-intentioned writers and critics to use phrases like "unfortunate creatures" when speaking of dwarfs, if only to follow by softening the description.

44. For an analysis of this painting, see Elizabeth Du Gue Trapier, *Velázquez* (New York: Hispanic Society of America, 1948), 338–342.

45. Edouard Garnier, *Les nains et les géants* (Paris: Librarie Hatchette, 1884), 113.

46. Tietze-Conrat, *Dwarfs and Jesters in Art,* 17, 20, 90, 92, 93.

47. Rischbieth and Barrington, "Dwarfs," 460–461.

48. Daniel Howard, *The World of Jacques Callot* (New York: Lear, 1948), 20.

49. Wilhelm Fraeger, ed., *Callotto Resuscitato; or, Callot's Neueigerichtetes Zwergenkabinett* (1622; E. Rentsch: Erlenbach, Switzerland, 1921). This work contains fifty engravings of odd dwarf characters in different situations.

50. "The War of the Garden Dwarfs," *Fortune,* 20 February 1995, 17.

51. "Garden Gnomes Dominate the Art Market," *Economist,* 13 November 1997; available at http://www.expresindia.com/fe/daily/19971113/31755803.html.

52. After visiting and photographing the garden dwarfs, I corresponded with Linda McKee, director of Museum Library Services, inquiring about their origins. In October 2001, she sent me a folder containing unpublished letters, documentation of oral history, and museum brochures. Provenance was uncertain, except for the fact that John Ringling had purchased them in Italy and they resembled dwarf statuary at the Villa Valmarana, Vicenza. At first scattered around the grounds, these Callot-like figures were later reorganized into a dwarf walk, landscaped to resemble a d'Este villa.

53. Enderle, Meyerhöfer, and Unverfehrt, *Small People—Great Art,* 232–233.

54. Nancy Bruett, telephone and correspondence, 18 August 1999–28 September 2001.

55. J. Murdoch and V. J. Murrell, "The Monogrammist DG: Dwarf Gibson and His Patrons," *Burlington Magazine* 123, no. 938 (1981): 282–289.

56. Horace Walpole, *Anecdotes of Painting in England* (London: Henry G. Bohn, 1849), vol. 2, 533–535.

57. George C. Williams, ed., *Bryan's Dictionary of Painters and Engravers* (New York: Macmillan, 1903), vol. 2, 238.

58. Turner, *Dictionary of Art,* s.v. "Gibson, Richard."

59. Murdoch and Murrell, "Monogrammist DG," 287.

60. Turner, *Dictionary of Art,* s.v. "Gibson, Richard."

61. In a 1681, for example, he initiated a court case to resolve the matrimonial problems of his daughter, Anna. Daphne Forbett, *Miniatures: Dictionary and Guide* (Suffolk, England: Antique Collectors Club., 1987), 547.

62. Lillian Langseth-Christensen, "The Amalienberg: A Perfect Pavilion," *Gourmet Magazine,* November 1976, 38–112.

63. Alaistair Lang questions whether Cuvilliès was a dwarf ("Palace Architecture in the Empire," in *Baroque and Rococo: Architecture and Decoration,* ed. Anthony Blunt [New York: Harper and Row, 1978], 281–287); he is referred to as a dwarf in Turner, *Dictionary of Art,* s.v. "Cuvilliès, (Jean) François (Vincent Joseph) de I."

64. Henry Channon, "The Frenchman, Cuvilliès," in *The Ludwigs of Bavaria* (London: Methuen, 1933), 226–234.

65. Turner, *Dictionary of Art,* s.v. "Cuvilliès, (Jean) François (Vincent Joseph) de I."

66. "Who's Who in Architecture from 1400 to the Present," vol. 1, 78–79.

67. One notable exception is Wolfgang Braunfels, *François Cuvilliès* (Munich: Suddeutscher Verlag, 1986). Most biographical accounts are in German or French.

68. Channon, "The Frenchman, Cuvilliès," 226–34.

69. Langseth Christenson, in "The Amalienburg," describes the interior, whose rooms contain imitation Delft paneling, an octagonal hall of mirrors, blue gray walls with silver decoration and exquisite doors, and elaborate scenes depicting hunts, nymphs, birds, cornucopia, and sea spray. The kitchen is covered with glazed tiles made at the Rose factory in Delft under Cuvilliès's supervision.

70. Garnier, *Les nains et les géants,* 238. My thanks to Aviva Breifel for translating this passage from the French.

71. Friedrich von Boetticher, *Maler Werke des neunzehnten Jahrhunderts* (Dresden, Germany: Boetticher's Verlag , 1891–1901; BOCO-Druck, 1969), vol. 1, s.v. "Lehnen, Jacob."

72. The two most comprehensive works in English are Marie Reimann-Reyer and Claude Keisch, eds. *Adolph Menzel: 1815–1905: Between Romanticism and Impressionism* (New Haven: Yale University Press, 1996) and Michael Fried, *Menzel's Realism: Art and Embodiment in Nineteenth-Century Berlin* (New Haven: Yale University Press, 2002).

73. Turner, *Dictionary of Art,* s.v. "Menzel, Adolph (Friedrich Erdman)."

74. Lucius Griesbach, "Moltke's Binoculars, Lena the Cook's Comb, and the Ink Pot on the Academy Table: Menzel's Eye for the Concrete," in *Prints and Drawings of Adolph Menzel,* ed. Lucius Griesbach, exh. cat. (Cambridge, England: Fitzwilliam) 8–10.

75. Enderle, Meyerhöfer, and Unverfehrt, *Small People—Great Art,* 294.

76. For an analysis of this painting, see Sigrid Achenbach and Ingeborg Becker, "Catalogue of Prints," in *Prints and Drawings of Adolph Menzel,* 190, fig. 131.

77. Gustav Kirstein, *Das Lebens Adolph Menzels* (Leipzig, Germany: EOT Seeman, 1919).

78. Russell, "The Truth of Feelings Joins the Truth of Fact," *New York Times,* 16 September 1990, H49.

79. Fried, *Menzel's Realism,* 5.

80. Jacques Lassaigne, *Lautrec: Biographical and Critical Studies,* trans. Stuart Gilbert (Cleveland: Albert Skira, World, 1953), 11, 13.

81. I am grateful to Nancy Bruett, who has written an unpublished novel in which a character is based on Lee, for this publicity brochure that Lee had used.

82. A clipping from the New York Public Library Art Division from *Art Digest,* 1 January 1947, has an advertisement for the show and a brief review from the *Herald Tribune* of 12 January 1947, n.p.

83. Provincetown Banner Staff, "History Highlights: Rosa Lee, World's Tiniest Portrait Painter," *Provincetown Banner,* 19 September, 2002, http://provincetownbanner.com/history/9/19/2002/1. They had a successful career as Les Petite Sisters, the world's smallest sister team, in vaudeville and nightclubs in the United States and Canada (ibid.).

84. For a reproduction of Erastus Salisbury Field's *Dwarf Boy in Red Dress Holding a Yellow Rattle* see "Important American Folk Art," *Antiques,* 127 (1985): 1249. The portrait (c. 1830) also appears in Mary Black, *Erastus Salisbury Field: 1805–1900* (Springfield, Mass: Museum of Fine Arts, 1984), plate 4. Although Black discusses Field's life and art, no mention is made of this painting.

85. John Russell, "Cézanne's Sketchbooks: Secrets and Surprises," *New York Times,* 13 March 1988, sec. 2, 1.

86. Critic Michael Gibson senses in the portrait Cézanne's strong identification with Emperaire's situation: "Emperaire, ten years older than Cézanne, had a dwarf's body and the fine head of a gentleman by Van Dyck. One may well imagine that Cézanne's large (6 ft. 6 in.) portrait—patterned on Ingres official icon of Napoleon I on the imperial throne—was also, in a sense, a melancholy image of the thirty-year-old Cézanne himself, who, with his tremendous, imperial urges, still felt powerless to accomplish" (Michael Gibson, "Cézanne: A Tenuous Triumph"; available as article 14934 in *The World and I,* June 1966, 1, http://www.worldandi.com/archive/arjune.htm.

87. Gerolamo Induno is a noted painter of historical themes, portraits, and landscapes. A political activist, he was implicated in the 1848 insurrection against Austrian rule. Induno's paintings are included in some of Italy's most important collections, and an exhibition of Induno and his circle was held in Rancate, Switzerland in 2002. He is little known in the United States.

88. H. R. Wiedemann, "Historical Case of Dwarfism: Attempted Diagnosis," *American Journal of Medical Genetics* 47(1993): 805–806.

89. Menzel's painting, however, showing him seated with others at a table, offers only a rear view of the artist.

90. The work is discussed in a catalog for an exhibition held in Rancato, Switzerland, in 2002. See Lucia Pini, "Gerolamo Induno, Sciancato che suona il mandolino, 1852," in *Intorno agli Induno: Pittura e*

sculptura tra genere e storia nel Canton Ticino, exh. cat. [Pinacoteca Cantonale Giovanni Zust, Rancate, Switzerland, 13 September–1 December 2002] (Milan, Italy: Skira Editore, 2002), 68.

91. Ibid. Both nineteenth-century critic Carlo Tenca and contemporary critic Lucia Pina, with slightly different emphases, seem to see the dwarf as an unhappy cripple, overcoming his environment through his music. The modern viewer may not necessarily assume that he is unhappy—and compensating for body or poverty—but simply captured at a happy moment, enjoying playing his music.

92. This work can be searched out in a hand-bound book published in 1926. See Michael Viladrich, *Work of the Artist in Eighty Four Engravings* (Buenos Aires: Caras y Caretas, 1926).

93. Cited by Dan Holm (curator at Pohjanmaan Museo, in Vasa, Finland), e-mail to the author, 26 June, 2003.

94. This image taken alone can been seen as an evocation of unrequited longing; Picasso drew a number of other figures in a similar relationship. See *Pablo Picasso: The Artist and His Model; 180 Drawings* (New York: Dover, 1994).

95. See Marilyn Kushner, *A Voice of Conscience: The Prints of Jack Levine,* unpublished label copy (New York: Brooklyn Museum, 1999); Kenneth W. Prescott and Emma Stina Prescott, *The Complete Graphic Works of Jack Levine* (New York: Dover, 1984), plates 18–20, 27.

96. These images are not readily available; I was able to view them in photocopies of Laurence B. Chollet, *Barks and Bite: The Paintings of Alan Loehle* (n.d.), which Bruce Johnson kindly sent me.

97. Ibid.

98. Alan Loehle, *"Walking Man," New American Paintings* 5, no. 3 (2000): 103–105.

99. Alfredo Triff, "Modern Wonders," *Miami New Times,* 19 October 2000, 1, http://www.miaminewtimes.com/issues/2000–10–19/art.html.

100. Kathryn Jacobi, "Artist Pages," *New Art Examiner,* December 1989, 38. Jacobi's Web site offers a more complete picture of her work (www.kathrynjacobi.com).

101. Kathryn Jacobi, e-mail to the author, 19 November 2001.

102. Mary Ellen Mark, *Indian Circus* (San Francisco: Chronicle Books, 1993), 11.

103. Ibid., 9.

104. Ibid., 13.

105. Bruce Davidson, *Bruce Davidson* (New York: Pantheon Books; Paris: Center National de la Photographie, 1986).

106. Bruce Davidson, *Bruce Davidson: Photographs* (New York: Agrinde/Summit Book, 1978), 6.

107. Bruce Johnson had seen a major show of Moriyama's in San Francisco in 1997 that included photographs of LPs. Several years later, Johnson succeeded in tracking down the 1967 article that includes the descriptions translated here. Moriyama was kind enough to grant permission for the use of this material.

108. Hiromichi Moriyama, "Actor," *Camera Mainiche Magazine,* no. 5 (1967). Translation by Glen Yamanoha.

109. André Kertész, *Kertész on Kertész* (New York: Abbeville Press, 1983), 99.

110. Robert Gurbo, curator of the Kertész estate, noted Kertész's method of waiting for a "photographic moment" (telephone conversation with the curator, 22 January 2004); Kertész's photographic approach often led him to remain at a site, anticipating an event that his intuition told him was about to unfold. Gurbo also noted that Kertész had photographed circus dwarfs—perhaps that is how the photographer knew the occupation of the dwarf benefactor.

111. Thomas Frederick Arndt, "Man on Bar," in *Men in America* (Washington, D.C.: National Museum of American Art, 1994), 21.

112. Alan Porter, "William Klein Apocalypse (Photographic Essay)," *Camera* (1981): 9.

113. Germano Celant, *Witkin* (Zurich: Scalo, 1995), 49.

114. Virginia Wageman, "Witkin Photographs Make a Provocative Show," *Honolulu Advertiser,* the.honoluluadvertiser.com./2001/Mar/04/islandlife.html.

115. Colin Westerbeck and Joel Meyerowitz, *Bystander: A History of Street Photography* (Boston: Little, Brown), 385; available at Wysuwyg://47/http://masters-of-photography.com/A/Arbus-articles3.html.

116. Diane Arbus, *Diane Arbus: An "Aperture" Monograph* (Millertown, N.Y.: Aperture, 1972), 1. This work was published in conjunction with a major exhibition at the Museum of Modern Art in New York.

117. Arthur Lubow, "Arbus Reconsidered," *New York Times,* 14 September 2003, 28–44, 63–69. A three-year traveling exhibition of Arbus's work opened in San Francisco on 25 October 2003; the catalog (Diane Arbus, *Diane Arbus Revelations* [New York: Random House, 2003]), containing two hundred full-page photographs, many never before published, includes essays by Doon Arbus, Sandra S. Phillips, et al. and excerpts from Arbus's autobiographical writings.

118. Doon Arbus and Marvin Israel, eds., *Diane Arbus: Magazine Work* (Millertown, N.Y: Aperture, 1984).

119. Arbus, *Diane Arbus,* 3;

120. Ibid., 291.

121. Ibid., 313. Notable among such photographers is Daniel Margulies, whose images appear in Joan Ablon, *Little People in America: The Social Dimensions of Dwarfism* (New York: Praeger, 1984); *Living with Difference: Families with Dwarf Children* (New York: Praeger, 1988); and Charles I. Scott et al., *Dwarfism: The Family and Professional Guide* (Irvine, Ca.: Short-Stature Foundation, 1994). Les Krims, for a time the official Little People of America photographer, published a set of sepia photographs of the 1971 convention.

122. Ingrid Bengis, introduction to *Women See Men,* ed. Yvonne Kalmus, Rikki Ripp, and Cheryl Wiesenfeld (New York: McGraw-Hill, 1977), 52–53.

123. George Dureau, *New Orleans: 50 Photographs* (London: GMP, 1985.) Unfortunately, this book is out of print.

124. Alice Hicks, "Images from Alain Gerard Clement and George Dureau," http://www.publicnews.com/issues/813/art.html.

125. Valerie Smith, "King of the Dwarfs: A Conversation with Milan Knizak," *Arts Magazine* 65, no. 9 (1991): 60–64.

126. There are ten thousand mentions of smurfs on the Internet. See, in particular, J. Marc Schmidt, "Sociopolitical Themes in the Smurfs," http://www.geocities.com/Hollywood/Cinema/3117/sociosmurfs2htm.

127. Jean Dobbs, in an article highlighting several professional artists, discusses the disadvantages of being labeled a "handicapped artist," as well as the controversy surrounding the organization Very Special Arts (VSA), which aims to increase self-esteem among young people and others with disabilities. See Jean Dobbs, "State of the Arts: Looking Beyond Labels," *New Mobility* 8, no. 47 (1997): 22–35; also at http://www.newmobility.com/review_article.cfm?id=3&action=browse. While efforts such as those of VSA are extremely important, they need to be distinguished from those of groups composed only of professional artists.

128. Bruce Johnson, telephone conversation with the author, 30 August 1999.

129. Leslye, a writer and gardener, has also served in LPA as vice president and its first director of development.

130. I first came upon some of Gil's photographs and reviews of his shows on the Internet in 1999. Gil and I became acquainted through e-mails, phone calls, and a meeting in New York in 2003.

131. Note, for example, two of the most famous of all portraits of female dwarfs, both titled *La Monstrua.* The youthful seventeenth-century court dwarf Eugenia Martinez Vallejo is painted by Juan Carreno de Miranda, who showed her both nude and in a red-and-white brocade dress. She is enormously obese, and her expression is sullen and guarded (Enderle, Meyerhöfer, and Unverfehrt, *Small People—Great Art,* 222–223).

132. See, among the articles and videos in which Gil has been profiled, Marcy Sheiner's "The Discreet Charm of a Dwarf," wysiwyg://5http://www.cando.com/cgi-bi…/cd- article.html?section=139&record=682.

133. Like Johnson, Gil had had an earlier marriage.

134. Ricardo Gil, telephone conversation, 21 September 1999.

135. *Corban Walker,* exh. cat. (Dublin: Dogbowl+Bones; Belfast: Nicholson and Bass, 1997), n.p.

136. Luke Clancy, "Corban Walker Green on Red Galleries," *Irish Times,* 23 October 1997, http://irishtimes.com/irish-times/paper/1997/1023/fea6.html.

137. Corban Walker, e-mail to the author, 6 January 2002.

138. See Fire Station Artists' Studio, www.firestation.ie.

139. Jacqueline Ann Clipsham, "Obstacles and Opportunities: Careers in the Visual Arts for People with Disabilities," paper presented at the National Forum on Careers in the Arts for People with Disabili-

ties, 14–16 June 1998, Kennedy Center for the Performing Arts, Washington, D.C; available at http://artsedge.kennedycenter.org/forum/papers/clipsham/html; also available at www.artslynx.org/heal/vis.htm. In 1986, at Johns Hopkins University, at a symposium for dwarfs, their families, and medical professionals, Clipsham spoke on the topic of dwarfs in art, and I spoke about dwarfs in literature. In 2001, I interviewed her at her home and studio in New Jersey.

140. Sam Fleming and Linda Dennis, *Certain Conditions*, exh. cat. [*Belfast + New York*, Belfast Waterfront Hall, Belfast, Ireland, 3–28 March 2003], (Belfast and New York: n.p, n.d), unpaginated.

141. Joel Selvin, *Photo Pass: The Rock and Roll Photography of Randy Bachman* (Berkeley, Calif.: SLG Books, 1994).

142. Rod Stringer, "Mark Gash Dies January 15 of Post-surgical Complications," *L.A. Weekly*, 21–27 January 2000; and in *Ebola Music*, http://www.ebolamusic.com/news/01.00/.

Chapter 8. Literature

1. *Stones from the River* was an Oprah's Book Club selection, guaranteeing its becoming a best seller.

2. Sir Thomas Malory, *Le Morte Darthur by Sir Thomas Malory*, ed. Charles R. Sanders and Charles E. Ward (New York: F. S. Crofts, 1940). For a good overview of the tradition, see the introduction.

3. Vernon J. Harward Jr., *The Dwarfs of Arthurian Romance and Celtic Tradition* (Leiden, Netherlands: E. J. Brill, 1958.

4. *Ysaie le Triste* (sometimes spelled *Isaie le Triste*) is a fifteenth-century French romance, originally published in 1522.

5. For an examination of the character of Troncq as symbolic of the human condition, see Barrington F. Beardsmore, "Ysaie Le Triste: An Analysis and a Study of the Role of the Dwarf, Troncq" (Ph.D. diss., University of British Columbia, 1969). Microfilm copy available from the National Library of Canada at Ottawa.

6. Oliver Goldsmith, *The Vicar of Wakefield* (1791; reprint, New York: Airmont, 1964), 67.

7. Alexander Pope, "Of a Dwarf Courting a Bright Lady," in John Dryden, *Poetical Miscellanies* (London: Jacob Tonson, 1709), 545–46.

8. Christopher Smart, "The Author Apologizes to a Lady for His Being a Little Man," in *The Collected Poems of Christopher Smart*, ed. Norman Callen (Cambridge: Harvard University Press, 1950), vol. 1, 112.

9. Johann Wolfgang von Goethe, *The New Melusina*, in *Selections: The Sorrows of Young Werther; The New Melusina; Novelle* (1774; reprint, New York: Holt, Rinehart and Winston, 1949), 143–167, 166.

10. See Monroe Stearns, *Goethe: Pattern of Genius* (New York: Franklin Watts, 1967).

11. Sir Walter Scott, *Tales of My Landlord: Old Mortality; The Black Dwarf; A Legend of Montrose; The Surgeon's Daughter* (1816; reprint, New York: John Wanamaker, 1917), xvi.

12. Benjamin Barker, *The Dwarf of the Channel or the Commodore's Daughter: A Nautical Romance of the Revolution* (Boston: Gleason's Publishing Hall, 1846).

13. Fergus Hume, "The Dwarf's Chamber," in *The Dwarf's Chamber and Other Stories* (London: Ward, Lock and Bowden, 1896).

14. William Shakespeare, *The Tragedy of Richard III*, in *The Yale Shakespeare*, ed. Jack R. Crawford (New Haven: Yale University Press, 1957), act 1, scene 1, lines 18–30.

15. James Rees, *The Dwarf, a Dramatic Poem* (New York: F. Saunders, 1839), 13.

16. George Darley, *Thomas à Becket: A Dramatic Chronicle* (London: Edward Moxon, 1840). For an analysis of this work, see Leslie Brisman, "George Darley: The Poet as Pigmy," *Studies in Romanticism*, 15 (Winter 1976): 119–141.

17. Charles Dickens, *The Old Curiosity Shop* (1841; reprint, New York: Oxford University Press, 1987), 42, 523.

18. Herman Hesse, "The Dwarf," in *The Fairy Tales of Herman Hesse* (1904; reprint, New York: Bantam Books, 1995), 1–26.

19. James G. Gamble, "Charles Dickens Gets a Lesson in Sensitivity: Mrs. Jane Seymour Hill's Reaction to David Copperfield," *Pharos* 61 (Summer 1998): 8–12.

20. My thanks to Dr. Gamble for his review of and comments on this chapter.

21. G. Storey and K. J. Fielding, *The Letters of Charles Dickens,* vol. 5 [1847–1849] (Oxford: Clarendon Press, 1981), 674–675.

22. Gamble, "Charles Dickens," 10.

23. Charles Dickens, *David Copperfield* (1849–1850; reprint, New York: Everyman's Library, Alfred A. Knopf, 1991), 461, 464–465.

24. Toby Olshin, "The Hawk's Eye: Dwarfs in the Works of Charles Dickens" (master's thesis, Adelphi University, 1967).

25. Gamble was convinced she had rickets; Olshin suggested spinal tuberculosis. See James G. Gamble, "Charles Dickens: His Quaint Little 'Person of the House' and the English Disease," *Pharos* 59 (Fall 1996): 24–28; Olshin, "The Hawk's Eye," 126 n. B.

26. Oscar Wilde, "The Birthday of the Infanta," in *The Complete Works of Oscar Wilde* (1889; reprint, with an introduction by Viviane Holland, New York: Harper and Row, 1989), 234–247, 247.

27. Edith Oliver, *Dwarf's Blood* (New York: Literary Guild, 1901).

28. Walter de la Mare, *Memoirs of a Midget* (New York: Alfred A. Knopf, 1922; reprint, with a foreword by Carl Van Doren, New York: Readers Club, 1941).

29. Storm Jameson, "Walter (John) de La Mare," 1922, quoted in *Twentieth Century Literary Criticism* (Detroit, Mich: Gale Research, 1981), vol. 4, 72.

30. Aldous Huxley, *Crome Yellow* (London: Chatto and Windus, 1923).

31. Francine Prose, *The Glorious Ones* (New York: Atheneum, 1974).

32. Barbara Jefferis, *The Tall One* (New York: Morrow, 1977).

33. Ruth Park, *Swords and Crowns and Rings* (New York: St. Martin's Press, 1978), 273.

34. Vesper Hunter, *Jacon* (Worcester, England: Square One, 1989).

35. Kathleen Robinson, *Dominic* (New York: St. Martin's Press, 1991).

36. George R. R. Martin, *A Game of Thrones* (New York: Bantam Books, 1996).

37. Ibid., 123.

38. David Madsen, *Memoirs of a Gnostic Dwarf* (Cambs., U.K.: Dedalus, 1995).

39. Chris Bunch, *The Empire Stone* (New York: Warner Books, 2000).

40. "Interview: Chris Bunch," http://www.twbookmark.com/authors/80/179/interview/7938.html.

41. Pär Lagerkvist, *The Dwarf,* trans. Alexandra Dick (1945; reprint, New York: Farrar, Strauss and Giroux, 1973); Elias Canetti, *Auto-da-Fé* (New York: Stern and Day, 1946).

42. Dorothy Canfield, quoted on back cover Lagerkvist, *The Dwarf.*

43. Lagerkvist, *Dwarf,* 28, 98.

44. George Herman, *A Comedy of Murders* (New York: Carroll and Graf, 1994).

45. Knut Hamsun, *Mysteries,* trans. Gerry Bothmer (1921; reprint, New York: Farrar, Strauss and Giroux, Condor, Souvenir Press, 1971).

46. Canetti, *Auto-da-Fé,* 176, 180.

47. Iris Murdoch, quoted on front cover of Canetti, *Auto-da-Fé.*

48. Jose Domoso, *The Obscene Bird of Night* (Boston: Non Pareil Books, 1970).

49. Ibid., 186.

50. Katherine Dunn, *Geek Love* (New York: Alfred A. Knopf, 1989).

51. See, for example, David Mitchell, "Modernist Freaks and Postmodern Geeks," in *The Disability Studies Reader,* ed. Lennard Davis (New York: Routledge, 1997), 348–365.

52. Carson McCullers, *The Ballad of the Sad Café* (Boston: Houghton Mifflin, 1951; New York: Bantam Books, 1964).

53. John Gardner, *In the Suicide Mountains* (New York: Alfred A. Knopf, 1977), 158.

54. J.R.R. Tolkien, *Lord of the Rings* (Boston: Houghton Mifflin, 1967). See also Tolkien, *The Annotated Hobbit: The Hobbit, or, There and Back Again,* introduction and notes by Douglas A. Andrew (Boston: Houghton Mifflin, 1988).

55. For a guide to identifying all the characters and categories of little people and for explication, see J.E.D. Tyler, *The New Tolkien Companion* (New York: St. Martin's Press, 1979).

56. Günter Grass, *The Tin Drum* (New York: Pantheon Books, 1962; reprint, New York: Crest, 1964); originally published as *Die Blechtrommel* (Darmstadt, Germany: Hermann Luchterhand, 1959).

57. H. Wayne Schow, "The Functional Complexity of Grass's Oskar," *Critique: Studies in Modern Fiction* 19, no. 3 (1978): 5–19.

58. Grass, *Tin Drum*, 423.

59. Ray Bradbury, *Something Wicked This Way Comes* (New York: Simon and Schuster, 1962; New York: Avon Books, 1998); Tama Janowitz, *A Cannibal in Manhattan* (New York: Crown, 1987); Martin Cruz Smith, *Gorky Park* (New York: Random House, 1981); Katherine Anne Porter, *Ship of Fools* (Boston: Little Brown, 1962). In the movie version of *Ship of Fools,* Michael Dunn, who plays the role of the dwarf character, transforms him, endowing him with dignity.

60. Lilli Palmer, *Night Music* (New York: Harper and Row, 1982).

61. Chesbro has written thirteen Mongo mysteries, published between 1977 and 1996, including *In the House of Secret Enemies* (New York: Mysteries Press, 1990), a short-story collection that contains "The Drop," which first introduced the Mongo character.

62. George Chesbro, *The Language of Cannibals* (New York: Mysterious Press, 1990).

63. Chesbro, *In the House of Secret Enemies,* 216.

64. George Chesbro, *Dark Chant in a Crimson Key* (New York, Mysterious Press, 1992), 194.

65. George Chesbro, "The Birth of a Series Character," in *In the House of Secret Enemies* (New York: Mysterious Press), 5, 6.

66. Ross Thomas, *The Eighth Dwarf* (New York: Simon and Schuster, 1979).

67. C. J. Koch, *The Year of Living Dangerously* (New York: St. Martin's Press, 1979).

68. Armistead Maupin, *Maybe the Moon* (New York: HarperCollins, 1992; New York: HarperPerennial, 1993).

69. Amy Rennert, "Interview with Armistead Maupin," http://www.literarybent.com/mtm_04_behind.html.

70. Simon Mawer, *Mendel's Dwarf* (New York: Harmony Books, 1998).

71. Ursula Hegi, *Stones from the River* (New York: Simon and Schuster, 1994; Scribner Paperback Fiction, 1995), 1.

72. Ursula Hegi, *Floating in My Mother's Palm* (New York: Poseidon Press, 1990).

73. Some readers have criticized Hegi as being inattentive to the Germans' extermination of dwarfs. In fact, except for institutionalized dwarfs with severe disabilities, dwarfs were generally safe, especially in rural areas. When the extremely disabled did end up in concentration camps, it was more on the grounds that they were Jews than because they were dwarfs. To understand the complexity of German and German American attitudes about the Holocaust, see Hegi, *Tearing the Silence* (New York: Simon and Schuster, 1997). Steve Colman, a Hungarian Jew, survived World War II because he was hidden from the Nazis by Karolina Reszeli (Csöpi), an eighteen-year-old dwarf, and her mother. For his memoir, see Steve Colman's home page (www.stevecolman.com).

74. John Irving, *The Hotel New Hampshire* (New York: Dutton, 1981; New York: Simon and Schuster, Pocket Books, 1982).

75. John Irving, *A Son of the Circus* (New York: Random House, 1994).

76. John Irving, *A Prayer for Owen Meany* (New York: Ballantine Books, 1989).

77. My curiosity about Irving's development of these characters, as well their early demise, led me to question the writer after a reading he gave (92nd Street Y, New York, May 2001). What follows is based on his responses.

    When I inquired about Lily's suicide, he responded by saying that she had killed herself because she was a writer. This reply, tossed off casually, should probably not be taken at face value: Irving's reading and comments were impressive and absorbing. He explained that his work tends to move from comic to dark; he likes to disarm readers into thinking that everything will be fun, and thereby cause them to be less guarded about events to come in the plot.

78. Anne Finger, "The Artist and the Dwarf" *Southern Review* 26 (Autumn 1993): 691–705.

79. John Sayles, *The Pride of the Bimbos* (Boston: Little, Brown, 1975).

80. Chet Raymo, *The Dork of Cork* (New York: Warner Books, 1993).

81. Bartle Bull, *The White Rhino Hotel* (New York: Viking, 1992); *A Café on the Nile* (New York: Carroll and Graf, 1998); *The Devil's Oasis* (New York: Carroll and Graf, 2001).

82. Cathryn Alpert, *Rocket City* (Aspen, Colo.: MacMurray and Beck, 1995).

83. My thanks to Ethel Ruben for drawing my attention to *Dvaergene's Dans* and providing a synopsis in English. The description here is drawn from her account.

84. James Thurber, "You Could Look It Up," first published in *The Saturday Evening Post* on 5 April 1941,

is republished in Charles Einstein ed., *The Fireside Book of Baseball*, (New York: Simon and Schuster, 1987.)

85. Alice Jane McVan, "Spanish Dwarfs," *Notes Hispanic* 2 (1942): 99. The verses I obtained from the Biblioteca Nacional in Madrid were badly printed; their condition and archaic language made translating them daunting. The poems, reflections on love, were written as songs of the young Sir Fernando de la Torre; they end with the poet passionately cursing the earth, wishing on it the same suffering as her own—as well as the "things of love" of which she has too much.

86. Bruce Clayton, *Forgotten Prophet: The Life of Randolph Bourne* (Baton Rouge: Louisiana State University Press, 1984); *The Lichtenberg Reader*, ed., trans., and with an introduction by Franz H. Mautner and Henry Hatfield (New York: Beacon, 1959); Gert Hofmann, *Lichtenberg and the Little Flower Girl*, trans. and with an afterword by Michael Hofmann (New York: New Directions, 2004). A good synopsis of both Lichtenberg's life and the novel appears in Gabrielle Annan, "Lichtenberg in Love," *New York Review of Books*, 12 August 2004, 43–44.

87. It has been claimed that he was crippled in a street accident that left him a hunchbacked dwarf. This unlikely scenario is attributed to Curtis Peebles, author of *Watch the Skies!* and Carl Sagan, author of *The Demon-Haunted World*, in an article titled "UFO's: Amazing Connections," http://ufos.miningco.com/library/weekly/aa061797.htm. Peebles and Sagan supposedly credit Palmer with being one of the first sources of the flying-saucer myth. My account is drawn from the preceding article.

88. Philip K. Dick, quoted in "Judy-Lynn Benjamin," *Spacelight*, http://members.tripod.com/~gwillick/delrayju.html.

89. "Judy-Lynn del Rey," in *I. Asimov* (New York: Doubleday, 1994), 316–340.

90. *Grimm's Fairy Tales*, 198.

91. Diane Stanley, *Rumpelstiltskin's Daughter* (New York: Morrow Junior Books, 1997).

92. Barbara H. Baskin and Karen H. Harris, *Notes from a Different Drummer: A Guide to Juvenile Fiction Portraying the Handicapped* (New York: R. R. Bowker, 1977); Barbara Baskin and Karen Harris, *More Notes from a Different Drummer: A Guide to Juvenile Fiction Portraying the Disabled* (New York: R. R. Bowker, 1984). These landmark works still provide the best general background.

93. Baskin and Harris, *Notes From a Different Drummer*, 41–42.

94. M. E. Kerr, *Little Little* (New York: Harper and Row, 1981), 179. Marijane Meaker (Kerr is her pen name) has published adult fiction under several names; she is best known, however, for her young-adult books. She received the Margaret Edwards award for lifetime achievement in 1993. During my visit with her in Long Island, New York, she discussed her life as writer, teacher, and lesbian. She indicated that her familiarity with the young people who visit her, as well as her close relationship with her own adolescence, had enabled her to capture their emotional lives in writing.

95. I have not annotated these works in the endnotes; precise references are obtainable online. With the exception of *Ginny's Backyard*, now out of print, they are readily available in libraries and bookstores.

96. During the first few months of 2004, *Stones from the River* was featured at events at Gettysburg College, in the town of Gettysburg, and in surrounding Adams County. Ursula Hegi was invited to lecture, and members of the dwarfism community were asked to participate; Cara Egan, Little People of America health care policy advisor, and I took part in the events.

Chapter 9. Theater, Film, and Television

1. Michael Dunn, quoted in "Milestones," *Time*, 10 September 1973, 60.

2. Robert Bogdan, *Freak Show* (Chicago: University of Chicago Press, 1988), 165.

3. *LPA District 2 Newsletter* (New York, New Jersey, Pennsylvania), January 1998, 6. This film, a suspense story featuring a deaf clairvoyant (Manganelli's wife, Terrylene), was released as *After Image*.

4. Because repetitions of the phrase *actors who are dwarfs* seems overly cumbersome, *dwarf actors* is used here for the sake of economy—I am nevertheless sensitive to the fact that professional actors may be put off by this term.

5. Alfred Enderle, Dietrich Meyerhöfer, and Gerd Unverfehrt, *Small People—Great Art*, trans. Karen Williams (Bremen, Germany: Artcolor Verlag, 1994), 237–39.

6. Martin Monestier, *Les nains: Des hommes différents* (Paris: Jean Claude Simeon, 1977), 170.

7. Barry Anthony, "Who's Who of Victorian Drama: Little Tich (Harry Relph)," www.victorian-cinema.net/tich.htm.

8. See, for example, Bernard Grebanier, *Then Came Each Actor: Shakespearean Actors Great and Otherwise* (New York: Julian Press, 1975). It is possible that some of the actors who were discussed in the literature may have been dwarfs without reference having been made to their stature. Nevertheless, it seems likely that an actor's unusual stature would have been mentioned.

9. Alvin Goldfarb, "Giants and Minuscule Actors in the Nineteenth Century American Stage," *Journal of Popular Culture* 10, no. 2 (1976): 267–269.

10. Ibid., 268–69.

11. This troupe spelled its name without the double *l*.

12. Goldfarb, "Giants and Minuscule Actors," 275.

13. Most are not available in general video stores. For a Web site listing twenty-five hundred feature films, see "Films Including Disabilities," at www.disabilityfilms.co.uk. The site is divided into fifteen categories, one of which is *dwarfism*. Although it is valuable because it lists more than 130 films in this category, its ratings of whether a film is "major" or "minor" may be disputed.

14. *Living in Oblivion* (1995), directed by Tom DiCillo.

15. *Twin Peaks,* American Broadcasting Company, 9 October 1990.

16. *Freaks* (1931), directed by Todd Browning.

17. David J. Skal, *The Monster Show: A Cultural History of Horror* (New York: W. W. Norton, 1993), 156.

18. Ibid.

19. For a discussion of the work of Arbus, see Chapter 7.

20. Capsule Film Review, *Even Dwarfs Started Small,* http://www.phx.com/alt/archive/movies/fi...ps/EVEN-DWARFS-STARTED-SMALL-196970.html.

21. Hal Erickson, "Even Dwarfs Started Small," in *All Movie Guide Review,* at video.barnesandnoble.com/search/product.asp?wrk=3620832. This excerpt was originally part of a longer one that appeared on a Web site that is no longer available.

22. For this and other recollections garnered in interviews of the surviving members of the group, see Stephen Cox, *The Munchkins Remember: "The Wizard of Oz" and Beyond* (New York: E. P. Dutton, 1989) and Aljean Harmetz, *The Making of "The Wizard of Oz"* (New York: Alfred A. Knopf), 1978.

23. Cox, *Munchkins,* 47.

24. Harmetz, *Making of "The Wizard of Oz,"* 202.

25. Ibid., 188.

26. *Under the Rainbow,* directed by Steve Rash.

27. Mark A. Satern, ed., *Illustrated Guide to Video's Best* (Phoenix: Saturn Press, 1995), 40.

28. "Kenny r2-d2 Baker from Star Wars—Official Website!" wwwkennybaker.co.uk/.

29. The Web site that contained the most complete information about Baker's film performances is no longer extant. However, his biography is expected to appear shortly.

30. Armistad Maupin, *Maybe the Moon* (New York: HarperCollins, 1992).

31. "Jesus Fernandez," http://www.aat.es/curricul/jfernandez.htm.

32. "Films Involving Disabilities: A Woman for Joe," http://www.disabilityfilms.co.uk/dwarf1/WomanforJoeA.htm.

33. Peter Brunette, "Political Subtext in a Fairy Tale from a Feminist," *New York Times,* 25 September 1994, H14–16.

34. Margaret A. McGurk, "'Simon Birch' a Sentimental Winner," *Cincinnati Inquirer,* http://www.cincinatti.com/freetime/moviesmcgurk/simonbirch.html.

35. M. V. Moorhead, "Little Big Man," http://www.houstonpress.com/1998/091098/film/.html. This movie elicited unusually polarized responses from reviewers and was not a great box office success. One reviewer called it "so relentlessly maudlin that even a distinguished supporting cast can't save it from becoming a preachy, misguided sugar rush about an unlikely child hero" (*Mr. Showbiz Movie Guide: Simon Birch, 1998,* site removed from Web.) But another wrote, "Odd, sweet, funny and surprising [with] the year's most unlikely and likable hero" (Tom Long, "Simon Birch, "*Detroit News,* http://www.detnews.com/SCREENS/9809/11simon/simon.htm). It received favorable reviews in the *Village Voice* and the *Montreal Gazette,* and the Broadcast Film Critics Association voted Ian Smith the best child performer of 1998.

36. David Denby, *New Yorker,* 5 July 1999, 90–99.

37. Mini-Me, http://cgi.pathfinder.com/ew/features/990625/itlist/minime.html.

38. Live chats transcripts, http:www.etonline.com/html/ChatSchedule/1122.2html. In the films, Mini-Me is a clone of the character Dr. Evil.

39. Susan Jacobs, Sharon Kahn, Rebecca Federman, East Coast Press, *Samuel Goldwyn Films Presents "The Red Dwarf" (Le nain rouge),* 3. Promotional brochure prepared by Kahn and Jacobs Public Relations, 27 West 24 Street, Suite 10C, New York, NY 10010, kahnjabos@aol.com.

40. Varying critical opinions on *The Embalmer* may be found at www.metacritic.com/video/titles/embalmer/.

41. Letter from Billy Barty soliciting for the Billy Barty Foundation, June 1998.

42. The dates of a selection of Barty films are *Alice in Wonderland,* 1932; *A Midsummer Night's Dream,* 1935; *Nothing Sacred,* 1937; *The Day of the Locust,* 1975; *Foul Play,* 1978; *Willow,* 1988; *Life Stinks,* 1991.

43. Barty made this comment in *Vaudeville* (1997; produced by American Masters), a television special on the era of vaudeville made by Gregg Palmer, in which three dozen veterans of the vaudeville stage, including Barty, were interviewed.

44. *AMG All Movie Guide,* http://205.186.189.2/cgi-win/avg.exe.

45. "Billy Barty Never Let a Few Inches Get Him Down," Columbia Broadcasting System, press release, 8 September 1972.

46. The remarks in this and following paragraph are from Billy Barty, telephone interview with the author, 17 December, 1998.

47. "Died, Michael Dunn, 38," *Time,* 10 September, 1973, 45.

48. Ibid.

49. Elisabeth Thomas-Matej, "What's in a Diagnosis: A Medical Biography of Michael Dunn," http://www.nctc.net/~hazard/conrad/michaeldunn/biography/. Thomas-Matej explores aspects of Dunn's life, his diagnosis, and the circumstances of his death; she corrects earlier assertions that his condition was achondroplasia or caused by a chemical imbalance during gestation.

50. Diana Lurie, "Dwarf's Full Size Success," *Life,* 14 February 1964, 43–44.

51. "Weaver, Interview with Dorin," 1, http://www.nctc.net/~hazard/conrad/dorin/. Dorin was also a close friend, and this interview is revealing.

52. *AMG All Movie Guide,* http:/205.186.189.2186.189.2/dcgi-win/avg.exe.

53. Patricia Bosworth, "Just an Ordinary Guy, All 3 Feet 10 of Him," *New York Times,* 25 September 1965.

54. For exaggerated accounts that Dunn made to gullible reporters, see Thomas-Matej, "Tall Tales," in "What's in a Diagnosis," 2.

55. "Weaver, interview with Dorin," 4.

56. Although alcohol and cigarettes may have contributed to Dunn's poor health, the cause of his death was likely "respiratory depression due to the prescribed drugs, with or without alcohol, frank right heart failure due to thoracic constriction, some type of chronic obstructive pulmonary disease, or both, or pneumonia" (Dr. John Hain, board-certified forensic pathologist in Carmel, California, consulted by Thomas-Matej, quoted in Thomas-Matej, "What's in a Diagnosis," 4).

57. Lurie, "Dwarf's Full Size Success," 43.

58. Pieral, *Vu d'en bas* (Paris: R. Laffont, 1976), 1.

59. Herve Villechaize, *AMG All Movie Guide,* http:/205.186.189.2186.189.2/dcgi-win/avg.exe.

60. Tom Gliatto and Todd Gold, "Laying Down the Burden," *People Weekly,* 20 September 1993, 50–51.

61. *New York Times,* 5 September, 1993, I54.

62. Sue Rositto, telephone conversation with the author, 28 May 2000. Martin Monestier has asserted that suicides are abnormally prevalent among dwarf performers; however, there is no statistical evidence for this (*Nains,* 176). Villechaize suffered from painful, debilitating medical problems, as well as alcohol addiction. Both Rappaport and Villechaize were known to have histories of depression; in this, they were not unique, as depression is also prevalent in the general population. I have spoken with a number of dwarf actors who have large circles of friends and acquaintances in theater and film, and they were aware of only one other suicide among dwarf actors.

63. Gliatto and Gold, "Laying down the Burden," 50.

64. David Van Biema and Mary Ann Norbom, "The First Little Person to Star on TV, the Wizard's David Rappaport, Plans to Set the World on Fire," *People Weekly,* 6 October 1986, 54.

65. Charles Moritz, ed., *Current Biography Yearbook, 1988* (New York: H. W. Wilson, 1988), 255–259.

66. Louis Beale, "Little Big Man," *Los Angeles Daily News,* 11 January 1987, 26.

67. Hank Gallo, "Short Change," *New York Daily News,* 26 August 1985, 35.

68. Cynthia Zarin, "Profiles: Linda Hunt," *New Yorker,* 30 July 1990, 37–54.

69. Ibid., 42.

70. Ibid.

71. Personal communication during meeting with the author, Los Angeles, 22 January 1999. The personal comments included in this chapter are drawn largely from that meeting and another in New York City on 8 April 1999.

72. Zarin, "Profiles," 37.

73. Ibid., 54.

74. For an interesting account of the making of the film, see Leslie Rubinstein, "A Hunt for the Rose," *Horizon,* December 1986, 49–50.

75. *Fame* was shown on NBC on 30 November 1978.

76. Zarin, "Profiles," 38

77. Ibid., 38.

78. Chad Connecky, "Twinkle, Twinkle, Little Star," *Boston Herald,* 3 July 2003, http://www.townonline.com/lynnfield/news/local_regional/nss_feanstwinkle07032003.htm).

79. Linda Hunt, personal communication, 22 January 1999.

80. Lisa Abelow Hedley, "Lives: A Child of Difference," *New York Times Magazine,* 12 October 1997, 98. Also reproduced by LPA Library (www.lpaonline.org).

81. Linda Hunt, "Letters to the Editor," *New York Times Magazine,* 2 November 1997, 18.

82. When I met Hedley several years after these events, she commented on Hunt's response, saying that she believed that the *New York Times'* omission of parts of the article she had originally submitted had distorted some of its content and consequently created the impression of nonacceptance that some readers were left with.

83. Letter to the author, 8 December 1998.

84. The comments that follow are drawn largely from these meetings, which took place on 22 January 1999 and 8 April 1999.

85. Jerry Della Femina, "Jerry's Ink," *East Hampton Independent,* http://www.indyeastend.com/jerry/120298ji.htm.

86. Sue Rossito, telephone conversation with the author, 28 May 2000.

87. Regina Murray, of the affirmative action department of the Screen Actors Guild, letter to the author, 26 April 1999.

88. Regina Murray, telephone conversation with the author, 19 April 1999.

89. When *People Weekly* organized a contest in April 1998 to select the ten most beautiful people, Kevin Renzulli, a Howard Stern fan who ran a Web site for other Stern enthusiasts, organized a campaign to choose Hank. Hank, whose real name was Henry Nasiff, won with 229,620 votes, more than ten times as many as those for Leonardo DiCaprio, who was in third place. Nasiff's own employment (apart from at the Stern show) had consisted of entertaining at parties, lap dancing, bartending, and delivering insults; however, he had had some contact with Little People of America members. Although they deplored his having been a partner to his own exploitation, they mourned Hank's passing; in an ironic footnote, Hank's Web site asked that gifts be sent in his honor to Little People of America and the Billy Barty Foundation. For a sample of Hank's patter, see Dan Wagner, "Hank the Angry Drunken Dwarf: THE INTERVIEW," 5 May 1998, http:www.danwagner.com/pages/hankqa.html.

90. Arturo Gil, telephone conversation with the author, 26 May 2000.

91. Dominick A. Miserandino, "Coleman, Gary—Originally of Different Strokes, Now Actor, Spokesman, Columnist," http://www.thecelebritycafé.com/interviews/gary_coleman.html.

92. Dean E. Murphy, "Los Angeles Hogs the Ballot and Spotlight," *New York Times,* 17 August 2003, sect. 4, 4.

93. "Heal Thyself," *Northern Exposure,* Columbia Broadcasting System, 15 November 1993; "Grand Prix," ibid., 9 May 1994.

94. Susan Schindehette, "Cryptic Dreams, a Dead Prom Queen, Dwarf Back Talk—Here at Last Is a Guide to What "Twin Peaks" Is All About," *People Weekly,* 14 May 1990, 87.

95. "Mister Dreeb Comes to Town," *Picket Fences,* Columbia Broadcasting System, 12 October 1992.

96. *Fool's Fire, American Playhouse,* Public Broadcasting System, 27 February 1992.

97. "A Clown's Prayer," *Touched by an Angel,* Columbia Broadcasting System, 7 May 2000.

98. See the comments of an enthusiastic fan of Fondacaro's in such roles in "Ghoulies II," http://www.angelfire.com/film/lookhot/reviewfilms/ghoulies2.html.

99. "Carnivale.Org: The Unofficial Carnivale Fan Web Site," http://www.carnivale.org/cast/Samson.htm.

100. Noel Holston, "Stepping into a Big Role: Michael J. Anderson, star of HBO's 'Carnivale,' Hopes to Show 'Little People' Have Serious Acting Chops," *Newsday,* 31 August 2003, http://www.newsday. co…'ny-fftv3431958.story?coll=ny=television-highl. Anderson has not been discussed at greater length because *Carnivale* began to air just as this manuscript was being completed.

101. David Capper, "Hank Dingo," http://www.thrillingdetective.com/eyes/dingo.html.

102. These quotations are from Leslie (Hoban) Blake, "Living Outside Oblivion," review of *I Want to Be Adored,* 17 May 2000, http://www.theatermania.com/news/feature/index.cfm?story+692&cid+1.

103. The production benefited also from other fine acting performances and the strong direction of Lee Breuer and Martha Clarke. It received prominent coverage in the *Village Voice* and positive reviews in the *New York Times* and *Newsday.* See Charles McNulty, "Lee Breuer's Radical Vision of Ibsen's 'Dollhouse,'" *Village Voice,* 12–18 November 2003, 1, 34–36.

104. Tekki Lomnicki and Lauri Benz, "Talent and Creativity Have No Restrictions when You Are Led by Your Heart," *LPA Today,* April–September 1993, 9–10. Also published in *Hot Wire Magazine,* September 1993. My thanks to Lomnicki for providing me with videos of her performances.

105. Tekki Lomnicki and Lotti Pharris, *Genetic Material,* 1999, video.

106. In "Let the Dead Rest," a presentation about her father, who had died ten years earlier, Lomnicki describes him as "a swearing superhero in polyester with a tape-measure—he could do anything, fix anything, save us from any peril." In *Genetic Material,* she mugs and coughs as she smokes a cigarette and gruffly proclaims, "After my first heart attack in 1960, I made up my mind I wasn't going to let people shit on me anymore!" Despite the many differences between her father and herself, she recognizes both his face and his force in her own being.

107. Lomnicki and Benz, " Talent and Creativity," 10.

108. Catey Sullivan, "LG Girl Pairs with Professionals for Performance," *The Surburban LIFE Citizen,* 7 October 1998, 17.

109. Lynn Garrett, "A Miracle of Art and Faith: Tekki Lomnicki Overcomes Hurdles to Find Niche in Theater, Friends' Hearts. *Chicago Tribune,* 25 September 1995, 3.

110. Steve Robles, "Steve Robles, "Little People, Big Bucks: 'Dwarf' Films Cast a Strange Spell on the Culture," Gettingit.com, 14 September 1999, www.gettingit.com/article/33.

111. Jan Krawitz is a documentary filmmaker who teaches at Stanford University. She has made insightful films whose environments range from subway to drive-in to traveling circus; their subject matter includes the experiences of blind and elderly individuals, as well as enlightening accounts of women's body images. In a film called *In Harm's Way,* Krawitz focuses on how her personal experience with violence has shattered her worldview.

112. Ann S. Lewis, "The Texas Documentary Tour: Jan Krawitz," *Austin Chronicle,* http://www.auschron. com/issues/Vol18/issue46/screens.doctour.html.

113. Unlike most of the others, this work is not available for purchase. It first appeared on KCTA, in Minneapolis and St. Paul, Minnesota, and was distributed by the Public Broadcasting System's *Independent Lens.*

114. Barbara Duncan, "Short Stories: Documentary Film Review," http://www.disabilityworld.org/10–12 _00/arts/shortstories.htm.

115. The transliterated Hebrew title is *Ee Efshar Lehasteer et Zeh.*

116. In the discussion with Witkowski and filmmaker Shahan Rozan following the film's New York premiere, the American audience applauded enthusiastically; the German audience, the filmmakers said, had responded with silence.

117. "The Wait Out," *Seinfeld,* National Broadcasting Company, 9 May 1996

118. "The Yada Yada," ibid., 24 April 1997. In this episode, before the show concludes, Karen says to Kramer, "I really wanted you," making Mickey's marriage something less than convincing as the stuff of romance.

119. Corey Sulcey, "13 Inane Questions With Danny Woodburn," http:www.sove.edu/ALESTLE/library/ spring 1998/apr.30/life2.html.

120. Ibid.

121. Danny Woodburn, address given at a benefit for Silver Springs Little People research, 5 October 1998.

122. Kathie Huddleston, "Special Unit 2," in *On Screen*, 30 November 2002, http://www.scifi.com/sfw/issue207/screen2.html.

123. "Celebrity Chat," AT&T Worldnet Service, 24 October 2001, http://community.att.net/chat/transcript_woodburn.html.

124. "Tracey Takes on Romance," *The Tracey Ullman Show*, Home Box Office, 24 January 1996.

125. "Tracey Takes on Fantasy," ibid., 25 January 1997.

126. "Love Fore Little Ones," *Pierre House Happenings* (biannual newsletter of the Little People's Research Fund, Inc., 80 Sister Pierre Drive, Towson, Md.), Fall/Winter 1998, 1. A former patient of orthopedic surgeon Steven Kopits, in 1998 he gave a funny and insightful talk at a fund-raiser for the Little People's Research Fund, crediting Kopits with giving him not only mobility, but also "a voice." Unfortunately, Dr. Kopits died in 2002; Woodburn wrote one of the eulogies delivered at his memorial service.

127. "The Station Agent, directed by Tom McCarthy," press release and biographies, http://thestationagent.com/press.doc.

128. Leslie (Hoban) Blake, "Living Outside Oblivion," TheaterMania.com, http://www.theatermania.com/news/feature/index.cfm?story=692&cid+1.

129. Karen Durbin, "The Scene Stealers: Six Actors to Watch this Fall (and Long Thereafter)," *New York Times*, 7 September 2003, Arts sec., 49.

130. Daniel Fierman, "Quick Take: Peter Dinklage," *Entertainment Weekly*, October/November 2003, 61.

131. Rebecca Murray, "Peter Dinklage Talks about the Station Agent," http://romanticmovies.about.com/cs/thestationagent/a/stationagentpd.htm.

132. Jason Zinoman, "Small, Dark, and Handsome," *Time Out*, 4–11 May 2000, 175.

133. Nick Paumgarten, "The Big Time: Pleasantville," *New Yorker*, 29 September, 2003.

134. *Family Law*, on CBS, originated in 1999, with Eaton joining the cast in 2001; her part was created for her by Paul Haggis, who had seen her in *Who Killed Victor Fox*. *Unconditional Love* appeared on foreign television in 2002 and in the United States in September 2003, when it was shown repeatedly as a "made for TV" film on the Starz channel. It was originally conceived as a motion picture. Production began in 1999.

135. Meredith Eaton, interview with the author, telephone, 28 August 2003.

136. Ibid. The observations in this paragraph and the one following are from this interview.

137. She has been featured on *CSI, Dharma and Gregg, L.A. Law, Martin, Saturday Night Live, Late Night with Conan O'Brien*, and *Late Show with David Letterman*. Her movie appearances include those in *Giant, Teen Witch*, and *Among Friends*.

138. Meredith Eaton, e-mail to the author, 14 September 2003.

139. Susan Wloszczyna, "Little People Get Big Movie Opportunities," *Lansing State Journal*, 4 February 2002, http://www.lepconnie.com/articles/lansingstjournal.html.

140. *Current Biography Yearbook 1988*, s.v. "Hunt, Linda," 259.

141. Lauri E. Klobas, *Disability Drama in Television and Film* (Jefferson, N.C.: McFarland, 1988), xi–xii, quoted in Martin Norden, *The Cinema of Isolation: A History of Physical Disability in the Movies* (New Brunswick: Rutgers University Press), 3.

142. Paul Darke, "Understanding Cinematic Representations of Disability," in *The Disability Reader: A Social Science Perspective*, ed. Tom Shakespeare (London: Cassell, 1998), 181–200.

Chapter 10. Music

1. Clemens M. Gruber, "Zwerge in der Oper," in *Die Zwerge kommen!* ed. Volker Hanzel and Diether Kramer (Trautenfels, Austria: Verein Schloss Trautenfels, 1993), 129–132.

2. My thanks to Laura Eppy for this information (telephone conversation with the author, 12 April 2001).

3. See Joseph Horowitz, "The Specter of Hitler in the Music of Wagner," *New York Times*, 8 November 1998, AR1, 38. The 1997 biography he refers to is Richard Weiner's *Richard Wagner and the Anti-Semitic Imagination*.

4. *New York Times,* 8 November 1998, 38.

5. Christopher Rouse, *"Der gerettete Alberich*—Press and Program Notes," http://www.Christopherrouse. com'gerettetepress.html.

6. Paul Griffiths, "Making the Case for an Odd and Anxious Romantic," *New York Times,* 16 August 1998, AR 29–30.

7. Georg C. Klaren, quotation from libretto for Alexander Zemlinsky's *The Dwarf,* in performance program, Avery Fisher Hall, Lincoln Center, New York, 9 June 2002, 57.

8. *Roctober Comics and Music* 13 (Summer 1995). Publication available from *Roctober,* 1507 E. Fifty-third Street, #617, Chicago IL 60615.

9. K. J. Evans, "Harvey Diederich: Touting His Town," *Las Vegas Review Journal,* 1999, http://www. 1st100.com/part2/diederich.html.

10. See, for example, Edith Piaf with Jean Noli, *Edith Piaf: My Life,* ed. and trans. Margaret Crossland (London: Peter Owen, 1990); "Biography: Edith Piaf," http://194://194.117.210.41/siteEn/biographie/biographie_6057.asp.

11. Steve Voce, Re: Kenton live/Trivia, http://merchant.book.uci.edu/lists/kenton-l/1998-03/msg00147. html.

12. Richard S. Ginell, "Chick Webb," *AMG All Music Guide,* wysiwyg://55/http:www.allmusic.com/cg/x. dll?p=amg&sql=B9908.

13. "Gene Krupa: Influences," http://crash.simplenet.com/influence.html.

14. Geoffrey Fidelman, *First Lady of Song: Ella Fitzgerald for the Record* (New York: Birch Lane Press, 1994), 20.

15. Stuart Nicholson, "Michel Petrucciani: Concerts inédits," *Jazz Times,* January/February 2001, 101–2.

16. "Michel Petrucciani, Jazz Pianist Born with Bone Disease," *Los Angeles Times,* 7 January 1999, A19.

17. Mike Zwerin, "Michel Petrucciani: Victory of the Spirit," *International Herald Tribune,* http://www.iht. com/IHT/SOUND/99/mz011299.html.

18. Ibid.

19. For a videotape showing Petrucciani in concert, see *Michel Petrucciani Trio* (60 mins.), directed by Eric Ebinger. Ebinger filmed Petrucciani playing his own compositions and a selection of jazz classics during his 1998 tour in Germany. Aired on educational television channels from time to time, this video is often paired with *Non-Stop: Travels with Michel Petrucciani,* a documentary that follows him to the major cities in which he has lived.

20. Elliot Zigmund, telephone interview with the author, 13 August 2001.

21. "Petrucciani Shines," *Breakthrough: The National Newsletter of the Osteogenesis Imperfecta Foundation, Inc.* 10, no. 3 (1988), 1.

22. Joseph Hooper, "The Ballad of Little Jimmy Scott," *New York Times Magazine,* 27 August 2000, 28–31.

23. For Scott's personal history, see his interview in Chip Deffaa, *Blue Rhythms: Six Lives in Rhythm and Blues* (Urbana: University of Illinois Press, 1996), 73–101.

24. Ibid., 75.

25. Joel E. Siegel, *Mood Indigo: NPR Jazz CD Review,* 2001, http://www.nprjazz.org/reviews/jrcd.jscott. html.

26. Hooper, "Ballad of Little Jimmy Scott," 30.

27. Susan Slattery, "Something Different: Jimmy Scott's Life and Times," http://www.berkshire.net/ ~cosmo/susan/music/Scott.html; also in *The Optimist,* 14 November 1996.

28. Allan Kozinn, "Playing Both Sides, Zesty and Serene," *New York Times,* 14 August 1999, B13.

29. Steven Moss, "The Sublime Voice of Thomas Quasthoff," *Guardian,* 20 October, 2000, http://www.guardianunlimited.co.uk/friday_review/story/0,3605,384884,00.html.

30. The performance was greeted with what a reviewer described as one of the most tumultuous ovations in his memory. See Janos Gereben, "TQ's Sound of No Hand Clapping: If This Be Pop, Play On!" http://www.gopera.com/quasthoff/reviews/2000625.html.

31. Anthony Tommasini, "It's the Vocal Chords That Matter Most," *New York Times,* 28 January 2004, E1, 6. Quasthoff's wish not to be judged specifically as a disabled musician led him to reject my request to use a Web site photograph of him in this present volume.

32. Moss, "Sublime Voice of Thomas Quasthoff," 4.

33. Some of the most interesting discussions of Quasthoff's feelings about his disabilities have appeared

in German publications. See, for example, "Seit Ihr alle krank?" *Stern,* 13 April 2000, http://www.gopera.com/quastoff/interviews/stern-2000-16.html. The following discussion is based on this article.

34. Melani Eskanazi, "St. Matthew Passion in London," http:www.gopera.com/quasthoff/reviews/20001022.html.

35. "Geto Boys," Rolling Stone.com, wsiwyg://18/http://www.rollingstone.co…sts/text/bio.asp?afl=&LookUpString=5159.

36. Ibid.

37. For the preceding description I am indebted to Steve Delano, the filmmaker who made *No Bigger Than a Minute,* a documentary about his identity journey as a dwarf (telephone conversation 18 July 2003).

38. The complete lyrics of "Size Ain't Shit" are available on sing 365.com, Internet music community, http://www.sing365.com/music/lyric.nsf/SongUnid/472947EBE6B1710448256A25002B6A13.

39. "Bushwick Bill," *Artist Direct,* Music Urban Showcase, http://imusic.artistdirect.com/showcase/urban/bushbill.html.

40. Steve Delano, telephone conversation with the author, 18 July 2003.

41. "Bushwick Bill," *Artist Direct.*

42. Nelson Ned, *Pequeño gigante de la canción* (Zondever: Jefferson Magno Costa, 1998).

43. Brush's Web page includes articles from the *Hamilton Spectator, Burlington Post,* and other publications (http://www.shawnbrush.com/start.html).

44. "Graham Rockingham, "Brush Stages Release of Two CD's," *Hamilton Spectator,* 24 October 2003.

45. Bethany Broadwell, "Shawn Brush: Performing Bluegrass Tunes as the Krooked Cowboy," Ican, 1 November 2001, http://www.ican.com/news/fullpage.cfm/articleid/44A56C18-420A-441B-9173…/article.cf.

46. "Shawn Brush (The Krooked Cowboy), Biography," Broten Sound Project, 1–3, www.brotensound.ca.http.

47. For comments by R. Broten, see ibid., 3.

48. Shawn Brush, telephone conversation with the author, 3 September 2003.

49. The list is at www.lpaonline.org/resources_discuss.html.

50. George Tabb, "Article/Interview," *New York Press,* 13–19 December 2000, http://www.comoddent.com/press2.htm.

51. Scott Strasbaugh post to Dwarfism List, 23 January 2001.

52. Frederick Nolan, *Lorenz Hart: A Poet on Broadway* (New York: Oxford University Press, 1994), 16, 243.

53. Michaela Kuzia post on Internet Dwarfism List, 23 January 2002.

Chapter 11. Lives Today

1. Julie Rotta, quoted on cover design of Joan Ablon, *Little People in America: The Social Dimensions of Dwarfism* (New York: Praeger, 1984).

2. The Rehabilitation Act of 1973 prohibited any federally funded agency from discriminating against persons with disabilities; the Individuals with Disabilities Act of 1975 guaranteed every child the right to a free and appropriate education in the least restrictive environment; and the Americans with Disabilities Act (ADA) of 1990 barred physical and social barriers in schools, jobs, and public places and provided legal recourse against offenders. For a history, see Doris Zames Fleischer and Frieda Zames, *The Disability Rights Movement* (Philadelphia: Temple University Press, 1999). For descriptions of advocacy relevant to dwarfs, see Cara Egan, "LPA, Inc.: Coming of Age in the Policy Arena" (master's thesis, School of Hygiene and Public Health, Department of Health Policy and Management, Johns Hopkins University, 2001). For implications of the ADA for dwarfs, see C. Angela Van Etten, "Little People and Disability from a Personal and Legal Perspective," *LPA Today,* May–September 1999, 50, http://gate.net/~vanetten/ergochair.htm.

3. Four works were examined: Joan Ablon, *Little People in America: The Social Dimensions of Dwarfism* (New York: Praeger, 1984); L. Stace and D. M. Danks, "A Social Study of Dwarfing Conditions, *Australian Pædiatric Journal* 17 (1981): 167–182; A. G. Hunter, "Some Psychosocial Aspects of Nonlethal Chondroplasias," *American Journal of Medical Genetics* 78, no. 1 (1998): 1–29; S. E. Gollust et al., "Living with

Achondroplasia in an Average-Sized World: An Assessment of the Quality of Life," *American Journal of Medical Genetics* 120A, no. 4 (2003): 447–58.

4. Bethany Jewett, "Watson Final Report," 1988, twenty pages, photocopy. Jewett's married name is Bethany Stark.

5. Hanna Beech, "High Hopes," *Time Asia,* 17 December 2001, 1–3, http://www.time.com/time/asia/news/magazine/0,9754,187654,00.html.

6. On 12 September 2004, the Chinese consulate in New York held its first formal reception for any publication. The book being honored was a history and criticism of women's issues (Tao Jie, Zheng Bijun, and Shirley L. Mow, eds., *They Hold up Half the Sky* [New York: Feminist Press, 2004]).

7. For a commentary and a discussion of changes for the disabled in Japan, see Nicholas D. Kristof, "Outcast Status Worsens Pain of Japan's Disabled," *New York Times,* 7 April 1996, L3; and Stephanie Strom, "Social Warming: Japan's Disabled Gain New Status," *New York Times,* 7 July 2001, B7. People with disabilities have become more visible on both television and city streets; Hajimi Sen, a man with cerebral palsy, has been elected to the Kamakura city assembly.

8. Etsuyu Enami Nomachi, e-mail to the author, 13 December 2001.

9. I exchanged many e-mails with George Sofkin throughout 2001. In extreme distress and requiring surgery, he finally underwent successful treatment in Holland; his surgeon visited Bulgaria to share his expertise.

10. E-mail from the Pretous to the author, 20 April 2001. The Pretous have a Web site on LPA Online.

11. E-mail from Honor Rawlings of the Restricted Growth Association, 21 January 2000.

12. "Dwarfs Lament Prejudice against Them," *This Day* (Lagos), posted 16 May 2003, http: allafrica.com/stories/200305160514.html.

13. Susan Orlean, "Fertile Ground," *New Yorker,* 7 June 1999, 64.

14. Dan Kennedy, *Little People: Learning to See the World through My Daughter's Eyes* (New York: Rodale Press, 2003); Betty Adelson, *Dwarfism: Medical and Psychosocial Aspects of Profound Short Stature* (Baltimore: Johns Hopkins University Press, 2005); Ablon, *Little People in America*; Ablon, *Living with Difference: Families with Dwarf Children* (New York: Praeger, 1988).

15. Only a small number of investigations have been carried out on marriage rates; between 1934 and 1995, these rates were cited as between 22 percent and 43 percent (the latter figure is in Hunter, "Some Psychosocial Aspects"). Higher figures are documented in Judith Hall, "Results of the Survey of Medical Complications in Classical Achondroplasia," photocopy, 1974–75. In this survey of 150 LPA members, Hall found that 75 percent of the women and 60 percent of the men had been or were married. This discrepant higher percentage may have resulted from the sample: the respondents were all diagnosed with the same condition (achondroplasia), and they were volunteers, that is, a self-selected group.

16. Ablon, *Little People in America,* 60.

17. Tom Shakespeare, in an unpublished study of members of Great Britain's Restricted Growth Association (RGA), found that more short-statured than average-sized couples said that they would not want to have short-statured children. Some German attendees at a convention in the mid-1990s indicated that they did not want to have short-statured children; perhaps partly as a consequence of this, they had decided not to have children at all (e-mail communication from Simon Minty, RGA member, 23 February 2002).

18. Walter Bodin and Barnet Hershey, *It's a Small World* (New York: Conrad-McCann, 1934), 89–90.

19. In 1968 sociologist Marcello Truzzi relied on its data, calling it a somewhat sensational but valuable journalistic report (Marcello Truzzi, "Lilliputians in Gulliver's Land: The Social Role of the Dwarf," in *Sociology and Everyday Life,* ed. Marcello Truzzi [Englewood Cliffs, N.J.: Prentice-Hall], 197–211).

20. Ernst Trier Morch, *Chondrodystrophic Dwarfs in Denmark* (Copenhagen: Einar Munksgaard, 1941).

21. Dave Elsila, "*Solidarity*: Little People with Big Jobs," October 1997, http://www.uaw.org/solidarity/9707/06_1.html.

22. Charles I. Scott Jr., "Medical and Social Adaptation in Dwarfing Conditions," *The National Foundation Birth Defects Original Article Series* 13, no. 3C (1977): 29–43; quotation is at 34.

23. The biography of Kitchens is based primarily on an interview with the author at the LPA conference in Portland, Oregon in July 1999.

24. Charles (Charley) Lockhart (1875–1954) served from 1931 to 1941, when he resigned because of

poor health. A 1937 Texas news item pictures one dwarf on either side of a tall depository manager. The two dwarfs were employed as clerks by Lockhart during the depression, when they must have found it especially difficult to obtain work. The caption reads, "Charles Lockhart, smallest treasurer of the biggest state in the Union, now has two employees he doesn't have to look up to." Lockhart was married with two children.

25. William Wheaton, e-mail to the author, 13 November 1999.

26. Ibid.

27. Wieder worked on the health-care effort with pediatrician Harley Gordon, who introduced me to Wieder. This section is based on my interview and later acquaintance with Wieder.

28. "Nothing Stops Harry When He Raises Hell," *New York Newsday,* 12 September 1993, A2.

29. I am grateful to Wieder for his contributions to this volume through his suggestions of fiction with dwarf characters.

30. Tom Shakespeare, "Tom Shakespeare," in *Invented Identities: Lesbians and Gays Talk about Migration,* ed. Bob Cant (London: Cassell Press, 1997), 29–38.

31. Ibid., 30.

32. Ibid., 35.

33. For a complete description, see his Web page (http://www.windmills.u-net.com/home.htm). Among his published works are Tom Shakespeare, Kath Gillespie-Sells, and Dominic Davies, *The Sexual Politics of Disability: Untold Desires* (London: Cassell, 1996); Tom Shakespeare, *Disability Reader*; Tom Shakespeare and Ann Kerr, *Genetic Politics: From Eugenics to Genome* (Cheltenham, U.K.: New Clarion Press, 2002).

34. Tom Shakespeare, "Last Words Mmmm Mmmm Mmmm: More Thoughts on Monogamy," *Bifrost* 38 (1994), http://bi//bi.org/~bi-arch/bifrost/38/lastword.html.

35. The New Jersey Developmental Disability Council, " Colleen L. Fraser," http://www.njddc.org/colleen-l-/fraser.htm.

36. Maryann B. Hunsberger, "The Workshops: Planning for Change," *Families* (New Jersey Developmental Disabilities Council) 10, no. 2 (2001): 51.

37. Colleen L. Fraser, "The New Millennium: Getting to a Better Place," *People with Disabilities Magazine,* April 2000, http://www.njddc.org/a_better_place.htm.

38. Angela Van Etten, *Dwarfs Don't Live in Doll Houses* (Rochester, N.Y.: Adaptive Living, 1988), 111–112.

39. Robert A. Weisberger, "Profiles of Working Professionals Who Have Accepted the Challenge: Problem Solving from a Different Perspective," in *The Challenged Scientists: Disabilities and the Triumph of Excellence* (New York: Praeger, 1991), 1–5.

40. Tricia Mason, "ANSI A117.1: Making Things Happen," *LPA Today,* Fall 2003, 36.

41. Sir William Shakespeare, *Walking through Leaves,* prepared and with an introduction by Tom Shakespeare. Available through the Restricted Growth Association of Great Britain, www.rgaonline.org.uk.

42. Ibid., 34.

43. Sir William Shakespeare, "Social Implications of Achondroplasia: A Public Health View," *Human Achondroplasia, Basic Life Science* 48 (1988): 453–5.

44. "Judith Badner," in *Journeys of Women in Science and Engineering: No Universal Constants,* ed. Susan A. Ambrose et al. (Philadelphia: Temple University Press, 1997), 41–43.

45. Mark Leibovich, "The True Measure of a Man: Robert Reich Rises above the Height Issue in His Run for Governor," *Washington Post,* 14 March 2002, CO1; available online at http://www.washingtonpost.com/wp-dyn/articles/A24219-2002Mar13.html.

46. For more on Fairbank disease, see the NORD Web site: http://www.rarediseases.org.

47. Robert Reich, e-mail to the author, 12 December 2001.

48. Robert B. Reich, *Locked in the Cabinet* (New York: Alfred A. Knopf, 1997).

49. "The AllPolitics Interview: Robert Reich-April 25, 1997," http://www.cnn.com/ALLPOLITICS/1997/04/25/reich/interview/.

50. Robert Reich, *The Future of Success: Working and Living in the New Economy* (New York: Alfred A. Knopf, 2000); Reich, *I'll Be Short: Essentials for a Decent Working Society* (Boston: Beacon Press, 2003.)

51. Reich, *Locked in the Cabinet,* 31.

52. Ibid., 24, 82.

53. Ibid., 82.

54. Pam Belluck. "Ex-Labor Secretary Outlines Race to Lead Massachusetts." *New York Times,* 10 January 2002, A23.

55. "Jennifer Mechem and Paul Steven Miller," *New York Times,* 25 May 1995., Society sec., 44.

56. "Paul Steven Miller Sworn-in for Five-Year Term as EEOC Commissioner," http://www.eeoc.gov/press/11-23-99.html.

57. Paul Steven Miller, "The Changing Face of Civil Rights," *LPA Today,* July–October 1998, 47–49. Delivered to the graduating class at the University of Iowa Law School.

58. "Jury Awards $13 Million in Disability Discrimination Case," *The US Equal Opportunity Commission Press Release,* 6 November 1999, http://www.eeoc.gov/press/11-06-99.html.

59. Rebecca A. Doyle, "No Employer Has the Right to See Your Genotype along with Your Resume," *University Record,* 25 September 2000, http://www.umich.edu/~urecord/0001/Sep25_00/17.htm. See Paul Steven Miller, "Genetic discrimination in the workplace," *Journal of Law, Medicine, and Ethics* 26, no. 3 (1998): 189–197; "Statement of Commissioner Paul Steven Miller, U.S. Economic Opportunity Commissioner before the Committee on Health, Education, Labor and Pensions," 20 July 2000, http://www.nhgri.nih.gov/Policy_and_public_affairs/Legislation/miller_testimony.htm.

60. Paul Steven Miller, interview with the author, 7 January 2002. Unless otherwise indicated, the quotations that follow are from this interview.

61. Uraya Shavit, "The Things That Really Matter," *Ha'aretz Magazine,* 22 February 2002, 18.

62. Ibid.

63. Gregg Rice, telephone interview with the author, n.d., 2000. The quotations included in this section are from this interview.

64. Carlos Vidal Greth, "Chaplain's Tall Order," *Austin American-Statesman;* reprinted in *LPA Today* supp., May 1999, 1–3, 14, 15.

65. Mary G. Hare, "God's Door Just Opened Up," *Pierre House Happenings* (The Little People's Research Fund), Spring/Summer 1996, 3; excerpted from *Baltimore Sun,* 18 April 1996. Quotation that follows is from this source.

66. Tom Zucco, "How Demeaning: Devil Rays Dropped the Ball on Dave," *St. Petersburg Times,* 19 April 1999, reprinted in *LPA Today,* March–April 1999.

67. The umpire Harold Schulman, four feet four inches in height, officiated at 180 games during his first year as a member of the United States Slo-pitch Softball Association/Rockland County Umpires Association, and worked in the county's top leagues. Eddie Morgan was first-base coach of the Walla Walla Bears, a Northwest League team.

68. Donald Davidson with Jesse Outlar, *Caught Short* (New York: Atheneum, 1972).

69. Leslie J. Low and Mary J. Knudsen, "Dwarfism: New Interest Area for Adaptive Physical Activity," *Adaptive Physical Activity Quarterly* 13 (1996), 1–15.

70. See the video created by Pam Prentice, available from Pam Prentice, 6539 Sunnyland Lane, Dallas, TX 75214–3124. *LPA Today* generally carries advertisements for it.

71. I wrote two letters to Westheimer's office about interviewing her for this volume, mentioning our mutual acquaintances, but she did not respond.

72. Ruth Westheimer, *All in a Lifetime* (New York: Warner Books, 1987), 90, originally written 16 January 1946.

73. Matt Roloff with Tracy Sumner, *Against Tall Odds* (Sisters, Ore.: Multnomah, 1999).

74. Joan Ablon, *Little People in America* (New York: Praeger, 1984).

75. Chris Lydgate, "Dwarf versus Dwarf: The Little People of America Want Respect and They're Fighting Each Other to Get It." *LPA Today,* May–September, 1999, 46–47. First published in *Willamette Week* (Portland, Ore.), 30 June 1999.

76. Danny Black, telephone conversation with the author, 27 November 2000.

77. Quoted in Dan Kennedy, *Little People: Learning to See the World through My Daughter's Eyes* (New York: Rodale, 2003), 216.

78. Steve Rukavina, correspondence and telephone interviews with the author, January 2000. The match had taken place in May 1999; he sent me his personal tape of the event.

79. Anthony Condello, telephone interview with the author. I am grateful to Steve Rukavina for facilitating this contact with Condello, and with Lord Littlebrook, discussed below.

80. Eric Tovey, speaking on Steve Rukavina CBC radio tape, May 1999.

81. Eric Tovey, interview with the author, by telephone from his home in St. Joseph, Missouri, 28 January 2000. The comments included here are from this interview.

82. "Bad Boys of Wrestling, News and Releases," http://www.bbow.com/news.html.

83. *Why My Saturday Night Was Ruined* includes articles from the *Washington Post* and the *Chantilly Times* and a press release from the Indy Pro Wrestling Alliance (http://www.ddtdigest.com/features/pca-muck.htm).

84. This event was shown on *The Real World*, MTV, 1 February 2000.

85. Van Etten, *Dwarfs Don't Live in Doll Houses*, 221.

86. Paul Hemp, "In Europe the Outcry Is Loud over a Sport Called Dwarf-Tossing," *Wall Street Journal*, 4 November 1985, 1.

87. Ibid.

88. Van Etten, *Dwarfs Don't Live in Doll Houses*, 237, 224.

89. Beth Tatman and Nancy Mayeux, "Little People Respond," *St. Petersburg Times*, 9 October 1988.

90. Associated Press, 27 November 1991.

91. Ron Strauss, "You Gotta Be Dopey," *Long Island Voice*, 5–11 August 1999, 5. Frank and his little-person trainee, Beetlejuice, currently advertise on the Internet that they are available for dwarf tossing, bachelor parties, and so on. They also sell a sexually explicit video online.

92. Douglas Martin, "James S. Moran Dies at 91; Master of the Publicity Stunt," *New York Times*, 24 October 1999, sec. 1, 5.

93. Peter Suber, "Paternalism," in *Philosophy of Law: An Encyclopedia*, ed. Christopher Grey (New York: Garland, 1999), vol. 2, 632–635; available at http://www.earlham.edu/-perers/writing/paternal.htm.

94. Robert W. McGee, "Dwarf Tossing Bans Violate Human Rights," *Policy Analysis* (Dumont Institute for Public Policy Research) 2 (1996), http://gaiafriends.com/ethics/Authors/MCGEE/Bans.htm. See also Robert W. McGee, "If Dwarf Tossing Is Outlawed, Only Outlaws Will Toss Dwarfs: Is Dwarf Tossing a Victimless Crime?" *American Journal of Jurisprudence* 38 (1993): 335–358.

95. "U.N. Backs 'Dwarf-Tossing' Ban," http://www.cnn.com/2002/WORLD/europe/09/27/dwarf.throwing/index.html.

96. Cara Egan, "Dismaying Profile," *Jersey Journal*, letter to the editor, 6 July 2001, http://www.nj.com/news/jjournal/index.ssf?/letters/jjpournal/letu6a.html.

97. Martin Monestier, *Les nains: Des hommes différents* (Paris: Jean Claude Simeon, 1977) 155, 149.

98. Daniel P. Mannix, *Freaks: We Who Are Not as Others* (New York: Pocket Books, 1976; San Francisco: Re/Search Publications, 1990), 9. Page number is from 1990 edition.

99. Martha Undercoffer, "Peer Support: Joint LPA/University of Cincinnati Project, *LPA Today*, May–September 1999, 12–13.

100. *The Oprah Winfrey Show*, National Broadcasting Company, 20 October 2003.

SELECTED BIBLIOGRAPHY

This bibliography has been arranged to provide an overview of major early references and an introduction to contemporary sources. In an effort not to duplicate voluminous endnotes, I have cited here only a small percentage of the works referred to in the text. Most notably, I have omitted fictional works altogether, trusting readers to use the discussion in Chapter 8 to guide their choices.

HISTORY, BIOGRAPHY, AND STIGMA

The Early Tradition

The following works are essential resources, but they must be approached with some caution. They focus primarily upon court dwarfs, exhibiting dwarfs, and entertainers, and they contain some inaccuracies.

Bodin, Walter, and Burnet Hershey. *It's a Small World: The World of Midgets*. New York: Coward-McCann, 1934.

Drimmer, Frederick. "The Little People." In *Very Special People*, 175–268. New York: Amjon, 1973.

Fiedler, Leslie. *Freaks: Myths and Images of the Secret Self*, 1–90. New York: Touchstone Press, 1977.

Garnier, Edward. *Les nains et les géants*. Paris: Librairie Hatchette, 1884.

Gould, George M., and Walter L. Pyle. *Anomalies and Curiosities of Medicine*, 335–343. Philadelphia: W. B. Saunders, 1896. Reprint, New York: Bell, 1973. Online: tanayanet/books/aacomio/.

Havard, Jean-Alexandre. *Les nains célèbres depuis l'antiquité jusques et y compris Tom-Pouce* [par A. Albanés (pseud.) et Georges Fath]. Paris: G. Havard, 1845.

Monestier, Martin. *Les nains: Des hommes différents*. Paris: J. C. Simeon, 1977.

Roth, Hy, and Robert Cromie. *The Little People*. New York: Everest House, 1980.

Thompson, C.J.S. *The Mystery and Lore of Monsters*. London: Williams and Norgate, 1930. Reissued as *Giants, Dwarfs, and Other Oddities* (New York: Citadel Press, 1968); then as *The History and Lore of Freaks* (London: Senate, 1996).

Wood, Edward J. *Giants and Dwarfs*. London: R. Bentley, 1868.

Contemporary Scholarly and General Works

Ablon, Joan. *Little People in America: The Social Dimensions of Dwarfism*. New York: Praeger, 1984.

———. *Living with Difference: Families with Dwarf Children*. New York: Praeger, 1988.

Bogdan, Robert. *Freak Show: Presenting Human Oddities for Amusement and Profit*. Chicago: University of Chicago Press, 1988.

Dasen, Veronique. *Dwarfs in Ancient Egypt and Greece*. New York: Oxford University Press, 1993.

Edwards, Martha. "Construction of Physical Disability in the Ancient Greek World: The Community Concept." In *The Body and Physical Differences: Discourses of Disability*, edited by David T. Mitchell and Sharon L. Snyder, 35–50. Ann Arbor: University of Michigan Press, 1997.

Egan, Cara. "LPA, Inc.: Coming of Age in the Policy Arena." Master's thesis, School of Hygiene and Public Health, Department of Health Policy and Management, Johns Hopkins University, 2001.

Fleischer, Doris Zames, and Frieda Zames. *The Disability Rights Movement: From Charity to Confrontation*. Philadelphia: Temple University Press, 2001.

Kennedy, Dan. *Little People: Learning to See the World through My Daughter's Eyes*. New York: Rodale Press, 2003.

Koren, Yehuda, and Eilat Negev. *In Our Hearts We Were Giants: The Remarkable Story of the Lilliput Troupe—A Dwarf Family's Survival of the Holocaust*. New York: Carroll and Graf, 2004.

McVan, Alice J. "Spanish Dwarfs," *Notes Hispanic* 2 (1942): 97–129.

Thomson, Rosemarie Garland. *Extraordinary Bodies: Figuring Physical Disability in American Culture and Literature*. New York: Columbia University Press, 1997.

———. *Freakery: Cultural Spectacles of the Extraordinary Body*. New York: New York University Press, 1996.

Tuan, Yi-Fu. *Dominance and Affection: The Making of Pets*. New Haven: Yale University Press, 1984.

Memoirs

Boruwlaski, Josef. 1788. *Memoirs of the Celebrated Dwarf, Joseph Boruwlaski, a Polish Gentleman*. Translated from the French by Mr. Des Carrieres. London, 1778.

Donaldson, David, with Jesse Outlar. *Caught Short*. New York: Atheneum, 1972.

Hathaway, Katherine Butler. *The Little Locksmith: A Memoir*. New York: Coward-McCann, 1942. Reprint, with a foreword by Alix Kates Shulman and an afterword by Nancy Mairs, New York: Feminist Press, 2000.

Magri, M. Lavinia, with Sylvester Bleeker. *The Autobiography of Mrs. Tom Thumb*. Camden Conn: Archon Books, 1970.

Moskowitz, Elizabeth. *By the Grace of the Satan: The Story of the Dwarves Family in Aushvitz in Dr. Mengele's Experiments*. Ramat Gan, Israel: Rotem, 1987.

Ned, Nelson. *Pequeño gigante de la canción*. Jefferson Magno Costa: Zondevan, 1998.

Pieral. *Vu d'en bas*. Paris: Laffont, 1976.

Prosch, Peter. *Leben und Ereignisse des Peter Prosch*. Munich: Anton Franz, 1789. Reprint, with preface by Walter Hansen, Pfaffenhoffen: W. Ludwig Verlag, 1984.

Roloff, Matt, with Tracy Sumner. *Against Tall Odds*. Sisters, Ore.: Multnomah Publishers, 1999.

Phillips, Sue. *Small Portion: A Dwarf Finds God in the Struggle for Normality*. Godalming, England: Highland Press, 1997.

Saint-Macary, Jean-Brissé. *1 Metre 34*. Paris: Julliard, 1975.

Shakespeare, Tom. "Tom Shakespeare." In *Invented Identities: Lesbians and Gays Talk about Migration,* edited by Bob Cant, 29–38. London: Cassell Press, 1997.

Shakespeare, Dr. William. *Walking through Leaves*. Prepared and with an introduction by Tom Shakespeare. Available through the Restricted Growth Association, P.O. Box 4744, Dorchester, England DT2 9FA; www.rgaonline.org.uk.

Van Etten, Angela. *Dwarfs Don't Live in Doll Houses*. Rochester, N.Y.: Adaptive Living, 1988.

Mythology

Appenzeller, Tim. *Dwarfs*. Alexandria, Va.: Time-Life Books, 1985.

Gray, L. H., and G. F. Moore, eds. *Mythology of All Races*. 13 vols. Boston: Marshall Jones, 1916–1933.

Meyers, Fritz. *Riesen und Zwerge am Niederrhein, ihre Spuren in Sage, Märchen, Geschichte und Kuntz*. Dusberg: Mercator Verlag, 1980.

Radin, Paul, Karl Karenyi, and C. G. Jung. *The Trickster: A Study of American Indian Mythology*. New York: Schocken Press, 1956.

Thompson, Stith, ed. *Motif-Index of Folk Literature*. 6 vols. Bloomington: Indiana University Press, 1955–1958. Published in a revised edition in 1989 and on CD-ROM in 1993.

MEDICAL ASPECTS

Adelson, Betty. *Dwarfism: Medical and Psychosocial Aspects of Profound Short Stature.* Baltimore: Johns Hopkins University Press, 2005.

"Medical Resource Center." LPA Online. LPAonline.org/resources_library.html.

Online Mendelian Inheritance in Man (OMIM). 2000. McKusick-Nathans Institute for Genetic Medicine, Johns Hopkins University (Baltimore, Md.) and National Center for Biotechnology Information, National Library of Medicine (Bethesda, Md.). Http://www.ncbi.nlm.nih.gov/omim.

Parker, James N., and Philip M. Parker, eds. *Dwarfism: A Medical Dictionary, Bibliography, and Annotated Guide to Internet References.* San Diego, CA: Icon Health Publications, 2004.

PubMed. National Library of Medicine. Http://www.ncbi.nlm.nihgov/entrez/query.fcqi?db=PubMed.

Scott, Charles I., Nancy Mayeux, Richard Crandall, and Joan Weiss. *Dwarfism: The Family and Professional Guide.* Irvine, Calif.: Short-Stature Foundation, 1994.

ARTS

Books

Charcot, Jean Martin, and Paul Richer. *Les difformes et les malades dans l'art.* Paris: Lecrosnier et Babe, 1889.

Darke, Paul. 1998. "Understanding Cinematic Representations of Disability." In *The Disability Reader: A Social Science Perspective,* edited by Tom Shakespeare, 181–200. London: Cassel, 1998.

Dasen, Veronique. 1993. *Dwarfs in Ancient Egypt and Greece.* Oxford: Oxford University Press, 1993.

"Dwarfs." In *Films Involving Disabilities.* 2003. Http://www.disabilityfilms.co.uk.

Enderle, Alfred, Dietrich Myerhöfer, and Gert Unverfehrt. *Small People—Great Art.* Translated by Karen Williams. Hamm, Germany: Artcolor Verlag, 1994.

Goldfarb, Allan. "Giants and Minuscule Actors in the Nineteenth-Century American Stage." *Journal of Popular Culture,* Fall 1976, 267–269.

Hansel, Volker, and Diether Kramer. *Die Zwerge kommen!* Trautenfels, Austria: Verein Schloss Trautenfels, 1993.

Kunze, J., and I. Nippert. *Genetics and Malformations in Art.* Berlin: Grosse Verlag, 1986.

Norden, Martin. *The Cinema of Isolation.* New Brunswick, N.J.: Rutgers University Press, 1994.

Rischbieth, H., and A. Barrington. "Dwarfism." In *A Treasury of Human Inheritance.* Vol. 1, 355–573. London: Francis Galton Laboratory of Human Eugenics, University of London, 1912.

Schele, Linda. 1997. *The Hidden Faces of the Mayas.* S.A. de C.V.: ALTI, Impetus Comunicacion, 1997.

Tietze-Conrat, Erica. 1957. *Dwarfs and Jesters in Art.* Translated by Elizabeth Olson. London: Phaidon, 1957.

Video Documentaries

Big Enough. 2003. Produced and directed by Jan Krawitz. Available at Amazon, www.amazon.com.

Dwarf: Little People—Big Steps. 2003. Produced and directed by Gerard Issembert. Available from Discovery Channel.

Dwarf: Standing Tall. 2001. Produced and directed by Gerard Issembert. Available from Discovery Channel.

Dwarfs: Not a Fairy Tale. 2001. Written by Lisa Abelow Hedley; codirected by Lisa Abelow and Bonnie Strauss. Available from HBO or Children of Difference Foundation.

Four Foot Ten. Produced by Peter Mauro. Available from Aquarius Health Care Videos.

Little People. 1981. Produced by Jan Krawitz and Tom Ott. Available from Amazon, www.amazon.com.

INDEX

Note: Page number in italics indicate illustrations.

ABOUT THE AUTHOR

Betty Adelson is a psychologist, formerly on the counseling staffs of New York University's School of Education and Queens College. She has spent most of her career as a psychotherapist in private practice in Brooklyn. After her daughter, Anna, was born with achondroplasia thirty years ago, Dr. Adelson became active in the dwarfism community. Since her retirement, she has focused on doing research for this volume and for *Dwarfism: Medical and Psychosocial Aspects of Profound Short Stature,* to be published by Johns Hopkins University Press in 2005.